That's Entertainment

ALSO BY TIGHE E. ZIMMERS
and from McFarland

Lyrical Satirical Harold Rome: A Biography of the Broadway Composer-Lyricist (2014)

Tin Pan Alley Girl: A Biography of Ann Ronell (2009)

That's Entertainment
A Biography of Broadway Composer Arthur Schwartz

Tighe E. Zimmers

McFarland & Company, Inc., Publishers
Jefferson, North Carolina

Library of Congress Cataloguing-in-Publication Data

Names: Zimmers, Tighe E., 1949– author.
Title: That's entertainment : a biography of Broadway composer Arthur Schwartz / Tighe E. Zimmers.
Description: Jefferson : McFarland & Company, Inc., Publishers, 2021. | Includes bibliographical references and index.
Identifiers: LCCN 2020057843 | ISBN 9781476678818 (paperback : acid free paper) ∞
ISBN 9781476641652 (ebook)
Subjects: LCSH: Schwartz, Arthur, 1900-1984. | Composers—United States—Biography. | Film composers—United States—Biography. | Musicals—New York (State)—New York—20th century—History and criticism.
Classification: LCC ML410.S418 Z56 2021 | DDC 782.1/4092 [B]—dc23
LC record available at https://lccn.loc.gov/2020057843

British Library cataloguing data are available

ISBN (print) 978-1-4766-7881-8
ISBN (ebook) 978-1-4766-4165-2

© 2021 Tighe E. Zimmers. All rights reserved

No part of this book may be reproduced or transmitted in any form or by any means, electronic or mechanical, including photocopying or recording, or by any information storage and retrieval system, without permission in writing from the publisher.

Front cover image: Arthur Schwartz watching rehearsals for Inside U.S.A. (Harry Ransom Center, University of Texas at Austin / New York Journal American photograph)
© 2021 Shutterstock/blinkblink

Printed in the United States of America

*McFarland & Company, Inc., Publishers
Box 611, Jefferson, North Carolina 28640
www.mcfarlandpub.com*

Acknowledgments

Special thanks to the following: for editorial assistance and reading early stages of the manuscript: Gail Porter Mandell; my sister, Malilee Elis Zimmers; and my wife, Noreen McDermott; Mark Horowitz, senior music specialist, and the staff at the Musical Division of the Library of Congress which houses the Arthur Schwartz Papers; Richard Schwegel, director, Performing Arts Library, Roosevelt University; the friendly staffs at the Starbucks Coffee stores where I wrote the majority of the book.

Thanks to the personnel of libraries, collections, and various institutions: Alamy, Inc.; Broward County Libraries; Edward M. Burns, trustee of the Carl Van Vechten Trust; June Can and Nancy Kuhl, Beinecke Rare Book and Manuscript Library, Yale University; Maryann Chach Vallillo, director of the Shubert Archive and her staff; Mark Chester, photographer; Chicago Public Libraries; Columbia University Libraries, Columbia Center for Oral History; Ned Comstock, USC Cinematic Arts Library; Emily DiLeo, Special Collections, Irving S. Gilmore Music Library, Yale University; Fran Smith, American Discography Project, University of California, Santa Barbara; Sheri Dolfen and Lisa Marine, Wisconsin Historical Society Archives; Kevin S. Fleming, archivist of Special Collections and Archives, Georgia State University Library; my daughter, Therese Fontana, for IT assistance; J. David Goldin Collection, radio archive; Howard Gotlieb Archival Research Center of Boston University; Louise Hilton, research specialist, and the staff of Special Collections Department, Margaret Herrick Library, AMPAS; Library of Congress, Prints and Photographs Division; Dr. bruce d. mcclung, College of Visual and Performing Arts, UNCG; Dr. Dominic McHugh, the University of Sheffield; Linda Briscoe Meyers, research associate, Harry Ransom Center, the University of Texas at Austin; Newberry Library; Park Ridge Public Library; Vicky Peterson, photographer; Photofest, Inc.; Manuscripts Division, Department of Special Collections, Princeton University; MGM; Lauren Robinson, reproductions specialist, Museum of the

City of New York; New York Public Library for the Performing Arts; Marcia L. Schiff, AP Images; Daniel Stetzel, Chicago College of Performing Arts, Roosevelt University; Warner Bros. Archives, School of Cinematic Arts, USC; Warner Bros. Pictures; my proofreaders: Katie Hickey, Bridget Joyce, Ellen McDerrmott, and Kathy Meierhoff.

Table of Contents

Acknowledgments — v
Preface — 1
Introduction — 5

1. Early Life — 9
2. Early Songwriting — 18
3. Howard Dietz — 28
4. *The Little Show* and "I Guess I'll Have to Change My Plan" — 33
5. The London Shows — 41
6. *Three's a Crowd* and "Something to Remember You By" — 46
7. *The Band Wagon* and "Dancing in the Dark" — 61
8. *Flying Colors* and "Alone Together" — 75
9. *The Gibson Family* and Radio — 84
10. *Revenge with Music* and "You and the Night and the Music" — 97
11. *At Home Abroad* — 105
12. Late Thirties: C.B. Cochran and *Follow the Sun* — 112
13. *Between the Devil*: "By Myself" and "I See Your Face Before Me" — 117
14. *Virginia* and the Rockefellers — 130
15. Dorothy Fields and *Stars in Your Eyes* — 140
16. Movie Songwriting: Frank Loesser and Johnny Mercer — 153
17. Movie Producing and Hollywood — 164
18. Songwriting — 179

19. *Park Avenue*: Ira Gershwin and George S. Kaufman — 188
20. *Inside U.S.A.* and Leo Robin — 196
21. More Producing: Television and *Inside U.S.A. with Chevrolet* — 210
22. *A Tree Grows in Brooklyn*: Shirley Booth and "Make the Man Love Me" — 219
23. *Schwartz v. Broadcast Music, Inc.* — 233
24. *The Band Wagon*: The Movie and "That's Entertainment" — 241
25. *By the Beautiful Sea* and More Dorothy Fields — 256
26. The Mid-Fifties: Odds and Ends and *Mrs. 'Arris Goes to Paris* — 267
27. *The Gay Life*: Barbara Cook and "Magic Moment" — 280
28. *Jennie* and Mary Martin — 287
29. Later Life — 297

Appendix A. Arthur Schwartz Chronology — 311
Appendix B. Chronology of Produced Shows — 317
Appendix C. Songs Composed by Schwartz with Various Lyricists — 319
Appendix D. Tribute Albums — 328
Appendix E. Schwartz Songs on Your Hit Parade — 330
Chapter Notes — 331
Bibliography — 371
Index — 377

Preface

Composers of the American Popular Songbook have always caught my attention. I grew up hearing their music on recordings and television, and in movies, concerts, and cabaret. I became especially interested after hearing singers like Bobby Short and Andrea Marcovici perform cabaret shows devoted to a specific composer or lyricist. These shows put these songs into context while entertaining and educating audiences along the way. I began collecting autographs in the area of American Popular Song which led to a large collection of 26 boxes of the papers of composer Ann Ronell. Between my collection and a similar one at the New York Public Library for the Performing Arts, I was able to write a biography of Ronell, *Tin Pan Alley Girl*, which came out in 2008.

A few years after that, I discovered the Harold Rome Papers at the Irving S. Gilmore Music Library at Yale University. These were extensive and together with information from his son, Joshua, provided the basis for *Lyrical Satirical Harold Rome: A Biography of the Broadway Composer-Lyricist*, published in 2014. These books brought into focus two composers, especially Rome, who had been lost in the shuffle and had not received proper credit among musical historians. I wanted to find another such composer.

To find a new subject, I looked at who of these popular composers had not had a book written about them. Many of the prominent popular composers of the first half of the twentieth century had one or more biographies / autobiographies. Among these were:

Harold Arlen   Duke Ellington
Irving Berlin   Dorothy Fields
Leonard Bernstein   George Gershwin
Hoagy Carmichael   Ira Gershwin
George M. Cohan   Oscar Hammerstein II
Howard Dietz   E.Y. Harburg
Vernon Duke   Lorenz Hart

Jerome Kern	Sigmund Romberg
Alan Jay Lerner	Harold Rome
Frank Loesser	Harry B. Smith
Frederick Loewe	Billy Strayhorn
Hugh Martin	Jule Styne
Jimmy McHugh	Jimmy Van Heusen
Johnny Mercer	Harry Warren
Cole Porter	Kurt Weill
Richard Rodgers	Vincent Youmans

Those who had been overlooked included Anne Caldwell, Walter Donaldson, Al Dubin, Gus Kahn, Burton Lane, Leo Robin, Arthur Schwartz, and Rida Johnson Young. Of these, Schwartz most caught my interest. I was first aware of him in 1987 from a cabaret show performed by Julie Wilson devoted to the songs of Schwartz and Howard Dietz. They did several revues in the thirties, and Schwartz had done book shows with Dietz, Dorothy Fields, and Ira Gershwin. Schwartz had also written songs and produced movies in Hollywood, working with lyricists Frank Loesser, Johnny Mercer, and Leo Robin, among others.

The Arthur Schwartz Papers were available at the Library of Congress. These are extensive and served as the foundation of my research. There was also material at the New York Public Library, mostly in the collections of Howard Dietz and Dorothy Fields. Dietz had written his autobiography, *Dancing in the Dark*, which spoke much of Schwartz. Because he had worked with so many other lyricists, bits and pieces of information were available in their biographies and personal and professional papers. The memoir of his son Jonathan, *All in Good Time: A Memoir*, was also helpful. With all this information at hand, Arthur Schwartz was a good subject for a biography.

Arthur Schwartz may not be a household name like some of the above composers, but he wrote a great deal of excellent theater and film music. I hit a gold mine that was deeper than I imagined. My biography of Schwartz focuses on his songwriting and shows, as well as his various collaborators. It also discusses what was generally going on in the theater and his personal life at various times. There are chapters on his early life and career and his later life, but most of the chapters are headed with show titles. There are others with topics that include Howard Dietz, the art of songwriting, and Schwartz's work in Hollywood as a songwriter and producer. I did no musical analysis of his songs, often seen in musical biographies. Though I play piano and have had plenty of music lessons, I never studied music theory, harmony, etc., and do not feel qualified to do such song analysis.

I have gone into much detail regarding Schwartz's professional life.

Each chapter has numerous notes, drawn from the Arthur Schwartz Papers, numerous biographies of other songwriters, encyclopedic entries, newspaper articles of the day, and other primary sources when available. Fortunately, Schwartz submitted to numerous interviews over the years. Dietz, besides his *Dancing in the Dark,* wrote much about his partner. Schwartz's sons, Jonathan and Paul, are working on a biography of their father and were not willing to contribute anything to my efforts. It is a significant deficit but one which could not be avoided.

This book should serve as a resource for anyone interested in Arthur Schwartz, theater and Hollywood music, revue, musical comedy, and American Popular Song. I would like to think that my biography of Arthur Schwartz would become an important reference work for those interested in the above topics and focus a brighter light on one of the premier composers of popular music in the twentieth century.

Introduction

In September 1958, Arthur Schwartz was featured on *The Perry Como Show*, a one-hour variety show starring the popular singer. Como introduced Schwartz as "one of America's most distinguished composers of the songs our nation has been singing for many years." The two meet at the piano, where Schwartz is sitting among a scattering of sheet music. Their discussion begins:

> COMO: Arthur, this is quite an impressive stack of songs for one man to have written.
> SCHWARTZ: If you think that's impressive, you should see the stack of songs I have at home that didn't make it.
> COMO: Let's talk about the winners. And you've got so many of them here.[1]

* * *

Musical entertainments of the American stage have had a long evolution. Starting with minstrel shows in the 1830s, other forms of an "American musical" have included burlesque, vaudeville, revue, operetta, musical comedy, book shows, concept musicals, and jukebox musicals. Each of these had early proponents, practitioners, and artists who perfected the genre and ultimately changed it. Each form had a run of twenty-five years or more, and along the way, there was plenty of overlap, imitation, and non–American influence. It has been an interesting evolution and secured for America its own place in the history of music and theater. Jazz may be the country's most unique contribution to music, but the American musical can also claim a strong standing.

Arthur Schwartz was a student of the theater and aware of how it had evolved. He was bitten by the "theatre bug" in his teenage years and could not rid himself of it. His English studies as an undergraduate at Columbia University as well as a Master of Arts from that school served to cultivate his interests. Despite success as an English teacher then as a practicing attorney, the pull of the theater was strong. Even with his English training, it was the music of the theater that most attracted him, rather than lyrics, scripts, or design elements. He had had little piano instruction but played well, thanks mostly to an excellent "ear" and a wonderful memory. In his early twenties, he began writing melodies, and like most beginning songwriters, his earliest efforts were often imitative. At the time, Irving Berlin, George M. Cohan, George Gershwin, and Jerome Kern, among others, had made their marks on American music. It was all but impossible not to be influenced by these talented men.

In the early twenties, the revue was in full bloom. The abovementioned songwriters as well as dozens of others were filling the American stage with hundreds of songs, many of them quite remarkable. The revue had developed into a recognizable form and a lucrative enterprise. The most prominent producers included Florenz Ziegfeld, Jr., J.J. and Lee Shubert, George White, Earl Carroll, John Murray Anderson, and Lew Leslie. The typical revue featured elegant costumes and scenery, chorus girls in provocative outfits, and elaborate production numbers. Songs took a back seat. But as the revue evolved, the formula grew stale. Audiences wanted a bit more substance in the book and definitely better songs. Lesser known American producers worked to improve the revue, like Max Gordon and Dwight Deere Wiman, and there were influences from Europe, most importantly André Charlot and C.B. Cochran.

In 1929, Schwartz teamed with lyricist / librettist / publicist Howard Dietz and producers Wiman and Tom Weatherly. They created *The Little Show*, a hit revue in 1929 that ran for 321 performances. Over a six-year period, Schwartz and Dietz had four more successful revues that included *Three's a Crowd* (1930), *The Band Wagon* (1931), *Flying Colors* (1932), and *At Home Abroad* (1935). Not only did these shows enjoy good runs, but Schwartz and Dietz redefined a genre that was getting stale. Their shows were smarter, more intimate, and led the way for other songwriting teams. Each show also included one or two hit songs from the young songwriting duo. During the thirties, Schwartz was writing revues for the London stage as well and became a favorite of those audiences and critics. In 1948, not yet finished with the genre, Schwartz and Dietz had their longest running revue with *Inside U.S.A.*

In the forties, Schwartz spent a fruitful period in Hollywood, writing songs with Johnny Mercer and Frank Loesser, then producing two successful musical films. He returned to Broadway to write a show with Ira Gershwin, *Park Avenue* (1946), then two musicals with Dorothy Fields, *A Tree Grows in Brooklyn* (1951) and *By the Beautiful Sea* (1954). Schwartz and Dietz joined forces once more in the early sixties for two unsuccessful shows, *The Gay Life* and *Jennie*. Again, these films and shows, while not all hits, produced several great songs. In 1953, a movie musical *The Band Wagon* was released, using Schwartz / Dietz songs from the original show and prompting them to write their famous show business anthem, "That's Entertainment."

Many of the best-known composers of the American Popular Songbook wrote shows that ran well over 500 performances, some over 2,000. Schwartz shows did not have such lengthy runs, but that was the nature of revue, for which a run of 200 or more was considered a success. More importantly, each revue held two or three gems from the Schwartz / Dietz songbook. They may have been light-hearted revues, but they contained some of the best ballads in the American Popular Songbook, as well as up-tempo and comedic numbers. The same can be said of their early attempts at book shows in the late thirties, including *Revenge with Music* (1934) and *Between the Devil* (1937). More than one critic commented that it was seldom the Schwartz score that failed a musical, but rather an inadequate book.

In addition to his composing, Schwartz became involved in various guilds and associations involving the arts and songwriting, always trying to improve the lot of composers and the theater in general. He was on the board of directors at ASCAP for twenty-five years and was the lead plaintiff in a 1953 suit against BMI, Inc., and several broadcasting companies and music publishers. Although he had discontinued his law practice in 1928, his law degree did not go unused. He also raised two boys, Jonathan and Paul, both of whom are still involved in the music world.

The names, facts, and stories of the songwriting world of Arthur Schwartz make a good biography. If the reader is interested in Broadway, Hollywood, and American Popular Song, this book should be of interest to him or her.

1

Early Life

"I think that I started very slowly, and very poor in my first efforts, and I grew, as many people grow."¹

According to almost all biographical sources, Arthur Schwartz was born November 25, 1900. But his birth certificate, issued by the Bureau of Records and Statistics of the City of New York, clearly states that his birthday was November 4 of that year.² Either way, over the next eighty-three

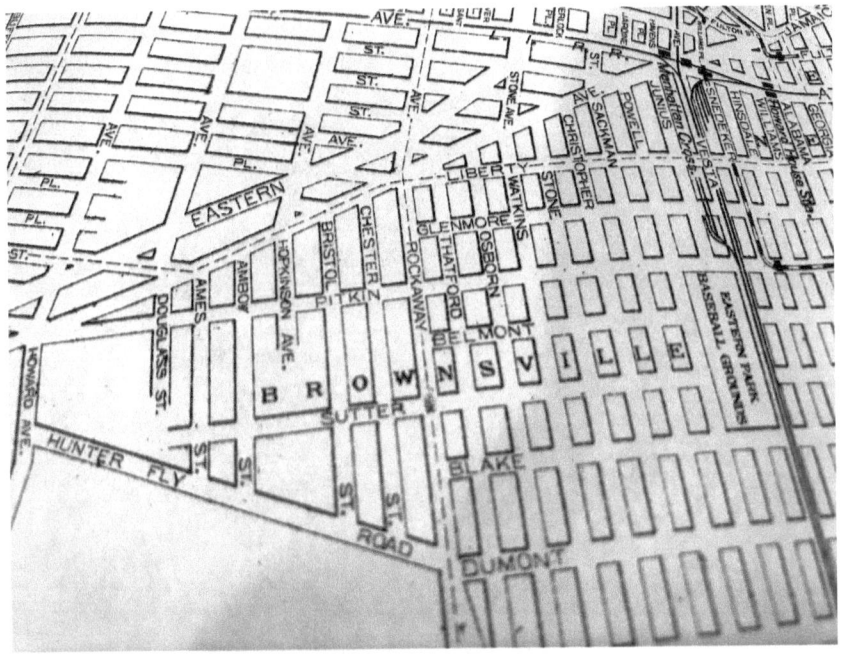

Solomon and Dora Schwartz were living in the Brownsville section of Brooklyn in 1900, the year that son Arthur was born, November 4. Brownsville was an outlying ward of Brooklyn. Their address was 69 Thatford Avenue between Pitkin and Gilmore avenues (courtesy Newberry Library).

years, he would establish himself among the elite of American Popular Song composers.

Arthur was the youngest of the four children of Solomon Samson Schwartz and Dora Grossman Schwartz. At the time of his birth, they lived at 69 Thatford Avenue in the Brownsville section of Brooklyn. In 1906, the family moved within the same borough of New York to 312 Rugby Road in the Flatbush neighborhood. At age six, Arthur was ready for school, and his family's move had put them only a few blocks from PS 139. He turned out to be a great student and always would be. He "skipped" a few grades and completed elementary school at the age of twelve.[3] From there he went to Boys High School of Brooklyn in the Bedford-Stuyvesant section, where competition was stiffer, and there was no skipping. Nonetheless, with his head start, he graduated from high school at age sixteen.

Despite his penchant for academics, Arthur had music on his mind. Solomon Schwartz did not. As was common in those days, families who could afford it would have a piano. The Schwartz family did, but Solomon thought music was a frivolous pastime and would only allow the oldest boy, William, to play music and take lessons. But things worked out: "What happened was that his brother got the lessons and Arthur got the natural

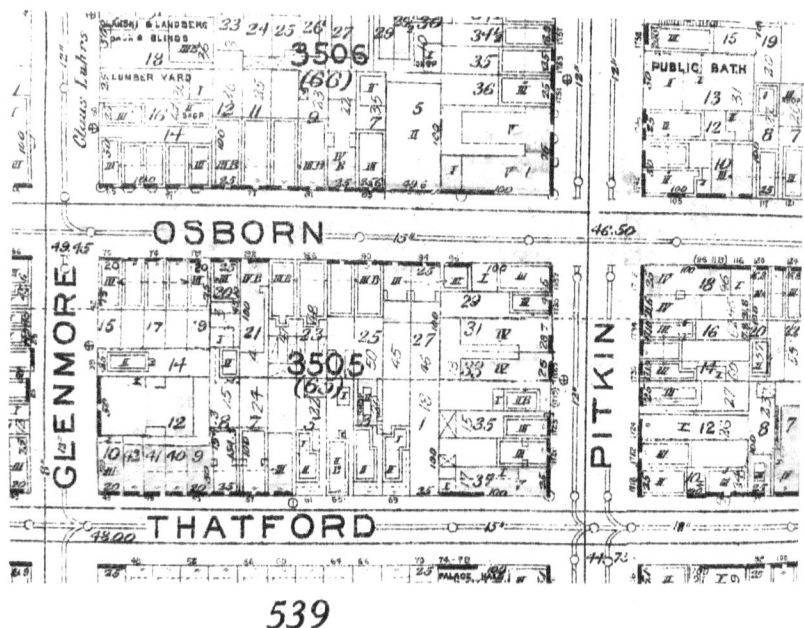

In 1900, the Schwartz family lived at 69 Thatford Avenue, about one-third of the way from Pitkin and Gilmore avenues, in the Brownsville section of Brooklyn (courtesy Newberry Library).

ability."[4] As much as Solomon disliked music, Dora encouraged it, aiding and abetting young Arthur, who had to sneak to the piano when his father was at work.[5] At the same time, Schwartz learned to play the kazoo, then taught himself the harmonica, instruments easy to play on the sly. Schwartz showed an aptitude for music, explaining, "I played piano by ear from the age of four and at the age of six or seven could play whatever I heard with fairly accurate harmonies."[6] As for composing, "At the age of six or seven, Arthur was writing songs, humming them first, and then successfully picking them out on the piano."[7]

Because of his talent and ear, lessons were not vital, but his mother also saw to it that these were provided, also on the sly. Still, Schwartz was mostly self-taught, which bothered him at times in a musical theater world where many composers had extensive formal education. In 1976, he told interviewer Gene Lees, "You see, I never had any music lessons in my life … and that worried me very much, because I was just an intuitive writer. I learned how to do everything myself."[8] Years later, in a radio series devoted to songwriters, composer / conductor André Previn put Schwartz's talent into perspective: "Fortunately for posterity, Arthur had the kind of instinctive musical awareness that transcends lessons and practice. In any case, his surroundings were giving him a different kind of instruction. A man with no formal musical training who yet managed to write music with an almost scholastic gravity about its finer ballad movements. When you ask him for an explanation he ducks out of it, like all self-respecting creative workers."[9]

Whichever way he learned, Schwartz forged his own style and workable techniques on the piano. Lorenz Hart's biographer, Frederick Nolan, referred to Schwartz as "a fine, instinctive pianist."[10] Son Jonathan thought, "My father at the keyboard was fluent and unafraid."[11] As for those other composers, well-trained or not, a *Collier's* writer said, "However, he is proudest of his playing, knowing that most popular composers are no better."[12] There were exceptions. Among the composers of American Popular Song, there were two child prodigies, Jule Styne and Cy Coleman, both of whom had performed classical music publicly at an early age. When they would meet at ASCAP functions, Styne was in the habit of telling Coleman, "You and I are the only real pianists here."[13]

Using his talent and a wonderful memory, Schwartz made his first money as an artist at the age of thirteen, playing piano at the Cortelyou Theater, a Flatbush movie house: "I was hired at $15 a week to play the accompaniment to silent movies. I had to audition and almost lost my opportunity when the proprietor found out I couldn't read notes, but played by ear. I clinched it though when he hummed his favorite song, a waltz I'd never heard before, and I instantly played it for him. I think I kept the job because every time I saw him come into the theatre that summer, no matter what was going on on the screen, I'd break into his favorite."[14] Years later, Schwartz told lyricist Howard Dietz that the piano playing job at the theater was never mentioned to his father, as the elder Schwartz "might have brought suit against the movie house for corrupting youth with a piano."[15]

The academic career of Schwartz flourished when he received a four-year scholarship to New York University (NYU). During that tenure, he was a member of ROTC and in June 1918, joined a Yale Naval ROTC unit, although he never enlisted. He stayed in the unit until the Armistice in December and saw no action during World War I. To facilitate his college degree, Schwartz took classes in summer and graduated with the class of 1920, several months before his twentieth birthday. He graduated with a Bachelor of Arts in English, a New York Public School teaching certificate, a Phi Beta Kappa key, and with a membership in Pi Lambda Phi fraternity.[16] During this time, he composed when he could and was always looking to get his name and songs known. He told Dietz about one of these early efforts:

> When in college I wrote words and music of a song called "I'm Getting Better Every Day," based on the Coue vogue of the moment. It was a very bad song, but I thought it was great. Someone introduced me to Elliot Shapiro of Shapiro Bernstein, a tough, stoney-face, tin pan alley character (today he's even tougher and stonier). I played him the song with the same enthusiasm as if it were "Alexander's Ragtime Band" or something equally revolutionary. When I finished I looked at him. He was silent for sixty seconds or more and then fixed his eye on me and almost whispered incredulously, "Are you kidding?"[17]

Such were the disappointments of the budding songwriter. In that comment to Dietz, Schwartz's referral to the Coue vogue referred to the French psychotherapist, Emile Coue, who espoused a method of self-help stressing autosuggestion. It was popular in the twenties and featured the slogan, "Day by day in every way I am getting better and better."[18]

Schwartz also wrote an NYU fight song, "Smash, Crash Right Through," with classmate Alexander Slavitt as lyricist.[19] For years, it was used whenever the Violets scored a touchdown—a rarity—so the song got little play. He and Slavitt also composed a fraternity theme, "Shine on Pi Lambda Phi," as well as songs for the 1920 NYU *Junior Show*, including a title number, "There's a Whole Lot of Moonlight and a Pretty Rustic Seat."[20] In addition to music and composing, Schwartz was busy with extracurricular activities, being at various times an editor of school publications, debater, actor, glee club member, and class officer.[21]

His education continued with a Master of Arts in English at Columbia University during the 1920–21 school year, and because this curriculum afforded him more free time, he pursued songwriting more diligently. He explained to Dietz years later, "It was during this year at Columbia that song-writing first seemed a possible career in [my] remote future, for between classes, I went constantly to Earl Hall and worked at the piano early mornings before other students arrived. The pain of groping for melodies that year is still vivid to me, but several tunes seemed good to me. (None that I ever used later.)"[22] To this scenario, he added, "Not till three years later did I write the first melody I thought was any good."[23]

After his Master of Arts at Columbia, he went back to NYU in September 1921 to work on a law degree. But it was not just school that occupied his time as he was also teaching high school. In his first years of law school, he would go to morning class at NYU, leave fifteen minutes early, and with any luck, catch a subway to arrive at the High School of Commerce by 12:10 p.m.[24] During these years, he had music and songwriting on his mind all the time. He would wake up early and have to decide between studying law, correcting papers, or writing melodies. Frequently, melody writing would win out.

His first published song came in 1923, during his law school years, when he teamed with lyricist Eli Dawson on "Baltimore, Md., You're the Only Doctor for Me," earning eight dollars for the effort. Schwartz would later say that it was "so bad even *he* wouldn't play it at parties."[25] However, he believed it to be "the funniest song" he had ever written.[26] In the year 1923 Schwartz began writing songs at Brant Lake Camp in the Adirondack Mountains of New York, a boys' camp where he was a counselor. These camps had the usual outdoor activities like tennis, swimming, baseball, and hiking, but there was also an emphasis on songs and entertainment. In *We'll Have Manhattan*, his examination of the early works of Rodgers and Hart, Dominic Symonds detailed this aspect of camp life:

> Camaraderie was encouraged, and campers would champion the identity of their own camp while jibing other camps in the area ... much of this camaraderie was generated in camp singsongs around the fire, and a tradition of revue-type performance developed, featuring songs and skits, and burlesquing the events of the week.... Such shows—often modeled around the popular minstrel show and featuring boys and counselors in drag or blackface—gave plenty of opportunities for creative sparks to fly. For young campers like Lorenz Hart, Richard Rodgers, and Herbert Fields, the shows were the sine qua non of camp life.[27]

Prior to the Brant Lake Camp, Schwartz had been a counselor at Camp Kiawah in Pennsylvania, but on the advice of Milton Bender, would change to Brant Lake a year later in hopes of working with Lorenz Hart. Bender and Hart were good friends, and Bender was an enthusiastic supporter of Hart's lyrics.

At Brant Lake, Schwartz first worked with Ted Goodman, writing songs for *Surprises of 1923*, a show for the campers and visitors. These were done at the camp every two weeks to welcome newcomers and to send off those leaving. Camp shows usually contained about ten songs, mostly humorous, as evidenced by these songs in *Surprises of 1923* by Schwartz and Goodman: "Candy Contrabandit," "Ding Dong," "Post Office Blues," "Seenyah!" and "Twilight."[28] They collaborated on another fortnightly show, *Palula Island*, this one a play with music. Also contributing to lyrics was Arthur Freund. *Palula Island* played in late July 1923, and the following songs were used and copyrighted[29]:

Adirondack History	Mountain Trail
Injuns of the Togo Togo	Palula Moon
Let's Whoop It Up for Brant Lake Camp	Spooks
Let's Wish	Trip, Trip, Trip!

After the summer hiatus, Schwartz was back at law school in the fall of 1923, interested in the law and studying hard, but now with music on his mind more than ever. In summer 1924, he returned to Brant Lake, remembering it fondly years later: "I got myself a job at Brant Lake just for the chance to meet Larry. It turned out to be a much better camp. I got more money, food—and I got to work with Larry Hart, who put on the camp show every other Saturday. ... From the start Larry seemed to have an interesting knack for staging things. He knew instinctively the right moments for a song number. He was not only a brilliant lyricist; he was a brilliant theatre man."[30]

Hart had been going to Brant Lake as a counselor since 1917, directing camp shows and writing lyrics.[31] Most frequently for these show songs, his collaborator was Mickey Thomashefsky, who would later become famous in New York's Yiddish theater and for a well-publicized, attempted murder / suicide in 1931.[32] While not yet a success, Hart and his composing partner, Richard Rodgers, were becoming known, and would break through in 1925 with "Manhattan" in the *Garrick Gaieties*. For now, Schwartz saw a chance to work with Hart.

Schwartz and Hart hit it off at Brant Lake and were soon working together. Among their best efforts was the show *Dream Boy*: "*Dream Boy*, about a fellow who doesn't care for the energetic, athletic activities of summer camp, but would rather stay in his camp and read books all the time—a character not all that far from Hart's own. They decided they needed a theme song for him, and Hart suggested the title 'I Love to Lie Awake in Bed.' Then Schwartz remembered: 'I wrote the melody to that title, and it was the first melody that I wrote that I felt was any good at all.'" For the same show, they also wrote "Last Night," about saying goodbye and another that "utilized the camp initials, B.L.C., where everyone was h-a-p-p-y as a k-i-d. The opening chorus, 'Down at the Lake,' was performed in bathing trunks and towels by the youngest kids, who were called 'midgets.'"[33]

But it was "I Love to Lie Awake in Bed" that later drew attention. The song would have a short life at Brant Lake, but Schwartz kept the melody in his trunk and employed it years later for *The Little Show,* a 1929 revue which was his first collaboration with Howard Dietz. For that show, Dietz re-titled it "I Guess I'll Have to Change My Plan" and reworked the lyric. It was their first hit and became known as "The Blue Pajama Song." Of the original song and Hart's lyrics, "They also are the only lyrics of any consequence written by Hart to any songwriter other than Richard Rodgers."[34]

Schwartz and Hart would go on to do further work at Brant Lake Camp that summer of 1924 and as these camp shows were performed every two weeks, there were presumably many more songs and skits from their collaboration. No Schwartz / Hart manuscripts were available in the Arthur Schwartz Papers at the Library of Congress. It is known that Max Dreyfus, head of T.B. Harms Music Publishers, visited Brant Lake Camp and heard their material. Why he was there is uncertain, although it may have been at the request of Hart, who had established some relationships on Broadway. What is clear is how Dreyfus reacted to their material: "Dreyfus was frankly pained at the entire performance and said so. Schwartz was dashed. Hart, on the other hand, veteran of many such rejections, was not the least bit disturbed."[35] A few years later, Hart and his new partner, Richard Rodgers, presented several songs to Dreyfus, including "Manhattan." After listening for some time, Dreyfus declared, "There is nothing of value here."[36] Dreyfus would become the principal publisher of Broadway songs with "a discriminating eye for talent" and "wielding an acumen that set him above his competition."[37]

To compare their careers at this point, Schwartz was a novice, and Hart had been toiling at songwriting for several years with only minor success. But the older and savvier Hart understood the game. Schwartz, of course, would learn the ups and downs of the songwriting business soon. In 1976, he told a Canadian interviewer, "No matter what, if you're a tunesmith in Tin Pan Alley, you must be prepared to take the bitter with the bitter."[38]

After Brant Lake in 1924, Schwartz and Hart wrote a song at the behest of their friend, Eddie Ugast. He was acquainted with vaudeville entertainers Besser & Amy, who needed a song for their show. Schwartz recalled the event, but less the details of the song:

> So Larry and I stayed up most of the night. The act consisted of a straight man and a Jewish comic. The song's title was "I Know My Girl by Her Perfume." The lyrics I have forgotten—something like "I know my girl by her perfume, Estelle has the breath of a

Rose...." That was the straight man's line. The Jewish comedian had girls with peculiar smells: Becky smells from herring, some other girls smell from garlic and so on.

They wanted it in their act the next day. It must have been three or four in the morning when we had a verse and straight chorus and a comedy chorus ... after one reading they said, "We'll take it!"[39]

Ugast brokered the deal for the song, seventy-five dollars in all, one-third to each of the songwriters and one-third for himself. Schwartz added, "That was the first money I had ever got for a song. But isn't it terrible—or maybe it isn't—that I can't remember that lyric."[40]

Schwartz was not naïve. While appreciative of the opportunity to write with Hart, he had no illusions of their teaming up. Schwartz had the greatest respect for Hart and knew that Hart's future lay with Richard Rodgers. The summer's experience and subsequent friendship with Hart were invaluable. Years later, Schwartz said, "I think that I started very slowly, and very poor in my first efforts, and I grew, as many people grow. But I think Larry was already full-grown. ... I don't think he advanced any. His gift never improved—it didn't need to. All he needed to do was practice his craft and do more work: he was an absolute genius."[41]

After that summer, Schwartz continued to do well at NYU Law School, graduating with the class of 1924. He passed the New York State Bar in 1924 and began practicing in Manhattan at 299 Broadway, working with an older gentleman, Mr. Schoenfeld. He had a large practice and being impressed with Schwartz's "Phi Bete [sic] key and my serious mien," hired him, turning over routine cases and the day-to-day running of the office. Early on, Schwartz made an error that cost a client $8,000 which caused the young lawyer great stress and necessitated his admittance to Briarcliff Lodge for recuperation. Schoenfeld was sympathetic, paying Schwartz's bill and bringing him back with higher pay and position. Of the whole experience, Schwartz remembered, "While at Briarcliff ... [I] wrote reams of tunes, and resolved that after I had established myself as a lawyer of experience, I would gamble on a year or so of time-off for show biz. Never let Schoenfeld know I was interested in music."[42]

Through the mid-twenties, his law practice flourished. Schwartz took on Hart's father, Max, as one of his clients. Dietz explained, "Pere Hart would start a new business every few months and had to have a new lawyer for each project because he never paid his old ones."[43] More to the point: "There was always action from Max and money to be made, but Schwartz wanted, more than anything, to make *music*."[44] During all this, Schwartz and Hart remained close, and the latter kept watch over Schwartz's composing. Hart's biographer, Frederick Nolan, explained: "He [Schwartz] kept on seeing Larry Hart, who listened to his tunes and told him which were promising and which were not. He also told Schwartz he couldn't go around trying to get jobs in the musical theatre while he was practicing law.... He [Schwartz] saw now that Hart's idea had been completely practical: if he failed in the songwriting business, he could always go back to the law. 'In advising me,' he said, 'Larry was like a big brother who was very careful not to make a mistake.'"[45]

2

Early Songwriting

> "I was a split personality ... and the company wasn't getting a fair split! I called it 'Schwartzophrenia.'"¹

In mid-1926, two things happened in the world of Arthur Schwartz to further his songwriting career. First, Lorenz Hart thought Schwartz's composing skills had developed to the point that he should try to make a go of it in the theater world. According to Hart's biographer, Dorothy Hart, he declared, "I think you're ready, if you've saved enough money to gamble awhile in the theatre—because you can't do both."² From their earliest days at Brant Lake Camp, Hart had been impressed with Schwartz and had mentored the younger composer, five years his junior. Years before, a confident Hart had told songwriter Henry Myers, "Don't worry about Arthur Schwartz getting there!"³ Of equal importance to talent in setting out as a composer was that Schwartz had saved up enough money to allow it to happen.⁴

To initiate Schwartz, Hart arranged for him to be rehearsal pianist for the latest Rodgers and Hart show, *Peggy-Ann*.⁵ The show was to be written by Herbert Fields and produced by his father, Lew. From the vantage point of the piano bench, Schwartz would get insights into the evolution of a show and the art of songwriting. George Gershwin biographer Rodney Greenberg discussed the importance of Gershwin having served as a rehearsal pianist: "His days as a lowly rehearsal pianist had allowed him to observe at firsthand how a musical was put together, how songs needed to be planned according to their position within the score, the mechanics of a show's overall structure, the distinction between opening numbers, finales, dance-routines, filling-in material under dialogue, transitional music, reprises of earlier tunes as the story developed, and so on."⁶ As musical shows were created, songs were added, dropped, or modified as scenes and dialogue were adjusted. Rodgers and Hart were a facile team and could create a song at a moment's notice, provided Hart was available. At the time of *Peggy-Ann*, they were among Broadway's hottest songwriting teams, having had hit shows with *The Garrick Gaieties* (1925), *Dearest Enemy* (1925), and *The Girl Friend* (1926). Exposure to the art of Rodgers and Hart was exactly what a new composer like Arthur Schwartz needed.

Even before *Peggy-Ann*, Schwartz had been working with other neophytes at the Neighborhood Playhouse on the lower east side of Manhattan, a group that would be considered Off Broadway today. The Playhouse had been organized in 1915 doing serious dramas and an occasional ballet. In 1922, led by Agnes Morgan, Helen Arthur, and Albert Carroll, the Playhouse assembled a revue to compete with the better known ones uptown, calling their production a "low-brow show for High Grade morons."[7] The show had been planned as a bonus to their subscribers and was to be a burlesque of the year's events at the Neighborhood Playhouse. To everyone's surprise, it was a hit: "Suddenly, from all over the city, people who had never heard of the Neighborhood Playhouse flocked to Grand Street. They stormed the doors to gain admission; tried even the subterfuge of pretending they had been subscribers."[8]

The Grand Street Follies of 1922 was such a success that an annual one was produced every year until 1929 with the exception of 1923.[9] By the second edition in 1924, word had spread, and the show was "received by the satiated critic and Broadway audiences as an innovation which neither the long pilgrimage to Grand Street nor the sweltering heat could mar."[10] These shows were a breath of fresh air to Broadway and important in the evolution of the revue. Rodgers and Hart biographer Dominic Symonds explained, "The *Grand Street Follies* was a benchmark for the company. This was another revue, conceived by Albert Carroll in 1922 and responding to a sea change as small-scale revues rich in singing and dancing but lacking any pretence of a plot or theme began to emerge, contrasting with the grandiose perennials mounted by the big impresarios."[11] The early *Grand Street Follies* would encourage the Junior Group—students and apprentices within the Theatre Guild—to launch the *Garrick Gaieties*.

Schwartz started with *The Grand Street Follies* on their fourth edition, 1926. This was a red-letter year for the revue genre as the Shuberts, John Murray Anderson, George White, Earl Carroll, and Lew Leslie all produced editions. Only Ziegfeld was missing from this roster. Historian Steven Suskin summarized the situation: "*The Grand Street Follies of 1926* was an intimate revue providing amusing, contemporary competition to the uptown annuals."[12] Cecil Smith described the concept behind *The Grand Street Follies* as "a conceit in which ideas were more important than surfaces."[13]

Schwartz wrote songs with three different lyricists for the 1926 show. Agnes Morgan, the show's book writer and principal lyricist, did words for Schwartz's "Little Igloo for Two" and "Uncle Tom's Cabin." The latter song was co-composed with Randall Thompson who would go on to distinguish himself in classical choral music.[14] Agnes Morgan had been with the *Follies* since its initial 1922 edition—a jack-of-all-trades—and would team again with Schwartz for *The Grand Street Follies of 1929*. After the *Follies* ended, she concentrated on playwriting and in 1940 joined the Paper Mill Playhouse in Millburn, New Jersey, as associate director.[15]

For "If You Know What I Mean," Schwartz's lyricists were Theodore (Ted) Goodwin and performer Albert Carroll. For one song in *The Grand Street Follies of 1926*, "The Polar Bear Strut," Schwartz was his own lyricist. None of the songs were memorable but of these early efforts, Steven Suskin concluded, "The Schwartz contributions were entertaining, if not over-whelming."[16] These *Follies* ran for fifty-five performances and provided Schwartz with much needed experience but provided no lyricist as a steady partner. Of his first encounter with *The Grand Street Follies*, he said, "My great fear was that Schoenfeld [law partner] might read the notices and come across my name. He didn't."[17] As Howard Dietz saw it, "They may have seen the name in the paper but didn't associate the composer with 'their' Arthur Schwartz in the glass cubicle."[18]

To further aid his composing friend, Lorenz Hart arranged another meeting between Schwartz and Max Dreyfus, by then the principal music publisher for Broadway. Schwartz felt that he had progressed enough that Dreyfus might have a different opinion of his music than the one from their disastrous meeting at Brant Lake Camp. As Schwartz remembered, "I went there walking on air. When I had finished playing my best dozen tunes, Dreyfus asked, 'Mr. Schwartz, what did you do before you were a song writer?' 'I was a lawyer,' I said. He answered: 'Go back and practice law.'"[19]

But in Schwartz's mind, the time had arrived that he would part ways with the law and his understanding senior partner, Schoenfeld. Howard Dietz explained, "Rude little rhythms would bother his head and on his desk would be notations on sheets of music paper that lived secretly in a drawer."[20] There was little doubt that Arthur Schwartz was an excellent lawyer—erudite, literate, and engaging with clients. Despite setbacks early on, Schoenfeld and clients had much respect for Schwartz. By the summer of 1928, he had been in practice four years and had developed a strong clientele. He took a six-week vacation and by the time he returned, had made up his mind to give up his law practice and concentrate on music for a year. He approached his senior partner, and as Schwartz recalled, "when I told Schoenfeld what I was planning, he actually thought I was out of my mind. My income as a lawyer in [my] last year of practice was $12,000—and that wasn't hay in 1928."[21] Schoenfeld was not alone in his opinion, as Schwartz admitted, "All my relatives were sure I had gone suddenly quite insane."[22] But to Schwartz, it was a matter of fairness to his clients and Schoenfeld:

2. Early Songwriting

"I was a split personality ... and the company wasn't getting a fair split! I called it 'Schwartzophrenia.'"[23]

His next step was to inform his clients, many of whom had been loyal. Howard Dietz claimed years later, in an unpublished essay titled "Aboard the Band Wagon: A Few Verbal Snapshots from an Album of Long Association with a Popular Composer," that Schwartz wrote the following letter to his personal clients: "Clients often leave lawyers but this time it's vice versa. For years I've had an ambition to become a composer. I can't write tunes and briefs at the same time so I'm giving up the practice of law. I may be making a mistake and if so I'll come crawling back to the office ringing your doorbell on the way. Thanks for past patronage. If I ever write a musical show or any part thereof I'll send you tickets for the opening night."[24] In the same essay, Dietz claimed the tickets were sent, and two clients who attended the show suggested Schwartz go back to the law. This claim and some of the facts may be apocryphal.

The transition from law to music took place over several months and, by early 1929, Schwartz was doing whatever he could in show business. When he left the law, his intention was to be "a writer of show music—not popular music, not film music."[25] He felt it was important to focus his work rather than dabble in various fields of music. Of course, Broadway producers were not exactly chasing him down to be their principal composer, so he wrote what he could when he could. The changeover was not as abrupt as it may have sounded because, as he readily admitted, from at least 1926 on, Schwartz had been splitting time between composing and his law practice—"Schwartzophrenia." Over many years, including his time spent as a rehearsal pianist for *Peggy-Ann*, Schwartz had been schooling himself in musical theater. With his formal education at Columbia University in English, bachelor and masters, he had a strong theater foundation. His masters concentrated on theater, and his thesis was a study of the plays and novels of Irish writer Saint John Greer Ervine.[26] This post-graduate training was designed to prepare him for a career in playwriting, directing, and other aspects of the dramatic stage.[27] He would try his hand at most anything, as long as it was theater-related, including ghostwriting, composing songs and scores, and at times, even functioning as a "show doctor." He worked on amateur productions, vaudeville, tabloid shows, and individual acts.

Tabloid shows were condensed versions of musical comedies that were "sent out on vaudeville circuits and the ideas were stolen directly from the reigning successes of the day." They were "a rather special segment of musical theatre in America from the early 1900s to the 1930s. ... They always carried a line of girls, a chorus line."[28] Produced by tabloid musical companies, these shows were usually performed in movie theaters between screenings of movies and might play several times a day. These tab shows were not satires or burlesques of current musicals but rather honest imitations, not unlike a student painter copying a masterpiece at the Louvre. An occasional one could be considered "a masterpiece of plagiarism."[29] Even the esteemed *Show Boat* was drastically shortened and used briefly as a tab show in 1933.[30]

Schwartz detailed one such tabloid show assignment: "In the year before *The Little Show,* when I was writing lyrics and music for tabloid musical comedies for vaudeville, the producers Sam Shannon (né Rifsky) and Ed Keller, a prominent vaudeville booker, commissioned me to imitate successful Broadway shows such as *Sailor Beware* and *Good News.* Our titles were *Sailor Be Good* and *Glad Tidings.* In the latter there was, of course, the title song 'Glad Tidings' which was a faint carbon copy of 'Good News,' and I also wrote a number 'College Hop' in faithful imitation of 'The Varsity Drag.'" For "Glad Tidings," Schwartz received a fifty-dollar royalty. Of his work on these shows, he admitted to Howard Dietz years later, "I gave up lyric writing when I met you. Up to that time I had written lyrics and music for vaudeville acts which were commissioned by a producing firm in the Palace Theatre—Sam Shannon and Ed Keller. My lyrics were painfully adequate."[31]

After his initiation in *The Grand Street Follies of 1926,* Schwartz continued contributing to shows. For two years, starting in March 1927, Schwartz participated, in varying degrees, as a composer for the following shows[32]:

Show	Opened	City	Performances on Broadway
The New Yorkers	March 10, 1927	New York	52
Good Boy	September 5, 1928	New York	253
Well! Well! Well!	December 10, 1928	New Haven	Closed in New Haven
The Red Robe	December 25, 1928	New York	167
Ned Wayburn's Gambols	January 15, 1929	New York	31
The Little Show	April 30, 1929	New York	321
The Grand Street Follies of 1929	May 1, 1929	New York	93
Wake Up and Dream	December 30, 1929	New York	136

The New Yorkers was a revue that began at the Intimate Playhouse in the Bronx and was originally titled *1928*. It played for only a week with a predominantly amateur cast, then was taken over and supervised by Milton "Doc" Bender who revamped and re-casted it, re-opening at the Intimate on February 19, 1927.[33] On March 10, he brought it to the Edyth Totten Theatre on Broadway. Bender, a close friend of Lorenz Hart, was a dentist by day, a theater denizen by night, and by most accounts, an unsavory character. Steven Suskin claimed, "'Doc' Bender held Machiavellian power over Hart."[34] Bender eventually left his dental practice and became an agent for several well-known Broadway talents, including George Balanchine, Vivienne Segal, and Wynn Murray. Hart's sister-in-law Dorothy knew Bender well, saying, "He would have been very successful indeed had it not been for the arrogance and even vituperativeness his new-found importance brought to the surface."[35]

Probably at Hart's behest, Schwartz was brought into the show to which he and book writer Henry Myers—a friend of Hart from Columbia—contributed nine songs:

A Song About Love	I Can't Get into the Quota
Floating Through the Air	Indian Chant (instrumental)
He Who Gets Slapped	99% Pure
Here Comes the Prince of Wales	Romany
	Self-Expression

The reviews were mixed, with most criticism aimed at its cast. A few weeks into the Broadway run, the show was reworked again, but ran a total of only fifty-two performances. As for the songs, *The New Yorker* critic claimed the show to have "better music and far better lyrics than many shows in town."[36] A few of the Schwartz / Myers efforts were singled out for praise. "Romany" was described as "a lilting tune that is reminiscent of Victor Herbert."[37] Audiences were amused by two of their songs, "99 Per Cent Pure" and "Here Comes the Prince of Wales." *Variety* declared, "Schwartz is a lawyer, but suggests potentialities as a composer."[38] Myers would go on to a career writing short stories, plays, poetry, five novels, and numerous screenplays, but would suffer badly from blacklisting in the fifties.

On a more personal basis, Schwartz began dating cast member Dorothy Daye during the run of *The New Yorkers*.[39] Of all the cast, she was singled out as most talented, particularly her dancing, stage presence, and attractiveness. One reviewer wrote of "a sprite by name Dorothy Daye, who has the charm and skill and youth of Ann Pennington and Marilyn Miller in embryo."[40] Quite stellar company. It would not be the last time the handsome, urbane Schwartz would date a theater beauty.

Schwartz had little to do with *Good Boy*, a revue with numerous interpolations. With longtime Jerome Kern collaborator, Otto Harbach, Schwartz contributed "You're the One," but it was cut before the Broadway opening. One hit emerged from *Good Boy*, "I Wanna Be Loved by You," by principal songwriters Harry Ruby and Bert Kalmar. Sung by Helen Kane, it brought her to fame as the "Boop-Boop-a-Doop Girl."[41] In the 1950 film

Three Little Words, based loosely on the careers of Ruby and Kalmar, Kane dubbed the song for Debbie Reynolds. It was also done on screen by Marilyn Monroe in *Some Like It Hot* in 1959. Kane and her song were enough to give *Good Boy* a run of 253 performances.[42]

Well! Well! Well! was a lesson in futility and humility for Schwartz. The show was a musical version of *Potash and Perlmutter*, a 1913 hit play by Montague Glass and Charles Klein. This had been based on short stories written by Glass. *Well! Well! Well!* held some promise at its onset and toured for ten weeks, although it was constantly changing. Howard Dietz detailed the evolution of the show: "It was a plotty charade … and was bad bad bad. Each day, a little of the plot was eliminated and a new song was interpolated by a new songwriter. By the time the show opened in New York, all the plot had been removed and also all of Schwartz's songs."[43] But the show never did make it to New York, closing in New Haven, Connecticut, during tryouts. To add insult to injury, it was reconfigured as *Pleasure Bound*, opened in New York, and managed 136 performances, still with none of Schwartz's songs.[44] This theater business could be more brutal than a hostile jury.

Schwartz then tried to get a song interpolated into the Shuberts' *The Red Robe*. The show was an adaptation by Broadway's busiest librettist, Harry B. Smith and Edward Delaney Dunn, of a novel by Stanley Weyman, *Under the Red Robe*. Smith wrote most of the songs with composer Jean Gilbert, but interpolations were made by Dunn, J. Keirn Brennan, Mann Holiner, Alberta Nichols, Maurie Rubens, and Robert Stolz. Schwartz did compose one song, "Believe in Me," with principal lyricist Smith.[45] On the Christmas night in 1928 that *The Red Robe* opened, a total of seven shows opened on Broadway. Despite such competition, *The Red Robe* was described as "a very tolerable entertainment of its kind" and managed a run of 167 performances.[46]

Only a month later, Schwartz interpolated two songs into a 1929 revue, *Ned Wayburn's Gambols*. Ned Wayburn had been a dancer and turned to choreography with the 1903 show *The Billionaire*. He was also a staff director for several revue producers including Lew Fields, Florenz Ziegfeld, Jr., and the Shuberts, working in New York, London, and Chicago. Through his own Headline Vaudeville Production Company, he produced his own revues, albeit not on the grand scale of his bosses. In 1915, he signed an exclusive agreement with Florenz Ziegfeld, Jr., as producing director for both the *Midnight Frolics* and the *Follies*.[47]

Between 1919 and 1922, Wayburn and Ziegfeld had a falling out, during which time Wayburn wrote his textbook, *The Art of Stage Dancing*, a codification of dance techniques. He is credited with refining tap dancing as it emerged on Broadway and was also a proponent of rapid pacing of dances and staging. Wayburn refined the chorus line and the ensemble tap dance, codified the vocabulary of choreography, and pioneered geometric choreography used so effectively years later by Busby Berkeley.[48] During these years, Wayburn also helped introduce a new genre to theater, the prolog, described in *Ned Wayburn and the Dance Routine*: "A form of live performance, designed to introduce a feature film and tour with it. Prologs made their appearance just after the war and were produced on contract from film studios."[49] Between 1919 and 1933, Wayburn created prologs for several major studios.

Ned Wayburn's Gambols premiered in Springfield, Massachusetts, in November of 1928 as a prolog for Paramount-Publix.[50] It was produced by Wayburn's own Headline Vaudeville Production Company and was brought to Broadway two months later. Besides lots of dancing, *Gambols* showcased the talent of Libby Holman who used her sultry voice on two audience favorites, "Salt of My Tears" and "Mother o' Men," neither of them by Schwartz.

For his contributions to *Gambols*, Schwartz teamed with writer Morrie Ryskind, whom he had known since 1924, when they would attend Saturday evening "concerts" by George Gershwin at the home of Lou and Emily Paley. These impromptus were remarkable not only for the playing of young George, but for the talented people they attracted, including playwright Marc Connelly, publisher Dick Simon, and songwriters Buddy DeSylva, Vincent Youmans, Yip Harburg, Harold Arlen, and Howard Dietz. Of these get-togethers, Gershwin's sister Frances Godowsky said, "People were drawn as if by magnets. Everybody was interesting, he or she in his own way. Each had something to give."[51] It was around this time that Schwartz had made his way into the Gershwin circle and was asked by George to play some of Schwartz's tunes, although not at one of the impromptus. As Schwartz remembered, "He [Gershwin] was very warm and very encouraging. ... And he gave me the feeling that perhaps I did have some talent and to persevere."[52]

Schwartz and Ryskind contributed two songs to *Ned Wayburn's Gambols*, "Gypsy Days" and "The Sun Will Shine." Steven Suskin said of the latter song, "The totally unknown and unjustly neglected 'The Sun Will Shine' was the first of Schwartz's beautiful ballads."[53] Historian of the revue, Lee Davis, explained that the two Schwartz / Ryskind interpolations were used "for production numbers that utilized, in the fashion of the time, either elaborate costumes or no costumes ('Two nearly nude gentlemen tossed a nearly nude lady back and forth in the air for several minutes,' observed one critic)."[54] The show ran only thirty-one performances.

Wayburn went on to produce numerous prologs and did his last editions of the *Ziegfeld Follies* in 1922 and 1923. Morrie Ryskind went on to fame as a book writer for George and Ira Gershwin for *Strike Up the Band*, *Of Thee I Sing*, *Pardon My English*, and *Let 'Em Eat Cake*. He and George S.

Kaufman won the Pulitzer Prize for Drama in 1932 for *Of Thee I Sing*. It was the first time the Drama Pulitzer was given to a musical. Interestingly, Ryskind had worked with Howard Dietz two years before Schwartz ever did, contributing lyrics along with Dietz to the show *Merry-Go-Round* in 1927.

Schwartz and Ryskind would work together again in 1934, writing an incidental song, "Down on the Old-Time Farm," for *Bring On the Girls*. This was a comedy written by Ryskind and George S. Kaufman, produced by Sam H. Harris, and starring Jack Benny, who is featured on the sheet music cover.[55] From the title, one would have thought that the show would be filled with music and beautiful chorus girls. But as they told the press, Kaufman and Ryskind "never had any intention of making this play a musical and were baffled by the public's confusion."[56] The Schwartz / Ryskind song was "a parody of badly dated vaudeville numbers."[57] Neither the song nor the show caught on with audiences, and *Bring on the Girls* closed during tryouts in Washington, D.C.

Dietz had become friends with Libby Holman and when *Gambols* closed in February 1929, he arranged for her to do a three-week singing engagement at a drab honky-tonk, the Monsignor, on West 47th Street. As her accompanist, he suggested his friend, Arthur Schwartz, a former lawyer and tyro composer. Since both were unemployed, Holman and Schwartz were enthusiastic and rehearsed at length. But their act was not to the liking of the crowd at the Monsignor. They were dismissed summarily, turning Holman livid, and causing her to throw her meager wages back at the club's manager. She added, "You god-damned gorilla, go out and buy yourself a stripper."[58] Shortly, Holman, Schwartz, and Dietz would work together under the much happier and more appreciated setting of *The Little Show*, which would open April 30, 1929.

At about the time Schwartz and Dietz started on *The Little Show*, Schwartz was writing for *The Grand Street Follies of 1929*. Agnes Morgan was still doing it all—director, sketch writer, lyricist, and performer—and the cast still included Albert Carroll. Like 1928, the 1929 cast included Paula Trueman and James Cagney. Sharing composing duties with Schwartz was Max Ewing, although each man did his own songs. Schwartz wrote several, including[59]:

Song	*Lyricist*	*Song*	*Lyricist*
The ABC of Traffic	Instrumental / sketch	Age of Innocence	Instrumental / dance
The Amoeba's Lament	Instrumental / sketch	Don't Do It	Agnes Morgan
The Double Standard	Agnes Morgan	I Love You and I Like You	Max and Nathaniel Lief

Song	Lyricist	Song	Lyricist
I Need You So	Howard Dietz and David Goldberg	The Jolly Troubador	Sketch / instrumental
My Dynamo	Agnes Morgan	The Vineyards of Manhattan	Sketch / instrumental
What Did Della Wear (When Georgie Came Across?)	Agnes Morgan and Albert Carroll		

By then, *The Grand Street Follies* had moved uptown to the Booth Theatre. Like the previous editions, the 1929 version was well-received, running ninety-three performances. No Schwartz song had any life after the show, but composing these songs, including instrumentals, was good experience. One song of his popular with audiences was "What Did Della Wear (When Georgie Came Across?)," sung by lyricist Albert Carroll impersonating Fanny Brice.[60]

As 1929 was drawing to a close, Schwartz and Dietz worked on songs for *Ripples*, a Charles Dillingham production. This was a showcase for the Stone family, Fred and Mrs. Stone and their daughters, Dorothy and Paula. It was much anticipated as comedian Stone was returning from serious injuries he had suffered in the preceding year. Principal composers were Oscar Levant and Albert Sirmay and lyricists were Irving Caesar and Graham John. Other interpolators were Jerome Kern and J. Fred Coots. None of the Schwartz / Dietz songs made it to the Broadway edition of *Ripples*, and the show lasted only fifty-five performances.[61]

More importantly in December 1929, Cole Porter's revue *Wake Up and Dream* opened on Broadway. The show had premiered in March in London as *Charles B. Cochran's 1929 Revue* and had a run of 263 performances. Jessie Matthews was the star of the show on both sides of the Atlantic. Porter's career was hitting its stride, and British audiences fell in love with "What Is This Thing Called Love?" and "Let's Do It." Two performers— multi-talented Jack Buchanan and choreographer / dancer Tilly Losch— were involved in both the London and New York versions of *Wake Up and Dream*. They would later play important roles in Schwartz shows.

As for Schwartz, he was able to interpolate one song into the Broadway version of *Wake Up and Dream*—"She's Such a Comfort to Me"— borrowed from an earlier 1929 London show, *The House That Jack Built*. Lyricists for this number included Douglas Furber, Donovan Parsons, and Max and Nathaniel Lief. In New York, *Wake Up and Dream* ran for 136 performances, and for Schwartz, having a song included in a Cole Porter show was another feather in his cap.[62]

3

Howard Dietz

> "Coming into contact with Dietz's brilliant versification and wit, Schwartz knew he had found the man with whom he wanted to work."[1]

From the mid-twenties on, Arthur Schwartz felt he needed a steady lyricist. He wanted one who was talented, educated, clever, and committed to doing theater—a Lorenz Hart. Unfortunately, Hart was already partnered with Richard Rodgers. In 1924, Schwartz made an attempt to collaborate with Howard Dietz, a newcomer to lyric writing. Dietz's first hit of any kind had been an interpolation into the show *Poppy* in 1923. The song was "Alibi Baby," and the composer was Arthur Samuels.[2]

What most attracted Schwartz to Dietz were his frequent entries in *The Conning Tower*. This was Franklin P. Adams' column in the *New York World* that included poems, one-liners, anecdotes, and brief commentaries from contributing readers. It has been called "the cradle of American lyricists."[3] The contributors were many: humorists Marc Connelly, Dorothy Parker, Morrie Ryskind, James Thurber, Louis Untermeyer, and E.B. White; lyricists Ira Gershwin, E.Y. Harburg, Lorenz Hart, and Albert Stillman; and playwrights George S. Kaufman, Newman Levy, Herman J. Mankiewicz, and Nate Salisbury.[4] Schwartz would explain years later that not all of the "poets" contributing to *The Conning Tower* could do what Dietz could: "VERSE writing is another matter. The many contributors to FPA just couldn't write lyrics. Newman Levy, George Macy are examples. You are the real exception."[5]

Wit and cleverness were valued in Adams' choices for *The Conning Tower*, and Dietz, writing as "Freckles," caught Schwartz's attention. Thinking he might have found his lyricist, Schwartz made a plea to Dietz in a letter in early 1924:

> This is what's on my chest: I'd love to work with you on songs for the Neighborhood Playhouse annual show, the *Grand Street Follies*. I am developing contacts which are, I think, going to lead to something worthwhile. As I told Beans [Bennett Cerf], I think

you are the only man in town to be compared to Larry Hart, and from me that's quite a tribute, because I know almost every line Larry has written. I think that three or four tunes of mine will be riots in the *Grand Street Follies* this year IF they have lyrics such as only Larry and you can write. Don't be too amused at the fact that I speak of tune-writing under a lawyer's letterhead. I'm giving up the law in a few months to spend all my time at music.[6]

Schwartz was not to give up the law until 1928, as it was not financially feasible, and because of the counsel of Lorenz Hart, who felt Schwartz was not ready. But from the above letter it is clear that the young lawyer had more on his mind than the law. However, it was a moot point as Dietz declined politely, stating that he had already written his first show with an established composer and suggested Schwartz do the same. Dietz closed, "In that way, we will both benefit by the reputation of our collaborators, then when we both get famous, we can collaborate with each other. It's nice to hear from you."[7]

The established composer to whom Dietz referred was Jerome Kern, who had also taken notice of Dietz's contributions to *The Conning Tower*. In early 1924, Kern, at the suggestion of Max Dreyfus, asked Dietz to contribute lyrics for Kern's latest show, *Dear Sir*. Music publisher and Kern associate Dreyfus had been trying to pair Kern with younger lyricists, having teamed him first with Buddy DeSylva for *Zip, Goes a Million* in 1919. Despite closing in out-of-town tryouts, the show included the Kern/DeSylva hit "Look for the Silver Lining."[8] In 1923, Dreyfus had put Kern and Noel Coward together. Songs that emerged from their brief union include "Tamarind," "If You Will Be My Morganatic Wife," and an early version of the song "Where's the Mate for Me?" later to be included in *Show Boat*, with Oscar Hammerstein II lyrics. No show came of the Kern/Coward union.[9]

As an audition for *Dear Sir*, Dietz was given a sheaf of melodies, worked on them for a week, and presented lyrics for a dozen or more songs to Kern. The composer took a liking to several of them, especially "My Houseboat on the Harlem" and "If We Could Only Lead a Merry Mormon Life." The latter was a reworking of the Kern/Coward song mentioned above, "If You Will Be My Morganatic Wife." Kern took Dietz on for *Dear Sir*, but the show closed after two weeks; they never collaborated again.[10] In 1927, Dietz worked with Jay Gorney and Morrie Ryskind on *Merry-Go-Round*, which ran much longer than *Dear Sir* and again brought attention to Dietz from Arthur Schwartz.

There are various times and scenarios as to when and how Schwartz and Dietz finally teamed up. One version, by biographer David Ewen, focuses on 1927, about the time of *Merry-Go-Round*: "Coming into contact with Dietz's brilliant versification and wit, Schwartz knew he had found the man with whom he wanted to work on a permanent basis. He badgered Dietz until the latter finally agreed to write lyrics to his music."[11] This would seem reasonable since both men were involved in the theater and had many mutual friends, including Dietz's Columbia classmate Lorenz Hart. The time was plausible for their joining up.

What time seems more probable is 1928, when Schwartz decided to give up his law practice and concentrate on music. The names of Schwartz and Dietz on a song or in a program were first to appear in April 1929 in *The Little Show*; they started work on that revue in the latter months of 1928. When exactly the two men joined forces is not nearly as important as the fact that they *did*. Schwartz would tell an interviewer in 1934 that his biggest thrill in the music business was the day he teamed with Dietz and "decided that he had discovered at last the man who could write the words to his songs much better than he."[12]

Dietz had a way with words, yet he tried to keep his lyrics simple. Looking back on his career and lyric writing, he explained in his autobiographical *Dancing in the Dark*: "The best lyric writers are the ones who write the most singable words. They need not be fancy words ... but words you can lean on, which is to say solid substantial words you can put your teeth into."[13] In *Lyrics on Several Occasions*, Ira Gershwin summed up the qualities of a good lyricist: "A fondness for music, a feeling for rhyme, a sense of whimsy and humor, an eye for the balanced sentence, an ear for the current phrase."[14] In program notes for *At Home Abroad* in 1935, Schwartz echoed Gershwin's thoughts, delineating his concept of the ideal collaborator: "a slightly mad sense of humor, a reasonably poetic spirit, a bottomless well of crisp ideas."[15]

Howard Dietz was perfect for the job and possessed the traits that Schwartz described. He had a "slightly mad sense of humor" which stood out, even in the theater crowd. He could be the funniest man in the room and held his own at the Round Table of the Algonquin Hotel. However, he did admit that at first, things did not go well with that group: "Although I rubbed elbows with the famous wits and playwrights, they didn't rub elbows with me. I was regarded as a publicity man, not as a creative artist. It was a frustrating relationship."[16] Eventually, he was a regular visitor at the Algonquin. An anecdote illustrating his mad sense of humor emerged during Dietz's college days. Students in the Columbia School of Journalism were given the assignment to write a brief, sensational, but fictional headline. Dietz topped them all with "Pope Elopes."[17]

A "poetic spirit" came through in his lyrics, particularly ballads. Schwartz commented years later, "His depth made 'Dancing in the Dark' one of the most poignant lyrics of our time."[18] Gene Lees, Canadian critic, biographer, and himself a lyricist, said of Dietz and his poetic talent: "He has maintained a dazzling quality in the use of language, particularly rhyme.... And yet, for all the strictures imposed by our language, Dietz never seems constrained in either imagination or diction. It is this quality of ease, of beauty or cleverness attained effortlessly, that makes his lyrics a perfect match for Schwartz's music."[19]

As for a "bottomless well of crisp ideas," it was Dietz who had numerous inclusions in the humorous columns of Franklin P. Adams' *The Conning Tower* and Don Marquis' *Sun Dial* in the *New York Sun*. All this had started during his undergraduate days and continued for years.

Dietz was born in lower Manhattan on September 8, 1896. He was a street kid and never happy with his father, but he and his four siblings were close to their mother. Dietz attended public schools and at age fifteen, worked as a copyboy for the *New York American*, and entered Columbia University in 1913. He became an advertising copywriter at the Philip Goodman Company after winning a $500 prize for the best entry in an ad contest sponsored by Fatima cigarettes.[20] His work in the advertising world prompted his dropping out of Columbia in his third year because, despite his facility with the English language, he was not much of a student. Dietz took a leave from the ad world to serve in the Navy in World War I, and although not combat material, became editor of *Navy Life*.[21]

Dietz parlayed his early success in copywriting into a career in the burgeoning motion picture industry. One of his first assignments was the account of Goldwyn Pictures Corporation, a new company that needed a trademark. Inspired by the mascot of Columbia University—the Columbia Lion—Dietz created Leo the Lion, which to this day roars at the opening of productions of M-G-M Studios, successor to Goldwyn Pictures. In addition to Leo, Dietz also created a classical slogan for Goldwyn, "Ars Gratia Artis"—"art for the sake of art"—which is also used to the present day.[22] Dietz broadened his advertising assignment at Goldwyn into a position with the company, working in publicity. When he left Goldwyn to work for M-G-M, he took Leo the Lion and the slogan with him.

By the time he and Dietz joined forces, Schwartz had freed himself from his "second" job, the law, but Dietz continued to lead a life as both publicist and lyricist. Dietz admitted, "Holding two jobs, what is now called moonlighting, was to become my way of life."[23] This double life would evolve as he became an executive in the motion picture industry, requiring him to be bi-coastal. But as of 1928, they were a new team and facing their first assignment in New York City. Historian Benny Green summarized the basis of the partnership and offered a possible explanation for their future success: "Rarely could two more compatible partners have ever found each other than Schwartz and Dietz, who were products of the same university in the same town in the same epoch, and who shared the same social and ethnic backgrounds, the same experience of the popular arts, and more or less identical views as to what might or might not divert the average musical comedy audience."[24]

With a new songwriting team in town, Broadway was in for a change.

4

The Little Show and "I Guess I'll Have to Change My Plan"

"There was a movement, with Schwartz at the vanguard, toward intimate revues."[1]

For many Broadway observers, the revue form had peaked in the mid-twenties. Emerging in the early twentieth century, revues had evolved from burlesque and vaudeville. Burlesque placed an emphasis on comedy and skits satirizing the events and personalities of the day, and vaudeville relied more on individual entertainers and acts. For a few decades, burlesque and vaudeville had shared the attention of audiences, but neither was ever presented in a Broadway theater. Each form had its own separate venues. The highest quality vaudeville was offered at the Palace on Times Square. As the two genres faded, Broadway revues took over. They offered satire, skits, and featured performers, and attempts were made to unify the material and place greater emphasis on songs.

Although hints of the revue form go back to the mid–nineteenth century, the first production to use the term "revue" in its description was *The Passing Show* in 1894. This revue was unrelated to *The Passing Shows* done two decades later by the Shubert brothers. Jonas Westover, in his biography of the Shuberts, described that "first" revue: "The show combined timely references with spectacular scenery and a parade of young chorus girls, and many of the songs made mention of other shows or events. The name 'passing show' referred to the dizzying movement of the world paraded before the eyes of anyone in a fixed position, an excellent title choice for a show that used seemingly unrelated events that moved on and off a stage. The popularity of *The Passing Show* was enough to spawn imitators, and in doing so, the revue found its theatrical footing."[2] Over the next several years, the "imitators" would include Joe Weber and Lew Fields, Florenz Ziegfeld, the Shuberts, George White, Earl Carroll, and others.

Revues were described as "shows more sophisticated and structured than vaudeville without the cohesive 'book' of an operetta or musical comedy."[3] From approximately 1910, they had attracted increasingly more theater-savvy audiences. But as the genre persisted on Broadway, revue creators often fell back on tried-and-true, albeit stale formulas which were wearing thin on audiences. Many revues had devolved into what New York critic George Jean Nathan referred to as "a second-rate, old-time vaudeville show."[4] Lorenz Hart "had become wary of revues consisting of numbers by several writers, even if some terrific songs had come out of these revues."[5] By the late twenties, the consensus of the theatrical crowd was that it was time to move on.

Arthur Schwartz and Howard Dietz did not hold this view. They took their cues from Londoner C.B. Cochran and Frenchman André Charlot, two producers who had popularized the intimate revue in London. The latter man had started in Paris, managing theaters including the Folies Bergère and the Palais-Royal, but had relocated to London in 1912. In following Cochran and Charlot, Schwartz and Dietz ushered in a period of American revues that were intimate and sophisticated: "Dietz called it 'high class vaudeville.' …when Dietz and Schwartz applied their minds to it they wittily superseded the elephantine entertainments against which they were reacting—the *Follies* of Ziegfeld, the *Scandals* of George White, the *Vanities* of Earl Carroll—with light, sleek, elegant, mocking songs and sketches."[6]

But Schwartz and Dietz did not reinvent the revue on their own. It would take a creation called *The Little Show*. In late 1928, producer Tom Weatherly and partner James Pond had been presenting small shows—*Divertissements*—on Sunday evenings at the Selwyn Theatre. In Weatherly's own words: "They were really nothing more than high-class vaudeville shows, but they were far more artistic than the Sunday night variety programs then being offered at the Winter Garden. They became so successful that I was convinced there would be an audience for a really smart and sophisticated revue."[7] His mention of Winter Garden shows referred to the more lavish, garish revues produced by the Shuberts. Schwartz happened upon Weatherly and mentioned that he had written several melodies; hearing them, Weatherly was impressed.[8] He explained to Schwartz that he and Pond wanted to expand their *Divertissements* into something larger, smarter, and more sophisticated and thought perhaps Schwartz could contribute. He, in turn, wanted Howard Dietz to get involved, an idea agreeable to the producers.

To hear Dietz tell the story, he brought the creative team together. Weatherly initially asked Dietz to do the lyrics, guaranteeing him $100 per week against ½ percent of the gross. Dietz then showed Weatherly and another producer, Dwight Deere Wiman, the letter he had received from Schwartz a few years back, asking to collaborate with Dietz. Dietz suggested they hire Schwartz, an unemployed composer; the producers agreed, and the team was set.⁹ Another account had Dietz overhearing Wiman and Weatherly at a speakeasy in the West Forties. He advised them to not do the new show, but they informed him that they had already signed Clifton Webb, Fred Allen, and Libby Holman. With this information and a few more drinks, Dietz agreed to do join the effort, suggesting Schwartz as composer.¹⁰

Whichever account is correct, Schwartz and Dietz began work on *The Little Show*, collaborating in the evening as Dietz had his daytime job at M-G-M. They found their best working environment to be hotel rooms, an arrangement which Dietz elaborated on in his 1974 autobiography, *Dancing in the Dark*:

> To suggest where our scores were written would sound like a guide to the hostelries of Manhattan. "Hostileries" would be more like it.... Working into the night, the sound of the piano, however muted, endlessly repeating the same strain, penetrated the walls to an unwilling audience. We worked on borrowed time waiting for the manager to knock on the door. We became wandering minstrels, moving from room to room, hotel to hotel.... "They don't like what I'm playing," said Arthur sadly. "That must be it," I replied. "They never complain about the lyrics."¹¹

In such a manner was *The Little Show* born and "cut the pattern for the intimate revue."¹² It was given its adjective "little" because the eventual cast was only twenty-nine in number, little by any Broadway measure of that period.

Although Dietz and the producers may not have been aware of it at the beginning of their work on *The Little Show*, Schwartz was being lured to Tinseltown. He admitted to Dietz years later:

> During the first week of my first collaboration with you, Jack Robbins, whose office I was also haunting, called me very late one night saying, "Pack your bags. You're going to MGM tomorrow afternoon along with six other writers. Your salary will be $250.00 for three months. If your option is picked up, it will be $500.00 and there are further options at higher salaries. This is what you've been waiting for." In spite of the certainty of income and a probable Hollywood career, I turned down this offer because I felt (a) the beginning of a collaboration with you would do me more good in the long run and (b) *The Little Show*, even in its formative stages, sounded good. I wanted the stage and not the picture business at that time.¹³

Jack Robbins was head of Robbins Music Corporation, a well-known music publisher, in New York and Hollywood. In 1934–35, M-G-M would acquire Robbins Music, Leo Feist, Inc., and Miller Music Publishing Company and consolidate them into Robbins, Feist, Miller Music Company, becoming the premier publisher in Hollywood. Robbins knew there would be plenty of work in Hollywood and, recognizing the talent of Schwartz, tried to lure him out West. However, the young composer stayed true to Dietz and their mission.

As *The Little Show* was a revue, it would involve song interpolations from several songwriters. Still, Weatherly was relying on the new partnership of Schwartz and Dietz for many of the songs. Among the first ones they completed was "Hammacher Schlemmer, I Love You," a send-up of movie title songs that always ended in "I Love You," no matter what. Dietz said, "It was a burlesque of the movie theme songs that were cluttering the air waves at the moment and making the air difficult to breathe."[14] He would later add, "It was the kind of number that didn't belong in musical comedy but was suitable for a revue."[15] The song was eventually cut from *The Little Show*, but it got the Schwartz and Dietz partnership off to a good start. Hammacher Schlemmer, the hardware company of the title, was pleased with the song and that Christmas, sent the duo a box of tools and a card reading, "Dietz and Schwartz, we love you." Years later, the company used the song in a commercial.[16]

In all, the new team wrote seven songs for *The Little Show*:

Get Up on a New Routine	I've Made a Habit of You
Hammacher Schlemmer, I Love You	Little Old New York
	Man About Town
I Guess I'll Have to Change My Plan	The Theme Song

Of all these songs, only "I Guess I'll Have to Change My Plan" would make its mark as one of America's best popular songs, and it deserves discussion. The melody had originated years before in a Brant Lake Camp show with a lighthearted lyric by Lorenz Hart, "I Love to Lie Awake in Bed." Although it never advanced beyond that camp, Schwartz said that it was "the first melody that I felt was any good at all."[17] He brought it out of his trunk for the star of *The Little Show*, Clifton Webb. Dietz explained, "He wanted a number that was more perverse, a number he could deliver all alone in a full-dress suit and a spotlight ... a lyric with suave romantic frustration."[18] He added, "Clifton Webb needed a lyric which had more bite and sophistication. He wanted a song that was tinged with acid."[19]

Dietz liked the melody but had to rework the lyric entirely, explaining, "I made it into a song about a different kind of bed, which sang of blue pajamas and forbidden fruit, comparatively poisonous."[20] It became a high point in the show for the debonair Webb, who sang it in white tie, top hat, and tails. The "suave romantic frustration" came across, and the song gripped "the listener with its juxtaposition of lighthearted music and downhearted lyric."[21]

As detailed in *America's Songs* by Philip Furia and Michael Lasser: "The opening words, 'I guess,' capture disappointment with a stoical, urban shrug as the key word, 'guess,' falls on the downbeat and registers the singer's frustration at learning the woman who has caught his eye is married. … Schwartz's melody thus went from a wholesome camp song to a sophisticated, salacious meditation."[22] Dietz was able to take a song with original

Sheet music cover for "I Guess I'll Have to Change My Plan," from *The Little Show* in 1929, the first production with Arthur Schwartz and Howard Dietz as a songwriting team. The song, their first hit, was often called "The Blue Pajama Song." Dietz had reworked the lyric from the original one by Lorenz Hart written at Brant Lake Camp in 1924, "I Love to Lie Awake in Bed." The Schwartz melody remained the same (courtesy Wisconsin Historical Society. WHi-142386).

lyrics reflecting "high jinks at a Boys' Camp" and make it an integral part of a Broadway revue: "Dietz had switched the approach of the words from the particular to the general, which is of course the first requisite for any song aspiring to a life beyond theatre walls."[23] This was not the last Schwartz melody that would assume two different forms on the circuitous route to becoming a hit.

Although popular in the show, "I Guess I'll Have to Change My Plan" did not become an immediate hit. As Dietz put it, "We thought it was lost in that Sargasso Sea of songs that have popular quality but no popular success. It seemed to have made the Flop Parade."[24] The song attracted more listeners in Europe and especially England, where the Prince of Wales repeatedly requested the song.[25] Three years after *The Little Show* opened, Schwartz heard the song in a British night club act of a cabaret duo, De Lys and Carter. They referred to the tune as "The Blue Pyjama Song," a direct reference to one of Dietz's lyrics. Schwartz related the club encounter in his appearance at the *Lyrics and Lyricists* series in 1978:

> The first time I heard that song in a night club, the singer came to my table and said: "Wait till you hear this next number—it's great." I asked: "Who wrote it?" He said: "I don't know—someone like Noel Coward." When the song was over, he asked me how I liked it. I said: "It's the best song someone like Noel Coward ever wrote."[26]

Fred Astaire sang "I Guess I'll Have to Change My Plan" in *The Band Wagon*, the 1953 movie derived partly from the Schwartz / Dietz revue *The Band Wagon*, but which included a great many of their other songs. Astaire sang it as a duet with Jack Buchanan, two debonair performers like Webb. Frank Sinatra, on his 1957 album *A Swingin' Affair*, put a good swing into it. Owing to these two stellar performances, "I Guess I'll Have to Change My Plan" became a perennial hit for Schwartz and Dietz.[27] Schwartz recorded it in 1976, an RCA album titled *from the pen of ... Arthur Schwartz*, eliciting these comments in a *Los Angeles Times* article: "The voice on the record sounds something like Fred Astaire, light and wary, and when you mention it the owner is delighted, because to tell the truth he was imitating Fred there, who always did do that song better than anybody. Glad it came through!"[28]

Besides writing their own songs, there was more work for Schwartz and Dietz in *The Little Show*. The composer worked with three other lyricists on song interpolations. With Henry Myers, his partner from *The New Yorkers* in 1927, Schwartz wrote "What Every Little Girl Should Know." He was also the composer with Lew Levenson on "Song of the Riveter" and with Harry Ruskin on "High Finance." Years later, when asked what his greatest thrill in the music business had been, Schwartz pointed to opening night of *The Little Show*, "when his 'Song of the Riveter' established him as a man who could make money in song writing."[29]

4. The Little Show *and* "I Guess I'll Have to Change My Plan" 39

Dietz ended up writing words to the show's biggest hit, "Moanin' Low." Schwartz had been having trouble coming up with a song for the star, Libby Holman, a singer who could deliver a torch piece. There were two pianists in the pit orchestra—Ralph Rainger and Adam Carroll—and Dietz, hearing Rainger improvising on a melody at a rehearsal, cornered the young composer. Within a short time, Dietz and Rainger completed "Moanin' Low."[30] Danced by Clifton Webb and sung by Holman, it was a showstopper. She sang another audience favorite of the evening, "Can't We Be Friends?," by Kay Swift and her husband, Paul James, better known as banker James Paul Warburg.

The two Holman hits, along with "I Guess I'll Have to Change My Plan" and several lesser songs, gave *The Little Show* musical credibility seldom seen in the revue genre. Gerald Bordman said of the score, "All the songs have a certain introverted quality as opposed to the more brash, gusty, or pontifical songs so dear to the huge annuals."[31] The producers wanted to publish them but were new in this arena. They turned to Dietz and Schwartz, the latter recalling, "You may not recall this but Wiman and Waverly [*sic*] did not know anything about publishers and asked our advice since we were musical editors as well as contributors. In spite of my resentment at Dreyfus, I recommended that they publish with him. In fact, I called Dreyfus myself and brought the show to him."[32] Dreyfus agreed to publish the songs. For Schwartz, finally an encounter with Max Dreyfus—he of the critical ear—ending with a good result.

The Little Show opened in Asbury Park, but Schwartz and Dietz missed the opening because of train delays. The performance did not go well, and by the time the composers arrived, they were facing a pessimistic Clifton Webb and despondent producers. They had decided to close the show by week's end and told the songwriters to go back home.[33] But audiences could be fickle and what might be jeered one night could bring loud applause the next—especially during tryouts. New at this, Schwartz and Dietz insisted on staying for the next evening's performance. The atmosphere of the following night's performance was a 180-degree turnaround, and the half-empty house was enthusiastic. "Hammacher Schlemmer, I Love You" and "Moanin' Low" stood out that evening, and Libby Holman stole the show with a dramatic "Can't We Be Friends," sung in front of the curtain. The previously disconsolate Weatherly declared, "All I can say is that what was a flop last night looks like a hit tonight." Schwartz added, "That's all you're allowed to say."[34] The remainder of the tryout run continued successfully.

With Libby Holman, Clifton Webb, and Fred Allen headlining the cast, *The Little Show* took another step away from the old revue form. Beyond the intimacy and sophistication, this newer revue relied on a talented cast that could do it all—sing, dance, and act—as well as project a stage presence and attractiveness. Gone were the specialty acts of vaudeville and burlesque. Gone were the performers insisting that they be allowed to perform their individual song, no matter how irrelevant to the show. These practices had made it difficult for the book writers of musical comedies in the early days of that genre.

Now, a performer might sing a duet in one scene and in the next, be asked to dance in front of a chorus. In *Sing for Your Supper*, his analysis of the Broadway musical in the thirties, Ethan Mordden explained the importance of *The Little Show* in this evolution: "What the new approach introduced was a complete integration of talent, so that the specialty stylists were dropped in favor of versatile performers. Intimate revue doesn't like impressionists who make no other contact with the audience.... Before *The Little Show*, revues were assemblies of performing spots, bridging them with some interaction among cast members but too often observing the limits of vaudeville: a sequence of independent acts."[35] These newer revues were to rely heavily on these "versatile" principal performers, and the composers would write to their talent. The producers of *The Little Show* discovered soon enough that their new formula had to be trusted as *The Second Little Show*, ignoring its roots, faltered. More on this show later.

With these three stars plus a parcel of good songs, *The Little Show* moved on to New York at the Music Box Theatre on April 30, 1929. Weatherly was joined by Dwight Deere Wiman and William A. Brady, Jr., in producing it. The critics were nearly unanimous in their raves. *The Little Show* ran for 321 performances and created "a vogue for sophisticated revues on Broadway."[36] It put Ziegfeld, the Shuberts, and the other producers of lavish revues on notice that there had been a sea change on Broadway, "a movement, with Schwartz at the vanguard, toward intimate revues."[37]

5

The London Shows

"Mr. Schwartz's music always comes to the rescue of an otherwise uninspired piece."[1]

When word of the success of *The Little Show* reached England, interest was shown in its young composer, Arthur Schwartz: "There is, unless I'm greatly mistaken, a marked tendency on the part of musical and theatrical London to 'take him up.' ... They tell me that the American Mr. Schwartz is an oncoming composer, and perhaps there's reason aplenty for such belief ... [*The Little Show*] gave him his start, as they say in show circles, and London is pushing him along."[2]

But finding work in England could still be difficult. Schwartz had been in touch with producer Julian Wylie but could not get a commitment from him. Schwartz had a book for a musical he thought perfect for the London stage. His account of what then happened was told to Howard Dietz years later: "My first complete score was not written in America at all.... Without letting him [Wylie] know, I took the next boat to England with a book written by Edgar McGregor [sic], *Here Comes the Bride*. When I turned up at his office in London, he was baffled. 'I thought I told you not to come over.' I explained I came over on a pure gamble with a book I thought he would like."[3] Wylie was impressed by Schwartz's effort and initiative, and more importantly, he liked the script the young man was proposing.[4] Schwartz had actually brought Wylie three, but the one that had been of most interest to the producer had been *Here Comes the Bride*, subtitled *A Modern Musical Comedy in Two Acts*.[5] The book had been written by R.P. Weston and Bert Lee, adapted from a play by MacGregor and Otto Harbach. This would be Schwartz's first opportunity to be the sole composer for a show— no interpolators. However, he would be without Dietz as his work as a publicist was keeping him in the States.

The lyricist with whom Schwartz was teamed in London was Desmond Carter, regarded by George Gershwin as "a promising young lyricist." The Gershwins frequently used Carter when they would move a show to London and the lyrics "required a certain localizing of the rhymes."[6] John Murray Anderson believed, "He [Carter] was comparable to the late W.S. Gilbert, with an up to the minute point of view and certain qualities of America's own Larry Hart."[7] Carter's lyrics had been heard in several London productions including the Gershwins' *Lady, Be Good!* and *Tell Me More!*, Jerome Kern's *Sunny*, and Vernon Duke's *The Yellow Mask*. Carter was principal lyricist with Ira Gershwin for *Primrose*, the 1924 Gershwin London hit.[8] Lew Fields employed Carter when Fields moved *Peggy-Ann*, the Rodgers and Hart musical, to London. Carter was friends with Hart and for *Peggy-Ann*, had changed Hart's "A Little Birdie Told Me So" into "Country Mouse."[9] Although he had worked on over thirty musicals in London, Carter was little known in America. When not involved directly with a show, he was a staff lyricist for the London office of Chappell, headed by Louis Dreyfus, the firm that published much of Broadway's best material. Carter would be the last lyricist George Gershwin would work with before George and Ira teamed up exclusively. Carter died in 1939 at age 43.

Here Comes the Bride opened in London in February 1930. Schwartz wrote twelve songs that were used in the show[10]:

Bang! There Goes My Heart	I'm Like a Sailor
Congratulations	Impossible Men
High and Low	No One to Blame but You
Hot	Nothing
I Love You and I Like You	A Rose in My Hair
I'll Always Remember	Why Not Have a Little Party?

Desmond Carter was the principal lyricist, but Howard Dietz, Lew Levinson, and Max and Nathaniel Lief also contributed. The two songs that stood out were "I'll Always Remember," a ballad for Jean Colin, and "High and Low," "a warmly swinging duet" for Ms. Colin and Clifford Mollison.[11] Both songs were reprised. "High and Low" went on to achieve minor hit status and was given a few recordings. It was used a year later in *The Band Wagon*. The *London Daily Mail*, after singling out Schwartz for "three excellent musical numbers," added that "everyone will be humming 'High and Low.'"[12]

One critic confessed, "The music by Mr. Arthur Schwartz did not delight my ear, but it acts powerfully as a foot-loosener," which was fortunate, as the star, Clifford Mollison, "can always score with his footwork when there is nothing else to be done."[13] The supporting cast, dancers Vera Bryer and Richard Dolman, were featured in "two routinely dance-y duos,"[14] "I Love You and I Like You" and "I'm Like a Sailor." Over the years, Schwartz became adept at writing instrumental dance numbers.

5. The London Shows

The *New York Herald Tribune*, in a synopsis of the London theater season and potential shows for New York, credited Schwartz with carrying *Here Comes the Bride*: "The book is conventional and the dances are staged with little imagination, but Mr. Schwartz's music always comes to the rescue of an otherwise uninspired piece."[15] Whoever was responsible for its success, *Here Comes the Bride* managed a run of 175 performances but was not taken to New York.

A sidelight to Schwartz's London visit emerged in an interview in the *London Daily Chronicle* about a month after *Here Comes the Bride* opened. Himself an impeccable, fashionable dresser, Schwartz engaged in a discussion with the reporter regarding the recent change in women's fashions and its effect on song composing:

> Women's long trailing evening frocks are altering the whole character of popular dance music. When long skirts returned to fashion, women found that they made dancing to the fast, quick rhythms of what we call "hot jazz" very difficult. Knee length dresses gave women freedom on the dance floor, but these trailing skirts hamper movement.
>
> So in America composers are completely revolutionizing their style of composition. For some time there has been a tendency to return to more melodic tunes, and now dance numbers are much slower, quieter, more easy flowing and graceful. This is definitely due to the influence of women's fashions.
>
> If the present fashion continues, it will probably lead to dance bands ceasing to feature the saxophone, and bringing back the wood winds and string instruments.[16]

In the interview, Schwartz did not explain if this change in fashion had affected his recent compositions.

Less than two months after *Here Comes the Bride* opened, Schwartz songs were heard in another London production, *The Co-Optimists of 1930*. The *Co-Optimist* series had begun in 1921 as a simpler alternative to the dominance of the revues of C.B. Cochran and André Charlot. In some ways, these were a London version of the *Grand Street Follies*. Robert Baral explained, "Basically, economics figured as a major cause of this marked change in London revues—the Cochran-Charlot fashion was too expensive to operate. Everything had to be done on a cheaper scale."[17] The initial *Co-Optimist* offering in 1921 ran 500 performances, and the series developed into a nearly annual occurrence, becoming somewhat of a "National Institution." Starting in 1921, featured players, known as "Co-ops," included David Burnaby, Phyllis Monkman, Elsa MacFarlane, Gilbert Childs, Melville Gideon, and Stanley Holloway, long before *My Fair Lady*. A few of the cast were involved in the entire ten-year run.[18]

Co-Optimist presentations relied on a much smaller cast: "*Co-Optimists* had no chorus, but relied solely upon the novelty of its libretto, the personality of its performers, and the tunefulness of its score. Upon the play, the actors, and the music devolved much of the task usually carried by the chorus—the duty of keeping the audience keyed up to a high pitch of emotional excitement."[19] These smaller productions—cast, sets, costumes—had an immense effect on the revue as it was evolving in America, including *Garrick Gaieties* and the *Little Shows*.[20] Exemplary of this was the reduced cast in *The Little Show* in 1929, where the triumvirate of Clifton Webb, Libby Holman, and Fred Allen shouldered the bulk of the entertainment and created a big hit. The 1930 *Co-Optimist* edition remained true to the blueprint of the series and was described by one critic as "a kind of Cochranesque revue, with 'produced' scenes, sketches, and little ballets, which seemed to be none the less brilliant for the fact that there was no chorus and that it was done by one small band of versatile principals."[21]

As with *Here Comes the Bride*, Schwartz was the principal composer, working with sketch writer / lyricist Greatrex Newman. Schwartz's songs and their performances that were singled out included Stanley Holloway singing "The Steeplechase"; "The Moment I Saw You," the hit of the evening, a duet sung and danced by Cyril Ritchard and Mimi Crawford; and "Sunday Afternoon," "a clever and melodious contrast between the manners of yesterday and today," sung by Elsa MacFarlane.[22] Newman was lyricist for all three of these with help from Howard Dietz. Schwartz wrote two instrumentals, "The Stuff to Give the Troops" and "Nothing Up Our Sleeves." Overall, Schwartz's music was described as "graceful and melodic."[23] In addition to praise for Schwartz, the choreography earned high praise, as did most of the cast. Nonetheless, *The Co-Optimists of 1930* could sustain a run of only 129 performances, well below the *Co-Optimist* average of 200.[24]

One week after that show opened, Ward Morehouse from the *New York Sun*, under a London dateline, summarized the theater career of Arthur Schwartz: "Two years ago Arthur Schwartz of Rugby Road, Flatbush, was a young lawyer with more ambition than clients and maintaining limited office space at 299 Broadway. And now look at him. He's quit the bar, he's written the music for two productions current in the London theatre, is writing a score for a third, is wearing Bond Street clothes and at this instant he's boarding the Golden Arrow for a brief holiday on the Continent. Cannes, most likely."[25]

By the time of this trip, Schwartz was at work on *The Second Little Show* and *Three's a Crowd*, both for Broadway, and had also done limited work on *Little Tommy Tucker*, his third London show. All three of these would open in the fall of 1930. The lyrics for *Little Tommy Tucker* were by Desmond Carter, but most of the music was composed by Vivian Ellis. "Out of the Blue" was penned by Schwartz and Ellis and was the principal ballad for the star, Ivy Tresmand.[26]

Schwartz wrote a melody that was used both in *Little Tommy Tucker*

5. The London Shows

and in *Three's a Crowd*. For the British show, Desmond Carter took Schwartz's tune and wrote "I Have No Words," a lighthearted duet for Tresmand and Gene Gerrard. It was a song described as "an ingenious blend of impudence and facetiousness,"[27] and as "a fast foxtrot with a comic lyric."[28] For New York, Dietz changed the tune into "Something to Remember You By," and had Schwartz play it with a slower tempo and more somber tone. Libby Holman made it a hit and a standard.[29] In later life, when giving a talk or recital, "Schwartz would make a point of demonstrating how a tune might be transformed by the work of a lyricist," comparing Carter's "I Have No Words" and Dietz's "Something to Remember You By."[30] *Little Tommy Tucker* would sustain a run of only eighty-three performances, and by the time it closed, Schwartz was back on Broadway.

6

Three's a Crowd and "Something to Remember You By"

"It was a grown-up revue, entirely free from banality and largely free from routine usages."[1]

Arthur Schwartz and Howard Dietz had been instrumental in advancing the revue genre with *The Little Show*, their 1929 revue that ran for 321 performances. What had been at the heart of the success of that show? Producers Dwight Deere Wiman and Tom Weatherly were betting on the format—the intimate revue: "Wiman and Weatherly wanted the title *The Little Show* to be the star."[2] At that time, there were eponymous revues produced by the likes of Earl Carroll, George White, Florenz Ziegfeld, and others. Although Wiman and Weatherly did not want their names on the title, they wanted to establish a franchise of *The Little Show* label for their subsequent revue efforts. In doing their next revue, *The Second Little Show*, they ignored their three stars from *The Little Show*, thinking that casting was less important than the intimate revue style. They didn't think that Clifton Webb, Libby Holman, and Fred Allen could repeat their success, pointing to the early *Charlot's Revues* of André Charlot which had starred Beatrice Lillie, Gertrude Lawrence, and Jack Buchanan. Even when all three appeared in Charlot's second edition, it ran less than half the number of performances of the first.[3] The producers were also afraid that the rising popularity of Webb, Holman, and Allen might require significant salary increases for the three.

The producers were not necessarily wrong on any of these accounts, nor were they naïve. Wiman, an heir to the Deere fortune, brought a lot more than money to a show. He was described as "a tasteful man and little inclined to meddle with composer, lyricist, or choreographer—he just let them get on with what they were doing."[4] Jo Mielziner, who would become a predominant Broadway set designer, worked on all three of *The*

Little Show editions. Although Mielziner thought Wiman to be "unusual," he saw him as one of the rare producers who were "highly creative and willing to take a loss on an artistically worthwhile property." Wiman would score big hits in the late thirties teaming with Rodgers and Hart for *On Your Toes*, *Babes in Arms*, and *I Married an Angel*. Of *The Little Show* series, Mielziner said, "These revues aimed at a much more sophisticated level of dialogue and lyrics than their contemporaries in the field of musical comedy; the sketches were no longer the burlesque or vaudeville blackout type; tableaux, girlie numbers, sentimental love scenes in rose-covered bowers, all were out."[5] While believing in the intimate revue, Schwartz and Dietz were not as confident of the new form, thinking their star trio had been the key to the success of *The Little Show*. They told this to Wiman and the other producers, who held to their position but still hired Schwartz and Dietz to do songs for *The Second Little Show*.

For this second edition, Dietz wrote only lyrics, leaving the sketches and limited book to several writers: Donald Blackwell, Norman Clark, James J. Coghlan, Marc Connelly, Bert Hanlon, and William Miles.[6] Schwartz and Dietz wrote numerous songs, adding or cutting them as needed. Eventually, nine made it to Broadway[7]:

Foolish Face	My Intuition
Good Clean Sport	New New York
I Started on a Shoestring	Swing Your Tails
Lonely Hearts' Ball	What a Case I've Got on You
Lucky Seven	

Of the Schwartz and Dietz entries, a Boston critic found the lyrics "amusing and sophisticated" and said of Schwartz's efforts that there were "plenty of tuneful torch melodies." The same scribe singled out "My Intuition" and "You're the Sunrise" as songs that "are bound to be danced to and whistled."[8] The latter song may have sounded good in Boston but never saw the lights of Broadway. None of the Schwartz / Dietz songs caught on with audiences nor had a life beyond the show. Only Herman Hupfeld's song, "Sing Something Simple," succeeded. Ruth Tester stopped the show with her singing of the Hupfeld melody, a song that "swept the nation."[9] A year later, Hupfeld would pen "As Time Goes By," which would languish until it surfaced in 1942 in *Casablanca* and became an American classic.

Ruth Tester was the principal female singer in *The Second Little Show*, replacing Gloria Grafton, who had opened in Boston. Grafton had been hired over a lesser known talent about whom Dietz remembered: "We took time out to hear an audition and were thrilled by a dark-eyed dynamo with the most positive delivery. In breathless excitement we told Dwight Wiman we had a 'find' for *The Second Little Show*. She sang 'Sing You Sinners' for Wiman. It was an event but the producer shook his head. 'Off-key' was the word he used. So Ethel Merman went into *Girl Crazy* by the brothers Gershwin. A girl named Gloria Grafton got the part in *The Second Little Show*."[10]

One reviewer referred to Grafton as a "lithographic brunette with a flat, unmusical voice."[11] Another, though saying little of her voice, painted a rosier picture: "Miss Holman's successor, judging by the somewhat lugubrious lyrics for her oh-so-blue tunes, is Miss Gloria Grafton, whose severely classic coiffure and revelatory gowns go a long way."[12] Although replaced in *The Second Little Show*, Grafton would make her mark on Broadway in 1935 in Rodgers and Hart's *Jumbo*. In that show, she introduced "Little Girl Blue" and in duets with Donald Novis, sang "My Romance" and "The Most Beautiful Girl in the World."[13] As good a Broadway song trio as could be imagined.

The Second Little Show was a revue with plenty of sketches and songs. In the Boston tryouts, there were a total of thirty-three scenes, but by opening week on Broadway, this had been reduced to twenty-four.[14] Only one sketch stood out, Marc Connelly's "The Guest," which had originated as a short piece for *The New Yorker*. "The Guest" was played by classic vaudevillian Al Trahan, the lead comic. Boston critic Edward Harold Crosby described the show as "not the typical 'revue' nor yet a vaudeville program, but rather a combination of the two."[15] This did not bode well as Broadway audiences were becoming used to intimate revues, and this revue did not pass muster. More importantly, Schwartz and Dietz had divided their efforts between this show and Max Gordon's *Three's a Crowd*, and it showed: "Mr. Gordon got the 'best of the bunch' of material and *The Second Little Show* ran only eight weeks."[16]

While agreeing to do *The Second Little Show* for Wiman and Weatherly, Schwartz and Dietz had hedged their bets and signed on to do a separate show with Max Gordon—*Three's a Crowd*. Dietz had formed an alliance with Webb, Holman, and Allen to do a show to be supervised by Dietz. He then enlisted Broadway agent Walter Batchelor to find a producer. Batchelor found Max Gordon who had the backing of the Erlanger group, and the deal was done.[17] This show was to be Gordon's first effort as an independent producer. Gordon had been a vaudeville booker for the Keith-Orpheum Circuit, then in 1918 began producing plays with Albert Lewis, often in association with Sam H. Harris. Gordon and Lewis had a hit in 1925 with the Samson Raphaelson play, *The Jazz Singer*.[18]

Gordon was aware of the simplicity, economy, and tastefulness of such shows as the *Greenwich Village Follies*, *Garrick Gaieties*, and the *Grand Street Follies*. In his autobiography, *Max Gordon Presents*, he explained how he, Schwartz, and Dietz viewed *Three's a Crowd*: "It was agreed that we would strive for an intimate revue of the finest quality, surpassing, if

6. Three's a Crowd *and* "Something to Remember You By"   49

possible, even that of *The Little Show*. What we desired was a production that would delight the eye and yet not be ostentatiously elaborate, whose content would be sharp, witty, sophisticated and intelligent ... it also represented our determination to underscore and widen the break *The Little Show* had made with the big revues of the twenties."[19]

Around this time, Schwartz worked briefly in Hollywood for Paramount Pictures. The first film was *Queen High*, which premiered August 1930 and starred Stanley Smith, Ginger Rogers, Charles Ruggles, and Frank Morgan. Schwartz collaborated with another composer, Ralph Rainger, and lyricist Edward Eliscu to write "I'm Afraid of You," a duet for Smith and Rogers. Also for *Queen High*, Schwartz, Rainger, and E.Y. Harburg created "Brother, Just Laugh It Off." The latter song was used in another 1930 Paramount picture, *Follow the Leader*, which also starred Rogers as well as Ed Wynn and Ethel Merman.[20] Although Schwartz would spend more time in Hollywood years later, it was back to Broadway after his work for Paramount.

Schwartz had been working on a much different show, an operetta, anchored to the European traditions which had been popular on Broadway for decades. He had become acquainted with Dr. Albert Sirmay among a circle of composers—veteran and new—who met frequently to share ideas and exhibit their latest work. Historian David Ewen described the setting:

> One of the most celebrated of these professional parlors in the 1920's was the one at Harms at 62 West 45th Street. There held sway such kings of Tin Pan Alley as Kern, Gershwin, Rodgers, Youmans—and, later on, Cole Porter. Important composers and lyricists of that day made it a habit to drop in at Harms during the noonday hour for some music, shoptalk, social palaver. George Gershwin could be found there several times a week. Harry Ruby, Bert Kalmar, Joe Meyer, Buddy DeSylva, Vincent Youmans, Irving Caesar, Paul [*sic*] Charig—later on, Arthur Schwartz, Vernon Duke and Harold Arlen—hovered around Gershwin like satellites.... The younger composers and lyricists would sometimes use this social period at Harms to discuss new projects with the Harms editor, Dr. Albert Sirmay, and their patron saint, Max Dreyfus.[21]

After some discussion, Schwartz and Sirmay agreed to collaborate on the music for an operetta, *Princess Charming*.

Operettas had originated in Western Europe, written mostly by Europeans, and many of these composers had traveled to America to continue their work. The best known of them included Rudolf Friml, Victor Herbert, and Sigmund Romberg, whose most successful shows include[22]:

Composer	Birth	American Operetta
Rudolf Friml	Czechoslovakia	*The Firefly* (1912); *Katinka* (1915); *Rose-Marie* (1924); *The Vagabond King* (1925); *The Three Musketeers* (1928)

Composer	Birth	American Operetta
Victor Herbert	Ireland	*Babes in Toyland* (1903); *Mlle Modiste* (1905); *The Red Mill* (1906); *Naughty Marietta* (1910); *Sweethearts* (1913); *Eileen* (1917)
Sigmund Romberg	Hungary	*The Student Prince* (1924); *The Desert Song* (1926); *My Maryland* (1927); *The New Moon* (1928)

Operetta arose in the mid-nineteenth century as an alternative to *opera comique*, which was a more serious form of opera that had been evolving at that time, more "humanistic" and meant to portray "real life." The creation of operetta is credited to French singer / composer / librettist Hervé in the 1840s. The successful development of it can be attributed to Jacques Offenbach in Paris, Johann Strauss II in Vienna, and Arthur Sullivan and W.S. Gilbert and their comic operas in England. Examples of their works include[23]:

Composer	Operetta (year)
Jacques Offenbach	*Orphée aux enfers* (1858); *Genevieve de Brabant* (1859); *La Perichole* (1868)
Johann Strauss II	*Die Fledermaus* (1874); *Prinz Methusalem* (1877); *Der Zigeunerbaron* (1885)
Arthur Sullivan and W.S. Gilbert	*H.M.S. Pinafore* (1878); *The Pirates of Penzance* (1879); *The Mikado* (1885)

Operetta audiences wanted lighter fare than was being offered by the traditional opera companies in Europe: "As a popular form of entertainment, the operetta reflected contemporary taste in the nature of its plots and moral attitudes as well as in topical references. As the predominant form of popular musical theatre of its time, it attracted composers, librettists, performers, managers, directors and designers."[24] Operettas were shorter than operas and lighter, both in subject matter—often set in fictional kingdoms—and in tone, usually amusing and even satirical.

Mounting an operetta on Broadway in 1930 was risky business. The genre in America had peaked in the first decade of the twentieth century, although as clear from a previous chart, Friml and Romberg had great success well into the twenties. Of this, composer Vernon Duke commented, "the old lady took a long time dying."[25] World War I and anti-German sentiments were partly responsible for the demise of the genre. Beyond this, Alan Jay Lerner surmised, "the theatre-going public was no longer in the mood to see the world through the rose-coloured spectacles of operetta."[26] Moreover, operetta was slowly evolving into the modern musical, the former being described as "light opera with acting" while musicals were "plays with singing and dancing."[27] Operetta often employed opera singers while musicals cast singers who could act and dance as well. Revivals met with success in the early forties, but ultimately, musical comedy spelled the doom of operetta.

By 1930, few operettas were being written, but Schwartz teamed with Dr. Albert Sirmay, a Hungarian operetta composer, to do just that. He had been trained in Budapest and came to the United States in the early twenties, as operetta was fading here. Born Szirmai, he Anglicized it to Sirmay. Well-trained in composition, orchestration, and editing, as were so many of the European operetta composers, Sirmay soon found work with Max Dreyfus at Harms. He was hired as a staff writer and editor of publications for the likes of Jerome Kern, George Gershwin, and Richard Rodgers. He worked closely with Cole Porter as a musical secretary, often helping him with chords and harmony. Sirmay became close with Gershwin and became editor of his musical estate. The Dreyfus family was the premier publisher for Broadway compositions and had numerous composers in their stable, all of whom kept Sirmay busy.[28]

The Schwartz / Sirmay operetta had a long gestation, starting in 1925 when Hungarian playwright, Franz Martos, wrote a play titled *Alexandra*, and asked his friend, Albert Sirmay to put a score to it. Sirmay was most willing, and wrote, "in what amounted to a frenzy," the entire score and a few extra songs. Martos and his producers were able to put the show together by November of that year, and it proved quite successful. The operetta was picked up by producers in London, who changed the name to *Princess Charming* because the Lord Chamberlain decided, "the name of the Dowager Queen Alexandra should not be taken so lightly, especially by an operetta in which royalty did not take itself too seriously."[29]

A British version of the script was done, and the show opened in England as *Princess Charming*, starring Evelyn Laye and Alice Delysia, and enjoyed a good run. The main idea was taken to America by producers Bobby Connolly and Arthur Swanstrom, who had just had a hit with *Sons o' Guns*. Connolly would direct, Swanstrom would do lyrics, and Jack Donahue would write the book. The original story by Martos evolved into a more American version from Donahue's pen. Sirmay's original score was used as a basis, and the majority of the songs were to be composed by Arthur Schwartz, who "up to then had been fooling only with revues and lighter comedies."[30]

The American *Princess Charming* was beset with a series of problems: difficulties in casting; a fire prior to the dress rehearsal in Boston ruined Joseph Urban's scenery; a tercentennial celebration in Boston that distracted everyone; and Jack Donahue's collapse while touring with *Sons o' Guns* and his death within the week. The production regrouped, veterans Evelyn Herbert and Robert Halliday joined the cast, and the show opened to enthusiastic audiences in New Haven. It was taken to New York and premiered on October 13, 1930, two days before *Three's a Crowd*.[31]

Portions of Sirmay's music from the 1925 edition of the show were incorporated into the American version of *Princess Charming*. Schwartz and Sirmay wrote sixteen songs used in the show, but it is unclear if both men worked on each song. The songs, credited to both of them with lyrics by Arthur Swanstrom, included[32]:

First Sunbeam	One for All
Here Is a Sword	Palace of Dreams
I Must Be One of Those Roses	The Panic's On
I'll Be There	Take a Letter to the King
I'll Never Leave You	Trailing a Shooting Star
I'm Designed for Love	Wings of the Morning
Just a Friend of Mine Never Mind How	A Wonderful Thing for the King You

Hartford critics were favorable to the show. The score was described as "tuneful and attractive."[33] Another reviewer found the songs "sufficiently sonorous and interesting in the romantic parts," and "catchily pleasing in a couple of modern dancing numbers."[34] Songs that were singled out included "Trailing a Star," "You," "I Love Love," "Palace of Dreams," and "I'll Never Leave You."[35] Another critic also cited this last song favorably, placing it on a par with "Lover, Come Back to Me," the 1928 ballad from *The New Moon*, written by Sigmund Romberg and Oscar Hammerstein II. That operetta included the same stars as *Princess Charming*, Evelyn Herbert and Robert Halliday.[36] In addition to the positive reviews of the songs, the overall show received much praise, labeled as "a sumptuous business"[37] and "musical entertainment which has real class."[38]

Most of these favorable reviews came from out-of-town critics, but Broadway scribes saw a different show. John Mason Brown of the *New York Evening Post* was no fan of operetta in general and *Princess Charming* in particular. He discussed the "trappings" of the show, all part of the genre: "its regulation fable of the two mythical kingdoms … its hordes of ardent revolutionaries, its brisk spick-and-span soldiery … its heart pressings … and all the hundred and one tarnished Prisoner-of-Zendarisms."

Brown adds, "it comes as something of an ordeal for those who do not take too readily to their operettas even when they are of the best." However, he concludes his comments by admitting that many in the audience were not in agreement with him and expressed such "by the warmth of their applause."[39]

The critic of *The New Yorker* held feelings similar to Brown, taking specific issue with the encores taken by the soprano, Evelyn Herbert, and the tenor, Robert Halliday, a common practice in operetta: "The whole charm of the thing was dissipated, the theatre got warm, watches were consulted, and it finally got so that as soon as it became apparent that another encore was to be indulged in, large sectors of the audience began racing up the aisles. The music was good and the voices were good, but there was too much of them. There ought to be a law against sopranos and tenors taking encores. They hold their notes too long."[40]

Despite this swing of the pendulum away from operetta, Schwartz maintained a love of it, telling Douglas Gilbert of the *New York Telegram*: "I really would rather do operetta stuff because I like melody, and I guess that's why I prefer *Princess Charming* of all my work." Referring to Schwartz as "the newest—and the best currently represented—of Broadway's torch tuners," Gilbert added, "The muted melody of 'Princess Charming' is his [Schwartz's] idea of music."[41] As always, the ultimate critics are the audiences who make known their reviews at the box office. Their response was tepid, and *Princess Charming* ran only fifty-six performances. For the young "torch tuner," it was back to the revue.

As *Three's a Crowd* progressed, Gordon, Schwartz, and Dietz became a most compatible triumvirate, agreeing on almost everything except an early big decision, the hiring of a director. Gordon had wanted Hassard Short. Schwartz and Dietz were reluctant to work with him, thinking he might not be up to an intimate revue. His previous directorial work had included *Sunny* and the 1921–1923 versions of the *Music Box Revues*. It was Short's expertise with these bigger shows that made Schwartz and Dietz uncomfortable. Gordon explained, "They said they thought he might not be able to fit into their younger and more modern ideas, that he might be too chichi and extravagant."[42]

Rodgers and Hart and Herbert Fields had endured a clash of generations when working with Fields' father, Lew, on *Poor Little Ritz Girl* in 1920. Shortly before the premier, the elder Fields, relying on tried-and-true formulas, rewrote the book, cut seven of the Rodgers and Hart songs, and replaced them with songs by Sigmund Romberg and Alex Gerber. The latter man had been a lyricist for numerous revues in the twenties. Fields' daughter, lyricist Dorothy Fields, explained the clash of generations on another show a few years after *Poor Little Ritz Girl*: "He [Lew] didn't want a coherent libretto or a book show. He wanted music, yes, but the rest should just be gags, black-outs, and belly laughs, whereas Herb, Dick, and Larry were obsessed with the necessity of having a strong story."[43] Like Lew Fields, Gordon overrode his younger collaborators; Short was hired.

With this settled, the composers headed to the Warwick Hotel where they set up their headquarters, Schwartz at a new Steinway as "composer-in-chief" and Dietz as "compiler-in-chief."[44] From their midtown hotel, the two met with other composers and lyricists who were hoping to get a song or two interpolated into the new show. Those ultimately successful included Eddie Brandt, Philip Charig, Vernon Duke, Henry Myers, Charles M. Schwab, and Alec Wilder.[45]

Getting a big break in the show was an eighteen-year-old Burton Lane who was recommended to Dietz by publisher Jack Robbins. Schwartz was hospitalized for an acute appendicitis, and Dietz wanted to keep the show moving forward. Lane played several songs for Dietz, who singled out two and put lyrics to them, "Forget All Your Books" and "Out in the Open Air," both added to the show. Schwartz was discharged from the hospital on August 13, took a liking to the young pianist's playing, and asked him to be rehearsal pianist for *Three's a Crowd*. Lane said of it all, "I loved the idea because it gave me a chance to see how a show is put together." Rehearsal pianist was not an uncommon position for budding songwriters: Schwartz had done so for *Peggy-Ann*; George Gershwin for Jerome Kern's *Miss 1917* and the *Ziegfeld Follies of 1918*; Vincent Youmans for Victor Herbert's *Orange Blossoms*; and Harold Arlen for Youmans' *Hit the Deck* and *Great Day!*, *Miss 1917* was little remembered except for the fact that George Gershwin had been the rehearsal pianist. Lane remembered the experience, explaining that Max Gordon "had me at all the meetings—kind of adopted me."[46]

For an interpolation into *Three's a Crowd*, Schwartz had been impressed with a song then popular in England, "Body and Soul." It had been composed by Johnny Green with lyrics by Edward Heyman and Robert Sour. At the time, Frank Eyton was also given credit for the lyrics, but as Green himself explained: "Frank Eyton was CHAPPELL'S in-house lyricist. His name went on the song. Need I say more? Did he write any part of the lyric? Not a word." The torch song seemed a natural for Libby Holman, but there were problems with it from the start. Holman did not like the original lyric, but a version worked out by Dietz was not the answer either and created friction among Dietz and the originators, as detailed by Green:

> Howard Dietz, who, with Arthur Schwartz, was in charge of music and lyrics for the production, decided that Heyman's and Sour's already international hit lyric was not classic enough for "THREE'S A CROWD" and wrote his own lyric, which he, in his position of authority, was able, despite Eddie's, Bobby's and my protests, to force into the show during the pre–New York Philadelphia try-out. We had no idea that he was

going to take it on himself to rush it through for print. End result:—the song bombed in the show with Dietz's lyric, and was a smash ... when Heyman's and Sour's lyric went back in.[47]

Nonetheless, some early copies of the sheet music had Dietz listed as lyricist, much to Green's annoyance.

There were problems with Green's orchestration of "Body and Soul." Gordon even had Green conduct the orchestra himself, but by Green's own admission, his orchestration "bombed."[48] Unhappy with the song, a distraught Holman threatened to quit and cried, "Instead of calling it *Three's a Crowd*, you can call it *Two's Company*."[49] Dietz was convinced that a better arrangement was needed. He shanghaied Ralph Rainger to Philadelphia to work on a new one. Rainger and Dietz had written Holman's hit from *The Little Show*, "Moanin' Low," and Dietz felt the young composer / arranger "had a special feeling for this type of dark number."[50] Rainger used a simple piano arrangement for the verse, then slowly brought the orchestra in on the chorus, achieving a dramatic effect with a rising crescendo. When coupled with Hassard Short's spotlight upon her, in front of the curtain, Holman and "Body and Soul" brought down the house.[51]

Schwartz and Dietz contributed five songs to *Three's a Crowd*[52]:

The California Collegians	Right at the Start of It
Je T'aime	Something to Remember You By
The Moment I Saw You	

"The Moment I Saw You" had come directly from the London show *The Co-Optimists of 1930* with the original words done by Greatrex Newman with assistance from Dietz. The song, a duet for Cyril Ritchard and Mimi Crawford, had been a favorite of British audiences. For *Three's a Crowd*, Dietz wrote an updated American lyric, sung by Clifton Webb and Amy Revere.[53]

For Schwartz and Dietz, their big song was "Something to Remember You By," borrowed from *Little Tommy Tucker*, originally titled "I Have No Words." The song had been done as a fast foxtrot with a comedic lyric by Desmond Carter.[54] While they were working at the Warwick Hotel, Schwartz played the original London song for Dietz, who wanted his partner to slow it down. Schwartz tried to dissuade him: "Howard, you don't make a something tune out of a nothing tune by slowing it down."[55] But Dietz, who could be stubborn, remembered the moment of creation:

> "You can't make a ballad out of that," Arthur said, "it's a tinkly chorus number." "No, it's just right," I said stubbornly, "play it again as slowly as you possibly can, you'll see." He had to repeat it many times before I got him to slow down to the pace I had in mind. Finally, he got the tinkly tempo out of his system, and I wrote the words to "Something to Remember You By."[56]

Sheet music cover for "Something to Remember You By," the Schwartz and Dietz hit from *Three's a Crowd*, the Max Gordon revue of 1930. This cover art features *left to right*: Fred Allen, Libby Holman, and Clifton Webb (collection of the author).

Sung longingly by Holman to her sailor going off to war, Fred MacMurray, presentation of the song was less of a problem than with "Body and Soul." "Something to Remember You By" was the hit of the first act and a particular favorite of Max Gordon. He had taken quite a liking to his composers, referring to Dietz as "a tireless worker, fastidious and exacting," and Schwartz as "lean and intense." Gordon said that the song "gave me chills every time it was sung by Libby Holman."[57] Dinah Shore recognized the sense and setting of the song and had a hit with it on Victor midway through World War II.

John Bush Jones, in *The Songs That Fought the War: Popular Music and the Home Front*, discussed "Something to Remember You By" as one of the better "songs [that] expressed thoughts of parting." He also mentioned "I'll Pray for You" by Arthur Altman and Kim Gannon, recorded by the Andrews Sisters, and "I'll Keep the Lovelight Burning" by Harold Levey, introduced by Kate Smith. Both songs had several recordings. Jones singled out "Something to Remember You By": "One truly great song from the girl's point of view surfaced in 1943 ... tailor-made for the situation of a girl sending her sweet-heart off to war.... Whoever recalled the song to revive it must have had a keen eye for timing, since everything in it resonates with the war years ... all this set to the gorgeously legato melody composer Schwartz excelled in."[58] In his commentary on American Popular Song, critic Wilfrid Sheed singled out the song for its timeless qualities: "there is a classic quality to Schwartz's best tunes that separates them from the crowd and seems to qualify him for his own statue and his own book. 'Something to Remember You By' is a song my grandmother used to sing, and that one, along with her other favorites, Berlin's 'What'll I Do' and Romberg's 'When I Grow Too Old to Dream,' form their own little timeless repertoire in my head dating back to the Garden of Infancy, when all the songs were young."[59]

A few paragraphs in the *New York Morning World* three months after the opening of *Three's a Crowd* discussed "Something to Remember You By" as a "delayed hit."[60] The reporter explained that often, when a musical opened, the producers will have decided on a "hit song" from their show and see to it that it gets properly plugged. They keep charts on its radio plays and urge orchestra leaders to entertain their audiences with the show's "hit song." In *We'll Have Manhattan*, Dominic Symonds explained: "Getting their work performed meant pleasing the money guys, and it was very often a producer's whim that made key decisions, making the producer in effect a collaborative partner.... In particular, the focus on marketing the hit songs of each production would cause interesting and sometimes problematic choices."[61] Not infrequently, the designated, "plugged" song does not take off as hoped and is superseded by another one from the show. An example given by the *Morning World* journalist was the success of "I'm Just Wild about Harry" in *Shuffle Along* when its producers had initially touted "Bandana Days" and "Love Will Find a Way." From *George White's Scandals of 1926*, "Birth of the Blues" emerged as the big hit after others had been anointed. For *Three's a Crowd*, "Body and Soul" had been the favored song for promotion, but "Something to Remember You By" quietly took the lead and after a few months, was the second most broadcast song on the air. The article concludes of the song, "A hit, a hit, a most palpable (if delayed) hit."[62]

So two great ballads came along in this show, one an interpolation, the other from the principal songwriters of the show. Perhaps it was the talented Ms. Holman who simply put them over so well that neither song could be ignored. Adding to their impact was the staging and lighting of Hassard Short, who opted to minimize the footlights and enhance the view of Holman with lighting hung from the balcony and by utilizing spotlights and pin lights. So unique was his lighting for "Body and Soul" that it was "patented and protected."[63] For his expansive lighting, which future shows emulated, Short received a medal from the General Electric Company, the first ever for stage lighting.[64]

Besides these two hits, there was a lot to like in this show. The *New York Sun* critic, Richard Lockridge, was the most effusive: "*Three's a Crowd* is so nearly all that a revue should be that any discussion of it is almost certain to end in an undignified outburst of superlatives."[65] A rave in the

Scene from the 1930 revue *Three's a Crowd* starring Libby Holman, Clifton Webb, and Fred Allen. In this setting, Holman sings "Something to Remember You By" to her departing sailor, Fred MacMurray (photographer unknown / courtesy Museum of the City of New York. F2013.41.8022).

6. *Three's a Crowd and "Something to Remember You By"*

Brooklyn Citizen declared, "It is novel, it is clever, it is sophisticated, it is bright, it is tasteful, it is gay, it is tuneful. What more could one ask for?"[66] The show was "devoid of conventional routines and … surpassed *The Little Show* in quality, style, humor and song."[67] Years later, musicologist Cecil Smith said, "It was a grown-up revue, entirely free from banality and largely free from routine usages."[68] The principal performers—Holman, Webb, and Allen—were all reviewed favorably, as were Short, choreographer Albertina Rasch, and the dancing of twenty-three-year-old Russian ballerina Tamara Geva. Of Rasch's work, the *Evening Wall Street Journal* concluded, "Albertina Rasch has extended the ordinary limits in her dance arrangements. None of them lapses into mere routine."[69]

As for the other Schwartz / Dietz songs, "Je T'aime" had been used in *The Second Little Show*, which had opened a month earlier, but had been "mishandled" and had to be "retailored" for Clifton Webb. He did it successfully in a comedic vein for *Three's a Crowd*.[70] Webb performed another, "Night after Night," compared by one reviewer to the Noel Coward song, "Dance, Little Lady," from his 1928 show, *This Year of Grace*.[71] Except for these two and "Something to Remember You By," the remainder of their score met with mixed reviews.

To audiences, *Three's a Crowd* was a hit. It advanced the revue form by doing things differently from its forerunners. It did not open with a lavish production number, but rather with a farcical sketch, "Bedroom Scene." The lighting and choreography were groundbreaking. Its principal performers were onstage together only for the finale, "Right at the Start of It." Overall, much credit was given to Dietz, who had also served as sketch writer and coordinator: "This new way of presenting a revue is the idea of Howard Dietz and it found instant favor last night. There is at last something new in the theatre."[72] But there was plenty of credit to be spread around for a job well done, and the audiences showed their appreciation, giving *Three's a Crowd* a run of 272 performances, excellent by any standard for a revue.

As for Arthur Schwartz, good things were happening in threes. The composer of *Three's a Crowd* had three shows on Broadway, an uncommon feat at that time or any time. The writer of a brief piece for the *New York Sun* mentioned that Jerome Kern had been the last to do it. With perhaps a bit of hyperbole, the *Sun* article pointed out that Schwartz had three hit songs, one from each of his three shows that "represent almost every example of light music." These included "I'll Never Leave You," a waltz from *Princess Charming*, for Evelyn Herbert and Robert Halliday; the "melancholy tune" from *Three's a Crowd*, "Something to Remember You By"; and "Lucky Seven," from *The Second Little Show*, described as "one of those blue rhythmic numbers that are in the style of 'St. Louis Blues.'" The piece ends: "A hasty computation shows that Mr. Schwartz has written an average of one show every two months since July, 1929."[73] While these were not all hits and in many cases represented only minor interpolations, for someone who had been a full-time practicing attorney only two years earlier, Mr. Schwartz was doing well in his new occupation.

7

The Band Wagon and "Dancing in the Dark"

> "Mr. Schwartz has accomplished this with characteristic wit and ingenuity and much musical invention of a high order."[1]

Consistency. It was what Max Gordon and his team of creators wanted for *The Band Wagon*. Consistency of the script, to be done only by George S. Kaufman and Howard Dietz, not the usual hodgepodge of sketches scattered around most revues. This would be the "revue with a single point of view."[2] Dietz and Arthur Schwartz "felt strongly that a revue should have the same homogeneity of style as a book musical."[3] They made this a stipulation for doing the show when Max Gordon approached them.[4] Gordon explained that Dietz felt confident about this, that it "would help create a definite unity instead of trusting to luck in assembling the show."[5]

There would be consistency in the songs as well, as they would be composed only by Schwartz and Dietz. There would be no hopeful composers trying to interpolate a song into *The Band Wagon*; there would not be "the customary battalion of conflicting tunesmiths."[6] Schwartz and Dietz had done their share of interpolations into other shows with varying degrees of success. *The Band Wagon* was to be pure Schwartz / Dietz.

Consistency would be enhanced by continuity. Fresh from their hit that had opened in October 1930, *Three's a Crowd*, Gordon, Schwartz, and Dietz wanted the same group that had created that show: choreography and dance direction by Albertina Rasch; stage sets by Albert Johnson; costumes by Kiviette with assistance from Constance Ripley; and stage direction and lighting design by Hassard Short.[7] Revues were a collaborative effort, and each piece of the puzzle had to fit to make a good show.

Albertina Rasch had been a leading choreographer on Broadway for years, often using her own Albertina Rasch Dancers in a show. She would do for *The Band Wagon*. Rasch was a smart businesswoman from Vienna and had been a founding member of the Russian Tea Room. She was married to Russian concert pianist / film composer Dimitri Tiomkin, who had toured with her company as an opening act.[8]

Rasch was fortunate to have another Viennese, Tilly Losch, as her principal dancer. She had started her training as a child at the Vienna

The sister-brother team of Adele and Fred Astaire in 1932, during the run of their hit revue, *The Band Wagon*. She was 35; Fred was 32. Adele retired from the stage when the show closed and married Englishman Lord Charles Cavendish (courtesy Everett Collection Historical / Alamy Stock photo).

7. The Band Wagon *and "Dancing in the Dark"*

Opera School, eventually moved to London and worked in shows for C.B. Cochran and Noel Coward. She then came to America as a dancer / choreographer for Max Reinhardt's school and repertory. Losch "lifted modern ballet to fresh popularity."[9] Cochran, the premier British producer of the period, appreciated both her dancing and choreography. Of the former, in his memoir, *I Had Almost Forgotten...*, the old showman compared her to "a flame in her movements—now calm and lambent, now flickering and darting like a tongue of fire."[10] Of her dance creations, Cochran declared they "appear so effortless that it is seldom realized that behind the poetry of her movements is a lifetime of training."[11]

The terpsichorean talents of Rasch and Losch complemented the stars of the show, Fred and Adele Astaire, no slouches themselves at dancing. Besides the pre-condition that there be only three writers for *The Band Wagon*, Schwartz and Dietz had also stipulated that the brother / sister duo be headliners.[12] Although the Astaires were at the pinnacle of their careers, Adele had wanted to retire as she was in love with Englishman Lord Charles Cavendish, and they were to be married. She had been performing since early childhood and had had enough. Adele wanted to do one more show and told Cavendish that "she couldn't retire on a flop. There would have to be one more good show—and she knew there was one in the offing."[13] *The Band Wagon* would provide the Astaires a phenomenal showcase with multiple characters to play.

Procuring the services of the Astaires and George S. Kaufman did not come cheaply.[14] Although Gordon had allied himself with Erlanger Productions, among the biggest and most powerful producers on Broadway, he still found himself scrambling for financing. This led Kaufman to confront his producer about running in the red. As Gordon remembered it in his memoir, *Max Gordon Presents*:

> "One of the boys at the *Times* told me," Kaufman replied. "Is it true?" "Don't worry about the money," I stalled. "The Erlangers have plenty of money." I was sorry I said that but it was too late. "I'm not dealing with the Erlangers," Kaufman snapped. "I'm dealing with you."[15]

Gordon had been co-producing shows since the early twenties but was unfamiliar with the practice of "buys" on Broadway. These were important in the financing of a show and were explained to him by the treasurer at the New Amsterdam Theatre, Louis Lotito. Again, from Gordon's memoir: "Lotito said he would get the money for me. The big brokers would advance the money, in return for which I would agree to let them have certain designated tickets each week, choice locations, of course. And each week, before paying for the tickets, they would deduct a portion as payment for the loan. Within two weeks Lotito handed me checks totaling ninety-nine thousand dollars."[16]

Although his creative team and financing were in place, Gordon still found himself uncertain of his young composer, Arthur Schwartz, and wanted to hear parts of the score. Howard Dietz said that Gordon "was not yet confident of Schwartz's ability to deliver a complete score."[17] Fortunately for Schwartz, he was adept at song presentations. Robert Russell Bennet, the orchestrator for *The Band Wagon* and the dean of Broadway orchestrators, recalled Schwartz as "quite young and enormously talented." Bennet continued regarding Schwartz's ability to present a song: "He is my choice for the best song demonstrator of the whole lot. He sings every word of the lyrics without hesitating over a syllable, even though he may be giving a performance of the whole show. His piano accompaniments are well arranged and always played the same way."[18]

For their early work on the show, Schwartz and Dietz were holed up at the St. Moritz Hotel, continuing their practice of working in the evenings after Dietz had done his day job. To keep Gordon hopeful, they would play him a song or two and won him over with "I Love Louisa." As Gordon remembered it:

> I shall never forget the Sunday Schwartz telephoned. "Max," he yelled, "we've just finished a knockout." "Sing it for me," I said. "I can't wait." Schwartz sang "I Love Louisa." I nearly jumped through the mouthpiece. In my exuberance, I proclaimed, "Boys, it's a pleasure to go broke with you."[19]

During that same phone call, Schwartz also played "New Sun in the Sky" and "Dancing in the Dark," adding to Gordon's confidence in his songwriting team.[20] Gordon explained that "what I was trying to tell them over the telephone was that the way things were going, even if the show failed, I would be happy having had the pleasure of being associated with it and its talented people."[21]

As the songwriting progressed, so did the sketches. When not working with Schwartz, Dietz would spend his evenings going over sketches with Kaufman. When work on *The Band Wagon* began, Kaufman was still in the cast of *Once in a Lifetime*, his hit comedy, co-authored with Moss Hart in their first collaboration. Dietz would meet with Kaufman at the theater after the evening performances, and although there was much give-and-take, Kaufman had final say on script matters. By this time, Kaufman had a stellar reputation on Broadway, comfortable writing both comedies and revue, though often uncomfortable with music. For him, it was all about the words, mostly comedic. Schwartz recalled the normally calm Kaufman losing his temper while working on *The Band Wagon*. Kaufman's biographer and collaborator, Howard Teichmann, described the occurrence:

> During a rehearsal of *The Band Wagon*, Fred Astaire danced and accompanied himself on an accordion in one number. At the end of the number, the orchestra came up with a

strong finish. "George was wild with rage because he couldn't hear the words," Schwartz said. All present hustled George out of the theatre, the orchestra stayed as it was, so did the number, and so did Fred Astaire. After that, they simply didn't rehearse the orchestra when George was around.[22]

Another Kaufman biographer, Malcolm Goldstein, corroborated this view of his subject and his behavior at rehearsals: "For some members of the cast his presence during rehearsals was unnerving, since he sat in unbroken silence, his head in his hands, giving no sign of approval whatsoever. Tilly Losch and the Astaires, though seasoned performers, were convinced that he did not care for their work."[23]

Kaufman himself was aware that he neglected the musical side of a show. Kaufman felt that "he failed to provide 'real musical opportunity' to his composers because his shows 'never have been primarily romantic, and the composer has thus been psychologically handicapped from the beginning. It is probably the reason that there has never been a real song hit in any show with which I have been connected.'"[24] Irving Berlin had wanted his song "Always" in *The Cocoanuts*, but it never made it in as Kaufman "didn't like the words that much."[25] Later in his career, while directing *Guys and Dolls*, Kaufman would butt heads with composer Frank Loesser over musical issues. According to theatrical lore, Kaufman told Loesser that he could reprise his songs if he, Kaufman, could reprise his jokes. Despite this story and Kaufman's own opinion of himself, plenty of good songs came out of shows Kaufman had written or directed. Among them was Loesser's *Guys and Dolls*.

Music and rehearsal behavior aside, *The Band Wagon* was coming together. Fred and Adele Astaire had been doing a failed musical comedy, *Smiles*, prior to *The Band Wagon*. Fred wrote years later in his autobiography, *Steps in Time*, that he and Adele "liked a revue for a change." Fortunately for them, Kaufman and Dietz, two intelligent and clever writers, came up with sketches and a show that Fred Astaire declared to be "new and original."[26] It was a show that he and Adele were happy to be part of. The writing efforts of Kaufman and Dietz led to a show with "the most elaborate eliminations" and "clichés that would not be seen."[27] In other words, this was not just any old revue. It would be called the "most sophisticated and imaginative revue ever mounted on Broadway."[28]

The "imaginative" began with the opening curtain, or rather, the lack of one, where the incoming audience witnessed cast members on stage, in formal attire, taking seats in a similar fashion as the audience. The cast mirrored its incoming audience. The opening number, rather than a well-worn, large chorus number, had the onstage "audience" singing a lively Schwartz/Dietz melody, "It Better Be Good."[29] At one point, Dietz had wanted to do an opening number dealing with the producer's difficulty financing the show. Instead of "It Better Be Good," the lyricist envisioned "Max Gordon Raised the Money."[30] Fortunately, director Hassard Short, Schwartz, and others prevailed, and "It Better Be Good" got the show off to a solid start.

As the creation of the show progressed, the sketches continued to surprise and delight and were well integrated with the music, sets, and lighting. It is here that the team assembled by Gordon, Dietz, and Schwartz proved their mettle. In the preceding few years, Hassard Short had been transforming the art of stage lighting on Broadway. In *Three's a Crowd*, he had avoided traditional footlights, preferring to illuminate the stage from the balcony, a technique which would be adopted by other Broadway lighting designers and become the standard. For *The Band Wagon*, he abandoned foot lighting entirely,[31] providing illumination from lamps mounted in front of the balcony.[32] Perhaps the show's most dramatic moment came as Tilly Losch performed "Dancing in the Dark," rendering "a haunting interpretation on a slanted, mirrored floor with varicolored lights,"[33] all of Short's invention. He had used equally dramatic lighting in *Three's a Crowd*, using a pin light to enhance Libby Holman's performance of "Body and Soul." Although his stage direction was more than adequate, it was in lighting that Short excelled and added to the imaginative sum total of *The Band Wagon*.

To complement Short's lighting, designer Albert Johnson, only twenty-one at the time, created imaginative sets with the help of a new device, the revolving stage. It had been first been used in Berlin theaters and became common in Wagnerian opera at the Bayreuth Festival.[34] One had been seen in *Ned Wayburn's Town Topics* in 1915, among others, and the technology had been improving. Lorenz Hart had convinced C.B. Cochran to build one for *Ever Green*, the London show composed by Rodgers and Hart. The Yiddish Art Theatre had one but on Broadway, revolving stages were all but unheard of as the stage floors of most theaters were neither strong enough nor large enough.[35] But the stage of the New Amsterdam Theatre had neither limitation, giving Johnson and Short the ability to utilize a revolving stage for the first time in an American revue.[36] But they took the idea a step further, creating two revolving stages, one inside the other.[37] They would patent this invention and notice of this was made in the program of the show: "NOTE: The double revolving stage and all scenic and lighting effects are protected and patented, as 'The Band Wagon' will be produced in London, Paris and Berlin."[38] Max Gordon, who had to approve the expenditures, was on board with the idea from the start: "Short had charged the atmosphere with excitement by suggesting that we use twin revolving stages to enhance our effects, making them part of the action instead of using them for changing scenery. I bought the idea on the spot. Never before had a revue in America used a revolving stage, much less two of them."[39]

7. The Band Wagon *and "Dancing in the Dark"* 67

So imaginative was the use of these stages that they "sometimes became a partner in the action."[40] The stages enhanced several scenes, including: "White Heat," where the dancers in full dress and high-hat are carried off by the stage[41]; "I Love Louisa," the first act finale, where the cast emerged on a working merry-go-round; "Hoops," in which the Astaires romped in a Parisian park as *enfants terribles*, "wreaking havoc on everyone and everything in sight"; and "The Beggar Waltz."[42] In this last one, Fred Astaire, as a beggar on the steps of the Vienna Opera House, dreams of romance with the prima ballerina, Tilly Losch, and the scene is transported from the streets to the theater and back, all in a dream sequence.

Max Gordon raved about these revolving stages: "Short and Johnson had integrated them into the action in all sorts of imaginative ways until they seemed to create a poetry of their own. In the finale [Act I] they turned in opposite directions, one of them bearing a carousel while on the other the Astaires danced as they had never danced before, and the orchestra played the contagious polka, 'I Love Louisa.'"[43] Historian Cecil Smith added this thought about the revolving stages: "A part of the delight of *The Band Wagon* lay in its transmutation of stage machinery into something approaching lyric poetry. The first American revue to take full cognizance of the revolving stage, it had two of them, and used them in all sorts of imaginative ways as an integral part of the bright Albert Johnson settings and the action and business devised by Short."[44]

Schwartz and Dietz, working their evening shifts at the St. Moritz and other Manhattan hotels, came up with a score described as "varied, gorgeous and imaginative,"[45] making "pop tunes into the cream of theatre songs."[46] Going further, Gerald Bordman opined, "the passage of time has suggested that the music was the crowning jewel of the evening. Schwartz created one of the greatest of all revue scores."[47]

When *The Band Wagon* opened on June 3, 1931, the songs were as varied as the sketches in the show. The Astaires carried them all off well as singers, dancers, and comedians. Fred especially shone as a comedian in the show. Journalist Lincoln Barnett described this in a biographical sketch of Fred twenty years later: "It was *The Band Wagon* that first proved to the Astaires and the public that Fred was separable from Adele. In the interest of economy the producers of *The Band Wagon* hired only a small cast and relied on Fred and Adele to do a great many things besides dance. Skits were varied, and with some misgivings the producers handed Fred a fantastic assortment of character parts. The morning after the opening ... there was ... an unexpected chorus of astonishment and delight at Fred Astaire's newly revealed talents as a comedian."[48]

An interesting song was "New Sun in the Sky," about which musical historian Larry Stempel wrote, "Sung and danced by Fred Astaire, the song exhibits the kind of optimism musicals cultivated during the Depression. It celebrates a newfound love, which so colors the singer's world as to make everything else in it new as well."[49] The Dietz lyric is simple but complements Schwartz's tune well. Of the song, Alec Wilder said, "It had to be a great deal of fun to write, and it sounds as if it all happened quickly, with no panic or brain cudgeling, while the writer was feeling particularly well, confident, and hopeful."[50] Between June and October of 1931, Fred and the Leo Reisman Orchestra recorded "New Sun in the Sky," "I Love Louisa," "White Heat," and "Hoops," the last with Adele, her final recording.[51]

Four months after the show opened, the RCA Victor Company chose to do a long-play version of *The Band Wagon* selections. This October 5, 1931, recording was at 33⅓ rpm, on a twelve-inch disc, with ten minutes of music on each side, and required a special turntable. Victor labeled this a "Program Transcription" and while not strictly a full cast-recording, it was a prototype of later full cast recordings which would be perfected by Columbia Records on LP recordings.[52] On the recording of *The Band Wagon*, the program is introduced by Leo Reisman who elicits a hello from the Astaires, Schwartz, and Dietz. Schwartz plays piano on one cut with a jazzy introduction and accompaniment to Fred's singing.

As a recording artist and the lead male singer in a show, Fred Astaire was often viewed with surprise or puzzlement, much as was Ethel Merman. But both could put over a song—Merman with her projection and Astaire with his phrasing—and composers knew it. Schwartz discussed this issue with a Canadian journalist forty-five years later: "Fred had a small voice. But every Broadway musical composer agrees with me that Fred's phrasing was best if you were introducing a new song. He always did sing closest to the composer's intention."[53] In close agreement, Astaire held fast to his singing of a song: "I like to do the songs just the way they were written. There's a tendency for a good many singers to take and mutilate a melody the minute it's given to them."[54]

Schwartz and Dietz included another optimistic song in their score, "High and Low," a hit song recycled from *Here Comes the Bride*, their 1930 London show. Both Dietz and Englishman Desmond Carter wrote the lyrics. It was performed early in Act I by Roberta Robinson, John Barker, and The Girls, a twenty-member chorus. It would be the only song not written specifically for *The Band Wagon*. Schwartz also wrote instrumental music for the show, one piece for a Frank Morgan and Helen Broderick sketch titled "When the Rain Goes Pitter-Patter," and another for a ballet sequence, "The Beggar Waltz." The latter instrumental was later given lyrics by Dietz to create a popular song, "Is It All a Dream?"[55]

One song in the show, "Confession," was sung as a dialogue between

7. The Band Wagon and "Dancing in the Dark" 69

The Girls and The Boys. The males wish to be confessors to the females and urge them to confess their "innermost thoughts." After an extended verse, the refrain is done in a standard thirty-two bar form in which The Girls quietly admit that: they would not kiss a man unless they knew his name; preferred the taste of gin over wine; and may go to bed early but then go home late. The bridge, sung by The Boys, asserts that virtue is its own reward.[56] It is all quite tongue-in-cheek. This was the only song from the show that was performed on Broadway but not cleared for broadcasting. Alec Wilder had much to say about "Confession": "It conveys a kind of humorously arch innocence, lyrically proven suspect, and though the lyric reveals less than innocence, the melody remains virginal.... The juxtaposition of viewpoints was what made 'In the Morning, No' by Cole Porter so effective. The lyric of the latter, however, made the delicacy of its melody ludicrous. In the case of 'Confession,' the lyric doesn't become gamey."[57]

In her 1956 album, *Censored*, theater and cabaret singer Martha Wright recorded Broadway songs that had all been banned from the air waves. Ms. Wright, who "imparts a certain class to the saucy wordage," sings "Confession" and eleven others.[58] Well-known songs on the album include: Porter's "Let's Do It," "Let's Misbehave," and "Love for Sale"; Rodgers and Hart's "Bewitched, Bothered and Bewildered"; and Berlin's "Doin' What Comes Naturally" and "Moonshine Lullaby."[59] "Confession" fits well into the collection of naughty songs.

Another light-hearted number and a perfect first act closer was "I Love Louisa," the song Schwartz had sung to Max Gordon over the phone, convincing Gordon that he, Schwartz, was the man for the job. More than any other song from *The Band Wagon*, "I Love Louisa" was a product of Schwartz and Dietz's hotel collaboration. As with many of their songs—and those of other songwriters—"I Love Louisa" began with a title, this one thrown out to Schwartz as Dietz left the St. Moritz Hotel for his daytime advertising job.[60] Their German chambermaid, Louisa, would often linger on her cleaning chores to listen to the songs Schwartz and Dietz were working on. As *The Band Wagon* needed a rousing Act One finale, the lyricist told the composer "I Love Louisa" might work, and according to Schwartz, Dietz then left "a dummy lyric of eight measures.... That morning I set the song and we finished it that night."[61]

Dietz simplified the matter years later in the *Lyrics and Lyricists Series*: "Yes, if you're working with Arthur Schwartz on a score for a Broadway show, and if you're staying at the Essex House [sic] and if your chambermaid happens to be named Louisa, what do you [do]? You write a song called 'I Love Louisa.'"[62] For that same presentation, in response to a question regarding the effect of revues on his lyric writing, Dietz answered:

Lyrics for a revue must be a complete story. Since each revue idea (whether lyrics or sketch) was an entity unto itself, the songs did not have to relate to each other. <u>Disadvantage</u>: difficult to come up with ideas that were self-contained. <u>Advantage</u>: <u>Any</u> idea or subject was fair game. More comedic.[63]

A German chambermaid named Louisa fit the bill—fair game, self-contained, and comedic. Years later, Schwartz recalled to Dietz George Gershwin's reaction to "I Love Louisa": "Gershwin came to the Philadelphia opening of *The Band Wagon*. I watched him all during the first act, hopeful he was approving my music and, at intermission, I followed him up the aisle hoping he would say something attractive. All he said was: 'That melody, "I Love Louisa" ... where did you get it from. It sounds like a real German folk tune.' I was crushed."[64] With the revolving stages and Fred Astaire's perfect German on one of the choruses, "I Love Louisa" became an audience favorite. *The New Yorker* critic complimented "the very nice music by Arthur Schwartz," then added, "is at his best in the simple peasant tunes such as 'Hoops' and 'I Love Louisa.'"[65]

While one critic may have appreciated Schwartz's "peasant tunes," it was his more serious melodies that caught the attention of the audience and critics. He wrote a beguiling waltz, "The Beggar Waltz," that accompanied a dream / dance sequence that best exemplified the synergistic talents of the creators of *The Band Wagon*. Ethan Mordden makes a case that it was the first dream sequence in the history of the musical, long before "Laurey Makes Up Her Mind" in *Oklahoma!* or "Peter's Dream" from *Babes in Arms*.[66]

The Johnson / Short revolving stage with Short's lighting changed the scene from the beggar's darkened street to the world of the premiere danseuse, a "brilliantly illuminated opera house ... done with rapidity and exquisite taste."[67] Within this setting, Albertina Rasch's waltz ballet was danced by Tilly Losch and Fred Astaire; "Astaire's handling of balletic chores was a new field for him to conquer."[68] Though a stage dancer and hoofer up to that time, Astaire comported himself well in the ballet, making a worthy partner for the classically-trained Losch. Her remembrances of working with the mild-mannered Fred Astaire on that show were bitter: "She thought Fred was dictatorial and used to call him Mussolini because at the time (1930–1) 'we thought Mussolini was the bossiest thing in the world.'"[69] Of the music for "The Beggar Waltz," a friend of Schwartz telegrammed him: "IT HAS THE SAME QUALITY OF LEHAR AND STRAUSS MUSIC ITS GREAT YOU SOUNDED JUST LIKE YOU."[70] In 1953, the melody would be used in the film, *The Band Wagon*, which incorporated a number of Schwartz / Dietz songs. Cyd Charisse, as ballerina Gabrielle Gerard, performs in *Giselle*. For the scene, the original ballet music of *Giselle*, written by Adolphe Adam, was replaced by "The Beggar Waltz."

Olin Downes, classical music critic of the *New York Times*, had high praise for the composer of "The Beggar Waltz": "Mr. Schwartz does not ape Messrs. Gershwin, Berlin or other current and successful writers of light music today. He dares to write in other rhythms than that of jazz. He is perfectly willing and able to pen a sensuous waltz and do it with unhackneyed sentiment, or write in other dance rhythms known to previous generations, and this with extraordinary verve and temperament—even feeling—which runs at precisely the depth required by his subject. Witness the scene of the Beggar waltz…"[71] Dietz commented on the interest Downes had shown Schwartz's work: "Olin Downes, the critic of the *New York Times*, was the first serious fellow to recognize Schwartz's 'musical invention of a high order,' 'the diverting variety of his style,' 'his graceful melodic vein.'"[72]

For Schwartz and Dietz, the crowning achievement in the score was "Dancing in the Dark," another song that had its origins in a title. At Dietz's home one evening, the lyricist "said he wanted to write a song that had more than just a romantic meaning, something that said more than 'Darling I Love You,' something about Man and his existence."[73] Along those lines, Schwartz had felt that "we needed a dark, somewhat mystical song to relieve the pace."[74] Dietz began looking along the titles of his shelved books, looking for an idea, and came across *Dancers in the Dark*: "'That's it,' he [Dietz] said, '"dancing in the dark,"' and I got his meaning immediately. I said that in a sense you mean all of us are dancing in the dark, yes, that is what I [Dietz] mean."[75] From that point on, Schwartz recalled the writing of the melody: "It was very late by now, but I went straight to the piano and I played this melody as if I had known it all my life. It took one minute or so to play. It took me one minute to write the tune and it took Howard two or three weeks to write the lyrics. … I'll tell you what I was aware of, not that it was going to be a hit. I regarded it as something fascinating and different, different from what I had heard anywhere else in form and in mood."[76]

Songwriter / conductor André Previn agreed with Schwartz that the song was different: "The truth is that with 'Dancing in the Dark' they'd stumbled on a kind of approach to ballad writing that was (a) completely original and (b) very touching and poignant in a way that popular songs are not usually expected to be."[77] Son Jonathan Schwartz corroborated the account of the quickness of the writing, describing it as an "insistent melody" for his father, who wrote it so swiftly, it was "as if it already existed."[78]

At first glance, "Dancing in the Dark" is about dancing and romance: "Slow, sensuous, mystical, and muted, with a definite impression of tentativeness and anticipation, 'Dancing' is a superb representation of two close together lovers passionately moving around a dance floor. No other American popular song has as capably captured the blend of dance, trance, and romance."[79] It also became a favorite of the jazz crowd, being recorded by the likes of Cannonball Adderley, Tony Bennett, Bill Evans, Ella Fitzgerald, Diana Krall, and Charlie Parker. Artie Shaw made a recording in 1941, arranged by Lenny Hayton, that sold over one million copies.[80] Frank Sinatra recorded it in 1958 "as if it were simply about dancing."[81]

Before all these artists, however, Bing Crosby recorded a version in 1931, soon after *The Band Wagon* had opened. It was the nadir of the Depression as well as his personal life, and according to Morris Dickstein in his *Dancing in the Dark: A Cultural History of the Great Depression*, Crosby's recording "spoke for the nation's mood as much as for his own."[82] Though considered a crooner at the time and not far from his days as one of "The Rhythm Boys," he took command of the song, recording a definitive version:

> But Crosby gave full play to its darker shadings. His version encompasses, yet goes beyond the dance floor; vividly, it evokes a sense of the darkness surrounding our lives. Working on many levels, it could refer just as easily to the darkened ballroom, our own darkest feelings, the existential limits of the human condition, or the ongoing troubles of the Depression. The range of emotion that Crosby brought to this song, the mixture of melancholy and hope, could not have been better keyed to the moment. The feeling is not simply in the lyric but in the surging melody that enforces the rhyme....[83]

This was a new decade—dominated by the Depression and looking at the Roaring Twenties in the rear view mirror—and Arthur Schwartz was a good fit as its composer: "He brought a sound of unusual elegance to the Broadway theatre and left a half-dozen standards that still evoke the svelte era that replaced the raucous twenties. 'Dancing in the Dark' is the perfect emblem of the new decade."[84] Dickstein described it as "a song about a community of two surrounded by a great darkness, a moment of tenuous joy whose backdrop is impermanence and insecurity...."[85] Ethan Mordden went further, calling the song "fatalistic."[86]

Perhaps all this is making too much of "Dancing in the Dark," but it became the crown jewel not only of the show but of the Schwartz and Dietz oeuvre. It has been recorded over a thousand times.[87] It was listed as one of *Variety* magazine's "Golden 100 Tin Pan Alley Songs, 1918–1935."[88] Whether sung as a song for dancing or a reflection of the burdens of a nation, performed solo by John Barker or danced mysteriously by Tilly Losch in *The Band Wagon*, it was an instant—and perennial—classic. Alec Wilder gave it high praise: "It is of conventional thirty-two measure length, and mysteriously gives the illusion of being a very rangy melody, whereas it is only one and a half tones more than an octave. Its principal characteristic is the use of repeated notes, which, because they are interrupted by stepwise, sinuous phrases, never become overinsistent."[89]

The creators of *The Band Wagon* were an inventive group, and none more so than the composer, Arthur Schwartz. While nearly every review of the show was complimentary of various performers and creators, classical music critic of the *New York Times*, Olin Downes, devoted a great deal of his commentary on the show to Schwartz's score. Downes' opening paragraph was not equivocal: "If we are not mistaken, this is the first time Mr. Schwartz has come fully into his own as a composer. He has collaborated in other diverting material, as in 'Three Is a Crowd,' [sic] and his signal ability evidently led to his being entrusted with the very difficult and exacting task of writing music for more than two hours of entertainment in the form of various pieces for a kaleidoscopic revue. Mr. Schwartz has accomplished this with characteristic wit and ingenuity and much musical invention of a high order."[90]

Downes admits that although Schwartz "deliberately imitates conventionality," he does it "with a twist and a sting in the music which shows a temperamental as well as an objective grasp of the spirit of the piece." Turning his focus to the future of American music, Downes expresses hope: "Who knows? Who dares to breathe the hope that the show which opened last week may constitute promise of a distant day when we shall have a school of American musical revue, comedy, operetta or what not, with characteristics as truly distinguishing as those of operetta schools of Paris or Vienna or other representative centres of art? Best of all, if the indications of Mr. Schwartz's music are trustworthy, ours will not be a school which casts its ideas in any one mold, or limits its forms by any fixed tradition."[91]

Three days before this June 7, 1931, Sunday commentary, Downes had written Schwartz a note, telling him of the upcoming article. The critic tells Schwartz that "if it has any effect in shaking other composers for the theatre out of their lethargy I shall be more than happy—but I should use the subjunctive, for nothing of the kind can possibly happen." After thanking Schwartz for tickets, Downes wanted "still more to thank you for the originality and esprit and, I think, far-reaching effect of your excellent music. To thank the artist is so much more pleasurable than only to thank the man!"[92]

Audiences and critics alike raved about *The Band Wagon*, Arthur Schwartz, and his collaborators. They had raised the revue to a new level with their exclusive trio of writers—Schwartz, Dietz, and Kaufman—producing "light, sleek, elegant, mocking songs and sketches." In doing so, "they wittily superseded the elephantine entertainments against which they were reacting."[93] Cecil Smith put the issue into a broader context: "Broadway producers quickly learned that they might as well spare their energy and save the money of their backers if their shows were not equipped to outwit the motion pictures with more intelligent and fresher ideas, more pungent or subtle wit, better casting and direction, and superior tastes in costumes and designs. *The Band Wagon* established a new level of discrimination."[94]

Despite the best efforts of all involved, *The Band Wagon* ran for only 260 performances in 1931–32 but may have run for 400 or more in the preceding decade when everyone had more money. Schwartz reminded his interviewer in a 1958 oral history: "People don't remember now how short runs were of great hits. … Less than a year, on a musical show, was considered a great, big smashing success."[95]

Schwartz was happy and proud with the direction of his professional development. He had been part of the redirection and rejuvenation of the revue form: "In the *First Little Show* [sic] he saw the gestation of a new idea for the American musical stage, an idea which reached the greatest point of its development in *The Band Wagon*."[96] This show issued in a new era for Broadway entertainment, and more specifically, the revue. Despite his sudden success, Schwartz was well aware that this new kind of revue did not just happen but was "the culmination of a long development."[97] He intended to continue along this same course and write even better songs for revues and other forms of musical theater. For now, it was London calling for two more successful shows.

8

Flying Colors and "Alone Together"

"Its brooding minor key reflects the novel lyrical contradiction of 'alone' and 'together.'"[1]

Success can be hard to follow: making a sequel to a hit movie; following the act that brought down the house; improving on the Broadway revue that set the standard for the genre. That is what Arthur Schwartz and Howard Dietz faced after their hit, *The Band Wagon*. Not only that show, but their two previous successes—*The Little Show* and *Three's a Crowd*—added to the difficulty. A Philadelphia critic would later conclude of *Flying Colors*: "Its greatest handicap is that it follows in the trail of such distinguished musical-comedy pathfinders."[2]

The producer for their new revue was again Max Gordon. Schwartz, Dietz, and Gordon, along with George S. Kaufman, had created a sleek, intimate revue in *The Band Wagon*. But now it was the middle of the Depression, and Gordon wanted to be able to attract a bigger audience, afraid that revues for small, sophisticated audiences might bring small, unprofitable results: "Because of the economic climate we decided that although we would try to do another, sophisticated, modern revue for essentially the same audience that had admired *Three's a Crowd* and *The Band Wagon*, we could not afford to make it too restricted for the general taste. Hence the decision to present the revue on a larger scale than *The Band Wagon*."[3] So Gordon made *Flying Colors* "a bigger affair, spectacular in mounting yet stylish and 'modernistic,' as they used to say, in treatment."[4]

To ensure success, they hired Tamara Geva to dance; Charles Butterworth, Imogene Coca, Patsy Kelly, and Philip Loeb to elicit laughter; and Clifton Webb to do everything. Webb, in particular, was a favorite of Max Gordon: "He could dance, act, clown and sing. Indeed, one critic had said of him, 'Little or no scenery is needed when Webb is on the stage—he is his own production.'"[5] These were Broadway veterans, giving Schwartz and Dietz freedom to experiment with sketches and songs. Less known to Broadway audiences was harmonicist Larry Adler. A virtuoso of his instrument, the eighteen-year-old Adler was also known for his chutzpah. Schwartz asked Adler to audition for *Flying* Colors. Adler recounted the audition in his autobiography, *It Ain't Necessarily So*: "I went to their studio in the Essex House in Central Park South. Schwartz played the score and somehow I got the idea that, not only was I already *in* the show, but that the whole thing was being built around me. This seemed to me entirely logical. I liked 'Alone Together,' said I'd do that as my main solo, but let on that I'd be cooperative about playing the other tunes as well. Schwartz and Dietz looked at each other; they'd never come across such a big-headed *schmuck* in their lives." Adler left a distinctly "unfavorable impression,"[6] but the songwriters recognized his talent and convinced Max Gordon to hire him.

Adler was to accompany a young brother / sister duo, Buddy and Vilma Ebsen, in their big number, "A Shine on Your Shoes." The harmonicist was impressed with the Ebsens, describing them as "a team who, even in rehearsals, stole the show."[7] After *Flying Colors*, the Ebsens worked in Hollywood and were a hit in *Broadway Melody of 1936*. Vilma returned to New York, and her last Broadway show was another by Schwartz and Dietz, *Between the Devil*, which opened in late 1937. Buddy would continue on in movies and then enjoy a big career in television. In that medium, he co-starred as George Russell in *Walt Disney's Davy Crockett: King of the Wild Frontier* (1953–54); as Jed Clampett in *The Beverly Hillbillies* (1962–71); and as the title character in *Barnaby Jones* (1973–80).[8] A third newcomer for *Flying Colors* was Jean Sargent, a radio singer from Philadelphia. Her first Broadway role had been in *Face the Music*, for which she had drawn wide attention.

On the creative side, Schwartz and Dietz would be the only songwriters, the latter also being the principal sketch writer and stage director. This led to labeling *Flying Colors* as *The New Howard Dietz Revue*.[9] Going for their fourth consecutive success, Gordon and his songwriters sought new talent "for a change of pace." For lighting and set design, they hired Norman Bel Geddes, who had worked in opera, theater, and even ice shows. He was also making a name for himself in industrial design with projects that were streamlined and looking to the future. Gordon appreciated "his heralded flair for the spectacular," but ultimately found him "overbearing and unsympathetic."[10]

The other "change of pace" hire was Agnes de Mille, an experienced ballet dancer and choreographer, new to Broadway assignments. Rarely had she and her associate, Warren Leonard, choreographed for a group larger than two. De Mille encountered numerous problems working on the show. Her biographer, Carol Easton, detailed the issues: "*Flying Colors*, so-called

8. Flying Colors and "Alone Together"

because half of the chorus girls were 'colored,' was an answered prayer. ... The sixteen African-American girls were talented but inexperienced, and their Caucasian counterparts were not dancers but showgirls, foisted on the choreographers by Gordon, Dietz, and Schwartz. The day had not yet come when more professional dancers / ballet dancers were used on Broadway, a practice pioneered by de Mille, George Balanchine, and Albertina Rasch. Due to a lack of communication and Agnes's lack of assertiveness, the costumes and sets were designed with no regard for the fact that dancers would be required to move in them."[11]

After disputes with Gordon, Dietz, and Bel Geddes,[12] de Mille was eventually let go and replaced by Albertina Rasch, who had done excellent work for *The Band Wagon*. Although recognizing de Mille's talent, Gordon felt she was "unused to the pressures of preparing a Broadway show."[13] De Mille would write years later that Schwartz had been especially kind to her at the time of the firing: "when he had fired me from *Flying Colors* last summer he had tried so hard to cheer me up: kissed me as I wept and advised me to start troupes of girls in out-of-town nightclubs."[14]

While personnel could often cause problems in mounting a Broadway show, financing was always a problem. Many Broadway producers were forever hustling for financing and trying to forestall bankruptcy. The Depression, which reached its nadir in early 1932, was a major factor. As Gordon saw it: "getting money for the new show, *Flying Colors*, was impossible. Bankrolls—what there were of them—had gone into hiding. Brokers on whom I had counted were in trouble. There was talk of surprisingly few new productions. My own personal financial position deteriorated."[15] Because he had made good profits on *The Band Wagon* and Jerome Kern's *The Cat and the Fiddle*, Gordon would spend heavily, convinced that "it was necessary to keep up appearances." He was also burdened by stocks he had purchased on margin. Three-fourths of the initial $100,000 investment for *Flying Colors* came from Gordon, Dietz, and Lee Shubert, each of whom contributed $25,000. Biographer of the Shuberts, Jerry Stagg, described the next development: "The remaining unsold fourth was owned by all three. Lee without discussion sold his part of the 25 percent left for $25,000, which in effect meant that he was a quarter partner with no investment. It was the way Rockefeller began."[16]

Gordon was not as shrewd as Lee Shubert, and a mountain of problems emerged as *Flying Colors* neared its tryout in Philadelphia: the financial deficit remained; there was a large theft of money at the Globe Theatre, where Gordon's show, *The Cat and the Fiddle*, was playing[17]; Agnes de Mille had to be fired; a set collapsed, severely injuring two of the chorus girls[18]; and more than the usual pre-opening snags.[19] Gordon summed it up, "Nothing seemed ready—the dances, costumes, lighting—everything was out of joint. ... All that I had built and striven for in the last two and a half years was being washed away."[20]

This all worked adversely on Gordon's psychological health and came to a head at the Forrest Theatre, in Philadelphia, where he attempted to jump to his death twice. He was stopped both times at the last second by Ben Boyar, his general manager. In a candid discussion in 1963, the showman detailed his difficulties:

> All the way back I cried, berated those associated with me, repeated mournfully that I was bankrupt, dishonored, that life was useless and no longer worth living. I wished I were dead....
>
> In the end, each case is individual, and recovery depends to a considerable degree on the complexity of the disturbance and the patient's own will to recover and live. For what seemed like an eternity to those near me, I did not care. There was no use in telling myself that after a series of hits I was entitled to one failure.[21]

He was diagnosed with what today would be considered major depression, but at the time was called a nervous breakdown. After hospitalization, months of therapy, and the support of family and numerous theater friends, Gordon recovered—as did his *Flying Colors*.

The show developed a cohesiveness and style of entertainment that appealed to audiences, but not to critics, who appeared ready to pounce on the fourth Schwartz / Dietz revue. Brooks Atkinson's review, titled "Flying the Band Wagon Colors," gave the show its due for "incomparable agility," but, referring to the fourth of four, declared, "Now that the freshness of style has worn off in the fourth generation the aristocracy of musical entertainment needs new blood."[22] It was also said, "a note of sameness seemed to be creeping into their formula."[23] On the other hand, referring to the previous successful shows, the *Evening Post* felt, "*Flying Colors* embroiders and elaborates on the finer qualities of *Three's a Crowd* and *The Band Wagon*." However, Dietz's sketches came in for criticism as "too long," "echoes" [of previous shows], and "crude or sophomoric."[24] Another scribe said the sketches "seemed always to run down like an unwound clock before they finished."[25] Even if the sketches might have been weak, the performers were not. Charles Butterworth was singled out for praise in nearly every New York review, and the other cast members contributing to comic sketches—Coca, Kelly, and Loeb—were mentioned as well.

If the comics were put on a pedestal, Arthur Schwartz and his music were on the one next to them. From the tryout city of Philadelphia, the *Public Ledger* declared that one of the paramount attributes of *Flying Colors* was "the glowing, but under-accentuated score of Arthur Schwartz," suggesting that after out-of-town adjustments were made, "the score had nearly a half-dozen potential smashes."[26] New York critics called the music "seductive,"[27] and composed with "an unfailing nicety, ingenuity, daintiness."[28]

Franklin P. Adams said that "what I liked best was the musique of Arthur Schwartz's, which seemed to me lovely and unhackneyed and melodious."[29] Another member of the reviewing corps gave credit to both Schwartz and his orchestrators—Hans Spialek, Edward B. Powell, Arthur Schutt, and Robert Russell Bennett—pointing out that the show held "music which consists of complex harmonizations as a basis for a wandering melodic line ornamented with effective orchestration and skillful instrumentation."[30]

Schwartz's score displayed a spectrum of songs: slow to fast; lighthearted to melancholic; and hopeful to dire. A trio of light, up-tempo songs stood out. "Louisiana Hayride" closed the first act in a rousing manner, "a joyous recreation of old Negro gospel songs with lyrics in fitting Negro dialect."[31] Schwartz recalled to Dietz that it was the "fastest song I ever wrote ... with you. As I recall, words and music of the chorus were written in about a half-hour."[32] Remembrances by Dietz of the writing of "Louisiana Hayride" were available in unpublished background material for *Dancing in the Dark*, his autobiography:

> They were writing a musical which had a negro troupe. A folksy tune was indicated. What about a hayride, it's gay and colorful? Where do they have hayrides and colored people? Carolina is trite. Kansas is obvious but prosaic. Arkansas suggests hillbillys [*sic*]. Mississippi is hard to rhyme and sing. Louisiana has the locale and flows easily. Feeling for the mood, Schwartz hits a few chords, playing what comes to mind. Dietz say "Go down there," or "More punch there." Soon he is writing words on a pad. Then he sings some of them. Schwartz improvises and refines. And suddenly, like a puzzle the key to which is found, the snatches of words and music become whole. In a half hour "Louisiana Hayride" was conceived and completed.[33]

Alec Wilder was taken by the dichotomy of the song: "It's a deliberate country song with sophisticated handling. This is a special kind of song, not easy to write if both countrification and sophistication are desired. Arlen's 'Shade of the New Apple Tree' is one. So, to a degree, is Schwartz's own 'A Gal in Calico.'"[34] "Louisiana Hayride" was a hit with audiences as well as buyers of recordings and sheet music. It received a big production number featuring Nanette Fabray in the 1953 film, *The Band Wagon*.

Looking at another up-tempo number, "Smokin' Reefer," "one may wonder what a tribute to marijuana is doing in a Dietz / Schwartz musical."[35] This blues song was unabashedly about marijuana, which was popular in jazz circles and Harlem and not illegal in 1932. Not knowing how hip an audience they had, the producer and manager of *Flying Colors* wrote an explanatory note beneath the title of the song in the program: "Note: A 'reefer' is a narcotic cigarette, made from the mariahuana weed, frequently smoked in the tropics and recently popular in Harlem."[36] Songs about marijuana were not unheard of in the early thirties, as jazz band-leader Don Redman had an instrumental hit with "Chant of the Weed."[37] Bandleader /

singer Cab Calloway performed two reefer songs in 1932, "Have You Ever Met That Funny Reefer Man,"[38] by J. Russell Robinson and Andy Razaf, and "The Wail of the Reefer Man." The latter was written by Harold Arlen and Ted Koehler for the *Cotton Club Parade* (21st edition) in 1932 which starred Calloway and Aida Ward.[39]

"Smokin' Reefers" provided the creators of *Flying Colors* the opportunity to use the African American chorus, who gave the show a "primitive savor,"[40] and an "exotic" feel with "Harlem's smouldering sex and sin singers."[41] Schwartz was able to capture the spirit of the setting and the drug for the melody of "Smokin' Reefers," described as "a Harlemese down-beat—very intricate for a revue song—...executed with marked fervor."[42] It was the choreography for this song which was the only work of Agnes de Mille and Warren Leonard that was retained for *Flying Colors*.[43] Despite the popularity of the song with audiences, the cast and crew had mixed feelings about it. The Bel Geddes set for "Smokin' Reefers" was the one that had collapsed and seriously injured two chorus girls. Before the accident, the set had been objected to by de Mille and Adler.[44]

But if one fast tempo number and its performers stole the show, it was "A Shine on Your Shoes." With a simple Dietz lyric, the Schwartz melody was catchy and the kind of song the audience whistles leaving the theater. As the principals "cavorted merrily around a shoeshine stand,"[45] Monette Moore sang, Larry Adler played, and Vilma and Buddy Ebsen danced, the latter two cited as "an attractive team of youthful dancers who have a way with them that caught the crowd."[46]

Schwartz had taken the song out of his trunk, something most of the popular songwriters did on a regular basis. Writer's block was a common malady among songwriters, and Schwartz readily discussed the difficulty in getting started some days. He admitted, "it takes fortitude sometimes to approach a piano or music writing table at nine a.m. without an idea in the world and sit down in cold-blood to start working up some songs. But that's the way to do it, he insists."[47]

On such days, particularly when a song was needed at that moment, the trunk could be a good solution. In the case of "A Shine on Your Shoes," he found a melody line he had noodled around with in his law school days: "As usual, Schwartz looked back into his collection of old songs, unfinished songs, rejected songs, in his effort to complete the score for *Flying Colors*. He recalled that years before, during preparations for the bar examination, he had begun whistling in the classroom, much to the displeasure of Harold Medina, the eminent master of jurisprudence who was lecturing to the class. Schwartz refined this fragment, which became 'A Shine on Your Shoes.'"[48] Of the song, Alec Wilder said: "For there is wit as well as sinewy strength to this song. And besides, it swings."[49] Years later, Fred

8. Flying Colors *and* "Alone Together"

Astaire would do a solo of the song, dancing around a shoeshine stand in an arcade in the 1953 movie *The Band Wagon*. While adept with songs that could swing, Schwartz oftentimes found them difficult to create: "Sad songs are easier to write than the other kind. Rhythm songs, songs to be danced to, and happy songs that are good, are harder to write than ballads."[50]

But Schwartz and Dietz were masters of "sad songs"—ballads—and the *Flying Colors* score did not disappoint. Lesser known in the score was "Day after Day," a song of "frenetic melancholia,"[51] sung by Clifton Webb. But the hit of the show, described as a "companion piece to 'Dancing in the Dark,'"[52] was "Alone Together." Both songs were done with an air of mystery. "Dancing in the Dark" had been performed by Tilly Losch in *The Band Wagon*, and "Alone Together" was a dance duet for Clifton Webb and Tamara Geva. Two writers expressed similar thoughts about the Webb / Geva dance on "Alone Together." John Anderson of the *New York Journal* described it as a "curiously somber and ghostly dance,"[53] and Robert Baral felt it "became so eerie and weird that the total effect was macabre."[54] Like the mirrored set of "Dancing in the Dark," "Alone Together" had a unique appearance, a "specially devised stage that slowly receded into darkness"[55] and accentuated the mood of the song. At one point, the lighting of the mostly darkened stage permitted the audience to see all of Webb, but only Geva's legs. During their duet, Jean Sargent sang the song.

Schwartz said of the two songs: "They have a mood which is similar, yeah. They both have a rhythm sense as well as a melody sense but I think the rhythms are different from each other."[56] As with "Dancing in the Dark," the lyric for "Alone Together" builds along with the melody: "Schwartz provided a melody that, once again, climbs higher and higher in step-wise repetitions, and Dietz follows them with parallel phrases ... that become increasingly bathetic."[57] This feeling was captured by Jo Stafford in a 1944 Capitol Records recording, directed by her husband / arranger, Paul Weston: "Jo Stafford's performance has just the right touch. She sings so precisely at the center of the pitch, with so little vibrato, that there is a disembodied quality to her voice—a perfect tool for this occasion." Like "Dancing in the Dark," Dietz developed a lyric focused on a couple in love, isolated from the world, if not literally, at least in their own minds: "the feeling is one of present or imminent sadness, as though to stress the 'alone' rather than the 'together.'"[58] Historian Thomas Hischak in *Word Crazy*, his discussion of lyricists, commented on the tone of Dietz's lyrics in comparison to those of another lyricist capable of sadness, Lorenz Hart: "Hart's love songs have a painful subtext; Dietz's have a sense of mystery. Hart foreshadows heartbreak and despair; Dietz looks to the future wistfully."[59]

Schwartz's haunting melody is a perfect partner to Dietz's setting: "its brooding minor key reflects the novel lyrical contradiction of 'alone' and 'together' as well as the conditional nature of the lovers' strength. The lovers are portrayed as interdependent, clinging individuals who, despite a deep love, feel strongly only as a pair in seclusion."[60] Popular song historian Allen Forte, in *The American Popular Ballad of the Golden Era*, placed it among "the best of the popular love songs of the period ... comparable to Berlin's 'How Deep Is the Ocean,' Duke's 'April in Paris,' and Porter's 'Night and Day' and 'After You, Who'—all written in 1932. ... It is a song that reveals no flaws."[61] And again Wilder: "It's a very lovely and a very dramatic song, one which with less expert handling could have fallen into artiness and pretentiousness. It never does, and Schwartz deserves great praise for keeping in the genre of legitimate theatre music."[62]

As previously mentioned, the overall score of *Flying Colors*, led by "Alone Together," was highly praised. Although not quite on a par with *The Band Wagon*, *Flying Colors* did sustain a run of 188 performances, but ran smack into the depths of the Depression. Other leading composers of the time met with similar fates during this period[63]:

Composer	*Show*	*Opened*	*Performances*
Vincent Youmans	*Through the Years*	January 28, 1932	20
Irving Berlin	*Face the Music*	February 17, 1932	165
George Gershwin	*Pardon My English*	January 20, 1933	46

The decline in audiences for *Flying Colors* continued despite Max Gordon's facing financial reality and cutting the price of a top ticket in half, from $4.40 to $2.20.[64]

After the opening of *Flying Colors* in mid–September 1932, Schwartz had a short respite from songwriting, but as fall wore on, his interest was diverted to a Broadway beauty, Katherine Wright Carrington. Jonathan Schwartz said, "My mother had come to town no older than twenty-one, with a lively mind and a generous spirit."[65] Carrington had started her stage career with the Winthrop Ames Gilbert and Sullivan Opera Company in 1926, in the chorus of *Iolanthe*. She also appeared in vaudeville with Arthur and Morton Havel, played a featured role in the *Garrick Gaieties*, and was a member of the original cast of *The Desert Song*. She had made a name for herself on Broadway substituting for Jeanne Aubert in *The Laugh Parade* with Ed Wynn after only three hours' rehearsal.[66] Soon after that, she landed the role of Kit Baker in Irving Berlin's *Face the Music*, introducing his hits "Soft Lights and Sweet Music" and "Let's Have Another Cup of Coffee." Carrington had married novelist Clifford Dowdey in 1930, but they were divorced in 1931.[67]

How she and Schwartz met is subject to debate, with one scenario

8. Flying Colors *and* "Alone Together"

coming from Jonathan Schwartz: "Katherine Carrington had been an ingénue on the stage. Arthur Schwartz had spotted her in Jerome Kern and Oscar Hammerstein's *Music in the Air* singing 'I've Told Every Little Star' to a young Walter Slezak. My father had attended the opening on election night 1932, a secondary event to FDR's first plurality but not secondary to the composer of 'Dancing in the Dark.' He sought out the ingénue almost before the curtain went down."[68]

A more likely rendition of their meeting also involves *Music in the Air*, this one from Kern's biographer, Michael Freedland: "they [Kern, Hammerstein, and impresario Peggy Fears] sat listening to a beautiful girl called Katherine Carrington going through two or three numbers. They did not notice that Miss Carrington was being given frequent encouraging glances from the rehearsal pianist in the pit ... it was clear that the pianist was willing Katherine Carrington to get the part. Finally, Kern and Hammerstein told her that the role was indeed hers.... Turning to Jerry she said: 'Mr. Kern, I'd like you to meet my accompanist, Arthur Schwartz.'"[69]

Howard Dietz related this incident a bit more amusingly, and his claims are not all in agreement with the Freedland story: "Jerome Kern was auditioning for talent and asked Arthur to accompany her. He was a little fussed at playing for the great Kern but more fussed by the young lady who got the job with Kern and Hammerstein as a result of the audition. As well as a more permanent job with Schwartz."[70] Schwartz corroborated this in unpublished notes decades later, stating they met when he accompanied her for the *Music in the Air* audition.[71]

One other complicating issue on this topic is that Carrington was understudy to Libby Holman in *The Little Show*, some time during its 1929–30 run. Carrington was involved with and then married to author Clifford Dowdey during this time.[72] Schwartz would at least have been aware of the understudy of the star of his first big hit, lending support to his role as her accompanist for her *Music in the Air* audition.

Though there might be questions here, what is not in doubt was that Schwartz had fallen in love with Katherine Carrington. According to Jonathan Schwartz, she was "adored, it seemed, by everyone around *Music in the Air*," and she considered Arthur to be "a very pleasant nuisance." Jonathan added, "In the year to follow, Arthur leapt upon every stage that Katherine traversed. Here was a blond woman with a white round face, a curvaceous form, a delightful laugh, and a clarion voice with a song inside."[73]

9

The Gibson Family and Radio

"He had given himself until September of 1934 to either be gainfully employed or return to the law, perhaps once and for all."[1]

The press release began: "Radio's first million-dollar program, 'The Gibson Family,' the first original radio musical comedy ... will be heard over a coast-to-coast NBC network starting Sept. 15 ... Procter & Gamble Co. will sponsor the program for their product, Ivory Soap."[2] The Cincinnati soap company was paying the Broadway composing team of Arthur Schwartz and Howard Dietz to do the songs and author Courtney Ryley Cooper to create an ongoing book for the radio serial. Up to this time, almost all music on radio, especially on serial programs with continuous stories, was derived from other sources—Tin Pan Alley, theater, and movies. Then Schwartz and Dietz agreed to take on the task of new weekly songs for *The Gibson Family*.

Prior to this, Schwartz had been underemployed and restless. From approximately February of 1933 to June of 1934,[3] he had been able to find only scattered work in London and had written a song here and there with lyricists other than Dietz. Mid–1933 found Schwartz working with book writer / lyricist Douglas Furber who was well-established in British musical comedy. Furber had written several shows for Jack Buchanan, the English comedy star.[4] Furber had been a co-lyricist with three others on a Schwartz melody for the song "She's Such a Comfort to Me," which had been interpolated into Cole Porter's 1929 show *Wake Up and Dream*. Helping Furber with the lyrics for the new show, *Nice Goings On*, would be Frank Eyton.

Nice Goings On was a return to musical comedy by producer / stage comedian Leslie Henson, a co-producer with Firth Shephard. Also involved was Percival Mackey, who was orchestrator for the show, and as

9. The Gibson Family *and* Radio

musical director, would conduct his Percival Mackey's Band. When Leslie was involved with a show, it would often be more farce than musical, and this production was described as a "farcical-play-with-songs-and-dances."[5] Farce shared top billing with songs as Schwartz and his lyricists penned ten of them[6]:

I Know the Kind of Girl (cut)	We've Got to Get On
The Life-Saver's Song	What a Young Girl Ought to Know
My Sweet One	
Nice Goings On	Whatever You Do
Place in the Sun	With You Here and Me
'Twixt the Devil and the Deep Blue Sea	Here

As testimony to Schwartz's growing reputation in England—"famous throughout two Continents for his irresistibly lilting tunes"[7]—there were only two interpolated songs, including "You're an Old Smoothie." This was written by Richard Whiting, Buddy DeSylva, and Nacio Herb Brown and had first been heard on Broadway in *Take a Chance*.[8]

Nice Goings On was given a tryout week in Birmingham in August 1933, then opened in London in mid–September at the Strand Theatre, enjoying a run of 221 performances there. One critic referred to Schwartz's "up-to-date" music and "catchy numbers," singling out "What a Young Girl Ought to Know," sung by Zelma O'Neal, as "one that should not be missed."[9] Also successful were Henson's amusing rendition of "The Life-Saver's Song," and a duet by O'Neal and Henson on "'Twixt the Devil and the Deep Blue Sea."[10]

That same August, Dietz wrote a letter from California to Schwartz in London, discussing current work and future possibilities. Although Dietz was comfortable and firmly established in his studio job at M-G-M, it is clear that he was sensitive to Schwartz's lack of work and had thought much about it and their partnership. He expressed all of this with sincerity and the Dietz wit:

> I have a strange feeling that your return to America will synchronize with my return to New York, which is also a return to America. As for your future, might I suggest that you don't tie yourself up too definitely without some communication with me, and I will do the same as regards you. I am not a bit dubious about the prospects of making a great deal of money. I am a little concerned about clearing the way to do distinguished work. Good business offers continually drift in and the radio ante has been raised, so anxious are the radio people to get new talent.[11]

Dietz's mention of "the radio ante" refers to their negotiations with NBC for songwriting on *The Gibson Family*.

Later in 1933, Schwartz and lyricist Edward Heyman teamed up for incidental songs in the nonmusical play *She Loves Me Not*. On the title page of the program, their credit reads, "A SONG OR TWO BY ARTHUR SCHWARTZ AND EDWARD HEYMAN."[12] They wrote "She Loves Me Not" and "After All You're All I'm After" for the show; the latter was introduced by John Beal in the play but garnered little attention. The chorus of "After All You're All I'm After" has an easy going melody, marked "slowly and gracefully."[13] Historian Thomas S. Hischak referred to Schwartz's music for the song as "both mystifying and animated."[14] Recordings were made by the Eddy Duchin Orchestra with Lew Sherwood, McKinney's Cotton Pickers, Don Redman, and Ray Noble with a vocal by Al Bowlly.

Schwartz was also writing songs on spec during this time, mostly with little success. The exception was "Then I'll Be Tired of You," which he penned in late 1933, "when things were slow in show business."[15] In a radio script years later, he recalled the song's development: "I think that's probably the only song I ever wrote that was not attached to a film or play. I wrote the melody one day and thought it was good enough to submit to somebody on the quiet, and I gave it to Yip Harburg, an old friend, and he wrote this lyric very quickly and we went to the publisher and they published it and it became a mild success. No great success but it was not connected with any show at all, just a song on its own."[16] Schwartz also pointed that is was "a love song that never uses the word love."[17] "Then I'll Be Tired of You" was recorded by Freddie Martin and His Orchestra in August 1934 and would go on to enjoy at least two dozen recordings. Jazz musicians were particularly taken to record the song, including John Coltrane, Paul Desmond, Ahmad Jamal, John Pizzarelli, George Shearing, Mel Tormé, and Stanley Turrentine.[18]

Despite these odd jobs, Schwartz considered his composing career to be at a standstill. He headed for Europe in late 1933 and wrote Katherine (Kay) Carrington from onboard a ship, shortly before reaching Gibraltar. It is a one-page letter detailing a dream he had regarding their visit to a marriage license bureau. His love for her is clear and overwhelming: "Sweet Kay, I do miss you. Be well, won't you, and don't live that fast night life you can so easily fall into when your ability to say NO gets you into dates. Read and practice and think of me…. And are you thinking of me? Are you happy? Be. I love you. You are love. You are beautiful. You are life."[19]

January 1934 found Schwartz in Hollywood, again corresponding with Carrington back in New York. They had been mostly inseparable since meeting in the fall of 1932, when she starred in *Music in the Air*. It had run until September 1933, and she had not been in a show since it had closed. His letter to her, dated January 14, is filled with love and insecurity: "Darling, darling, assure me constantly that you adore me with all my frequent

9. The Gibson Family *and Radio*

spinelessness and introspective nonsense and self-pity…. Keep those men at a distance. I am so much yours that there isn't anybody in the world who'd have a chance to steal into your place. And I want to know you too are mine." His insecurities relate not only to their relationship, but to his precarious work situation. He continues in the same letter: "I guess I haven't been meeting the right people, and Dietz doesn't extend himself to see that I should. But what the hell—he's so generous in many other ways with me, and is trying to get a Metro picture for him and me to do…. And my physical atrophy (it almost seems that way) is definitely connected with my lack of productivity in music and both will be changed when somebody gives me a job."[20] The insightful Dietz was able to view the problem from Schwartz's perspective, at least in later years: "the insecurity of living from show to show had an effect on a young man of orderly habits and none of the eccentricities that go with talent. He could not rely on me as my movie job came first."[21]

Schwartz had given himself until September 1934 to be either gainfully employed or return to the law, perhaps once and for all.[22] Just in time, the radio work to which Dietz had alluded materialized in the form of *The Gibson Family*, the weekly radio show mentioned at the beginning of the chapter. Donald Voorhees, the multi-talented orchestra leader for the new show, had been looking around for a composer willing to write at least three songs a week for a thirty-nine-week show. He eventually came upon Schwartz, "who was ready for anything."[23] With a country still in the Depression, regular employment on a radio show was appealing to Schwartz, and Dietz had agreed to do it to keep his partner solvent. It was reported that Schwartz and Dietz were each to make a weekly salary of $1,250 to turn out four new songs for each weekly show.[24] It should be noted that at the time, Dietz was also making $1,000 per week as publicity director for M-G-M.[25] $1,250 per week in 1934 was excellent money and since work on the show would begin before September—Schwartz's self-imposed deadline—there was no need for him to return to the practice of law.

With the promise of steady, lucrative employment, Schwartz and Katherine Carrington could afford to get married, which is what they did on July 7, 1934, at the Great Neck, Long Island home of Lawrence Fertig, an advertising executive, journalist, and friend of Howard Dietz. The latter acted as a witness for the ceremony as did the Fertigs. Jonathan Schwartz set the scene in his memoir: "Kay and Arthur were married in 1934 amid the theater's elite. A photograph from around that time reveals a slim, young man, dark complexioned, dark-haired, handsome, sitting on the grass in front of a country house with his arm around a beautiful, round-faced, light-skinned girl—a young woman—exhibiting a thoughtful smile." Later on, Jonathan added, "My mother, so clearly Christian, had no idea in the world what she was. Yip Harburg called her 'Arthur's shiksa.'"[26] After a brief honeymoon, Schwartz began his composing for *The Gibson Family*.

Schwartz and Dietz were not the only songwriters of the period venturing into radio. At the time, George Gershwin had been working on *Music by Gershwin*, a radio series advertising Feen-A-Mint, a chewing gum laxative.[27] In spring 1934, Gershwin was engaged in writing *Porgy and Bess* and under a time constraint, but the radio show was a steady income for him and helped support the Gershwin / DuBose Heyward opera. Heyward was appreciative and amused at the whole operation: "And with the authentic medicine-man flair, the manufacturer distributed his information in an irresistible wrapper of Gershwin hits, with the composer at the piano. There is, I imagine, a worse fate than that which derives from the use of laxative gum. And, anyhow, we felt that the end justified the means."[28]

Gershwin had always been interested in popular composers, mentoring younger ones and following their careers, and *Music by Gershwin* allowed him to exploit this. His biographer, Howard Pollack, explained: "Popular composers and lyricists flocked to George and Ira in part because of the sympathetic interest they showed toward colleagues. Whereas Gershwin stood somewhat apart from his more serious colleagues, from the mid–1920's to the end of his life he reigned as Broadway's central composer, the epicenter of a circle."[29] Those within this circle included:

Milton Ager	Jerome Kern
Harold Arlen	Burton Lane
Irving Berlin	Oscar Levant
Rube Bloom	Cole Porter
Irving Caesar	Richard Rodgers
Hoagy Carmichael	Ann Ronell
Phil Charig	Harry Ruby
Buddy DeSylva	Arthur Schwartz
Howard Dietz	Dana Suesse
Vernon Duke	Kay Swift
Johnny Green	Harry Warren
Yip Harburg	Vincent Youmans

Another Gershwin biographer, Wilfrid Sheed, pointed out, "Gershwin's embrace of other songwriters was, in short, universal, reaching back into the past and forward into the future."[30] Gershwin parlayed this into his *Music by Gershwin* program, hosting composers and discussing songs and songwriting with them.

Richard Rodgers and Lorenz Hart worked on a live CBS radio network show, *Let's Have Fun*. The plot was based on a modern-day crooner being transported to another time. The composers provided only two songs for the initial show—"A Little of You on Toast" and "Please Make Me Be Good"—and had singers Helen Morgan and Lois Long and the Freddie Rich Orchestra to get the songs across. Both songs were frequently reprised in that first show. Apparently the star, Ken Murray, was poorly prepared, causing lines and songs to be muffed. *Let's Have Fun* premiered on October 22, 1934, was described as an "unmitigated disaster,"[31] and was promptly cancelled.

Rodgers and Hart were also involved with an NBC radio show, *The Jumbo Fire Chief Program*, derived from their show *Jumbo*. The star of that show, Jimmy Durante, also starred in this circus-related radio program, a soap opera with songs. No new Rodgers and Hart songs were used, as most of the program was a transcription from the stage show. Producer Billy Rose spared no costs, and despite all the talent, the show could only garner mediocre ratings. It ran four months, closing in February 1936.[32]

From 1933 through 1937, there was a successful musical variety show, the *Maxwell House Show Boat*. It had been inspired by the success of Kern and Hammerstein's *Show Boat* and even starred Charles Winninger, the original Cap'n Andy. On this show he played Captain Henry, and a thin plot was employed. The *Maxwell House Show Boat* was described as "a pure radio fantasy of music and sound effects."[33] The show launched careers for Lanny Ross and Muriel Wilson and also included singers Annette Hanshaw and Jules Bledsoe. Later in its five-year run, *Maxwell House Show Boat* relied less on story and more on guest celebrities.[34]

During a press promotion prior to the first episode of *The Gibson Family*, Schwartz and Dietz were asked the oft-repeated question posed to songwriters, "Which comes first, the words or music?" Dietz denied either one was first, but rather that it was the "sponsor's check that was always the initial step."[35] Faced with that same question often, Ira Gershwin would answer, "The contract."[36] During that same promotional gathering, Schwartz was asked if writing so many tunes over such a short period would take a lot out of him, he replied, "Yes, but not as much as it will take out of Bach, Beethoven, and Brahms."[37]

Procter & Gamble and the Blackman Advertising Agency envisioned *The Gibson Family* as a new art form—radio musical comedy. It would be developed within the confines of a thirty-minute show and the promotion of their product. The print promotional ads prior to the show featured fictional daughter Sally Gibson. She extolled the virtues of Ivory Soap, which she used on her face, and Ivory Flakes, which she used for her washing. The idea was that both were gentle and "99 and 44/100% pure"—a catchphrase of the ad campaign. During the show's intermissions, the announcer would occasionally talk to Sally backstage, and in one instance, she gave her maid, Hilda, complexion advice. Of course, Ivory Soap was the answer.[38]

About the three principal creators of *The Gibson Family*—Schwartz, Dietz, and Cooper—an upstate New York journalist wrote: "Schwartz is an old hand at composing show hits. Howard Dietz wrote the lyrics and he is an old hand at that. Courtney Ryley Cooper wrote the story—another old hand."[39] Cooper was indeed an old hand, having held several jobs in the circus and rodeo fields as a clown, press agent, and manager. He then turned to writing, creating thirty novels, fifteen movie scripts, and 2,000 short stories, mostly for magazines. He had begun radio work only in 1933, writing scripts for *Circus Days*, an NBC radio drama.[40]

Donald Voorhees was the musical director and conductor for *The Gibson Family*, leading the Ivory Orchestra and the all-male Ivory City Quartet.[41] Voorhees would go on to be director / conductor for the *Bell Telephone Hour* on radio from 1940 to 1959, then on television from 1959 through 1968, for a run of twenty-eight years.[42] The vocal arrangements and direction were to be done by another member of the Voorhees musical organization, Ken Christy.[43] Those involved in the casting included Schwartz, Dietz, Cooper, Ivory Soap representatives and Blackman Advertising Agency executives.[44] Casting was complicated by the fact that not all of the radio actors could sing, requiring double casting. Like the movies, but unlike theater, radio actors could be dubbed. Ultimately, the cast was as follows[45]:

Character	*Voiced by*	*Sung by*
Mr. Gibson	Jack Roseleigh; Bill Adams	Unsung role
Mrs. Gibson	Anne Elstner	Unsung role
Sally Gibson	Adele Ronson	Lois Bennett (soprano)
Bobby Gibson	Jack Clemens	Jack Clemens (tenor) Al Dary (tenor)
Jack Hamilton	Warren Hull John McGovern	Conrad Thibault (baritone)
Dotty Marsh	Loretta Clemens	Loretta Clemens (contralto)
Theophilus ("Awful")	Ernest "Bubbles" Whitman	Unsung role

Cooper's story line revolved around the Gibsons—Pa, Ma, Sally, and Bobby—and principal antagonist Jack Hamilton, a local dude rancher who has taken a liking to Sally. In turn, Hamilton draws the ire of her father. A secondary romantic line was provided by Bobby Gibson and his girlfriend, Dotty Marsh.[46] For comedic relief there was Theophilus, a character for which the *Variety* critic took the writers to task: "the veteran colored valet, butler and general man o' the house who alternatingly reminds of Stepin

Fetchit's delivery and that of a minstrel end-man. That character jars a bit, being discordantly unreal whenever he asserts himself." Of the initial plot and characters, *Variety* summarized: "Heralded as a typically American cross-section of family life, it's all predicated on a homely, romantic premise, patently designed to catch maximum audience appeal in that its pattern is primed to embrace drama, music, comedy—and suspense."[47]

The songs were designed to entertain and advance the plot as well, much as was occurring in Broadway musical comedy. It had been the convention of radio shows of all types—dramas, comedies, variety shows—to make use of current and not-so-current songs. With *The Gibson Family*, the idea was to have new songs for each week's episode, all "brand new to radio listeners."[48] Jack Brinkeley of the *Radio Guide*, expanded on this: "Heretofore listeners have been forced to lend an ear to broadcasts composed largely of second-hand musical numbers … created for the stage and photoplay and offered, in part, to the broadcasters. These same compositions have worn thin by being played on many programs, until they are close to boring from repetition."[49]

The musical format, which had to accommodate commercials, intermissions, and song reprises, dictated four new songs each week. Pointing out the burden facing Schwartz and Dietz, *Variety* explained: "They, too, have no mean task, as the exigencies of the hour necessitate the creation of almost instantaneously appealing ditties, unfortified by prior radio or other exploitation. Each number must click with the auditors pronto and, when reprised, take on the added appeal of mellowness."[50] Samuel Kaufman of the *New York Sun* added, "As in standard stage musical comedy, there will be frequent recourse to reprises in order to convey an atmosphere, established when the song was first introduced on the program."[51] A look at the program and the four Schwartz / Dietz songs for the premier gives a clear idea of the format[52]:

First Act	Second Act
"Overture"	"Overture"
"Absent Minded"	"Hi De Home Sweet Home"
"Cowboy, Where Are You Riding?"	Reprise: "Under Your Spell"
"Under Your Spell"	Reprise: "Absent Minded"
Reprise: "Under Your Spell"	Reprise: "Cowboy, Where Are You Riding?"; "Under Your Spell" (theme music)

Of these four, only "Under Your Spell" was ever used again on the show, becoming the theme song for *The Gibson Family*. Four new songs were the standard procedure from week to week, and Dietz recalled, "In that period, it seems to me, I never came out of the shower without a new lyric. And Arthur always had a tune for it."[53]

Schwartz and Dietz worked closely with radio script writer Cooper, reading his weekly scripts in advance, discussing where to place the four songs, and deciding how these might advance the plot; these were songs that Cooper referred to as "self-interlocking." It would be expected that songs be fit into the plot, but with Schwartz and Dietz, the cart often came before the horse, as detailed by Cooper:

> Sometimes they get a sudden song idea and ask me if I can use it. Then I can write a dramatic situation leading up to the song. Occasionally a suggestion by Dietz and Schwartz leads to a considerable altering of a script's action or the inclusion of new characters. For example, Schwartz called me on the phone one day and said he worked up a number called "Tell It to Aunt Eliza." I heard it and thought it was quite suitable for the series. But I told Schwartz I would have to hold it until the third script so that, by that time, I could plausibly work in a character to be known as "Aunt Eliza," even though I did not have any intention to do so until his song suggestion reached me.[54]

Whichever came first, plot or songs, all were in agreement that songwriting for the radio had its problems. Despite the urgency of the situation, Schwartz and Dietz wanted to maintain the quality of their output, and Dietz was aware that his composer would not let him down. In a 1971 interview, he discussed this with Joan Taylor:

> **J:** Well, that [*The Gibson Family*] was a show in which you wrote a song a day, wasn't it, and you were working at MGM at the time. How did you manage to schedule that in, how much time did it take you?
> **HD:** I could write a song every five minutes, that would be enough time for me to go to work on.
> **J:** If you could get a fast enough composer.
> **HD:** Yes, and a rhythmic title. You have a sort of telepathic feeling. I couldn't write a song with Romberg....
> **J:** And when you were saying that Schwartz was the most demanding composer you ever worked with, that implies that if he really liked a lyric it meant something
> **HD:** Yes, I agree with you. Now Jerome Kern, put up with a lot, he'd settle for something that was second best.[55]

Well-versed in songs for the theater, Schwartz was aware that they could be enhanced by stage direction, sets, costumes, lighting, and choreography. He told an interviewer that this was not true of the air waves: "On the radio there is but the single medium of sound to put the number over. The gain or loss of eye appeal is a thing that makes the major difference between stage and air renditions."[56] Because of this limitation, Schwartz felt that the songs for *The Gibson Family* should stand on their own and not merely play second fiddle to the story and end there: "The new songs must have some sophistication ... enough to prove that there is mentality behind them. Radio has developed intricate and colorful harmonic treatment of themes. It has opened a great field for music rich in structure. These indications will be apparent in our new series, which will contain a minimum of so-called hot music. I believe people are more interested in melody."[57]

In the same article, Jack D. Brinkeley discussed Schwartz's talent and versatility: "Why was Arthur Schwartz chosen from all American composers to write the music for this milestone in radio production? The reason is obvious when it is realized that one recent show score by this writer contained music in the distinct styles of six different countries; and that, in addition to his reputation for composing successful popular songs, he holds the distinction of being the only composer of the 'popular' school to receive consideration for a serious theme from the classical music columns of the *New York Times*. The composition was the 'Beggar's [sic] Waltz.'" Schwartz was always happy to get a compliment, be it from the *Radio Guide* or the *New York Times*, but he was also quick to give credit to others, especially his songwriting partner. In that same Brinkeley interview, Schwartz praised his friend and co-worker: "Mr. Dietz is far above the average lyric writer, in my humble opinion. He is musically inclined, and the creator of melodic pattern as well as actual lyrics. I sometimes help him with the words; but his donation is greater. Dietz is capable of writing anything for the stage. I mean libretto and drama as well as lyrics. His contribution to our work is inestimable."[58]

Schwartz and Dietz often discussed their songwriting techniques. Due to the exigencies of *The Gibson Family* and the four-songs-per-week dictum, they worked quicker than ever during this period. Their process was detailed in an article in the *New York Sun* approximately three months into the run of the show. The setting is a small room on the third floor of 1540 Broadway with walls and a small piano and bench—all painted apple green—a couch, and an armchair. Their discussion follows:

HD: What are they doing Saturday Night?
AS: They're all going out skating.
HD: Then we'd better write a skating song.
AS: You bet.
HD: The trouble with a skating song is that both "ice" and "skating" are difficult words. They're kind of thick and hard to rhyme.
AS: What's wrong with "nice" and "mating"?
HD: Go easy—this is for the radio. Give me a minute. I've got a title, "Dancing on the Lake."
AS: A honey.
HD: Please give me a phrase. Now this is to be a simple song—a song of simple charm.
AS: O.K. [He plays a phrase.]
HD: That's good. Go on. [Schwartz continues on with occasional interruptions from Dietz such as:]

HD: Go down! I want a down note there. A change of rhythm here. Make your phrases parallel. Put a trick at the end of the middle. [All this time, Dietz is jotting down lyrics, as the two of them haggle over lyrics and melody.]
HD: That's where I needed the down note.
AS: I knew it.
HD: Well, that's the pants done. [Reporter questions this.]
HD: Yes, a song has a coat, vest and pants. The coat's the beginning. The vest is the part of the verse leading into the chorus. The pants is the chorus. [Dietz gives examples.]
HD: Now we've got to do the coat and vest of this skating song.

The reporter, Michel Mok, sums up: "They do. The entire operation—coat, vest and pants—has taken forty minutes by the reporter's watch."[59] The song, "Skating on the Lake," is used on the next episode of *The Gibson Family*.

Schwartz and Dietz held ownership of the copyrights of *The Gibson Family* songs along with Harms, Inc. Only the three of them benefited from sheet music sales. A month into the show, sheet music for several of the songs was "selling at what is regarded an excellent pace." Those mentioned as doing well included "How High Can a Little Bird Fly?" (2,732 copies); "Under Your Spell" (2,156); "Absent Minded" (1,400); and "Hi De Home Sweet Home" (1,128).[60] These sales numbers were surprising since, with the exception of the show's theme, "Under Your Spell," songs from *The Gibson Family* had only had one or two airings on the program on any given week. Then the next week's show would feature four new songs. It was admitted that "the Program 'plugged' the life out of 'Under Your Spell,' but it seems worthy of the 'plugging.'"[61] Another critic said the show has a "tendency to 'overplug' the music."[62] For the radio critics, "Under Your Spell" was the best of the songs of the first episode. The song would later be sold to 20th Century–Fox for Lawrence Tibbett to perform,[63] as was "My Little Mule Wagon," also from *The Gibson Family*. The movie was also titled *Under Your Spell* and opened in 1936 starring Tibbett and Wendy Barrie.

The Gibson Family premiered on September 15, 1934, a Saturday night, at 9:30 p.m. (EST). This late hour was designed so that West Coast listeners would hear it around dinner time, 6:30 p.m. (PST).[64] It got off to a good start its first few weeks, but then for reasons unclear, the ratings went into a steady decline. A "vital spark" was missing. Some felt there could have been more dramatic action. There also may have been too much Ivory Soap and not enough of the Gibson family. As they had invested $500,000 in the development of the show, the Procter & Gamble executives chose to pull it off the air six months into its initial run and revamp it.[65]

Re-opening on March 31, 1935, the new and improved version de-emphasized Sally Gibson's role and essentially eliminated her romance with Jack Hamilton as well as the singing they did. The bulk of the plot focused on a traveling carnival in the Gibson's hometown and the new show was renamed *Uncle Charlie's Tent Show*. New songs were no longer used. To play Uncle Charlie, the producers brought in Charles Winninger, who had just severed ties with the successful *Maxwell House Show Boat* program. Script writer Cooper was replaced by Owen and Donald Davis. The new version never caught on, and *Uncle Charlie's Tent Show* was canceled after its September 8, 1935, airing.[66]

The promoters of the show had touted it as a new art form. One critic agreed: "If telling a credible story—certainly as credible as the plot of the average musical comedy—...to the accompaniment of catchy songs, then 'The Gibson Family' is a new art form."[67] But as well thought out as it appeared to be, audiences never took to it. It was unclear why. If the songs were the problem, it was never mentioned. Despite its brief and interrupted run, from its premier on September 15, 1934, until its last airing, June 2, 1935, *The Gibson Family* provided Schwartz and Dietz a good income and the opportunity to write over 100 songs. Several of these had been taken from previous projects, and in turn, several others were used in later shows or movies. Media critic Leonard Maltin suggested that of all the songwriters who turned to radio, Schwartz and Dietz had done it most successfully: "Still, the medium remained a mixed blessing for songwriters. Tunesmiths who worked on Broadway were often approached to write for radio—the prestige they brought with them was unbeatable—but few if any could conform to radio's voracious appetite.... They [Schwartz and Dietz] survived the entire season, and ... they were smart enough to use the show as a kind of proving ground."[68]

During work on *The Gibson Family*, Schwartz became involved in a lyric writing contest in *Melody* magazine, a monthly for and about songs and songwriting. But rather than being a contestant, he was the judge. The contest was titled "Dollars for Words," and Schwartz would decide the winner. For prospective lyricists, he wrote a twenty-bar melody, marked "Slowly (with expression)" which was printed in the May 1935 issue of *Melody*. He offered advice to contestants about setting lyrics: "To simplify the task of writing a lyric to the melody I have submitted for the contest, I suggest that the finding of a suitable title is half the battle. In my opinion, this title should fit the phrase of music contained in the first two bars since this is the phrase most repeated and most characteristic."[69] The contest was so popular that another melody without words was printed in the July 1935 issue, this one written by Dana Suesse, famous for her "You Ought to Be in Pictures."[70] In August, another melody was provided by Vernon Duke.[71] The winning lyrics and lyricist for the Schwartz melody were printed in the August issue. The winner was Merle Lundvall of Davenport, Iowa, who received the $25.00 First Prize.[72]

During all this, Schwartz and Dietz managed to contribute a few songs to a London revue, *Stop Press*. A stop press was a primitive device that teletyped bits of news onto the corner of the front page of newspapers.[73] This London show, using fictional stop press messages as sources for sketches and songs, opened on the West End in February 1935. It was a descendant of the Irving Berlin hit, *As Thousands Cheer*, which had used news headlines for sketch material. *Stop Press* included several Berlin songs and Moss Hart and Greatrex Newman sketches, but also had song interpolations with contributors including Noel Gay, E.Y. Harburg, Johnny Green, and Newman, as well as Schwartz and Dietz songs from *The Band Wagon* and *Revenge with Music*.[74] Among the contributions was Schwartz's "The Beggar Waltz," renamed "The Beggar's Dream," and danced by Florence Chumbecos. She had been in the original chorus of *The Band Wagon* and replaced Tilly Losch for the national tour.[75] *Stop Press* ran afoul of the Lord Chamberlain's censorship rules. This shortened its run to 148 performances and incurred fines for producer Clifford Whitley, director Hassard Short, general manager John Greenhill, and sketch writer Greatrex Newman.[76] As for Schwartz and Dietz, having finished a national radio program and placed a few song interpolations into a London show, they were ready for more Broadway.

10

Revenge with Music and "You and the Night and the Music"

"I was just standing there on the deck when the complete melody came to me."[1]

Schwartz and Dietz had proven to be masters of the revue, but could their songs and Dietz's book writing progress in the direction Broadway was going? As historian Thomas Hischak put it: "Just as the Depression was sealing the fate of operetta, the musical revue seemed to be in its waning days as well. Everyone was turning to the book musical, so Dietz and Schwartz did also."[2]

After Schwartz had completed a trans-Atlantic boat passage in spring of 1933, he had pleaded with Dietz to collaborate on a book show, i.e., to go beyond the revue genre.[3] The proposed show, ultimately called *Revenge with Music*, was based on a Spanish folk tale which had become a novel, *El sombrero de tres picos*, by Pedro A. de Alarcón. This story had been used for Hugo Wolf's opera, *Der Corregidor*, and for Manuel de Falla's ballet for the Ballets Russes, *The Three-Cornered Hat*, produced by Sergei Diaghilev, choreographed by Leonide Massine, and costumed by Pablo Picasso.[4]

The approach of Schwartz and Dietz to such a show was to be different from their revue work: "The two had selected *The Three-Cornered Hat* with some care. It had long been a great Spanish classic, and it offered a chance for all the color they felt was so essential to a big Broadway production. Several months of research preceded the writing, with the two men immersing themselves in Spanish literary history and the musical styles of the time. There was little of the trial-and-error, shooting-from-the-hip approach to the writing that had worked so instinctively and successfully for them in putting together the revues."[5]

Despite several months of work, it was unclear how they would present the story. In a long letter to Schwartz on August 9, 1933, it is clear that

Dietz was still uncertain about the project: "As for 'The Three-Cornered Hat,' I have a slightly changed viewpoint on it which can best be expressed in the copy. The fact that I am still confident of this property must mean something in relation to its merit. So, altogether, I feel that there is a lot to be done, and a great deal depends on which direction we want to turn towards it."[6] By this time, no songs had been written, no casting had been done, and the rest of the creative group—other than producers Harold B. Franklin and Arch Selwyn—had not been signed on.

At the time Schwartz and Dietz found themselves in a new venture, their friend Libby Holman was looking for work on Broadway. Her last work there had been in 1930–31 in *Three's a Crowd*. She had heard that other old acquaintances, producers Franklin and Selwyn, were working on a new show. Holman had just gone through tumultuous legal problems, most notably an indictment for the murder of her husband, R.J. Reynolds Tobacco heir Zachary Smith Reynolds. Although the case was eventually dismissed for lack of evidence and the coroner's determination that the death of Reynolds had been a suicide, Holman gained notoriety and attracted more than a few skeptics. Schwartz would be witness to this in the opening night audience at *Revenge with Music*: "Arthur Schwartz was assigned to mingle with the crowd to eavesdrop on any criticisms or comments concerning the performance of their benighted star. Schwartz lingered in the lobby.... No one mentioned Libby. Schwartz was about to return to his seat when he overheard Libby's name. Unobtrusively, he backed up to the woman who had spoken of her; but she was not commenting on Libby's performance. In tones of pure and unmistakable conviction, she was saying: 'I *bet* she killed him. I just *bet* she killed him.'"[7]

Arthur Schwartz, after four years as a successful revue composer, pictured on November 23, 1933, during work on *Revenge with Music*, his first book musical. Schwartz is seldom photographed in glasses, even in later life (courtesy Beinecke Rare Book and Manuscript Library, Yale University / photographer Carl Van Vechten / ©Van Vechten Trust).

10. Revenge with Music *and "You and the Night and the Music"* 99

Holman tried to talk Dietz into casting her for the show, telling him "how much she wanted to come back, though frankly she was a little scared." Dietz had always been her advocate, but he was apprehensive as well, as he and Schwartz now viewed the work as more of an operetta, a genre Holman was not accustomed to. She had, however, sung a secondary lead as Lotta in the 1929 operetta *Rainbow*. As her biographer Hamilton Darby Perry put it, the show and the casting of her was "a long outfield throw from the bright, brittle revues and the slinky, sexy roles that had gained Libby her reputation." But Holman was determined and had even been taking voice lessons to be ready for whatever problems the score of an operetta might present. After all, she was the star who had sung "Body and Soul," "Moanin' Low," and "Something to Remember You By" into hits. She eventually persuaded Dietz of her fitness for the role, and he convinced producers Selwyn and Franklin.[8]

The songwriters continued to have reservations about her reputation, thinking that the presence of her name on a marquee might not hold sway. As insurance, they hired Charles Winninger, famous on Broadway for his role as Cap'n Andy in the original 1927 *Show Boat* and its 1932 revival. He had garnered popularity on the national radio program *Maxwell House Show Boat*. Also brought in was Georges Metaxa who had appeared in Noel Coward's 1929 play, *Bitter Sweet*, and Kern's 1931 musical, *The Cat and the Fiddle*. More importantly, the Romanian-born Metaxa had a Continental persona that was important to his character, the Spanish bridegroom.[9] The producers hired Broadway veterans Robert Russell Bennett to do orchestrations and Victor Baravelle as musical director. Of equal importance, they tapped Albert Johnson for sets and lighting. He had worked brilliantly with Hassard Short

Arthur Schwartz at age 33, after successes with *The Little Show, Three's a Crowd*, and *The Band Wagon* with lyricist Howard Dietz (courtesy Library of Congress, Prints and Photographs Division, Carl Van Vechten Collection [LC-USZ62-139393] / photographer Carl Van Vechten).

on the lighting and double revolving turntables on *The Band Wagon*. Johnson would again employ the revolving turntable and create seventeen separate sets for the Spanish-inspired show.[10]

The initial choice of stage director, Theodore Komisarjevsky, caused problems early on for *Revenge with Music*. He was a disciple of Stanislavski and had done his directing in plays and operas in Moscow, St. Petersburg, and London.[11] Difficulties developed with Komisarjevsky during tryouts, necessitating changes of directors and some degree of show doctoring. Subsequent directors included Marc Connelly, Worthington Miner, and even Dietz.[12]

Revenge with Music was not an operetta, as Dietz had first viewed it, but was described as a "romantic play with music."[13] He and Schwartz had a formidable task, assembling a score that could advance the plot of a romance yet maintain the freshness of songs of the thirties. The Schwartz / Dietz score, which contained both ballads and playful numbers, was well-liked by audiences. Historian Ethan Mordden admitted that while "the music feels right for the story," the songs were limited, as "the lyrics are very thirties in their lack of references specific to the plot and characters."[14]

Schwartz and Dietz wrote twelve songs that made it to the stage for *Revenge with Music*[15]; six were published in sheet music form, indicated with an asterisk[16]:

Flamenco
If There Is Someone Lovelier Than
    You*
In the Middle of the Night
In the Noonday Sun
Maria*
My Father Said

Never Marry a Dancer
That Fellow Manuelo*
Think It Over
Wand'ring Heart*
When You Love Only One*
You and the Night and the Music*

In its print advertisement for the sheet music, Harms singled out one of the songs: "We Believe—'IF THERE IS SOMEONE LOVELIER THAN YOU' IS NOW ON THE WAY TO BECOMING A STANDARD BALLAD ALONG WITH THE GREAT HARMS NUMBERS."[17] The song had been written for *The Gibson Family*, although it is unclear if it was ever aired.[18] It was placed into *Revenge with Music* to be sung by Georges Metaxa as the miller, to his wife, played by Libby Holman: "Although melodically it may have lacked the proper Spanish coloration, Mr. Metaxa's European accent and the orchestral arrangement combined to give it just the right atmosphere for the locale."[19]

In 1975, Dietz appeared in the *Lyrics and Lyricists Series* in New York at the 92nd Street YM-YWHA. Preparation for that program included a taped interview which he did with the creator of the series, Maurice Levine, but which was not part of the public presentation. When their conversation turned to the creative process and development of a song, Dietz and Levine focused on "If There Is Someone Lovelier Than You." Levine summarized the process: "In other words, you did the title first, he wrote a melody that incorporated that title, it was a complete melody of itself and you had to then go back and add lyrics for the rest of the song [and] the song was more or less dictated by the rise and fall of the melody, rhythmically and melodically in terms of high and low."[20] The song rests in the upper echelon of popular ballads and the Schwartz / Dietz songbook. Alec Wilder said, "It has exactly the tender, lyric quality that its title suggests. It moves gracefully, uncontrivedly [sic], and with true creative inevitability."[21] Schwartz himself "often claimed that this was his favorite among his own compositions."[22]

Beyond "If There Is Someone Lovelier Than You," another ballad became a hit for Schwartz and Dietz. Sung by Libby Holman, "You and the Night and the Music" took a circuitous route to end up in *Revenge with Music*. It began on a ship bound for England, was sung in an English movie, came back to America, and was altered to fit a Broadway show. Schwartz begins the story with a shipboard account:

> I was on a ship coming to England, and on the ship were Maurice Chevalier, Georges Carpentier the prizefighter, Helen Morgan the musical comedy star, and one or two other people. Chevalier and Carpentier and Morgan were doing a concert for the passengers, and one morning I was standing on the deck while a rehearsal was going on nearby. Suddenly this melody came to me. It always sounds phoney when a composer says a melody "came to him" but that's the only description I can give you. I had made no effort to write it. I wasn't sitting trying to find something. I was just standing there on the deck when the complete melody came to me. I was afraid I would forget it, so I burst into this rehearsal of Chevalier and the others and said, "Would you let me play something on the piano before I forget it?" They must have thought I was some kind of a nut, but they knew I was a songwriter. I played the melody four or five times and they all said, "What is that? That's great! What is that?" I told them it was just something I had composed. Later I found some music paper and put it down.[23]

Once he got to England, Schwartz teamed up with Desmond Carter, his partner from the 1930 production *Here Comes the Bride*. They took Schwartz's shipboard melody and turned it into a song, "Tonight," for the mostly nonmusical film *The Queen's Affair*. It was a 1934 British production starring Anna Neagle and Fernand Gravey, and in America, it was released as *Runaway Queen*, only a month after *Revenge with Music* opened.[24] The only solo in the movie is by a young man, Trefor Jones, singing the song. The Schwartz / Carter tune garnered no attention in the film, but as historian Benny Green explains: "'Tonight' may be sung with complete confidence to the tune of 'You and the Night and the Music.'"[25] Soon after his work with Carter, Schwartz put that melody into his trunk—literally and figuratively—and returned to America.

When work began on *Revenge with Music*, Schwartz resurrected the "Tonight" melody and played it for Dietz. While liking the melody, "the lyricist sensed that a longer title would capture the dark, swirling melody, and suggested 'You and the Night and the Music.'"[26] It was a duet for Libby Holman and Georges Metaxa and a hit with audiences. Holman's subsequent recording "was temporarily banned on the radio. The lyrics of the song, particularly the manner in which Libby sang them, were considered risqué and immoral, and added to her already notorious reputation."[27] Schwartz took a dim view of this, revealed in a script for the *Lyrics and Lyricists Series* years later: "Censorship also existed in radio. Imagine Howard Dietz's words: 'You and the night and the music fill me with flaming desire' knocking that song off the air. It was reinstated only after the publisher threatened to remove his entire catalog."[28] Despite the temporary setback on the airwaves, the song became a "perfect vehicle for the seductive baritone of Tony Martin,"[29] who had a hit with it. The diverse, stellar list of others recording it included Chet Baker, Nelson Eddy, Clark Ingram, Julie London, Louis Prima, Jonathan Schwartz, Frank Sinatra, Barbra Streisand, Mel Tormé, Joe Williams, and the Phil Woods Quintet.[30]

Schwartz discussed the song years later in answers to queries by Dietz, making a comparison of the composing styles of Richard Rodgers and himself: "Rodgers and I once discussed classical composers. I asked him what he felt about Tschaikowsky [sic]. 'He cries constantly,' said Dick. This is perhaps an explanation of Dick's MAJOR-ness. I find nothing lacking in his music, but my music differs from his (I mean my range) in that I seem not to fear crying. 'You and the Night' is a melody I don't think Dick would write. His Teutonism as against my Slavicism is what I think I'm trying to state."[31] Schwartz's minor key "crying" song did well and became another evergreen in the Schwartz / Dietz songbook. But "You and the Night and the Music" and "If There Is Someone Lovelier Than You" were not enough to carry *Revenge with Music*. It opened November 28, 1934, sustained a mediocre run of 158 performances, and was neither a critical success nor an audience had-to-see. From an initial investment of $120,000, only $45,000 was recouped.[32]

Overall, while not regretting the casting of Libby Holman, Dietz put a portion of the blame on her. Holman biographer Jon Bradshaw explained: "She had been miscast, and her singing lessons, rather than improving her voice, had ruined it. In Dietz's view, Libby now lacked the ability to project her lyrics, and worse, her voice had lost its raw, untrained sensuality. It had become merely grand, pretentious." Corroborating this was Steve Wiman, wife of producer Dwight Deere Wiman, who told Dietz during tryouts: "If Libby doesn't stop acting so goddamned piss-elegant, she's going to wreck our show. For God's sake, tell her to speak American."[33] But Holman was

10. Revenge with Music *and* "You and the Night and the Music"   103

only a small part of the problem with *Revenge with Music*, and after all, she still brought down the house every night with "You and the Night and the Music."[34]

Although Schwartz and Dietz had considered doing *Revenge with Music* as an operetta early on, this never materialized. Historians of popular song and musical theater weighed in on this issue of operetta and Schwartz and Dietz. Operetta called for music with a distinctive ethnic flair—Vienna or Spain or Ruritania—but Schwartz's melodies were just beautiful and "peculiarly un–Spanish in tone."[35] Caryl Brahms and Ned Sherrin were more general in their criticism of the songwriting duo, explaining that "others have laid the blame at the door of Dietz and Schwartz, suggesting that the premise of the show was operetta, that Dietz's lyrics were uneven and that Schwartz's work, though often graceful, lacked the rich flamboyant effects which Romberg or Friml might have supplied for this sort of

Composers gathered around a piano at an ASCAP dinner, circa 1935. *Left to right*: Laurence Schwab, Richard A. Whiting, Arthur Schwartz, George Gershwin, unidentified man, Sigmund Romberg, unidentified man, Jerome Kern seated at piano (courtesy Richard A. Whiting Collection, M209_28, Popular Music and Culture Collection, Special Collections and Archives, Georgia State University Library / World Wide Photos / photographer unknown).

subject."[36] Gerald Bordman put the issue into the context of Schwartz, the thirties, and the evolution of the Broadway song: "While, ten years before, Rudolf Friml or Sigmund Romberg might have filled just such a tale with rich, arioso passages, Schwartz was of a different school. True, his melodic line was longer and more graceful than that of most of his competitors, but his chromatics were strictly of the decade and his range within a song carefully restricted. At best he approached Jerome Kern in Kern's latest efforts to re-create the obsolete operetta in modern, native terms."[37]

But with those great songs, "un–Spanish" or not, the score can only be assessed a small amount of blame. The main impediment went back to the beginning, to the decision to do a book show. Book writer Dietz was perhaps not ready to take one on, having just come off several popular revues. Schwartz's assessment of *Revenge with Music*: "It had good songs, and a basically sound story, but not one which was great."[38] He told Dietz years later about a conversation he had had with leading London producer C.B. Cochran. When Schwartz asked him what he thought of the show, Cochran's reply was simple: "Sir, it's DIRE!"[39] The opening night critic for the *New York Times* summed it up: "It was Miss Holman, the dancers, and the music that won the most applause, and the book won least."[40] A close friend of Dietz, Alan Jay Lerner, surmised that Dietz "was not at home in dramatic story-telling."[41] Ethan Mordden was more direct and critical: "Dietz's script lies on the dull side. ... Dietz never gets out of the rut of cliché, functional rather than interesting dialogue, and dumb jokes."[42]

With two hits and a few lesser known songs, Schwartz and Dietz could still be proud of their songwriting. Within the year, they would be back where they belonged, writing a revue with a few Broadway heavyweights.

11

At Home Abroad

"*At Home Abroad* gives me more scope than the usual musical."[1]

The prolific Shubert Brothers from Syracuse, J.J. and Lee, achieved much success presenting revues on Broadway. They produced shows on an almost annual basis, first with *The Passing Shows* from 1919 through 1924, then overlapping with the more risqué *Artists and Models*, presented from 1923 through 1927. Their revue competitors were formidable and included[2]:

Revue	Years	Producers / Creators
Ziegfeld Follies	1907–1925; 1927; 1931; 1933; 1936; 1943; 1956; 1957	Florenz Ziegfeld, Jr.
The Passing Shows	1912–1919; 1921–1924	J.J. and Lee Shubert
Hitchy-Koo	1917–1920; 1922	Raymond Hitchcock
Artists and Models	1923–1925; 1927; 1943	J.J. and Lee Shubert
Greenwich Village Follies	1919–1925; 1928	John Murray Anderson
George White's Scandals	1919–1926; 1928–1929; 1931; 1936; 1939	George White
Music Box Revues	1921–1924	Irving Berlin and Sam H. Harris
Earl Carroll's Vanities	1923–1928; 1930–1932	Earl Carroll
Lew Leslie's Blackbirds	1926; 1928; 1933–1934; 1936; 1939	Lew Leslie
New Faces	1934; 1936; 1943; 1952; 1956; 1962; 1968	Leon Sillman

The Shuberts could fill a house, but their taste and creativity could be questioned. Their revues featured elaborate costumes and scenery and plenty of young women in various stages of undress. Words, music, and sketch material were an afterthought. They had presented successful operettas in the twenties, including *Blossom Time* and *The Student Prince*. By the mid-thirties, the brothers had been seeking other quality entertainment to present and had success with *Life Begins at 8:40*, a 1934 show written by Harold Arlen, E.Y. Harburg, and Ira Gershwin. When the Shuberts heard that Arthur Schwartz and Howard Dietz were working on a new revue, they were interested. This songwriting team had become masters of the intimate revue and was creating another one, *At Home Abroad*. They had struck gold with *The Little Show*, *Three's a Crowd*, *The Band Wagon*, and *Flying Colors*. Opening between 1929 and 1932, these four shows had logged over one thousand performances in total. The Shuberts believed that *At Home Abroad* could elevate the overall quality of their productions and add another hit to their empire.

By this time, the Schwartz / Dietz label on a show could attract pre-opening sales and a top-flight cast; *At Home Abroad* was no exception. For this show, they had a triumvirate of female stars—Beatrice Lillie, Ethel Waters, and Eleanor Powell. These three talents were happy to do the Schwartz and Dietz revue as the two songwriters were known to give "performers a chance to shine."[3] Schwartz and Dietz knew that as good as their songs might be, they had to be sure they showcased a star's voice, enhancing the performance and the song in a bit of theatrical synergy.

Beatrice Lillie had been performing in London since 1914, debuted on Broadway in *André Charlot's Revue of 1924*, and did her first movie in 1926, *Exit Smiling*. Her Broadway shows up to that time included *This Year of Grace* (1928), *The Third Little Show* (1931), and *Walk a Little Faster* (1932). London producer C.B. Cochran said that she was "one of the few living players to whom I dare apply the word 'genius' in its proper sense without apology."[4]

Ethel Waters had entertained in vaudeville, night clubs, movies, and at the Plantation Club and Cotton Club. On Broadway, she had appeared in *Africana*, *Lew Leslie's Blackbirds*, and *Rhapsody in Black*, among others. As a featured performer in *As Thousands Cheer*, Irving Berlin's hit of 1933, Waters had introduced "Supper Time" and "Harlem on My Mind." In many of her roles, "She had changed the very concept of what a Negro woman could do on Broadway."[5]

Eleanor Powell had been dancing on Broadway since the late twenties and would go on to a successful career in Hollywood. Her first big film roles were in *George White's 1935 Scandals* and *Broadway Melody of 1936*, both released in 1935. Around this time, she was given the title of "World's Greatest Feminine Tap Dancer" and had a famous pair of legs. The program notes for *At Home Abroad* would say of Powell: "Her style of tap dancing has never been attempted proficiently by any other girl and by few men, the main feature of it being a successful combination of ease and precision."[6] Powell would be Fred Astaire's first film partner after Ginger Rogers, starring in *Broadway Melody of 1940*. He would say of Powell: "Her tap work was individual. She 'put 'em down' like a man, no ricky-ticky-sissy stuff with Ellie. She really knocked out a tap dance in a class by herself."[7]

As director for *At Home Abroad*, the Shuberts hired Vincente Minnelli; this would be his first full-length show as a director on Broadway. To convince him to do the show, Lee Shubert—seeking "respectability"—told Minnelli: "I want to move on to quality shows ... and I think you should be with us."[8] Minnelli brought a refreshing view to directing on Broadway, one that was artful with emphasis on sets and costumes, both of which he would also be doing for this show. Minnelli had started as a billboard painter and window dresser in Chicago and soon became involved there in the theater, mostly for the chain of Balaban and Katz. After a few years in the Midwest, he moved to New York and Broadway, finding his niche in the revue genre. He did sets and costumes for *Earl Carroll's Vanities*, Radio City Music Hall shows, and the *Ziegfeld Follies of 1936*. Ultimately, he became master of the movie musical at M-G-M, scoring huge successes with *Cabin in the Sky* (1943), *Meet Me in St. Louis* (1944), and *An American in Paris* (1951).

As the projected opening of September 1935 neared, there were problems with the *At Home Abroad* sketches. The bulk of them were to be done by Howard Dietz, based on an idea of Raymond Knight, but because writing had progressed slowly, Dietz received assistance from Marc Connelly, Don Titheradge, and Knight. J.J. Shubert was concerned with the sketches and the lyrics, compelling him to write William Klein, principal attorney for the Shubert Organization: "I wish you would ask for a manuscript yourself of AT HOME ABROAD and read it yourself. I read it and believe me when I tell you there wasn't one outstanding thing in the play. ... I did not see anything outstanding in the lyrics or sketches." J.J.'s conclusion to Klein on the matter is emphatic: "If you asked me to invest a five cent piece in the proposition I would absolutely refuse to do so." Despite his negative comments, Shubert belies his own doubts for *At Home Abroad*, expressing praise for the cast and composers later on in the letter: "They have a lot of favorites—as good a cast as you can get; they also have Howard Dietz and Arthur Schwartz who have patterned their show after a great many things they have done before, and you have Bee [*sic*] Lillie."[9]

As with most Broadway shows, *At Home Abroad* had more than sketch or lyric writing problems during its preparation. With two major stars involved, billing on the program was one of these. Waters insisted on placement above the title, a sure sign of star status. But Lillie had already been placed there. After wrangling among their representatives, both ladies' names were to be above the title, but Lillie's was a bit higher. Throughout the run of the show, the two remained cordial but never became close friends.[10] Waters and Powell enjoyed a much warmer relationship as Waters, age forty at the time, took the younger woman under her wing as one of her "babies." She had done this often over her career with younger, less experienced entertainers.

There was another impediment after the opening of the show. Lillie had been unhappy with her role, and as a well-established star, she could dictate song and skit choices. She could also be temperamental and had erupted early in the run. In a frank letter to her, Dietz addressed her complaints, but at the same time chastised her for her behavior:

> To review what must be unpleasant—for the sake of getting to the better part—it all started after the show Saturday when you came to the party and made three statements. 1. That we'd let you down from the standpoint of material, 2. That you <u>must</u> come before the show, and 3. That—or else—you were going to pack up and go to England next week. With these three strong points I was deeply hurt and Arthur exploded. At which you rose and left the room. In all fairness you could not expect us to take these remarks lying down. I do not feel that we have let you down in the show. Quite the contrary. The public and critics declare that you are at your very best in your career. A new number would not change this fact and any number that is not as good as Paree or Mitzi might be and serve to do the very thing that you have expressed to me yourself, to wit; the danger of being on stage too often…. I have always admired and adored you and my heart is broken at the statements you made. I do hope it has been due to the strain we have all been under and I hope that anything unsocial that I may have done will be construed in that light.[11]

Good Broadway songwriters would not merely write a song they thought would fit a scene and hope for the best. Rather, they designed songs for specific talents and voices. When Lillie accused them of letting her down "from the standpoint of material," it was not surprising that Dietz was hurt and Schwartz became angry. Ultimately, Dietz's charm and forthrightness resolved the problems, and Lillie stayed for the run of the show.

Although interest in revues may have been waning, Schwartz and Dietz were confident that with Minnelli, their three stars, and plenty of good songs, they could pull off a successful revue. Early titles included *A Nautical Revue* and *Not in the Guidebook*, but these were replaced by *At Home Abroad*. Schwartz liked the fact that it was a loosely-knit travelogue with international settings. In the souvenir program for the show, Schwartz explained, "*At Home Abroad* gives me more scope than the usual musical, because the songs, in conjunction with the book, are supposed to be international."[12] This gave designer Minnelli plenty to work with. His settings for *At Home Abroad* included a papier-mâché Matterhorn, a gilt baroque setting, and a bullfight ring. He would be praised for "an extremely good looking show."[13]

In the musical travelogue, an American couple, the Hatricks—Herb Williams and Vera Allen—embark on a round-the-world cruise. The global scenes and songs created for the show included

London	Lillie in a department store ordering double damask dinner napkins
England	Powell toe-tapping in an Eton costume to "That's Not Cricket"
African Congo	Waters singing and dancing to "Hottentot Potentate"
French Riviera	Williams and cast members in "The Gigolo Business"
Paris	Lillie singing "Paree"
Harlem	Waters singing and Powell dancing to "Got a Bran' New Suit"
Japan	Lillie as a chorus girl / geisha in "Get Yourself a Geisha"
Spain	Paul Haakon's toreador dancing to "Death in the Afternoon"
Balkan country	Powell as a Balkan spy tapping coded messages in "Lady with the Tap"
West Indies	Waters singing "Loadin' Time" on a cargo ship
Alps	Lillie, as bride of an Alpine guide, singing and yodeling "O Leo"

Because *At Home Abroad* was a light-hearted revue, the political unrest in Ethiopia, Germany, Italy, and Russia precluded "travel" to these countries. A few weeks before the show opened, an isolationist United States Congress had passed the Neutrality Act forbidding arms trade with belligerent nations. Moreover, Adolf Hitler had issued his Nuremberg Race Laws, rescinding the citizenship of all German Jews,[14] and Italy had just invaded Ethiopia. Such areas would be avoided by *At Home Abroad* travelers.

The variety of scenes was complemented by the diversity of the stars with whom Schwartz worked. "Death in the Afternoon" allowed the composer to create something in a more serious vein, a tango danced by Paul Haakon. A supporting cast member, Woods Miller, had a wonderful baritone which Schwartz put to good use in "Farewell, My Lovely," described as "one of Schwartz's most deviously haunting melodies ... made of a constantly repeated or varied cell of two or three notes in ascending pattern."[15] More up-tempo numbers were assigned to the tap dancing of Eleanor Powell, including "The Lady with the Tap," a spoof on an Ernst Lubitsch spy drama, where Powell tapped out spy messages in code. Interestingly, Dietz had wanted to cut both "Death in the Afternoon" and "Lady with the Tap." Fortunately, director Minnelli prevailed, and both songs remained in the show, both audience favorites.[16]

Beatrice Lillie had her usual comic songs, most notably "Get Yourself a Geisha" and the Alpine-inspired "O Leo." Her funniest skit, "Dinner Napkins," was done with Reginald Gardiner, he as a store clerk and she as the customer attempting to buy double damask dinner napkins. Schwartz wrote songs for Ethel Waters to sing as only she could: bluesy, as a "soignée playgirl in Paris reminiscent of Josephine Baker,"[17] in "A Thief in the Night"; sizzling and shouting in "Hottentot Potentate"; and jazzy in "Got a Bran' New Suit." The last of these was aided by Minnelli's brilliant costuming of her in a checkered, masculine suit while Powell tapped it out. For "Hottentot Potentate," Minnelli designed an elaborate costume with gold bands, a blue gown, and an elegant headdress. Waters had worn an exotic costume for "Heat Wave," and Minnelli took the idea and improved on it: "As over-the-top as the outfit was, Ethel, just as she had done with her costume for 'Heat Wave' ... [knew] how to move in it, to bring the design itself to life."[18] Schwartz had appreciation for a star of Waters' caliber, knowing that if the songs he wrote were good, she would make them better.

When *At Home Abroad* traveled to Boston for its tryout, seven railway cars were needed to carry costumes, lights, and scenery, an unheard of amount for a musical, but important to Minnelli's overall designs. When the show opened in Boston, it was an hour too long, and several scenes and songs were cut prior to Broadway. Boston audiences loved the show and tolerated the $3.00 top ticket, a record price then for a Shubert show. This meant a gross of $26,500 per week. In New York, best seats would go for $4.40, which could mean a weekly gross of $39,000.[19] Boston audiences and critics alike were so favorable toward the show that the other planned tryout cities were cancelled, and the show went directly to Broadway. After that, the show was taken on a national tour that included Washington, D.C., Philadelphia, Chicago, and Cincinnati.[20]

During that tour, a Washington, D.C., critic referred to the songs as "bright, informal and funny."[21] A Philadelphia scribe referred to the "haunting swing of the Arthur Schwartz melodies."[22] Minnelli, who had been pleased with the work of Schwartz and Dietz, would say in his autobiography, "No huge hits came out of *At Home Abroad*, but the songs worked well within their context."[23] Robert Baral pointed out in *Revue*, "The press declared that as long as they came like this, 'Revue was not passé.'"[24]

Schwartz told a New York journalist that of the twenty-two songs written for the show, four of them resonated with the Tin Pan Alley trade, where sheet music still held sway: "Farewell, My Lovely"; "Love Is a Dancing Thing"; "O Leo"; and "A Thief in the Night."[25] Several of the songs were recorded on Gramophone Records by members of the cast including: Beatrice Lillie, "Paree"; Ethel Waters, "Thief in the Night" and "Hottentot Potentate"; and Eleanor Powell, "Got a Bran' New Suit" and "That's Not Cricket" (singing / tap dancing).[26] Lillie liked "Paree" well enough to sing it ten years later in a smaller revue, *Better Late*.[27] None of the *At Home Abroad* songs became hits. Schwartz addressed this point in an oral history interview for Columbia University: "It didn't have any hits to speak of. I think it was our fault for not producing the songs in a way that would call attention to them."[28] In this oral history, recorded twenty-two years after *At Home Abroad*, Schwartz's memory may have failed him somewhat, overlooking the staging given these songs by Vincente Minnelli and the performances of the three stars.

At Home Abroad closed March 7, 1936, running 198 performances, respectable for a topical revue. It probably would have run longer if not facing such strong competition during the 1935–1936 Broadway season[29]:

Show	Composers	Performances
Porgy and Bess	George Gershwin / Ira Gershwin	124
Jubilee	Cole Porter	169
On Your Toes	Richard Rodgers / Lorenz Hart	315
May Wine	Sigmund Romberg / Oscar Hammerstein II	213
Ziegfeld Follies of 1936	Various	115
Jumbo	Richard Rodgers / Lorenz Hart	233

Nearly the entire original cast went on the national tour except for Eleanor Powell, who was excused for vague health reasons. On February 7, 1936, one month before the Broadway closing, she signed an agreement with the Shuberts getting out of her contract and recompensing them $25,000.[30] She and her Hollywood producers were anxious for her to continue her film career. Powell went directly to a starring role in *Born to Dance* which was released in November 1936.

There was discussion of taking the show to London. English producers, including C.B. Cochran, were reluctant to stage the show, thinking many of the numbers and sketches not presentable to English audiences. Schwartz disagreed, feeling that he knew London audiences and that most of the songs would appeal to them. He had done several London shows and had worked closely with English lyricists, most notably Desmond Carter. But to do the show meant securing foreign song rights, which was often problematic; the songwriters had to rely on their producers to do it. Schwartz wanted to keep the bulk of his *At Home Abroad* score if the show were presented in the West End. As he cabled the Shubert Theatre in New York in October 1935: "AM PRAYING YOUR TERMS REASONABLE ELSE WILL BE PERSONALLY TERRIBLY INCONVENIENCED WRITING NEW NUMBERS DO YOUR BEST."[31]

Schwartz was not called upon to write new tunes. The show Cochran produced was a composite based on songs and sketches from both *At Home Abroad* and *The Show Is On*. The latter was another Shubert revue to which Schwartz and Dietz contributed, to be discussed in the next chapter. Cochran's revue, with director Eddie Dowling, was titled *Happy Returns* but did not open until May 1938. It failed to find an audience.[32] Conversely, *At Home Abroad* had been a success for its songwriting team and young director, keeping the revue form in the forefront of Broadway entertainments.

12

Late Thirties
C.B. Cochran and *Follow the Sun*

"Mr. Schwartz provides a brilliant piano medley and interpolates his own vocal choruses."[1]

With *At Home Abroad* off to a strong start in September 1935, Arthur Schwartz and Kay Carrington left for England on October 9, 1935. She had just finished a month's run at the Municipal Opera of St. Louis in *Madame Sherry*, a musical farce by Karl Hoschna and Otto Harbach.[2] In London, Schwartz was to write the entire score for the latest C.B. Cochran revue with lyrics to be provided by both Howard Dietz and Englishman Desmond Carter.[3] The show was to open in Manchester in late December. Cochran and his book and sketch writers, Ronald Jeans and John Hastings Turner, were aware of the success of *At Home Abroad*. They wanted to use a musical travelogue format and were going to *Follow the Sun*.

Schwartz held Cochran in high regard, telling Dietz years later, "Of all the theatrical producers I have written music for, Cochran undoubtedly was the greatest. He knew more about every department of the theatre. He was rightfully known as the Ziegfeld of England, but he was much more than that."[4] While revue producers and their creators borrowed from each other frequently, it was Cochran who could put his individual stamp on a show, even with a borrowed idea: "Mr. Cochran's revues stand in a class apart. It has always been his method to gather round him artists of real talent and discrimination and to weld their combined genius into a pattern of beauty."[5]

For *Follow the Sun*, Cochran had a cast of 90 requiring 1,200 costumes for twenty-five scenes, all at an initial layout of 25,000 pounds ($60,000), enormous by the standards of the day on either side of the Atlantic.[6] The cast included Americans Claire Luce and Nick Long, Jr., an actor / dancer. Luce's work on Broadway had included *Dear Sir*, *Ziegfeld Follies of 1927*, and *Gay Divorce*. In *Follow the Sun*, she performed "Lady with the Tap," the Eleanor Powell number from *At Home Abroad*. Luce also danced *The Last Shoot*, a ballet choreographed by Frederick Ashton with music by William Walton.

Cochran and the Shubert brothers had an agreement whereby Cochran could use any and all material from *At Home Abroad* in exchange for 1 percent of the gross receipts from *Follow the Sun*.[7] In addition to their *At Home Abroad* songs, Schwartz and Dietz also included work from *The Gibson Family* and *Flying Colors*. Their numbers in *Follow the Sun* included:

Previous Show	Song(s)
The Gibson Family (radio show)	How High Can a Little Bird Fly?; Sleigh Bells
At Home Abroad	Love Is a Dancing Thing; Lady with the Tap
Flying Colors	Mein Kleine Acrobat

Several recordings of songs from the show were made by Columbia, notably by Schwartz himself. He played a "brilliant piano medley"[8] and sang a few of his songs. Hildegarde sang "Love Is a Dancing Thing." Henry Hall and the BBC Dance Orchestra also did this one, along with "Got a Bran' New Suit" and a rumba called "Nicotina." Also heard on Columbia was the star comedian of the show, Englishman Vic Oliver, who recorded several of the songs. The recordings are no longer available.

Although the show enjoyed great reviews and initial audience enthusiasm, Cochran was not happy with the run of *Follow the Sun*. Five weeks after the February 4, 1936, opening, the showman voiced his complaints to Schwartz: "It [personal matter] has hit me pretty hard, particularly as 'Follow the Sun' is proving a disappointment. Nothing in London is doing capacity although there are six or seven hits. This is poor consolation and it is not one of the usual excuses; this time it is a fact."[9] Despite Cochran's dim view, *Follow the Sun* ran a respectable 204 performances and solidified the reputation of Schwartz and Dietz with English audiences.

Several months after the opening of *Follow the Sun*, Katherine Carrington fell ill on a tennis court on Long Island. Jonathan Schwartz described the incident in his memoir: "I'm told that she dropped to her knees, then to her back, complaining of dizziness, of 'swirling.' ... In the hospital it became apparent that my mother's disorder was grave. There was nothing to be done for 'malignant hypertension.' In later years, my father would use the word 'catastrophic' to describe my mother's sickness."[10]

Within twenty-five years, such uncontrollable high blood pressure was readily treatable, saving its victims from episodes such as Carrington experienced, as well as decreasing the occurrences of the strokes, myocardial infarctions, and various neurological symptoms. Only twenty-six at the time, malignant hypertension would plague Carrington until her death in 1953 of a cerebral hemorrhage.

Following *At Home Abroad*, the Shuberts directed their efforts to another revue, *The Show Is On,* again employing Vincente Minnelli as director, costumer, and set designer. Always looking at the bottom line, the brothers must have figured paying one man to do three jobs was cheaper than paying three separate people, even if rates were now a bit higher for the popular Minnelli. Several of the *At Home Abroad* cast were retained as well, including Beatrice Lillie, Reginald Gardiner, Paul Haakon, and Vera Allen. Starring with Lillie were comedian Bert Lahr and Mitzi Mayfair as principal dancer. Mayfair had replaced Eleanor Powell when she left *At Home Abroad* early.

Also taken from *At Home Abroad* was the idea of world travel, but in this show, the traveling would be around the world of show business, taking every opportunity to skewer its artists and practices. To do this, two of Broadway's best sketch writers were employed, David Freedman and Moss Hart. Freedman had been writing for Broadway since 1926 and also had a successful career in radio. Hart had teamed with George S. Kaufman since 1930 and would win the Pulitzer Prize for Drama in 1937 for *You Can't Take It with You.*

While the principal songwriters for *The Show Is On* were to be Vernon Duke and Ted Fetter, this production incorporated numerous interpolated songs. These were written by other composers and lyricists, then fit into a show as the director and book writer saw fit. This had been the usual practice in assembling revues over the previous twenty years. Robert Baral called the Shuberts' *Passing Shows* "a melting pot for interpolated songs that quite frequently carried a show."[11] Among others, George Gershwin and Andy Razaf both had interpolations in *Passing Shows* in the early days of that series. This practice of interpolations provided young composers not only with exposure to New York theatergoers but to national audiences as well if the show went on a cross-country tour. For Shubert shows especially, the national exposure was extensive as their empire included theaters across the nation.[12]

The interpolation of individual songs was probably the most common route for aspiring composers and lyricists to get an introduction to Broadway theater. A few prominent interpolations that boosted careers include[13]:

12. Late Thirties

Songwriters	Song	Show	Year
Jerome Kern / Edward Laska	How'd You Like to Spoon with Me?	*The Earl and the Girl*	1905
Irving Berlin	Alexander's Ragtime Band	*Friar's Frolic of 1911*	1911
George Gershwin / Arthur Frances (Ira Gershwin)	The Real American Folk Song (Is a Rag)	*Ladies First*	1918
Harold Arlen / Ted Koehler	Get Happy	*Nine-Fifteen Revue*	1930

In the case of *The Show Is On*, the lineup of song interpolators was anything but newcomers. It included Herman Hupfeld, the Gershwins, Hoagy Carmichael, Stanley Adams, E.Y. Harburg, Harold Arlen, Will Irwin, Norman Zeno, Schwartz and Dietz, and Rodgers and Hart.

For this revue, Schwartz and Dietz wrote the first number, "Shakespearean Opening." This was a scene featuring Reginald Gardiner as Shakespeare with cast members portraying, with broad humor, more than a dozen of the Bard's best-known characters including Cleopatra, Marc Antony, Rosencrantz, Guildenstern, Shylock, Romeo, Juliet, Three Witches, Desdemona, Othello, Brutus, Ophelia, and King Lear. The take on Shakespeare was to see what the characters would be doing if he had written his plays for Broadway instead of the Globe Theatre. Schwartz and Dietz also collaborated on a song for Lillie titled "Josephine Waters," but it was cut during the pre–Broadway run. A song of the same title was added to the New York run but was listed as written by Arlen and Harburg.[14] Two hits emerged from *The Show Is On*. The Gershwins' "By Strauss" was sung by Gracie Barrie. The second, "Little Old Lady," was written by Hoagy Carmichael and Stanley Adams. It was described as "a delightful, old-fashioned number,"[15] sung and danced by Mitzi Mayfair. Characterized as "a charming if atypical Carmichael tune,"[16] "Little Old Lady" became a national hit and was recorded by several artists.

After pre–Broadway weeks in Boston, Philadelphia, Washington, D.C., and Pittsburgh, *The Show Is On* opened at the Winter Garden on Christmas of 1936 and ran for 237 performances. Lillie and Lahr earned rave reviews as did Paul Haakon, dancing in "Casanova." In one show-stopping scene— "Buy Yourself a Balloon"—Lillie entered perched on a crescent moon, swung over the audience via crane, and dropped garters onto unsuspecting men.[17] She would use her moon number years later in *An Evening with Beatrice Lillie*. Not to be outdone by his English castmate, Lahr did a burlesque of burlesque in a sketch titled "Burlesque."

There was a summer hiatus for cast members to vacation or work in Hollywood. When the show returned to Broadway in September 1937, the cast had changed greatly and was headlined by Willie and Eugene Howard. Although this group was well-received critically, the show ran for only seventeen performances and then went on a national tour which began in Chicago on October 5, 1937.[18] *The Show Is On* had been an unequivocal hit and a revue of which Schwartz and Dietz were proud to have been a small part.

13

Between the Devil

"By Myself" and
"I See Your Face Before Me"

"A new high, even for this talented composer."[1]

Schwartz and Dietz knew that Broadway was moving in the direction of book shows, and despite problems with their first such show, *Revenge with Music*, they wanted to attempt another. Their efforts in 1936–37 were focused on *Between the Devil*, which had a plot based on accidental bigamy. When it opened, a souvenir program book exclaimed that Schwartz and Dietz had created "a musical triangle," conceiving "an unique 'design for living' idea for a musical."[2]

This latter phrase was clearly a reference to the Noel Coward play *Design for Living*, which had been a success on Broadway in 1933, after it was determined to be too risqué for most London audiences. That production involved a delightful trio of artistic characters—just two men and one woman—in a complicated, three-way relationship. The play had been written specifically for Alfred Lunt, Lynn Fontanne, and Coward. Dietz took the idea of three people but added two marriages and changed the principals to become just two women and one man. It was, critic Robert Coleman said, Dietz's "sophisticated idea of what a French farce should be."[3]

During work on the *Between the Devil*, Schwartz promoted himself as a songwriter available for other assignments. Work with Dietz, his "part-time lyricist,"[4] could be haphazard due to the latter's day job at M-G-M, which demanded more of Dietz's time. Schwartz knew that there were other talented lyricists looking for a songwriting partner, long-term or otherwise. He affiliated himself with the William Morris Agency, and the following promotional brochure was among the agency's efforts[5]:

117

118 That's Entertainment

ARTHUR
SCHWARTZ
Composer

LILY PONS IN AN R.K.O. PRODUCTION
Now in Production
LYRICS BY EDWARD HEYMAN

"UNDER YOUR SPELL"—20TH Century-Fox
Starring LAWRENCE TIBBETT
Now in Production
LYRICS BY HOWARD DIETZ

"The Mark of Zorro"— 20th Century-Fox
(To be produced shortly with an all-star musical cast)
LYRICS BY IRVING CAESAR

In Preparation for Broadway:

Max Gordon's Production, **"BETWEEN THE DEVIL"**
PLAY AND LYRICS BY HOWARD DIETZ

NEW YORK PRODUCTIONS	LONDON PRODUCTIONS
"The First Little Show"	"Here Comes the Bride"
"Three's a Crowd"	"The Co-Optimists"
"The Band Wagon"	"Flying Colors"
"Revenge with Music"	C.B. Cochran's Revue
"At Home Abroad"	"Follow the Sun"

Represented Exclusively By **WILLIAM MORRIS AGENCY INC.**

    The RKO production starring Lily Pons became *That Girl from Paris*, one of a few films she made in the mid–thirties. Famous as a coloratura soprano with the Metropolitan Opera and other international opera houses, Pons had the looks and presence to extend her career to Hollywood. In the film, she also showed a comic side and was nicknamed "High C." Her supporting cast for the film included Jack Oakie, Gene Raymond, Mischa Auer, and Lucille Ball. When the film was in production, Schwartz had busied himself in Hollywood, complaining to his wife, Katherine Carrington, back in New York, "Naturally, I haven't had a minute to think of a tune for Lily Pons, and she'll be out here in about two-and-a-half weeks!"[6] Nine days later, Schwartz wrote again, missing his young wife and still having problems with the songs for Pons:

> Do you love me more than ever? Do you know I have improved as a person because of you? In every way? Do you know that I am crazy about you and that I also like you? I have no lyricist as yet for the Pons picture. Dorothy Fields may not be available. Ira Gershwin can't come. Maybe Leo Robin   remember him![7]

13. Between the Devil

For the songs for *That Girl from Paris*, Schwartz eventually re-teamed with Edward Heyman, with whom he had written "After All You're All I'm After" for *She Loves Me Not* in 1933. For Jack Oakie, Schwartz and Heyman wrote two up-tempo swing numbers for Oakie's character, the drummer for Windy McLean and His Wildcats. Both numbers—"Love and Learn" and "Moon Face"—were catchy and perfect for a swing quartet. The songwriters wrote two songs for Pons, "The Call to Arms" and a waltz, "Seal It with a Kiss," both romantic ballads.[8] Critic Howard Barnes was complimentary of Schwartz's work on the film:

> You may thrill to her [Pons'] eloquent rendering of the Rossini opera, but you are more likely to be captivated by the magnificent contretemps effected by Arthur Schwartz, in which the star executes cadenzas against a jazz background of the "Blue Danube" waltz. Mr. Schwartz has done a resourceful job of composing for the film. His original songs are engaging and his arrangements are captivating. He has had to divide his attention between an opera star and the mad doings of a perambulating "hot" orchestra and he has effected a nice musical compromise.[9]

Unfortunately for Schwartz and Heyman, Pons, who had a huge following across the world, never recorded any of their songs from *That Girl from Paris*.

The second reference in the William Morris Agency promotion was to *Under Your Spell*, an Otto Preminger film that starred Wendy Barrie in addition to Lawrence Tibbett. Two Schwartz / Dietz songs from *The Gibson Family* radio show—"Under Your Spell" and "My Little Mule Wagon"— had been sold to 20th Century–Fox for *Under Your Spell*. They also wrote an additional song for the film, "Amigo." Schwartz was in Hollywood dealing with "Tibbett's fussiness" and the baritone's demand that he be allowed to sing an interpolated song for the movie, one written by Johnny Green. When producer Darryl F. Zanuck was in agreement with Tibbett and his agent, Schwartz had to explain to the three of them that "for seven years I hadn't allowed an interpolation in any score that I wrote and to do so would be equivalent to allowing another baritone to sing an important song in a Tibbett picture."[10] It was hard to argue against Schwartz.

Tibbett also requested a new verse for "Under Your Spell," most importantly in a lower register than the one used in *The Gibson Family*. As Dietz was occupied with other matters at the time, Schwartz wrote a new verse—melody and lyrics—for "Under Your Spell" for the movie. Dietz had high praise for him: "Your verse on 'Under Your Spell' was perfectly fine. I couldn't have done better and I almost believe (again that 'almost') that you could write your own lyrics successfully. You really understand metric schemes and certainly know songs thoroughly. Also you would be one who would continually improve because you know so much more than the lyric writers you're supposed to work with."[11]

Schwartz was pleased with Tibbett's recording of "Under Your Spell" for the movie but thought that the various orchestrations provided by Donald Voorhees for the song on the radio were more "potent" than the one in the movie. There was also an issue trying to get Tibbett to do another Schwartz / Dietz song, "I'm Going to Buy Low and Sell High." The singer won that round, and it was never in the film. With all these Hollywood machinations, which Schwartz had detailed to Dietz in a letter, he ended, "This all sounds very boring but I thought you ought to know what you escaped by not being born a composer. You hit and run, and I have the baby!"[12]

Another 20th Century–Fox film was mentioned in Schwartz's list of current work, *The Mark of Zorro*. He had signed a ten-week contract with producer Darryl F. Zanuck to do the music for that film. He headed to Hollywood in March 1936 to begin, although at that time, neither a director nor a cast had been selected. Schwartz was teamed with veteran lyricist Irving Caesar, renowned for lyrics for "Swanee," "Tea for Two," and "Just a Gigolo." Caesar had also been a prolific book and lyric writer for revues, especially the *Greenwich Village Follies*. Schwartz and his new collaborator wrote six songs for the film:

Dancing Conversation	My Saddle Is My Throne
I Remember a Dream	The Night Has Lost the Moon
Lolita Love Song	Serpentine

All for naught as the film went unproduced.[13] There was a 1940 movie, *The Mark of Zorro*, but it contained no Schwartz / Caesar songs and featured a score by Alfred Newman.

From the beginning, Dietz had problems with the book of *Between the Devil* and by August 1936, he had been working on the script for over three months. But his regular job in Hollywood as well as smaller writing chores had consumed his time and made it difficult for him to put together a cohesive story. Later that month, Schwartz wrote Dietz a long letter with comments on the script, implying that Dietz had a long way to go:

> While I like it [second act], I feel that it lacks the punch that it should have in places and that structurally it may need repair to heighten the climax.... My feeling is as it was when you were plotting this act: that you build and build up to and including his two farewells and that the last scene is a letdown, except for the actual finish.... I know that it is tough to construct anything past the gendarme scene which really belongs to the story and has comedy or suspense contribution. All of these difficulties I am aware of and yet I feel you ought to seriously dig for an answer to my reservations.[14]

13. Between the Devil

Principals of the show listening to Arthur Schwartz play the score of *Between the Devil*, 1937. *Left to right*: Schwartz at piano, Evelyn Laye, and Adele Dixon (in the shadows, Jack Buchanan) (Photofest / photographer unknown).

Schwartz wrote another letter a day later with suggestions for some of the script problems.[15] A few days later, Dietz responded to Schwartz:

> I am disappointed to hear that you did not think the second act as good as the first, for I had hopes (but doubts) that it was.... You are the second person who has thought so, and I am confident there will be a fourth and a fifth and so on. Perhaps I can improve it, either by radical tactics or by perfecting what it has. Just at present I don't feel like sitting down to rewrite. I have been working very hard on all other matters and I am a little sick of the play. The futility of it all.... If I'm going to write I'd better write a straight play ... or try fiction.

To these overall comments, he added suggestions of specific changes that he might make. In the same letter was the recurrent theme of delays in the casting: "You know it is difficult to write a play that looks so doubtful of early casting. Yet I know that if it were really sensational it would solve itself."[16]

Dietz's story line was based on bigamy, where the protagonist / bigamist employs two names: Peter Anthony, when he is with his English wife, Natalie Rives, and Pierre Antoine with his French wife, Claudette Gilbert. According to historian Gerald Bordman, the confusion and plot twists conceived by Dietz were described as a "really old French bedroom farce streamlined for modern consumption." Perhaps it was all too modern, for

Rehearsals for *Between the Devil*, which opened December 22, 1937. *Left to right*: Arthur Schwartz, Jack Buchanan, and Adele Dixon. In 1953, Buchanan would co-star in *The Band Wagon*, the M-G-M movie musical featuring the songs of Schwartz and Dietz (Photofest / photographer unknown).

when *Between the Devil* opened in Philadelphia on October 14, 1937, the bigamy situation was met with "Howls of outrage and threats to close the show for indecency."[17] Audiences were said to be "rather shocked."[18] George S. Kaufman told Dietz, "I understand your new play is full of single entendre."[19] The show closed ten days later, October 23, not really because of the "indecency," but as Edwin H. Schloss, critic for the *Philadelphia Record*, put it, "the situation lacks authentic wit, the pseudo-sophisticated lyrics often fail to come off and the score lacks tunes."[20]

Even before the show closed, those involved knew that it was in trouble, prompting the Shuberts to employ show doctors, including Edwin Gilbert, John Kenley, and Jake Wilck, and to avail themselves of the advice of Broadway star Clifton Webb.[21] Also involved in this process was E.R. "Ma" Simmons, the longtime Shubert casting and wardrobe director, often referred to as "J.J.'s right hand."[22] These various critics focused on many of the same points, mostly Dietz's book, but several other issues deserved mention as well[23]:

(1) the premise and details behind the bigamy were not clear; (2) the use of the word "bitch" three times in an early scene was vulgar, as was Dietz's habit of using Broadway gags in lieu of good comedy; (3) scenes such as the second act trial scene bordered on burlesque rather than farce or comedy; (4) Leo G. Carroll as a competing suitor to

the star, Jack Buchanan, is too old and not handsome enough; (5) the end of the show is confusing and unresolved; (6) director Edward Clark Lilley was unable to direct the book scenes adequately.

Criticism of the score was mixed, and most felt the need for a title song, "Between the Devil." Edwin Gilbert held to that idea and made other cogent comments. However, he also demonstrated that show doctors, like theater critics, are not infallible, telling the Shuberts, "There is not one strong song that can be remembered."[24] John Kenley was also hard on Schwartz, saying that songs for Evelyn Laye were not a good fit: "They must write a melodic number for her, one that the auditor can enjoy and follow," adding, "The score is pathetic."[25] J.J. Shubert himself was critical of the Schwartz score as well, focusing on the songs Schwartz had written for Laye: "The music of Miss Laye does not fit her voice at all. It is too heavy and operatic for her to sing. The one song she sings at the piano is absolutely a dirge, and the consensus of the opinion of everybody in the theatre last night was the same. The same thing applies to most of the music she has to sing."[26]

What was not criticized, by the show doctors or the critics in Philadelphia through New York, were the principals of the cast—Jack Buchanan, Evelyn Laye, and Adele Dixon—all British. Buchanan had been discovered by French impresario André Charlot and became a favorite of Broadway audiences in 1924 with *Charlot's London Revue*. He embodied "the epitome of British sophistication."[27] Buchanan was considered perfect for the role, but the path to his hiring had been circuitous. Dietz had had a discussion with him as early as June 1936, even giving him an early draft of the first act.[28] But Buchanan was much in demand and could not commit at the time.

Two months later and still without a leading man, Schwartz expressed frustration with the casting process. As he told an interviewer years later, "Inspiration is all very well … but I find that I write songs best when I have to write them for a specific performer and a specific show."[29] This had been true during Schwartz and Dietz's revue days and continued into the writing of book shows. Schwartz complained to his partner, "How the hell can we get this god-damn show on without a leading man? I imagine you feel exactly as I do about the foolishness of making compromises in cast just to get a show on. After reading the revised version of the First Act I believe the show, when correctly cast, will be a knockout. Why court disaster with compromised casting?"[30]

Several names for the Peter / Pierre role were tossed around in discussions for *Between the Devil*. Artists mentioned included Czech-born Francis Lederer, Belgian Fernand Gravey, Frenchmen Maurice Chevalier and Henri Garat, as well as Rex Harrison, William Gaxton, and Hugh Sinclair.[31] It took a veteran showman, Max Gordon, to settle the issue.

He had become involved with *Between the Devil* in spring of 1936, negotiating with Schwartz and Dietz for their initial contracts.[32] After six months of discussion regarding casting the male lead, Dietz telegrammed Schwartz: "MAX GORDON CRAZY ABOUT SCRIPT BELIEVES NO ONE BUT JACK BUCHANAN SHOULD DO IT STOP HAS GOTTEN IN TOUCH WITH BUCHANAN."[33] Although he was responsible for the signing of Buchanan, Gordon did not ultimately produce *Between the Devil*, as the Shuberts assumed control of the production in fall 1936. Gordon became more involved in non-musical dramas and comedies, including *Pride and Prejudice*, *Ethan Frome*, *St. Helena*, and *The Women*, as well as most of George S. Kaufman's plays.

Once Buchanan was signed, focus was on securing the two female leads. From the start, Dietz had wanted Evelyn Laye to play the English wife.[34] She had begun her stage career in the choruses of George Edwardes, a proving ground for many stars including Gladys Cooper, Gertrude Lawrence, and Jessie Matthews. Critic John Anderson referred to Laye as the "golden prima donna who captivated the town in *Bitter Sweet*," Noel Coward's operetta that had starred Laye in both the London and New York productions.[35] Dietz had to do some work convincing Laye to do the part because she wanted him to "write a new play for her"; additionally, she was pursuing a Hollywood career.[36] Convince her he did, which turned out to be beneficial for all involved, as she received glowing reviews for her singing, comedy, and beauty.[37] The role of the French spouse was played by a Broadway newcomer, Adele Dixon, and the critics liked her as much as Evelyn Laye. Boston writer Elinor Hughes described her as "a combination of Lila Damita and Ina Claire yet with a definite personality and charm of her own."[38]

Although Buchanan, Laye, and Dixon were new to Schwartz and Dietz shows, the songwriters had assembled many of their regulars for the creative team: overall director Hassard Short, set designer Albert Johnson, costumer Kiviette, musical supervisor Donald Voorhees, and choreographer Robert Alton. Short was assisted by Edward Duryea Dowling. There were multiple orchestrators: Hans Spialek, Conrad Salinger, Ardon Cornwell, Edward B. Powell, and Phil Wall.[39]

During the six-week hiatus between Philadelphia and an opening in Boston, a good many of the changes recommended by the show doctors were made: Leo G. Carroll was replaced by a younger and more handsome William Kendall; John Hayden replaced Edward Clark Lilley as director of dialogue; and Evelyn Laye was given more lighthearted songs.[40] As for the book, the edge was taken off the bigamy: "In the new, or Boston version, he thinks the French wife has been drowned at sea and doesn't find out she is still alive until he has married the Briton. It's still bigamy, but involuntary bigamy, and that makes all the difference."[41]

13. Between the Devil

The show that opened in New York had the same songs as in Boston except for one exclusion, "I've Made Up My Mind," which had been sung by all three principals. Also, Schwartz and Dietz never did see fit to write a title or theme song, even though Schwartz had penned a melody as early as March 1936 that he felt would make a good one. Schwartz in California sent it to Dietz in New York, and the lyricist raved about it: "First off, let me tell you that I was crazy about the songs you sent me, particularly the theme.... The theme is marvelous and simple. Whether it is perfect as the theme itself or would be better in some other part of the score I haven't decided. But that it is in, there is no doubt." It is unclear if this melody did make it into the show under a different title. Dietz does mention in the same letter, "There will be a place in the second act where this will fit perfectly."[42]

What never made it into the show was a coherent story ending, as well as a definitive answer as to whether *Between the Devil* was a farce or a musical comedy. As to the former, critic John Anderson found problems with the inability of the book to have the Buchanan character ever make a choice between the two ladies: "For the life of Mr. Dietz, Mr. Buchanan can't make up his mind, and the thing ends in a draw with the audience asked to take its choice."[43] Years later, historian Ethan Mordden concurred: "The problem with this subject matter is that unless it is given an emotional foundation ... there's no logical way for the story to end. It remains a naughty jest without a punch line. *Between the Devil* all but admitted that it didn't resolve the narrative's problem, but simply asked the public to imagine an ending of its choice."[44] As for the show being a farce or not, the critics did not care so much, as a few of them felt it was a genre that had run its course. These sentiments were best expressed by Brooks Atkinson: "Mr. Dietz and Mr. Schwartz have saddled it with one of those musical stage imbecilities that were risqué in 1917, piquant in 1927 and are only a pain in the first and second acts today."[45]

The show eventually opened on Broadway on December 22, 1937, after long delays in the first half of that year, then the Philadelphia closing and show doctoring, a six-week hiatus, and a Boston re-opening. Anderson referred to it as "the musical comedy that has been announced and withdrawn, tried-out, re-written and tinkered into its present shape."[46] Despite all this, the book of the show was still considered vulnerable, prompting the Shuberts in January 1938, to employ two more show doctors / writers. Elmer Harris was to do a "revision of the script,"[47] and Tom McKnight was brought in "to furnish new material and make suggestions and changes in the book."[48] What changes each man suggested is unclear.

During all this, the cast and crew of *Between the Devil* were asked to give a Command Performance at the National Theatre in Washington, D.C., in honor of President Franklin D. Roosevelt's birthday.[49] The celebration was a fundraiser for the National Foundation for the Prevention of Infantile Paralysis, a cause dear to Roosevelt's heart as he himself was a victim of the disease, better known today as polio. The Messrs. Shubert were reported to have spent $6,000 transporting all personnel and scenery to D.C., no small undertaking: "Nine baggage cars were required to haul the settings and properties while the stage hands agreed to do without sleep for 24 hours in order to make it possible for the musicale to be moved from New York to Washington and back between the Saturday and Monday evening performances."[50] A similar effort had been put forth by the management, cast, and crew of *Pins and Needles*, the Harold Rome revue, performed by the International Ladies' Garment Workers' Union and a favorite show of First Lady Eleanor Roosevelt. That performance was also given at the White House and was a big hit there, as was *Between the Devil*.[51]

Between the Devil closed in March 1938 after only ninety-three performances. One gets the feeling that it did not have to end that way. As mentioned previously, Buchanan, Laye, and Dixon all received high praise. The choreography of Robert Alton was well-received, as were the dancers—The Debonairs, Charles Walters, and Vilma Ebsen. She was the focus of several favorable paragraphs among all the reviews. She and her brother, Buddy, had stopped the 1932 Schwartz / Dietz show, *Flying Colors*, with their dancing duet of "A Shine on Your Shoes." Compliments for Ebsen in *Between the Devil* included "a wholly attractive dancer—humorous and refreshingly animated"[52] and "pretty enough and talented enough to star in a show on her own right."[53]

But the three talented principals and all the wonderful dancing were not enough to sustain the show. Dietz confessed, "I didn't make it hilarious enough."[54] But he may have missed the point as the plot ultimately floundered, jokes or not. As Dietz's friend Alan Jay Lerner put it: "Arthur Schwartz and Howard Dietz again tried their hand at a book show ... and again found the form elusive."[55] Brooks Atkinson ended his review and the debate as follows: "If it were not for the book, 'Between the Devil' would probably look and sound as frisky as it pretends to be. But, oh, these bigamists! Oh, these wicked Parisian chanteuses! Oh, these improper situations! Oh!"[56]

Except for a few minor criticisms, the Schwartz score was not found wanting. Reviewers cited several songs as probable hits, including:

By Myself	I See Your Face Before Me
Celina Couldn't Say No	I'm Against Rhythm
Don't Go Away, Monsieur	I've Made Up My Mind
Experience	Triplets
Fly by Night	

13. Between the Devil

Robert Coleman of the *Daily Mirror* opined: "Mr. Schwartz has outdone himself this time. Each and every one of his songs has that catchy swing which assures popularity with radio and dance bands."[57] Boston critic Elinor Hughes declared that the "songs set a new high, even for this talented composer,"[58] and a Philadelphia writer added, "This is a musical score with fetching swing and go, and it struck a warmly responsive chord in the audience last night."[59]

With previous shows, successful or not, Schwartz and Dietz had managed to come away with one or more songs which would endure beyond the life of the show. *Between the Devil* was no exception and provided them with three such songs—a novelty number and two ballads. They had written "Triplets" for their 1932 revue, *Flying Colors*. Sung in the early tryouts of that show by Clifton Webb, Philip Loeb, and Imogene Coca, it was cut before New York. It was to be a solo for Beatrice Lillie in *At Home Abroad* three years later, but again it was cut out of town. With *Between the Devil*, the right combination came along in the persons of Andy Love, Jack Lathrop, and Bob Wacker, who billed themselves as The Savoy Club Boys, but were re-named in the program as The Tune Twisters. Dietz wrote a scene that involved a cocktail party and for the latter part of it, conceived a spot to have The Tune Twisters perform as three infant boys—brats—to deliver the song. As preposterous as it sounds, the trio pulled it off, and "Triplets" became an audience favorite.[60] Boston critic Elliott Norton described it as "3 men who did a lunatic scene about triplets till the Shubert chandelier shook from the laughter beneath."[61] Decades later, Schwartz would say of "Triplets," "That song was written for just no purpose, just around the piano writing a crazy song. And we threw it out of several shows before it got into *Between the Devil*. It is not related to the plot at all."[62] In the 1953 movie *The Band Wagon*, featuring the music of Schwartz and Dietz, it would be performed by three "infants" in pink outfits and bonnets, sitting in highchairs—Fred Astaire, Nanette Fabray, and Jack Buchanan. It would not have fit the character Buchanan played in *Between the Devil*, but in the movie, he and his co-stars pulled it off.

An evergreen ballad of *Between the Devil*, "By Myself," was slow in reaching that status. It was the hit of the second act, if not the entire show, done as a solo by the Buchanan character and important to that role. The song was called "a triumph of economy; tightly controlled, shifting accents and stresses articulate its succinct melodic line."[63] It needed "only 24 bars to tell its lovelorn story—a minimalist gem."[64] Per Alec Wilder: "First, it accomplishes so much with so little. Its range is only an octave, yet it's so well conceived it has the effect of wide range." Wilder made similar comments about "Dancing in the Dark" and "Alone Together" as songs with deceptively narrow ranges.[65]

Schwartz and composer / conductor André Previn discussed the evolution of "By Myself" in a radio interview years later:

> **AS:** In fact the plot in the second act was that the bigamist Buchanan was trapped, of course he was going to jail and he sang this song, because he had to go his way all by himself and there was a policeman standing behind him and as he sang the policeman danced along with him like a shadow and at the end put his handcuffs on him and went off.
>
> **ANDRÉ PREVIN:** [that song] turned out to be one of the great symbolic songs of Fred Astaire's career. You can almost see him as the music begins, with his hands in pockets, doing that saunter that isn't really a walk at all but a piece of natural choreography. Now that song, that beautifully finished, highly sophisticated song was dumped on the rubbish heap of the music business for 15 years before Astaire rescued it.[66]

Previn's reference is to Fred Astaire's performance of the song in 1953 in *The Band Wagon*, singing as he walks along after deboarding a train.

Of the two important ballads that emerged from *Between the Devil*, "I See Your Face Before Me" had been the dark horse. It was the first song in the show, sung in the opening scene, first by Evelyn Laye, then by Adele Dixon. In Boston tryouts, Laye reprised it with Jack Buchanan in the second scene, but this was cut by the time the show reached New York.[67] Music historians have identified it out as yet another only-Schwartz-could-have-written melody. Gerald Bordman pointed out, "It used effectively a device Schwartz generally ignored, the repeated note."[68] Alec Wilder went further on this point: "The song is a beauty, all of it, words and music. The repeated note, which Schwartz hitherto has not made a point of, is here in strength. The song is based on it. And there is nothing of the aggressiveness with which I usually associate the repeated note device."[69] Despite all the praise, Schwartz admitted in a 1976 interview that it did not come as easy as its beauty and fluidity might suggest:

> "I See Your Face Before Me" took Schwartz months, the last phrase coming first, the first coming last. "A good song, but a totally manufactured song," he says, not without pride. "A craftsman has to know how to solder."[70]

In a remembrance of the song, Jonathan Schwartz mentioned that in his days at school away from his parents, "They kept in touch with me by phone and even by phonograph record. These were no amateur amusement park contrivances. Arthur took Kay into professional recording studios.... Katherine Carrington sang Arthur's well-known 'I See Your Face before Me,' with a 'Jonathan' thrown in before 'face.'"[71]

One critic singled out "I See Your Face Before Me" as "a song that will soon be popular in night clubs and on the radio,"[72] but it was slow to gain popularity. Within months of the opening of *Between the Devil*, it had been recorded by Guy Lombardo and His Royal Canadians and Glenn Gray and the Casa Loma Orchestra, both to some success on the charts; from there it languished.[73] André Previn also commented on "I See Your Face Before Me" in his radio discussion with Schwartz, puzzled by its delay in reaching hit status, much like "By Myself": "What's even more remarkable, and very, very depressing, is that in the very same show there was another outstanding song, and the same thing happened.... Fortunately there was an identical denouement. Several years pass and then another unusually perceptive performer picks the song up and restores its ruffled dignity."[74]

The restoration of the song's "dignity" came about in 1955 with a recording by Frank Sinatra on his *In the Wee Small Hours* album. This was fitting as Schwartz considered Sinatra the best, relating this in a 1976 interview: "I like Tony Bennett and Jack Jones. But Frank is still the champ. His technique for delivering a ballad that moves you is incomparable. Sinatra told me at a party once that he swims underneath the water regularly to increase his breath control, so he can hold notes longer than any other singer in the business."[75] Within that same year, several other recordings were made: Bing Crosby for his radio show; Miles Davis on *The Musings of Miles*; and Johnny Hartman on *Songs from the Heart*. With all this, "By Myself" and "I See Your Face Before Me" became entrenched in the American Popular Songbook. *Between the Devil* was never brought to the stage again.

14

Virginia and the Rockefellers

"Schwartz felt so bad about it that one of the Rockefeller boys came around to keep him from self-destruction."[1]

Having the support of the Rockefeller family was a good thing in the post–Depression thirties. During that time, the family was involved in two large building projects that would have a bearing on Arthur Schwartz's career. The first was a multi-million dollar restoration of the town of Williamsburg, Virginia, to its colonial splendor, a project completed by 1937.[2] The other was a much bigger work-in-progress—Rockefeller Center— which had broken ground in July 1931.[3] The complex included offices, retail space, and two theaters, Radio City Music Hall and Center Theater.

Center Theater was to be a movie house, because films were attracting more and more audiences. But films did not show well there, partly because the 65-foot high front stage wall extended well above the movie screen, forcing upper balcony patrons to look down with a distorted view. Beyond this, the acoustics were not conducive to the performance of music, an opinion given to the Rockefellers by conductor Walter Damrosch.[4] To add insult to injury, movie audiences were more attracted to Radio City Music Hall, which held 6,200 seats, even though that venue had not been intended for the cinema.[5] Critic Richard Watts, Jr., summarized the problem: "Obviously it is no easy task to find a show suitable for the Center Theater. This handsomest of New York playhouses, the smaller brother of the nearby Radio City Music Hall, has always been the problem child of Rockefeller Center."[6] But Center Theater was a beautiful venue, "dignified and cheerful and commodious,"[7] and Rockefeller Center management could not abandon it. They decided to use it to stage "vast musical spectacles,"[8] like those at the Earl Carroll Theater or the Hippodrome. At the latter venue, Rodgers and Hart and Billy Rose had great success with *Jumbo* in 1935.

14. Virginia *and the Rockefellers*

In presenting large shows at Center Theater, producers could take advantage of the large proscenium and the 3,500-seat capacity of the Center. The first such show was produced by Max Gordon, a "spectacular production of the Strauss-filled *The Great Waltz*,"[9] that ran for 289 performances. The second Center Theater show, *White Horse Inn*, was based on a successful German play and operetta of the same name. In New York, it was directed by Erik Charell with the original Ralph Benatzky and Robert Stolz score re-orchestrated by Hans Spialek, new English lyrics by Irving Caesar, and a book by David Freedman. It had a run of 223 performances and encouraged the Rockefellers to do more of the same.[10]

They began looking for another large musical, and into this void stepped Arthur Schwartz. He had recently seen *White Horse Inn* at the Center and had an "infatuation" for the venue.[11] Moreover, he was looking to do a book show, preferably one with a historical theme: "In those [revue] years, 'sophisticated' was the nicest thing to be said about one's music, and I'd be a liar to say I didn't like mine called that. Yet I was restless to break away from it. Perhaps, I thought, I might write a score of rather more substance if only I could align it with a sustained story—a 'book show.' A book show permits a composer greater scope than he finds in the patchwork structure of a revue. ... I made the agreeable discovery that American history was admirable source material."[12]

Schwartz approached John Kenneth Hyatt, managing director of Center Theater, and proposed a show. Schwartz would later claim, "I persuaded the Rockefeller family to invest $250,000."[13] Hyatt urged Schwartz to engage a book writer; he responded with Laurence Stallings. He had achieved his greatest success in 1924, co-authoring with Maxwell Anderson, *What Price Glory?* which became a movie in 1926 and again in 1952. Stallings had also written the book and lyrics for *Deep River*, a 1926 musical composed with Frank Harling and starring Jules Bledsoe. Ethan Mordden described it as "probably the most inventive of all the black musicals" of the period and "a serious show, steeped in history and folklore."[14] Stallings had worked with Oscar Hammerstein II and Vincent Youmans on *Rainbow*, a 1928 musical. Both it and *Deep River* were unsuccessful, although Gerald Bordman speculates that they "had failed as much because they were ahead of their time as for any other reason."[15] After these stage efforts, Stallings had been drawn to Hollywood.

Because Schwartz wanted a book derived from American history, he had chosen Stallings, known for a historical bent to his writings. Schwartz saw the hiring of Stallings in practical terms: "Laurence Stallings, I felt, was the one for that task. He knows history; once at work we didn't relish pausing for research, and Stallings's memory was insurance against such delay."[16] When Hyatt agreed that a historical story would be perfect for the third show at Center Theater and that Stallings would write the book, *Virginia* went into production.

Stallings' idea was to place the show in Williamsburg, Virginia, just before the Revolutionary War. The choice was an accommodation to the Rockefellers, who had just finished their restoration of that town. As the *New York World-Telegram* put it, "The two enterprises—the restored village and the musical romance—expect to publicize each other."[17] When asked about this, a Rockefeller executive initially replied that it was "sort of coincidence," then concluded, "The authors selected this locale because the richness of life in the American colonies on the eve of the Revolution impressed them as admirably suited to the sort of robust romance they had in mind."[18] *Variety* took a more cynical view, claiming that it was the Rockefellers who chose the setting: "An operetta with a story anent Virginia in Colonial times, and with Williamsburg the particular locale was apparently a must by the Rockefellers since they had but recently completed the restoration of that historical spot."[19]

From Radio City Music Hall, staff director Leon Leonidoff, choreographer Florence Rogge, and staff lyricist Albert Stillman were to be used for the show.[20] Alumni from *The Gibson Family* were hired to work on *Virginia*, including musical supervisor Donald Voorhees and vocal arranger Ken Christie. Other positions included John McManus, musical director; Edward Clark Lilley, book director; and Irene Sharaff, costume designer. Orchestrations were to be done by Schwartz / Dietz veterans Hans Spialek and Phil Wall, as well as Will Vodery, Ardon Cornwell, and Maurice Baron.[21]

Schwartz never did his own orchestrations, admitting, "I haven't got the experience for it."[22] He had great respect for orchestrators, singling out Robert Russell Bennet, Hans Spialek, and Don Walker and what they did: "The best kind of illustration is what an orchestrator does with a long sustained note at the end of a composer's main strain. Inventiveness of this kind is still demanding, but not as much as is required for inventing the main strain itself."[23] Although shying away from orchestration, Schwartz would develop a piano part of his melodies: "Now what I do, and other people do, is make very elaborate piano parts with many suggestions for figurations, some of which are better than others, giving the orchestrator a choice, and then saying to him, 'If you don't like these, try your own and let me see whether I like them.'"[24]

Most important to Schwartz was lyricist Albert Stillman. He had graduated from New York University and had been working for Radio City Musical Hall since 1933 and would remain there for forty years. Stillman wrote lyrics for whatever show was being produced in the Rockefeller complex, including ice shows which became popular. He would go on to success with numerous pop songs in the fifties, including[25]:

14. Virginia *and the Rockefellers*

Artist	Songs
Perry Como	Home for the Holidays; I Believe; You Alone (Solo Tu); I Love You and Don't You Forget It
The Four Lads	Moments to Remember; No, Not Much
Frankie Laine	I Believe
Johnny Mathis	Chances Are; It's Not for Me to Say; Teacher, Teacher

Schwartz and Stillman worked well together, though differently, as Schwartz explained in an article for the *New York Herald Tribune*: "Stallings closeted himself with the book, away from his several other jobs. I stalked melody in the streets, with Albert Stillman, the lyric writer. He is skeptical of the inspiration to be found in footwork, and he frequently darted indoors to come to closer grips with his rhymes. But I like the street. The traffic cacophony of Fifth Avenue, and its layers of carbon monoxide, are tonic to a composer."[26] There is a wonderful photo of Arthur Schwartz walking down the street, dressed in one of his fashionable suits, cigarette in right hand, and slightly stooped over. Although it is shot from behind, it is clear he is deep in thought, perhaps searching for his next melody.[27]

For *Virginia*, Schwartz took on more of the work than for many of his previous shows. Of all the production people on *Virginia*, he alone "was footloose at the time."[28] His availability had developed as a result of ongoing delays with *Between the Devil*, his show with Howard Dietz that would open December 1937. These holdups included Dietz finishing the book, several late casting issues, and changes in stage direction. In any case, Schwartz had taken on much of the work for *Virginia*. He had convinced the Rockefellers that a historical musical would fit well into their plans for the Center Theater, then found the book writer and several musical personnel for them. The casting chores were heaped on him as well. He explained, "I had become a traveling man. Since a piano is available almost anywhere, I was burdened with casting chores as well as music-making."[29]

Casting had become more difficult as actors were scattered to all corners of the earth as modes of travel had improved, especially air travel. For performers, doing a show in London or running out to Hollywood for several weeks to work on a film could now be fit around their Broadway work.[30] One executive complained, "Some of the English players just got in under the wire for rehearsals. The cast was scattered all over the world and it took a lot of cabling to assemble them."[31] In a column written prior to the opening, Ward Morehouse of the *New York Sun* detailed Schwartz's efforts in casting: "Of pressing need was the prima donna, and a survey of America proved it barren of girls measuring up to Schwartz's ideas of beauty and singing prowess. England was indicated. In London the composer, hopeful of casting five roles, interviewed 100 Britishers in a hurried three weeks. He inspected 130 reels of film and saw fifteen stage shows, Old Vic and Sadler's Wells theaters drawing him to repeated visits."[32]

Schwartz eventually met with success. Early on in London he had been able to convince film actress Bertha Belmore to play a supporting role. She was known to New York audiences from the role of Parthy Ann Hawkes in *Show Boat*, succeeding Edna May Oliver in the 1932 revival. The big delay for Schwartz was in finding the female lead who would play the prima donna of the fictional Drury Lane players in *Virginia*: "For three weeks I knew futility. 'The Evening Standard' ended my frustration by publishing a photograph of Anne Booth. Next morning she sang for me, and I had no further search."[33] On returning from England, Schwartz visited Minneapolis and Detroit, then spent a few weeks in Hollywood. His efforts yielded a cast of principals mostly from the British Empire: "two English women; two Englishmen; one Canadian; an Australian; a South African; and a Scotsman."[34]

With cast and creative team in place, *Virginia* began to take shape. Set in Williamsburg in 1775, the plot revolved around delivery of a letter to General George Washington by the leader of the Drury Lane players. Despite attempts by loyalists to the Crown to prevent this, it passed from Fortesque, the leader of the players, to his friend and prima donna of the troupe, Sylvia Laurence. From there, the letter went to Colonel Richard Fairfax, a member of Washington's forces and an admirer of Laurence. The latter two roles were played by Anne Booth and Ronald Graham, and their romance—plus the letter—constituted the bulk of the plot.[35]

Almost from the start, the book was in trouble. Schwartz could see that Stallings could not finish the work: "He could not make the script revisions, write the added dialogue and perform the literary tidying up necessary to plays in preproduction state."[36] Stallings was preoccupied with other work and a second marriage, having just wed his secretary from Fox Studios. Soon after being taken on as book writer, Stallings had left for an extended European honeymoon. The composer had interrupted Stallings' trip, asking him to come to London to help audition Anne Booth. Stallings was understandably reluctant to come, saying, according to Schwartz, "If I liked Miss Booth he liked her, too. But his conscience told him casting was more painstaking than that."[37] Ultimately, Stallings came that morning to the Queen's Hall, where just he and Schwartz listened to her, then hired Miss Booth on the spot.[38]

Stallings was ultimately replaced as book writer, then recommended Owen Davis, another prolific writer with historical leanings. Schwartz was well-acquainted with Davis as the two of them had worked together in 1935 on *Uncle Charlie's Tent Show* radio show, successor to *The Gibson Family*.

14. Virginia *and the Rockefellers*

The efforts of Stallings then Davis never produced a workable story for *Virginia*; the critics were nearly unanimous on this point. Robert Coleman described the book as "overly long, strangely undramatic and lacking comedy, it does not represent Messrs. Stallings and Davis at their best."[39] Richard Watts, Jr. was harder on Stallings, as he considered him to be a book writer of great promise: "I wish Mr. Stallings had been able to bring to his libretto some of the heartiness, vitality and romantic color that he got into his splendid book for the ill-fated musical show called 'Rainbow,' ... the best period American musical play next to 'Show Boat.'... I still think he could have done it again if he had worked a little harder."[40] John Mason Brown echoed these sentiments, believing that the choice of Stallings held much promise, but concluded, "Mr. Stallings has ... been faithful only to the sleepiest conventions of outmoded musical comedies and to what tradition says is possible at the Center."[41]

This was not the first time Arthur Schwartz had been burdened with a poor book, nor would it be the last. After writing several successful revues and their sketches, Howard Dietz had fallen short addressing the books of musicals, the first time with *Revenge with Music* in 1934. Then, as Schwartz was working on *Virginia*, Dietz was struggling with *Between the Devil*. His struggles with that script through a good part of 1937 caused it to open on Broadway in mid–December, much later than planned. Fortunately for Schwartz and Dietz, they emerged from these two flops—*Revenge with Music* and *Between the Devil*—with a sheaf of hit songs. Historians David Jenness and Don Velsey commented on this point in their *Classic American Popular Song*: "Arthur Schwartz is seldom mentioned in the same breath as the other top-tier composers, still active in 1950, like Berlin, Porter, or Arlen. One reason surely is that his songs, many written with lyricist Howard Dietz, were often better than the shows he wrote them for."[42]

Saddled with a weak book, it was up to Schwartz and the cast and co-creators to salvage *Virginia*. Chief among these was Irene Sharaff, whose period costumes drew critical raves. She had been working on Broadway since 1932 and had worked on *As Thousands Cheer*, *Jubilee*, *On Your Toes*, and *White Horse Inn*, among others. Of her work on *Virginia*, it was said: "poetically faithful to this exquisite period"[43]; "costumes calculated to catch the eye"[44]; and "a visual delight and might easily be rated the show's standout."[45] Animating Sharaff's costumes was the choreography of Florence Rogge, house choreographer for Rockefeller Center. *Virginia* included more ballet than most musicals of the day. Of the ballerinas, Patricia Bowman was singled out. She had made a career in both musical theater and the classical ballet world and had been appointed prima ballerina at Radio City Musical Hall in 1932.[46]

Vital to this musical spectacle were the elaborate sets of Lee Simonson.

The stage of Center Theater was deep and wide and had to be artistically filled. Albert Johnson and Hassard Short had seen to that in *The Great Waltz*, and Ernst Stern and Eugene Braun had done the same for *White Horse Inn*. The grandeur and scope of these two shows had convinced the Rockefellers to produce *Virginia*.[47] One critic of the book felt that its deficits could be overlooked, concluding, "the piece is so opulent, so painstakingly staged, so beautifully costumed and danced and so striking a spectacle at large that criticism of the plot becomes quibbling."[48] Curbside comments on opening night included "It is gorgeous"; "impressive, but only as a spectacle"; and "Almost knocks your eye out."[49]

With costumes, sets, and dances ensuring the eye appeal of *Virginia*, the next step in overcoming the book was to elicit great performances from Schwartz's hand-picked cast. He had gone to Detroit to sign Avis Andrews, a big band singer who had started out at the Cotton Club and had appeared in the 1935 Broadway show *Parade*. Named "The Sepia Prima Donna," she had appeared in New York with Cab Calloway in the spring of 1937.[50] In *Virginia*, Andrews played a maid, a role made interesting because she was also a British spy and an untrustworthy servant. Richard Watts, Jr., was especially taken with Andrews and her singing of the Schwartz / Stillman songs: "the show is at its happiest when the plot stops—as, heaven knows, it has a way of doing—and the singing begins. This is particularly true when the singer happens to be the gay and good looking Negro girl named Avis Andrews, who not only plays the role of a maid spying for the British with high-spirited charm, but proves that she can put over a song with exceptional skill and individuality. I think the dusky Miss Andrews is quite the find of 'Virginia.'"[51] She stood out in two songs, "Send One Angel Down" and "I'll Be Sittin' in de Lap o' de Lord," the latter done with Ford L. Buck, John W. Bubbles, and a black choir.[52] Bubbles, the original Sportin' Life in *Porgy and Bess*, was praised for his softshoe dancing.[53] Although the black talent was cast in typical subservient roles, Ethan Mordden felt the musical "included a strong dose of race relations."[54]

The other cast discovery of Schwartz was Anne Booth. He had auditioned her in London and raved about her to everyone in America. She had several songs including duets with Ronald Graham. Described as having "a fragile look, a graceful presence and a pleasant voice,"[55] Booth was a soprano "whose sweet song-birding does so well by the Schwartz score."[56] If there was a problem, it was that her "pleasant lyric soprano was slightly smothered by the size of the theatre."[57]

Booth was not the only one "smothered" by the house. Gerald Bordman summarized the problem with the show: "It was overwhelmed by the house. The Center, like the Hippodrome or the Earl Carroll, was adequate for spectacle, but intimate, spoken dialogue and the low-ranged, croonable melodies of the American musical were lost in its vastness."[58] These sentiments were echoed by Richard Watts, Jr., along with some insight into the evolution of the musical at that time: "You cannot lean too heavily on dialogue because the theater is a bit too large. ... You cannot indulge in the extreme simplicities of plot and dialogue that are the easiest to hear and handle on so large a stage without going in for a naïveté embarrassing in these partially sophisticated days."[59]

As these comments suggest, Schwartz and his co-creators could not overcome the cumbersome book of *Virginia*. The show flopped, costing the Rockefellers approximately $175,000, if not more, and leading them to rethink their use of the Center Theater.[60] However, there was another immense flop at Center Theater two years later, *Swingin' the Dream*. It was produced, directed, and co-written by Erik Charell, who had done *White Horse Inn* at the Center. Despite a cast of 100 that included Louis Armstrong and Maxine Sullivan and music by Jimmy Van Heusen and Eddie De Lange, *Swingin' the Dream* lasted only thirteen performances.[61] From 1940 on, the Center Theater was used mostly for ice shows, using a proscenium rather than an arena, the usual venue for such presentations. They were produced by Olympic champion figure skater / film star Sonja Henie and Arthur Wirtz.[62] Center Theater was later used as a television studio and then finally razed in 1954.

While Schwartz had done much for the show—engaging the Rockefellers, then casting and hiring—it was still his music that critics looked to for his contribution. He had been faced with writing the score for a period piece, a spectacle, and even an operetta—all three and none of the three. At the same time, audiences expected thirties songs—tuneful and rhythmic—from Schwartz. As for the latter requirements, his songs from *Virginia* were described as "typically attractive Arthur Schwartz,"[63] and "generally excellent, with several superior songs which will linger longer than the show."[64] Six months after the show closed, Brooks Atkinson opined, "the best score Arthur Schwartz ever wrote did not save *Virginia* from the bailiffs."[65]

The Schwartz / Stillman songs that pleased audiences most were "If You Were Someone Else," "An Old Flame Never Dies," and "You and I Know." Laurence Stallings contributed lyrics to the last of these. These were written for Anne Booth and sung mostly in duet with Ronald Graham. "An Old Flame Never Dies" was described as "a prettily haunting love call, delicate and persuasive,"[66] and became a favorite of opera sopranos wanting to do a crossover melody on radio or in concert.[67]

Years later, in preparation for a piece about his partner, Howard Dietz sent Schwartz a number of questions about his songwriting and their work together. Out of the blue, "You and I Know" came up, a song with a non–Dietz lyric:

MY MOST PLAYED SONG
You'd never guess. It's "You and I Know" from *Virginia*, a flop operetta. How come? It's the theme song of a radio soap opera coast to coast five days a week and, under the ASCAP system, it is credited with more performances than "Dancing in the Dark."[68]

"You and I Know" made it to #10 on *Your Hit Parade* on November 6, 1937, with a recording by the Glenn Miller Orchestra, sung by Ray Eberle.[69] "You and I Know" and "An Old Flame Never Dies" were recorded by the orchestras of Tommy Dorsey, Ozzie Nelson, and Claude Thornhill.[70]

Of interest in the preceding quotation, Schwartz refers to *Virginia* as an operetta, a term which must have emerged as the show developed, as he had not used it in his early discussions of the show. It is unlikely he would have sought to write an operetta at this point in his career—a book show was enough. Also on his mind may have been *Princess Charming*, the 1930 operetta written by him with Albert Sirmay that met with little success.

Gerald Bordman, while acknowledging that Schwartz had written "a fine score" with "small-scaled and tender" songs, thought there was a bigger problem with *Virginia*: "In selecting Schwartz to write the songs, the management made a major error. Schwartz had a long, romantic musical line, much like Jerome Kern's at his most intimate, but he was not given to the more full-bodied melodies the large house required."[71] But Bordman may have been too harsh in his assessment. Schwartz and Stillman wrote "Meet Me at the Fair," a song befitting Colonial times and staged lavishly, extolled by Burns Mantle as an "authentic theme song." He suggested it might be used for the upcoming World's Fair of 1939.[72] The roles of the black cast members called for "full-bodied" songs. Avis Andrews, John Bubbles, Ford Buck, and the black choir were not singing love duets. As mentioned previously, Andrews was praised for "Send One Angel Down," a "full-throated spiritual." The same critic felt "the Negro choruses are full of life."[73] From the standpoint of meeting the requirements of the show, Schwartz's score was labeled "varied"[74] and "invariably skillful and attractive."[75]

Virginia (The American Musical Romance) lasted only sixty performances, a great disappointment to Schwartz. Even if consensus was that the book and the venue had brought the show down, he felt responsible, giving rise to two incidents after the closing of the show. The first was related in *Collier's* magazine seven years later in a Schwartz interview with Kyle Crichton:

> Schwartz felt so bad about it that one of the Rockefeller boys came around to keep him from self-destruction. "Despite what you think," he told Schwartz, "we still have breakfast money. We're a sturdy people, we Rockefellers."[76]

The other story was directly from Schwartz's notes in his personal papers at the Library of Congress:

14. Virginia *and the Rockefellers*

When the show failed, Kay and I took a trip to Williamsburg and in going through the Governor's Mansion spotted John D. Rockefeller, Jr. talking with one of the superintendents of the building. This was the one Rockefeller I had not dealt with in my negotiations. The show had just closed after eight losing weeks. I pointed Rockefeller out to Kay. She said, "Why don't you go over to him and tell him who you are?" I said, "I don't happen to have $250,000.00 on me at the moment."[77]

Schwartz got over the failure of *Virginia*, diverting his efforts to *Between the Devil*, another book show. The Rockefellers got over it, too.

15

Dorothy Fields
and *Stars in Your Eyes*

"It starts you wondering whatever became of the idea with which you began."[1]

Who would have guessed that a sophisticated composer of the revue would conceive of a book musical about leftists in Hollywood? Or that a well-known writer would join the composer? Then, a successful lyricist? And finally, that a wealthy, independent Broadway producer would buy into this triumvirate's ideas? That's what happened, and their names were Arthur Schwartz, J.P. McEvoy, Dorothy Fields, and Dwight Deere Wiman. As Schwartz explained at the time: "When the notion struck me that a very funny show might be written about a Hollywood musical picture produced by the forces of the Leftist theatre it generated enough enthusiasm to buoy me up all the way from Hollywood to New York. The more I thought of social criticism rendered in terms of cinematic splendor the more hilarious it seemed."[2] Schwartz refined the idea to where it revolved "around the idea of having a leftist composer like Harold Rome go to Hollywood on a movie contract; the comedy would grow out of the situation of a flaming liberal trapped inside Hollywood's capitalist machinery."[3]

Composer / lyricist Harold Rome was a liberal among liberals in the Broadway theater world. He had made a name for himself in 1937 writing songs and sketches for *Pins and Needles*, an in-house entertainment for the International Ladies' Garment Workers' Union. The show was such a success that it moved to Broadway and ran until 1940, 1,108 performances, a record at the time. Rome was smart, satirical, and engaged. His songs for *Pins and Needles* included "One Big Union for Two"; "Doing the Reactionary"; "Britannia Waives the Rules"; and "Chain Story Daisy." He would go on to more Broadway success with *Call Me Mister*, *Wish You Were Here*, *Fanny*, *Destry Rides Again*, and *I Can Get It for You Wholesale*.[4]

Schwartz, McEvoy, and Fields had all recently been in Hollywood,

15. Dorothy Fields and Stars in Your Eyes

Arthur Schwartz and wife Katherine Carrington, late 1938, several months after the birth of their son, Jonathan. At this time, Schwartz was writing the score for *Stars in Your Eyes* with lyricist Dorothy Fields (courtesy Harry Ransom Center, the University of Texas at Austin / *New York Journal American* photograph).

coinciding with Schwartz's idea that the show would "be a satire drawing on everyone's recent experiences in Hollywood, a 'what would happen if' ... notion surrounding a left-wing writer (an Orson Welles genius type) getting involved with the making of a Hollywood plantation epic."[5] While Hollywood could be a gold mine for song and scriptwriters, it was a different world than New York theater and could be tough on its writers. On Broadway, plays and especially musicals were more collaborative in their creation. In Hollywood, songwriters would submit their songs or turn their musicals over to directors and producers and hope for the best. Kurt Weill and Ogden Nash's *One Touch of Venus* and Rome's *Fanny* are examples of distinguished musicals that were cut to the bone by Hollywood. The list is long.

There was always a problem with song submissions, and only Irving Berlin could dictate what was kept. For *Holiday Inn*, there was "a stipulation that not a note of his music would be changed once filming started." When a movie was made of his World War II revue, *This Is the Army*, Berlin said, "Don't change the songs, that's all I ask."[6] Richard Rodgers was particularly disenchanted with Hollywood, and he and Lorenz Hart left there around 1935. They returned in 1937 to write a score for Ethel Merman in *Fools for Scandal*, only to have most of their songs and Merman eliminated from the film. Rodgers returned to New York and would write most of his award-winning *State Fair* score back in New York, avoiding the Tinseltown fray. To this point, historian Wilfrid Sheed noted, "as Cy Coleman explained to me, while you were home arranging your songs, the producer and director were quite likely removing the scenes your songs were in and hence the songs too."[7] According to J.P. McEvoy, "In Hollywood too much time is wasted 'pulling punches.'"[8] These Hollywood trials, which Schwartz, McEvoy, and Fields had all experienced, might make good musical comedy.

As for left-wing writers, Hollywood had plenty of them. When the cinema industry grew, so had the number of left-wing writers. Script writers such as Ring Lardner, Jr., John Howard Lawson, and Dalton Trumbo had gravitated to Hollywood to work in the lucrative film industry. These three and seven others would become known as the Hollywood Ten, and years later, would suffer personal and professional setbacks as a result of their politics. Testifying in front of the House Un-American Activities Committee, they would deny communist affiliations and refuse to "name names" of those involved in the Communist party. Broadway and East Coast writers were less at risk for this harassment, as it came down to money and power, and most of that was in Hollywood. There were noted leftists and shows on Broadway: Marc Blitzstein and *The Cradle Will Rock*, a play with music in 1937, sponsored by the Federal Theatre Project; E.Y. Harburg and Fred Saidy, whose 1947 musical, *Finian's Rainbow*, took on bigotry and big politics; and Rome's *Pins and Needles*.

Blitzstein had been on the radar of Schwartz and McEvoy in the early stages of their show. Broadway columnist Leonard Lyons reported the following conversation:

> Schwartz said, "If you're still interested in being an actor, Marc, I'd like to use you in our new show." "What's it about?" Blitzstein asked. "Frankly, it's about you." "Well, I won't act in it, but I'll take the job of research director."[9]

But it was Hollywood not Broadway that Schwartz and McEvoy were interested in, and the rise of left-wing writers in Hollywood was perfect fodder for their show.

McEvoy was a true jack-of-all-trades among writers, described in the show's program as "a writing dynamo capable of turning out a movie scenario or musical comedy at the drop of a hat while he knocks off a best seller with his left hand."[10] He began as a sports writer in South Bend, Indiana, then moved on to the *Chicago Tribune*. He wrote greeting cards for the P.F. Vollard Company in the early twenties as well as advertising copy, including Burma-Shave signs. Gravitating to New York, he began writing vaudeville routines then contributed sketches to revues including the *Ziegfeld Follies of 1925*, *No Foolin'*, *Allez-oop*, and *Americana*. His most successful novel was *Show Girl* in 1927 which was developed into the movies *Show Girl* and *Show Girl in Hollywood*. McEvoy also used this story line in 1929 to create a comic strip, *Dixie Dugan*. The 1929 Ziegfeld show, *Show Girl*, starred Ruby Keeler as Dixie Dugan. McEvoy wrote scripts for Hollywood, radio, and television and numerous articles for *Reader's Digest*. When he joined Schwartz, he had just completed work in Hollywood on *Just Around the Corner* and *Artists and Models Abroad*.[11]

After enlisting McEvoy, Schwartz needed a lyricist, and with Howard Dietz otherwise engaged at M-G-M, he hoped to collaborate with Dorothy Fields. Schwartz and Fields had never worked together but were old friends and well-acquainted with each other's talents. In 1935, she had begun collaborating with Jerome Kern in Hollywood. They succeeded as a team, first on *Roberta*, with the Oscar-nominated "Lovely to Look At," and *I Dream Too Much*, which starred Lily Pons. These were followed by the 1936 Academy Award for Best Song, "The Way You Look Tonight" from *Swing Time*. Later on, they composed songs for the movies *Joy of Living*, *When You're in Love*, and *One Night in the Tropics*.

During her time in Hollywood, Fields was carrying on a bi-coastal relationship with blouse manufacturer Eli Lahm, and she was anxious to get back to New York. They would marry in 1939 and settle down in a 57th Street apartment across from Carnegie Hall.[12] Schwartz was anxious to get her in the fold, so he made a call to the West Coast: "She was taking a health retreat at the Arrowhead Springs Hotel [San Bernardino] when Schwartz reached her; the telephone was brought to her while she was having a mud bath, and she instantly said yes."[13]

Fields had both lyric and book writing experience, working with composer Jimmy McHugh with whom she had started at Harlem's Cotton Club. They were the sole songwriters for *Blackbirds of 1928*, which ran 519 performances and included their hits "Diga-Diga-Doo," "I Must Have That Man!" and "I Can't Give You Anything but Love." As a book writer, she had teamed with her brother Herbert on shows produced by their father, Lew. The entire Fields family was engaged in the theatrical business, including patriarch Lew, mother Rose, Herbert, and brother Joseph, also a playwright. At the time, the close-knit Fields family was more dispersed than usual and not entrenched in New York. Dorothy missed having frequent visits and meals with them.[14] Fortunately, she would be working with her old friend, Arthur Schwartz.

When Schwartz, McEvoy, and Fields got started in New York in the latter half of 1938, McEvoy wrote the bulk of the script, adhering to Schwartz's original idea of a leftist in Hollywood. Fields made contributions to the story but focused on lyrics. She brought her own viewpoint to the story and the writing of songs. As Schwartz saw it in an article for the *New York Herald Tribune* only a few days after the opening: "Dorothy came to her task fresh from a collaboration with Jerome Kern. Freed of the gyves [shackles] that limit the rhyming range in the cinema, she allowed herself a truly noble lyric flight. This was expressed in her verses for 'Swing to the Left,' a song so full of mischief and wit, and so serviceable to our theme, delighted McEvoy and myself agreed it should give title to the show."[15]

With Schwartz's original idea, parts of the book, a few songs, and the title—*Swing to the Left*—producer Dwight Deere Wiman became involved. He and Schwartz had collaborated on the first two editions of *The Little Show*. Although Wiman liked the idea, he had other reasons to get involved. He was "more concerned that the show provide a good showcase for his new protégé, the beautiful Ballet Russe de Monte Carlo star Tamara Toumanova."[16] She had been one of the "baby ballerinas" discovered in a Paris dance studio by George Balanchine when she was twelve and employed by him when he became resident choreographer for Ballet Russe de Monte Carlo.[17] She had also been a principal dancer with Les Ballets 1933, the short-lived ballet company formed by Tilly Losch and her husband, Edward James. Already a prima ballerina, she was only nineteen and known for "amazingly perfect technique, her compelling grace and the persuasive charm of her beauty and personality."[18] Beyond a role for Toumanova, Wiman "wanted to have a show running to take advantage of the influx of tourists in town for the World's Fair."[19] He was hoping that the throngs expected for the 1939 exposition would spill over onto Broadway and not confine themselves to the fairgrounds.

In anticipation of this, Wiman had hired two Broadway stalwarts, Ethel Merman and Jimmy Durante. Merman had been the toast of Broadway for years now, starring in shows like *Girl Crazy*, *Anything Goes* (show and movie), and *Red, Hot and Blue!* Durante had flourished in vaudeville with the trio Clayton, Jackson and Durante then made a successful transition into musical comedy and film. He had great success on stage in *Billy Rose's Jumbo* and appeared in *Red, Hot and Blue!*

Completing the creative staff were Schwartz regulars Hans Spialek and Don Walker doing the majority of the orchestrations with help from Al Goodman.[20] He and his orchestra also provided the musical accompaniment. Goodman had quite a resume, having conducted more than 125 Broadway musical productions up to that point, including *The Band Wagon*. He was also conductor for *Your Hit Parade* for Columbia Broadcasting. As the program explained, "Virtually every musical comedy star and radio headliner of the past decade have stood on the stage or before the microphone awaiting the Goodman cue."[21] Choreographer Carl Randall's dancers included Alicia Alonso, Nora Kaye, Maria Karnilova, and Jerome Robbins in his chorus, as well as the principal dancer, Toumanova.

For director, Wiman turned to another one of his protégés, *wunderkind* Joshua Logan. He was fresh from two successful musicals, *I Married an Angel* and *Knickerbocker Holiday*, with runs of 338 and 168 performances, respectively.[22] He had also directed a play for Wiman, *On Borrowed Time*, which had nearly a year's run. Logan had been working on *Knickerbocker Holiday* just prior to this show and came late into the development of *Stars in Your Eyes*. Never shy, Logan did not buy into the McEvoy / Schwartz / Fields story—no matter what their recent experiences had been—thinking that the leftist-in-Hollywood theme had been overdone. As he recalled in his memoir, *Josh*:

> Nothing on the red side sounded funny to me. I told Dwight so, quite emphatically.... He told me, "If you don't like the way it is, change it; only make sure it's a hit." "All right," I said. "Let's throw all the unfunny Communist stuff out the window and just do a show about the crazy way Hollywood people mix sex and movies?"[23]

In the article previously cited, Schwartz discussed Logan's attitude toward the original book and songs. It should be noted that this piece by Schwartz, titled "The Evolution of a Gay Musical: Collaborators Hardly Know It," was written tongue-in-cheek or with much sarcasm, or both. Schwartz related his view of Logan's initiation into the material: "He celebrated his alliance with us by throwing his icy disapproval all over our work. He conceded our socio-politico-colossal dabblings were very funny—but not for our particular medium.... Left themes are fine for a revue, Joshua granted, since it is a revue's right to criticize. But why clutter up a gay musical narrative with weighty commentary? Why class angle the moon when it can be put to the better service of romance?"[24]

Fields' biographer, Charlotte Greenspan, surmised, "Since no one involved in the show had the socialist zeal of, say, Yip Harburg or Marc Blitzstein, Logan's attitude prevailed."[25] Schwartz felt that McEvoy and Fields, "after the first instinctive resistance," surrendered to the young director gracefully. Schwartz implied that his own transition did not go as smoothly, and as a composer, he admitted to "a twinge or two at the extinction of my numbers, but it passed." He added: "I have evidence ... in a sheaf of songs written expressly for the show and now locked away with other unheard melodies. My associates also have waddings of typescript as testimony to their lost labor."[26]

From there on, the script was in a steady state of revision, and no song previously written was safe. Most notable among these was "My New Kentucky Home," in which "the sun, stars and grass functioned only on union hours." Logan explained that, "As often happens, it was such a bright, witty song that we didn't realize it was killing the show until almost too late."[27] But "Schwartz was mad to have it in,"[28] liking Fields' "sprightly lyric on the Southland's new economy ... and ... the garnishing of melody that I had accorded it."[29] It took Logan's best powers of persuasion to convince Schwartz and Fields to drop it. With the new focus on Hollywood and away from the union, one of their other favorites was also axed, "Swing to the Left." With these two songs eliminated, *Swing to the Left* became *Stars in Your Eyes*, and "the social commentary disappeared."[30] Durante's role went from union organizer to Hollywood trouble shooter and studio "idea" man, and Merman's became more romantic. As Logan had pitched Wiman, the show became "a combination of sex and Hollywood"[31] and "a vehicle tailored to the talents of Merman and Durante."[32]

Writing for Ethel Merman at this point in her career was done in the shadow of Cole Porter, as the duo had teamed up for several hit songs. For *Anything Goes* in 1934, Porter had written four high energy numbers for Merman's character, Reno Sweeney: "I Get a Kick Out of You," "You're the Top," "Anything Goes," and "Blow, Gabriel, Blow." This was followed by "Ridin' High" in 1936 from *Red, Hot and Blue!* Ethan Mordden explained, "She was so Merman by now that one had to write Merman numbers if one wanted her to sing them."[33] Moreover, she had developed "unerring instincts about whether new material was going to work." Case in point was the aforementioned "My New Kentucky Home." It had been written for the original show, *Swing to the Left*, and did not fit the new story line. Logan was strongly against the song, but Merman, agreeing that "it was dragging the show down," consented to do it in the New Haven tryout: "She was a good sport to do it, although she herself knew, better than Arthur did, that it wasn't going to work."[34]

Fields and eventually Schwartz got the point and wrote a replacement number—"A Lady Needs a Change"—which was "a hit from the instant it went in."[35] Fields' lyric was a "list" of laments, each resolved as the "lady" made a change. Schwartz, quick to give his lyricists their due, referred to "the full, rich expression of Dorothy's release of censored [Hollywood] versifying, and by common agreement Miss Merman's best song in the show."[36] Logan concluded that "it was bawdy and wonderful and turned the show into a hit."[37]

In Cole Porter shows, Merman played comic and bawdy, but with *Stars in Your Eyes*, she was able to do more dramatic work. Her role as Jeanette Adair (Queen of the Lot) "gave her a dignity and glamour that her sidekick and goodtime-gal roles had thus far failed to."[38] Merman appreciated this movement away from typecasting, which may have been the case had the original *Swing to the Left* story remained. With this major change, the script was in constant flux, as was her character. As she remembered it: "We sometimes had to suspend rehearsals while McEvoy and Josh rewrote scenes. Still I was happy as I saw my character grow as grand as Norma Shearer, as tough as Carole Lombard and as pampered as Joan Crawford.... It was my best shot at acting yet."[39]

Accompanying her more dramatic role was a more somber song, "I'll Pay the Check." It was a "heartbreaking torch song," putting Schwartz in his element and creating a dramatic mood change in a heretofore comic scene. Again, Merman remembered, "in it, as a rich, worldly-wise woman, I assure the young director that he owed me nothing. In our relationship I might be heading for an enormous wreck, but he was not to worry. It was my party and I'd pay the check."[40] With a torchy Schwartz melody, Merman pulled off the change of tone flawlessly, going from comic to dramatic without missing a beat, a talent not lost on Logan: "To Logan, Ethel seemed a consummate actress who moved easily from the comedy scenes to the tender moments. In the Schwartz-Fields song 'I'll Pay the Check' in which Jeanette Adair realizes that she can never make the young writer fall in love with her, Ethel was achingly poignant."[41]

Another big song for Merman was "This Is It." This was a number for her character to express confidence, and one that Schwartz and Fields labored over more than usual. Schwartz recalled, "Dorothy Fields was one of the most brilliant lyric writers and one of my dearest friends. She once gave me a title with a similar problem. The show was 'Stars in Your Eyes' for Ethel Merman. Dorothy's title was 'This Is It.' I wrote 7 or 8 versions of that title phrase—adding dummy lyrics of my own.... I soon realized that the word 'this' must be given more musical space. I also realized that I'd better write a better tune."[42] Another source reported that Schwartz and Fields together "wrote and discarded five versions of the song before reaching satisfaction."[43] Their efforts were well-rewarded as the song was an audience favorite, later recorded by Merman, Judy Garland, and Helen Forrest with the Artie Shaw Orchestra.

Schwartz and Fields wrote a duet for the second act—"It's All Yours"— which became the climactic song of the show and a tour de force for Merman and Durante. Logan liked the song, saw it as the eleven o'clock number for the show, and contacted composer / voice arranger Hugh Martin. Martin had attracted attention with his arrangement of "Sing for Your Supper" in Rodgers and Hart's *The Boys from Syracuse* in late 1938. He had pushed Rodgers to put more emphasis on the vocal arrangements, and it had paid off. To present the song, Logan, Merman, and Durante settled into a small room with Martin at an old upright piano. Martin recalled the moment in his memoir, *Hugh Martin: The Boy Next Door*:

> I played it and we all sang. It registered big, and I could feel myself itching to tailor it for these two show biz icons.... I came back the next day with a complete duet arrangement for two of Broadway's brightest. When I sang it for them, the reception was polite.

But when it found its way into the Merman-Durante throats, Josh whooped and hollered. He tracked down Dorothy Fields and Arthur Schwartz and forced them to listen. They whooped and hollered. Opening night at about eleven o-clock on a cold February evening, the audience whooped and hollered and made them repeat the tag two or three times.[44]

For "It's All Yours," Merman and Durante would begin the chorus, then, in the middle of it, he would stop and do a notorious / corny / vaudevillian joke. Durante had done a similar number—"(Everyone Knows I Can Do Without Broadway, But) Can Broadway Do Without Me?"—in *Show Girl* in 1929.[45] Logan referred to "It's All Yours" as "the wildest I've ever tried," noting that their routine went on for ten choruses, "but the audience was so happy we could have gone on for twenty-four."[46] The success of the song depended not so much on the music or lyrics, "but on Miss Merman and Durante's horseplay."[47]

Schwartz and Fields ended up with fourteen songs for the show[48]:

All the Time	Never a Dull Moment
As of Today	Okay for Sound
He's Goin' Home	One Brief Moment
I'll Pay the Check	Places, Everybody
It's All Yours	Self Made Man
Just a Little Bit More	Terribly Attractive
A Lady Needs a Change	This Is It

A song titled "Mr. Blake," sung by singers on an offstage microphone, was either cut or not listed in the final program. In addition, Schwartz wrote the "Night Club Ballet" and "Court Ballet" for Tamara Toumanova, one in each act, for Dwight Wiman to show off his protégé. Brooks Atkinson did mention that there were "a number of good music hall songs for which Miss Fields has written salty lyrics." Kelcy Allen referred to Schwartz's music as "richly tuneful." Richard Watts felt "Schwartz fell below his own normal high level in this show." Overall the lyrics met with more favor than the music.[49] Either way, no hits emerged from the show.

Early in the run, the show was struggling, mostly from a mediocre book, the bane of Broadway musical comedy. Critics felt that neither Broadway musical comedy nor any other art form needed another satire of Hollywood.[50] The principals agreed to take a 50 percent pay cut in hopes of giving the show time to build an audience, but to no avail; the show closed after 127 performances. Ironically, the very event that Wiman had hoped to capitalize on worked against him and the success of the show. Merman spelled it out in her autobiography: "But patrons of the 1939 World's Fair spent their money to see Eleanor Holm and Johnny Weissmuller in Billy

15. Dorothy Fields *and* Stars in Your Eyes

Rose's *Aquacade*, attended Mike Todd's all-black *Hot Mikado* or went to the *Frozen Alive* and other Flushing Meadows sideshows. They had no money left for Broadway."[51]

Stars in Your Eyes, a.k.a. *Swing to the Left*, had originated with its composer, Arthur Schwartz. He had been involved with story lines in his earlier shows, of course, but story and script were always in someone else's hands, usually those of Howard Dietz. *Stars in Your Eyes* had been Schwartz's baby and had developed with the help of J.P. McEvoy and Dorothy Fields. Then it was taken from them—for better or for worse—by Joshua Logan. Schwartz had mixed emotions about all this, expressed in his extended *Herald Tribune* piece, "The Evolution of a Gay Musical: Collaborators Hardly Know It." He opened the piece with a speculation: "It is always a little chastening to peer back over a finished play. It starts you wondering whatever became of the idea with which you began."[52]

Schwartz then summarized the evolution of the show, especially that of the story line. Although respectful of Logan's reputation, hard work, and creativity, he noted that Logan had kept rehearsals and work on the show in a state of flux. Schwartz marveled at writer McEvoy's ability to "equip his characters with new identities and feed them onto Joshua's ravenous assembly line."[53] By Logan's own admission, "often I had to break rehearsal to ask Mac to rewrite the very scene we were rehearsing. There was little time for sleep."[54] Merman biographer Brian Kellow believed that Logan's cuts and changes during tryouts in New Haven and Boston were too much: "Logan made more drastic cuts, but this time his hacking seemed to inflict significant damage on the show's delicate balance of humor and pathos, and it never quite recovered."[55]

What kind of show *Swing to the Left* might have been cannot be known. With the original three creators, how bad could it have been? Schwartz and Fields wrote at least two songs that garnered much attention, "Swing to the Left" and "My New Kentucky Home," "bright" and "witty" in Joshua Logan's own words.[56] Two big songs could go a long way in making a Broadway musical a hit. But it never happened, and despite initial anticipation by most involved in the show, *Stars in Your Eyes* did not do well. Oddly enough, Schwartz would recall the show more favorably in an oral history interview twenty years later, saying, "It was Josh Logan who made the show successful. He has a magical touch. Great theatre man."[57] By most standards, the show was a failure, and "after this expensive failure, Schwartz remained away from Broadway until 1946."[58]

How he ultimately felt about Logan and *Stars in Your Eyes* is uncertain, but Schwartz did end his piece about the show with a bit of sarcasm: "Now that I've pretty well shifted the responsibility for 'Stars in Your Eyes' onto Joshua, I confess I'm bothered by a recurring speculation. I keep wondering if social significance could be superimposed on Hollywood grandeur to make a hilarious musical show. I must talk it over sometime with Dorothy and Mac."⁵⁹

Shortly after all this, Schwartz faced two more projects, one personal and one theatrical. The first involved the American Society of Composers, Authors and Publishers (ASCAP). Formed in 1914, ASCAP is a performing rights organization that protects the copyrights of its members, collecting fees from broadcast media and performing artists. Its earliest members included Victor Herbert, Irving Berlin, Rudolf Friml, Otto Harbach, Jerome Kern, and John Philip Sousa. As ASCAP grew, it developed a multi-tiered system of payments. The most senior members were classified AA, lesser ones A, on down to D. Songwriters were paid by the number of uses one or more of their songs had had. All members were then paid out of a large fund accumulated at ASCAP through payments from those using ASCAP songs. But the system favored the better known, more successful songwriters, those in the AA classification. They got paid more for each use of a song than lesser known writers. The rich got richer, a sore point for those in lower classifications.

Many complained but did little about it. Not so Arthur Schwartz. In 1940, despite numerous hits from his revue work, his classification was only A, with fifty-two songwriters above him at the AA level. Years later, he explained to Howard Dietz what he had to go through to improve his status: "I felt that ... I rated as well as at least half of those fifty-two. Under the system at the time performers' records were not available to writers, but I forced the Classification Committee to allow me access for the purpose of making comparisons.... It ... took me a total of approximately 150 hours in the file rooms of ASCAP to complete my study and prepare charts for presentation.... I succeeded in proving what I set out to; namely, that my record in all respects was <u>superior</u> to twenty-six of the fifty-two above me in rating and income."⁶⁰

Schwartz met with the committee and, despite his facts and charts, was turned down. Perhaps forgetting that Schwartz had practiced law before turning to songwriting, the committee was presented with a lawsuit from the young songwriter. As Dietz put it: "Schwartz wasn't mean, he was just firm. And a little impatient with stupidity. He had a determination to be a success despite publishers and producers. If he doesn't get his rights, he's apt to sue."⁶¹ The case was settled before trial, winning for Schwartz an AA classification, a one-year retroactive increase, and legal expenses. Schwartz was pleased with the outcome, explaining to Dietz that it meant even more for ASCAP's young writers: "This case cracked the classification system, causing at least a dozen other writers to follow my pattern and resulted in a Government Consent Decree in '41 defining an entirely new set of classification rules based upon performance of songs."⁶²

Schwartz's theatrical project was not on Broadway, but entailed working with Oscar Hammerstein II. Ironically, it would be an assignment for the New York World's Fair, the same one that had doomed *Stars in Your Eyes*. The World's Fair of 1939 had ended in late October with mixed success. Because of growing interest in the later months, led by *Billy Rose's Aquacade*, the World's Fair Corporation had decided to extend the Fair another season. Their Entertainments Director, John Krimsky, thought that another cultural exhibit, "in the nature of a pageant of American history," should be added for the second season.⁶³ The show, eventually called *American Jubilee*, was first offered to Rodgers and Hart. Krimsky, however, was "looking for something nearer Radio City than Broadway," and the two of them turned it down.⁶⁴

Krimsky then enlisted Oscar Hammerstein II to work with producer Albert Johnson to create "an elaborate musical show."⁶⁵ One early idea was to do a 45-minute version of *Show Boat*, but both Hammerstein and Jerome Kern were averse to this. It was then decided to do a show consisting of a series of events and personalities in American history. For this, Hammerstein chose to collaborate with Schwartz.⁶⁶ Among the historical events and personalities chosen were George Washington's inauguration, Abraham Lincoln at Gettysburg, Teddy Roosevelt and his Rough Riders, Swedish soprano Jenny Lind and her affiliation with P.T. Barnum, Diamond Jim Brady, Lillian Russell, as well as a collection of antique automobiles.⁶⁷ *American Jubilee* was not so much a historical show as it was an exhibition of Americana. Just as the show was a *Who's Who* of American life, the roster of creators of the show was a *Who's Who* of Broadway: songwriters Hammerstein and Schwartz; producer Johnson; costume designer Lucinda Ballard; stage director Leon Leonidoff; orchestrator Hans Spialek; conductor Donald Voorhees; and vocal arranger Ken Christie.⁶⁸

Schwartz and Hammerstein wrote nine songs for *American Jubilee*⁶⁹:

Another New Day	My Bicycle Girl
By the People	One in a Million
The Firemen's Serenade	Tennessee Fish Fry
How Can I Ever Be Alone?	We Like It Over Here
Jenny Lind	

For the most part, the score "was in keeping with the pageant," and none of the songs achieved great success. "My Bicycle Girl" was a number perfect for the large stage at the Fair. Twenty-four girls rode around on bicycles, a configuration difficult on the average Broadway stage.[70] "How Can I Ever Be Alone?" was a ballad Schwartz was fond of.[71] "Tennessee Fish Fry" was an easy-going Schwartz melody with a colloquial lyric by Hammerstein referring to fishing for your dinner and cornbread drowned in butter.[72] Sung rousingly by Wynn Murray, the song appealed to audiences at the World's Fair and several recordings have been made of it. *American Jubilee* was a success from the re-opening of the Fair on May 11, 1940, until its closing in late October.[73]

As *American Jubilee* was running, Schwartz was interviewed by a reporter from the *New York Times*, Benjamin Welles, and his impressions of Schwartz are worthy of note: "In openness and cordiality Schwartz strikes the newcomer as eminently un-'theatrical,' and the usual hesitation so typical to non-theatre folk in the presence of those of the stage passes almost at first contact."[74] After *American Jubilee*, Schwartz moved to Hollywood to work with other lyric writers for films. It would be six years before he had another Broadway opening.

16

Movie Songwriting
Frank Loesser and Johnny Mercer

Schwartz and Loesser "seemed unable to escape the pervasive wartime psychology in their music."[1]

After the failure of *Stars in Your Eyes*, Broadway slowed for Schwartz, and he began looking for other work. He told a New York journalist years later, "My getting to Hollywood was just one of those freaks. I'd written the score for a musical comedy—it was six years ago—and somehow it didn't open on Broadway. I was advised to peddle my songs to pictures, and MGM bought them at a nice price—and I got a bid to stay on and write music for Metro musicals."[2]

Schwartz's light-hearted comment on becoming involved in Hollywood songwriting belies the problems inherent in that profession, as it was a tradeoff. There was more money out West—usually paid up front or as a salary—and the weather was better. Filmdom had attracted the likes of Harold Arlen, Irving Berlin, Richard Rodgers and Lorenz Hart, E.Y. Harburg, Jerome Kern, Oscar Hammerstein II, and plenty of others. But the advantages to writing in Hollywood ended there. On Broadway, where songwriters shared in a percentage of profits, a long-running show meant a steady paycheck for the duration. Not so in Tinseltown. While composers would earn royalties on songs if they had a life beyond a film, there were no royalties to composers—unless you were Berlin—if the movie was successful. He had demanded a percentage of the gross for *Easter Parade*, and when Twentieth Century–Fox turned him down, Louis B. Mayer at M-G-M obliged. Berlin made a killing.[3]

Moreover, one was an employee or independent contractor in Hollywood, not a collaborator. Songwriters would turn in their songs and hope for the best. As a biographer of the Gershwins put it, "once your songs were accepted by the studio, you were rarely consulted on the arrangement and performance of your material. Too often, good songs

Left to right: Arthur Schwartz at piano and a skeptical Johnny Mercer watch Ann Sheridan and Martha Raye rehearse a song for *Navy Blues*. It was a 1941 film from Warner Bros., and the lyrics for a few of the songs ran afoul of the Production Code Administration censors (courtesy M221x_1190, Stephen Taksler Collection, Popular Music and Culture Collection, Special Collections and Archives, George State University Library).

were truncated or poorly performed in mediocre movies."4 Songwriters were at the mercy of producers, directors, choreographers, orchestrators, and musical conductors. Even Berlin had to put up with this: "I wrote *Holiday Inn* in 1941 and it wasn't until 1942 or later that people saw it. All that time the songs are hidden away and you have no way of knowing whether the songs will be accepted or rejected." A composer might conceive of his song in a certain setting or production, but it was out of his hands. Berlin added, "And when you do a picture score, you may find that one of your best has been killed by something someone else wrote in the meantime."5 Input was often limited, unlike Broadway, where discussions were constant during rehearsals and tryouts. Even composers who worked exclusively in Hollywood were not protected. Multi-Oscar winner Dimitri Tiomkin learned early on what might happen to his music: "Music he had imagined as quiet and expressive was drowned out by sound effects and his expansive, *fortissimo* passages were faded almost to a whisper."[6]

Knowing all this, Schwartz set his sights on composing in Hollywood. Howard Dietz was well-entrenched at M-G-M, deep into publicity and administration at that studio. He was not in a lyric writing mode. Fortunately, there were numerous composers and lyricists in Hollywood, and it was reasonable that Schwartz would collaborate with one or more of them. In a few short years in the early forties, he worked with several prominent lyricists. A summary of these writers and their movie songs with Schwartz is as follows.

Year	Movie	Lyricist(s)	Song(s)
1941	Navy Blues	Johnny Mercer	In Waikiki; Navy Blues; When Are We Going to Land Abroad?; You're a Natural; The Strip Polka (censored and cut); Turn Out the Light (and Call the Law) (censored and cut)
1942	All Through the Night	Johnny Mercer	All through the Night
1942	Cairo	E.Y. Harburg	A Man Without a Woman (cut); Cairo (The Moon Looks Down on Cairo); In Times Like These (cut); The Waltz Is Over; Keep the Light Burning Bright
1942	The Moon Is Down	Frank Loesser	The Moon Is Down (not in film)
1942	Crossroads	Howard Dietz	'Til You Return
1943	Princess O'Rourke	E.Y. Harburg / Ira Gershwin	Honorable Moon (originally written for United China Relief)
1943	Thank Your Lucky Stars	Frank Loesser	Thank Your Lucky Stars; I'm Riding for a Fall; We're Staying Home Tonight (My Baby and Me); I'm Goin' North; Love Isn't Born (It's Made); No You, No Me; The Dreamer; Ice Cold Katy; How Sweet You Are; That's What You Jolly Well Get; They're Either Too Young or Too Old; Good Night, Good Neighbor

Among Schwartz's first efforts in the early forties was a song written with E.Y. Harburg and Ira Gershwin. Titled "Honorable Moon," it was written for a fund raiser for United China Relief which had been founded in New York in 1941 to consolidate the efforts of various organizations doing relief work in Asia. The mission of United China Relief was to provide ongoing aid to China, often struck with famine and at that time, engaged in the Second Sino-Japanese War, which had begun in 1937.[7] The song was launched on a national radio broadcast, sung by Connie Boswell.[8] "Honorable Moon" was used two years later in the movie *Princess O'Rourke*, starring Robert Cummings and Olivia de Havilland. It was sung by Nan Wynn at a Chinese restaurant.[9]

In 1941, Schwartz was teamed with lyricist Johnny Mercer at Warner Bros. for *Navy Blues*. Mercer had roots in the South and his hometown of Savannah, Georgia. He had struggled in New York first as an actor, then as a songwriter. During his time in the East, Mercer met most of the popular songwriters of the day through Max Dreyfus, head of Harms. Mercer explained: "I began to hang around Harms, who published my first song and there I caught glimpses of all the great writers of the day—George Gershwin, Vincent Youmans, Brian Hooker, Harry B. Smith, Victor Herbert's lyricist, Sigmund Romberg, Oscar Levant, Jerome Kern and Oscar Hammerstein. Quite a team—all presided over by that shrewd and wise old publisher, Max Dreyfus. I met Herman Hupfeld, who gave me advice. Phil Charig and Richard Myers, who were kind enough to write with me. Arthur Schwartz, who listened with a critical ear to my first efforts."[10] Mercer biographer Gene Lees was more emphatic about Schwartz and young Mercer: "And so when Johnny says in that casually dismissive way of his that Arthur Schwartz listened with a critical ear to his early work, it is not to be taken lightly. His advice to John goes unrecorded, but that this connection was ever made is significant."[11] Mercer broke through writing lyrics to "Lazybones," with music by Hoagy Carmichael. By 1941, he had achieved success in Hollywood, writing with numerous composers. His hits up to that time included "Too Marvelous for Words," "Hooray for Hollywood," "Jeepers Creepers," "Day In, Day Out," and "Fools Rush In," among others.

Navy Blues was a lighthearted take on Navy life in Hawaii with the comedy derived from shore romances and wagering on a gunnery competition. Schwartz and Mercer provided four songs for the movie: "Navy Blues," "When Are We Going to Land Abroad?," "In Waikiki," and "You're a Natural." The last three were published in sheet music form by Warner Bros. with the stars on the cover—Ann Sheridan, Jack Oakie, Martha Raye, and Jack Haley.[12] The title number was sung by Raye, Sheridan, and the Navy Blues Sextette. There was also a duet, "You're a Natural," about which one blogger on old movies said, "Miss Sheridan surprises, however, by being quite a good singer and dancer, and her alto duet with oh-shucks-ma'am Herbert Anderson (with quite a decent baritone himself) in 'You're a Natural' is silly and sweet."[13]

The other song attracting attention was "When Are We Going to Land Abroad?," with the title words employing an "obvious Code-skirting pun about landing 'abroad.'"[14] The Code was the Motion Picture Production Code which existed in Hollywood as a means to censor cinematic words and visuals and was administered by Will Hays. In 1934, the Production Code Administration (PCA) was created by Hays to enforce the Code, and he appointed Joseph I. Breen to head the PCA. There was a bit of a game in Hollywood trying to get one past Breen and his censors. For most films, there would often be numerous letters exchanged between the movie studio and Breen's office, whose staff would go over lyrics word by word. For the title song, "Navy Blues," Breen's office objected to the following several words and phrases: "Who sits upon <u>her</u> davenport"; "givin' me the finger"; "Cigars, cigarettes, <u>Nuts</u>"; "I need <u>launching</u>"; and "Or <u>laying</u> a little tarpaulin."[15] Breen considered these all vulgar or suggestive. As Schwartz remembered it years later:

> Another great lyricist famous for his wit was the brilliant Johnny Mercer. He and I wrote a score for a film called *Navy Blues*. In those days in Hollywood, censorship was a problem. It affected not only scripts but also lyrics, as Johnny and I found out with this song: "When Are We Gonna [*sic*] Land Abroad?" The censor blue-pencilled this lyric. When Johnny and I went to protest, the censor said to us: "To my mind, this is a dirty lyric." Johnny replied: "I think your mind could use a little soap and water, sir."[16]

Ironically, the lyric of "When Are We Going to Land Abroad?" mentions Japan as a dreamy port of call. The attack at Pearl Harbor took place less than three months after *Navy Blues* was released.

Two other songs written for the film were never used because of Breen's objections to lyrics. "Strip Polka" had words and music by Mercer, and Breen told Warner Bros., "The entire lyrics for 'The Strip Polka' are unacceptable because of their low moral tone." Less offensive but still objected to was the Schwartz / Mercer "Turn Out the Light (and Call the Law)."[17] None of the Schwartz / Mercer songs had any life beyond the movie.

Still with Warner Bros., Schwartz and Mercer wrote a title song for *All Through the Night*, a 1942 wartime murder mystery with Humphrey Bogart, Kaaren Verne, and Conrad Veidt. The song, sung by Verne at the Duchess Club, was the only credited song in the movie. It was recorded by the M-G-M Strings, Hi, Lo, Jack and the Dame, and years later, by Meredith D'Ambrosio, but it never achieved popularity.[18] The last of these performers did a beautiful job with the pretty melody, not rushing it. This song is not to be confused with the Cole Porter one of the same title from *Anything Goes* which enjoyed great success.

From here, Schwartz moved on to a different studio, M-G-M, and a new lyricist, E.Y. Harburg. *Cairo* was a Jeanette MacDonald / Robert Young film set in Egypt during the early days of World War II. It utilized well-worn arias and recital songs to showcase MacDonald's voice and beauty. But it was also a spoof on spy dramas and "irreverently dedicated" to these authors. Much of the plot revolves around mistaken identities and covert activities. One lighthearted device involved MacDonald's character, a touring operatic soprano, being able to open a secret tomb by hitting a high C.[19] It may have been the forties, but this was not film noir.

Two scenes stood out with Schwartz / Harburg songs. The first was MacDonald with a five-piece combo and four backup singers, The King's Men, all in rehearsal. She and Ethel Waters, playing MacDonald's maid, each do a chorus of "Waiting for the Robert E. Lee," then everyone, including Young, sings "Avalon." The scenes ends with MacDonald singing "Keep the Light Burning Bright," a patriotic song by Schwartz, Dietz, and Harburg,[20] tuneful and typical for the period. In the other scene, MacDonald sings "The Moon Looks Down on Cairo," a romantic ballad. She had quite the soprano and plenty of screen presence. The other Schwartz / Harburg song was "The Waltz Is Over," sung behind the camera by MacDonald in a hotel scene, but barely audible. Two other songs—"A Man Without a Woman" and "In Times Like These"—did not make the final cut.

The most successful song in *Cairo* was "Buds Won't Bud." Harburg had convinced M-G-M to allow him to interpolate the song into the score, one he had written with Harold Arlen that had been dropped from their Broadway show, *Hooray for What!* In the film, Ethel Waters put it over in her "light and witty singing style," and it "provides one of the few musically valid reasons for watching *Cairo*."[21] Within the scene, Waters briefly reprises the song with Dooley Wilson, soon to be famous as Sam in another North African film.

As *Cairo* closes with "The End" on the screen, there appears onscreen a plea for the audience to buy war bonds and stamps, available at the theater, a reminder of what was going on in the real world of Europe and North Africa. Within the year, Schwartz and Frank Loesser wrote "Buy a Bond," a title that needs no explanation and was not written for any film. Jonathan Schwartz remembered the song and his father's pleasure with it: "My father, with Frank Loesser, wrote such a masterwork.... My father played it and sang it, with gusto: 'Buy a bond, give a dollar, and we'll hear the people holler' is the one line left in my mind. ... My father, singing it, had such a wonderful time, way up there on the high notes: 'And we'll hear the people holler!' when he performed 'Buy a Bond' on a demonstration record and at parties downstairs. He sang it as if trying to differentiate the song from his other material by lending it a patriotic glow, his fervor unbounded. The audiences in the living room were the Beverly Hills elite."[22]

Despite the lack of success of the score, *Cairo* provided an amusing anecdote of the nonsense that songwriters had to tolerate in Hollywood. Gossip columnist Sidney Skolsky related a discussion of a piece of instrumental music written by Schwartz for the movie. When he played it for director Major W.S. Van Dyke, he did not like it. Their discussion ensues:

MVD: It isn't right. Now I remember a song that was popular some years back. A peach of a song. And it fits the scene. "Hindustan."

AS: I think it's wrong for the character to play an old song at that point in the story. Besides I'm doing all the music for the picture, and I should have my music in that spot too.

MVD: But "Hindustan" strikes me better there than the music you wrote. [Later that night, an angry Schwartz phoned Van Dyke at home, asking him to listen to a new melody.]

AS: Maybe you're right.... I think you'll like it.

MVD: That's it. That's more like what I want. I knew you could do it if you had to.... I know music. It'll be bigger than "Hindustan."[23]

In Hollywood, everyone was an expert, taking credit whenever they could. It seemed that the less informed they were, the more patient Schwartz would be with them. It let him go far.

Partnering with Ira Gershwin, E.Y. Harburg, and Johnny Mercer—all in his first two years in Hollywood—was a credit to Schwartz's reputation as a composer. But his best connection and most successful film score was with Frank Loesser. Loesser had come to Hollywood via New York after struggling on Tin Pan Alley with composers perhaps a bit too classical. When Loesser did hit Hollywood in 1937, he teamed with Hoagy Carmichael, who found him "so packed with ideas, he was overloaded."[24] Loesser achieved his first success with "Moon of Manakoora," writing lyrics for music by Alfred Newman, a classically-trained composer. Like Johnny Mercer, Loesser also collaborated with Hoagy Carmichael, writing "Two Sleepy People" and "Heart and Soul," both in 1938.

Schwartz and Loesser first worked together on "The Moon Is Down." This had been a novelette by John Steinbeck about the German occupation of Norway during World War II. It then became a play, not well received by the critics. A 1943 movie, starring Cedric Hardwicke, Lee J. Cobb, and Henry Travers, fared better. Loesser "proposed to write what he called an oratorio." His piece is lengthy, equating the Norwegians with an absent moon which, like Norway's people, would rise again. Steinbeck liked the lyric, leading Loesser to enlist Schwartz to put it to music. Schwartz and Loesser both believed in this piece, even though it was not their usual stock and trade. After much wrangling, they got a recording made, which required an operatic singer and a good-sized orchestra. Steinbeck "loved it," but the piece was never published. Loesser's daughter, Susan, said of it: "Jonathan Schwartz remembers that it sounded rather pompous, with an operatic voice—possibly Tibbett's—singing a 'dark' melody. I've never heard it myself, and the demo seems to be lost."[25] Schwartz and Loesser wrote no songs for the film, *The Moon Is Down*. Alfred Newman wrote the score.

From this, Schwartz and Loesser moved on to *Thank Your Lucky Stars* at Warner Bros. This was a star-studded revue with lots of musical talent to work with: Eddie Cantor, Dennis Morgan, Ann Sheridan, and Dinah Shore. In addition to singing talent, actors in this celebrity-filled extravaganza included Joan Leslie, S.Z. Sakall, Edward Everett Horton, Humphrey Bogart, Bette Davis, Olivia de Havilland, Errol Flynn, Ida Lupino, and Alexis Smith. Leslie was dubbed in her singing by Sally Sweetland and de Havilland by Lynn Martin.[26] In the story, the Hollywood stars are assembled for a benefit program, *Cavalcade of Stars*, organized by Eddie Cantor. During the *Cavalcade*, Cantor's character is kidnapped to keep him from meddling; then he is mistaken for a psychiatric patient. All far-fetched. The original story had been written by Schwartz and Everett Freeman, but the screenplay was done by Melvin Frank, James V. Kern, and Norman Panama. Schwartz had worked with Freeman on writing several stories years before, but only this one made it to the screen or stage.

Thank Your Lucky Stars was reminiscent of the thirties and a more care-free time and "seemed to have little or nothing to do with the contemporary situation." However, as World War II expanded, attitudes in Hollywood had changed, and "the consciousness of the war had altered the Warners' musical." Likewise, Schwartz and Loesser "seemed unable to escape the pervasive wartime psychology in their music."[27] *Thank Your Lucky Stars* was described as being "typical of the seemingly hundreds of motion pictures that were turned out in assembly line fashion for one purpose: entertain the soldiers and those left behind during the war."[28]

Their twelve songs for the movie and the performers included[29]:

Song	*Sung by*	*Song*	*Sung by*
Thank Your Lucky Stars	Dinah Shore	The Dreamer	Dinah Shore
I'm Ridin' for a Fall	Dennis Morgan, Joan Leslie (dubbed by Sally Sweetland), and Spike Jones and His City Slickers	Ice Cold Katy	Hattie McDaniel, Willie Best, Rita Christiani
We're Staying Home Tonight	Eddie Cantor	How Sweet You Are	Dinah Shore
Goin' North	Jack Carson and Alan Hale	That's What You Jolly Well Get	Errol Flynn and pub chorus
Love Isn't Born (It's Made)	Ann Sheridan and chorus girls	They're Either Too Young or Too Old	Bette Davis
No You, No Me	Dennis Morgan and Joan Leslie (dubbed by Sally Sweetland)	Good Night, Good Neighbor	Dennis Morgan

16. *Movie Songwriting*

Rationing songs were popular during the war, with titles that included "Take the Door at the Left"; "Don't Forget There's a War Going On"; and "You Can't Get That No More."[30] The last of these charted for Louis Jordan. *Thank Your Lucky Stars* opens with Dinah Shore singing the title song, advising her listeners not to worry about rationing as long as they have romance. Love was the one thing that could not be rationed. It is an easy-going song done in the movie on Eddie Cantor's radio show in Shore's effortless style. More in the rationing vein was "We're Staying Home Tonight (My Baby and Me)," sung by Cantor at his poolside mansion. It is pure Cantor, and stresses a lot of saving, all for the betterment of the war effort.

There were plenty of love songs written during the war, but there was also a genre of songs encouraging girls on the home front to oblige the boys going off to war or on leave. These titles include "You Can't Say No to a Soldier"; "He Loved Me Till the All-Clear Came"; "I'm Doin' It for Defense"; and "On Leave for Love."[31] These songs were "slightly suggestive" and done in fun. Schwartz and Loesser's contribution to this was "Ice Cold Katy," whose soldier is camped outside her door. The chorus encourages Katy to marry her soldier before he has to leave. This was an all-black production number featuring Hattie McDaniel and Willie Best, and after "several choruses, three dance breaks, and the arrival of a preacher, Katy Brown finally marries Private Jones."[32] One rhythmic melody by Schwartz had a perfect Loesser lyric, also suggestive. It was sung by Ann Sheridan, as herself, advising a group of young chorus girls that "Love Isn't Born (It's Made)." Sheridan was a Texas beauty queen turned actress and sang in her own sexy alto. The song was later recorded by Gloria Campbell and Elaine Stritch.

As would happen with Broadway shows, Hollywood film producers would designate songs they thought should be plugged to encourage radio play and sales of recordings and sheet music. Sometimes they would get fooled. An extreme example of this occurred with the Irving Berlin film *Holiday Inn*. The producers and music director Walter Scharf were confident that "Be Careful, It's My Heart" would be "the big, big hit." Scharf related what then happened: "But a few days after he gave me that song, he came up with another one. It seemed a nice enough song—but no one thought it would be much else." That "nice enough song" was "White Christmas."[33]

For *Thank Your Lucky Stars*, the title song was at first singled out for promotion, but the first line of the lyric, asking about the listener's love life, ran afoul of the censors. The next two chosen for popularity were "The Dreamer" and "How Sweet You Are," both done by Dinah Shore. The former was a tuneful ballad, sung beautifully by her in a farm setting. The problem was, "The Dreamer" was "almost unsingable except by someone with a voice whose quality and range equaled Miss Shore's."³⁴ "How Sweet You Are" was given a big dance number with Shore and the chorus in Civil War garb. She tells her Yankee soldier that she will wait for him. Again, Loesser's lyric reflecting the war theme. But even Shore could not rescue the rather drab ballad. Although it fared well in early sales, it simply was not hit material.

That left "They're Either Too Young or Too Old" to lead. Producers and publishers considered this unlikely, as the song was viewed as "special material." That was a song that was not the customary thirty-two bars but usually longer, might tell a story, and was written specifically for a stage or screen star. "They're Either Too Young or Too Old" fit this description, making it commercially unfeasible for sheet music.³⁵ Moreover, its lyrics were suggestive in many phrases. To be done by Bette Davis, the songwriters presented her "with a strange alternative; she must date men below the age of puberty or men so old that she must carry them around the dance floor."³⁶ Davis's singing of it did not particularly sell the song. How she was chosen was a mystery. She sings it to a group of old men at their club, and the comic sense that Schwartz and Loesser put into it does not come out. As Jonathan Schwartz put it, "Bette Davis singing. Sort of."³⁷

There was little commercial hope for the song, but then the title kept appearing on salesmen's request slips because it was what the public wanted to hear. Those supposedly in the know, including publisher M. Witmark & Sons, had "failed to reckon with the mood of young men going off to war, who wholeheartedly approved the song's idea that the men left behind to date their girls were either too juvenile or too senile to be a romantic threat."³⁸ But Loesser saw it ahead of time as he had been in the Army Air Force and was attuned to the plight of G.I.s: "As he did so often and so well, Loesser imbued a richly comic lyric with genuine feelings, in this case the girl's pledge of constancy to her man away."³⁹

"They're Either Too Young or Too Old" took off. It was soon recorded by Jimmy Dorsey and His Orchestra with the vocal by Kitty Kallen, staying on the *Hot Charts* for four months and peaking in seventh in December 1943. Likewise, the same rendition spent twelve weeks on *Your Hit Parade*, reaching the #2 position twice.⁴⁰ In sheet music, it was among the top fifteen sellers for thirteen weeks. For the 1944 Academy Awards, it received a Best Original Song nomination. The competition that year included "Happiness Is a Thing Called Joe"; "My Shining Hour"; "That Old Black Magic"; "You'd Be So Nice to Come Home To"; and "You'll Never Know." The last one took home the Oscar.⁴¹

"They're Either Too Young or Too Old" was used in the Jane Froman film biography, *With a Song in My Heart*, sung by Susan Hayward who was dubbed by Jane Froman. In 1980, the song was selected among hundreds of Loesser songs to be included in *Perfectly Frank: Frank Loesser Revived*, a Broadway revue organized by his widow, Jo Loesser.[42] The song has been recorded by Pearly Bailey, Rosemary Clooney, Hildegarde, Andrea Marcovici, Maureen McGovern, and KT Sullivan—an evergreen in the Schwartz songbook.[43]

Schwartz and Loesser maintained a friendship and mutual respect for each other over the years. In 1948, five years after their Hollywood work, Loesser wrote *Where's Charley?*, a musical starring Ray Bolger. Despite good reviews, the box office got off to a slow start. Appalled by the response, Schwartz wrote an unsolicited article in the *New York Times*, stating that Loesser was "the greatest undiscovered composer in America."[44] This commentary, and Ray Bolger's singing "Once in Love with Amy" with audience participation and encores, tipped the balance and led *Where's Charley?* to a run of 792 performances. Loesser was forever grateful to his Hollywood friend.

17

Movie Producing and Hollywood

"It was like Gandhi against the British Empire, and we know who won."[1]

It started with a visit in 1944 to Harry Cohn, the autocratic head of Columbia Pictures Corporation. Arthur Schwartz was attempting to buy back rights to *A Young Girl's Fancy,* a story he had collaborated on with Everett Freeman. Schwartz remembered being paid $25,000 by Columbia for it and that the studio "engaged over a period of a year four different screen writers to develop this story with no luck."[2] Schwartz wanted to retrieve it and make a musical play out of it, but when he and Cohn met at a Manhattan hotel, the producer turned down the idea. The two then proceeded with a conversation[3]:

> **HC:** I like your work. How would you like to be the producer of the new Rita Hayworth film, *Cover Girl*?
> [Schwartz protested that Cohn must have the wrong guy. He had never produced a film in his life.]
> **HC:** That doesn't matter, and I want you to write the score, too.
> **AS:** I couldn't write the score *and* learn how to be a producer. I'll get someone else.
> **HC:** Who'll you get?
> **AS:** I'll get the best—Jerry Kern

Getting Jerome Kern to write a movie score and songs would be a feather in the cap for a new producer. Since he and Kern were longstanding friends, Schwartz was confident he could do it. He called Kern, who said yes. Schwartz was delighted, but with some trepidation: "Schwartz was somewhat fearful of working with a man whom he idolized, but also whom he had heard could be 'provoking.' He soon found that Kern could be irritating, but more often than not was amiable, understanding, and accommodating."[4]

Schwartz was fifteen years younger than Kern and had learned much

17. Movie Producing and Hollywood

from him. Kern's influence on Schwartz was apparent, and the younger man's melodies were at times described as Kern-like. Schwartz wrote of Kern, "His creations are bound by the same forms which govern other songs, and they appeal to the same sentiments. Yet they aren't Tin Pan Alley at all. In them is a deep intrinsic feeling. About them is no hint of the contrived, no taint of the manufactured." Schwartz said that Kern was "the daddy of the modern musical comedy"[5] and that "he can't think of 10 operatic arias as good as Kern's 'All the Things You Are' or Kern's 'They Didn't Believe Me.'"[6] To Schwartz, "All the Things You Are" was "the greatest song ever written."[7]

To complement Kern, Schwartz was able to sign Ira Gershwin to do the lyrics. Kern and Gershwin had great respect for each other, but they also had their differences. Kern wanted to work at his Beverly Hills home. Gershwin preferred to work at his own home, surrounded by his books and reference sources; Kern prevailed. Gershwin found himself listening to Kern's latest melodies, setting a dummy lyric to them, then returning to his own study "to wrestle with the real words."[8] Beyond this, they worked at different speeds: "Ira liked to work slowly, while Kern demanded instant responses to his melodies."[9] On this topic, Schwartz would comment years later about Ira and his work with brother George: "Knowing [Ira] personally so well, I have often wondered how his leisurely temperament ever managed to keep pace with George's supersonic velocity."[10]

Saul Chaplin did arrangements and incidental composing for *Cover Girl* and was an admirer of Kern. As for the man and his lyricists, Chaplin said, "His reputation as a collaborator, however, was another thing. He was difficult to work with because he was so inflexible about his music. It is not uncommon for a lyricist to ask a composer to add a note to a phrase so that it will fit a particularly good line that he thought of. Kern very rarely cooperated."[11] By this time in his career, Kern would negotiate advantageous financial arrangements when collaborating, and *Cover Girl* and Ira Gershwin were no exceptions. Kern biographer Michael Freedland explained, "Even with this acknowledged master of words, Jerry still made it clear that it would be *his* score and that he was the chief. And a very fussy one at that, insisting on the usual 55–45 percent share of royalties in his favour."[12] The final word on Kern and his collaborators may have come from Harold Arlen. When asked by writer Wilfrid Sheed about why so few anecdotes about Kern circulated, Arlen explained, "Maybe because he was such a son of a bitch that nobody wants to talk about him."[13]

Despite all this, Schwartz was glad to be working with Kern and Gershwin as well as with his three stars—Rita Hayworth, Phil Silvers, and Gene Kelly. Hayworth was just coming into her own at Columbia after small parts for several years. She was an excellent dancer and "a major-league beauty if ever there was one."[14] Although she and Cohn were often at odds, he recognized the star in her and promoted her heavily. Silvers was a veteran comic actor of burlesque, vaudeville, and theater. He would go on to win a Tony Award in 1952 as Best Actor in a Musical for *Top Banana*, then enjoy success on television as Sargent Bilko in *You'll Never Get Rich / The Phil Silvers Show* in the fifties.[15] To complement Silvers' comedy, Schwartz hired Eve Arden. She had been working steadily in Hollywood since the late thirties, usually in comic roles, often as a wise-cracking, supporting character.

It was with the casting of Kelly that things got complicated. His career was suffering following a blowup with Louis B. Mayer at M-G-M after the filming of *Pal Joey*. Fortunately for Kelly, none of the usual leading men of the time were available for *Cover Girl*, and although most insiders considered Kelly not right for the role, Schwartz thought him perfect. When he suggested Kelly to Harry Cohn, the producer exclaimed, "What? That tough Irishman with his tough Irish mug? You couldn't put him in the same frame as Rita! Nothing doing. Besides, I saw him in *Pal Joey* and he's too goddamn short!" For Schwartz, time was at a premium; he needed and wanted Kelly. Using his skills as a negotiator, Schwartz bypassed Cohn and worked out a deal with M-G-M to release Kelly to work on *Cover Girl*. The parties agreed to four weeks. When Schwartz faced Cohn to announce his leading man, he fully expected to be fired. But the studio mogul, well aware of time constraints, replied, "Thank God!"[16] Years later, Kelly gave Schwartz his due at a posthumous tribute to the composer on October 22, 1984, several weeks after his death. Kelly said that Schwartz's intercession with Cohn on Kelly's behalf had revitalized his career, adding, "It was like Gandhi against the British Empire, and we know who won."[17]

Kelly was excited to begin, not only because it was a good role, but also because Schwartz had asked him to do the choreography. Although he had done some for films, this would be his first credit for it. When the two discussed Kelly's involvement in *Cover Girl*, they discovered a mutual appreciation for Agnes de Mille's work, as she had just had success with the ballet *Rodeo* as well as *Oklahoma!* Kelly thought de Mille was "extraordinarily creative, very much the way he wanted to go, integrating dance into the body of the story." In full agreement with his star and choreographer, Schwartz emphasized, "God knows, we need you, Gene!"[18]

Before the choreography, however, there had to be music, and Kern and Gershwin were hard at it. They began to enjoy working with each other, "Jerry reclining on a leather couch while Ira sang his lines to the composer from a foot-stool at his side."[19] Although Schwartz was the producer for this film, his experience as a composer induced him to be more involved with the songs—as critic and cheerleader—than most producers. It was common for Hollywood producers to meddle in the scores of their composers,

17. Movie Producing and Hollywood

but few had the credentials of Schwartz. Regarding all this, Schwartz said, "People who work in the theater as writers—authors, composers, lyricists—know a great deal more about production than the people in Hollywood who are doing the same things. They give approval to the cast, the director and are really co-producers without the title. It's just surprising that more songwriters don't become producers, although there's certainly a trend that way."[20]

Musically, Schwartz's first test as a producer involved a song for Gene Kelly, "Put Me to the Test." The song had been written by George and Ira Gershwin for *Damsel in Distress* and danced in a scene by Fred Astaire, Gracie Allen, and George Burns with no lyrics. Ira gave it to Kern as an "inspiration." What happened next is explained by Ira Gershwin biographer Philip Furia: "Kern performed an unusual feat of musical alchemy: he substituted new notes—but in exactly the same rhythmic pattern—for the ones George had written. 'I gave him the lyric,' Ira observed, 'I didn't think he'd take the tune too.'"[21]

Schwartz became involved with the song at its first rehearsal and was not enthusiastic. Kern saw this and left the room. Kern wanted the song to be given a big production, but Schwartz thought that within the context of a small club, in which the film was set, it would be "patently ridiculous."[22] A few days later, Kern called Schwartz, an edge in his voice:

> **KERN:** Look, I'm now up at Metro for another film and if you don't like it, I'll use it here.
> **SCHWARTZ:** Jerry, it's up to you ... but I think it's very practical for what we have in mind....
> **KERN:** I have a feeling you don't like it, and I don't want to do anything with it.
> **SCHWARTZ:** No, I like it. But I think my idea of its value outside the film is a little different from yours.[23]

There was "a distinct coolness—bordering on unpleasantness—between them, simply because Schwartz had the temerity to speak his mind and express a tiny doubt about the master's work." Schwartz and Kern patched up differences quickly, but it became Kern's practice that if Schwartz expressed negative opinions about a song, Kern would mark the manuscript "ADL," which Schwartz found out meant "Arthur Doesn't Like."[24] Fortunately, "Put Me to the Test" remained in the film and was made the most of by Kelly.

Schwartz proved his mettle as a producer with "Long Ago and Far Away," a sweeping ballad composed by Kern. When he played it for Schwartz, Kern so embellished it with chords that the producer could not judge it. Schwartz then did something only a composer might do: "He asked Jerry to play the melody with one finger. Jerry did and Schwartz instantly recognized the song for the masterpiece it is."[25] Schwartz later explained, "Irving Berlin picks his tunes out with one finger, Jerome Kern seems to get sick of the melodies, because when he plays them, he embroiders them so much you have a hard time telling whether they're Kern or Bach."[26]

More problems ensued with "Long Ago and Far Away" as Gershwin's procrastination was delaying its completion. He had an "antipathy to romantic ballads," and in the case of this one, "No melody ever gave Ira more difficulty. From the very first he was stumped over what to do with the long opening phrase of seven notes."[27] In his *Lyrics on Several Occasions*, Gershwin explained, "this one took a lot of experimenting. (I have before me a dozen crowded worksheets; there must have been thirty or forty others I tore up at the time.)"[28] He wrote a lyric for Kern's melody that he titled "Midnight Music," thought it too complicated, and discarded it. Impatiently, Kern provided Gershwin with a dummy lyric that began, "Watching little Alice pee."[29] Delays continued until Schwartz intervened, needing the song for filming. He insisted that Gershwin read whatever he had to him over the phone. He read him his new lyric; Schwartz liked it and put it into the film as dictated.[30] "Long Ago and Far Away" became a hit, and by Gershwin's account, "Dept. of You Never Can Tell, Who Knows?, &c.: It turned out that this number was the biggest hit I'd had in any one year, with sheet-music sales over six hundred thousand."[31]

One reason producers were reluctant to hire Gene Kelly was his tendency to control a project, "involving himself in every facet of the production, not just his dances, wanting to convert every production into a Gene Kelly film—the Orson Welles syndrome."[32] Director Charles Vidor resented Kelly's interference and more than once, Vidor and Kelly had their disputes—one an actual fistfight—settled by Cohn.[33] Another time, Kelly had worked hard to perfect a dance scene, but when Vidor viewed it, he turned and walked away, saying nothing. That time, Cohn got involved, telling Vidor, "that was a hell of a way to treat an artist."[34] Kelly even took on Kern and Gershwin, mediation of which "took all of Schwartz's tact." Kelly protested that their songs were too long, had too many choruses, and slowed down the pace, which on the big screen had to be faster than on a Broadway stage. Fortunately for Schwartz, "the two legends of stage musicals came to trust his [Kelly's] instincts for what would play."[35]

As filming progressed, those on the set could see that *Cover Girl* was turning into a good story, one which only Schwartz and a handful of others had first believed in. Eventually, most everyone considered it "a little genius of a script."[36] The reluctant Harry Cohn could also see this and "had the sense that *Cover Girl* was no longer a lemon being improved to lemonade; thanks to Kelly's talent, even genius, there was now the possibility of a winner here."[37]

Kelly's genius was no more apparent than in his staging, filming, and performance of the "Alter Ego Dance," where he used trick photography to dance with his own reflection—his alter ego. At times, they dance in unison, at other times, the alter ego steps back to take a critical look at what is going on. At some angles, the image of Kelly's alter ego looks much like a hologram. The scene ends as Kelly shatters a store window, and the alter ego disappears. Schwartz had high praise for it:

> The dance in the dark street … was Gene Kelly's idea; he called it the "Alter Ego Dance." It was his whole conception, and the question was how we could make it part of the story, which we did, because he told it to me early enough to weave it into the story. I think that's one of the cardinal rules of musical story-telling: make everything in the musical phase of the story connected and interdependent with the story.… It's called "integration" now.[38]

This matter of integration and storytelling had weighed on Schwartz's mind as he had approached *Cover Girl* in the role of producer. He was aware of the lack of success with book shows that he and Howard Dietz had had. On his first cinematic effort, he wanted to make sure the film told a story and integrated the songs and dances. Schwartz had taken on Kern, Gershwin, and especially Kelly because they were all sensitive to this.

Schwartz need not have worried as *Cover Girl* was a rousing success and one of the most original movie musicals of the forties. Kelly's biographer, Alvin Yudkoff, attributed the film's success to three factors: "The driving influence of Gene Kelly on the entire production team; the presence and persona of the spectacular Rita Hayworth; and a Kelly dance masterpiece, with, quite possibly, his favorite partner: himself."[39] While Hayworth and Kelly were not the best actors in Hollywood, they both had great screen presence, and could they dance! Kelly's voice, though never great, fit his character. Hayworth was dubbed by Martha Mears, probably Hollywood's premier song dubber or "ghost singer" at the time. The list of actresses Mears dubbed includes Loretta Young, Hedy Lamarr, Sonja Henie, Claudette Colbert, Eva Gabor, Veronica Lake, Lucille Ball, and Marjorie Reynolds. For the last of these, Mears was the ghost singer for "White Christmas" in *Holiday Inn*. For Hayworth in *Cover Girl*, Mears dubbed "Sure Thing" and "Long Ago and Far Away."[40]

As Harry Cohn counted his money and Schwartz basked in his initial success, the two had a rancorous split. It went back to their initial negotiations of Schwartz's contract. Attorney Schwartz had insisted on a one-picture deal, refusing to give Cohn options for a second one, a ploy used by producers to establish more control over their employees. Cohn resented this stipulation by Schwartz, causing negotiations to languish. What then followed is in Schwartz's own words: "Cohen [*sic*] finally gave in when I told him I could not be happy working with anyone difficult and I heard he was difficult. He assured me he wouldn't be with me, and to show his good faith, took me on with no option."[41]

But Schwartz was never comfortable with Cohn or with Hollywood, for that matter. He knew that with *Cover Girl* a hit, his stock was on the rise; he wanted to move on. Before *Cover Girl* was released, Schwartz signed with Warner Bros., a shock to Cohn: "Harry had felt that Schwartz was to be his boy, and now Arthur fled. He claimed that he had discovered Schwartz and given him his big chances—and this was his reward!" If Schwartz made a mistake in his Warner Bros. deal, it was in signing too early. Cohn was able to get revenge by keeping Schwartz's name out of all advertising for *Cover Girl*, and on the screen credits, "it appears *below* the assistant producer's."[42]

During his time producing in Hollywood, Schwartz busied himself with other projects. He was as comfortable writing words as putting down notes, and he did a few articles for *The Hollywood Reporter*. One of these was an essay defining American music, while at the same time, explaining why there was "the lack of a classical music culture in America." He admitted that Americans, for the most part, were not writing operas or symphonies like the European composers. However, he declared Americans to be "among the most musical people in the world," pointing to our eclectic American musical tradition which included hymns, work-songs, blues, spirituals, and backwoods ballads. He pointed to American composers as diverse as Stephen Foster and Victor Herbert. He then made a pitch for popular songs and Tin Pan Alley:

> Tin Pan Alley, so-called, has taken a lot of abuse as being cheap, brash, and vulgar and its products shallow and in bad taste. At the expense of seeming to be defending my own, since I wrote many popular songs before I became a motion picture producer, I believe that Tin Pan Alley has contributed much really good music to the public. It has turned out songs that people whistle and sing songs that have kept up public morale and helped win wars. But I do know that in America, commercial songs are written that have such a wide appeal and strike such a common denominator that within a few weeks of their introduction they are being hummed and whistled by millions of people. It may be only a simple melody, but when a popular song has that wide an appeal, it is bound to have something of the quality of living music.[43]

In his discussion, Schwartz makes a good case for American Popular Song, although the phrase was not in existence at that time. Songs of this ilk were still under the umbrella of Tin Pan Alley, and Schwartz was touting its popular songs. But at that moment, he was still a movie producer.

For his next assignment, Schwartz went from the imaginary world of a small night club to the real world of theater and Broadway. Aware of the work Schwartz had been doing on *Cover Girl*, Jack Warner asked Schwartz to produce *Night and Day*, a rendering of the life of Cole Porter. Warner thought that Schwartz, the composer / producer, could do justice to the story of a fellow songwriter. Since the beginning of World War II, Irving Berlin had been pushing Warner Bros. to do a Porter biopic. Berlin felt "a film based on Porter's life—how he managed to triumph over the pain and crippling effects of breaking his legs—would be a tremendous morale booster for the troops wounded in action."[44]

Schwartz and Porter had never worked together, but they had been friends since 1931, when Porter had called the younger man to compliment his revue work. Schwartz felt that Porter had "a tremendous interest in young composers." Porter had provided twelve letters of introduction to friends in Paris, Cannes, Nice, and London for him when he traveled to Europe. Of these letters, Schwartz exclaimed they "worked like a charm."[45] He later admitted in the Introduction to a Cole Porter biography: "I was overcome by his thoughtfulness and generosity, but when I made the trip I found I was unwilling to impose upon more than three of his friends. It was a wise decision. Had I met all of them, I surely would have needed a holiday to recuperate from their hospitality."[46]

Porter had been working in Hollywood on and off since the mid-thirties having done songs for *Born to Dance* (1936), *Rosalie* (1937), *You'll Never Get Rich* (1941), and *Something to Shout About* (1943).[47] He and Schwartz had taken on a new movie for Warner Bros., *Mississippi Belle*, with Schwartz in his first producing effort for Warner. Schwartz commented then that Porter was "a great chap in addition to being just about the best there is among popular composers."[48] This early amity dissipated as Schwartz and Porter butted heads over Porter's songs for the movie. He had written nine songs which Schwartz felt were inferior. When he asked for more, rancor ensued. As Porter biographer Charles Schwartz put it: "Possibly if Schwartz himself were not a songwriter, Cole might have taken more kindly to these suggestions. But since inherent in Schwartz's carpings [sic] and Cole's negative responses were ego factors heightened by artistic differences, it was perhaps inevitable that a blowup should occur."[49]

Porter called for a meeting with Schwartz and other executives, demanding that the bulk of his now thirteen songs be retained. In the meeting, Porter had suggested that rather than *Mississippi Belle*, what they were trying to produce should be called *Mississippi Cover*, an obvious reference to Schwartz's recent film, *Cover Girl*. Porter was so angry that Schwartz and the others backed off, agreeing to keep ten of the Porter tunes. Eventually, the entire project was shelved, probably to everyone's relief.[50] Oddly enough, a few years later, Jack Warner proposed *Mississippi Belle* as a stage musical. Schwartz informed Warner that he had given the material a careful look but felt that it was not right for a musical. He gives Warner his reasons and at the same time gets in a dig on the Broadway critics: "Since I have been wrong many times before, it's quite possible I am wrong again this time, but my reaction is probably based on the view that the locale and characters of 'Mississippi Belle' would probably seem dated to those hatchet boys on the New York press, without whom it is just impossible to have a success."[51] Then Schwartz and Porter turned to *Night and Day*, previous offenses forgotten.

A film biography of Cole Porter was in keeping with the then current Hollywood practice of producing biopics of famous composers. Movies of this genre between 1938 and 1954 included:

Movie	Year	Songwriter	Portrayed by
Alexander's Ragtime Band	1938	Irving Berlin*	Tyrone Power (as Alexander)
The Great Victor Herbert	1939	Victor Herbert	Walter Connolly
Yankee Doodle Dandy	1942	George M. Cohan	James Cagney
Rhapsody in Blue	1945	George Gershwin	Robert Alda
Words and Music	1945	Richard Rodgers / Lorenz Hart	Tom Drake / Mickey Rooney
Till the Clouds Roll By	1946	Jerome Kern	Robert Walker
Deep in My Heart	1954	Sigmund Romberg	José Ferrer

* *This film was not a biography of Irving Berlin, but was filled with his music, as were* This Is the Army *(1943) and* Blue Skies *(1946). Tyrone Power played Alexander. Berlin refused to have his life story filmed while still alive.*[52]

These screen treatments were problematic. To begin, there had to be an effort to make these films biographic but avoid idolizing the subject. One reviewer of *Night and Day* would refer to the "unbelievable hero worship of the Gershwin yarn."[53] Beyond this, the screen writers had to be sure there was enough in the subject's life to warrant a story that would hold the interest of audiences. If the composer's life came up short, writers and producers never shied away from using fictional scenes. Usually, with a number of beautiful songs to surround them, story lines could be manipulated. Schwartz was well aware of all this, declaring, "The difficulty of making a film about a person who is alive today is that you not only have to get that person's entire approval but you have to be sure his biography is entertainment. In the case of Cole Porter we were lucky. His real life road very much like a piece of fiction in many places."[54] Schwartz would later say that there was "enough substance to make a couple of great pictures."[55] Porter had lived a life filled with anecdotes, adventures, and eccentric companions. The writers were more worried that if they told the truth, it might be viewed by the audiences as improbable. In this vein, "the writers threw away dozens of real incidents that actually happened to Porter."[56]

17. Movie Producing and Hollywood

When Porter had agreed to a film treatment of his life, he insisted on final script approval. Once that was given, he received $300,000 for these rights. With contracts signed, Schwartz and his team could move ahead.[57] After he read the initial script, Schwartz wrote an interoffice communication to Jack Warner that began, "Dear Boss, I believe that NIGHT AND DAY has perfectly enormous possibilities. I must say that my first reading of the script was unfavorably colored by the 'FINAL' label placed upon it. So many ideas occurred to me for improvement as I went along that I could not believe anyone could regard this version as anything better than temporary." The suggestions Schwartz made included:

(1) improvement of the love story "by relieving some of its heaviness"; (2) inclusion into the story of Monty Woolley, Porter's long-term friend from Yale days, as well as other personalities like Elsa Maxwell and Charles B. Cochran; (3) appearance of performers who had starred in Porter productions including Fred Astaire, Jimmy Durante, Gertrude Lawrence, Victor Moore, Bob Hope, Mary Martin, Ethel Merman, Eve Arden, and Fred Waring; (4) "relieving the terrible monotony of Cole Porter singing and

Producer Arthur Schwartz (left) with director Michael Curtiz on the set of *Night and Day*, Warner Bros. production of 1946. This was Schwartz's second major film. He had already done the musical *Cover Girl* in 1944, working with Jerome Kern, Ira Gershwin, Gene Kelly, and Rita Hayworth. *Night and Day* starred Cary Grant as Cole Porter and Alexis Smith as Linda Porter (Warner Bros. Pictures / Photofest ©Warner Bros. Pictures).

playing at the piano"; (5) more scenes in London and fewer in Paris; (6) "Improve the dialogue throughout. There are many scenes which I believe to be badly written. The characters in the story demand topflight writing."[58]

Three months later, Schwartz wrote Porter, asking him to personally contact the various stars mentioned above and ask that they perform in his movie biography: "The many stars who are deeply indebted to you because of your great contribution to their success would surely be more receptive if approached by you."[59] Of all the stars associated with Porter shows, only Mary Martin performed in the movie, singing "My Heart Belongs to Daddy." Eve Arden, Jane Wyman, and Ginny Simms were cast in roles which represented a composite of several stars and personalities in Porter's life.[60] Simms' character mostly paralleled the career of Ethel Merman.

Casting of the principals went with surprising ease. Porter had always wanted Cary Grant to portray him on film if the opportunity presented itself. Grant was a big fan of Porter's music which made contract negotiations easier than expected. Nonetheless, the tall, handsome Grant hardly resembled the short, balding Porter. As for Linda Porter, "lovely and elegant" Alexis Smith looked much like her and was already part of the Warner Bros. stable of stars.[61]

Night and Day received a mixed reception from the critics. Grant was credited with giving his Porter character warmth. Grant's voice had been suspect from the start, and the *New Yorker* critic was hard on him: "Mr. Grant is forced to break into song now and then, which is rather too bad, since his voice, though resonant, is no more mellifluous than the average subway guard's."[62] Ginny Simms, who was given six songs to sing, was praised for doing "a deeply satisfying job on the best of the Porter tunes."[63] Several critics singled out her rendition of "I've Got You under My Skin." The score for the film, done by Ray Heindorf and Max Steiner, received an Academy Award nomination for 1947.

Schwartz and director Michael Curtiz were mentioned favorably in several reviews. Of Schwartz's production, *The Hollywood Reporter* cited complimentary reviews:

> When Arthur Schwartz, the producer, a song writer himself and a man who knows how to put on a musical number, decides to make a production out of a song, he does it in the grand style.... Producer Arthur Schwartz and Director Michael Curtiz, backed by Warners resources of sound and set, have spared nothing to make the magnificence of production match the splendid sounds.[64]

Another showbiz weekly, *Hollywood Review*, was equally impressed by Schwartz's efforts:

> This is the first production from the genius of Arthur Schwartz since his "Cover Girl" several years ago. It is just as well that the intervening years were not given to anything

routine. One expects nothing but the best from Arthur Schwartz. "Cover Girl" made film history and "Night and Day" will repeat. Warners and Arthur Schwartz have omitted no single entertainment factor to make it so exciting and thrilling; it is an extraordinarily fine picture.[65]

Not all was wonderful during the production of *Night and Day*. There was a strike in the middle of filming, the second week of October 1945, causing delays and a shutdown that cost the studio half a million dollars. Script development also went over budget. The eventual cost of production was well over three million dollars.[66] These extra expenses and delays precluded the hiring of stars from Porter shows that Schwartz had pushed for. As mentioned, among a host of Broadway stars who might have been cast, only Mary Martin was on-screen. Other stars in the film—Ginny Simms, and Jane Wyman—had not been in Porter shows.

Also during 1946, Porter had been fighting a plagiarism suit that had first been filed in 1944. At that time, Schwartz and Harry Warner had received a letter from plaintiff Ira Arnstein. He claimed that Porter had pirated "Night and Day" from Arnstein's "I Love You Madly," and made allegations regarding other songs as well. Accusations from Arnstein against songwriters were not new. In 1928, he claimed that he had submitted a song to Irving Berlin's publishing house titled "Alone," only to have it stolen by Berlin for his "Russian Lullaby." The case was thrown out of court. Like Berlin, Porter was found innocent of plagiarism.[67] But in February 1946, a higher court reversed the jury's decision; the Arnstein case was reinstated. Finally in May, a federal court ruled in Porter's favor. Despite the outcome, the lawsuit had been an ordeal for Porter.[68]

Schwartz was involved in another production delay, albeit a preposterous one. Douglas Watt of the *New York News* explained that Jack Warner objected to Porter's lyric "You're the top, you're Mickey Mouse" during the filming of "You're the Top." At the time, Bugs Bunny was the Warner Bros. cartoon star, and Warner wanted to avoid publicity for Mickey Mouse, the longtime Disney cartoon character. Watt continued the story:

> Schwartz said he couldn't ask Porter to change it, so Warner said he would and forgot. The scene was recorded with Mickey's name and, during the rushes, Warner blew his top. He called Schwartz and said, "I gave you a perfectly good line—'You're funny like Bugs Bunny.'" Schwartz said, "You didn't but I wish you had. It would have made all the difference."[69]

Despite the favorable reviews, great box office, and the blessings of Cole Porter and Jack Warner, *Night and Day* failed as a film biography. It was notoriously inaccurate. As *Halliwell's Film and Video Guide* described it: "The life of Cole Porter. Or rather, a fictitious story about a composer who happens to be called Cole Porter."[70] The inaccuracies pile up as Porter is portrayed: living at the family mansion in Peru, Indiana, staffed by black servants; working as an ambulance driver in World War I, badly injured in a bomb explosion; and composing "Night and Day" in the presence of Linda, while the rain lands softly on the window panes. The biggest departure from the truth was the relationship between Porter and Linda. Although they were in love, the marriage was often one of convenience. In the film, the topic of Porter's bisexuality is never discussed nor are his multiple affairs. This was all common knowledge in Hollywood, but such exclusions would be expected for that era.[71] A 2004 film, *De-Lovely*, focused more on Cole and Linda's relationship and his sexuality. The film starred Kevin Kline and Ashley Judd.

Schwartz, despite making a beautiful picture in sight and sound, had dropped the ball on a truthful biography. He wrote of Porter and all of this a few years later:

> He was phenomenally gifted and very rich, he had an indescribably beautiful wife, his name was the proverbial household word, and celebrated people the world over sought his companionship. He and I both knew that these were not quite elements of great story-making. But we also knew that fictionalizing was out of the question. Audiences wanted to meet the real Cole Porter. So we settled for the truth.... Cole and I weren't satisfied, but the public was.[72]

Schwartz was either trying to hide the facts or was naïve. The latter is unlikely as he was no stranger to the ways of Broadway and Hollywood and close enough to Porter to know the truth. Perhaps Schwartz was simply trying to hide the facts, portraying *Night and Day* as something it was not. Faced with a successful film, nobody at the studio cared that much and least of all Cole Porter. Shortly after the premier, he telegrammed Schwartz: "DEAR ARTHUR I SAW A SHOWING OF NIGHT AND DAY AND I COULD NOT HAVE HAD A BETTER PRODUCER. LOOK FORWARD TO SEEING YOU AND HEARING YOUR NEW SCORE WHEN I HIT THE COAST. ALL MY BEST. COLE."[73]

Porter led audiences and the press to believe that he liked the film. Most probably, he loved the idea of being portrayed by Cary Grant. With friends, however, Porter admitted, "None of it is true." When it started to be shown on television, "Cole would watch it at every opportunity so that he could have a good time laughing at the many plot absurdities concocted by a string of Hollywood hacks."[74] Perhaps the biggest critic was Schwartz's son, Jonathan. Over fifty years after the movie opened, he wrote, "Starring Cary Grant, *Night and Day* was as hollow a film as you could imagine, held afloat only by Porter's songs. It allowed me the first inkling, however it came to me, that up on that screen the truth wasn't being told. The whole thing was in cartoon language and not to be taken seriously."[75]

Controversy with *Night and Day* did not stop with the end of filming. Finished in late 1945, it was not released until July 1946. By this time,

Schwartz had been disengaging himself from Hollywood. As mentioned before, he was averse to multi-picture deals. A Hollywood journalist explained, "Now that Jack Warner has seen *Night and Day* and given it his blessing, Schwartz has cut loose from that studio. He does not enjoy the feeling of slow strangulation that comes with tight contractual bonds."[76] Like Harry Cohn, Jack Warner did not like employees leaving him, and Schwartz was no exception.

Again like Cohn, Warner gave Schwartz short shrift in advertisements for the film. Schwartz detailed this in a letter to Warner in July 1946. Schwartz first admitted, "Throughout our entire association together, your attitude toward me was so fair and generous." He then details his complaint, saying it was more a matter of fairness than legality, a redress which he wanted to avoid despite his experience as an attorney: "It's the question of my billing in the 'Night and Day' advertisements. The recent ones announcing the opening reduced my name to a size type which I do not consider fair.... If you have any particular reason for discriminating against me, I should like to know what it is. All I know is that I gave my very best effort to the job, and that the job turned out respectable. You and I know from the notices and the reactions of everyone who has seen the picture that it is going to be a great success."[77] It is unclear if Schwartz ever got satisfaction and a larger billing. It is clear that Hollywood producers of the day were happier when they could control employees with a multi-picture deal.

Despite the success of his two movies and frequent offers to produce, Schwartz had had his fill of Hollywood and producing. He did not like how the movie industry operated, telling Howard Dietz: "I'm strictly a piece-work guy. One job at a time. The idea of preparing four or five scripts simultaneously seemed abhorrent, and that's the Hollywood system, except for independents."[78] In a similar vein, he concluded to an oral historian years later, "I think that's an insane life." But it was not just Hollywood pushing him out, it was Broadway pulling him back. As he told the same interviewer, "My only love is the theatre.... In the New York theatre, the group of authors has some control. In Hollywood you are an employee."[79] Schwartz frequently talked about the freedom of working on Broadway and the spirit of cooperation among the creators, a phenomenon often lost in Hollywood. His was an intelligent, creative mind, and he needed the freedom to exercise it. A Hollywood journalist surmised, "Arthur Schwartz, who makes a fetish of unorthodoxy, is again turning down all Hollywood contract offers in order to freshen his mind on the Broadway front. Also maintain his own freedom, and I suspect the latter motive is the more compelling."[80] His departure from Hollywood had been in the offing. He would continue producing, but it would be on Broadway for his own revue, *Inside U.S.A* (1948), and a dramatic play, *Hilda Crane* (1950). For Schwartz, no more autocrats and multi-picture deals. No more assembly lines. He left Tinseltown with few regrets and a composing and producing record to be proud of.

By the time *Night and Day* opened, Schwartz was back in New York and working on *Park Avenue*, which would open in November 1946. He was taking care of wife Katherine and would suffer an occasional recurrence of his depression, but he was still a presence in his profession. Three brief sketches of him about this time were all quite favorable:

Jonathan Schwartz: "My father in his forties cut a suave path. He was cultivated, as suggested by his unaccountable, ever-so-slight British accent. He was always wonderfully dressed. He moved gracefully with cigarette in hand, a man in honorable thought. His dark hair was turning gray, his light blue eyes held no venom. He was alive and ready for conversation, by all accounts a marvelous listener."[81]

Hollywood journalist Florabel Muir: "Dapper, sophisticated, practical with a dash of the elf. He asserts that he takes life easily, likes to eat and drink and wear the best, and feels at ease among stimulating and interesting company, preferably show people."[82]

Howard Dietz: "Arthur's looks then, as now, were good. Tall—about six one, thin—a good clothes prop, a face that sunburns well, eyes slanting like an Egyptian's, teeth as even as though they were false, jet-black hair—now graying at the temples, high brow, horn-rimmed glasses, a Phi Beta Kappa key."[83]

18

Songwriting

"But you have to do it every day and keep it up until you live, breathe and dream pop songs."[1]

Late in his career, Arthur Schwartz began writing a book on how to become a songwriter. A sort of *Songwriting for Dummies*, but not with that tone. He first considered titles:

Proposed book on songwriting, possible book titles:

Are You a Song-Writer?   How to Write Song Hits
How to Write Popular Songs   I Feel a Song Coming On[2]
How to Write Better Songs

It is not clear what prompted him to start the book. Although it was never published, his notes on the book provide insight into his working methods and what was important to him in. First off, he posed the following questions:

How to decide whether you are a song-writer
1. What and how much have you written?
2. Is there any work you would rather do? (Then do it.)
3. Honestly, how do you rate your work when comparing it to the best and most successful songs over the years? (Self-editing tough job)
4. Who, besides you and your friends, likes your songs?[3]

At this point in his career, Schwartz could have given some good answers to his own queries. As to how much he had written, there are titles for over 650 songs, done with various lyricists, listed in the Appendix of this book. Not all were published, fewer were recorded, and still fewer became hits, but this is quite an output. This is to say nothing of the hundreds of song snippets tossed aside after the composer decided they were unfit to be played or presented to his lyricist. Schwartz wanted budding songwriters to realize that one did not write a few songs and hope for the best. One had to work at it: "the first step along the path of writing tunes is to write tunes.

Jerome Kern taught me to write something every day. Not everything he wrote was useful; but he kept on writing—not just thinking of tunes but setting them down."[4] Similarly, Schwartz told a publicist: "In the first place, you don't write <u>A</u> popular song. You simply write popular music continually day in and day out, and if you are talented enough and lucky enough, you get a certain amount of hits over a period of time. Probably what happens is that when you work at it enough, your subconscious gets into the act and you start coming up with good musical ideas. But you have to do it every day and keep it up until you live, breathe and dream pop songs."[5]

Schwartz's second query to prospective songwriters regarded other employment. He felt that if a person was happy and successful in another profession, songwriting was too risky to count on. As early as 1924, Schwartz wanted to team with Howard Dietz and wrote him a letter to that effect. Schwartz wanted to make a career of the theater and give up his practice of law. Dietz discouraged their union, but understood Schwartz's dilemma and ability: "If it weren't for the persistent melodies that entered his ear without knocking, Arthur Schwartz might have climbed to some dizzy height, even to Attorney General."[6] At the time, Schwartz was successfully engaged as a lawyer, and no less a judge than Lorenz Hart told him he was not ready to take up songwriting full time. Hart told him he would let him know when the time was right. It came in 1928, and Schwartz abandoned the law. His family, friends, and senior law partner all thought him daft. Years later, Schwartz revealed that writing music required "digging and logic, and there is no better training for assembling material logically than law training."[7]

The third question detailed by Schwartz asked how, in honest self-appraisal, the songs of the songwriter held up against the hits of the day. Self-criticism was crucial to Schwartz in the songwriting process: "Eminent success, of course, supposes outstanding talent, but a small gift can go far—provided (and here comes point two) that it is coupled with a keen sense of self-criticism. This, alas, most tunesmiths lack."[8] This was not just an overall appraisal of one's song when it was finished, but rather an ongoing evaluation as the song was being composed. Jonathan Schwartz recalled listening to his father composing: "Downstairs, Arthur was composing with the door closed. I often sat outside that door, as the audience, and heard him repeat a melody over and over again, adding to it, subtracting, changing keys, experimenting with tempo. It seemed to me that he could stay in there forever."[9] This ability to self-criticize also applied to the collaborative process with his many lyricists over the years. Howard Dietz recalled their process, which produced over 400 songs by his count: "Arthur and I got along well.... Sometimes I would suggest a title and even a rhyme with a melody. But most often he would write a tune first. We weren't touchy about criticism. I would say 'The tune stinks' he would say 'The lyric is lousy.' We aimed to please each other—we figured that if we succeeded there were a lot of people like us. Schwartz was a great judge of lyrics, an editorial mind, an ear for the fitness of sound."[10]

Finally, Schwartz asked songwriting neophytes: "Does anybody like your songs?" Early on, Schwartz had had limited success, and there were lots of songs he wrote that never saw the lights of a stage. He and his lyricists were beginners, and they knew it. His first published song, "Baltimore, Md., You're the Only Doctor for Me," earned him eight dollars, but he admitted it was "so bad that even *he* wouldn't play it at parties."[11] But Schwartz persisted. In the above-mentioned letter, he proposed to Howard Dietz that they form a songwriting partnership. Dietz declined the offer, focusing on their lack of experience and the need to work with more veteran partners before they teamed up. Even after they did get together in 1928, Dietz was not impressed with Schwartz's early work:

> At first I didn't get excited about his music. It was too much like everybody else's and pretended to be commercial. Most of his songs sounded like "Among My Souvenirs." But when he risked playing songs he had written for himself and not for an imaginary market, the real Schwartz came through. The first number we completed together was a satire on the very type of corn that he had first played.[12]

That song was "Hammacher Schlemmer, I Love You," written for *The Little Show* in 1929.

Schwartz would have readily agreed with his partner's assessment, knowing full well that it took him years to find his own voice. Dietz asked Schwartz what composers had most influenced him, to which he answered, "Kern above all, and somewhat Gershwin." Then he conceded, "Having no actual signature as a composer myself (no false modesty), and having started with you in the revue field where your conceptions threw us into a highly varied musical canvas, I adapted myself as well as I could to the style demands dictated. This at first was imitation, and then as I went along it seemed slightly more original."[13] Dietz bore witness to Schwartz's influences in melody writing: "Having familiarized myself with almost every note that Arthur has written, I find his relationship closer to such classic ancestors as Mozart and Haydn, particularly in the major key. In the minor key, Tchaikovsky may have contemplated a sepulchral action for 'Alone Together' and 'You and the Night and the Music.' But, for the most part a spirit closer to the popular field, that of Jerome Kern, often crept into the piano."[14]

Like Kern, Schwartz wanted to write songs that were fit for an American theater. Well-versed in opera and operetta, he wanted to break away from that tradition. Although operetta lingered on American stages until the thirties and in Hollywood into the forties, the songwriters of revue and musical comedy were offering audiences something different. It has been said that Jerome Kern's "They Didn't Believe Me" in 1917 was the song that broke through. Historian / critic Benny Green wrote of that song: "What has that song got that Romberg and Friml and Herbert don't have? The word that occurs to me is—Intimacy. It is non-pretentious, not flamboyant, not to be sung too loudly, not to be shouted."[15] Other writers quickly followed Kern, including Schwartz. Alec Wilder said of Schwartz: "Arthur Schwartz wrote some splendid songs…. None of these songs concern themselves with anything but the American musical atmosphere of the time. Schwartz never looked over his shoulder at Europe or operetta or the concert hall. He wrote with total self-assurance and high professional skill and never lingered by the wayside to gaze with longing at the musically greener grass of Culture. He rolled up his sleeves and went to work."[16]

To Schwartz, the "American musical atmosphere" applied to any song that might improve a show or a sketch. His range of successful songs was wide and included up-tempo numbers, dances / ballets, ethnic melodies, duets, comic songs, and ballads. These are songs which "have a wide appeal, and are as melodious and as singable as anything that has come out of this century's popular music."[17] He was writing "show music," that which he liked best: "I've an idea that show music ranks a step ahead of separate songs; it represents a more sustained creative effort. Show music means writing to the book which, in turn, involves continuity of mood and pace; characterization; and the use of larger forms."[18] Wilder felt that Schwartz's songs had "the character and sinew of the best of theater music."[19]

Compliments like these, while encompassing a variety of Schwartz's songs, invariably come down to his ballads, which "are simply the epitome of the form."[20] At a posthumous tribute to Schwartz, arranger / conductor Nelson Riddle commented, "He was the master of the haunting melody," and his songs were "golden grist for the arranging mill."[21] Schwartz had a "brooding soulfulness that is perhaps matched only by some of Cole Porter's works,"[22] most famously, "In the Still of the Night." Although Schwartz did not compose as many songs as some of the other great songwriters, there are several ballads of his in the pantheon of American Popular Song:

Alone Together
By Myself
Dancing in the Dark
Haunted Heart
I See Your Face Before Me
If There Is Someone Lovelier Than You

Magic Moment
Make the Man Love Me
Then I'll Be Tired of You
You and the Night and the Music
Something to Remember You By

18. Songwriting

Of these songs, musical historian William Zinsser wrote, "Nobody wrote melodies as sensuous. ... They are grandly constructed songs, soaring at exactly the moment when they need to take flight and then returning to earth, all musical issues resolved."[23] While each of these has a wonderful lyric, it is the melodies that may have kept them popular. Schwartz said of this: "Lorenz Hart used to say that a song won popularity because of its title or its lyric, or both; and that it remained popular because of its music. I incline to agree with this."[24]

There are other ballads, not as popular as those above, which deserve mention. Written with various lyricists, they cover over thirty years of Schwartz's career:

Song	Lyricist	Year	Show
All Through the Night	Johnny Mercer	1941	*All Through the Night* (film)
Alone Too Long	Dorothy Fields	1954	*By the Beautiful Sea*
Before I Kiss the World Goodbye	Howard Dietz	1963	*Jennie*
Blue Grass	Howard Dietz	1948	*Inside U.S.A.*
Goodbye to All That	Ira Gershwin	1946	*Park Avenue*
How Sweet You Are	Frank Loesser	1943	*Thank Your Lucky Stars* (film)
I'm Part of You	Howard Dietz	1956	*A Bell for Adano* (television)
I Still Look at You That Way	Howard Dietz	1963	*Jennie*
I'll Always Remember	Max & Nathaniel Lief	1928	*Well! Well! Well!*
I'll Buy You a Star	Dorothy Fields	1951	*A Tree Grows in Brooklyn*
More Love Than Your Love	Dorothy Fields	1954	*By the Beautiful Sea*
Oh, But I Do	Leo Robin	1946	*The Time, the Place and the Girl*
Something You Never Had Before	Howard Dietz	1961	*The Gay Life*
This Is It	Dorothy Fields	1939	*Stars in Your Eyes*
Where Do I Go from You?	Dorothy Fields	1939	Independent song
Where You Are	Howard Dietz	1963	*Jennie*
You and I Know	Albert Stillman / Laurence Stallings	1937	*Virginia*

Almost all of these have been recorded, but for the most part, are seldom performed. Fortunately, they emerge in an occasional tribute show or cabaret act. Historian Wilfrid Sheed discussed Schwartz and other songwriters who never achieved top status—although their work warranted it—and are for the most part forgotten:

> Walter Donaldson and Arthur Schwartz remain head-scratchers. "Hmm, the name sounds familiar. Give me a clue." The drive to amnesia is mighty strong, and even Vincent Youmans, whose name seems close to unforgettable, remains shrouded in fog.... Of Arthur Schwartz as much as anyone, it could be said that in any less crowded time and place, he would surely have been deemed a grand master, but that in any such normal circumstances, he might not have become a songwriter at all.[25]

To look again at Schwartz's "How to" book on songwriting, he attempted to answer a long-standing question in the field:

> What makes a song a <u>hit</u>
> 1. Something <u>distinctive</u>
>   A. title
>   B. lyric—novel <u>or</u> beautiful
>   C. melody
>   1. a <u>front</u>-phrase
>   2. sheer beauty
> 2. <u>Construction</u>
>   A. form, no matter how loose ("Begin the Beguine")
> 3. Simplicity even though there are many exceptions
> 4. Wedding of words and music (so you can't tell which came first)[26]

Without launching into a speculative analysis of individual songs, the ballads listed above fit this outline well. Schwartz believed in songs being "distinctive." To this point he said, "I find I place a great emphasis on freshness. There are dozens of songs I like very much (and I wish I had written), but only a couple of handfuls strike me as especially original."[27]

Another adjective for Schwartz's melody writing would be "different ... that seems to be the catchword of Arthur Schwartz's every endeavor. The unexplored bypaths of musical interpretation alone are for him, the old trodden paths to be used only incidentally in his quests."[28] Whatever descriptor one might use—distinctive, freshness, original, different—Schwartz had a unique brand of songwriting. Alec Wilder, in a final analysis of Schwartz: "I admit that it's fun to find devices which begin to crop up, devices which cause you to be certain the song is by so-and-so and no one else. One might, in the case of Schwartz, accomplish this by the method of eliminating certain writers and assuming that if you're left with skill, wit, sophistication, sinew, and drive, it might well be he."[29]

Schwartz had received little formal training, an aspect that bothered him from time to time. He wrote nothing that could be called classical, but did have success with short ballets and other dance pieces within his revues, including "The Beggar Waltz" (*The Band Wagon*), "Death in the Afternoon" (*At Home Abroad*), and "Tiger Lily" (*Inside U.S.A.*). As his career flourished in the early thirties, particularly after the opening of *The Band Wagon* in June 1931, Schwartz wondered if he should pursue more formal study. Among popular songwriters, George Gershwin, Vernon Duke, and Kurt Weill had had extensive classical training. Schwartz brought the matter up to orchestrator Robert Russell Bennett: "He said that if I wanted to continue to do shows of the type I was doing, study of theory was not necessary since I was getting along all right. He advised me to study only if I wanted to write in larger and different forms."[30] Bennett had "feared that such a study might destroy his [Schwartz's] melodic spontaneity."[31] George Gershwin received similar advice from fellow songwriter Buddy DeSylva. When conductor Walter Damrosch encouraged Gershwin to write orchestral works, DeSylva countered to the young Gershwin: "Further study will cramp your style; stick with songs."[32] Likewise, the classically educated Victor Herbert, appreciative of Irving Berlin's brand of songwriting, "advised him not to learn any more about music."[33]

What Schwartz lacked in formal education and piano lessons, he made up for in other areas. Howard Dietz was quick to point out: "He had a light touch, a gift for improvisation and could pick out any tune he heard."[34] As with most composers, melodies would often just come to him, "Rude little rhythms [that] would bother his head," according to Dietz.[35] Along the same line, a Hollywood reporter explained, "He gets sudden inspirations at ungodly hours and never makes the mistake of ignoring them."[36] With these melodic inspirations, Schwartz would put together a song, organizing and structuring it with techniques mostly self-taught. As he told a Canadian interviewer, "I believe that music ... is structure and form. Without it, it wouldn't be very good, in my opinion."[37] Son Jonathan was acutely aware of Schwartz's construction of a song, listening often to his father at work: "Although I never told him, I could identify his edits, his inclusions, or a new line or two that he's made up right then. I was able to hear the architecture of a melody, to feel it whole, a complete thing, with no words yet. Just my dad. Just his handiwork."[38]

On a lighter note regarding song structure, Schwartz and Dietz shared their techniques with a New York reporter. It was 1934, and they were immersed in *The Gibson Family*, writing four new songs a week for this national radio show. Each song had a coat, a vest, and pants, a phrase employed by Tin Pan Alley tunesmiths. In the article, detailed earlier in *The Gibson Family* chapter, Schwartz and Dietz demonstrated their writing of the song "Skating on the Lake" for an episode of the show. Thirty years later, they again shared their method with a reporter, who summarized it well: "The coat is the lead-off verse, which sets the pace of the tune and words. The vest is the climax couplet which audiences are supposed to remember and the pants symbolize, of course, the chorus."[39] Much of this was tongue-in-cheek, but it did give an idea as to how a composer and lyricist would put a song together. Although Dietz was the lyricist, Schwartz would always have input into that component of a song. Schwartz pointed out that he and Dietz were of similar minds on most aspects of lyrics. As an example, he explained the issue of false rhymes: "He and I both hated false rhymes. There was a famous lyricist, Benny Davis who wrote a tremendous number of false rhymes. One of them was home and alone, which don't rhyme, and together and forever; they don't rhyme. And Howard said, … heaven save us from Benny Davis."[40]

Because of the hurried pace of *The Gibson Family*, Schwartz and Dietz developed techniques that moved the process along. As Schwartz put it, "When you've worked together so long, there's a kind of shorthand you acquire that saves time."[41] Essential to this was their ability to critique each other's work and not worry about feelings. On occasion, Dietz might come up with a few measures of melody and Schwartz a line or two of lyrics. The point was to get a good song written.

In most discussions of songwriting, the issue comes up as to what comes first—words or music. Asked around the time of *The Gibson Family*, Dietz answered that it was "the sponsor's check."[42] Each team of popular songwriters worked differently. Richard Rodgers wrote the music first when working with the mercurial Lorenz Hart, but reversed this and wrote the melody after Oscar Hammerstein II had done a lyric. Jerome Kern insisted on writing his music first. Each team of songwriters had its own methods.

Dietz claimed that most often Schwartz provided a melody first, but this contradicts other claims he made. Frequently, there was a lyric, even if just a few lines, but then they agreed that most often, they worked from a title first.[43] All this being said, Schwartz and his lyricists, especially Dietz, had no set pattern: "Most people interested in songs want to know how they were written. Music first? Lyrics first? In our case, there was no rule. 'You and the Night and the Music,' music first. 'That's Entertainment,' title first, then tune, then lyric—all within one hour. 'If There Is Someone Lovelier Than You,' the entire lyric first."[44] Whatever devices they used, Schwartz and Dietz made it work, and they did so over a thirty-five-year span. There was little doubt what Schwartz felt about his most frequent collaborator: "Although I have gone to California and written shows with other people, Dietz is my favorite collaborator, and I think the most able one that I have ever come across."[45]

Wilfrid Sheed commented on their collaboration: "I am struck by the fact that while he obviously could write good songs with anyone, they only sounded like genuine Schwartz songs if they had genuine Dietz lyrics. And the rapport cut both ways. Dietz was a firm believer that how the words sounded was more important than what they meant."[46]

The catalogue of great Schwartz / Dietz songs is proof of their process and needs no further analysis. Jonathan Schwartz gave the final word on their efforts in the Preface to the anthology, *That's Entertainment: The Great Songs of Dietz & Schwartz*: "My father's melodies poked around in the wounded corners of the heart while presenting themselves impeccably.... Some of their songs are among the greatest ever written, original documents that speak for human feeling and regret. They will always help to identify the first half of the 20th Century in America. 'So that's how it was, people will say, when they come across the Schwartz-Dietz songbook.'"[47]

19

Park Avenue
Ira Gershwin and George S. Kaufman

"He would rue the day he'd taken on *Park Avenue*."[1]

It was 1946, and George S. Kaufman was bothered by the turns the American musical had been taking. For him, it had all become too folksy with period musicals like *Oklahoma!* (1943), *Bloomer Girl* (1944), *The Song of Norway* (1944), *Up in Central Park* (1945), and *Carousel* (1945). Despite the success of these shows, Kaufman and screenwriter Nunnally Johnson felt "that Broadway was ripe for a 'smart' show."[2] For the two of them, "the spate of home-spun Americana period-pieces ... had run its course."[3]

Johnson had started out as a reporter for various newspapers, including the *Brooklyn Daily Eagle* and in New York, the *Herald Tribune*, then the *Evening Post*. He also wrote fiction, especially short stories, for the *Saturday Evening Post*, *The New Yorker*, *Smart Set*, and *American Mercury*. By the early thirties, he had moved to Hollywood as a screenwriter, adept at converting novels to screenplays. His successes there included *The Grapes of Wrath* (1940), *Tobacco Road* (1941), *The Moon Is Down* (1943), and *The Keys of the Kingdom* (1944). Eventually, he got into movie producing and directing. Although seldom a writer on Broadway, he did pen a movie musical, *Rose of Washington Square*, in 1939. He and Kaufman had been friends for years, knowing one another from New York newspaper circles.[4]

Although a brilliant playwright, revue sketch writer, and show doctor, George Kaufman remained at odds with the book musical. To him, a song was only filler between his dialogue and jokes. As for Richard Rodgers and Oscar Hammerstein II, who had perfected the book musical, "nothing could ever persuade him that the famous team's kind of musical was a genuine contribution to culture."[5] There had to be some professional jealousy, as Kaufman saw their show and song royalties skyrocket. When *South Pacific* opened, Kaufman wrote a friend, "*South Pacific* only grossed fifty-two hundred dollars tonight. Of course, since it's Sunday there was no performance, but passersby threw fifty-two hundred into the lobby anyway."[6]

Kaufman's topic for this new book musical was divorce among the wealthy, "a tale about multiple marriage in the Smart Set."[7] To be called *Park Avenue*, it would be "concerned with nothing more serious than the compulsion of socialites to shed their mates with as much frequency as possible."[8] Kaufman discussed the book with Arthur Schwartz, who was enthusiastic to be back on Broadway. Their meetings took place in late 1945, and by January 1946, Schwartz was all in. He wrote to Max Gordon, his old friend and the show's producer, "I am leaving this afternoon and have instructed Howard Reinheimer to get in touch with you early in the week and work out all the clauses. He knows exactly how I feel on all points, and I'm sure there will be no trouble."[9]

Even as early as this and without a contract, Schwartz was engaged in the creative process for the show. Thinking like a producer as well as a songwriter, Schwartz adds advice to Gordon:

> Regarding size of orchestra, you will recall what I said in Philadelphia about the need for a slightly larger group than was needed in previous years. This is because radio has accustomed everyone to fuller sound. I think that 27 men for the first four weeks and 25 thereafter would be O.K. As for orchestra on the road, I think we should take the maximum allowed by the various cities we play in because the extra expense is counter-balanced by the saving in rehearsal time.[10]

Around the same time, Nunnally Johnson presented the idea to Ira Gershwin in Hollywood and convinced him of the soundness of the idea. Agreeing with Kaufman and Johnson, Gershwin felt Broadway needed something new. These discussions took place in late 1945 to early 1946, leading Kaufman to write Gershwin, "I was overjoyed to hear from Nunnally that you liked the idea, and I think that the four of us ought to make a hell of a musical out of it. Sorry we didn't come to you and get one of George's scores, but of course we never knew that such a thing existed. However, Arthur's grasp of the book delights me, and he is looking forward to working with you."[11]

Kaufman's mention of "one of George's scores" referred to the use of Gershwin melodies for *The Shocking Miss Pilgrim*, a Betty Grable movie musical set in the 1870s in Boston. Ira had created the score with extensive help from Kay Swift, who had been musical secretary to George and was a composer in her own right. Ira and Swift had cobbled together George's unfinished or never used melodies to create a Gershwin score for the movie: "By Ira's own account, he had a staggering amount of musical material to work with—100 songs, fifty of them complete ... there was plenty of material that could be used for the film—as well as future musicals." Ira and Swift emended the melodies and lyrics to fit the period of the film, and occasionally, Swift "added some 'grace notes' to the melody, lengthening various lines of the chorus to give Ira extra syllables." On other songs, she did "more extensive musical excavations and reconstructions."[12] When Ira first got wind of the Kaufman / Nunnally project, he assumed that the same would be done with this show. While disappointed with the new arrangement, he was happy to be teamed with Schwartz. They were long-time friends and had recently worked together on *Cover Girl*, the Rita Hayworth / Gene Kelly film hit.

Despite the enthusiasm of his letter, Kaufman, like Gershwin and Schwartz, was not in a good place personally or professionally. He was still grieving the death of his wife, Beatrice, in 1945. He had become more introverted and had turned bitter towards those who had not attended her funeral. The normally prolific Kaufman was entering an unproductive five-year period.[13] Ira Gershwin had just endured a flop with *Firebrand of Florence*, a show written with Kurt Weill that ran only forty-three performances.

But it was Arthur Schwartz who most needed this musical to come through for him. His last Broadway hit had been *At Home Abroad* in 1935, and he was no longer teamed with Howard Dietz, who was busy in Hollywood. Working with Dorothy Fields in the late thirties on the middling *Stars in Your Eyes* had helped. He then occupied himself in Hollywood for the first half of the forties, moving his family to California for six years. While there, he was songwriting and producing but in the long run, he was a theater man. For him, the film industry was too disjointed, impersonal, hectic, and not appreciative of composers. According to Jonathan, his father was pinning a lot on this new show: "He was telling me that he would write great music for a smash and he was feeling great about it. He had mentioned in the car that Ira Gershwin would do the lyrics and two other guys would work on the smash show. The smash would put him back in business in New York." Jonathan described Arthur as having "a mischievous smile" and being "exhilarated" as he spoke that evening.[14] *Park Avenue* had taken on great importance for Schwartz.

The book of *Park Avenue* was to be based on Nunnally Johnson's short story, "Holy Matrimony," published in the *Saturday Evening Post*. To Kaufman, this was the perfect basis for a "smart" musical. Schwartz would later add, "It's like a Noel Coward play with music. No ballets, no big production numbers."[15] When Kaufman had a premise, he ran with it, diving headlong into his satire of marriage and divorce. Discussing the early scripts of *Park Avenue*, Kaufman biographer Malcolm Goldstein came right to the point: "There was, first of all, too much of it; Kaufman, with his usual indifference to musical numbers, wrote so much dialogue that the numbers appeared as digressions."[16] His aversion to music had been well known for years. In a 1938 article titled "Music to My Ears," Kaufman readily admitted, "Broadly speaking, I should say that I never like a song the first time I hear it."[17] When he and Irving Berlin were working on *The Cocoanuts*, Kaufman did not like a particular song and refused to have it in the show, despite Berlin's protesting. The song: "Always." In another show, a songwriter requested to do a reprise of a song later in a show; Kaufman consented, but only "if you let me reprise some of the jokes."[18] In the same article, Kaufman did give his composers—Berlin, Gershwin, Rodgers, and Schwartz—their proper due: "Without exception, they have been delightful and considerate collaborators—fond of their music, of course, but keenly sympathetic to the problems of the book writer. In the main, I should say that their concern over the book has been far greater than mine over the music."[19]

Such disinterest in music may make for good anecdotes, but it made collaboration on a musical comedy difficult. The songwriters are dependent upon the book writers of a show not only to provide slots for songs to be used, but to precede these moments with some characterization or story line that allows the lyricist to expand on the idea. Comparable to this would be the good piano accompanist who leads a singer up to her opening note or a difficult phrase with a gradual series of chords. But such was not Kaufman's *modus operandi*: "Bent upon gags, his script outline gave Ira little inspiration in the way of character or situations. For an opening number, the playwright suggested 'fast dancing goings-on' with 'some such title' based on what was to become the show's one and only joke: 'When I Was Married to Your Mother (I Remember Her Well).' Ira tried other titles but they only reflected the script's permutations on its single theme.... When it came to suggesting a theme for a 'straight love song,' however, the anti-romantic Kaufman was at a loss: 'a wedding, the nature of their lives together—God knows what. Anyhow—NUMBER.'"[20] Gershwin would later say, "Funny thing about Kaufman, it's very funny, considering he did so many musicals—he hated music you know."[21]

With this unsympathetic script and Kaufman as director, Schwartz and Gershwin forged a score. For the most part, Schwartz deferred to Gershwin, allowing him to pen lyrics first. To Schwartz it mattered little, as he and Howard Dietz had written songs in any which order during their revue days and in the hectic months of the four-songs-a-week pace of *The Gibson Family* radio show. By May 1946, Schwartz and Gershwin had written one-half dozen songs, some of the work being done at Kaufman's Bucks County, Pennsylvania, farm.[22] In early August, the four settled in there for "a few polishing weeks together."[23]

As rehearsals approached, Schwartz and Gershwin had written at least sixteen songs for *Park Avenue*[24]:

The Dew Was on the Rose	My Son-in-Law
The Dinner Song*	Remind Me Not to Leave Town*
Don't Be a Woman If You Can	Stay as We Are
For the Life of Me	Sweet Nevada
The Future Mrs. Coleman*	There's No Holding Me
Goodbye to All That	There's Nothing Like Marriage for People
Heavenly Day*	
Hope for the Best	Tomorrow Is the Time
The Land of Opportunitee	

Those with an asterisk were never used, and "Stay as We Are" was cut after tryouts in Boston. In addition, Schwartz wrote two melodies for dances, "Echo" and "In the Courtroom," one in each act.

The reviewers would turn out to be critical of the Kaufman / Johnson book, using phrases that included "thin and quite labored satire," "mirthless," and "a violent maltreatment of a lonely gag."[25] So it had been up to the Schwartz and Gershwin songs to put some life and mirth into the show—and they delivered. John Chapman of the *Daily News* concluded, "Schwartz and Gershwin seem to be livelier than Johnson and Kaufman, and their musical numbers are excellent."[26] Others referred to the "chi-chi lyrics ... and serviceable score"[27] and "a handful of catchy songs."[28]

There was a quartet of up-tempo numbers that were cited favorably by many of the critics. "There's No Holding Me" is a "happy song of young love" from the first act that moves along "as a rather jaunty ditty." All this is accomplished with the musically economical Schwartz "using mostly the first five tones of the scale."[29] Similarly, "For the Life of Me" was described as "nicely jaunty,"[30] a song that "starts right in with melodic enthusiasm on an upbeat figure and doesn't stop for reflection."[31] It is a serviceable, plot-specific number, never to be a hit, that craftsman like Schwartz and Gershwin would create to advance the plot and improve a show. This number and "There's No Holding Me" were sung by ex-band singer Martha Stewart, the most capable voice in the show.

Although well-regarded for ballads, Schwartz may have been given too little credit for his quicker tempos and specialty songs. One such number was "Land of Opportunitee," a "caustic calypso,"[32] targeting rumbas, private enterprise, the stock market, the race track, and quiz programs. Performed by four gentlemen in dinner jackets singing Trinidadian rhythms and dialect, it was a number that Gershwin particularly liked. He shared credit for it with Schwartz in *Lyrics on Several Occasions*: "The improvised calypso, with its odd syllabic stress and loose rhyme, can narrate, advise, philosophize, fulminate, use this morning's headlines—and any theme goes, including the political and the sexual. Thanks to subject matter and Schwartz's varied rhythms, our longish 'Land of Opportunitee' sat well with the audience."[33]

Finishing the quartet of up-tempo songs was another group number, "Don't Be a Woman If You Can," a "proto-feminist" satire.[34] Like "Land of Opportunitee," lines were distributed among several singers. Gershwin had written plenty of lyrics, and as he put it, "*unisono* [performed in unison], they'd soon have been out of breath in the patters."[35] In the scene, three un-liberated young women complain about expectations others have of their lives on Park Avenue and as women—"An Upper-Bracket Litany." Considering the era, "Don't Be a Woman If You Can" was "before-its-time."[36] Women's Liberation was a movement that had not yet taken hold in America in the late forties, but it could not be ignored. Dealing with a sensitive topic, Ira Gershwin would do it in his kinder, gentler way. As historians Caryl Brahms and Ned Sherrin explained: "Ira Gershwin's lyrics show no fangs; indeed, it is difficult to see why they should have been expected to, it was not his style; nor did they reveal the wounds that a more emotional, open lyric writer might have uncovered for the brittle subject in hand. His 'Don't Be a Lady If You Can' invades the same territory as Sondheim's 'The Ladies Who Lunch'—but without the same bitter relish."[37] The song got more to the core of the marriage / divorce lifestyles of the principal characters than the laborious script had. Gershwin managed to conceal "the 'bad taste' in the plot beneath wit, good humor, and that winningly naïve attitude toward life that has made his friends elect him Vice-President of the Sweet Fellows Society."[38] Gershwin and Schwartz made the problem more complex than Kaufman saw it, and the song "displayed a hint of each writer's flair."[39]

In the forties, Las Vegas was known as "the divorce capital of America" due to its favorable divorce laws. Schwartz and Gershwin—in a musical about divorce—had a ready-made topic for a song. But the two veteran songwriters added a nice twist; they did it as a waltz, "in an ultra-Viennesy style." When "Sweet Nevada" was first written and rehearsed, they were pleased with the song and the leading lady performing it, Leonora Corbett. But singing was not her forte. In New Haven, it was clear that the song was too much for her, and things had to be changed: "By the time the show reached Philadelphia the song had been completely rewritten. It was no longer a solo but a number with several participants plus a satirical courtroom ballet."[40]

With all these integrated songs, including a waltz, was there room left for a Schwartz ballad? Of course. He and Gershwin created "Goodbye to All That," a late second act ballad, described as "heart-breakingly beautiful." It is quintessential Schwartz, with a range of only one octave and two-measure phrases that alternate between major and minor. The song had no life beyond the show, but "there are few songs that describe love lost as poignantly as this one."[41]

During tryouts, Gershwin wrote that "*Park Avenue* is better than it was when it opened in New Haven, we're still working hard to get it in first-rate shape. The principal trouble was, and is, vocal."[42] One important role, divorce attorney Mr. Meachem, had to be re-cast three times. It ended up in the capable hands of David Wayne, soon to star as leprechaun Og in *Finian's Rainbow*. On top of this, the original choreographer Eugene Loring was replaced by Helen Tamiris after the Boston run.[43] There were lesser casting problems along the way, some involving Kaufman's judgment. His biographer, Malcolm Goldstein, stated, "Max Gordon was astonished to find Kaufman so obviously faltering in his casting sense and so hesitant to make substitutions as the rehearsals went on."[44] Whether this was due to Kaufman's personal state or his distaste for musicals is unclear. With the show in constant flux, Gordon chose to keep it on the road for almost six weeks.

Despite the efforts of numerous Broadway veterans onstage and off, *Park Avenue* did poorly. It opened November 4, 1946, and closed by early January. There had been strong advance ticket sales due to the names of Kaufman, Johnson, Gershwin, and Schwartz, but then poor reviews and a lack of hit songs failed to attract further audiences. As previously mentioned, the biggest complaints of the scribes were the book and its "lonely gag."[45] The highest praise went to Ira Gershwin. Schwartz got caught somewhere in the middle, but in the integrated songs of a book show, it can be difficult to separate lyricist from composer. Gershwin biographer Edward Jablonski defended Schwartz, "Arthur Schwartz was roughly handled by the critics; since his music is perfectly wedded to the acclaimed lyrics, however, it is somewhat difficult to understand why the praise accorded the lyricist could not have been extended to the composer as well."[46] In a later piece, "What about Ira?," Jablonski added, "The music, by Arthur Schwartz, was ... poorly received, though many of the truly smart songs (that is, those with intricately rhymed and pointed lyrics) were noted."[47]

In 1999, *Park Avenue* enjoyed a revival at Theatre 1010, a small venue located at 1010 Park Avenue in Manhattan. The creative team, headed by director David Fuller and musical director Allan Greene, re-worked the show from a script recovered from George Kaufman's family and papers from the Max Gordon Collection at Princeton University.[48] The revival ran nineteen performances. This may have been planned, or perhaps audiences were still averse to divorce musical comedy.

Park Avenue earned a listing in *The Musicals No One Came to See*, a book by Rick Simas cataloging "musical-comedy casualties."[49] Although it may seem an unfair ending to a musical with a score by songwriting luminaries Arthur Schwartz and Ira Gershwin, so it is. As for why it ultimately failed, there is no better source than Gershwin himself: "Novelty or not, there were two reasons for our flopping: (A) charm wasn't enough to sustain the second act; (B) evidently divorce is a ticklish subject to be funny about for an entire show. In Boston during the first week of our tryout, Arthur Schwartz told me that a friend of his, whom he had invited to see the show, cried through most of it. She had recently been divorced and just couldn't take it."[50]

The songwriters each responded differently. Gershwin, after *The Firebrand of Florence* and *Park Avenue*, had had it: "Heigh ho—guess I can't afford to do any more flops—two in a row is about six too many."[51] He retired to California, never to do another Broadway show. As for Schwartz, when he came back to Beverly Hills after the *Park Avenue* failure, he was fighting depression, a problem which had plagued him intermittently for much of his life; son Jonathan referred to it as "the man with the pitchfork." In addition, Katherine Carrington, Arthur's wife of twelve years, was in failing health. Only in her thirties, she suffered from severe high blood pressure, known in medical circles as malignant hypertension. The insidious disease had taken its toll, leaving her mostly bed-ridden. A rather somber picture of the Schwartz family at that time was described by Jonathan in his 2004 memoir, *All in Good Time*. At the time of *Park Avenue*, he was eight years old:

> Arthur Schwartz and his family were back in Beverly Hills for Thanksgiving. The man with the pitchfork had remained on Crescent Drive, awaiting Arthur's failure. My mother and father's two dark rooms now assumed a somber formality. Night into day, there they were, the man with the pitchfork downstairs with my father. I rambled between them, my mother far the more interesting of the two.... Funereally chained to his brown couch, my father said little. "Jonno boy, oh, Jonno boy," is what he had to offer. And occasionally: "Your mother is so sick. I can't do any more for her than I am." He would sleep and sleep. He would rue the day he'd taken on *Park Avenue*. He told me that he would never return to Broadway. He told me he *would* return to Broadway if only he had a "project." Then he would sleep again and not sleep again.[52]

Fortunately, that "project" would arise within two years in the person of Howard Dietz and, despite the dominance of book musicals on Broadway, it would be in the form of a revue.

20

Inside U.S.A. and Leo Robin

"Berlin was, along with Arthur Schwartz, our most successful composer for revues."[1]

Before returning to Broadway and Howard Dietz, Arthur Schwartz re-engaged in work in Hollywood. It was the production side of the film industry that he had disliked, but he wanted to do more composing. Fortunately, he teamed up with one of Hollywood's finest lyricists—Leo Robin, a talent who has been called "chronically underrated."[2] He and Schwartz had considered working together in 1936 on *That Girl from Paris*, starring Lily Pons, but Schwartz had ended up with Edward Heyman.[3] Robin was a native of Pittsburgh who had studied drama at the Carnegie Institute of Technology. He ended up in New York and Broadway in the early twenties, with his first hit, "My Cutie's Due at Two-to-Two Today," with Tin Pan Alley composer Albert Von Tilzer.

Robin was signed by Max Dreyfus from Harms Music, Inc. and from 1926 through 1928, worked on eight Broadway shows. Most notably, he and Vincent Youmans wrote *Hit the Deck* (1927); their "Hallelujah!" from that show became an international hit. Robin was held in high regard among theater songwriters as one of the nice guys in the business. Schwartz said of him years later, "Leo is renowned for his generosity to his colleagues. When a group of us were discussing a score written by two men who were not present, someone asked Leo what he thought of it. Leo said: 'I haven't heard it, but I'll bet it's great.'"[4]

As with many songwriters, Hollywood lured Robin, and again he found success. He first teamed with Richard Whiting, and two of their biggest hits were "My Ideal" and "Beyond the Blue Horizon." But in 1930, he met Ralph Rainger, and they clicked immediately. For twelve years, until Rainger's death in a plane crash, they wrote hundreds of songs. Their biggest hits included "Blue Hawaii"; "Here Lies Love"; "June in January";

20. Inside U.S.A. *and Leo Robin*

Left to right: sketch writer Arnold Auerbach, author John Gunther, composer and producer Arthur Schwartz at piano, and lyricist Howard Dietz during rehearsals for *Inside U.S.A.* The show had been the idea of Schwartz when he saw a copy of Gunther's recent book, *Inside U.S.A.* (Photofest).

"Love in Bloom"; and "Easy Living." The biggest hit for Robin and Rainger was "Thanks for the Memory" from *The Big Broadcast of 1938*, sung by Bob Hope and Shirley Ross, earning the Academy Award for Best Song of 1938. It became Hope's theme song. Robin and Rainger also wrote "Love in Bloom," which became the theme song for another comedian, Jack Benny.[5]

Schwartz and Robin wrote the score for *The Time, the Place and the Girl*, a Warner Bros. movie that opened in 1946. A rundown of the principal characters includes:

Role	Played by	Character Description
Steve Ross	Dennis Morgan	Songwriter, singer, co-owner of Bamboo Club
Jeff Howard	Jack Carson	Ross's friend and co-owner of the club
Victoria Cassel	Martha Vickers	Ross's girlfriend, soprano, and the film's ingénue

Role	Played by	Character Description
Sue Jackson	Janis Paige	Howard's girlfriend
Ladislaus Cassel	S.K. Sakall	Grandfather of Cassel and conductor
Elaine Winter	Angela Green	Howard's old girlfriend and investor in the club

Mostly a backstage story, Ross has financial problems with the club as he plans a big opening show. He meets young soprano Victoria Cassel, but besides not being able to win her over, meets resistance from her grandfather who does not want her classical singing career to be derailed. Despite numerous setbacks, all ends well with a big Hollywood finish. On the way, the audience is treated to six Schwartz / Robin songs.

"I Happened to Walk Down First Street" is done as a number at the Bamboo Club by four of the main characters. Their "walk" is achieved with use of a moving belt [treadmill] and moving backdrop as the stars sing and dance, a scene created by choreographer Leroy Prinz. For "I Happened to Walk Down First Street," Prinz estimated that his four principals "walked more than twenty miles a day while rehearsing dance routines on a tread-mill [sic] which was constructed on one of the stages of the studio."[6] The song is upbeat and was noted by historian Gary Marmorstein to be "under-recorded."[7]

This song is followed by an ensemble number fronted by Janis Paige and Jack Carson, "A Solid Citizen of the Solid South." This is a rousing number, first sung by the cast, then danced by the Condos Brothers—Frank and Harry—with tap dancers and a trumpeter in blackface. The reviewer for the *Brooklyn Eagle* was not fond of the Schwartz / Robin score, "turned out during some of their least-inspired moments." Oddly, he found this song the best of the lot, but with a caveat: "And the team's one good one—a black-face routine called 'A Solid Citizen of the Solid South'—is spoiled by its distasteful caricaturing of two Negro singers."[8] Watching the film in this century, a scene with characters in blackface is off-putting. In the forties, it was not uncommon, as entertainers like Al Jolson and Eddie Cantor still performed in that manner but not with malice. Cantor's 1941 musical, *Banjo Eyes*, included one of his blackface medleys as a closing.[9] Harold Rome's "Franklin D. Roosevelt Jones" was performed in blackface by Judy Garland in the 1941 film *Babes on Broadway*. There were many others.

The best ballad in *The Time, the Place and the Girl* is "Oh, But I Do," sung by Dennis Morgan as he dances with Martha Vickers. Not only was Morgan a handsome Irishman, but he had a pleasant tenor and did well with the small range of "Oh, But I Do." He had been praised for *Thank Your Lucky Stars*, the 1943 film with music by Schwartz and Frank Loesser, singing "I'm Ridin' for a Fall" and "No You, No Me." "Oh, But I Do" is a tuneful, romantic ballad and is reprised in the finale of the club show / movie, sung by Morgan, Paige, Carson, Vickers, and the chorus. "Oh, But I Do" was a hit recording for Margaret Whiting, remaining ten weeks on *Your Hit Parade*, mostly in the #3 slot.[10] In the film, Vickers was cast as the soprano and was dubbed in all her singing by Sally Sweetland, who had also dubbed Joan Leslie in *Thank Your Lucky Stars*. Another ballad, "Through a Thousand Dreams" is schmaltzy, sung by Morgan and a female chorus. However, it is of interest because as they finish, the scene fades to pianist Carmen Cavallaro seated at a piano raised high in the air, playing one of his pyrotechnic arrangements. The piano was custom-built in the studio shops, made of plastic reinforced with steel, and cost an estimated $7,000.[11]

"Three people gather around a piano," watercolor by Jaro Fabry. Used in *Town and Country* magazine with the caption "Beatrice Lillie (warming up) with Howard Dietz and Arthur Schwartz (cooling off)." This was early 1948, during rehearsals for *Inside U.S.A.*, which opened April 30 of that year (original watercolor by Jaro Fabry / collection of the author).

Two of the Schwartz / Robin songs stood out in the film and beyond. The biggest production number in the movie was "A Rainy Night in Rio." This gave Leroy Prinz the opportunity to stage a big south-of-the-border dance, lavish and colorful. The number included Carmen Cavallaro and His Orchestra and Chandra Kaly and His Dancers. Things South American had become popular in both musicals and movies from the late thirties on. In his 1946 post-war revue, *Call Me Mister*, Harold Rome had even satirized the craze in his "South America, Take It Away." "A Rainy Night in Rio" was a favorite of film audiences, and Dinah Shore made a popular recording of it the same year for Columbia.

An anecdote regarding the song involved another well-known singer, Doris Day, who used the song to audition for Michael Curtiz for the singing lead in *Romance on the High Seas* (1948). She was up against Janice Paige and Marion Hutton; the latter's sister, Betty, had been cast but dropped out due to pregnancy. As the audition story goes: "She [Day] sang 'What Do You Do on a Rainy Night in Rio?' [*sic*] while Curtiz tried to get her to do more than just stand there by taking her hips into his hands and pushing her side to side. Day commented, 'I don't bounce around, I just sing.'" Nonetheless, Curtiz liked the audition and ordered a screen test, and "when the test was screened in the projection room, the place exploded."[12] Day not only got the singing role but the opportunity to sing "It's Magic," which became her first hit.

The biggest song success of *The Time, the Place and the Girl* was "A Gal in Calico," sung by Morgan and Carson—in chaps—and Vickers (Sweetland). It was perfect for the Bamboo Club's revue with lots of rhythm and activity and included rope trick performers and dancers, mostly cowgirls. In reviewing *The Time, the Place and the Girl*, the *Los Angeles Times* said that the plot "is held up periodically ... for some pleasant melodic interludes composed by Arthur Schwartz to words by Leo Robin and staged with commendable Technicolor restraint by LeRoy Prinz."[13]

"A Gal in Calico" gave Schwartz his second Academy Award nomination for Best Song, his first being for "They're Either Too Young or Too Old" in 1943. For Robin, it would be one of ten nominations he earned, winning once for "Thanks for the Memory" in 1938. In the 1947 Oscars competition, "A Gal in Calico" lost out to "Zip-a-Dee-Doo-Dah" from Walt Disney's *Song of the South*. Numerous singers recorded the Schwartz / Robin song including Bing Crosby, Steve Lawrence, Tony Martin, Johnny Mercer, Louis Prima, and The Manhattan Transfer.[14] The recording by Johnny Mercer was on *Your Hit Parade* for thirteen weeks, reaching #1 in late February 1947.[15] The Schwartz / Robin collaboration had been a success.

As he was working on the score for *The Time, the Place and the Girl*, Schwartz found a Broadway project that would bring him back to Howard Dietz and the theater world he loved, as both composer and producer. The idea came from the pen of John Gunther, the best-selling author who had written a series of *Inside* books. Up to that time, he had done *Inside Europe*, *Inside Asia*, and *Inside Latin America*. His *Inside U.S.A.* had just been published and was already at the top of the bestseller list. Schwartz saw the book in the window of a book store during a cross-country automobile drive from California to New York. It had started out as a family trip but in Wyoming, Katherine had taken ill with a severe dizzy spell that lasted two days, a frequent occurrence associated with her severe hypertension. Schwartz had ultimately sent her and son Jonathan back to New York by train and continued the drive by himself.[16]

On seeing the book, the topic and title for a new show popped into

20. Inside U.S.A. and Leo Robin

his head. Gunther's books were laden with facts, but Schwartz only wanted the title: "I'm not planning to use anything from the book except the title, which is not only a great commercial asset, but a perfect label for the show I have in mind."[17] Schwartz would later add, "America has become the hottest topical subject for Americans everywhere."[18] He wanted to capitalize on the post-war boom and enthusiasm that had hit the country. From the idea of the book, Schwartz would take off on a pseudo-travelogue, much like he had done with Dietz in *At Home Abroad* (1935) and with Desmond Carter in London with *Follow the Sun* (1936). As Jonathan Schwartz remembered it: "He would do it in revue form; he and Howard Dietz would write songs that glorified unusual spots on the map, such as Rhode Island, Pittsburgh, Atlanta. He'd already written a title song with a complete melody and a partial lyric. Would we like to hear it?"[19]

With a revue format and all of America from which to choose, sketch topics were in abundance. Sketch writers were available too, which made Schwartz's job as producer much easier: "Instead of my having to contact writers for sketches, my Hollywood office was deluged with calls from top writers who wished to submit sketches for 'Inside U.S.A.' to me, without my

Howard Dietz and Arthur Schwartz watching rehearsals for *Inside U.S.A.* The show opened in April 30, 1948, starring Beatrice Lillie and Jack Haley. It was considered the best of the last great revues (courtesy Harry Ransom Center, University of Texas at Austin / *New York Journal American* photograph).

having to approach them at all. ... If our show fails, I can't imagine the reason being a lack of good sketch material."[20]

In the Arthur Schwartz Papers at the Library of Congress, there is correspondence regarding sketches for *Inside U.S.A.* from two dozen writers, the elite of Broadway and Hollywood, including[21]:

Goodman Ace	Charles Lederer
Fred Allen	Leonard L. Levinson
Allan Boretz	Joseph L. Mankiewicz
Irving Brecher	Groucho Marx
Abe Burrows	J.P. McEvoy
Edward Eliscu	Morty Offner
Julius Epstein	Dorothy Parker
Philip Epstein	Nat Perrin
Moss Hart	Don Quinn
Ben Hecht	Sidney Sheldon
George S. Kaufman	Robert Sherwood
Harry Kurnitz	Harry Tugend

Two months after all these letters, Schwartz received a submission from P.G. Wodehouse, a legend in Broadway sketch writing: "I wonder if the enclosed would be of any use to you for 'Inside U.S.A.' ... I wrote it in case Guy and I ever got around to doing a show with a Civil War ball scene in it, but it might fit better into a revue."[22] Schwartz, disappointed but no doubt flattered, replied: "I wish to God I could say that your notion fits in with our show, but it doesn't really."[23]

Ultimately, only Arnold Auerbach, Moss Hart, and Arnold B. Horwitt were credited with the sketches. Auerbach had recent success with *Call Me Mister*, his 1946 revue with Harold Rome, focused on re-mobilization of war personnel. Horwitt had written sketches for another Rome revue, *Pins and Needles*, the 1937 show of the International Ladies' Garment Workers' Union. Horwitt would go on to critical and popular success in 1955 as lyricist for *Plain and Fancy*, a musical about an Amish community, written with composer Albert Hague.[24]

In late summer 1947, Schwartz was in contact with Beatrice Lillie, because he felt she was the linchpin to the success of *Inside U.S.A.*, as she had been for his *At Home Abroad* in 1935: "Just as At Home Abroad toured Non-America, this show will tour America. Here is the $64 question: Will you star in it? I am writing the songs with Dietzy-boy ... and plan to go into rehearsal after you have had a White Christmas."[25] Six weeks later, Schwartz was still working on Lillie, although part of his multi-page letter discussed contract specifics, as she was close to signing. Even at this late date, he is assuring her of his and Dietz's commitment: "Howard is so excited and so rich in ideas these days, and I personally feel in a marvelous musical mood, in spite of all the business details I have taken on with the show, that I am terribly confident of turning out an outstanding score."[26]

Schwartz goes on to explain the rising costs of production and the improbability of his meeting her demands. He details the extent to which he and Dietz have taken cuts in their royalties for the show. As composer and lyricist, they would each normally get 3 to 3-1/2 percent of the gross receipts of a show, but for *Inside U.S.A.*, they had each agreed to 2-1/2 percent. The same 2-1/2 percent applied to royalties for all of the sketches, for a total of 7-1/2 percent for author's royalties. He emphasized: "I am sure you are aware that this is the lowest total royalty for 'name' authors in recent years." For *Seven Lively Arts*, Lillie had received $2,500 per week against 10 percent of the gross, extremely lucrative for that era. Of this, Schwartz declares, "Under present operating conditions, Bea, it just would not be practical for me to make this kind of deal with you."[27] Schwartz and his team must have wanted her badly for the show, for when her contract was completed and signed on January 9, 1948, she received $2,500 per week, increased to $2,750 after twenty weeks, then $3,000 for any road tour.[28] There is no mention made regarding percentage of the gross, perhaps her concession to the producers.

Another significant issue developed which involved Lillie as well as Schwartz and Dietz—approval of material. As a Broadway and West End star, Lillie not only had final approval of songs and sketches, but in certain circumstances, could bring a song or sketch into a show as an interpolation. But this was a Schwartz / Dietz show, and Schwartz made that clear to Lillie: "As to the song material, you may have the same right of approval—bearing in mind only that any substituted music or lyrics for songs of which you do not approve must be written by Dietz and me." In the aforementioned *Seven Lively Arts*, there had been disagreements between Lillie and Porter, as he had insisted on keeping songs despite her lack of approval. Schwartz ends his discussion of the matter with a re-assurance and comparison to Porter: "However, I can only remind you of your past experience with Dietz and myself, and I honestly think that not only does our record with you speak for itself but that we also understand you much better than Cole Porter did."[29]

Although difficult to sign, once she did, Beatrice Lillie was committed to and enthusiastic about her shows. *Inside U.S.A.* was no exception. Still in England in the early months of 1948, she would not be over to the States for another month or more, depending on the rehearsal schedule. Schwartz later recalled this situation and the need to discuss songs with her—over trans-Atlantic telephone:

I telephoned her from New York to London to assure her all was going well. She asked me to sing a couple of the songs we wrote for her, which I did at the rate of $15.00 a minute. When I finished, I asked Bea how she liked the songs. She said, "I love them. Sing them all over again." And I said, "I'll be glad to when you call me."[30]

In addition to Lillie, the cast included Jack Haley, principal dancer Valerie Bettis, baritone John Tyers, comedian Estelle Loring, big band singer Thelma Carpenter, and new to Broadway, a Will Rogers–type monologist, Herb Shriner. Most of the comical sketches were written for Lillie with Haley supporting. He had done Broadway work in the twenties as a comic and song-and-dance man, then had worked steadily in Hollywood for twenty years from 1930 on. His biggest film role was playing the Tin Man in *The Wizard of Oz* (1939).[31] Lillie had wanted Jack Buchanan to play opposite her as they were fellow Brits and had worked together early in their careers. Schwartz had known Buchanan since their work together on *Between the Devil* in 1937. Although Schwartz appreciated Buchanan's wide-ranging talent, he thought him not right for the part: "Because of the subject and scope of this show, I do not picture Jack Buchanan in it. We would assemble a cast around you, and there are some wonderful people available."[32]

The songs and their settings give a clear idea as to its travelogue scheme:

Song	*Sung by*	*Setting*
Inside U.S.A.	Company	U.S.A.
Come, O Come (to Pittsburgh)	Principals	Pittsburgh, Pennsylvania
Blue Grass	Thelma Carpenter	Churchill Downs, Kentucky
Rhode Island Is Famous for You	Jack Haley and Estelle Loring	Rhode Island
Haunted Heart	John Tyers; Danced by Valerie Bettis	San Francisco, California
First Prize at the Fair	Company	Kenosha County, Wisconsin
At the Mardi Gras	Beatrice Lillie	New Orleans, Louisiana
My Gal Is Mine Once More	John Tyers	Jackson Hole, Wyoming
Tiger Lily	Danced by Valerie Bettis	Chicago, Illinois
We Won't Take It Back	Lillie and Haley	Albuquerque, New Mexico

Locales for sketches included Miami Beach; Chillicothe, Ohio; Indiana; New York City; Massachusetts; and Off-Broadway.

The four songs that ended the first act were the strongest in the

Schwartz / Dietz score. "Blue Grass" was a bluesy lament of losing a boyfriend to the track life in Kentucky, sung by Thelma Carpenter. She had been discovered by John Hammond while still in high school, then given a job with Teddy Wilson's band. This led to work with the bands of Coleman Hawkins then Count Basie. The talented Carpenter debuted on Broadway in 1944 in *Memphis Band* with Bill Robinson. She would go on to numerous television and film roles and would understudy Pearl Bailey in *Hello, Dolly!* in 1967–68, going on over 100 times as Dolly Levi during the run. She was known for "a bubbling, buoyant personality, with a pleasant voice and polished sense of showmanship."[33] In short, she was perfect for the "wry 'Blue Grass'"—staged in the paddock at Churchill Downs—and made it one of the show's big hits.[34]

Another showstopper was "Rhode Island Is Famous for You," probably the best "list" song Schwartz and Dietz ever wrote. Although famous for his lyrics to Schwartz's superb ballads, it should not be forgotten what a wit and knowledgeable fellow Dietz was. He set out to include as many states as he could, each one with something to be proud of. Most were legitimate, but several—minnows from Minnesota; divorces from Nevada; vests from Vest Virginia; pencils from Pennsylvania; tents from Tennessee; and coats from Dakota—were the Dietz sense of humor at its best. Here was a true "laundry list" lyric, on a par with Cole Porter's "You're the Top" or Lorenz Hart's "Manhattan." When sung in performance or in recordings, the usual several stanzas are done. There is one stanza in the Arthur Schwartz Papers at the Library of Congress that went unpublished and is never sung, as the lyrics do not quite fit the meter of the melody. However, the lyrics are no less creative than many that are used:

> Hoosiers Come from Indiana
> Mormons Come from Utah
> And Sap Comes from Vermont
> The Hop Crop Is the Top Crop of Wisconsin
> One Sits There Drinking Schlitz There All You Want
> And Oranges Come from California
> Florida Will Scornya
> If They're Not Mentioned Too
> And You You Come from Rhode Island
> And Dance It
> You Enhance It
> More Than Newport, Providence, Narragansett
> Rhode Island's Famous for You[35]

In the summer of 1947, when he and Schwartz were turning out songs for *Inside U.S.A.*, and before Lillie and other cast members were signed, Dietz wrote his partner about a possible title song for the show:

As for the chanson americaine (I mean the song about the U.S.A.) I haven't come up with a good idea yet and then shall write you. I started out this way:

There are bales of cotton in Georgia
Lots of lumber in Maine
Maple syrup in Vermont
And corn on the Kansas plain
The U.S.A.
Has everything you could wish for
All the meat
You can eat
All the fish you could fish for
But I decided this was too much like "Rhode Island."[36]

What is a Schwartz / Dietz score without a classic ballad, preferably in a minor key? Late in the first act of *Inside U.S.A.*, the songwriters gave John Tyers such a song with "Haunted Heart." To add to the drama, it was then danced by Valerie Bettis, which stopped the show. This singing / dancing of their ballads had been used effectively in *The Band Wagon* where John Barker had sung "Dancing in the Dark," then Tilly Losch had danced it dramatically in front of a set of mirrors. "Haunted Heart" strived "for the same theatrical effects as 'Dancing in the Dark.'"[37] The setting was a beautiful scene on the San Francisco waterfront, adding mood to Tyers' smooth baritone. Always a Schwartz fan, Alec Wilder said of the ballad, "Maybe my eyes are too bright with memories, yet in the first three notes I find myself caught, lost, found, whatever it is."[38] Jo Stafford and Perry Como each had hits with "Haunted Heart" in 1948, and both Bing Crosby and Guy Lombardo and His Royal Canadians recorded it during the run of the show.

The last of the four songs from the first act was "First Prize at the Fair," which historian Gerald Bordman thought "deserved a better fate."[39] It was an ensemble song about a young man who loses whatever contest he enters at the fair, but comes away with a new girlfriend, "First Prize at the Fair" in his eyes. The song has a folksy melody complemented by Dietz's almost corny lyric, but a lyric distinguished enough to attract the attention of P.G. Wodehouse: "May a brother thrush (though one of much inferior singing qualities) congratulate you on your absolutely masterful lyrics for *Inside U.S.A.* ... and if there has ever been a neater lyric than 'First Prize at the Fair' I have yet to hear it. And all the others are just as good. It is a triumph."[40] Dietz considered "First Prize at the Fair" the best song in the show.

These four songs were all excellent, and it is surprising that they did not go further at the time. One reason was that ASCAP had gone on strike against radio and recording studios in 1948; composers and lyricists were demanding better terms for their music. At the same time, James Petrillo, head of the American Federation of Musicians (AFM), enjoined his members from entering recording studios.[41] As a result, *Inside U.S.A.* songs and many others from other Broadway shows did not get the usual radio play that would have accompanied at least the early weeks of a show. One upside of the AFM strike was that in anticipation of it, the cast had recorded the score in December 1947, four months before the opening, so audiences often came into the show familiar with the songs.[42] Since the recording was made before the pre–Broadway tryouts, two songs—"Protect Me" and Lillie's "Atlanta"—that had been cut and never heard on Broadway, live on in the recordings. The personnel chosen for the *Inside U.S.A.* score are interesting in that Lillie and Haley did their songs, but for all of the other numbers, non-cast members recordings were employed, including Pearl Bailey, Buddy Clark, Perry Como, and Billy Williams. Almost all of them were done December 31, 1947, with Russ Case and his Orchestra.[43]

Two other songs from the show should be discussed because they were commented on years later by Dietz and Schwartz, giving insight into their working methods. In the *Lyrics & Lyricists Series* program that Dietz did in 1974, he discussed the writing of "We Won't Take It Back," sung by Lillie and Haley as two Indians, set in a railroad station with a group of tourists. It was a song, but it had strong sketch elements as well. In the script for *Lyrics and Lyricists*, just prior to the singing of "We Won't Take It Back," there is a brief question and answer section with Dietz:

> Question: (1) We've seen that in the main, your work with Arthur Schwartz was truly a collaborative effort. (2) However, there were times that he presented you with a complete melody. (3) Did you ever present Arthur with a completely written lyric?
> Answer: Yes, but not often. When it did happen, it was always in connection with a Revue because that was the kind of situation where the lyricist, in effect, is writing a complete theatrical situation.[44]

In this case, Dietz had presented Schwartz with a lyric that fit the scene and had been outlined by Dietz and the other sketch writers.

On the opposite end of their process, Schwartz wrote the entire melody for an *Inside U.S.A.* number before it was set to a lyric. The melody came to Schwartz, and he acted on it: "I composed the whole song, 'My Gal Is Mine Once More,' while sitting in [attorney Howard] Reinheimer's office listening to him caution me, in emphatic and boringly repetitious admonitions, against agreeing to certain clauses in the agreement with Jack Haley. I heard what Reinheimer said while this tune took possession of me, and finally, fearing I might forget it, I let his words trail off as in a dream, and excused myself, pleading nature's call. I walked out of the office, out of the building, took a taxi home, and played the tune all day to remember it."[45] In such varied ways were Broadway scores composed.

Inside U.S.A., Schwartz's first solo attempt at producing a Broadway show, was met with raves. Most of them were heaped on Beatrice Lillie, whom critics seemed unable to get enough of. Her portrayals included: a choir director in Pittsburgh; an Indian selling souvenirs; a theater maid with a Ouija board; a muse of the great composers; and a mermaid on a rock off Massachusetts.[46] Monologist Herb Shriner was also singled out as he "strolled on alone before the curtain, commented on present-day happenings, and stopped the show."[47] Jack Haley sparkled with the song "Rhode Island Is Famous for You." Also outstanding was Valerie Bettis, the principal dancer performing the choreography of Helen Tamiris, "a departure from the usual balletic style." Bettis was a "modern dancer ... sensational as Tiger Lilly, a gun moll in the Chicago stop-over."[48] She also stood out in the dramatic San Francisco waterfront scene conceived for "Haunted Heart."

Reviews were mixed on the Schwartz's score, but it is unquestionably one of the best of the last of the revues. As Gerald Bordman explained: "Berlin was, along with Arthur Schwartz, our most successful composer for revues.... Berlin's score for *This Is the Army* [1942] can in retrospect be seen as the last great revue score, with only Schwartz's melodies for *Inside U.S.A.* in serious contention for the honor."[49]

Midway through the Broadway run, *Inside U.S.A.* switched theaters, going from the New Century to the Majestic. After a New York run of 399 performances, the show went on a successful national tour that included the East Coast, Chicago, and Los Angeles. Lillie, always in need of money to pay for a small entourage in her life, was glad to do the tour which paid her $3,000 per week.[50] As in New York, she was a phenomenal success across the country, receiving "a two-and-one-half-minute standing ovation opening night in Chicago."[51]

Because Schwartz was earning money from both composing and producing, and because of the successful Broadway run and national tour, the show was lucrative for him. Never one to shy away from the better things of life, he could always use the money. He and Katherine had just moved into a penthouse at 94th Street and Lexington Avenue. Son Jonathan's description: "It took up the entire top floor of the building, the twelfth floor, and was surrounded by a brick terrace.... It was a luxurious pad just off the Park Avenue loop. The fact of its being a penthouse allowed it a grand stature, despite Lexington Avenue's slight tilt to the east.... Arthur's spacious office ... included his Hamilton piano, a sturdy wooden desk, the brown couch for the man with the pitchfork to approach."[52]

Inside U.S.A. was a show Arthur Schwartz could be proud of. It was at a time that the revue genre was on its last legs, and there had been few successful ones in the forties. Ethan Mordden commented on the demise of the revue: "So the short of it was that, even now in the last faint gleam before television variety killed it off, the revue was commercial, attracting major talent and good houses. It was even influential, as the natural playing field for comics too special to work well in the story shows."[53] This demise of revues came about not only because of the emergence of book shows on Broadway, but also because of the growing medium of television. As Schwartz told an oral historian ten years later, "But I think that [*Inside U.S.A.*] was the last revue ... that made money for anybody, because television had taken over the revue medium."[54]

21

More Producing
Television and *Inside U.S.A.* with Chevrolet

"TV, of all the media, comes closest to the living theatre."[1]

Within a few years of the invention of television, programming on it included shows that featured a variety of performers—singers, comedians, dancers, acrobats, monologists—not unlike revues. Starting with *The Toast of the Town / The Ed Sullivan Show* in 1948, these programs included entertainers of every type, sometimes luring Broadway performers away for lucrative appearances. These shows would feature excerpts from current or upcoming Broadway shows, usually musicals. From the late forties on, numerous variety shows premiered, usually with a star attached. To name a few: *Texaco Star Theater* (1948); *Cavalcade of Stars / The Jackie Gleason Show* (1949); *The Garry Moore Show* (1950); *The Red Skelton Show* (1951); and *The Dinah Shore Show* (1951).[2]

Schwartz was well aware of the new medium of television. His producing in Hollywood gave him the experience and confidence to continue doing so for the small screen. As in Hollywood, Schwartz wanted creative freedom, and rather than sign on as the producer for a series which had been offered to him, he began with a one-shot program, *Surprise from Santa*.[3] It was presented live from New York over CBS-TV and starred Whitford Kane in the title role. The ninety-minute show was mostly a revue that included songs, sketches, and acts including the Bill and Cora Baird puppets and ice-skating routines on a rink adjacent to the main stage. Santa and two children used a "slight story line" to introduce them. One innovation was the use of a rear projection screen, fourteen by seventeen feet, which allowed scenes of Central Park to be shown, while in the foreground, Anne Jeffreys sang two songs from a carriage.[4] Schwartz pointed to the limitations of the medium, as the stage was too small, making several camera angles impossible, and lighting was too constricted. The audience at the theater was not large enough for much comedy and the live laughter needed. But after the screening on Christmas Eve of 1948, Schwartz told *Variety* he found the new medium "fascinating" and recognized the "gigantic opportunity for everyone in show business with talent."[5]

With *Inside U.S.A.* still running, Schwartz thought the format of his musical revue might adapt well to television. Just as he had been on the vanguard of the intimate revue in the early thirties, he was the "First of the leading Broadway showmen to go into television."[6] Schwartz appreciated what this new medium, in its infancy, would mean to the entertainment world:

> The advent of television is without precedent in the history of entertainment because it brings living theatre right into your own home. Now for the first time since the dawn of civilization you yourself can ring up the curtain not on one show, but on any of a large number of shows that may be on the air simultaneously. Television is, naturally, a big advance over the wonders of radio.... Television has the great advantage of variety that comes to you from innumerable sending stations and which in addition changes from hour to hour, or oftener.[7]

Schwartz concluded, "TV, of all the media, comes closest to the living theatre."[8] No less an authority than London producer C.B. Cochran had expressed similar thoughts years earlier in his memoir, *Showman Looks On*: "in television there will come—and I think quickly—a medium capable of presenting to perfection a combination of all the elements that draw dollars to the theatre, the music-hall, the concert room, the opera house, and the sports ground, a medium not limited in any way by cost of production and possibility of receipts."[9]

The new show Schwartz had in mind was *Inside U.S.A. with Chevrolet*, and like his musicals—*Revenge with Music, Virginia*, and *Inside U.S.A.*— it was mostly his idea. Howard Dietz gave his partner full credit: "*Inside U.S.A.* ran for two years and then Arthur invented a television program based on the idea. It used our songs."[10] It was to be a takeoff from *Inside U.S.A.*, but it would be expanded to the entire country on a state-by-state basis. As Schwartz outlined during the planning:

> It will bring to life in song, dance, comedy and drama the great glories of America today and yesterday. Going each week from State to State, the show will reproduce "everything great in the forty-eight." Creating a variety-show format all its own, "Inside USA" will weave together such colorful and contrasting items as these: Song-and-dance numbers relating to the particular locales of each state ... "Educational" lectures about the past and present of each state, being a burlesque of facts and figures.... Personalities in the news.... Short scenes from the great stage plays and motion pictures that have dealt with fascinating Americana.... A feature called "THE WAY WE LIVE." ... Showcase for outstanding musical amateurs, each week from a different state. In short, "Inside U.S.A." on television will present a weekly panorama of America itself.[11]

Tied in with the show was the Chevrolet Motor Division of General Motors Corporation, itself new in the medium of television, having sponsored up to that time only *Chevrolet on Broadway* (*The Chevrolet Tele-Theatre*) starting in 1948 and several football games.[12] The general sales manager of Chevrolet, W.E. Fish, delineated the artistic and commercial partnership of the show: "'Inside U.S.A.' seemed a natural to us. Not only does it contain the magic of Arthur Schwartz and top theatrical talent, but its basic theme is appropriate. Its broad scope permits us to present our product against a backdrop of the entire country, which has voted Chevrolet its preferred automobile."[13]

The format was designed around comedian Peter Lind Hayes as master of ceremonies and traveling minstrel, motoring across America, discovering its people and locales: "Audiences will see the great continent through the eyes of a typical American who will traverse rugged mountains, picturesque valleys and teeming cities as he travels with light heart across broad rivers and undulating plains into the horizon."[14] He would be traversing America often seen in a Chevrolet, and the theme song which closed the episodes was "See the U.S.A. in Your Chevrolet."[15] Hayes was considered perfect for the position as he was charming and glib, with boyish good looks and a sense of humor. Critics had used the term "'Chaplinesque' to describe his wistful, sadly human quality." He was only thirty-three at the time but had already had success with a night club act across the country, then with guest spots in television variety. It was hoped, "Television, which is easily as intimate as a cabaret, may be his dish."[16]

Assisting Hayes were his wife, singer Mary Healy, dancer Sheila Bond, singer Marion Colby, and Jay Blackton and His Orchestra. Blackton was well-known on Broadway as a musical director and conductor and had held that position for *Inside U.S.A.* Each episode of *Inside U.S.A. with Chevrolet* had a "Star of the Week," the first being film actress Margaret O'Brien, then Broadway / film star Celeste Holm, and Oscar Levant, pianist and humorist, the third week. A list of forty-three names had been drawn up as potential guests—a Who's Who of Hollywood and Broadway.[17]

Unlike the rigors of *The Gibson Family*, where Schwartz and Dietz had to create four new songs per weekly episode, Schwartz was not going to be writing new songs each week, but he would dip into his large catalogue of melodies. A list of thirty-five songs used or planned to be used were mostly Schwartz songs,[18] along with a smattering of those of other composers. One media critic commented, "just what he plans to do after he runs through all his Broadway musicals, I have no idea."[19] Credited in the program were Howard Dietz, Ira Gershwin, Oscar Hammerstein II, and Albert Stillman, all lyricists with whom Schwartz had worked. For the premier episode of *Inside U.S.A. with Chevrolet*, recorded in front of a live audience, Schwartz and Stillman wrote "I'm Looking Down on the Moon," sung by Mary Healy. Also used on opening night was "Tennessee Fish Fry," a Schwartz / Hammerstein hit from *American Jubilee* (1940), sung by Marion Colby and danced by Sheila Bond on television. It was the showstopper of the evening.[20]

The inside title page of the *Playbill* lists no sketch writers but an array of them were available. Sketch writers would submit an idea or a script on spec, and Schwartz kept them in an inventory of sorts. Writers listed in a later page of the television *Playbill* included Marc Connelly, Corey Ford, Moss Hart, George S. Kaufman, Newman Levy, and J.P. McEvoy.[21] Also in the Arthur Schwartz Paper regarding the show was a list of OTHER SKETCHES AVAILABLE, totaling over forty; whether these were used or not is unclear.[22]

The cost of production for a half-hour show was approximately $22,000 per week including talent and production costs, one of the most expensive on television at that time.[23] A full orchestra, dance chorus, weekly guest stars, and various and plentiful Americana sets did not come cheap. Chevrolet and their advertising firm, Campbell-Ewald Company, Inc., were new to this medium and while wanting to produce a quality show, were hesitant at the beginning. It was decided to run the show every other week—alternating with programming of a different nature—then move to a weekly schedule.

Inside U.S.A. with Chevrolet premiered Thursday evening, September 29, 1949, at 8:30 p.m. Reviews were favorable, *Variety* liking the show and its concept: "'U.S.A.'s' outstanding virtue lies in its approach to video [television]—in the fashioning of a musical revue generic to the medium. It bursts at the seams with originality.... If the sum total failed to emerge as something distinguished, the viewer was nonetheless alerted to the fact that here at least, TV was being treated as a mature entertainment medium."[24] *Variety* would later give much credit to Schwartz, who had "learned the knack of adapting the legit-type revue to video's facilities."[25] Hayes and other talent were praised, especially Mary Healy and Sheila Bond. The critic for the *New York Herald Tribune*, John Crosby, who was on the whole favorable to the show, found the commercials in verse read by Peter Lind Hayes to be an embarrassment to the star. Crosby also felt that they should have done away with "the audience on a show of this quality so that the actors could concentrate on the cameras."[26] Whatever the reasons were, *Inside U.S.A. with Chevrolet* lasted only thirteen episodes, ending in mid–March 1950. The final episode included guest stars Joan Blondell and Jack Haley, the latter a fitting visitor to a show inspired by the earlier *Inside U.S.A.* Haley had introduced "Rhode Island Is Famous for You" and "First Prize at the Fair" in that revue.

Ultimately, as with most television, it came down to the numbers, as "Chevrolet dropped the show because its top-heavy budget failed to pay off with the desired ratings."[27] General sales manager for Chevrolet, W.E. Fish, stated the case clearly to Schwartz: "We admit we are pretty much 'babes in arms' as far as our television programs are concerned and, frankly, blow both hot and cold about our future participation in it. The constantly increasing cost of television to merchandise an article as high priced as an automobile always is a constant check on the other side of the ledger." In closing, Fish complimented his producer, "We appreciate very much your interest and work in 'Inside U.S.A.' and feel that in many ways it was a very satisfactory arrangement in the overall television development. We appreciate particularly your personal endeavors."[28] One of the advertising executives from Campbell-Ewald was equally complimentary of Schwartz: "With the closing of 'Inside U.S.A. with Chevrolet,' may I say how very much we enjoyed working with you. Your television show reflected production know-how which has set a standard for television programs. Many thanks for a job well done."[29]

As so often happened during his career, *Inside U.S.A. with Chevrolet* left the Schwartz reputation for hard work and a quality product well intact. Schwartz was anxious to return to Broadway, and 1950 would offer him two chances to do so. The first was as producer of a dramatic play, *Hilda Crane*, the other as composer of a musicalization of *Grand Hotel*. His love of theatrical drama and his penchant for producing led Schwartz to take on the role of producer for the Samson Raphaelson play. Schwartz and Raphaelson had worked on the British film, *The Queen's Affair* [a.k.a. *Runaway Queen*] in 1932 with Raphaelson doing the screen play and Schwartz the songs along with Desmond Carter. Early on, Schwartz said of *Hilda Crane*, "It's a mature, adult play. Raphaelson's most serious one. The writing is exceptionally good."[30] The two shared a mutual respect, apparent as they began negotiations in June 1950. Raphaelson's letter to Schwartz regarding terms of the contract begins amicably: "I cannot tell you with what pleasure and peace of mind I go into this deal with you. May it be the beginning of a long and vital association. I will give it everything I've got, and I know you will, too." In the letter, Raphaelson gives his approval of Jessica Tandy in the title role, while at the same time, discouraging the hiring of E.G. Marshall for a lead role as he "doesn't seem right for that part."[31]

Compared to a musical or a film, producing a dramatic play was considerably less time consuming. For *Hilda Crane*, there were only ten cast members and no orchestra, songs, or dance numbers. The Howard Bay scenery was only two sets, both living rooms. The leading lady, Jessica Tandy, and the director, Hume Cronyn, were married, so even communication was simpler. Because of the lesser work load, Schwartz was able to keep other irons in the fire. Songwriting and producing were not enough theater for Arthur Schwartz. He had become involved in organizations of producers in New York: the League of New York Theatres (LNYT) and the Council of the Living Theatre (CLT). LNYT was an association of theater producers looking out for their own welfare and that of New York theater in general. Among the functions of the League was resolving issues with Equity, the union for stage actors in New York. Foremost was the periodic contract which LNYT signed with Equity, stipulating wages, benefits, and work rules.

In the summer of 1950, the overriding issue of the negotiations was the establishment of a pension fund. With his legal background, respect for performers, and the ability to see the issues from both sides as producer and creator, Schwartz was welcomed at the bargaining table. Schwartz himself said, "I speak both languages."[32] In an interview in *Theatre News Weekly*, he was quick to tell the reporter that he had been at all sixteen negotiating sessions, attempting to allay rumors that the League was not bargaining in good faith. As to the general state of the theater, he commented, "There is no doubt that the economic situation is critical in the theatre. It calls for a spirit of cooperation on the part of all concerned. Theatre costs can't be reduced without the cooperation of authors and unions." However, as to the major stumbling block, establishment of a pension, Schwartz came down firmly on the side of producers: "We feel that a pension plan at this time is not workable. It would add to production costs and mean fewer shows. Costs are so high already. Less than ten percent of major business organizations have the benefit of pension plans. Only two of the airlines have such plans. And, a pension presumes a continuity of employment."[33]

Concerning stability, the executive secretary of Equity, Louis M. Simon, felt just the opposite, stating, "Over the years, the stage employment of Equity members has decreased. The actor has been driven to other media. We don't know if a pension fund is a complete answer. But it is needed for the stability of the actor." Simon felt that Equity's demands had been "cut down to the bone," adding, "There are many ways in which extravagance and waste can be cut out without taking it out on the actor."[34] The pension issue remained unresolved during that period of negotiations as Equity chose, for the most part, to sign individual contracts with individual producers. Costs, pensions, and work rules were a never-ending battle, and despite mixed success at the bargaining table, the LNYT was pleased with the work of their committee and especially that of Schwartz. In October 1950, he was elected president of the League with Lee Shubert his first vice president. In an editorial shortly before the election, *Theatre News Weekly* was most complimentary of Schwartz and his negotiating efforts, stating that his "sincere interest and willingness to give freely of his time was fully equaled by his detailed knowledge of the theatre's economic plight and his keen awareness of the need for corrective action." In a small jab at the producers of old, the editorial concluded, "Arthur Schwartz definitely is part and parcel of the new-type trained and forward looking group in the theatre ... the arrival of a new day which offers not alone [sic] new problems but opportunity for new greatness in the theatre."[35] Schwartz knew, as well as anyone, that the producers, unions, and everyone else in the production of theater in New York had to give something or the theater world would suffer greatly. Over the next few years, changes were made, leading to the production of more theater and increased employment of authors, actors, and stage hands

Concomitant with his work with the LNYT, Schwartz became involved with another theatrical association, the Council of the Living Theatre (CLT). The CLT had been created for the purpose of promoting Broadway theater across the nation. Its first president, playwright Robert Sherwood, explained that the CLT was intended to "bring more people to the theatre and more theatre to the people."[36] Theater attendance had declined in New York circa 1950, as well as the prevalence of touring theatrical productions across the United States. Broadway producers had been reluctant to take their shows on tour because audiences could be spotty and there were few guarantees of success, even with shows that had been hits in New York. To remedy this, the CLT and producers and committees in various cities across the country established a subscription series. Schwartz explained, "The cities are deeply desirous of flesh-and-blood shows, and they embraced our proposal that 'you supply the audiences and we'll supply the plays.' Committees were organized, with civic and social leaders as chairmen, and in some of the cities as many as five hundred local men and women did the actual recruitment of subscribers."[37] Schwartz even traveled to several towns to promote the subscription program.

To raise money for the CLT, Schwartz and Hollywood producer Lester Cowan came upon the idea of a movie love story within the world of the theater.[38] Proceeds from the film, titled *Main Street to Broadway*, would go partly to the CLT and its efforts to promote theater nationwide. Schwartz engaged Robert Sherwood to write the story and Samson Raphaelson the screenplay. The movie included Mary Martin starring and singing, as well as numerous cameos by Hollywood stars. Those who eventually appeared gratis—included Tallulah Bankhead, Ethel and Lionel Barrymore, Gertrude Berg, Shirley Booth, Faye Emerson, Rex Harrison, Helen Hayes, Agnes Moorehead, Lilli Palmer, and Cornell Wilde. Most of these stars had done theater and had an appreciation for the need of a healthy theater environment in New York and the rest of the country.

The music for the movie was to be done mostly by Cowan's wife, Ann

Ronell, best known as composer of "Willow Weep for Me" and co-composer of "Who's Afraid of the Big Bad Wolf." For *Main Street to Broadway*, she wrote the score as well as the theme song, "Blue New York," and a number for star Herb Shriner, "Just a Girl." Schwartz induced Richard Rodgers and Oscar Hammerstein II to write a song to be sung in the film by Mary Martin, "There's Music in You." Ultimately, *Main Street to Broadway* did poorly at the box office. For its efforts on the project, the CLT had received an initial $50,000 from the producers, but netted little after that from the film.[39] Nevertheless, this money and a matching sum from the American Theatre Society had helped to finance subscriptions in ten of the twenty-one subscription cities. This, in turn, increased total touring weeks of New York shows to 251 and increased pre-sold ticket numbers by 185,000.[40]

In October 1953, the LNYT created a radio show, *Stage Struck*, to be played on the CBS Radio Network on Friday evenings. It was designed to give national audiences a behind-the-scenes view of Broadway theater and to celebrate the re-emergence of theater across the country. One scene included back-stage at the Winter Garden Theatre where *Wonderful Town* had been running. The stars, including Rosalind Russell, sang two of the show's hits, "Christopher Street" and "Ohio." Another scene brought the listener backstage at the Empire Theatre days before it was to be demolished. Shirley Booth played the last scene from *The Time of the Cuckoo*, the last lines to be heard at the Empire before its razing. At the close of *Stage Struck*, Schwartz spoke briefly about "the current vitality of the American theatre." The *Playbill* for *Stage Struck* included a brief page of commentary by Schwartz, echoing what he said on the radio program:

> Two years ago the legitimate producers and theatre owners decided to pump some oxygen into the fabulous invalid. We knew that over the many centuries it had proven to be more fabulous than invalid. We interested new people in producing plays. We joined with all the theatrical crafts and unions to make economic conditions more sound. We raised money to increase the support of the theatre on the road by package subscriptions. The oxygen treatment had begun to work. This past season, Broadway had a higher percentage of hits than in a long time—and there are more excellent shows touring the country now than in many years.... I am deeply gratified that theatergoers everywhere are leaving their TV sets with their baby sitters and are flocking back to us. Apparently they have discovered there is no substitute for the warmth of human contact from one side of the footlights to the other. Yes, it seems that audiences are just as stage struck as the actors.[41]

The radio show closed with the *Stage Struck* theme, "That's Entertainment," the show business anthem Schwartz and Howard Dietz had written for the film *The Band Wagon*.

As for *Hilda Crane*, it opened at the Coronet Theatre November 1, 1950, but did not do well from the start. Brooks Atkinson, while praising the acting, thought that Jessica Tandy's title character was "a tiring, irritating egotist" and Raphaelson's writing "not original enough."[42] With a rocky start, Schwartz convinced the principal actors and the director to take pay cuts while the show was finding an audience. But the star power of Jessica Tandy was not enough. The drama closed after only seventy performances, a disappointment to Schwartz and his investors.[43] It became a film drama in 1956 for 20th Century–Fox starring Jean Simmons. The musical score for the movie was by David Raksin, and Schwartz was not involved.

Schwartz's other Broadway project in 1950, turning *Grand Hotel* into a musical, never got off the ground. It was based on a 1929 novel and play by Vicki Baum, *Menschen im Hotel* (*People in a Hotel*) which then became an M-G-M film in 1932 starring Greta Garbo. There is correspondence from writer Luther Davis to Schwartz in fall 1950 regarding the musical. Davis opens the letter congratulating Schwartz on his success with *Hilda Crane*. Davis is enthusiastic about *Grand Hotel* and outlines a few ideas for the show's book to Schwartz. Davis admits that he has had problems with the Internal Revenue Service and was, at the time, nearly insolvent.[44]

Eleven months later, Davis sends an angry, disappointed, yet apologetic telegram to Schwartz: "AT YOUR REQUEST I STEP ASIDE WITH GROSS REGRETS, MUCH AFFECTION AND ADMIRATION, AS WELL AS, I MUST ADMIT, A FEELING OF GUILT. MY ONLY HOPE IS THAT YOU SHARE SOME OF THE LATTER." Apparently, Schwartz had decided not to go through with the show with Davis because he had done little work over nearly a year. Davis claimed that Schwartz had done little to help the project along, stating that he had had more input from Howard Dietz. There was also the issue of an advance Davis had been given which Schwartz, apparently, expected to be returned. Davis pled, "YOU OF COURSE KNEW THAT I WAS NOT RICH OR EVEN SOLVENT WHEN I SIGNED ONTO THIS AND YOU'LL UNDERSTAND THAT PAYING BACK SPENT MONEY IS NOT AN EASY BUSINESS FOR ME."[45] None of the Schwartz correspondence to Davis was available.

Ultimately, the Schwartz musical of *Grand Hotel* was never done. Davis, however, picked the project up in the late Eighties, working with songwriters Robert Wright and George Forrest. They had teamed up in 1953 for *Kismet*—based on the music of Alexander Borodin—which ran for 583 performances on Broadway and even longer in London. For *Grand Hotel*, the triumvirate worked with songwriter Maury Yeston as well as director / choreographer Tommy Tune. The show opened in 1985 and ran for 1,017 performances. It garnered twelve Tony nominations and won five of them, including two for Tommy Tune for direction and choreography. Davis was nominated for Best Book of a Musical.[46] Sweet revenge for Davis, no doubt.

22

A Tree Grows in Brooklyn
Shirley Booth and "Make the Man Love Me"

"[I]t was one of the most beautiful of all Broadway scores. The man couldn't help being a class act."[1]

Arthur Schwartz and Dorothy Fields wanted another shot at a book show. The two friends had collaborated in 1938–39, along with book writer J.P. McEvoy, on a musical about a leftist in Hollywood—*Stars in Your Eyes*. The project had been hijacked by director Joshua Logan, who turned the musical into a star vehicle for Ethel Merman and Jimmy Durante; the show fizzled. *A Tree Grows in Brooklyn* presented a new opportunity for Schwartz and Fields.

It began in 1950 with neophyte producer, Robert Fryer, who had bought the musical comedy rights to the best-selling novel of the same name, written by Betty Smith. Fryer had asked his friend George Abbott to co-produce. Abbott enlisted help from Leland Hayward, who provided advice and also invested in the show. Then Logan, Smith, and a star of the show, Johnny Johnston, did also. CBS assumed half of the initial investment for $200,000, with their deal including recording rights to the show.[2]

At the time, Abbott was among the busiest people on Broadway as director / producer / show doctor. He was "perceived as the grand master of 'good old-fashioned' musical comedy."[3] Abbott had wanted Irving Berlin to write the score; the two of them and Hayward had just had a hit with *Call Me Madam* in September 1950. Berlin declined, explaining that he was "temporarily dried up."[4] Jule Styne and Bob Hilliard were also mentioned, but the project was turned over to Schwartz and Fields. She had just gone through an unsuccessful show, *Arms and the Girl*, working with Morton Gould and her brother Herbert, but the hard-working Fields was always up for a project. Schwartz was flush with the success he and lyricist Howard Dietz were enjoying with their revue, *Inside U.S.A.*, and was looking for a book show.

Arthur Schwartz and lyricist Dorothy Fields working on *A Tree Grows in Brooklyn*, early 1951, "one of the most beautiful of all Broadway scores." It starred Shirley Booth, and the book of the show was written by George Abbott and Betty Smith. She had written the novel of the same name (Library of Congress, Prints & Photographs Division / Walter Albertin photograph, *New York World Telegram & Sun*).

By the fall of 1950, *A Tree Grows in Brooklyn* was taking shape, and Schwartz was turning fifty. He was still bothered by recurrent depression but remained enthusiastic about his life, family, and his work. Wife Kay, despite chronic illness, wanted to give him a proper fiftieth birthday party. Son Jonathan described the event which took place on a cold, rainy night in Manhattan:

> Kay really got herself up for Arthur's fiftieth birthday.... Theater people en masse and the two or three regular buddies my father had accumulated: an economist, Larry Fertig; a PR guy Sy Seadler; and the publishers Bennett Cerf and Richard Simon. Arthur was told about the party and asked what he thought should be done. His answer I remember still: "Bring 'em on!" he said. "I'll bet you no one shows up anyway." Through the howling storm they came, in their finery, soaked through and through, more than seventy-five, a crowd that took up the whole apartment.[5]

The celebration was no doubt an affirmation for Schwartz and could not but help him take on his latest show.

The book for that show was to be written by George Abbott, who wanted Betty Smith to get involved. Her novel, *A Tree Grows in Brooklyn*, had sold five million copies up to that time and had been translated into sixteen languages. She had turned down any involvement in the screenplay for the 1945 movie of the same name and was reluctant to do a stage treatment of her book. The movie had been a hit, directed by Elia Kazan and starring Joan Blondell, Dorothy McGuire, and Jamie Dunn. Despite Smith's noninvolvement, the screen adaptation was "an unusually sensitive and faithful adaptation of the book,"[6] a fact that would affect audience perception of the musical.

Her novel had started out as a play, *Francie Nolan*, while Smith was a student at the University of Michigan. She had expanded it to a full-length novel, which was published in 1943. After discussions with Abbott, "she found herself brimming with ideas about the adaptation, promptly changed her mind and decided to collaborate with Abbott on the show's book."[7] Of their collaboration, Smith would later say, "I think it was one of the most amiable collaborations in dramatic history.... We never disagreed on script.... We had one trait in common. Both of us were avid cutters."[8]

For their score, Schwartz and Fields were concerned that it retain the original flavor of the novel and turn-of-the-century Brooklyn. *A Tree*

William Auerbach-Levy ink drawing on paper of principal characters of *A Tree Grows in Brooklyn*, 1951. *Left to right*: Shirley Booth as Aunt Cissy, Marcia Van Dyke as Katie Nolan, and Johnny Johnston as Johnny Nolan (courtesy William Auerbach-Levy (1889–1964) / Museum of the City of New York. 64.100.2163).

Grows in Brooklyn was "an atypical show for Schwartz and Fields, who tended towards revues and comic musicals."[9] Nonetheless, the two Broadway veterans had worked on period shows before. Although throttled by a bad book, Schwartz had written a critically-praised score for *Virginia*, set in colonial Williamsburg; Fields had had success in 1945 with *Up in Central Park*, an 1870s New York musical written with Sigmund Romberg which ran for 504 performances.

Shortly before the April 19, 1951, opening of *A Tree Grows in Brooklyn*, Schwartz wrote an article in the *New York Herald* addressing the score and attempts to capture the flavor of 1900 Brooklyn: "Being born and brought up in Brooklyn probably was of some help in my job. It was there that I heard all the wonderful popular songs which Betty Smith's characters would have known. So any resemblance between the tunes you will hear in the show and those I remembered from my childhood is strictly not coincidental."[10] Schwartz was an avid walker and put this to good use for the show: "For Schwartz, it was an opportunity to return to the people and the places he had once known during his boyhood in Brooklyn, and he took long walks through the tenement areas of the city in order to steep himself in the proper atmosphere."[11]

The book of the show concerns the Nolan family. The mother, Katie, has high hopes for her husband, Johnny, who is charming and handsome but an alcoholic ne'er-do-well. The story follows their lives over thirteen years with their daughter Francie and Katie's sister, Cissy. In the end, Johnny dies, with Katie still loving him and hopeful for Francie. The story line of *A Tree Grows in Brooklyn* paralleled *Carousel*, the 1945 musical based on Ferenc Molnár's *Lilliom*. Both involve an innocent young woman and her no-account man. Both fathers want to do well by their daughters but do not know how. The endings of both musicals involve a graduation. In *Carousel*, Billy Bigelow descends from heaven to attend his daughter's ceremony and encourages her to believe in herself. In *A Tree Grows in Brooklyn*, Johnny has a similar effect on Francie, having arranged for flowers and a note to be given to her at graduation. Along the way, he also sings her a song, "Don't Be Afraid."[12]

The novel and the movie focused on Francie and the tumultuous relationship between her parents, the role of Cissy being minor. For the musical, Abbott and Smith enhanced this role, playing upon the many men in her life and turning the part into a comic one, perfect for Shirley Booth. In doing so, the plot of the novel—the life of Francie and her parents—was downplayed and got lost in the adaptation. Moreover, "it was difficult for the audience to shift from the Nolans' hopes and despairs to Booth's sitcom bits."[13]

The principal cast for *A Tree Grows in Brooklyn* was led by Booth, just ending a Tony Award-winning performance in William Inge's *Come Back, Little Sheba*, a dramatic role. She was known for her comedic abilities and stage sense but not for her voice. In 1940, she had played Ruth in *My Sister Eileen*, which ran for over two years. Her audition for that show for director George S. Kaufman and playwrights Joseph Fields and Jerome Chodorov was a brief one: "Picking up the script, Miss Booth read two lines, and Kaufman turned to the authors and asserted, 'That's it.' *He* knew that *she* knew her business. Her instinct for a line was perfect."[14] Revue producer Leonard Sillman went further: "Notice the extraordinary effects she gets simply by lifting an eyebrow, or by the fabulously economical use of her hands, or by shifting the pitch of her speaking voice the tenth of a quarter note. Watch how she gets all her effects with *little* things."[15] One more bit of praise for Booth came from Helen Hayes: "She has perfect timing and perfect reading, and always has complete control of herself, her part and her audience."[16]

From here, Abbott indulged in what he was best known to do—offbeat casting.[17] For Katie Nolan, the names of Ginger Rogers, Nanette Fabray, and Martha Wright had been discussed, but he cast Marcia Van Dyke. She was unknown to stage audiences, but was a swimming champion, some-time actress, and a violinist with the San Francisco Symphony. Van Dyke had played a minor role to Judy Garland in *In the Good Old Summertime* and had the look and voice Abbott wanted. *The Billboard* critic would later say, "while her voice is small, it has splendid quality."[18] For Johnny, Abbott chose Johnny Johnston, another stage newcomer but a handsome tenor, well-known to night club, radio, and recording audiences, who would be singled out as "the finest voice in the production."[19] Nomi Mitty was cast as Francie, and while a good actor, her lack of singing ability would cause a few songs to be transferred to other characters. Nonetheless, Abbott insisted on keeping her in the show.[20]

With three good singers, turn-of-the-century Brooklyn, and a book with both drama and comedy, Schwartz and Fields had plenty of openings for songs of several types. Their work began in early December 1950, and got off to a good start; both had strong work habits. On December 12, Betty Smith dropped a note to Schwartz: "Thanks for telling me about the progress. Four songs, sweetie, is a terrific output for one week. I know the melodies will hum and the lyrics shine. I can hardly wait until the 18th."[21] A week later, however, Smith, Abbott, and Fields had their first conference, and things did not go so well. In frustration, Abbott wrote to Schwartz:

> Last night, Betty and I had a long talk about the future of BROOKLYN BRIDGE. … Dorothy Fields is one of the most gracious and charming women I have ever known. But when it comes to her work, she seems to have a super sensitiveness which makes her resist and resent all criticism. … I cannot think of any suggestion that has been

made to her which she has welcomed. I don't think it is possible to get anything but mediocrity with this sort of an attitude.... I think you should be the one to talk to her about the wisdom of trying to accept our criticisms in the spirit in which they are intended ... the desire to get the show as perfect as possible.[22]

In his 1963 autobiography, *"Mr. Abbott,"* he echoed this theme: "Everyone is there for the same reason: to try to get the show in as perfect condition as possible. And the endeavor shouldn't involve emotions or personalities or pettiness."[23] It is unclear whether Schwartz talked to Fields about all this or showed her the letter, as Abbott had suggested. Presumably, Fields had such respect for Abbott that she acquiesced.

Whatever ensued, the show and score progressed well from then on. Schwartz wrote extensively about their score in his pre-opening article, starting with an explanation as to why he and Fields did not "begin at the beginning." He credited Fields with breaking the ice with a lyric for a second-act song, "Growing Pains." In it, the struggling Johnny Nolan explains to his twelve-year-old daughter the reason behind, as Schwartz called it, her "pre-adolescent pangs"—she was growing up. Schwartz explained, "When we finished the words and music, in a matter of hours, we had found the key to the whole score." The key was a song which engaged two main characters on an everyday level, in words and melody. Although Johnny Johnston sang it beautifully, it could easily have been spoken / sung, à la Rex Harrison. On the first of their songs for the score, Schwartz concluded, "I felt that if we could continue writing as simply and honestly, making the lyrics extensions into meter of the natural language of our characters, and find earthy melodies as accompaniments, we could achieve that 'whole-cloth' result, an integration between dialogue and song which audiences demand of the modern musical play."[24] To that end, Fields declared, "The characters told me what I should write—I didn't tell them."[25]

After this initial effort, Schwartz and Fields went back to the beginning and took each scene as it came, fitting their songs into the story of the Nolans and Aunt Cissy. To lead off, "Mine 'til Monday" describes the practice within the social milieu of the book of taking possessions—suits, dresses, jewelry—out of hock for the weekend, then returning them on Monday. Schwartz commented, "Ragtime had just come in. Should we try to imitate its exact degree of elementary rhythm, or add a measure of modernity? 'Mine Till [sic] Monday' attempts to establish the true rhythmic spirit of the time."[26] The song ends with Johnny and ensemble members in a pawn shop.

Schwartz knew the importance of song placement and the need for the book to indicate "the most satisfying places for them." He added, "Here we were immeasurably aided by Dorothy Fields' many years as librettist." This was exemplified in the show's strongest ballad, "Make the Man Love

Me." Schwartz credited his lyricist for not only the lyrics of the song but the development of a scene around it: "It was Dorothy's title, 'Make the Man Love Me,' which gave us our theme for Katie and eventually led to the writing of a touching love scene."[27] The song became an audience favorite, a duet for Marcia Van Dyke and Johnny Johnston. The cast recording is charming, as they join voices for the final chorus, and Johnston avoids upstaging her with his stronger voice.[28] It was a song that Alec Wilder called "a gem of tenderness and warmth."[29] It has attracted numerous recording artists including Vicki Carr, Barbara Cook, Maureen McGovern, Barbra Streisand, Dinah Washington, and Margaret Whiting.[30]

The songwriters then had two up-tempo numbers, "I'm Like a New Broom" and "Look Who's Dancing." The former was a solo for Johnston as his character wins Katie's heart and a new job. He sang a fine rendition of the song as did Schwartz's son, Jonathan, on his 1995 album, *Alone Together: Jonathan Schwartz Sings Arthur Schwartz*.[31] "Look Who's Dancing" was not in the show in Philadelphia but was included by the time the show reached New York, replacing "The Bride Wore Something Old," a ballad for Van Dyke.[32] "Look Who's Dancing" was a music hall-like number, perfect for the era, and was Shirley Booth's first song in the show. She and Van Dyke did a lively duet on it. Betty Smith's favorite song, "Tuscaloosa," was cut after Philadelphia.[33] The melody for "Tuscaloosa" would be used for Schwartz and Fields' next book show, *By the Beautiful Sea*, renamed "Old Enough to Love" with new lyrics.[34] Full lyrics for another song with a similar title, "I'm Old Enough," are in the Dorothy Fields Papers, written for a later show.[35] Also cut before Broadway was "Oysters in July."[36]

Besides "Look Who's Dancing," another period song, "If You Haven't Got a Sweetheart," was an ensemble number for singers and dancers. Schwartz recalled the genesis of the song: "On a lucky taxi ride through Central Park one day I thought of a gay waltz, as definitely 1905 as leg-of-mutton sleeves. With Dorothy's words, 'If You Haven't Got a Sweetheart,' it seems to capture the particular spirit of the girls and boys on a tenement roof in July."[37] This adherence to the flavor of the period was critical to Schwartz and Fields as well as the co-writer of the book, Betty Smith. As liner notes for the cast recording declare: "The entire score is flavored with a sense of the story's period, but it is very much in the musical-play style pioneered by Rodgers and Hammerstein in the early '40s that became the favored Broadway style in the late '40s and early '50s."[38] Brooks Atkinson echoed, "In many of his songs Arthur Schwartz has recovered the simple, hearty rhythms of old-fashioned picnic music."[39]

The big solo number for Johnny Johnston was "I'll Buy You a Star," capturing his love for Katie while exposing his impractical side. Again, Johnston's voice is perfect for the hope in the song, and it comes across especially well on the cast recording. It was the last song of Act I and a showstopper for Johnston. Despite his ample voice and stage presence, he went back to broadcast media and night clubs after this show, never to return to Broadway. The same for Marcia Van Dyke, who returned to classical violin and film work.

One principal cast member who did return to Broadway was Shirley Booth. She would go on to starring roles in another Schwartz / Fields musical, *By the Beautiful Sea*, as well as musicals *Juno* and *Look to the Lilies*. She would also win another Best Actress Tony Award for *The Time of the Cuckoo*. As the audience favorite of *A Tree Grows in Brooklyn*, she had stage presence and uncanny comic timing. Beyond this, she had developed a singing voice that allowed her to put a song over, even if nasal and nearly off-key. Betty Smith would say of her performance, "She knows more about Cissy than I do."[40] Booth did all this despite turmoil in her personal life. Her husband, Bill, suffered a heart attack and died on March 4, six weeks before the opening.[41]

"Love Is the Reason" was a late first act number crucial to the development of Cissy's character. Schwartz explained what confronted Fields and himself: "Our most difficult assignment was to find the appropriate musical expression for this delightfully amoral character. The danger was in going sophisticated or smart. Cissy was anything but. After making several false starts, we soon found a gay ditty called 'Love Is the Reason.'"[42] Booth's biographer, Jim Manago, described it as "the song critics considered a well-written number looking at the sharp side to love. With a fugue arrangement, Cissy's friends harmonize by interweaving comments and repeating Cissy's lines."[43] Booth's tour de force in the show was "He Had Refinement," a song in which Cissy humorously recalls the traits of her first husband. It required expert timing to get across the recurring lyric of the title, and with the song, Booth stopped the show every night. Schwartz said of the song, "The comedy of insult need not be as hackneyed as our radio comedians have made it. In a mock lament for love that has cooled off, we wrote a song for this situation which has respect for character as well as laughter."[44]

The success of the Cissy character was a two-edged sword for its creators. What had begun as a love story in Act I, with the story of Katie and Johnny Nolan and their travails in 1900 Brooklyn, evolved into a star vehicle for Shirley Booth as Katie's older sister who led a more entertaining life. As Ethan Mordden described it: "the contrasting halves of the show warred uncontrollably with each other, the sad marriage of Katie and Johnny Nolan with its moving ballads versus Aunt Cissie's [sic] uproarious carryings on—one to be taken seriously, the other guffawed at."[45] The Broadway newcomers, Johnston and Van Dyke, lost out: "Booth was a genuine star, and she was so wonderful that audiences tended to wait for her reappearances during the scenes focusing on Johnny and Katie, who were meant to be the central characters."[46] This dichotomy in the show was not missed by the critics, one saying, "*A Tree Grows in Brooklyn* is a splendid musical—or two musicals."[47]

After preview weeks in New Haven and Philadelphia, *A Tree Grows in Brooklyn* opened at the Alvin Theatre on April 19, 1951, to good reviews. Critic Linton Martin in Philadelphia felt "everybody concerned with creating it has sincerely tried to retain the flavor and effect of the original story,"[48] a sentiment sounded by several New York scribes. Booth captured all the critics, but Johnston and Van Dyke received praise as well. Booth would go on to win the Donaldson Award for Best Actress in a Musical (1950–51), beating out Gertrude Lawrence (*The King and I*), Ethel Merman (*Call Me Madam*), and Vivian Blaine (*Guys and Dolls*). Excerpts from the show were showcased on the *Ed Sullivan Show*, a distinction for a Broadway musical. Sullivan, a Broadway columnist and television host for over twenty years, would feature one or more songs from a show, sung live by cast members. These appearances would be done during the run of a show and often boost interest in it.[49]

Next to Booth, Schwartz and Fields received the highest praise. Fields' biographer, Deborah Grace Winer, said that the show led Fields to write "her best musical theatre score to date, and arguably the finest of her career," and "allowed him to sink his exceptional melodic gifts into a substantial vehicle."[50] Critics and historians heaped praise on the Schwartz / Fields score, fairly equally. Comments from the day after the opening and historians years later include[51]:

Critic / Historian	Of Schwartz	Of Fields
Vernon Duke	"best score for a 'book' show"	"a neat set of lyrics"
Gerald Bordman	"superbly lyrical … tied to traditional light opera forms"	"humorous, colloquial lyrics"
Mel Tormé	"tough and tender and touching"	
Ethan Mordden	"romantic, comic, and streetwise"	
Linton Martin	"easy on the ear"	
Brooks Atkinson	"richest score [Schwartz] has written in years"	"idiomatic lyrics to express the comedy and the pensiveness of the music"
Herbert H. Keyser	"best score he ever created for Broadway"	"finest show she had ever written"

Critic / Historian	Of Schwartz	Of Fields
Otis L. Guernsey, Jr.	"catchy, sentimental music"	"street-corner lyrics"
Deborah Grace Winer	"songs expressed the characters' inner thoughts in their own voices"	
Stanley Green	"strove for authenticity"	

It was clear that the warmth of the Schwartz / Fields friendship had carried over to their collaboration and score. Jonathan Schwartz described their relationship as "exceptionally warm and exceptionally loving. At the same time, they were wonderful, gossipy chums and literate collaborators. My father was particularly fond of Dorothy's ability to write comedy numbers, 'He Had Refinement' being a classic example. And he was able to supply her with some really beautiful melodies."[52] Of their relationship, Fields said, "It's never been anything but a pleasure. Arthur's very easy to work with, and we're close friends."[53] After their work together, Schwartz and Fields agreed that the book of the musical had lent itself to a score: "a perfect vehicle for a thoroughly integrated score. ... It was a great pleasure for us to translate their [characters'] emotions into words and music."[54]

Despite a good book, an integrated score, good choreography and sets, a star and talented supporting characters, *A Tree Grows in Brooklyn* ran only eight months—267 performances—respectable but not profitable. Schwartz and Fields were accustomed to such runs for their revues, but a good musical comedy of the era should have run longer. Despite earning a profit in its early months,[55] audiences stopped coming, and the show closed December 1951. There was a two-week run in Dallas in June 1952 with Shirley Booth, but with none of the other original principals.[56] She then had to leave the tour due to a movie commitment for *Come Back, Little Sheba*. The role for the road was offered to Ann Sothern and Gypsy Rose Lee, among others, but Joan Blondell got the part.[57] She had starred as Aunt Cissy in the 1945 movie, and as a Boston critic noted of Blondell, she "may have no voice to sing but you forget her vocal lack when she puts over ... the naughty lyrics of 'He Had Refinement.'"[58] The tour closed after two months. Subsequent non–Broadway revivals include: Players' Ring, Los Angeles (1956); Goodspeed Opera House, Connecticut (2003); Encores!, New York (2005); and Peccadillo Theater Company, New York (2011).

There were a number of reasons and speculations for the mediocre Broadway run. As mentioned before, the comedic character of Aunt Cissy gradually drew attention away from the Nolan family and diluted a good book. Betty Smith's agent Helen Strauss felt "the show had been revised too many times,"[59] including changes made by show doctor Jerome Robbins.[60] Ethan Mordden was especially tough on George Abbott as director, not book writer, in laying blame: "Somewhere in what he okayed for the Broadway premiere was one of the best of the musical plays not by Rodgers and Hammerstein, but it got lost in that darned 'let's get there' efficiency-without-sensitivity that Abbott favored—and this at a time when audiences were looking for intelligence, substance, consistency."[61] A Dallas critic concurred, "The pointed-up comedy and outrageous farcing is Abbottonian while the sentimentalities remain Miss Smith's."[62]

Perhaps most significantly, *A Tree Grows in Brooklyn* was faced with too much competition that theater season. At the time of its opening, the show was faced with what the *New York Sunday News* referred to as "The Golden Dozen." These were six dramatic plays and six musicals running at the time, all with 140 or more performances. *Kiss Me Kate*, *South Pacific*, *Gentlemen Prefer Blondes* and the play, *The Happy Time*, each had over 500, and *Guys and Dolls* and *Call Me Madam* would eventually join them.[63] There were only so many entertainments that Broadway audiences could attend, and despite Shirley Booth and the Schwartz / Fields score, *A Tree Grows in Brooklyn* lost out.

Around the time of their work on the show, Schwartz and Fields had been drawn back to Hollywood to do songs for *Excuse My Dust*. It was an M-G-M production described as "a charming and funny little Technicolor musical set at the turn of the century."[64] The production starred Red Skelton, then at the end of his contract with M-G-M, after which he would concentrate on his successful television career. Skelton plays the inventor of the "gasomobile," a horseless carriage, in 1900 Indiana. His love interest, Sally Forrest, is the daughter of a livery stable owner—William Demarest—who has little use for the young inventor and his idea. The story develops in a mostly light vein. Minor roles were played by MacDonald Carey, Guy Anderson, and Monica Lewis.

While always happy to work with Schwartz, Fields was reluctant to return to Hollywood. Since her heyday there in the late thirties working with Jerome Kern, the city and the industry had changed. More importantly, her family, circle of friends, and associates had mostly moved back to New York. Her father Lew, George Gershwin, Lorenz Hart, and Kern had passed away. She said of returning to California after thirteen years: "The subsequent trips to Hollywood, while they were all right, the business had changed, and the town of Beverly Hills had changed, and I must say I wasn't nearly as happy or as pleased to be working in pictures as I was in the old days. The period that I liked least was around 1950."[65]

Schwartz and Fields ended up writing nine songs for the film, six of which were kept—not a bad ratio for Tinseltown.⁶⁶ Those making it into the film included:

>   Get a Horse   Lorelei Brown
>   Goin' Steady   Spring Has Sprung
>   I'd Like to Take You Out   That's for Children
>   Dreaming

Most of these songs were done in outside scenes, at hayrides, picnics, and such. Fields biographer Charlotte Greenspan referred to them as "emotionally generalized and publicly performed." She did, however, feel that the duet, "Spring Has Sprung," had "some sense of intimacy."⁶⁷ Another song singled out was "That's for Children," described as "an amusing little love song ... with some priceless Fields lines."⁶⁸ Most of the singing was done by MacDonald Carey and Monica Lewis. Primarily a dancer, Sally Forrest's voice was dubbed by Gloria Gray for this film. Forrest did get to show off her dancing talents with scenes choreographed by Hermes Pan. *Excuse My Dust* opened late June 1951, ten weeks after *A Tree Grows in Brooklyn*. The film only did fair at the box office, and none of the songs had a life afterwards.

Several months later, Schwartz still had his attachments to Hollywood as he and Johnny Mercer were approached by M-G-M to write a few movie songs. They were for a light-hearted film—*Dangerous When Wet*—starring Esther Williams and Fernando Lamas. Williams had been a champion swimmer and parlayed her athleticism and good looks into a Hollywood career. She had been noticed by staff members of Billy Rose and was hired for the San Francisco run of *Billy Rose's Aquacade* in 1940. From there, M-G-M noticed her and the film offers poured in. By the time of *Dangerous When Wet*, she had appeared in over twenty movies, most notably in *Million Dollar Mermaid*, the story of Australian swimmer Annette Kellermann. That title became Williams' nickname at M-G-M. Also of interest was her appearance in *Neptune's Daughter,* in which she sang a duet with Ricardo Montalban of Frank Loesser's "Baby, It's Cold Outside," which won the Academy Award for Best Original Song in 1949.⁶⁹ Although not hired for her voice, Williams had sung that duet well, crediting her voice coach Harriet Lee: "She took whatever voice I had and taught me how to use it. ... She taught just enough vocal technique to handle a song."⁷⁰

The plot of *Dangerous When Wet* involves an Arkansas dairy farm family who are health conscious. The promoter of an elixir persuades the Higgins family to swim the English Channel, and complications ensue. André Lanet, a French vintner (Lamas) rescues Katie Higgins (Williams) during one of her practice sessions in the Channel, and a romance develops. The film also stars veterans William Demarest and Charlotte Greenwood as the parents, Jack Carson as the promoter, and Barbara Whiting, Margaret's sister, as Katie's sister Susie.

After listing several positive elements of the film, the *Motion Picture Daily* critic added: "If, with all this in its favor, the production needed anything else to guarantee its audience success, that could be songs by a couple of gentlemen as skilled in their art as Arthur Schwartz and Johnny Mercer, who supply four numbers high above filmusical [sic] level."[71] One song of note, "In My Wildest Dreams," made use of the cartoon expertise of Joseph Barbera, William Hanna, and Fred Quimby. In the scene, Katie Higgins dreams a Tom and Jerry cartoon where she is underwater with the cat and mouse duo and an octopus character in a beret, representing André. Williams' agility underwater is striking, and the cartoon characters follow her lead. The song is also done by Fernando Lamas in a romantic scene on his sailboat.[72] Gene Kelly had danced an animated scene with Jerry in *Anchors Aweigh* in 1945.

Two other Schwartz / Mercer tunes were "I Like Men" and "Ain't Nature Grand." "I Like Men" was sung by Susie Higgins, performed with a bluegrass quartet. The latter tune was a lively group number with multiple scenes that included duets by Williams and Lamas in a swimming pool as well as Demarest and Greenwood, who at sixty-three, could still sing and dance. Lamas was an excellent swimmer, a trait Williams had looked for in this film, as she had been burdened with a few non-swimmers in previous films, including Van Johnson, Ricardo Montalban, and John Bromfield.[73]

Musically, what attracted the most attention was "I Got Out of Bed on the Right Side." One reviewer noted that the song "is used by the swimming family somewhat as 'Hi Ho' was used by the Seven Dwarfs in Walt Disney's 'Snow White,' and with the same steadily-building effectiveness."[74] It opens the movie as the Higgins family sings it while doing calisthenics. The song is described in *Classic American Popular Song* as "a long song packed with energy and good humor. ... Schwartz's tune takes right off with successive phrases that step up one note each time ... until a high point is reached and the melody tumbles down in a favorite Schwartz device of intervals of thirds."[75] These songs made the Schwartz / Mercer effort "an underrated, delightful score" and led to another M-G-M musical hit.[76] The *Los Angeles Times* declared *Dangerous When Wet* "just about the best of the Ester Williams swimsings."[77] In a typical Hollywood ending, Ester Williams wins the English Channel competition, earning enough money to save the dairy farm, and then marries Lamas, which she did in real life sixteen years later.

Late into 1951, the possibility of another project for Schwartz had emerged briefly. There had been talk for years on Broadway about making a musical of George Bernard Shaw's *Pygmalion*. Shaw was against it, as he had always disliked Oscar Straus's 1908 operetta, *The Chocolate Soldier*, based on his *Arms and the Man*. As a result, he forbade any further musical creations from his plays. After he died in 1950, however, his estate was more open to the idea. Richard Rodgers and Oscar Hammerstein II were approached but thought the project unworkable. Alan Jay Lerner and Frederick Loewe worked on it briefly but abandoned the project. Most Broadway veterans were reluctant to take it on: "As one of the great Broadway legends has it, a musical adaptation of *Pygmalion* was viewed by the theatrical community as a nonstarter from the very beginning; a dramatic play so devoid of the conventions of traditional musical comedy that it could never be successfully musicalized, cast, or staged."[78]

Director Gabriel Pascal then acquired the rights to do a musical and approached the Theatre Guild to consider mounting one.[79] Over the next two years, Pascal and Lawrence Langner and Theresa Helburn of the Theatre Guild approached several songwriters. Frank Loesser and Cole Porter were considered, but both declined. The Guild then cast a wider net. Among the possible songwriters they considered were Richard Adler and Jerry Ross, Harold Arlen, Irving Berlin, Leonard Bernstein, Betty Comden and Adolph Green, Noël Coward, Yip Harburg, Gian Carlo Menotti, André Previn, Harold Rome, Fred Saidy, Schwartz and Dietz.[80] They all turned the project down, including Schwartz, who blamed it all on Dietz: "Howard told me it was a terrible idea. He said 'if the plot were about a Brooklyn girl being taught to develop a proper American accent, maybe it would work. But who cares about a London Cockney flower girl?' Now, whenever we meet, I tell Howard, 'You owe me $5 million.'"[81] Ultimately, the Theatre Guild relinquished their rights which were then acquired by Lerner and Loewe from the Chase Manhattan Bank which held the rights for the Shaw estate. After difficulties and false starts, Alan Jay Lerner and Frederick Loewe conquered *Pygmalion* and made Broadway history with *My Fair Lady*.

The songwriting team of Arthur Schwartz and Dorothy Fields moved on after *A Tree Grows in Brooklyn*. Fortunately, they would team up three years later for one more period musical, *By the Beautiful Sea*, again starring Shirley Booth. Fields went on to more book writing with her brother, Herbert, as well as film composing with Schwartz, Harold Arlen, and Harry Warren. Schwartz continued to have many irons in the fire—producing, composing, legal and administrative work—and would stay busy until *By the Beautiful Sea*. As for *A Tree Grows in Brooklyn*, historian William Zinsser put it best: "I particularly remember the musical *A Tree Grows in Brooklyn* (1951). With lyrics by Dorothy Fields ... it was one of the most beautiful of all Broadway scores. The man couldn't help being a class act."[82]

23

Schwartz v. Broadcast Music, Inc.

"A few of the boys ... began to believe that there was a conspiracy on the part of the broadcast companies which own BMI."[1]

The issues had developed over years and would end up in the courts and Congress. Animosity between ASCAP (American Society of Composers, Authors and Publishers) and BMI (Broadcast Music, Inc.) went back to the thirties. As the primary licensor of music in the country, ASCAP charged the radio broadcasters for performances of its songs, requiring them to buy a "blanket" license rather than just paying for the music they actually used. From 1932 on, ASCAP established a rate of 5 percent of a station's advertising revenue as the amount due to ASCAP for use of their songs on the radio.[2] BMI was formed in 1939 to combat these fees, as well as to provide an outlet for the alternative forms of music which ASCAP shied away from. These included "hillbilly" (country & western), folk, "race" (rhythm & blues), and Latin songs, as well as numerous other foreign compositions. In addition, BMI used a fixed payment fee per performance or airing of a song, rather than the complicated tier system of ASCAP that favored established composers.

BMI broadcasters, which included numerous local stations as well as the NBC and CBS radio networks, finally had had enough in 1940 when ASCAP attempted to double its licensing fees. Starting on January 1, 1941, BMI and its affiliates staged a boycott of all ASCAP songs and played only those of BMI. The number of songs in the BMI inventory was woefully inadequate, and broadcasters resorted to playing songs in the public domain or from the classical repertoire. "I Dream of Jeannie with the Light Brown Hair," a Stephen Foster song written in 1854, was one of the more popular ones on the airwaves that year. The boycott lasted until October 29, 1941, and the problem was resolved only when ASCAP reduced their fees, most of them ending up around 2.5 percent, about half of what they were getting before 1940.³

Bolstered by this, BMI redoubled its efforts during the forties to draw in composers and entertainers from numerous genres—country-and-western, rhythm & blues, jazz, swing, and novelty, then later, rock 'n' roll. As it evolved, BMI began incorporating music publishers, recording houses, and the networks, both radio and television, into their membership. The activities of BMI became synergistic—some would say monopolistic—as networks and their publishing arms would promote and play music mostly created by BMI songwriters. Moreover, BMI made membership easy, even offering financial inducements to small music publishing firms to join up. Arthur Schwartz, who had kept a watchful eye on BMI for years, explained, "BMI has been subsidizing new publishing firms literally by the dozens. If you or I at this moment wanted to have a BMI firm, all we would need to do would be to express interest to the proper BMI brass and we would be given no less than a two-year contract for $50,000 or $60,000 a year to start business."⁴ To this point, a suit against BMI which was to be filed in 1953, used even stronger language: "defendants, for the purpose of inducing publishers ... have paid and granted to them subsidies, guarantees and other valuable consideration. ... Defendants have induced, coerced and intimidated writers and publishers of musical compositions to vest in the BMI music pool performance rights in their musical compositions."⁵ The result of such subsidies was that BMI encompassed 1,300 affiliated publishers, whereas ASCAP had only 600.

These revelations had emerged at a July 1952 meeting of fifteen songwriters that included Schwartz and John Schulman, an attorney for the Songwriters' Protective Association. Schwartz said of that meeting: "The songwriters of all types—production, popular, and standard—began to notice about two and a half years ago that their performances [song plays] on radio and television were diminishing at an alarming rate. A few of the boys ... began to believe that there was a conspiracy on the part of the broadcast companies which own BMI ... to 'ration' the amount of ASCAP music performed." They had all had enough. For Schwartz, his moment of revelation had come a year earlier, when RCA Victor, the recording arm of NBC, had refused to record any of his songs from *A Tree Grows in Brooklyn*. Moreover, an RCA executive told Schwartz, "it was going to be his policy to favor hillbilly music and 'certain types' of popular songs as against motion picture and stage music." This was borne out in 1952 when only a few Hollywood songs received any significant media play, most notably Oscar winner "In the Cool, Cool, Cool of the Evening" and "Buttons and Bows." Well-acquainted with all entities involved, Schwartz explained, "Motion picture music has been a particular target. This has probably been due to the growing enmity between television and the motion picture industries."[6]

This all culminated in November 1953 when thirty-three songwriters, organized as the Songwriters of America, filed suit against BMI, the National Association of Radio and Television Broadcasters (NARTB), the major networks, publishing firms, and executives of these companies. The suit became known as *Schwartz v. BMI*, and although ASCAP was not listed as a plaintiff, those involved knew that ASCAP was firmly behind it. Songwriters like Irving Berlin and Cole Porter were not listed as plaintiffs, as the Songwriters of America wanted to leave the impression of representing a cross-section of composers and lyricists. Richard Rodgers and Oscar Hammerstein II, also not listed, issued a joint statement in support of the suit, stating: "All of these songwriters, we believe, deserve the continuing right to submit their music to the American public without restriction. Even more important, we feel, is the right of every American to hear ... the music of his choice, music which has become established in a free and competitive American market."[7]

The songwriters listed as plaintiffs were a formidable group:

Milton Ager	Robert MacGimsey
Samuel Barber	Gian Carlo Menotti
Walter Bishop	George W. Meyer
Paul Cunningham	Joseph Meyer
Mack David	Vic Mizzy
Milton Drake	Douglas Stuart Moore
Dorothy Fields	Don Raye
James Kimball Gannon	Arthur Schwartz
Ira Gershwin	William Grant Still
L. Wolfe Gilbert	Randall Thompson
George Graff	Virgil Thomson
Alex Charles Kramer	Charles Tobias
Jack Lawrence	Leonard Whitcup
Alan Jay Lerner	Joan Whitney
Edgar Leslie	Jack Yellen
Jerry Livingston	Victor Young
John Jacob Loeb	

The list of defendants, besides BMI, Inc., was more imposing and included, among others[8]:

ABC	RCA	NBC, Inc.	CBS, Inc.
Columbia Records, Inc.	Okeh Music Publishing	Paramount Theatres, Inc.	Mutual Broadcasting
BMI Canada, Ltd.	David Sarnoff	William S. Paley	Frank Stanton
Carl Haverlin	National Association of Radio and Television Broadcasters (NARTB)		

The suit was filed as a class action on November 9, 1953, charging the defendants with monopolistic practices under both the Clayton and Sherman Anti-trust Acts. The gist of the suit was best stated in Paragraph 29 / Section (a): "Defendants have acquired numerous musical compositions for publication and have directly and indirectly published musical compositions, but have refrained from acquiring and publishing, and have refused to acquire and publish, any musical compositions unless the performance rights therein were controlled by defendant BMI."[9]

The plaintiffs were suing for $150,000,000, making it one of the largest actions ever under the anti-trust acts.[10] At the press conference held at the Waldorf-Astoria Hotel on the day the suit was filed, Schwartz explained: "The $150,000,000 damage figure is not one that has been exaggerated simply for purposes of a law suit. Our evidence shows that damages suffered by the songwriters is the amount named, and that is what we aim to recover."[11] The suit would seek to recover $150,000,000, which represented trebled damages of $50,000,000 plus interest, court costs, and attorneys' fees. To finance their suit, a steering committee that included Schwartz had organized a system by which, "[e]ach of us has pledged a minimum of 5% of our ASCAP income over a period of the next three years. Many of us are giving much more than that."[12]

The issue of financing the law suit was an ongoing concern for Schwartz and his fellow plaintiffs. Early on, Irving Berlin had not been openly supportive of their efforts, behavior that rankled Schwartz. Berlin reacted unfavorably to "wise-cracks" Schwartz had made about Berlin which came out in "The Lyons Den," the daily Broadway column of Leonard Lyons. Berlin complained to Schwartz, "We [Berlin, Schwartz, and composer Edgar Leslie] had a very frank talk in my office regarding my feelings about joining the group in the B.M.I. law suit. I told you then that I was acting on the advice of my attorney. You should be the last person to find fault with that.... So until I make my decision where the B.M.I. law suit is concerned, it would be best for the cause and for our relationship if you stopped inventing wise-cracks at my expense."[13]

Schwartz replied quickly to Berlin that the plaintiffs needed not only Berlin's financial support, but his moral support as well. In a strongly worded paragraph, he told Berlin, "Your abstention thus far has already given comfort to our opponents. It obviously would. And it has raised serious questions in the minds of some of our writers. They are really asking, in their own terms: If the keystone is missing, will the building stand up? ... It [ASCAP] may possibly be broken up ... if we should lose our present writers' suit against BMI. In my opinion, we can only lose it if we falter in our financial support."[14] Never one to back down, the diminutive, veteran replied: "As for the rest of your letter, I am sure if you read it two weeks from now you will feel a little silly because frankly Arthur, it's pompous and lawyer-like. I will not bother to answer it.... In a nutshell, my interest in ASCAP is much greater than yours, so you can rest assured that I will fight anyone, including BMI, who tries to do anything to injure ASCAP without pressure from you or anyone else."[15] It should be remembered that Berlin had been there from the beginning and had a unique view of these matters. As historian Wilfrid Sheed pointed out, "Veterans like George M. Cohan and Irving Berlin had to fight so many small fights with small people—over copyrights, royalties, credits, survival—that they remained slightly crouched and suspicious for the rest of their days."[16]

Financing of the songwriters' legal efforts continued, as did their suit. It charged that "the defendants agreed and jointly undertook to establish and create a music pool to be operated under their domination and control for their joint use and benefit." This monopoly and restraint of trade was achieved through:

(a) ownership and control of radio and television broadcasting stations and networks....

(b) joint creation and operation of defendant Broadcast Music, Inc....

(c) boycott of and discrimination against the music written by plaintiffs and others....

The suit further charged a conspiracy among the defendants, going back to 1939, BMI's first year: "the defendants ... conceived, formulated and embarked upon a plan, scheme and conspiracy to dominate and control the market for the use and exploitation of musical compositions...."[17] Because of all this, in addition to the money, plaintiffs were asking for preliminary and permanent injunctions against and dissolution of BMI as well as the NARTB. The latter was a trade association with a membership of 1,099 radio stations and 192 television stations, whose personnel directed BMI operations.[18]

To all these charges, BMI president Carl Haverlin pointed out that all the songwriters listed as plaintiffs were members of ASCAP and added,

"The baseless conspiracy charges made in the complaint are a rehash of charges which ASCAP has been making for years and has never been able to substantiate." His view of BMI was diametrically opposed to that of the plaintiffs: "As a result of the competition created by BMI, music writing is no longer a monopoly of 'Tin Pan Alley.'"[19] It all depended on one's view of where, if any, the monopoly existed. As *Variety* concluded, "When and if this N.Y. Federal Court action reaches trial in a year or so, there will be plenty of dirty linen aired. If not sooner. As of now, to be precise."[20] Several weeks after the suit was filed, Schwartz wrote Miriam Stern, executive director of the American Guild of Authors and Composers and a close friend, not so much airing dirty linen, but rather getting personal about a few of the well-known defendants: "Good fellowship type discussions with Paley, Sarnoff and Sydney Kaye are about as useful as with Kruschchev [sic] ... pleasant talk about business morality is a naïve concept. You do not have drinks with bandits. You fight them."[21]

Schwartz v. BMI progressed as class action suits do—slowly. To ensure this, the BMI attorneys requested that they be permitted to examine the performance cards of 200,000 ASCAP songs going back to 1934. These cards held the number of plays for each song, listed by year, and to examine all of them was a daunting task.[22] Along the same lines, BMI sought to interrogate ten of the thirty-three plaintiffs / songwriters in detail regarding their songs and ties to ASCAP.[23] These two ploys, both agreed to by the courts, served to delay the legal action and weakened the songwriters' case.

These delays led the plaintiffs to seek redress through Congress, where they had an ally in Representative Emanuel Celler of New York, chairman of the House Judiciary Committee. In 1956, he called for subcommittee hearings on the issues. Stanley Adams, former president of ASCAP, set the tone for the songwriters' side, asserting that BMI and its affiliates "have sought to and do control the faucets through which music flows."[24] Various songwriters voiced complaints, some legitimate, others whiny. Showman Billy Rose and composer Jack Lawrence went so far as to accuse BMI of jamming the airwaves with an "electronic curtain ... to keep the music of America's best songwriters away from the public." Also cited was a brief note of advice in the *BMI Bulletin* from BMI to their broadcasters regarding a particular two-sided recording: "This is a BMI number—meaning it is your own music. ... Be careful of the other side of this disk, it is not a BMI tune." Among the better testimony read into the record was a statement by lyricist / librettist Otto Harbach, a founding member and past president of ASCAP: "A few years ago, when I first began to realize the enormity of the conspiracy launched against good music, it occurred to me that the greatest melodies of the past would never have had the chance to reach the public if they were written now instead of then. Would 'Smoke Gets in Your

23. Schwartz v. Broadcast Music, Inc.   239

Eyes' be allowed by the broadcasters to be heard instead of 'Be-Bop-a-Lulu' [*sic*]? Could 'Indian Love Call' penetrate the airwaves which are flooded with 'Hound Dog'? It is to me a shocking thing that the power of broadcasters has been used to debase popular music."[25]

But to BMI and their co-defendants, this was so much smoke and mirrors. Carl Haverlin testified that of the music played on radio in 1954 only 17.6 percent was BMI, with ASCAP accounting for 71.1 percent. There were even bigger differences between the two entities regarding television and motion picture music. Similar numbers were supported even by ASCAP's own investigations. After all had spoken, committee members went against chairman Celler and took no action, recommending only that the Justice Department undertake an investigation of the music industry. As *Variety* put it, "despite an apparent attitude of prejudgment and a sweeping subpoena power ... the networks acquitted themselves on virtually every score."[26]

The next glacial movement in *Schwartz v. BMI* was another round of hearings, these of the Committee on Interstate and Foreign Commerce. These had been convened as a result of the introduction by Senator George Smathers of Florida of a bill, "attempting to divorce broadcast stations and networks from publishing music or making records." Oscar Hammerstein II, who led off the hearings, acknowledged that while popular songs were popular, this was due mostly to the ploys used by BMI and its affiliates. Such popularity was due not to the merits of the music, but to the promotion of specific songs by the BMI-influenced industry. He concluded, "They die as soon as the plug stops."[27]

Schwartz testified at these Senate hearings, claiming that nothing good had happened since the House hearings two years before. He singled out Mitch Miller, the artists and repertoire (A&R) head of Columbia Records. Miller was one of the first executives to take an active role as a producer, helping to elevate that position to the dominant role it would have in the rock 'n' roll era. Miller had made a speech to disc jockeys and other members of the music industry criticizing rock music; he had passed on signing Elvis Presley, Buddy Holly, and even the Beatles. Yet Miller was responsible for creating dozens of inartistic novelty songs. He had produced such hits as "Come On-a My House" for Rosemary Clooney and "Mule Train" for Frankie Lane, adding the bullwhip as a sound effect. Of Miller, Schwartz said, "This is the man who was as instrumental as any single person in the recording industry for recording, promoting, encouraging this same brand of music."[28] It was Schwartz's contention that like many recording executives who were part of BMI, Miller controlled what was recorded and aired at the exclusion of better—read "ASCAP"—music. Schwartz and Miller were to butt heads on a related issue in the near future.

The BMI publishers had strong testimony of their own, most notably several country & western music stars, including Gene Autry, Pee Wee King, and Jimmie Davis. Their complaints are best summarized by what Autry admitted, "Well, I tried to get into ASCAP as far back as 1930, and could not get an audience, or could not even get in." Senator John Pastore of Rhode Island weighed in on the side of BMI: "I don't like rock and roll too much as a personal taste, but there are a lot of people who do. And I don't think it is within the province of Congress to tell people whether they should listen to *South Pacific*, or listen to some rock and roll."[29] The Smathers bill never made it out of committee.

Gradually, the suit unraveled for the songwriters. In December 1959—six years after the original filing—Judge Edward Weinfeld made a ruling, noting the 20,000 pages of testimony and 11,000 exhibits totaling 55,000 pages. He deemed that if there were a conspiracy, it was targeted at ASCAP and not the thirty-three songwriters. In his mind, this left the plaintiffs "without standing to sue." Three months later, Judge Sylvester J. Ryan did everything but dismiss the suit. He ruled that to be awarded damages, each songwriter would have to show exactly how much more money each would have earned from a particular song if the "conspiracy" had not been in place. This was essentially "an impossible proposition." Although this nearly killed the suit, many of the plaintiffs persisted, but to no avail. Eventually, in 1971, a Federal judge dismissed the suit with prejudice, meaning that it was dismissed permanently and could not be brought back to court. That was the end of *Schwartz v. BMI*.[30]

* * *

Songwriters in Washington, D.C., stating their cases led to an amusing incident regarding Arthur Schwartz and a few Senators. During these hearings, Schwartz traveled there with songwriters Burton Lane and Jack Lawrence. They were invited to a dinner party at the home of a prominent Republican. There was much drinking through the evening, and at the end of dinner, Schwartz sat down at the piano to entertain. Senator Barry Goldwater asked Schwartz to play "Tea for Two" in stop-time. Goldwater grabbed another senator and as Schwartz played, the two did a tap routine, soon falling down, whooping and laughing. Lawrence recalled what Schwartz, still at the piano, said to the guests: "You'll be interested to know, ladies and gentlemen, I studied the law, passed my bar—and then I told my father that I planned to be a songwriter and write for the theater. My father was shocked. 'The theater! You'll meet such a terrible class of people!' Well, folks, I just wish my father could be here tonight." Lawrence concluded, "Would you believe those senators madly applauded Arthur?"[31]

24

The Band Wagon
The Movie and "That's Entertainment"

"Some songs come hard, some come easy. 'That's Entertainment' was like—taking dictation."[1]

Arthur Freed had become the master of the movie musical. In the late forties, he had produced two musical film biographies—biopics—for M-G-M: the life of Jerome Kern in *Till the Clouds Roll By* (1946); and *Words and Music* (1948), the story of Rodgers and Hart. These films used the songs of particular songwriting teams to tell the story of their collaboration. It was said, "Freed gave more weight to the music and less to the bio."[2] In Freed's view, why worry about a biographical fact or two if one more great song could be fit into the film. Historian Wilfrid Sheed referred to these as films that "were laughingly called biographies but were more like music racks."[3]

In the early fifties, Freed's approach changed. He continued to focus on songwriters and their songs, but the screenplays were less biographical. The stories were overtly fictional and served as vehicles for the songs, more plausibly than some forced "biography." These "indirect musicals"[4] began with *An American in Paris* (1951), which employed the songs of George and Ira Gershwin. The next was *Singin' in the Rain* (1952), where Freed used the songs that he and Nacio Herb Brown had written. After these two hits, Freed wanted to do another "song catalogue musical."[5] He had always liked the songs of Schwartz and Dietz and was especially fond of their 1931 revue, *The Band Wagon*. Freed was a friend and co-worker with Dietz at M-G-M and had told him, "One day I want to do a picture with your songs!"[6] That day had come.

In 1949, Twentieth Century–Fox had produced a movie, *Dancing in the Dark*, starring William Powell, Betsy Drake, and Adolphe Menjou. Aspects of the original *The Band Wagon* were incorporated into the screenplay by Marion Turk.[7] The film involved a washed-up actor, a budding female star, and an autocratic studio chief. The last of these was played by

Left to right: composer Arthur Schwartz, star Cyd Charisse, and lyricist Howard Dietz during filming of *The Band Wagon*, 1953 M-G-M musical. The film featured several songs from their revue days as well as a new hit, "That's Entertainment" (MGM / Photofest ©MGM).

Menjou, who did a takeoff on Fox studio head Daryl F. Zanuck. The producers made good use of the title song, as it was "sung under the credits, was used as a recurring theme throughout, and was featured by Betsy Drake"—dubbed by Bonnie Lou Williams—"in a production number."[8] Other Schwartz / Dietz songs used in the film and dubbed by Williams were "I Love Louisa," "New Sun in the Sky," and "Something to Remember You By." Because Fox owned the titles to both *Dancing in the Dark* and *The Band Wagon*, Freed had to buy back *The Band Wagon* to replace the working title of his Schwartz / Dietz film, *I Love Louisa*.[9]

The Band Wagon had been a revue and contained few plot elements that could support a Hollywood screenplay. Freed turned to screenwriters / lyricists Betty Comden and Adolph Green who had just written the screenplay for *Singin' in the Rain*. Prior to that, they had written successful screenplays for *Good News* (1947), *The Barkleys of Broadway* (1949), and *On the Town* (1949).[10] Director Vincente Minnelli referred to them as "the brightest of the writing lights in theater and films."[11]

24. The Band Wagon

For several years, Freed had been working closely with Roger Edens, who served as both associate producer and musical supervisor. He had played in pit orchestras on Broadway and had met Ethel Merman when they were both working in *Girl Crazy*. Edens had also been her accompanist for a vaudeville act. The two of them ended up in Hollywood in 1932, where he wrote and arranged material for her in various Paramount productions. He did similar work for Judy Garland after befriending her in 1935. Before working on *The Band Wagon*, Edens had garnered eight Academy Award nominations for Best Score, winning three times: *Easter Parade* (1948) with Johnny Green; *On the Town* (1949) with Lennie Hayton; and *Annie Get Your Gun* (1950) with Adolph Deutsch.[12]

Freed and Edens, in consultation with Schwartz and Dietz, chose songs from their extensive oeuvre and asked Comden and Green to fashion a story to incorporate them. Years later, they recalled their writing of the screenplay:

> **COMDEN:** We were given a stack of music written by Howard Dietz and Arthur Schwartz.
> **GREEN:** They had style. They were terrific. But it didn't seem to fit into a story very easily.
> **COMDEN:** That's why we decided to pick a theatre background and just try to put in some of the things that actually happened to us, some of our experiences, and what we knew about a show and to be truthful about it, and to make the characters convincing.[13]

Eventually, the two screenwriters would insist that they be recognized for the originality of their story and screenplay as it in no way resembled the original *The Band Wagon*. Their agent, Irving Lazar, made the point clear to Arthur Freed: "They didn't want a credit 'Based on ------' because it would not be a fact."[14] They received the proper credit and would earn an Academy Award nomination for Best Story and Screenplay.

After mulling over the music and story ideas for several weeks, Comden and Green came upon a simple plot, show business people—dancers, singers, writers, and a director—attempting a Broadway musical. This would be a show-within-a-show. The screenwriting pair took the ordinary story and incorporated what the film people knew about putting on a show. For the writers, this meant numerous, long meetings sitting around listening to Astaire and Minnelli reminisce about their theatrical days.[15] Green explained, "We wanted to show all the clichés, ... how the troubles out of town can happen ... how it happens that friends can turn to you and ask, 'how can you smart people get together and turn out such a mess?'"[16]

A show-within-a-show was a device used in theater and film and provided leeway for using the Schwartz / Dietz songs. But in employing this well-worn tool, Comden and Green knew their story needed a hook, and they found it in the differences between the principals of the show: Fred Astaire as Tommy Hunter, a has-been song-and-dance man, and Cyd Charisse as Gabrielle Gerard, an up-and-coming ballet dancer. Howard Dietz described the eureka moment: "'That's it!,' shouted Adolph. 'We'll base the plot on the conflict between two dancers. Fred'll say she's too tall, Cyd will say he's too old. Fred will hate ballet dancing, she will hate hot rhythm. It'll be the first true show-business story.'"[17]

In the movie, Tony is reluctant to star with Gabrielle despite her talent and beauty. He is bothered by her height, refusing to dance with a woman taller than he. The idea for all this came about because Astaire had been reluctant to dance with Cyd Charisse for that very reason. As choreographer Michael Kidd explained: "In real life, Fred was concerned that Cyd was too tall for him, which bothered him a great deal. After we discovered that, and he mentioned it a few times, a scene was put in the movie where Cyd is standing on a lower rung of a staircase and Fred looks at her and steps up one rung, to see at what height he would match her height. He was also really uneasy about dancing with Cyd Charisse for the true life reasons that are incorporated in the story. She was, primarily, a beautiful ballet dancer, and … he was a hoofer, though a superb one and a graceful one."[18] Astaire's biographer, Michael Freedland, adds to the story: "It was while she was working on another M-G-M film that Astaire appeared on the set, without warning and proceeded to walk round and round like a fox sizing up a prey.... When Arthur Freed offered her the co-starring part in *The Band Wagon* she realized what the circling had all been about. Astaire had simply been trying to work out how tall she was."[19] Howard Dietz saw it all a bit more humorously: "Cyd was an inch taller and had longer legs; and her long legs made her look streamlined like the Chrysler Building. Fred was General Motors."[20]

In a brief profile of Arthur Freed, historian Hugh Fordin described him: "His emotional scale is limited and uncomplicated: admiration for some, respect for a few, rejection of mediocrity. Secure within himself, he has the courage, the daring to venture toward the unexplored."[21] Time and again, Freed had proven his ability to choose the right creative team and leave them on their own. For *The Band Wagon*, he hired Vincente Minnelli, who had been directing hits on Broadway and in Hollywood for years, beginning with the Schwartz / Dietz revue *At Home Abroad* in 1935. In his directing, Minnelli brought a sense of color and design to his work. He had just directed *Singin' in the Rain*. Set designer Oliver Smith was doing his first film, but had achieved fame on Broadway designing *On the Town*, *High Button Shoes*, *Gentlemen Prefer Blondes*, and *Paint Your Wagon*. Michael Kidd, another Broadway veteran with his first official assignment for Hollywood, was to do choreography. He and Smith had worked together at Ballet Theatre. Kidd had already won two Tony Awards for Best Choreography for *Finian's Rainbow* (1947) and *Guys and Dolls* (1951). He would go on to win three more—*Can-Can* (1954), *Li'l Abner* (1957), and *Destry Rides Again* (1960).[22]

Hollywood veteran Adolph Deutsch was musical conductor and in charge of the overall score, working with the arrangements of several orchestrators: Alexander (Sandy) Courage, Bob Franklyn, Skip Martin, and Conrad Salinger.[23] Salinger had done orchestrations for *Between the Devil* and was well-acquainted with Schwartz. All this musical talent was needed as there would be plenty of Schwartz / Dietz songs to be arranged, conducted, and choreographed. The final edition of their songs included[24]:

Song	*Performed by*	*As*	*Original Show*
By Myself	Fred Astaire	Solo	*Between the Devil*
Penny Arcade		Instrumental	New for film
A Shine on Your Shoes	Astaire and LeRoy Daniels	Song and dance	*Flying Colors*
Oedipus Rex	Jack Buchanan and chorus	Ensemble	New for film
That's Entertainment	Astaire, Buchanan, Nanette Fabray, Oscar Levant, Cyd Charisse (dubbed by India Adams)	Group number	New for film
The Beggar Waltz (part of ballet scene of *Giselle*)	Charisse and corps de ballet	Dance	*The Band Wagon*
Dancing in the Dark	Astaire and Charisse	Dance duet	*The Band Wagon*
You and the Night and the Music	Chorus / Astaire and Charisse	Song / dance	*Revenge with Music*
The Egg		Instrumental	New for film
Something to Remember You By	Party guests	Group number	*Three's a Crowd*
High and Low	Party guests	Group number	*Here Comes the Bride / The Band Wagon*
I Love Louisa	Astaire, Fabray, Levant, guests	Group number	*The Band Wagon*
New Sun in the Sky	Charisse (dubbed by India Adams)	Solo	*The Band Wagon*
I Guess I'll Have to Change My Plan	Astaire and Buchanan	Song and dance	*The Little Show*
Louisiana Hayride	Fabray and chorus	Solo and group	*Flying Colors*

| Triplets | Astaire, Fabray, Buchanan | Trio | *Flying Colors* |
| The Girl Hunt | Astaire, Charisse | Dance duet | New for film |

For use of their old songs, the Schwartz / Dietz team was paid $40,000, and for the new songs, $25,000. For their thirty weeks of work on the screenplay, Comden and Green were paid approximately $52,000 each, about $1,750 per week.[25] Other principals in the cast included Englishman Jack Buchanan as the pretentious director, Jeffrey Cordova; Nanette Fabray and Oscar Levant as Tony Hunter's writer friends, Lily and Lester Marton; James Mitchell as Paul Byrd, Gerard's mentor and fiancé; and Thurston Hall as Colonel Tide, the principal backer of the show.

The initial version of *The Band Wagon* ran two hours and twenty-nine minutes, too long for the ideal two-hour length that movie house operators preferred. Several of the Schwartz / Dietz songs from past shows had to be cut, including "Got a Bran' New Suit" (*At Home Abroad*); "Never Marry a Dancer" (*Revenge with Music*); "Sweet Music" (*The Band Wagon*); "Two-Faced Woman" (*Flying Colors*); and "You Have Everything" (*Between the Devil*). A portion of "The Girl Hunt," written for the film by Schwartz and Edens, was deleted as well. All these cuts left the final edition of *The Band Wagon* at a workable 112 minutes.[26] "Two-Faced Woman" had been performed by Cyd Charisse and dubbed by India Adams and would be heard that same year in *Torch Song* in which the Adams recording was used to dub Joan Crawford on that film. Adams explained, "It's the only time in motion picture history that two different actresses have lip-synched to the very same track."[27] M-G-M made a series of *That's Entertainment!* films based on the studio's musicals. In *That's Entertainment! III*, the omitted footage of Cyd Charisse and the frames of Joan Crawford that were used in *Torch Song*—both lip-synching "Two-Faced Woman"—are shown on a split screen segment.[28] On the DVD of *The Band Wagon*, there are several takes of Charisse singing and dancing the "Two-Faced Woman" scene, a lot of work that all ended up on the cutting room floor. "Alone Together" (*Flying Colors*) and "The Private Eye," written by Schwartz and Dietz specifically for the movie, were never filmed.[29] Lyrics for the latter song—a spoof by Dietz—are in the Roger Edens Collection at the University of Southern California Cinematic Arts Library.[30]

The opening scene in *The Band Wagon* reveals an auction house with items from Tony Hunter's life and career being unceremoniously sold off. He then returns to New York by train and after deboarding, strides rhythmically beside the train, singing "By Myself" while he is "neither dancing nor walking but something between."[31] Jonathan Schwartz said much about this scene: "One of the songs, 'By Myself,' had lain dormant for years. It had been written for a flop show in the late thirties and had never been discovered, never examined or embraced. Astaire himself remembered it, brought it forward, and began *The Band Wagon* by singing it in a melancholy understatement as if thinking aloud … it made 'By Myself' a standard. Its melody, as I hear it, comes closer than any other to identifying the true Arthur."[32] Edens and Freed were fond of the song, and Comden and Green had insisted on its inclusion as it was essential to their characterization of Hunter.

After "By Myself," Tony Hunter is met at Grand Central Station by his writer friends, the Martons, bearing the sign "Tony Hunter Fan Club" and lifting his spirits. The scene was reminiscent of a similar experience in the lives of Comden and Green. Their careers had hit a low in Hollywood, causing Comden to return to New York.[33] Green followed several days later and was met by Comden at the station, holding an "Adolph Green Fan Club" sign. Green explained, "It was a tremendous lift psychologically. In fact you could say it was a turning point in my life."[34]

Following this was one of the most entertaining scenes in *The Band Wagon*. In the performance of "A Shine on Your Shoes," Astaire insisted on doing the song with a shoe shine man. A dancing one—LeRoy Daniels—was found in downtown Los Angeles by assistant dance director Alex Romero. Romero had been hired for *The Band Wagon* because of his tap dancing experience, and he also served as Astaire's dancing stand-in. Leroy Daniels was in his early twenties and known as the "BeBop Bootblack," using his dance skills to attract customers. This was not his first claim to fame as he had been the topic of a 1950 song, "Chattanooga Shoe Shine Boy," recorded by both Bing Crosby and Red Foley. After *The Band Wagon*, he formed a nightclub act. Daniels would continue to appear several times on-screen, including the part of a shoe shine man in *Avenging Angels* (1985) and in a recurring role in television's *Sanford and Son* as Lucky LeRoy.[35] Astaire meshed well with his partner, and the untrained Daniels was up to the task, dancing and using his brushes and shoe shine cloth as props.

"A Shine on Your Shoes" was filmed in an arcade where Daniels' character worked. In addition to their duet, Astaire employs the props provided by the arcade setting, including a fun house mirror, shooting gallery, photo booth, and the shoe shine stand. As the scene closes, Astaire kicks a penny arcade machine—a combination calliope and rocket launcher—which erupts in noise and color, a Minnelli touch designed by Oliver Smith. It took Smith ten days, working with fifteen draftsmen, to come up with the complicated prop. It ended up costing $8,800 and was in the scene for thirty-five seconds.[36]

As the story evolves, Hunter and the Martons have convinced director

Jeffrey Cordova to do the musical they have envisioned. At this point, Freed wanted a new song from Schwartz and Dietz, nothing from their old shows. He told them, "In the script this director, Buchanan, is saying that practically anything you can do will work if it's entertaining. I want a 'There's No Business Like Show Business.'"[37] Over the years, there had been several good showbiz songs on stage and in film:

Song	Composer / Lyricist	From (medium)	Year	Introduced by
42nd Street	Harry Warren / Al Dubin	42nd Street (film)	1933	Ruby Keeler and Dick Powell
Hooray for Hollywood	Richard Whiting / Johnny Mercer	Hollywood Hotel (film)	1937	Frances Langford and Johnnie Davis
There's No Business Like Show Business	Irving Berlin	Annie Get Your Gun (musical)	1946	Members of wild west show
Another Op'nin', Another Show	Cole Porter	Kiss Me Kate (musical)	1948	Band of players
Make 'Em Laugh	Nacio Herb Brown / Arthur Freed	Singin' in the Rain (film)	1952	Donald O'Connor

Freed wanted his songwriters to capture the spirit of these songs.

Dietz remembered the emergence of the song differently, claiming that he and Schwartz had written several new songs for the film, but "the MGM powers that be didn't think that the songs were necessary for the picture." He then recalled that the song was more his and Schwartz's idea than Freed's, and the songwriters saw this as their chance to get a new song into *The Band Wagon*:

> Of course, we were determined to write a song that they just couldn't refuse. Since the movie was about Show Business, I hit upon the title "That's Entertainment." Arthur agreed. And we went to work. Arthur then wrote a melody that had a marvelous show biz, old time vaudeville feel to it. The middle part of this melody ... was so constructed that it seemed to call for those couplets and the title line "That's Entertainment." We realized that we had hit upon the essence of what we were trying to say.[38]

What all agree about is that the melody came quickly to Schwartz, as son Jonathan explained: "They were invited to write a song to define entertainment. My father wrote the melody in the length of time that it takes to play it. It's as if it had existed. Now the lyric took a long time. Think of those words. And Howard's lyric is so sophisticated. My father's distinguished, thrilling melody has a Conrad Salinger arrangement. Conrad Salinger was a stunning musician."[39] Other reports say it may have taken Schwartz as long as thirty to forty-five minutes. Two years after Dietz's recollections,

24. The Band Wagon

Schwartz told a Los Angeles reporter, "Some songs comes hard, some come easy. 'That's Entertainment' was like—taking dictation."[40] Whatever the time, Schwartz and Dietz had another hit on their hands, one that has stood the test of time. So popular was "That's Entertainment" in film circles that in 1974, M-G-M created a movie based on clips from their old musicals and titled it *That's Entertainment!* It was also used for sequels in 1976 and 1994. In 1990, it was given the ASCAP Award for Most Performed Feature Film Song.

Several scenes later, the music for *The Band Wagon* turns from anthem to ballad. Tony Hunter and Gabrielle Gerard have been cast for Cordova's show and are not happy about it. They are having troubles bridging their age and artistic differences. What better way to patch up their differences—in Hollywood thinking—but with a romantic dance. And what better song to do it with than the ultimate Schwartz / Dietz ballad, "Dancing in the Dark." Hunter and Gerard slip away by carriage to Central Park, wander through a crowd, and find a private place to dance through their differences. By the end of the scene, all is forgotten, and a bond is formed.

Much has been written about the scene. Historian Gerald Mast explained, "the dance is a conversion, turning a former enemy into a partner, merely because of the way they dance together." He points out that Astaire had two similar "conversion" scenes with Ginger Rogers during their long association. *The Gay Divorcee* (1934), they danced to "Night and Day," and in *Shall We Dance?* (1937), to "They All Laughed."[41] In *The Band Wagon*, the "Dancing in the Dark" scene captures the mystery of the song, the talents of the dancers, and Charisse's grace and beauty. It was choreographed by Michael Kidd with Astaire's influence and much credit to orchestrator Conrad Salinger. Historian Gary Marmorstein felt "for dreamy urban romanticism, Salinger's arrangement of 'Dancing in the Dark' is peerless."[42] Biographer of the Astaires, Kathleen Riley, concurred: "It is an extraordinary dance of emotional discovery, richly textured in its somatic phrasing and intricately responsive to Conrad Salinger's voluptuous but delicately modulated orchestration."[43] Jonathan Schwartz added, "The arrangement is as distinguished as the melody. The arrangement that Salinger provided for 'Dancing in the Dark' is the most thrilling writing for orchestra in a musical film ever."[44]

With things patched up, the inner show can go on. The plot moves along to include more Schwartz and Dietz songs, including another Astaire / Charisse duet on "You and the Night and the Music," as well as group numbers "Something to Remember You By," "High and Low," and "I Love Louisa." Then Charisse performs "New Sun in the Sky," in a colorful Minnelli / Smith setting, dubbed by India Adams.

This is followed by "I Guess I'll Have to Change My Plan," a song and dance by two veterans of the art, Astaire and Jack Buchanan. Clifton Webb had been Freed's first choice for the role but turned it down because he did not want to play second fiddle as the arty director Cordova. Webb, who recommended Buchanan for the role, opted for the starring role in *Stars and Stripes Forever*, playing John Philip Sousa. Vincent Price and Edward G. Robinson were also considered for Cordova, a role described as "a cross between Orson Welles and José Ferrer."[45] Buchanan was no stranger to Schwartz and Dietz songs, having taken the lead in *Between the Devil*, playing the accidental bigamist, Peter Anthony / Pierre Antoine. In that 1937 role, Buchanan introduced "By Myself."

Astaire and Buchanan performed "I Guess I'll Have to Change My Plan" in top hat and tails with canes. The scene is a department store window of pastel stripes designed by Oliver Smith and Minnelli, the latter having been a window dresser before his theater career. The Astaire / Buchanan duet has been described as "the most breezily comfortable soft shoe duet in film history."[46] Alec Wilder had seen the song that way: "It's in the 'soft shoe' genre.... It's a very sweet, warm song suggesting a dance as much as a song, as charming as the lyric is. It's only twenty measures long."[47] Although Michael Kidd had done most of the choreography for *The Band Wagon*, Astaire worked out the duet for this scene with Buchanan.[48] Orchestrator Alexander Courage was delighted when Edens asked him to do the arrangement: "The most elegant, imaginable pair of soft shoe artists doing the most elegant possible soft shoe song, so I did that. That was just heaven."[49] In the original presentation of the song in *The Little Show* in 1929, Clifton Webb had sung of "blue pajamas" and a "big affair." In 1953, the members of the Production Code Administration felt that a song lyric could not celebrate an illicit affair, and the lyrics were toned down for the film.[50]

Despite an opening night disaster, the inner show becomes a hit—of course—moving the film along. Nanette Fabray then performs two songs originally written for *Flying Colors*, the 1932 Schwartz / Dietz revue, "Louisiana Hayride" and "Triplets." By this time on the set, filming was moving along well, and the two songs were scheduled to be filmed a day apart. For "Louisiana Hayride," Fabray sang solo with support from the chorus. During the filming, she jumped onto a barrel that was not properly reinforced and tore up a leg. She was put on pain killers so that "Triplets" could be shot the next day. She had not been slotted to do the number until Oscar Levant claimed ill health, wanting no part of the dancing in the scene.[51]

"Triplets" had been cut from *Flying Colors*, then from *At Home Abroad*, but was finally kept in *Between the Devil*. Putting a song into a show, then deleting it before the show opened on Broadway, only to try it in another show, was common in musical theater. Famously, "Blue Moon" was cut three times by Rodgers and Hart. Jerome Kern's "Bill" had been withdrawn from a few productions before it landed up in *Show Boat* for Helen Morgan. The Gershwins did the same with "The Man I Love," omitted from *Lady, Be Good!*, *Strike Up the Band*, and *Rosalie*.[52] Knowing the value of this "song without a home," Gershwins' publisher, Max Dreyfus, issued "The Man I Love" as an independent publication.[53]

In *Flying Colors*, the performers had included Clifton Webb at six feet two inches, Philip Loeb at five feet eight, and Imogene Coca at five feet even, and the number failed.[54] For the movie, "Triplets" was to be performed by Astaire, Buchanan, and Fabray. To Kidd, it was important that the three "triplets" be the same size to accentuate their identical costumes. To achieve this effect, costumes were fashioned whereby custom-designed baby shoes were fit over the performers' knees. Their legs were then covered with black velvet, matching the black floor of the set. To carry the image off, the performers sang and danced on their knees, not an easy proposition. Because of this difficulty, filming could only be done twenty minutes at a time before the actors needed a break. The knee dancing coupled with her leg injury led Fabray to recall the filming as "a long day of pain, terror and anxiety."[55] To which Astaire added, "As a knee dancer, I'm a good singer. This could ruin me!"[56]

Fabray had a good singing voice for theater, having had principal roles in *High Button Shoes* (1947), *Love Life* (1948), and *Arms and the Girl* (1950), winning a Tony Award for her performance in *Love Life*. Singing on screen was a different art, but she acquitted herself well in her singing scenes, giving much credit to Roger Edens: "Roger developed my voice note for note and vowel by vowel. He found that my best note was a high B flat and my best sound was an open A: 'Hay—ride.' Hour by hour he worked with me to develop my lung strength."[57] She added in an interview, "Roger was a great strength and he was endlessly wonderful…. I think it was all Roger Edens what [sic] made that movie great."[58]

The climactic scene in *The Band Wagon* was a thirteen-minute ballet duet for Astaire and Charisse, "The Girl Hunt." The idea for the scene had begun as a brief note on a script which Comden and Green had intended to turn into a plot for the choreographer. Instead, Roger Edens asked Schwartz and Dietz to write a new number. They called it "The Private Eye," but it did not play well in rehearsals and was never filmed. During all this, Edens had seen a *Life* magazine article about mystery writer Mickey Spillane and thought a dance spoof of that detective genre might work. Schwartz was asked to compose several musical themes which Edens orchestrated into a ballet. Hugh Fordin explained the difficulty: "Edens had a big job on his hands. Unlike 'An American in Paris,' a tone poem, what he had to work with was a disparate ray [sic] of themes and motives which he actually had to compose into a musical continuity."[59] Edens pulled out all the stops for the filming of "The Girl Hunt." Adolph Deutsch explained, "In the recording of the ballet we used a greater variety of techniques available to us than I've ever seen used in any one number."[60]

To enhance the atmosphere of the noir spoof, a voiceover narrative was written by Alan Jay Lerner, uncredited, who had written the screenplay for Freed's *An American in Paris*. It was voiced in the film by Fred Astaire as private eye Rod Riley. One of the reasons Michael Kidd had been hired for *The Band Wagon* was because of the choreography he had done for *Guys and Dolls*. Freed and Edens thought that Kidd could "bring some of that show's lowlife flair to the piece."[61] In his memoir, *Steps in Time*, Astaire wrote, "'The 'Girl Hunt Ballet' in *Band Wagon*, patterned after Mickey Spillane's stories, I must make special mention of, because I liked it so much. Michael Kidd choreographed that one."[62]

The Astaire / Charisse duet for "Dancing in the Dark" was romantic and elegant. Wearing a plain white summer dress, she exhibited her ballet talents. With "The Girl Hunt," her beauty and famous legs were as much a part of the scene as her dancing. To accentuate this, she performed in a leotard cut quite high. Shocked at her thigh-baring costume, the National Legion of Decency rated the picture "Morally Objectionable in Part for All."[63] The scene was spectacular and shots of Charisse and Astaire were used for the film's promotion. She proved to be an able partner for Astaire, displaying modern dance and jazz abilities as well as her ballet background. Astaire played a great second fiddle to her. His biographer, Michael Freedland, explained, "It was the uncanny combination of Astaire and Charisse that impressed itself most on Kidd. Uncanny because they really did work together beautifully."[64] Astaire had high praise for his dance partner as well: "Cyd Charisse is a terrific dancer, a wonderful partner. She has precision plus—beautiful dynamite, I call it."[65] In her interview on the DVD of *The Band Wagon*, Charisse was proud to quote Astaire, who had said of her, "When you dance with Cyd Charisse, you've been danced with."[66]

Six weeks of rehearsals for *The Band Wagon* began in mid–August 1952, but filming did not begin until late September. While the overall mood of the film was one of a cooperative, friendly group of theater people, conditions on the set were "plagued with problems." Astaire's wife, Phyllis, was in the late stages of lung cancer and would die in 1954. Astaire's daughter, Ava Astaire McKenzie, would say of her father, "He was dealing with that through the whole time of making the picture. Working during that whole time was one of the biggest helps it could have been for him to get through it."[67] As for Schwartz, his wife Katherine continued to suffer from severe hypertension which kept her bed-bound and weighed heavily on him. Minnelli was worried about his ex-wife, Judy Garland, whose erratic behavior on the set of *A Star Is Born* was getting worse. Levant was recovering from

24. The Band Wagon

a heart attack, which aggravated his already acerbic nature, and Buchanan was going through extensive dental surgeries.[68]

Professional problems arose as well. Costume designer Mary Ann Nyberg butted heads with the wardrobe department—"a special conclave in the hierarchy of the studio"—finding them slow, costly, and unable to take directions. A simple white dress which Nyberg had in mind for Cyd Charisse to wear in the "Dancing in the Dark" scene ended up costing $1,000. She had bought a similar dress a few years earlier for twenty-five dollars. Likewise, set designer Smith, though fond of the head of the art department, Cedric Gibbons, found the rest of the department hostile and slow. Edens and Smith had poor rapport, which "they hid behind their excellent manners." Their dislike of each other related to disagreements over Leonard Bernstein's *On the Town*. Edens never liked the score of the original musical, and Smith did not care for Edens' work on the film of the musical, even though Edens won an Academy Award for Best Score. Smith also clashed with art designer Preston Ames and had to fight for final say over all set decorations.[69]

More importantly, Astaire and Fabray did not get along. Her smiling, charming manner carried over to her singing and dancing but belied an undercurrent of problems. She and Astaire were in numerous scenes together and three big musical numbers, including "That's Entertainment," "I Love Louisa," and "Triplets." What the exact problems were is unclear, but Astaire biographer Freedland was certain of the issue: "But she and Fred Astaire did not get on—and that is putting it mildly."[70] Fabray felt that most of the filming experience was difficult, saying, "Nobody talked to anybody—it was the coldest, unfriendlies[t], the most terrible experience I remem[b]er as far as being in show business is concerned."[71]

But the overriding problem on the set was Minnelli's perfectionism coupled with his obliviousness to things around him. While his results were not in question, his getting there affected many. Astaire explained, "When you work with the brilliant Vincente Minnelli as your director, you want to come through with everything he asks for and sometimes the order is a bit difficult to handle." One scene included several people crammed in a small hotel room. Astaire remembered, "Nothing seemed to play and Vincente kept changing lines and positions." Astaire became confused and walked off the set. After a discussion with Freed and a fifteen-minute walk, Astaire was able to clear his head and resume the scene. He concluded, "I went to Minnelli afterward and apologized, explaining my mental lapse, and Vincente said, 'Oh, that's perfectly all right, Fred, I drive everybody crazy.'"[72]

Despite all of the personal and professional problems on the set, filming of *The Band Wagon* ended in late January 1953. Editing and reshooting was done over the next few months, but there was little work for the songwriters. Although he had been off the set for much of the shooting in 1952,

Schwartz had come back to Hollywood late that year—at Freed's behest—to do additional work on "The Girl Hunt."[73] By January 1953, Schwartz was back in New York, and Dietz sent him a telegram: "SAW BAND WAGON ALMOST COMPLETE. IT IS JUST GREAT! LEAVING FOR NEW YORK TONIGHT. LOVE."[74]

Schwartz had left Hollywood to be with his wife, Katherine, who continued to suffer from her hypertension and died in Doctors Hospital, May 2, 1953, of a cerebral hemorrhage.[75] She was forty-six and had retired from the stage in 1937 due to her health. Although Schwartz knew she would probably suffer an early death, he was distraught when it happened. Son Jonathan was fifteen at the time. He recalled the incident:

> My father, weeping in the hallway, came to me. Standing in the middle of my room, he howled, put his palms to his face, his howl, a wail, a shout, a gurgle, a howl, so much more than grief. Standing there, his palms still on his face, he spoke, incoherently at first, about his love for his wife. He dropped his arms to his sides. His eyes were black. His clothes were caked in blood. He was fifty-three and a half years old, but he looked to me as ancient as human life, his gray hair knotted and tangled. His tentative cohesion left him. His howl returned. He sat down at the foot of my bed. "Jonno boy, Jonno boy," he said, his right hand on my ankle that was concealed under the covers. I recall that his moist fingers picked up lint from the blanket. I consoled him in some way. In time I sat and took his head in my lap and stroked his soaking brow. "She was so so so so sick," he said into the covers around my waist.[76]

Schwartz had a large group of friends who provided support, but Jonathan felt his father was "never psychologically intimate" with anyone. He added, "Even Howard Dietz, his collaborator, fell short of being a real confidant. Arthur, a gregarious, informed entertainer out in the world, had little access to naked honesty." Katherine's death left Schwartz raising his fifteen-year-old son alone. Gary Marmorstein remarked that, upon her death, "a deeply melancholy man, Schwartz plunged into even darker waters."[77]

One bright spot was a publicity tour for *The Band Wagon* upon which Schwartz and Dietz embarked after the New York premier on July 9, 1953. The idea was for the songwriting team to tour cities where their thirties revue had played and where the new movie would be shown. National release was set for August 7. The first leg of the tour found them in Boston the week of July 13. Mayor John B. Hynes designated it Dietz-Schwartz Week. When they were given the Mayor's guest book to sign, the ever-humorous Dietz penned, "No one declines Mayor Hynes," and Schwartz set a few bars of music to it. A *Boston Globe* reporter wrote, "They were so proud of their accomplishment in a matter of seconds that you might think they had just finished 'Dancing in the Dark,' one of their favorite songs."[78] For this summer tour, Schwartz was accompanied by Jonathan, no doubt a blessing for both. Moreover, young Schwartz was fond

24. The Band Wagon

of Dietz and enjoyed his humor. Other cities on the route included Philadelphia, Washington, D.C., Pittsburgh, and Cleveland. According to Dietz, advance staff from M-G-M had arranged luncheons, cocktail parties, radio and television appearances, and "shenanigans in general." He added, "Our role is merely to be gracefully receptive, cheerfully responsive, witty if possible, and wise enough to keep 'The Band Wagon' as the central note of every moment."[79]

Whether or not their promotional tour had much to do with it cannot be determined, but *The Band Wagon* did well at the box office. New York reviews were favorable; the music and Smith's sets came in for particular praise. Howard Dietz wired Howard Strickling, head of publicity at M-G-M: "NEVER HAVE PAPERS GIVEN ANY MOTION PICTURE MORE EXTRAVAGANT PRAISE THAN THAT ACCORDED BAND WAGON TODAY."[80] Schwartz had praise for Freed and Edens: "The whole placing of the songs—Roger Edens! Well, he was a giant in this field of choosing and arranging and rearranging things. He was a wonderful talent. And Arthur [Freed], being a songwriter, being the best producer of musicals who ever lived—they knew their way around."[81] Jonathan Schwartz was well aware of what *The Band Wagon* meant to his father:

> He was born in 1900, so therefore, when the film opened, he was a fifty-three-year-old man. What a wonderful thing to happen. My mother was very ill, and she had been ill all of her adult life with hypertension which was unsolvable at that time. There was a great deal of tension because of my mother's health, my father writing songs on the phone. He was melancholy, and he wanted really to do one thing in life, to write melodies. Everything took second place to the writing of the melody.[82]

With a cost of approximately $3 million and receipts of $5.7 million, the film was worth M-G-M's investment. It garnered three Academy Award nominations at the 26th Annual Awards in 1954: Comden and Green for Best Story and Screenplay; Adolph Deutsch for Best Musical Score; and Mary Ann Nyberg for Best Costume Design, Color. Despite critical praise, Smith was not nominated. "That's Entertainment" was ignored by the Oscars committee as well.[83] Over the years, *The Band Wagon* has been awarded other honors: the American Film Institute's No. 17 Greatest Movie Musical; *Entertainment Weekly*'s No. 6 Greatest Movie Musical of All Time; "That's Entertainment" as the No. 45 song in the American Film Institute's *100 Years ... 100 Songs*; and inclusion in the National Film Registry in 1995.[84]

Producer of the original revue, Max Gordon, had high praise for the film. He wrote to Fred Astaire after the opening, "I saw the full picture of 'The Bandwagon' [*sic*] twice, and the last hour three different times, and if it isn't the best musical picture ever made, it will certainly do til that one comes along."[85]

25

By the Beautiful Sea and More Dorothy Fields

"[I]t is a pleasure to encounter a melodious score, like the one Arthur Schwartz has written here."[1]

In 1953, Arthur Schwartz began working with Alan Jay Lerner on a few projects. The first was a screen version of *Paint Your Wagon*, the Lerner and Frederick Loewe musical that had a disappointing run from November 1951 to July 1952. Lerner always believed it would be a good screen vehicle, but Loewe declined to work on it. By October 1952, Lerner and Loewe again parted ways as they had done after working on *Brigadoon* in 1947, due much to Loewe's exasperation with Lerner's slow working methods.[2] In early 1953, Schwartz and Lerner had begun writing songs for the *Paint Your Wagon* film, to be added to the original ones from the show. As early as February, the *New York Times* reported that filming would begin in June, and the *Los Angeles Times* corroborated this, adding, "Lerner and Arthur Schwartz are to write eight new songs." Both papers noted that the film would be done in Cinerama, the film technology that had premiered in 1952.[3]

Within a few months, Schwartz and Lerner had written at least seven songs. They are in the Arthur Schwartz Papers in the Library of Congress in piano-vocal manuscript form, although two of them are lacking lyrics. Dominic McHugh, in *Loverly: The Life and Times of My Fair Lady*, noted that of these songs from *Paint Your Wagon*, two ballads stood out: "Over the Purple Hills" and "There's Always One You Can't Forget." McHugh said of the team, "At their best, one can see how the fruits of the Lerner-Schwartz alliance might have boded well for future collaborations … it is easy to understand why Lerner might have turned to Schwartz: as a composer, one of his stylistic facets was the ability to create a lot of expressive internal harmonic movement in a song, something that he shared with Loewe. Had the film come to pass, Lerner and Schwartz might have gone on to a string of works together."[4] Echoing this, another historian wrote, "In essence it would have been a felicitous collaboration, for Schwartz was an expansive and sensitive composer."[5]

However, the Schwartz / Lerner 1953 version of *Paint Your Wagon* never saw the lights of a soundstage, but according to Lerner biographer Edward Jablonski, their collaboration on that film did not end there. In mid–1957, Schwartz and Lerner were brought together by Louis B. Mayer and his nephew, Jack Cummings. Mayer had acquired the screen rights to *Paint Your Wagon* and wanted to renew the project. Work did not progress far, and when Mayer died in October 1957, the project was scrapped.[6] In 1969, Lerner would write another screenplay for *Paint Your Wagon*, engaging André Previn as composer. They wrote an additional four songs for the film and at the same time, were working on their musical, *Coco*, which opened December 1969. As always, Lerner was difficult to work with. Previn remarked of Lerner, "It drove people who worked with him kind of crazy that he could not release a lyric."[7] After working on projects with Lerner, Burton Lane and Richard Rodgers held similar feelings, and Lerner himself was well aware of his slow pace. The Lerner / Previn *Paint Your Wagon* was released October 1969 and did poorly at the box office, despite stars Lee Marvin, Clint Eastwood, and Jean Seberg.

Around the time of their efforts on *Paint Your Wagon*, Schwartz and Lerner had announced other projects: a play to be written by Lerner with Schwartz producing; a film version of *Kismet*, with screenplay and lyrics by Lerner and music by Schwartz; and a musical comedy based on the Al Capp cartoon, *Li'l Abner*, with songs by Schwartz and Lerner. Of this last project, the *New York Times* reported in March 1953 that the two songwriters had reached an agreement with Capp and would also serve as co-producers.[8] Problems must have ensued over the next few months, not only with Capp, but also between Schwartz and Lerner. The lyricist sent Schwartz an optimistic telegram on July 21, 1953: "JUST HAD AND [sic] EXHILARATING MEETING WITH AL CAPP CONTRACTS WERE SIGNED…I AM MORE ENTHUSIASTIC THAN EVER AND CANT WAIT TO GO TO WORK HOPE YOU WILL BRUSH ASIDE ALL NEGATIVE FEELINGS AND THROW YOURSELF INTO WHAT I AM CONVINCED CAN BE ONE OF THE MOST EXCITING EXPERIENCES OF BOTH OUR LIVES."[9] These "negative feelings" may have been conflicts over *Paint Your Wagon*, but this is not clear.

Although work on *Li'l Abner* continued into fall 1953, little was accomplished. During this time, Lerner's assistant Doris Shapiro was working with the two songwriters and referred to Schwartz as "a very sweet man." She did not always feel the same about her boss and could also tell that "he didn't have his heart in it."[10] As with *Paint Your Wagon*, Schwartz was unhappy with the progress Lerner had made on the book and lyrics. The other projects mentioned above—the Lerner play and the *Kismet* film—went nowhere. Moreover, it was announced on October 29, 1953, that Lerner had started work on a screenplay of *Green Mansions*, a novel by W.H. Hudson, to be filmed by Arthur Freed.[11] This may have been the last straw for Schwartz.

In early fall 1953, Dorothy Fields had approached Schwartz about writing another book musical with her. Like *A Tree Grows in Brooklyn*, it would be set at the turn-of-the-century and star Shirley Booth. Fields and her brother, Herbert, had written the book and had originally engaged Burton Lane to do the music. He quit the project, dissatisfied with the Fields' first draft of the book, which Lane felt had deviated too much from the original synopsis he had been given.[12] Dorothy Fields' offer came to Schwartz at an opportune time for him, as his relationship with Lerner was tenuous and his finances were suffering. He had not had a hit since *Inside U.S.A.* in 1948, and more importantly, his wife Katherine's medical bills were enormous. She had passed away in May 1953 after being sick for several years. Fed up with Lerner's procrastination, Schwartz told Lerner about accepting the Fields' offer. Jonathan Schwartz related the confrontation as he had heard it years later from his father:

> Alan's face turned red with anger. He said that by taking the Fields show, Arthur had ruptured their collaboration. "*What* collaboration?" Arthur told me he'd said. He [Lerner] left the office at once and never returned, though their companionship survived.[13]

Despite the rancorous parting, Schwartz and Lerner would remain friends over their lives.

In November 1953, Lerner would take on a new partner to write *Li'l Abner*—Burton Lane. Not only did Lane have to put up with the delay-ridden Lerner, but about this time, Lerner and Loewe began a second attempt at *Pygmalion*. The Lane / Lerner *Li'l Abner* faltered and was abandoned August 1954.[14] The Al Capp cartoon would not make it to Broadway until 1956 with the songwriting team of Johnny Mercer and Gene de Paul. Although not seasoned Broadway writers, their show ran for 693 performances.[15]

The story written by the Fields was titled *By the Beautiful Sea*. It evolved around the boarding house owner Lottie Gibson (Shirley Booth), an aging Shakespearean actor at her house, Dennis Emery (Wilbur Evans), and Lottie's maid and confidante, Ruby Monk (Mae Barnes). Each of these principals had prominent songs and interaction with the ensemble. Supporting characters included: a boarder's daughter, Baby Betsy Busch; her love interest and a waiter, Mickey Powers; Ruby's son, Half-Note; and Lottie's father, Carl Gibson.[16]

The book of *A Tree Grows in Brooklyn* had created a dichotomy in that earlier show. Aunt Cissy's carefree life overshadowed the tragic story of her sister Kate Nolan and her husband Johnny. Shirley Booth, as Cissy, dominated the show with her comedic presence and songs, causing the more serious aspects of the plot to suffer. With *By the Beautiful Sea*, librettists Dorothy and Herbert Fields created another tug-of-war. This one involved the story of a boarding house owner and her search for love and companionship set against the jovial atmosphere of 1907 Coney Island. Critic William Hawkins said of this theatrical dual, "Miss Booth is asked to follow thunderous numbers with subdued pathos."[17]

As with *A Tree Grows in Brooklyn*, Schwartz and Fields provided a score with variety and artistic confidence colored with turn-of-the-century charm. The first act provided Booth with two lively songs, "The Sea Song" and "Coney Island Boat." The first of these, an expansive, up-tempo waltz sung by Booth and the chorus, extolled the advantages of life by the beautiful sea. It was the title song without the title. "Coney Island Boat" was even more energetic. It was begun by the chorus, who were then followed by Booth singing "In the Good Old Summertime," the 1902 Tin Pan Alley hit. The two were then sung in unison, the chorus against Booth, a display of Schwartz's ability to write a counter melody.[18]

Another pair of songs, one for each act, was written for baritone Wilbur Evans. He was a classically-trained singer, comfortable on radio, in opera, and Gilbert and Sullivan. His first act ballad, "Alone Too Long," spelled out his problems as an aging man, not confident enough to approach Lottie. Historians David Jenness and Don Velsey said of the song, "First it expresses the fear of seeking love; then, in the bridge, it gathers courage (musically, if not verbally); and in the last A-section, it knows that the loved one understands.... The lyric is an example of very simple language with enormous impact."[19] The tuneful lament displayed Evans' voice to be "as rich and virile as ever," with a "warmth of personality."[20] "Alone Too Long" proved that Schwartz could still write a first-rate ballad. In act two, Evans had another ballad, "More Love Than Your Love," an audience favorite. A Boston critic described Evans as a "a good, solid foil for Miss Booth's emotion."[21]

Two songs, again one in each act, were created for Mae Barnes. She had begun her career on Broadway in the twenties, introducing the Charleston to Broadway in "Running Wild." She was nicknamed "the bronze Anne Pennington," and the legendary Bill Robinson called her "the greatest living female tap dancer" after seeing her in "Shuffle Along." Her dance career was curtailed by an auto accident which caused a fractured pelvis. This necessitated a change to singing. Barnes explained, "I took the rhythm from my dancing and put it in my songs."[22] She developed a popular club act, becoming "an animate fixture" at the Bon Soir in Greenwich Village. This evolved into cabaret work in London. A souvenir program for the show described her "special style of vocalizing," adding, "Now when she belts a tune in her inimitable rhythmic fashion, she sets her night club and musical comedy audiences stomping, shouting, cheering as they applaud."[23]

This uncommon ability to engage an audience manifested itself in both of her solo numbers, "Happy Habit" and "Hang Up," songs with "naughty and diverting lyrics."[24] Brooks Atkinson discussed her talent at length in a commentary on the show days after its opening: "Somewhere in the background of her style there seems to be a touch of the minstrel show—the casual prelude to a joke and then the sociable, unpredictable and funny climax. When Miss Barnes begins 'Happy Habit' she sings it straight, and the song belongs to.... Schwartz ... and Fields.... Half way through the song, Miss Barnes breaks out in a ludicrous dance for a moment and the song becomes hers in perpetuity."[25] Similarly, "Hang Up" in the second act brought "the show to life."[26]

These three sets of songs for the principals—Booth, Evans, and Barnes—boded well for the show. *By the Beautiful Sea* had good pre-opening sales and received a promotional preview on *Stage Struck*, the radio show hosted by Mike Wallace which focused on the world of theater. On April 4, four days before the Broadway opening, producers Lawrence Carr and Robert Fryer appeared on the show with cast members who performed a few songs.[27]

But from the beginning there were problems, and the seven-week tryout period—New Haven, Boston, and Philadelphia—was needed. Difficulties involved casting, direction, choreography, vocal arrangements, and songs for Booth. Joanne Woodward had been chosen for the ingénue role. She had been trained in the Group Theatre and "spent too much time in rehearsal questioning her motivation for every step she took, and not enough time learning her lines."[28] As Woodward told a reporter fifty years later, "Shirley Booth put up with this for about four days and then said, 'She's gotta go,' and I was fired."[29] Other changes included: director Charles Walters was replaced by Marshall Jamison; Richard France took over for the original Mickey Powers, Ray Malone; and the hiring of choreographer Helen Tamiris to replace Donald Saddler.[30] Why Saddler was replaced is unclear, as he had great credentials and had just won a Tony award for Best Choreography for *Wonderful Town*. Tamiris was credited with bringing life to the musical with her dances and overcoming the clumsy book.[31]

Problems between Schwartz and two artists in the show—dance composer and arranger Genevieve Pitot and Shirley Booth—lend credence to the idea that he had become difficult to work with. He was showing stress due to ongoing problems: recurrent depression, financial difficulties, and raising a teenage son. This was surprising because in his revue days, Schwartz was often the conciliatory member of the team. He mediated problems and showed kindness to the likes of Agnes de Mille and various singers and dancers. Controversy between Schwartz and Pitot went back six years to *Inside U.S.A.* For that show, Schwartz had wanted to write the ballets, but when he failed to attend rehearsals, Tamiris replaced him with her friend Pitot.[32] As for *By the Beautiful Sea*, most composers would give dance arrangers free rein with their music, but some became territorial, as Steven Suskin suggests Schwartz did, "perhaps self-conscious about the way the rest of the show was going." Donald Saddler, who thought Pitot a genius, saw Schwartz as the problem during dance rehearsals for *By the Beautiful Sea*: "At the orchestra reading in New Haven, all the musicians applauded Pitot. Arthur Schwartz was furious—particularly because they had all cheered, 'Bravo, Pitot.' He complained to me [Saddler], 'She has taken my music and changed it!' In all the revues he had done, they had just taken the songs and repeated them for the dances. Arthur was furious. 'By the time we get to New York,' he told me, 'every note that woman has written will be out.'"[33]

Another manifestation of the Schwartz mood occurred three months into the run of the show. Receipts had suffered in the summer months, leading to Schwartz waiving his royalties. During this time, Booth had approached Schwartz, feeling that an additional song or two for her role as Lottie might lift the show out of its doldrums. Although Schwartz had tremendous respect for Booth, this was apparently asking too much. As Schwartz's attorney, Lee Moselle, explained to Booth's, Arnold Weissberger, "For reasons heretofore discussed, Mr. Schwartz does not feel it appropriate to write additional songs for Miss Booth. He thinks doing this would harm rather than help the show."[34] Weissberger ended the discussion four weeks later, commenting, "Because of the inability of Miss Booth and Mr. Schwartz to see eye to eye in the matter of the additional songs, this request has now been abandoned."[35]

A non-show problem for Schwartz emerged in early 1954 in the form of the California Legislative Committee on Un-American Activities. He had been informed by the Screen Writers' Guild offices that he was on the Committee's list as "a person connected with organization of doubtful Americanism." He sent the committee a two-page, registered letter. He detailed anti–Communist groups with whom he was or had been affiliated, including the Council of the Authors League of America, the League of New York Theatres, and the Screen Writers' Guild as well as involvement in the campaign to elect Dwight D. Eisenhower to the Presidency in 1952. His strongest statement in the letter addressed his involvement in a Democratic organization:

> I lived in California from 1941 to 1947. The only organization of a political nature to which I belonged during that time was called either the Hollywood Democratic Club or the Hollywood Democratic Committee. Its specific purpose was to promote the election of Franklin D. Roosevelt in 1944. Upon the election of Roosevelt I resigned from that organization because several of its leaders wanted to continue it under another name. I felt, along with many other strong anti–Communists, that the proposed new set-up might be a cover for Communists and pro–Communists.

He closed by stressing, "I am shocked to learn from the Screen Writers' Guild that I am included in any list of persons suspected of pro–Communistic sympathies."[36] Nothing came of the allegations, and the matter appears to have blown over.

But this and the various show problems did not deter Schwartz, along with Fields, from writing a wonderful score. It was called by various critics, "robust," "lovely, skillful," and "melodious."[37] A longtime fan of Schwartz, Brooks Atkinson surmised, "After the banal sort of musical comedy Broadway has been afflicted with this season, it is a pleasure to encounter a melodious score, like the one Arthur Schwartz has written here, and original lyrics, like the ones Dorothy Fields has composed."[38]

There were several other contributors to *By the Beautiful Sea* who stood out. Mae Barnes and Wilbur Evans, as previously mentioned, acquitted themselves well. Irene Sharaff was in her element doing period costumes and was lauded by most of the critics. Also recognized was Jo Mielziner, who by this time in his career, had designed sets for over 150 shows. For this one, he created a boarding house, a tunnel-of-love ride, and a boardwalk on Coney Island. His best effort was for the first act finale, where "Shirley Booth appears to leap out of a hot-air balloon and parachute to the ground."[39] Also noted favorably were the orchestrations by Robert Russell Bennett and Joe Glover.

As with *A Tree Grows in Brooklyn*, the highest praise was saved for Shirley Booth. Besides the usual plaudits about her acting, comedy, and even her ability to get a song across, critics focused on the totality of her presence on the stage. Praise included: "Her acting [that] has become ... an instinctive form of expression"[40]; an ability to "take over any stage in town"[41]; and "musical comedy itself: bright, fetching, unpredictable."[42] Booth adapted to what was given to her and was able to go beyond the original concepts of the authors. It was what George S. Kaufman realized when hearing her read only two lines for an audition for *My Sister Eileen*, as previously mentioned. There was a gestalt to her performances, the whole more than the sum of its parts. As expected, she won the Donaldson award for Best Performance by an Actress (Musical) for the 1953–54 Broadway season.

Despite a lot of positives, *By the Beautiful Sea* ran only 270 performances, the same as *A Tree Grows in Brooklyn*. Enthusiasm over Booth,

25. By the Beautiful Sea *and More Dorothy Fields*   263

Schwartz, and Fields had attracted 178 financial backers, but in the end they were disappointed.[43] The problem: THE BOOK. Critics were almost unanimous that the story dragged the songs down. The Fields' book was called "desultory and lacklustre"[44] and "a perfunctory affair with as many loose ends as a session of Congress."[45] Fields' biographer, Charlotte Greenspan, found the show and score lacking in some aspects: "The whole score tends to be up-tempo, almost relentlessly cheerful, and surprisingly impersonal. It generally steers away from defining character. ... It is a pity that Shirley Booth was not given a chance to sing, without ironic distancing, about love."[46] As Ethan Mordden concluded, "So we have too little story and a not very integrated score."[47]

Early in the run of the musical, Schwartz did an interview with Lawrence Perry of the *Springfield* (MA) *Republic*. Their discussion dealt with musical comedy books—their pros and cons. While primarily a composer, Schwartz had been involved in all facets of the theater since the late twenties, working on tabloid shows and the *Grand Street Follies* at that time. He had written a few plays, but none had been produced. Except for occasional constructive criticism, he did not venture into book writing for his musicals. Faced with what he must have realized was the weak book of *By the Beautiful Sea* and what the critics had said about it, he demonstrated his understanding of this aspect of musical comedies in the Perry interview. Paraphrasing Schwartz, Perry wrote, "with everything else approximately perfect, it [the book] is apt to be open to faultfinding." To Schwartz, drama journalists found it easier to criticize the book rather than other elements of a musical. As evidence, he cited Otto Harbach, a librettist with a string of hits, who once told Schwartz, "he had never received a good notice about any of his plots." Victor Herbert, a composer, not a critic, said, "in all his career as a composer he was never provided with a good book."[48]

Schwartz believed that this increased criticism was occurring because the standards of musical comedy books had been improving since the late twenties, pointing to *Show Boat* (1927) and *Of Thee I Sing* (1932). He felt that better books became a necessity in the forties after shows like *Brigadoon*, *Finian's Rainbow*, *South Pacific*, and *Carousel* hit the boards. Schwartz believed, "It was after these productions that the critics really began to have their say." Surprisingly, he found fault with the book of *Oklahoma!*—"by no means good"—acknowledging that "other factors made it a fabulous success." He cited several other hit shows that he felt had inferior books: *Sunny*, *Sally*, *Roberta*, *The Cat and the Fiddle*, and *Lady, Be Good!*[49]

In defense of book writers, Schwartz explained that in musical comedies, songs could be intrusive to the flow of a story. Ideally, songs were supposed to advance the plot, but they often failed. According to Schwartz, "They can—and do—break up a plot into 20 pieces. Musicals that best can stand these diversions and interruptions are those endowed with a theme in which audiences are at once interested and with enough playable scenes to give the feeling of a story well told."[50] He did not mention it, but *By the Beautiful Sea* was plagued by this. The book was "flimsy and inconsequential," a reviewer in 1999 said, only "an excuse for a succession of set pieces for its star."[51] In the entire printed article, neither the interviewer nor Schwartz specifically brought up the book of his show. Perhaps he did not agree with the critics, or he thought that it was injudicious to bring it up.

Two months after *By the Beautiful Sea* opened, Schwartz married Mary O'Hagan Scott, who also went by the name of Mary Grey. She had been born and raised in New York and was a Broadway performer. Her most recent show had been a minor role in *Camino Real* in 1953, a Tennessee Williams play directed by Elia Kazan. Scott had been married to Edward Scott of Los Angeles, and they had a daughter, Madeleine. Grey and Schwartz had met at a gathering at the home of Betty Comden. They were married on June 13, 1954, by New York Supreme Court Justice Henry Clay Greenberg at the Sands Point home of Howard and Tanis Dietz.[52] They would have a son, Paul, born in 1956, who became a composer and conductor.

Through the years, Grey and her stepson, Jonathan Schwartz, would have a rancorous relationship. From his accounts, she was crude and condescending to him, even in his teens. Early in the Schwartz / Grey marriage, Jonathan had come upon love letters his father had written to Grey in 1951–52, well before his mother, Katherine Carrington, had died. He had brought them up to the two of them and caused quite a scene with Arthur caught in the middle.[53] There are several intimate letters from Grey to Schwartz, written in 1952–53, in the Arthur Schwartz Papers at the Library of Congress.[54]

In July 1953, months before the *By the Beautiful Sea* opened, Schwartz had a distasteful encounter while trying to get the score recorded. At the time, Mitch Miller had risen to the top of popular music as an artists and repertoire man for Columbia Records and was considered the "golden boy" in his field. Ironically, it was Goddard Lieberson, a music man of class and taste who was revolutionizing Broadway cast recordings, who had hired Miller. It was Miller's practice to see agents and songwriters on Monday afternoons and allow them to present their latest songs. He was quick to dismiss the people and their songs, and a steady stream went through his office all afternoon. Out of respect for Schwartz and his body of work, Miller gave him a private hearing for the music of the show. Nonetheless, the meeting still left Schwartz uneasy. Historian Ben Yagoda explained, "But the composer couldn't help approaching the meeting with mixed feelings. Private audience or no, it seemed less than respectful that he, Arthur Schwartz, was still forced to appear before this crass A & R man and depend on his good graces."[55]

Of all the songs from the show, only "More Love Than Your Love" interested Miller, and even then, he suggested an additional eight-measure section. Schwartz felt that incorporating these changes would make him beholden to Miller. For Schwartz, "It was a shakedown, pure and simple."

Wedding of Arthur Schwartz and Mary O'Hagan Scott, June 13, 1954. She also went by the name of Mary Grey. *Left to right*: O'Hagan Scott's daughter from her first marriage, Madeleine Scott, Mary O'Hagan Scott, Arthur Schwartz, and Jonathan Schwartz (courtesy Harry Ransom Center, the University of Texas at Austin / *New York Journal American* photograph).

As Yagoda concluded, "This goateed vulgarian ... having the nerve to tell Arthur Schwartz, friend and colleague of George Gershwin and Richard Rodgers, to write a song in AABA—the elemental form of American popular song since Irving Berlin and Jerome Kern were starting out—as if this were some kind of brilliant and original insight! And if the 'improvement' was accepted, no doubt expecting his palm to be greased!"[56] Schwartz would not make the changes and never saw Miller about it again.

Schwartz was aware that musical tastes were changing and that recording companies were favoring more "popular" music: rock 'n' roll, country & western, Latin, novelty, and rhythm & blues. Son Paul Schwartz explained: "He viewed himself as a theatrical writer.... He looked down on 'pop' songs, said they were for people like Jimmy Van Heusen and Sammy Cahn. I told him that was bullshit. 'No, no, no,' he'd say. 'I worked in the theater.' The music *business*, to him, was déclassé."[57]

26

The Mid-Fifties
Odds and Ends and
Mrs. 'Arris Goes to Paris

"We have a wholesome disrespect for philistine producers who care only for the dough and have no true appreciation for work well done."[1]

A few months into the run of *By the Beautiful Sea*, writer Jerome Weidman approached Arthur Schwartz with a proposal for a musical. Weidman had achieved fame with his 1937 novel, *I Can Get It for You Wholesale*, followed closely by *What's in It for Me?* the next year. Both novels featured anti-hero Harry Bogen and were set against the background of New York's Garment District. In a letter of July 1954, Weidman told Schwartz that he thought that the first of these novels could be "the basis for a powerful musical play in the great tradition of 'Guys and Dolls,' 'Pal Joey,' and 'The Pajama Game.'" These musicals featured protagonists with unsavory personalities like Bogen. Weidman stressed to Schwartz, "I believe you are the right composer. I believe, also, I am the right man to do the book, but if you disagree, or if you prefer somebody else, I would be willing to step aside to get the project underway."[2]

Schwartz replied to Weidman within ten days, showing interest. Weidman followed up on August 10, emphasizing that he did not want to shy away from the unlikable Bogen and his world: "I want to stick to the book like a mustard plaster." He went into specifics about his proposed musical, adding that *I Can Get It for You Wholesale* was his "favorite child" of all his works. Besides an outline and ideas for music and lyrics, he added words of encouragement and an admonition: "You are one of our most distinguished musicians. But I would like to tell you that I think this story might be for you the opening of a door to a whole new dimension in your work. I don't think ... you have ever tackled a subject like this. I think you should. ... I think in this story you may find the inspiration for a flood of completely new music, more powerful than your talents have given us thus far, and you have given us plenty." In closing, Weidman stressed, "I would like to add that I feel in myself the stirrings of a libretto that can be a landmark of the American stage. If you add to it the music I know you have in you, we can make it a monument."[3]

For Schwartz, the project never came to fruition. It may not have been a world that he was comfortable addressing, but why he turned the show down is unclear. Weidman went on to win the Pulitzer Prize for Drama in 1960 for *Fiorello!*, sharing the award with George S. Kaufman, Jerry Bock, and Sheldon Harnick. A year after this, Weidman joined forces with composer / lyricist Harold Rome to create the musical *I Can Get It for You Wholesale*. It was a successful David Merrick production directed by Arthur Laurents. The show starred Elliott Gould as Bogen, Lillian Roth as his mother, and Barbra Streisand in the supporting role of Miss Marmelstein, her first on Broadway. During its creation, Weidman and Rome had to battle with Laurents to keep the bite in the Bogen character. This often meant casting the Jewish community in the Garment District in a bad light.

Arthur Schwartz at the piano, circa 1957. The title of the song he is working on is not readable, but the sheet music for "Make the Man Love Me" from *A Tree Grows in Brooklyn*, 1951, rests on the music stand (courtesy Harry Ransom Center, the University of Texas at Austin / *New York Journal American* photograph).

Weidman had worked there in his earlier years and felt strongly about it.[4] *I Can Get It for You Wholesale* opened March 22, 1962, and ran for 300 performances.

In late 1954, Schwartz was again composing music for a Hollywood film. He was teamed with lyricist Sammy Cahn and was to be paid $25,000. In addition, Schwartz and Cahn were also able to negotiate a favorable deal regarding publication of their songs from the movie.[5] Schwartz was enthusiastic about working with Cahn, writing to son Jonathan, "Sammy's very commercially successful, and maybe he'll get me a hit song. He did 'Time After Time,' and I can't remember the others."[6] Cahn had started his career writing specialty material for vaudeville and night club acts in the thirties. His composing partners included Nicholas Brodszky, Saul Chaplin, Gene de Paul, Jule Styne, and Jimmy Van Heusen. Before joining up with Schwartz, Cahn had won an Academy Award with Styne for "Three Coins in the Fountain," from the 1954 movie. He would go on to win three more Oscars and receive twenty-three other nominations. Cahn was "famous for being able to come up at the spur of the moment with a lyric for any occasion."[7]

The Schwartz / Cahn assignment was a Dean Martin and Jerry Lewis comedy, *You're Never Too Young*. Lewis plays a young barber and Martin, a teacher at a girls' school. They accidentally become involved in a jewel heist. Except for Martin's several songs, the movie is mostly Lewis clowning around. Among the cast were Raymond Burr and Veda Ann Borg, as husband and wife jewel thieves, and Diana Flynn as Martin's girlfriend. For the film, Schwartz and Cahn were credited with six songs[8]:

Every Day Is a Happy Day	Love Is All That Matters
I Know Your Mother Loves You	Relax-Ay-Voo
I Like to Hike	Simpatico

The first song in *You're Never Too Young* is "I Know Your Mother Loves You," which Martin sings to his girlfriend at Union Station in Los Angeles. The handsome Italian has an easy-going screen presence and sells the song, accompanied by a strolling quartet at the station.[9] Martin's other notable song is "Simpatico," a Latin number which he sings at a formal dance at the girls' school. One critic said that of all the songs, it "appears to have the best chance of latching on."[10] The best of the Schwartz / Cahn score— "Relax-Ay-Voo"—was never filmed, but was later recorded by Martin and also by Line Renaud.[11] She was a French night club and concert performer who included the song in her act. Those who enjoy Martin's laid-back manner might like *You're Never Too Young*, but the film is mostly for Lewis fans and the French.

In the fall of 1955, Schwartz found himself in Los Angeles for more producing, working with CBS Television on three specials to be aired on *Ford Star Jubilee*, a monthly anthology series. One would be a drama, *Twentieth Century*, starring Orson Welles and Betty Grable and directed by Paul Nickell. It was an adaptation of the Ben Hecht/Charles MacArthur play and aired April 7, 1956.[12] The other two would be plays with music which Schwartz would write in addition to acting as producer. The first of these was a musical version of Maxwell Anderson's 1937 play *High Tor*, for which he had won a New York Drama Critics' Circle Award. Anderson was not interested in television but had agreed to do the teleplay with John Monks, Jr. The two writers and director James Neilson were looking to put "more warmth and heart" into the musical version.[13] Schwartz and Anderson were to write several songs for *High Tor*.

Bing Crosby would be starring as Van Van Dorn, an easy-going idealist who owns a small peak, High Tor, on the Hudson River. Julie Andrews was to play Lise, a phantom Dutch girl living on the peak since lost in a shipwreck 300 years before. Other characters included Dutch sailors lost in the wreck, their captain, his wife, and Van Dorn's girlfriend, Julie, who leaves him after a dispute over High Tor. Crosby had wanted Andrews cast as Lise after seeing her in *The Boy Friend*, her Broadway debut. He had also insisted that the ninety-minute performance be filmed, not shown live, as he did not yet trust the vagaries of live television. *High Tor* was considered by *The Guinness Book of World Records* to be the first made-for-television movie. It was filmed over twelve days in Hollywood with a plaster re-creation of the craggy peak. There was a second film unit sent to New York for shots of the actual mountain. The budget exceeded $300,000, a record for television at the time.[14]

In November 1955, Andrews came to Los Angeles for the filming during a three-month break between *The Boy Friend* and the beginning of rehearsals for *My Fair Lady*. Only twenty years old and new to Los Angeles and filming, she wrote that she was given a warm welcome by her producer and was a house guest at the Schwartz's: "Arthur Schwartz and his wife took me under their wing. They could not have been kinder—treating me as a young protégé about to be launched on a waiting world. They wanted to show me off and have me meet as many people as might help my career. A dinner was held for me at their house in Beverly Hills. It was a big gathering and I was asked to sing a couple of the songs from *High Tor*. Arthur played for me, and though I felt shy, everyone was friendly and appreciative."[15]

Schwartz and Anderson wrote six songs for the broadcast:

John Barleycorn	Once Upon a Long Ago
A Little Love, a Little While	Sad Is the Life of the Sailor's Wife
Living One Day at a Time	When You're in Love

Recorded by Decca, the show has been preserved on a Stage Door Records issuance. It begins with Crosby (Van Dorn) giving a brief account of what had happened on his mountain one night. His narration is interspersed among the six songs and three reprises. Van Dorn's girlfriend Judith, played by Nancy Olson, had grown impatient with Van Dorn for his reluctance to sell his mountain to developers. He sings "Living One Day at a Time," a melodic, easy-going song.[16] Van Dorn and Judith break up but he reaffirms his love for her, singing "When You're in Love," a lush ballad. Alone on his mountain, Van Dorn comes across the ghosts of an old shipwreck, the captain (Everett Sloane) and his wife, Dutch sailors, and a young woman, Lise (Andrews). She sings "Sad Is the Life of the Sailor's Wife." Lise and the captain then reprise "When You're in Love" as they wish to return to their past lives. Lise and Van Dorn meet and strike up a relationship, knowing it cannot last. He sings "A Little Love, a Little While." Van Dorn then finds the two developers stuck in the scoop of a steam shovel. In an up-tempo song, he blames their plight on "John Barleycorn"—intoxication. The song picks up the pace of the sometimes slow-moving telecast. More complications ensue with the developers, the Dutch sailors, and bank robbers who have happened upon the mountain.[17]

Lise and Van Dorn find themselves alone, and she sings a ballad of lost love, "Once Upon a Long Ago." They then play a tender scene, people from two different eras realizing they cannot be together. She tells him, "Your hurt's cured and mine's past curing. This is your age, your dawn, your life to live." As Lise disappears with the sailors, Van Dorn reprises "Once Upon a Long Ago." Eventually, he and Judy are reconciled, and the show closes with his reprise of "A Little Love, a Little While." The CD of *High Tor* also includes two other recordings of "When You're in Love," one by Leroy Holmes and His Orchestra and Chorus and the other by The Lancers. The Holmes rendition captures the haunting aspect of the Schwartz ballad.[18]

High Tor was broadcast on March 10, 1956, only five days before the opening of *My Fair Lady* on Broadway. Ms. Andrews had been a busy young woman. Television ratings were not disappointing because *Ford Star Jubilee* was a popular program, but the show received a tepid critical reception. Andrews wrote, "Alas, *High Tor* was not a memorable piece, and received only lukewarm reviews."[19] Andrews was given praise by those close to the show as seen in an Alan Jay Lerner letter to Andrews: "Nancy [Olson, Lerner's wife] tells me you are absolutely first-rate in *High Tor*—which comes as no surprise. And I also received a letter from Arthur Schwartz with a more gushing version of the same report."[20] Crosby was considered to be wrong for the part, and "that crucial scene between the man of the 1950s and the girl of the 1650s lacked feeling."[21]

In early 1956, Schwartz and Dietz wrote five songs for a television musical adaptation of *A Bell for Adano*. Like *High Tor*, it was a ninety-minute presentation of *Ford Star Jubilee* for CBS Television, the third of Schwartz's projects for the network. It was based on the 1944 Pulitzer Prize-winning novel by John Hersey about the reconstruction of a fictional town, Adano, during the invasion of Sicily. The novel spawned a movie with Gene Tierney, John Hodiak, and William Bendix, as well as a 1944 Broadway play starring Fredric March, which ran for 304 performances.[22] The protagonist is U.S. Army Major Victor Joppolo who comes to Adano as part of an occupation force. Hersey had participated in the invasion of Sicily and bore witness to the occupying forces and the conquered Sicilians. Joppolo represented his positive view of the occupation forces.[23] Despite resistance from a superior officer, he allows the villagers free movement of their water carts. These had been obstructing Allied troop movements in the town, but his permission for them to continue to move about was important to the villagers. He also introduces democracy, lifts fishing restrictions, and procures a new bell for the church. *A Bell for Adano* starred Barry Sullivan as Joppolo and Anna Maria Alberghetti as Tina Tomasino, the local woman with whom he falls in love.

Musicals written for television were still new. The first, *Satins and Spurs*, aired in September 1954. It starred Betty Hutton and was written by Jay Livingston and Ray Evans. In the late fifties, several other popular songwriters would compose television musicals, among them[24]:

Songwriters	Show	Year
Jimmy Van Heusen / Sammy Cahn	Our Town	1955
Arthur Schwartz / Maxwell Anderson	High Tor	1956
Burton Lane / Dorothy Fields	Junior Miss	1957
Richard Rodgers / Oscar Hammerstein	Cinderella	1957
Jule Styne / Leo Robin	Ruggles of Red Gap	1957
Hugh Martin	Hans Brinker and the Silver Skates	1958
Cole Porter	Aladdin	1958
Richard Adler	Gift of the Magi	1958
Alec Wilder / William Engvick	Hansel and Gretel	1958

These shows were done before the widespread use of videotape and presented numerous artistic and technical problems in their live presentations.

The ninety-minute restriction was difficult for the writers: "Economy of written expression—always a hallmark of good musical theater writing in the theater—became an unbending necessity for the medium of television."[25] This time limit affected both script length and number of songs: "Television's relentless dictator—the clock."[26] For *A Bell for Adano*, Schwartz and Dietz wrote five songs:

A Bell for Adano	Okay, Mister Major
Fish	Why Not Surrender?
I'm Part of You	(not recorded)

Most of the collaboration was done by phone with Dietz in New York and Schwartz in Hollywood.[27] It was decided by the creators of the show that the singing roles would be limited to the villagers, which allowed the songwriters to write more for Alberghetti's soprano. Singing was also done by tenors Edwin Steffi and Frank Yaconelli as villagers.

On the television recording, the first song is "A Bell for Adano," an ensemble number featuring a villager stressing to Joppolo and his soldiers the importance of the bell. It goes from ballad to up-tempo and back to ballad. This is followed by two lighthearted songs—"Okay, Mister Major" and "Fish"—the latter featuring a children's chorus. Described as a "very cute and Dietzy song,"[28] they sing of the importance of fish in their lives, explaining it is their "wish" and their "favorite dish." One critic said, "The expressions on the children's faces are refreshing and fascinating."[29] The casting of these children was not easy for producer Schwartz and his team. They auditioned 164 children, and the biggest problem was the "stage mothers" and their "stage-aimed children." According to Schwartz, the children were too often given audition songs by their parents more fit for "Ethel Merman or Johnny Ray." He continued that this killed "whatever natural charm or appeal their offspring might have." Schwartz was ultimately pleased with his young cast: "They are unspoiled and have the proper amount of shyness and restraint. But mainly they sing with a naturalness that is genuine."[30]

Another standout Schwartz / Dietz song was a ballad, "I'm Part of You." It is first sung in Italian by Frank Yaconelli. Alberghetti then interprets the song in English to Barry Sullivan, expressing how she feels about him. It is a wonderful Schwartz melody, and Alberghetti exhibits her soprano with much feeling.[31] The photogenic Alberghetti would continue her successful career with a Tony Award for Best Actress in a Musical in 1962 for *Carnival!* She would appear over fifty times on the *Ed Sullivan Show*.[32] *A Bell for Adano* was aired June 2, 1956. It was generally well-received, with praise for Alberghetti and Sullivan and the inclusion of filmed scenes from the Sicilian countryside. Critics did feel that although the music was good, the inclusion of it and the emphasis on the romance compromised the drama of the original Hersey story.[33]

Schwartz employed his producing skills and intimate knowledge of

Broadway and Hollywood to bring a show to fruition for the American Theatre Wing (ATW). He began work in September 1956, together with ATW president Helen Hayes and director David Alexander, to produce the second annual First Night Ball and Command Performance, *Serenade to the President*. It was an overview of music from the 1890s to the fifties, the years encompassing the life of then President Dwight D. Eisenhower.[34] The program was a benefit for the ATW's Professional Training Program, Community Plays Project, and Hospital Services Committee. Master of ceremonies was Oscar Hammerstein II. Schwartz said of the undertaking, "It's a headache, but I'm glad to be doing it. Our show covers the life span of President Eisenhower. ... It's not a political show, though. It's just great musical moments from all those administrations. We're going to have actors dressed up as the various presidents. The man who played Truman in 'Call Me Madam' will play him again. We haven't found anyone who looks like Eisenhower yet, but we're working on it."[35]

Serenade to the President was presented at the grand ballroom of the Waldorf Astoria in New York on January 27, 1957, at fifty dollars per ticket, raising a good sum for ATW. Due to pressing issues of his office, President and Mrs. Eisenhower were not able to attend. The attendees were a Who's Who of Broadway and Hollywood, and if a star was not on the stage, he or she was in the audience.[36] Among the performers were Helen Hayes, Lena Horne, Ethel Merman, Julie Andrews, Rex Harrison, Sammy Davis, Jr., Sid Caesar, Carl Reiner, Judy Holliday, and W.C. Handy. Hayes did a song-and-dance number, "San Antonio," with four dancers garbed as cowboys. Peter Gennaro and Ellen Ray, from the cast of *Bells Are Ringing*, performed "one of the danciest versions" of "The Carioca," bringing down the house.[37] The presentation was well-received by attendees and critics, one referring to Schwartz's production as "unbelievable."[38] *Serenade to the President* demonstrated once again the versatility of entertainment insider Arthur Schwartz.

Schwartz and Howard Dietz were adept at writing songs for special occasions. In March 1958, they were part of a group that honored drama and musical theater critic Brooks Atkinson, who had been doing reviews for the *New York Times* since 1922 except for a stint reporting on World War II. The surprise party was organized by Helen Hayes and Paula Strasberg, wife of Lee, and was held at Sardi's Restaurant, filled with 130 Broadway luminaries. Atkinson was truly surprised, admitting so in his two-minute speech. He ended his words saying, "I have tried to be on the level."[39] Oscar Hammerstein II was the emcee, and Atkinson was lauded by Ralph Bellamy, head of Actors' Equity. Then letters from playwrights Sean O'Casey and Moss Hart, read by Hammerstein and Kitty Carlisle, added more praise. Mary Martin sang "I'm in Love with a Wonderful Guy" with Richard

Rodgers as accompanist. Paula Strasberg said of the affair, "It was a party given with love, to let Brooks know what theater people think of him."[40]

For their part, Schwartz and Dietz came up with the comic relief of the evening by way of a song, "The Critic." Dietz's lyric declared that a critic has a mother and is a generous human being—in the daytime. The critic in the evening is different, undergoing a Jekyll for Hyde transformation. The song, with great wit and satire, was sung by the songwriters.[41] Hammerstein concluded the evening, saying, "We are here this evening to give Brooks Atkinson a good notice."[42]

This was not the last Broadway party for which the songwriting team would provide the entertainment. In 1959, Moss Hart came out with *Act One*, an account of his early theater days. For the publication party, Hart asked Schwartz and Dietz to contribute to the entertainment. As Dietz remembered it: "Moss suggested that Arthur and I write a musical comedy based on *Act One* and perform it at the party and we did. We wrote a miniature musical which even included a parody of the kind of interminable ballet resolving the plot, which has clogged up most musicals since *Oklahoma!*" Their short musical included a parody of "The Rain in Spain," called "De Oily Boid," accompanied by tambourines.[43] The grand finale was a Schwartz / Dietz original, "It Only Happens Once in a Lifetime," sung by Kitty Carlisle, who called it "a lovely song."[44] Among all the theater folk in attendance at the *Act One* party, it was Schwartz and Dietz who were selected by Moss Hart himself to provide the main entertainment. This had to be a source of pride for the old songwriting team, who were soon to embark on another book musical after twelve years apart.

A Broadway show in the making is a fragile entity and needs constant support until it finds its way. In getting there, the producer, director, and writers need to be on the same page. Arthur Schwartz and Howard Dietz, already well aware of this, were reminded of it in 1959. The show in question was *Mrs. 'Arris Goes to Paris*, based on a novel by Paul Gallico. Schwartz and Dietz had first been approached by set designer Jo Mielziner, who thought the story would lend itself to a musical. Mielziner had been in contact with television writer Michael Dyne, who had written a teleplay of the story that aired on *Studio One* on CBS in April 1958. It starred Gracie Fields in the title role. By the time Mielziner contacted Schwartz and Dietz, Dyne was already working on the book for the musical.[45]

Schwartz and Dietz were enthusiastic about the project, and both had a particular liking for Paul Gallico. A prolific author, he had started his career as a movie critic for the *New York Daily News*, then became a sports writer there. He achieved fame in the latter post when he boxed with Jack Dempsey, was knocked out within two minutes, and wrote a column about it. An early day George Plimpton, Gallico followed this with accounts of batting against Dizzy Dean and his fastballs, then playing golf with Bobby Jones. After years writing sports, Gallico became a free lance writer, penning short stories mostly for magazines, including *Vanity Fair* and the *Saturday Evening Post*. His most famous work was *The Snow Goose*, a novella written for the *Post*. It became a movie for British television starring Richard Harris and Jenny Agutter and was later shown on *Hallmark Hall of Fame* in America. Gallico's novel, *Mrs. 'Arris Goes to Paris*, came out in 1958 and became a bestseller. He wrote three subsequent stories about the "lovable charwoman." The original story was produced as a television movie in 1992 with Angela Lansbury in the title role.[46]

Early on, producer Arnold Saint-Subber (Saint Subber) had been involved but was abruptly replaced by Ray Stark of World Enterprises, Inc., in California.[47] By spring of 1959, Stark had engaged Schwartz, Dietz and book writer Howard Teichmann to create *Mrs. 'Arris Goes to Parris*, with all parties entering into a contract on April 21, 1959.[48] Teichmann had begun as an assistant stage manager for Orson Welles at the Mercury Theatre, later writing and producing for the Mercury Theatre of the Air. He did writing for radio and television, and in 1953, had a hit with *The Solid Gold Cadillac*, which he co-wrote with George S. Kaufman. He went on to author several plays by himself, most notably *Miss Lonelyhearts*, in 1957. *Mrs. 'Arris Goes to Paris* would be his first musical.[49] The contract stipulated that Teichmann would deliver a first draft of the book by July 1, 1959, and that Schwartz and Dietz would deliver "what they deem to be the major musical compositions of the play" by August 15. Stark was to produce the musical by February 1, 1960.[50]

Schwartz and Dietz began work on the songs within a few weeks, without the advantage of a book. Because Teichmann had intended to follow the novel closely, the songwriters felt they could approximate where songs might be placed and worked from there. By June 30, 1959, they had completed seven "principal songs," had them recorded, and sent the demonstration record off to Gallico in London. In the accompanying letter, Dietz gave a brief description of each song and cautioned Gallico, "Bear in mind these songs are not finally final, nor are they presented in ultimate running order. And we'd be pleased if you can keep them to your intimate self, as we do not want them loosed prematurely on a gossipy world."[51]

Gallico responded favorably by July 12, saying, "I liked the music, which seemed to me fresh, melodic and memorable, and the lyrics are loaded with amusing lines." He especially liked "Who Can? You Can!," and in his comments on that song, Gallico exhibited an understanding of what songwriters of a musical are up against: "Of course I am quite stiff with admiration for the ability and talent that it takes to write a song which not only is a part of the plot ... but which also can be lifted completely out of context and sung and enjoyed or listened to as a pop song quite on its own, and whose lyrics then take on still another meaning." Gallico continued in a complimentary vein, voicing a few minor complaints, and suggesting songs for specific characters. Even his strongest thought was expressed tentatively: "I was only wondering whether a slightly more Gallic idiom might not be developed in the music from time to time, to give one the feeling of Paris and France musically as well as visually." Dietz would later assure him that this would be taken care of with the orchestrations. Gallico told Schwartz and Dietz that after hearing their songs, "You both have now got me really excited over this."[52]

Within three weeks of the Gallico letter, Schwartz and Dietz had delivered twelve songs to World Enterprises and Ray Stark, well within their deadline[53]:

Au Revoir, Paree	I Don't Want to Go Home
Before I Kiss the World Goodbye	I Never Get Anywhere on Time
	I'll Make You Happy, Cherie
Diplomacy	Montage—Musical Scene
Don't Go Away, Monsieur	The Sewing Circle on the Seine
The Gendarme Never Loses His Head	Toujours Gai
	Who Can? You Can!

Two of these songs were taken from previous Schwartz / Dietz projects: "Don't Go Away, Monsieur" from *Between the Devil* (1937) and "I'll Make You Happy, Cherie" from *The Gibson Family* radio show (1934).

It is unclear whether Teichmann met his July 1 deadline for delivery of the first draft, but overall, it seemed that progress was being made on *Mrs. 'Arris Goes to Paris*. Behind the scenes, however, things had been grinding to a halt due to disagreements among the principals. From Antibes on the French Riviera, Gallico wrote a letter to Katharine (Kay) Brown, Teichmann's agent from MCA Artists, and courtesy copied Schwartz, Dietz, Teichmann, and Stark. His intention was "to clear the air, bring about an understanding, and contribute to what we all want: namely, to get this show on the boards." Gallico felt that despite being across the Atlantic, he had kept abreast of matters and had recently had a meeting with Dietz in London. Gallico said of their discussion, "Howard agreed that he and Arthur had been beastly to Tyke [Teichmann], and said that Tyke had likewise been beastly to him, or to them.... If I might suggest, no one has been entirely free from error or blame in this crack-up: if Howard and Arthur have been too demanding and aggressive, possibly Tyke has been too sensitive, and Ray has been too far away."[54] The aggressiveness on the part of the songwriters had come about as they pushed Teichmann to produce a book as soon as possible. Helen Hayes was still considering signing on to the show, but first needed something more concrete—like a book.[55]

Gallico further discussed the need for a strong director to pull everything together and "be boss," noting that Dietz "admitted that Arthur was a difficult man to boss." Later in the letter, Gallico added that he had received complaints that "Arthur tries to run everything." Gallico criticized the songwriters for writing ahead of the book, stating the obvious: "I had always thought that the book writer and song writers had to work together most closely on a show, step by step, so that the songs would be really integrated into the script, would grow out of the action and into the action, and would move that action forward." Gallico appreciated book writers, saying, "I doff my skimmer to those writers of good musical comedy books, who really have to practice literary economy." This he followed with praise for Teichmann as a dramatist, but added, "he would be helping himself and us if he listened to someone of experience in the musical field." In his letter to Brown, Gallico also found fault with Ray Stark and Kermit Bloomgarden, Stark's representative in New York, for not taking charge of the project, and especially for not hiring a director as yet. Within the eight-page letter, there are other complaints and observations, but with a conciliatory tone Gallico concludes, "all have been a little to blame, [and] no one is really out to do anyone in the eye."[56]

When the dust settled, the principal problem seemed to be Ray Stark. Dietz described him to Helen Hayes as "very manana."[57] Stark had been dragging his feet on selection of a director, even though he and all three writers had tentatively agreed, at a September 3 meeting, on pursuing Robert Lewis, Rouben Mamoulian, or Cyril Ritchard to direct the show. Stark was also slow in finding a new co-producer in New York as Kermit Bloomgarden had turned out to be unhelpful to the cause. Beyond this, Stark wanted to set back the date of production to autumn 1960, several months after the contractual February 1. On October 15, 1959, Stark had an extended conversation with Howard Reinheimer, attorney for Schwartz and Dietz. In that conversation, Stark expressed that he felt that the three writers could not get along and wanted to replace all of them. He believed that finding a new producer was not the answer "because of the incompatibility of the three authors." Stark admitted that his real intention for *Mrs. 'Arris Goes to Paris* had been to do it as a movie, but he had agreed to a musical as this was Gallico's wish.[58]

Hearing all of this from the Reinheimer / Stark conversation was the last straw for Dietz, and he wrote Gallico a ten-page letter on October 16. After detailing what had been going on, Dietz speculated to Gallico: "Stark's pattern of behavior convinced Arthur and me long before September that while he was occasionally making a motion toward producing the show, his real intention had been <u>not</u> to produce it but instead to force us by his tactics to lose our rights, and then hopefully to secure them once more from you for a motion picture. ... In short, his record of bad faith is clear as can be.... I am afraid, however, that his sole intention for a long time has been to sabotage the production." As might be expected, Dietz made a plea to Gallico for an extension of their rights: "To deprive us of the rights when they expire would be grossly unfair, and I think these rights should be given to Schwartz and me, and, of course, to Teichmann too unless he chooses to withdraw." Dietz closed the letter saying, "We have a wholesome disrespect for philistine producers who care only for the dough and have no true appreciation for work well done."[59]

The musical of *Mrs. 'Arris Goes to Paris* never came to be. A new co-producer was never found, no casting was done, and the writers ceased any further work together. Of Schwartz and Dietz, it might be said that they had not been writing a musical in a collaborative manner. Writing songs ahead of a book might work for revues, but not for an integrated musical. There is no doubt they had been difficult for Teichmann to deal with, seeming to be in a hurry to get things done. They were older and more experienced. Schwartz, especially, could have been more patient. Failure of the show was partly their doing. Conversely, Teichmann may have been too hesitant on the whole project. His limited experience in musicals was evident. If Stark or Bloomgarden and a strong director had been more involved, perhaps the show might have been salvaged.

The story was produced as a made for television movie in 1992 under the same title. It starred Angela Lansbury, Diana Rigg, Lothaire Bluteau, and Omar Sharif. The teleplay was by John Hawkesworth.[60] There were no songs. Schwartz and Dietz were able to salvage two songs from their ill-fated *Mrs. 'Arris Goes to Paris* for later productions: "Who Can? You Can!," sung by Barbara Cook in *The Gay Life* (1961), and "Before I Kiss the World Goodbye," performed by Mary Martin in *Jennie* (1963).

27

The Gay Life
Barbara Cook and "Magic Moment"

"I have seen shows in the past recover from a poor start and 'The Gay Life' may be one of them."[1]

The day before the opening of Arthur Schwartz's new show, his friend Johnny Loeb sent him a most encouraging telegram:

I HOPE THE CRITICS WONT BE ALONE TOGETHER DANCING IN THE DARK EITHER TOO YOUNG OR TOO OLD TO BE UNDER YOUR SPELL BUT INSTEAD WILL SAY THIS IS IT HOW SWEET YOU ARE AND SEAL IT WITH A KISS FOR YOU AND I KNOW AN OLD FLAME NEVER DIES AND AS I SEE YOUR FACE BEFORE ME OH BUT I DO WISH THE GREATEST OF SUCCESS TO YOU AND THE NIGHT AND THE MUSIC[2]

In addition to a heartfelt greeting, the telegram managed to incorporate twelve Schwartz song titles. The show was *The Gay Life* and like Loeb's telegram, it spawned hope and good feeling.

The show starred Barbara Cook and Walter Chiari. She was the leading ingénue of the day on Broadway and had had lead roles in *Plain and Fancy* (1955), *Candide* (1956), and *The Music Man* (1957). The last role garnered a 1958 Tony Award for Best Featured Actress in a Musical for her. In *The Gay Life*, she played Liesl, a naïve young woman who has a lifelong crush on Anatol, a well-known lothario. The book writers for the show, Fay and Michael Kanin, took the 1893 Arthur Schnitzler one-act play, *Anatol*, and instead of focusing on the title character, emphasized the role of Liesl. This allowed Schwartz and Dietz to write several songs for Cook. Also featured in the story were Anatol's past girlfriends played by Elizabeth Allen, Jeanne Bal, Yvonne Constant, and Anita Gillette, all good singers and beautiful. Jules Munshin played the comic role of Max, Anatol's best friend. Besides Schwartz, Dietz, and the Kanins, the creative team for producer Kermit Bloomgarden included director Gerald Freedman, set designer Oliver Smith, lighting designer Jean Rosenthal, and costume designer Lucinda Ballard, the wife of Howard Dietz.[3]

To audition Chiari, Schwartz had traveled to Italy at the request of Bloomgarden. The last overseas casting Schwartz had done was in the United Kingdom in 1937 for *Virginia*. Schwartz and Bloomgarden hoped that Chiari, known as "the Italian Danny Kaye," would fill the bill as the "comic foreigner" for the role of Anatol. To entice Chiari to sign, Schwartz played him songs from the score. Son Jonathan Schwartz described the trip: "Arthur set out alone, and what he found in the hills of Tuscany was an excitable, flamboyant leading man who drove Arthur through the mountains with ferocious speed in an Italian sports car, shouting at him happily in speedy Italian. My father hired him, I've always thought, just to get out of Italy alive."[4]

The development of the show was uncertain from the start. Director Freedman was found wanting by Chiari's agent, Eugene Lerner, who wrote to Bloomgarden the day after the opening in Detroit: "I do not believe that there is any doubt that the Director is gravely insecure about how to resolve his particular problems. His confusion is evident in his failure to recognize certain serious and fundamental principles in staging of his material and the direction of his principals. The heaviness of the book, its old-fashioned elements have weighed heavily on him."[5] Freedman retained program credit as director but was replaced during the Detroit run by Herbert Ross who was already doing the choreography. The show was in much better hands with him, as "Ross provided the wit that the Kanins too often didn't; he gave them class and sex appeal."[6]

The Kanins had problems with the book from the outset and could not decide on whether the show was about Anatol or Liesl, to which Lerner replied, "They are both terribly important, equally important. Audience adoration for Liesl must equal adoration for Anatol, and vice versa."[7] That decision was taken out of the hands of the Kanins when it was discovered that Chiari was a poor singer. Songs were gradually turned over to Cook, and it became her show. Jonathan Schwartz wondered about Chiari's casting, explaining:

> Chiari's singing voice was grating, unmusical, and deadly. Coaches arrived and huddled with Chiari for hours, improving Chiari's instrument only slightly. Why, how, please tell me, did Arthur, one of the better melodists in the United States, engage this guy without hearing so much as a note of his singing? Gradually, on the road, when it became obvious that Walter Chiari was, at best, a distressing singer, more and more songs were given to Barbara Cook, even one last-minute enormous production number called "The Label on the Bottle."[8]

This is not to say that Chiari was without assets. Favorable comments on him included "a looker," "a gifted comic, able even in slapstick," and "an Italian Cary Grant."[9] Cook said of her co-star, "He wasn't used to the kind of discipline that was needed. He had a great deal of charm, but it was lost on the audience because he was so hard to understand. He didn't sing terribly well.... But he had a great, great comic sense, and he was very sexy."[10] Perhaps because he had hired him and felt a bit defensive, Schwartz had praise for Chiari, writing to his agents seven weeks into the run, "Walter's performance has been consistently good, and at the curtain calls his applause usually exceeds that of Barbara Cook."[11] In light of the admiration critics had for Cook, this last statement seems doubtful and may have been Schwartz trying to prop up the mood of the star's agents.

The book had its problems, and major changes were being made at a pace greater than most Broadway musicals. Nine songs were cut along the way to Broadway. In Detroit, it was decided to cut the opening scene in which one of Anatol's girlfriends pretends to jump off a bridge. A Motor City critic lamented the change, saying, "It was an unconventional opening for a musical show, it had warmth and wit, and it broke with hide-bound tradition."[12] Along with that scene, Anita Gillette and her only song, "I Lost the Love of Anatol," were also taken out. Gillette remembered, "I had only one scene and one song, and the most beautiful gown in the whole show.... It was a beautiful song."[13] This scene was replaced by a more conventional opening, the chorus singing "The Gay Life," which was soon to be eliminated as well.

Major changes did not stop here. When the production hit Broadway, the first two songs in the show were "What a Charming Couple" and "Why Go Anywhere at All?" After opening, the decision was made not to do the story as a flashback, which eliminated these two numbers. "Why Go Anywhere at All?" was a definite loss, sung by soprano Jeanne Bal as one of Anatol's lovers. It is a rhythmic ballad, "filled with new melodic ideas; in fact, the song suggests a true renaissance of theater music."[14] Fortunately, it remained on the cast recording.[15]

It was clear that the Kanins, primarily screenwriters with little musical experience, could not get their book in order, an occurrence Schwartz had become accustomed to. His great scores with Howard Dietz or Dorothy Fields seldom led to hit shows if the books failed. Of *The Gay Life*, historian Ethan Mordden wrote, "The score, marking the reunion of Arthur Schwartz and Howard Dietz, was a dream; the book, a mess. They were still trying to fix the show after it opened, still fixing it when it closed, are perhaps fixing it now in Cain's Warehouse."[16] A critic for the *Wall Street Journal* declared, "its worst failing is that it never sets a genuine mood, and we have farce, romance and buffoonery pretty well scrambled."[17]

There is no doubt Schwartz had reservations about the book. As the show was struggling six weeks into its run, he displayed his frustration about it, as well as aggravation, with the listing of *The Gay Life* in *The New Yorker*. In doing so, he appears to reveal his opinion of the book: "Howard

Dietz and I wrote only the songs. The book was written by Fay and Michael Kanin.... I appeal to the fairness of The New Yorker to alter the wording so as not to make it appear to your readers that Howard Dietz and I wrote the entire show."[18]

The weakness of the book was unfortunate because the show had much to offer. Receiving frequent critical praise were the sets of Oliver Smith and the costumes of Lucinda Ballard. Of Ballard, one reviewer said, "She not only has re-evoked the flourish and elegance of an era, but she has recaptured the loftiest level of taste as well."[19] She would win the Tony Award for Best Costume Design; Smith received a Tony nomination. Little was mentioned of Herbert Ross's direction as Gerald Freedman was still listed as director despite his firing in Detroit, but the critics loved the choreography of Ross. Orchestrations by Don Walker and conductor / musical director Herbert Greene were appreciated, and of particular note was the instrumentation: "Walker built his score around the cimbalom, which is a sort of xylophone with strings (instead of metal bars), played with mallets, a mainstay of old-time Hungarian tearooms. Walker placed the cimbalom where the harp might usually be; what would otherwise have been the piano chair was split between accordion and celesta ... the orchestration—from the opening cimbalom cadenza in the overture—is suffused with unusual, vibrant colors."[20] The cimbalom was also prominent in the second act gypsy song and dance, "Come A-Wandering with Me."

As for the score, it was called "waltzy when it feels like it and incisive when necessary."[21] Another critic called it "an attractive score by Arthur Schwartz in the near-Viennese manner and Howard Dietz's characteristically sprightly lyrics."[22] Gerald Bordman surmised, "A number of musicologists have hailed Schwartz's score as one of his masterpieces."[23] With the score for *The Gay Life*, as with most of his previous works, Schwartz demonstrated an ability to write melodies for different styles, tempos, rhythm, and settings. As for lyrics, another reviewer said, "Mr. Dietz is seldom willing to be content with an obvious line or an easy rhyme."[24]

An early scene in Act One finds Cook's character, Liesl, realizing she is smitten with Anatol and declaring her love to him. This ballad, "Magic Moment," was cited by nearly every critic as the hit of the show. Composer / critic Vernon Duke called it "one luscious morsel of a love song, especially as served up by Barbara Cook."[25] One reviewer felt the song helped the slow-starting show gain "headway,"[26] and another felt it "will haunt us for a sweet long time."[27] The song is one of Schwartz's great ballads, and Cook delivers it perfectly, a prominent reason for the reviewers gushing over her. There are numerous theater songs that were excellent and the composers knew it, but then a great voice and performer comes along and elevates the song. One gets that feeling with Cook and "Magic Moment." In other

Schwartz shows, Libby Holman did it with "Something to Remember You By" in *Three's a Crowd* and Thelma Carpenter with "Blue Grass" in *Inside U.S.A.* As for Cook and *The Gay Life*, one New York critic declared, "She shapes a song into a delicate cup of life and … places notes precisely and modulates them into subtle meanings."[28]

"Magic Moment" is followed by a duet for Cook and Chiari—"Who Can? You Can"—probably the latter's finest musical turn in the show. It is Dietz at his best, "a catchy tune … based on the brave although illogical idea that anybody can do anything if he just sets his mind to it."[29] "Oh, Mein Liebchen" finds Schwartz in a waltz mode, where he was always comfortable, as he demonstrated on "The Beggar Waltz" (*The Band Wagon*), "Sweet Nevada" (*Park Avenue*), and "If You Haven't Got a Sweetheart" (*A Tree Grows in Brooklyn*). *The Gay Life* was, after all, a musical based in Vienna, and with "Oh, Mein Liebchen," "Mr. Schwartz caught the Straussian tempo and lilt."[30] Alec Wilder called it "a rousing waltz … which, in spite of the title, never uses it as an excuse to wallow in Viennese sentimentality. Rather is it simply a strong, honest waltz."[31]

Two second act songs deserve mention. "Something You Never Had Before" is another Schwartz ballad that gave Cook the chance to again bring down the house. Once more, Wilder: "it's as refined and distilled and in as high style as any great Kern song. It does unusual, unexpected things and deserves to be listed among the great theater songs."[32] The last big dance number involved Magda, a Hungarian night club singer, played by Elizabeth Allen. She sings "Come A-Wandering with Me" to Anatol who is attempting to hide behind a menu. It was Allen's only solo in the show, and her performance earned her a Tony nomination for Best Performance by a Featured Actress in a Musical. She would go on to another Tony nomination for Best Actress in a Musical in 1965 for *Do I Hear a Waltz?*, co-starring Sergio Franchi.

A Gay Life opened November 18, 1961, and despite mixed reviews, Schwartz was optimistic about the show. He wrote to Max Gordon three weeks after the opening, "As you can well imagine the road tour was purgatory but that's all behind us and I hope we're in for a run."[33] But despite the performances of Cook and Allen, the work of Lucinda Ballard and Oliver Smith, and a strong Schwartz / Dietz score, the show could not catch on. In a letter to Chiari's agents, Henry Kaufman and Eugene Lerner, Schwartz was at a loss to explain the lackluster audiences: "Our show mystifies me. I have seen most of the performances since we opened and with the exception of a few tough benefit audiences [*sic*] the great majority go out liking the show very much. But, we have not as yet shown signs of switching from the doubtful to the hit class."[34] He goes on to mention an appearance of the cast on the *Ed Sullivan Show* and upcoming coverage in *Life* magazine.

That article was brief, but complimentary, especially of the sets and costumes. *Life* mentions the show's rocky start but then declares, perhaps prematurely, that it was now "spinning like a musical top."[35] Schwartz stressed to Kaufman and Lerner that several cast members had appeared on media broadcasts to promote *The Gay Life*, and that he had done twenty-seven himself. He was also planning a six-day tour of the Midwest to promote the show and the Capitol Records cast recording, for which Capitol had invested $200,000 for the rights. In his final comment, Schwartz leaves a bit of hope, saying, "I have seen shows in the past recover from a poor start and 'The Gay Life' may be one of them, but as I said at the outset, we are puzzled by the failure to catch on in a big way considering audience reaction."[36]

The Gay Life would close in late February 1962, after only 113 performances. Speculations for the reasons were many, mostly focusing on the ever-changing book and its paucity of humor. Schwartz had maintained a close relationship with Chiari and his agents during work on the show. When closing of the show was imminent, agent Eugene Lerner wrote to Schwartz: "We know that you personally have done everything that a human being can do to make the show a success. Perhaps all the labor, all the creative energy expended was not sufficient to overcome the major flaws in the book."[37] Opinions were split on Chiari, but Dietz was rather hard on him: "Barbara Cook and all the singers liked their parts, but our leading man couldn't act, dance, sing or speak English, which was a handicap."[38]

There was also the ever-present competition on Broadway, particularly stiff during the 1961–62 season. The following musicals—total performances in parentheses—were playing on Broadway at the time: *Camelot* (873); *Carnival* (719); *Do Re Mi* (400); *How to Succeed in Business Without Really Trying* (1,417); *Irma La Douce* (524); *Milk and Honey* (543); *My Fair Lady* (2,717); *The Sound of Music* (1,443); and *The Unsinkable Molly Brown* (532).[39] As mentioned in other chapters, there are only so many shows a Broadway lover can attend. A musical about old Vienna could get lost in the shuffle among so many wonderful musicals.

More specific insight into the failure of *The Gay Life* was offered years later by James Maher, an associate of Alec Wilder:

> This score raises some interesting questions. I believe it to have been one of the finest of the Dietz and Schwartz scores. The music was tasteful, full of melodic invention, sophisticated, and, in another era, may well have found a wide audience outside the theater. But, it never had a chance to find such an audience. The rock era closed the door on all such music and its mature sensibilities. Further, the theater audiences may not have been aware of the consistent high quality of the score because of the casting. America had been charmed by Ezio Pinza's broken English; it turned an indifferent ear to Walter Chiari's. Another point: the modern musical theater audience no longer distinguishes between functional theater music and songs that merit an independent career as standard popular songs.

To these comments, Wilder added, "There is such sadness in the renaissance of Schwartz's high style just at the point when 'good taste' became an obsolete phrase.... Of course the most dramatic and ironic burst of talent occurred in 'The Gay Life' when the handwriting of the Beatles was on the wall."[40] This may sound like resentment, but Wilder and Maher were certainly not alone. Like it or not, rock 'n' roll was here to stay, and as for rock and musical theater, *Hair, Jesus Christ Superstar, Godspell, Grease,* and *Pippin,* among others, were on the horizon.

It should be mentioned what an effect the failure of *The Gay Life* had on its songwriters. In 1954, Howard Dietz had been diagnosed with Parkinson's Disease and would be bothered intermittently with tremors, weakness, spasms, and rigidity as his disease progressed. He referred to it as "unbearable, but not totally incapacitating." In the late fifties, he was still at M-G-M where there was upheaval in the executive offices. The extra work and stress of all this exacerbated the Parkinson's and led him to resign from M-G-M, as he planned to "devote my time to writing shows with Arthur Schwartz."[41] The effects of the disease took a toll on his participation in show preparation, as he explained to interviewer Joan Taylor in 1971:

> HD: Um. I had two flop shows because of Parkinson's.
> J: I assume one of them was *Jennie*, what was the other one?
> HD: *The Gay Life*
> J: Oh, I didn't realize that was a flop.
> HD: It played a bit.
> J: Well, you said that you did two, the last two shows which you characterized as flops because of Parkinson's, how did it enter in?
> HD: I didn't have the energy to make a show come out my way.... You go to the theatre, not feeling good, and something is changed in the show. You don't have the energy to complain until a week later. Then they say why didn't you speak up? It was very awkward.[42]

His statement speaks to the need for Broadway show creators to be hands-on, as opposed to Hollywood, where "you just shut up and write your nice songs and leave the rest to us." Wilfrid Sheed explained, "On Broadway, contrariwise, the more you could do for yourself the better, from picking the project ... to placing the songs and protecting them just by hanging around rehearsals and making a pest of yourself."[43] Dietz just did not have the strength to do this. Despite improved medications, the disease would continue to severely affect his life until his death in 1983.

As for Arthur Schwartz and *The Gay Life*, Jonathan concluded, "My father, ashamed and desperate, took to his couch, which I never visited."[44]

28

Jennie and Mary Martin

"Please, in the interest of turning our show into a possible success, show us the respect we have earned."[1]

The producer of a musical comedy is supposed to bring together a creative team and facilitate their efforts. The star of the musical should do his or her best to take what is written and work with it. When the producer and star are husband and wife and become overly involved in the creation of the show, it can mean trouble. With Arthur Schwartz and Howard Dietz's last show—*Jennie*—there were problems from the beginning, many of them due to star Mary Martin and her husband, producer Richard Halliday. This was unfortunate because Schwartz had always loved her work and "the acquisition of Mary Martin ... made him positively giddy. This was to be his moment, his Mary Martin time of life."[2] Schwartz believed in his star and initially invested $20,000—two percent—along with $5,000 from son Jonathan.[3] The majority of the beginning $500,000 investment was supplied by Martin, Halliday, co-producer Cheryl Crawford, and producer / director Alan Pakula, who had brought the idea to Crawford and Halliday. Martin and Crawford had teamed up successfully in 1943 for *One Touch of Venus*, but until *Jennie*, they had not found another project that appealed to both of them.

The genesis of *Jennie* was a biography by Marguerite Courtney of her mother, actress Laurette Taylor. Taylor had started her career in turn-of-the-century melodramas, had a hit with *Peg o' My Heart* in 1913, and finished her career in Tennessee Williams' *The Glass Menagerie* in 1946. Martin and Halliday had followed Courtney during the writing of her book, thinking that Martin would be perfect as Laurette Taylor if it were adapted for the stage. However, they could not get a director or another producer interested, and the project was dropped. Soon after that, Martin and Halliday were offered *Blood and Thunder*, the biography of Charles Taylor, Laurette's husband, an actor / manager known as the "Master of Melodramas."[4] This had been written by Taylor's son, Dwight.

Humorist / playwright S.N. Behrman was to write the book for *Blood and Thunder*, and Schwartz and Dietz would do the score. By January 1962, they had written three songs and Schwartz was enthusiastic about the project, declaring, "our show will bring back the flavor of the old melodramas, the incredible spectacles that they used to use on the stage, fires, train wrecks, the buzz saw getting closer to the heroine."⁵ But *Blood and Thunder* failed to develop as a musical. During this early attempt with Behrman, Schwartz and Dietz had been working in Barbados at the home of Claudette Colbert. As Dietz detailed, "So we went to Barbados, the blue water paradise, and there we met up with an old friend, the dazzling star off-stage or on, off-screen or on, Claudette Colbert.... She lives in Barbados, and we could have the use of her beautiful piano and her beach on one condition—that we play and sing for her charming guests, (those non-charming were absent)."⁶ Behrman also happened to be in the Caribbean at the time, but before he could do any work with the songwriters, there or back in New York, he was taken off the assignment. Again Dietz, discussing Behrman's treatment: "When we got back to town, we found out that the Dick-Mary-Donahue [*sic*] axis, had washed their hands of Behrman some weeks ago, but they hadn't told him or us. Such treatment he [Behrman] said, could not be surpassed even in the more insensitive reaches of Hollywood."⁷

Arthur Schwartz and Howard Dietz during their work on *Jennie*, the 1963 musical starring Mary Martin. Dietz had been suffering from Parkinson's Disease for nearly ten years, reflected in his appearance and posture (courtesy Harry Ransom Center, the University of Texas at Austin / Joseph Abeles Studio Collection, 1935–1975).

Despite this upheaval, Martin hoped to do the show, saying, "I wanted *Jennie* to be a big success because I loved Laurette Taylor. She was so close to me and really was very precious."⁸ Martin had turned down the roles of

Fanny Brice in *Funny Girl* and Dolly Levi in *Hello, Dolly!* to do the show. She and Halliday went back to the Courtney biography and at Pakula's suggestion, enlisted Max Shulman to write a book and focus on two years in Laurette Taylor's life. Shulman had troubles with the story and had to put up with interference from director Vincent Donehue, who had been hired early on. He was Martin's preferred director, having guided her through *The Sound of Music* and *Annie Get Your Gun* as well as *Peter Pan* on television.[9] Shulman wrote to Schwartz and Dietz, "The reason you haven't heard from me is that I'm still fighting with Donehue about Act II."[10] Within a few months, Shulman left the project. Problems with Donehue would continue, as his vision of the musical and the Laurette Taylor story differed from not only Schwartz and Dietz, but even from that of Martin. Soon after Shulman left, Arnold Schulman was taken on as book writer. He had just had his first success as a playwright with *A Hole in the Head* and found success later on as a screenwriter with *Love with the Proper Stranger*, *Wild Is the Wind*, and his own *A Hole in the Head*.[11]

By this time, Martin, Halliday, and co-producer Cheryl Crawford changed the name of the show to *Jennie*. They wanted to distance it from the play *Laurette*, which had opened in September 1960 starring Judy Holliday. It had closed out of town, due in part to Holliday's health. The producers of *Jennie* then hired choreographer Matt Mattox and costume designer Irene Sharaff. Lucinda Ballard, Dietz's wife and an award-winning designer, had been originally slotted for the job. At Martin and Halliday's insistence, Sharaff replaced Ballard. Martin biographer Ronald L. Davis said, "she was unceremoniously replaced and informed by letter that the producers had discovered a prior commitment with Sharaff."[12]

During these months, Schwartz and Dietz were working at one of three places: their suites in the Park-Shelton Hotel; Claudette Colbert's beach house on Barbados; and Dietz's home on Long Island, a 200-year-old farmhouse. The last of these was preferred by Dietz as his Parkinson's Disease had become worse. In a Detroit interview during tryouts of the show, Lucinda Ballard said, "They're sleeping about five hours a night now. Howard isn't in the best of health, so I see that he takes his pills, eats properly, and catnaps when he can."[13]

Progress was slow through most of 1962 and into the next year as Schwartz, Dietz, and Schulman endured Halliday's meddling. Typical of it was a letter from Halliday to Dietz in February 1963. After making two specific suggestions for changes in the lyrics, he goes on in a condescending tone: "You will try to understand, please, in case either hits you in a sensitive spot. It's just that we are so pleased and proud and happy, we so love what you and Arthur are doing, that we can't stop looking, seeking, and hoping that a soul won't find a single syllable that isn't top Dietz—top everything.... It does have the feel, the smell, the something that is worth cherishing, perfecting, working for, that can make exciting theatre."[14] This was only a sampling of Halliday's interference.

Martin engaged in similar behavior, especially when it came to lyrics. She and Dietz came to blows over one of the show's best songs, "Before I Kiss the World Goodbye." He discussed this years later in his appearance in the *Lyrics & Lyricists* series:

> Question: ...What does a lyricist do when, during the rehearsal of a new show, the star starts making word changes and then even line changes. OR when the star expresses disapproval and asks for a change. [sic]
>
> Answer: Actually you have asked two questions. When a star starts throwing her weight around by making lyric changes that cancel out the lyricist's style and content, that's a serious matter. However, when a star asks for a change and the reason for that change is logical, then the lyricist should do his or her best to supply the change. Sometimes, you even do it when the reason for the change is not so logical. In the show "Jennie," Arthur and I wrote a song for Mary called "When I Kiss the World Goodbye." Miss Martin objected to a couplet in the song. Here is what aroused her ire:
>
> Before I go to meet my maker I want to use the salt left in the shaker
>
> She thought these lines were filthy. She refused to sing them.
>
> Although I didn't agree with her reason (I certainly didn't plan this couplet to be filthy), I made the change.[15]

Schwartz threatened to take the matter up with the Dramatists' Guild but never did, although this caused him and Dietz to be barred from the theater for several days.[16] Of the whole incident, Dietz concluded, "Mary's nun had triumphed. Mary Martin was a great performer and fun. She was victimized by her lack of trust in anyone but herself."[17]

Only a week before the New York opening, she would go as far as omitting an entire chorus of a song. She did this on "Where You Are," a duet with Robin Bailey, and Dietz called her on it. Halliday and stage manager Randy Brooks were apparently in on it as well. To the latter, Dietz had stipulated, "Don't allow any deviations from the score without getting my or Arthur Schwartz's permission."[18] Nonetheless, she went on to do it at the next performance. Cheryl Crawford saw the incident differently and gave another perspective on Schwartz during this difficult time for all concerned: "Arthur Schwartz told me that if Mary cut any of the songs without first informing him or Dietz or their attorneys he would take it up at once with the Dramatists' Guild and we might lose the rights [to the songs]. He pointed out that he was a member of the Guild's Council and was prepared to make maximum legal trouble.... He was adamant about what he said were 'his rights.' I felt he was ready to 'cut off his nose to spite his face.' I found him unmovable by reason or anger."[19]

Martin's demands went beyond lyrics and affected the roles of minor players. In 1938, when Martin was new on Broadway, Sophie Tucker had a

Martin showstopper cut out of Cole Porter's *Leave It to Me*, not wanting to be upstaged by the younger singer. Similarly, Pearl Bailey tried to take Diahann Carroll's best songs from her during the creation of Harold Arlen's *House of Flowers*. Jerry Arlen, the songwriter's brother and conductor of the show, put a stop to it. During *Jennie* rehearsals, Martin reacted unfavorably to a newcomer and "had the promising Imelda De Martin's role in *Jennie* hashed to pieces."[20] De Martin ended up with no songs in the final productions of *Jennie*. When the show headed to Boston, Schwartz and Dietz were interviewed by Earl Wilson on the subject of Mary Martin, whom Wilson called "the greatest draw on the American stage." As usual, the two songwriters kidded around, but with a hint of negativity:

> WILSON: Is Mary tough to work with?
> DIETZ: Yes, all stars are tough.
> SCHWARTZ: I don't think so.
> DIETZ: Mary is—but it's hard for her to be tough with us—we give her such brilliant material.[21]

These problems with Martin, Halliday, and Donehue led to a difficult tryout period. Biographer Davis concluded, "the tension between the factions within the production team was such that all involved knew that they were in for a bumpy ride."[22] After rehearsals, which began June 1963, the plan was to take the show from Boston to Detroit to Broadway. After the July 29 opening, the Boston critics were unanimous, judging Martin and the first act wonderful and Schulman's book and the second act poor. Schwartz and Dietz were in strong agreement with them, writing to Halliday and Crawford during the Boston run:

> We had felt that in spite of the many flaws in Arnold's script as now being played, his basic talent <u>might</u> carry him through to a respectable revision of the entire script.... We now believe that he is not capable of doing this. Consider: the second act problems are far more severe than those of the first act.... We believe that if a fresh talent does not take over the rewrite of the script, then we all should be prepared for a failure. However, if Arnold is to continue as the writer, we will accept the situation resignedly—the situation of a sure-flop.... We are in enormous peril, and only heroic measures will pull us through.[23]

Davis surmised, "the author claimed that he was writing a serious play whereas the composer and lyricist insisted they were writing a light, entertaining score."[24] The two songwriters went on to criticize director Donehue and choreographer Matt Mattox, then concluded their memo on a more personal note:

> However, we urge you to alter the attitudes that you Richard, and you Cheryl, and you Vincent have consistently had toward us in the preparation of the show over the last year or more. Actually, you cannot afford NOT to change.... The fact that Dennis O'Keefe turned out the way we said he would should give you pause. Please, in

the interest of turning our show into a possible success, show us the respect we have earned.[25]

Boston Globe critic, Kevin Kelly, wrote two pieces on the show. The first one, after opening night, was harsher than that of his fellow Boston scribes, generally a patient and forgiving group. Kelly said, "It is scenically ponderous, painfully slow, romantically patronizing, and very nearly witless.... And the package is padded with easy, derivative songs by Howard Dietz and Arthur Schwartz. While the score is the best thing in the show, it is lyrically limp and far from original. In two numbers, Miss Martin seems to be singing the same songs she sang through the syrup of 'The Sound of Music.'"[26] Kelly's second column was critical of Schwartz, claiming that his score "poaches on the melodies of other composers, from Rodgers and Hammerstein to Meredith Willson, Frank Loesser, and Bob Merrill."[27] Within two weeks, Schwartz filed a $1,000,000 suit against Kelly and the Globe Newspaper Company, publisher of the *Boston Daily Globe*, charging that they had accused him of artistic plagiarism. The defendants denied the allegations.[28] A Chicago critic noted, "Such legal action as Schwartz has taken against Kelly is rare in theatrical history, especially when the sum involved is a million dollars—or, for that matter, even two dollars, which is about how much most producers think drama critics are worth."[29] Eventually, the suit was dropped, but the incident added to the ill-feeling surrounding *Jennie*.

As the show headed for Detroit, changes were made. Carol Haney replaced Matt Mattox but would be uncredited for her choreographic work. The role of one of Jennie's friends, played by Constance Carpenter, was written out. Dennis O'Keefe, referred to in the aforementioned Dietz / Schwartz letter, could not sing and was replaced by George Wallace.[30] New material was written for Wallace to sing. By the end of the Boston run, there had been some improvement. Elinor Hughes of the *Boston Herald* took a second look at *Jennie* one month after her initial review. She held out hope, writing, "Unquestionably, after last night's performance, I'd say that progress has been made and that the prospects are definitely better. Overall, the show has better pace and has been shortened, to advantage."[31]

In Detroit, it was clear that no one was happy with the show, most of all Schwartz and Dietz. In communications with Halliday and Crawford, they were still making wholesale suggestions for dialogue, staging, and plot changes. On September 7, two days before the Detroit opening, they pleaded with their producers:

> It is our opinion that the routining of last night makes our first act bog down so seriously that recovery may be impossible. Imagine for a moment that we are able to get advice on this problem from any or all of the following men: Richard Rodgers, George Abbott, Moss Hart, Abe Burrows, George Kaufman, Alan Lerner. With their known

attitude toward pace and tempo in musical shows, what do you think they would say? All of us know the darkness of the cloud we are under in Detroit at this moment. The public here as well as the critics have read the Boston notices.... Why gamble on the possibility of opening here with a first act worse than it was in Boston?[32]

The next day, Schwartz and Dietz continued, sending a two-page letter enumerating changes, especially song additions, designed to make use of the singing talent of George Wallace.[33]

On September 10, the day after the Detroit opening, Halliday responded to Schulman, Dietz, and Schwartz. By this time, Halliday was only communicating with the writers through his attorney, Herman Bernstein. Halliday sent "FOUR ALTERNATE PROPOSALS":

1. Halliday will turn over the entire production to Schulman, Dietz and Schwartz. Mary Martin will leave the show.

2. Halliday will assume complete responsibility of the show without using any material, whether book, lyrics or music by any other author.

3. Halliday will freeze the show as it played September 9th, and open in New York that way.

4. The producers will close the show at the end of the Detroit engagement October 5, 1963.[34]

The last of these proposals elicited a strong negative reaction from Schwartz and Dietz. The advance ticket sales for Broadway were estimated at $1,300,000 to $2,000,000 and the composers threatened to sue for much the same amount if the producers failed to open on Broadway.[35]

A day later, the three writers—through their attorneys—accepted proposition number three. Even with this acceptance, they proceeded to suggest several changes. They agreed to not attend any further rehearsals, and "On matters affecting the Play, we shall communicate directly with Cheryl Crawford." Their main stipulation was "that you will open the play in New York City with its present cast."[36] But then only two days later, the three asked Crawford to delay the New York opening by two weeks, and in the same communication, offered two changes in the book and numerous song changes. They added, "we propose that it be kept unfrozen even longer than had been planned, in order to give our director, our choreographer, and our cast additional time to work."[37]

Schwartz and Halliday had ceased communicating weeks before. It was precipitated by a "nasty confrontation" in a hotel lobby during the tryout period. According to Jonathan Schwartz, Halliday had "battled Arthur at every turn."[38] All along, Crawford had been more open to changes, advice, and discussions than Halliday. As late as September 26, Schwartz was proposing new songs, but only to Crawford: "Here is a recording of 'I THOUGHT I WAS FREE,' for Jennie to sing at the end of Act One. As you recall, Dick Rodgers suggested that we write a song in a slightly extended form, with a rising ending with dramatic power."[39] The song was not on the program for Broadway. Of all this, Crawford said, "I was still in the unpleasant position of being the only one to whom the others would talk. It was a dreary, exhausting time for me."[40]

With the third proposal in force—"Halliday will freeze the show as it played September 9th"—*Jennie* opened at the Majestic Theatre on October 17, 1963. Reviews were tepid at best, although Martin, Ethel Shutta as Jennie's mother, and Robin Bailey as dramatist J. Hartley Manners, Laurette Taylor's second husband, were cited favorably. Irene Sharaff dressed Martin in numerous period costumes and won praise for the effort. From the viewpoint of the critics, it was Schulman's book that dragged down the proceedings. Although the show was titled *Jennie*, it was based on the theater world of Laurette Taylor which Schulman "almost entirely failed to encompass."[41] Years later, historian Ken Mandelbaum concluded, "It was a remarkably unexciting book, one of the weakest ever to be accepted by a major star in the fifties and sixties ... the show had just three things going for it: Martin, as always irresistible to her audiences; an attractive score; and the physical production."[42]

Schwartz and Dietz composed thirteen songs for *Jennie* that made it to Broadway:

Before I Kiss the World Goodbye	The Night May Be Dark
Born Again	Over Here
For Better or Worse	See Seattle
High Is Better Than Low	Waitin' for the Evening Train
I Believe in Taking a Chance	When You're Far Away from New
I Still Look at You That Way	York Town
Lonely Nights	Where You Are

Nine others songs were cut early on. In addition, Schwartz wrote two dance numbers, "The Jig" and "Sauce Diable."[43]

There were great Schwartz / Dietz songs in this score. In Boston, the *Christian Science Monitor* critic had said, "the music and lyrics, redolent with the song styles of Lillian Russell's day, are tuneful enough to end up on a hit parade."[44] Among these were two duets for Martin and George Wallace early in the first act. "Waiting for the Evening Train" is lighthearted and breezy, and "I Still Look at You That Way," is "a wistful old-married-folks song," but a Schwartz ballad to be sure.[45] He spoke of its creation and his work routine: "I frequently walk downtown to think out an idea. One song in the show is called 'I Still Look at You That Way.' Howard Dietz had given me the title. Between 95th Street and 79th Street I finished the tune. For the most part, every song I've written was written to a title. That's the way we've been working all these years. I work fast, but not until the title comes from Howard. I usually walk on the side of the street that follows Central Park so I don't have to stop for traffic."[46]

Despite the controversy over the lyrics mentioned previously, "Before I Kiss the World Goodbye" became Martin's hit solo in the show. It was the song that had drawn her to Schwartz, Dietz, and *Jennie*: "They played it for me and I loved it from the moment I heard it. I couldn't wait to sing it."[47] This is followed by another, "Where You Are," a duet with Robin Bailey. Alec Wilder was complimentary of the song: "The ballad *Where You Are* is very direct and simple, made principally of imitative phrases. But it has that choke-up quality which it is impossible to find the melodic cause of, but which is always instantly recognizable. The very first phrase of this song has it."[48]

There was another Schwartz contributor to *Jennie*—son Paul—who was only seven at the time. The proud father told an interviewer, "He [Paul] wrote a theme about eight months ago. Without telling him, I developed it into a dance for harem girls, and it's being used in *Jennie*. He's getting program credit, too."[49] It is unclear into which song or scene it was included.

The cast recording of *Jennie*, done by RCA Victor and now available on BMG Classics, is worth a listen.[50] It is a wonderful collection of songs that deserved a better fate. Jack De Lon as company manager and George Wallace and Robin Bailey as Jennie's love interests all have strong voices. The same for Ethel Shutta as Jennie's mother, especially in "For Better or Worse," a lament that could easily have come from Aunt Cissy in *A Tree Grows in Brooklyn*. But like the Broadway show, the recording of *Jennie* is a tour de force for Mary Martin. She sings nine different songs with a wide variety of tempos, moods, and partners. She has a perfect theater voice and while getting her songs across, she never tries to bring down the house. She just does.

Despite Mary Martin, a good score, and substantial advance sales, *Jennie* could not sustain a steady audience. Halliday, having met his obligation to bring the show into New York, closed it on December 28, after eighty-two performances. He had trouble admitting defeat in the press and claimed that the original investment had been recouped. Many doubted this, although the 1963 year-end statements of the Jennie Company support Halliday's claim.[51]

In analyzing the failure of *Jennie*, Dietz pulled no punches. In *Dancing in the Dark*, he laid it out: "We had not foreseen that with Mary and her husband Dick Halliday as producers, we would have little to say. We were not protected contractually and I was ill and couldn't take a firm position.... *Jennie* had more operations than I did, but despite the surgery it had trouble talking, walking, and being entertaining. To flatter it, one would call it a flop."[52] In support of Dietz, his wife, Lucinda Ballard, no doubt unhappy about being removed as costume designer, "maintained that Dick Halliday was drunk all the time *Jennie* was going through its metamorphosis."[53] On the other hand, it is clear that Schwartz and Dietz, acting as a team, dug in their heels some place along the way during the creation of *Jennie*. They may have stepped beyond their artistic boundaries. Schwartz was particularly a problem and not in good spirits during most of the work. A member of the chorus, Bernice Saunders, wrote to her husband during out-of-town tryouts, "Mr. Schwartz is really the most humorless, almost ridiculous man ... a real cry baby about his music."[54] Collaborative discussion became non-existent among the principal creators. As for Halliday and Martin, her biographer David Kaufman concluded, "After years of putting shows together on their own terms, the Hallidays simply failed to appreciate the degree to which theater was, first and last, a collaborative art."[55]

Even though he could see it coming, Schwartz took the failure of *Jennie* extremely hard. Jonathan Schwartz remembered the scene:

> On the concrete steps outside the theater, I spotted my father, his elbows resting on his knees, as he faced Forty-fourth Street. I left the lobby and sat down next to him in the cold. For a while we didn't say a thing. When, finally, he spoke, he barely whispered. "We're not getting over," he said. That was all he said.[56]

The opening night party was not a happy affair; Mary Martin and Richard Halliday did not attend. Cheryl Crawford stated in her memoir that "*Jennie* turned into the toughest production I ever tackled," adding, "Everyone was relieved when *Jennie* closed."[57] The Tony Awards committee ignored *Jennie* in all categories. Those shows that Mary Martin turned down, *Hello, Dolly!* and *Funny Girl*, received numerous nominations. *Hello, Dolly!* ran away with the awards. Arthur Schwartz and Howard Dietz never attempted another Broadway show.

29

Later Life

"Their melodies, by my father, are romantic and original; they reveal the dignity and passion of the composer."[1]

While Arthur Schwartz was preparing *Jennie*, his last show on Broadway, he was a guest on the NBC-TV morning show, *Today*, on March 22, 1963. He was interviewed by hosts Hugh Downs and Jack Lescoulie, and several of his songs were performed. Skitch Henderson led an orchestra that accompanied singers Sally Ann Howes and Robert Carroll. How

Songwriters gathered at CBS Television for the 50th Anniversary of ASCAP, February 1964. *Left to right*: Harold Rome, Harold Arlen, Sammy Cahn, Arthur Schwartz, and Jimmy McHugh (courtesy Gilmore Music Library, Yale University).

popular the segment was is hard to know, but the Arthur Schwartz Papers contain several favorable letters to Downs. One listener commented, "Mr. Schwartz emerged not only as a great if hitherto neglected composer but as a warm, gentle person."[2] Another fan added, "Melodies by Arthur Schwartz were beautiful, how uplifting it would be to hear more of them."[3] This was the early sixties, and just as new listeners were discovering his music, rock 'n' roll was taking over the air waves.

Over the next two decades, Schwartz would continue to work on songs and ideas for musicals with various lyricists. A few of these shows even went into early production, while most went no further than the discussion stage. Those he worked on included:

Show	Year(s)	Lyricist(s)	Subject matter / Book writer(s)
Dragon Lady	1963–64	Howard Dietz	Ngo Dinh Nhu, sister-in-law of South Viet Nam president Diem and much in the news
Casablanca	1964–65	Howard Dietz	Based on the movie of the same name
Casablanca	1967–70	Leo Robin	Based on the movie of the same name
Nickleby and Me	1971–75	Caryl Brahms / Ned Sherrin	Charles Dickens' *Nicholas Nickleby* /Brahms and Sherrin
Vicky for President	1972	E.Y. Harburg	Stockbroker / feminist Victoria Woodhull in late 19th century / Burt Shevelove and Herb Sargent
The Adventures of Don Quixote and Sancho Panza	1977	Sammy Cahn	An animated film, derived from the Cervantes work
Our Man in Havana	1977	Sammy Cahn	Based on the Graham Green novel of the same name
YEAH!	1977–78	Sammy Cahn	Unproduced musical
Look Who's Dancing	1978	Dorothy Fields / Arthur Schwartz	Rewrite of *A Tree Grows in Brooklyn* /Mary O'Hagan
Nicholas Nickleby	1978	Arthur Schwartz	Charles Dickens' serialized novel / Mary O'Hagan
All About Love	1982	Arthur Schwartz	A couple's journey in life and love / Mary O'Hagan

A great deal of work was done on *Casablanca* by Schwartz, lyricist Leo Robin, and book writer Julius J. Epstein, who had written the screenplay for the 1942 film. Epstein and his co-authors, brother Philip G. and Howard Koch, had based their story on an unproduced play, *Everyone Comes to Rick's*, and won the Academy Award for their efforts. The producers of the musical were to be Schwartz and Epstein, and the initial capitalization was $500,000. Tryouts were planned for Detroit and Baltimore with a tentative Broadway opening date of October 23, 1967. Sidney Chaplin had been cast as Rick.[4]

Over the next three years, there were legal obstacles, contract delays, and artists coming and going on the project. Joshua Logan was interested in the project and had listened to several songs.[5] But he and Chaplin were busy in Hollywood and never followed through. The production languished into 1970, when Schwartz attempted to get British producer Hugh "Binkie" Beaumont to take it on. In a letter to Beaumont, he extols the talents of his book writer, Epstein: "Julie is probably the most flexible collaborator I have ever worked with. He's the opposite of the breed Mike Todd used to describe as believing everything they wrote was 'written in concrete.'"[6] Despite Schwartz's best efforts, including several songs he and Robin wrote, *Casablanca* was never brought to the stage.[7] Oddly enough, Schwartz told John S. Wilson of the *New York Times* that he and Dietz had

Members of ASCAP at a Muscular Dystrophy Association Benefit in New York, October 23, 1964. The dinner was a special tribute saluting ASCAP. *Left to right*: Arthur Schwartz, Jule Styne, Ned Washington, Johnny Mercer, Jimmy Rule, Ralph Blane, ASCAP President Stanley Adams, and J. Fred Coots (courtesy ©Mark Chester / M001_338, Johnny Mercer Papers, Popular Music and Culture Collection, Special Collections and Archives, Georgia State University Library).

written a musical version of *Casablanca*. This took place in the years immediately after *Jennie* (1963), but it had gone unproduced. Schwartz surmised, "But we couldn't find a satisfactory lead. No actor wanted to follow Bogart. Finally we just gave up."[8]

By 1969, Schwartz had moved to London at 83 Duke Street. It was a city he had always admired and which appreciated him as a composer. These feelings toward London and the United Kingdom may have partly explained "his unaccountable, ever-so-slight British accent," mentioned by Jonathan Schwartz.[9] For over ten years—1969–1979—Schwartz made the transatlantic round trip over 100 times, usually staying several days for ASCAP meetings and other business.[10] He had become a director for ASCAP in 1958 and held that post until 1983. He was also on the governing board of the Dramatists' Guild from 1967 to 1969 and became its London representative when he moved there. On at least two of these commutes, he went to New York on the Cunard Line's Queen Elizabeth II, not just as a passenger but also as a guest lecturer. During the crossing, he entertained in the ship's theater, playing and singing his songs, and was listed as a member of the Art, Culture and Entertainment staff. On a May 1979 crossing, also entertaining the passengers was actor Walter Slezak. He had starred with Katherine Carrington in *Music in the Air* in 1932, and Schwartz had been the rehearsal pianist for his future wife's audition.[11]

In 1970, Jonathan met with success with a collection of short stories, *Almost Home* published by Doubleday. Encouraged by his son and having had the idea of an autobiography on his mind for years, Schwartz approached editor Kenneth McCormick at Doubleday. In a two-page letter from London dated September 22, 1971, he introduced himself as "Jonathan Schwartz's father." He expressed several thoughts about autobiographies, his and others:

> Life-stories of show biz characters flood the market, it seems, and I imagine most of them have been duds. I have a feeling ... that mine could lift its head above the crowd. I would avoid the "and then I wrote ... and then I met" gambit, but not exclude material of that category if it had comic or dramatic value. Moss Hart's "Act One" would be my model chiefly because Moss's theatrical instincts made him think and write in terms of suspense. But my aim would be to include all the careers I've had: teacher of English in New York schools, practicing lawyer, composer, film scenarist, producer of plays, motion pictures and television. The construction would be aimed at propelling interest. Well, you say, why take on a book at such a time? Because I wake up every day far too early to disturb the neighbors with the piano, and pencils are silent. Besides, I've thought of two possible titles: "Best of Both Worlds" (I have lived and worked both in America and England)—"Pitkin Avenue to Piccadilly" (I was born in Brownsville Brooklyn and am now living in London.)[12]

Despite Schwartz's enthusiasm and availability, the book was never written. None of the Schwartz papers at the Library of Congress contains any

29. Later Life

unfinished book, chapters, notes, or further correspondence with McCormick or anyone else at Doubleday. Twelve years later, Schwartz was interviewed a few times by historian Benny Green, an Englishman. In their last meeting, Green said, "I asked him why he did not write his autobiography. His response was the most revealing thing I ever heard him say: 'Howard has already written it.'"[13] This was a reference to *Dancing in the Dark: Words by Howard Dietz: An Autobiography*, which had been published in 1974.

From 1971 and the following four years, Schwartz was involved in a musical version of *Nicholas Nickleby*, Charles Dickens' serialized novel published in 1838–39. Schwartz's first collaborators on the project, to be called *Nickleby and Me*, were Caryl Brahms and Ned Sherrin. Brahms had been a novelist, journalist, and critic, particularly for ballet. She teamed with Sherrin on several projects, as he had been an author, stage director, and broadcaster. Both, it seemed, were jacks-of-all-trades, and were going to do the book and lyrics.

In the available correspondence between the two Brits and Schwartz, while their association seemed amicable at first, disagreements developed regarding their conceptions of the score. Brahms and Sherrin apparently wanted music from the Dickensian period, whereas Schwartz wanted a period musical but with room for a modern score. He had had some success on such shows with *Virginia* (Colonial Williamsburg) and *A Tree Grows in Brooklyn* (1900 New York). These divergent views created acrimony among the principals after Brahms and Sherrin were critical of Schwartz's score, citing negative comments by friends in the theatrical community. Schwartz responded firmly:

> So I think you and Caryl should now decide if you want this collaboration to end.... However, if you feel you want to proceed with it, I think you must stick to the conception of the score we have agreed upon. Further, I think you must adhere to the policy of all the writers of lyrics and music in my acquaintance that no word or note stays in if there is an objection on the part of any collaborator. I am not prepared to write Dickensian music—whatever that is—in the year 1972. I think it would die, and the show along with it. I prefer to have a success and let the pedants carp. Pedants don't buy many tickets. They didn't buy many to "Oliver."[14]

Whatever transpired over the next several months is not clear, but nearly a year later, their show was still in the works. It was announced that it would be co-produced by Bernard Delfont and Robert Stigwood with a proposed opening in mid-1973. Schwartz, Brahms, and Sherrin were all still onboard.[15]

By July 1973, dissension re-emerged, this time over Schwartz's meddling with the lyrics. Again, Schwartz informed the lyricists how things used to be and still should be: "This is the first time any lyricist has ever taken the position with me that any contribution of mine was unwelcome.

Howard Dietz, Ira Gershwin, Dorothy Fields, Oscar Hammerstein, and others have gladly accepted titles, lines, and lyrics from me, as indeed you and Ned have frequently done. I am puzzled by your change."[16] Schwartz's interference with his librettists apparently intensified after this. Producer Henry Fielding had become involved, and in early fall, Schwartz submitted a new version of the first act to Fielding, unbeknownst to Brahms and Sherrin. By late October, when they found out about the Schwartz revisions, the relationship was over: "We are not new to the theatre and to have our book re-written by our (excellent) composer ... is a piece of unprofessional behavior which gives us no confidence in a continuation of our collaboration. We shall miss your fine tunes but we must preserve the qualities of our musical and we think that that will be best done by re-working it with another composer."[17]

Schwartz agreed that their relationship should be terminated, but did so in a five-page letter going into great detail about the book changes and several paragraphs about his behavior being "unprofessional." The last page focuses on the possibility of plagiarism and includes a thinly veiled threat by Schwartz: "Musical plagiarism is not limited to the melody line of a composition.... Consequently, it would appear that if you give your new composer lyrics or parts of lyrics you wrote after you heard my melodies, and if he re-sets them, or parts of them, with new music of his, I believe his task of avoiding infringement is something you and he should study most carefully."[18] The three continued their correspondence, mostly of the same tenor, into early 1974. Overall, Schwartz's letters have a defensiveness and bitterness that suggests the lack of a collaborative spirit, as if to say, "That's not how we used to do things." It is reminiscent of the rancor that developed during the creation of *Jennie* and the disputes Schwartz and Dietz had with Mary Martin, Richard Halliday, and director Vincent Donehue.

Over the next eighteen months, Schwartz was in discussions with producer Arthur Cantor at H.M. Tennent Ltd. in London for a different musical version of *Nicholas Nickleby*. Schwartz was going to do book, music, and lyrics. In July 1975, it was announced that *Nicholas Nickleby* would be produced by Cantor for the upcoming Broadway winter season.[19] Both this version with Cantor and another one Schwartz had worked on with Harold Fielding fell through.[20] No Arthur Schwartz musical based on *Nicholas Nickleby* was ever produced. Jonathan Schwartz, discussing his father's late efforts for the stage—*Casablanca* and *Nicholas Nickleby*—explained, "There were no workshop performances of either show, no readings or tryouts or out-of-town reviews or opening night."[21] Brahms and Sherrin did follow through with the project, teaming up with composer Ron Grainer. Their *Nickleby and Me* opened December 1975 at the Theatre Royal Stratford East in London and ran for six weeks.

ASCAP function, circa 1970. *Left to right*: Arthur Schwartz, Ethel Merman, Dorothy Fields, and ASCAP President Stanley Adams (courtesy ©Mark Chester).

In 1976, Schwartz worked on an album of his own songs. He said that the idea had grown out of a television special in London about George Gershwin. After Schwartz sang on that show, he was approached to do an album of his works.[22] It was an RCA recording done in London, conducted and orchestrated by Tony Osborne. Entitled *from the pen of ... Arthur Schwartz*, it included fourteen songs, all sung by Schwartz:

Alone Together	Love Is a Dancing Thing
By Myself	A Rainy Night in Rio
Dancing in the Dark	Rhode Island Is Famous for You
A Gal in Calico	A Shine on Your Shoes
I Guess I'll Have to Change My Plan	Something to Remember You By
	That's Entertainment
If There Is Someone Lovelier Than You	Triplets
	You and the Night and the Music

The album was released in February 1976 and elicited favorable critical comments. In London, Peter Hepple of *The Stage* said that Schwartz was "a joy, with a crisp, confident attack that belies his 75 years and the fact that he does not claim to be a singer."[23] Martin Bookspan was even more favorable: "How well does Schwartz sing his own songs? With splendid conviction. That he brings such conviction to his performance is not surprising; neither is the fact that he is meticulous about diction, phrasing, and rhythm. What does surprise is the ease and warmth and total professionalism of his singing."[24]

On listening to it, one is struck by Schwartz's enjoyment of his own songs. He has a limited tenor, but overcomes it with his sensitivity and diction. "Something to Remember You By" and "By Myself" are his best ballads on the album. He is most enthusiastic on "Rhode Island Is Famous for You." All the songs are Dietz lyrics except for "A Rainy Night in Rio" and "A Gal in Calico," both from Leo Robin and *The Time, the Place and the Girl*, a 1946 film. It was surprising that Schwartz recorded no Dorothy Fields' songs.[25] Schwartz wrote the album notes as well, discussing his long association with Dietz and making brief comments about Robin. Of those involved with him on the production of the album, he writes, "Tony Osborn's orchestrations of the songs in this album are outstanding. Modern in conception, but true to the spirit of each number, they are a delight to listen to.... Alan Dell, producer of this album, suggested that I sing them. Alan has always been known for his courage."[26]

Regretfully, Schwartz and Dietz had a bitter disagreement over the album. In a letter to Schwartz on June 22, 1976, Dietz comes across petty and cantankerous: "I believe your including 'Rio' and 'Gal in Calico' in the album was because you wanted to hedge against me. 'From the Pen of' was a gesture of possession."[27] Schwartz, while laying some blame on RCA-London for the title, content, and sleeve notes, did not back down from Dietz regarding the inclusion of the Robin songs. In a four-page letter, he points out the albums brought out by several songwriters—Harold Arlen, Alan Jay Lerner, Sammy Cahn, Johnny Mercer, and Stephen Sondheim—in which they included songs by other collaborators, not just their principal ones. Pointing out that when Dietz was given a *Lyrics & Lyricists* program at the YM-YWHA, several of the composers with whom Dietz had worked were included. Schwartz stated emphatically: "All those works are part of your repertoire. Why shouldn't the public know that? Similarly, then, why shouldn't the public hear the music I wrote with the many partners I have worked with? I have written about one hundred and fifty songs with collaborators other than you. So—do you think it is fair for you to feel that in any forum where a substantial body of my work is performed, I should exclude performance of all lyrics except yours."[28] In a conciliatory tone a few weeks later, Dietz replied, "You have gone to a great deal of trouble to prove your point, and I have been emotional. Let it rest."[29] The dispute seems to have ended there.

Only three months after this, Dietz wrote Schwartz suggesting they publish a songbook of their best works. Dietz told his partner, "I am told by a young composer, who makes his living mostly by arranging music for night club acts, that we are the only team of any importance, who does not have a song book available." He explained that according to this pianist / arranger, when such books come out, media people and singers and arrangers "pour over them." Dietz, whose condition with Parkinsonism was worsening, then concluded, "I don't have much influence, but you have. Is there no way you could press to have a Dietz / Schwartz song book printed? It needn't be expensive. I tried to get Warner and Chappell to issue such a book, but got nowhere."[30] How much work Schwartz may have put into it is unclear, but the songbook—*That's Entertainment: The Great Songs of Dietz & Schwartz*—was not published until 1990. It contained forty-five songs and included lyricists Dorothy Fields, Frank Loesser, and Leo Robin in addition to Dietz. Included was even a Dietz / Vernon Duke tune. The songbook was put out by Warner Bros. Publications with a preface by Jonathan Schwartz.[31]

In 1976, Schwartz was interviewed in America by Dan Sullivan of the *Los Angeles Times*. Sullivan's profile is complimentary: "it's hard to believe he's 75. … The man waiting for you in the lobby of the Beverly Hills in open shirt, denim jacket and blue sneakers is chatty, in touch and, at most, 55. He's glad to talk about his old songs—that's why he's here, plugging the record—but wait until you hear the ones he's writing for his new show, *Nicholas Nickleby*. Is there a piano around here?" Relevant to that show, the discussion touched on the current music climate and the difficulty in getting a song out there. Schwartz explained, "Let's say I have a great big score with *Nicholas Nickleby*. There are fewer people I can go to with it than in the old days. Streisand. Sinatra. Cleo Laine. Andy Williams. Jack Jones. Como, maybe. That's about all. It doesn't mean a good show song will die—look at Judy Collins with 'Send in the Clowns'—but it does mean it'll take longer to get around."[32]

One year after Arthur did his album, Jonathan Schwartz recorded *Alone Together: Jonathan Schwartz Sings Arthur Schwartz*. The LP recording on Muse Records included ten songs:

Alone Together
By Myself
I Guess I'll Have to Change My Plan
I See Your Face Before Me
I'm Like a New Broom

New Sun in the Sky
Something to Remember You By
Then I'll Be Tired of You
Where Do I Go from You?
You and the Night and the Music

The album was recorded with a five-piece jazz ensemble. Jonathan said of the songs chosen: "Here are ten songs of beauty and character. Their lyrics, by Howard Dietz, Dorothy Fields and Yip Harburg are wonderfully drawn.

Their melodies, by my father, are romantic and original; they reveal the dignity and passion of the composer. I have tried to sing them with the spirit in which they were written. It is my hope that I have not been intrusive."[33] He adds that he was proud to have done the first recording of "Where Do I Go from You?," a song by Schwartz and Fields written around the time of *Stars in Your Eyes* (1939) but never used in that show nor published. There is a great photograph on the album of Arthur at the piano, actively engaged in playing, while Jonathan stands proudly over him.

In early 1977, Arthur Schwartz and Sammy Cahn renewed a working relationship. They had written the score for the Martin and Lewis movie, *You're Never Too Young*, in 1954, but had not worked together since. Schwartz was in London and Cahn mostly on the West Coast. Both were involved with ASCAP and would see each other at meetings. They began kicking around ideas for songs and shows. Both were energetic with plenty of ideas, and Cahn was a fast worker. As Jimmy Van Heusen, frequent collaborator of Cahn said, "Sammy is as facile a man with words as there is in our business."[34] During 1977–78, Schwartz and Cahn worked on songs for a musical, *YEAH!*, and a movie, *Golden Memories*.

YEAH! never came to fruition, but there are lyric sheets in the Sammy Cahn Papers of the Margaret Herrick Library and in the Arthur Schwartz Papers. For *YEAH!*, Cahn had written lyrics to four songs dated April and May 1977: "I Would Have Bet Against It!," "The Today People!," "Yeah!," and "It's Love!" There are no melodies, musical notations, or related correspondence to go with them in either collection.[35] This may have been the musical mentioned by John S. Wilson in his 1978 interview of Schwartz, "a black revue that will star Cab Calloway and Judith Jamison."[36]

In the summer of 1977, Cahn completed lyrics on three songs for *Golden Memories*: "Golden Memories," "Astaire, Kelly and Me!," and "You Can't Win a War Without a Song!" These are in both the Cahn and Schwartz Papers, and again, there is no music to go with them. The movie was to be produced by Stepaul productions in California. In December 1977, Cahn wrote to Schwartz, "FLASH! Ed Traubner [business manager] has 'cahn-cluded' a deal with our boy producer for the three songs for GOLDEN MEMORIES! It isn't any munificent sum but it is a beginning for us. We got five thousand a song!"[37]

Although *Golden Memories* also fizzled, Schwartz and Cahn enjoyed their working relationship. Schwartz and Dietz had always worked on the supposition that if one did not like something the other had written and wanted to suggest a change, so be it. Yip Harburg spoke of this in his relationship with Harold Arlen: "I respected ... him to make the final decision musically, me to make the final decision lyrically. And lots of times we compromised when he didn't like a lyric or when I didn't like a tune."[38] Schwartz and Cahn appear to have worked similarly. In response to the lyrics of a song Cahn had sent him, Schwartz suggests word changes and explains them:

> Here is a cassette of the "WAR" song. I have taken a liberty which you should know about before you play the tune. In line 3 of each phrase I have ended the line with a two-syllable rhyme, disregarding your one-syllable rhyme. Dummy example: Needing Succeeding instead of Need Succeed. Two reasons, equally important, I think: One: The other lines of the lyric are ALL one syllable rhymes, which I think is monotonous. Two: I think I have found a melody for those lines which justifies the double-syllable. However, if you disagree, I'll go back to the drawing board.... I'm as flexible as you are so if you don't like these changes, just tell me, and I'll start all over again—that is, after I pick myself up and dust myself off.[39]

Cahn must have acceded to Schwartz's wishes and stayed with the double-syllable changes. In a letter three months later, Schwartz again sends a different cassette of the "WAR" song, telling his lyricist, "Sorry about the double-syllable changes I made. Simply couldn't solve the tune without them." He finishes on a complimentary note to Cahn about some other lyrics he had written that had impressed a friend of Schwartz: "I told him you found those lines in half-a-minute. He was astounded, as indeed I always am at your lightning brilliance."[40] Also during 1977–78, the two veteran songwriters were discussing other projects: a Broadway musical "with a Washington [D.C.] background" in collaboration with humorist Art Buchwald; *The Adventures of Don Quixote and Sancho Panza*, an animated musical film "in a broad popular vein as Cervantes originally intended it"; a musical version of Graham Greene's *Our Man in Havana*; and a Carol Channing revue.[41] None of these went very far. Realizing that their timing may have been wrong to get a musical produced, Schwartz concluded in a letter to Cahn, "I could only wish we had met and worked together sooner. Your skill and imagination are unique."[42]

In 1978, Schwartz was part of a *Lyrics & Lyricists* presentation at the 92nd Street YM-YWHA. *An Evening with Arthur Schwartz* was performed March 19–20 with singers J.T. Cromwell, Anita Darian, and Barbara Lea with piano accompaniment by Paul Trueblood. Twenty-nine songs were chosen and included nine of the lyricists with whom Schwartz had worked: Lorenz Hart, Howard Dietz, Johnny Mercer, Frank Loesser, Dorothy Fields, Leo Robin, Maxwell Anderson, E.Y. Harburg, and Ira Gershwin. The program ended with a Schwartz / Dietz medley. Schwartz played a bit and added commentary.[43]

During the late Seventies, Schwartz and wife, Mary O'Hagan, were working on *Look Who's Dancing*, a rewrite of *A Tree Grows in Brooklyn*. O'Hagan was to rework the book and Schwartz to add eight new songs, words and music, to the existing score. *A Tree Grows in Brooklyn*, despite

Shirley Booth and a wonderful score, ran only 267 performances. Schwartz explained to John S. Wilson the reason for taking it on again:

> When 'A Tree Grows in Brooklyn' was produced in 1951, it appealed to people but it was not a great success. It was based on an autobiographical novel by Betty Smith about the people in her life when she was growing up in Brooklyn. We had Shirley Booth play the Betty Smith role and, because she was a rising star, George Abbott and Betty Smith, who wrote the book for the show, decided to build her part. As a result, the musical got away from the focus of the novel. The new version goes back to the novel.[44]

Look Who's Dancing was presented at the Berkshire Music Festival in Stockbridge, Massachusetts, in the summer of 1978.[45]

In the late seventies, Jonathan Schwartz performed numerous times at Michael's Pub in Manhattan. Schwartz visited his son during one of these shows, and Jonathan remembered the evening: "I had called him up onstage to play 'Dancing in the Dark,' for which he'd received a standing ovation ... his blue eyes excited as people gathered around to shake his hand, to seek an autograph. He was seventy-nine ... his hair dyed boot black on behalf of youth, his frailty apparent in his cautious navigation of departure.... I watched him go. He was delayed once by a couple his age, Arthur's music in their bones, which is, I guess, what they wanted to tell him."[46]

Also during this period, O'Hagan devised a revue titled *Dancing in the Dark*, an anthology of her husband's music. The idea had been presented to Schwartz in London, but he was never happy with the format proposed. O'Hagan's concept was two couples, one in their mid-forties, the other twenty-something, and as Schwartz explained, "It's not a plot, just a thread that dictates a variety of songs."[47] It was produced at the Manhattan Theatre Club which had recently created *Ain't Misbehavin'*, the Fats Waller musical that went to Broadway for a long run. The singers for *Dancing in the Dark* were John Cunningham, Allyn Ann McClerie, Merilee Magnuson, and Donn Simione with Paul Trueblood as musical director and arranger. Schwartz wrote two new songs for it, "Love Should Be Free" and "The Jog."[48] The show had a successful one-month run, but was never taken to Broadway. Schwartz had hoped it might become "the white 'Ain't Misbehavin.'"[49]

Into his eighties, Schwartz was still working on musicals. He and O'Hagan created *All About Love*, which they referred to as "a new form of musical entertainment ... a revue-with-a-story." The book, written by O'Hagan, was an offshoot of the above *Dancing in the Dark*, "an intriguing tale of one couple, from the time they first met, to their marriage, cooling-off, swinging affairs, disenchantment, and reconciliation." The score was to employ songs from the Schwartz / Dietz songbook, as well as new songs with words and music by Schwartz. A promotional announcement for the musical explained, "Perhaps the most novel aspect about the show is that it has no dialogue at all. Instead, there are musical-and-lyrical bridges which propel the story with wit and warmth."[50]

Schwartz and O'Hagan pitched the show to prospective investors on stationery of Arthur Schwartz Productions at 1082 Park Avenue. Their letter described *All About Love* and its songs, adding that the cast required a sophisticated man and woman, as well as an ensemble of singers and dancers, four women and four men. In letters during the summer of 1982, they explained that Ann Reinking and Ken Howard had been cast as the principal couple and that the director / choreographer would be Michael Smuin, who had just directed the successful *Sophisticated Ladies*. The proposed budget was $1.25 million. Targeted investors included producer Norman Leary and hotel mogul Leona Helmsley.[51] Schwartz and O'Hagan could not generate enough investor interest, and the show went unproduced.

As mentioned earlier, Schwartz met a few times in London with historian Benny Green. Like Dan Sullivan from the *Los Angeles Times*, Green was favorably impressed by his subject:

> Everything about him seemed spry, alert, a man in full command of his powers. To meet Arthur in those later years was an experience which never failed to astonish the suppliant Englishmen who were granted an audience. The extraordinary thing was his physical appearance, especially his face. The reference books all agreed that he had been born in 1900, yet here he was, with the features of a man far too young to have written a Broadway show before the Wall Street Crash. When I left after the first meeting, I confirmed the relevant dates and was reduced to wonder. We lunched at a restaurant in St. Martin's Lane. It was a summer day and we were both feeling the heat. I noticed that when Arthur reached out for the menu, his forearm seemed scrawny, the forearm of a very old man. Yet he was only 83, and we all knew that Arthur was destined for a century.[52]

By the early Eighties, Schwartz and O'Hagan had moved back to New York. For several years, Jonathan and his stepmother, whom he referred to as Mary Grey, had an acrimonious relationship. At times, this kept him at a distance from his father. Arthur suffered a stroke in February 1984, which left him paralyzed on the right side and with loss of speech, aphasia. When Jonathan first visited his father that day, he and Grey nearly came to blows. Through tears and unintelligible speech, Schwartz asked his son about future piano playing, wiggling his left fingers. Jonathan answered, "Of course. More like Irving Berlin than Gershwin, but you'll do okay." Schwartz was taken to a rehabilitation center in White Plains, New York, but according to Jonathan, "refused to participate." His condition generally deteriorated from then on, but "his eyes remained alert and oddly youthful." Schwartz died seven months after his stroke, on September 4, 1984, in Kintnersville, Pennsylvania. Grey and son Paul were at his bedside.[53]

Jonathan and Paul, born in 1956, had not been particularly close. This was due in part to the eighteen years difference in their age, but more to the animosity between Jonathan and his stepmother. After she was killed in a car accident in 1994, things changed. As Jonathan saw it, "We'd been cautious half brothers until Mary Grey's car crash. We were then able to begin to talk." By 2001, they had become quite close. They were part of a celebration of their father's music at Lincoln Center, Jonathan as emcee and the classically-trained Paul as conductor of the thirty-five piece orchestra. Jonathan concluded of the two-day event, "For two hours on both of the evenings, the music of Arthur Schwartz filled, it seemed to me, *all* of Lincoln Center.... My father's music rose up into the winter night, rising ever higher into the sky."[54]

THAT'S ENTERTAINMENT!

Appendix A

Arthur Schwartz Chronology

Date	Occurrence
11/04/1900	Born in Brooklyn, fourth child of Solomon and Dora Schwartz (nee: Grossman). Family living at 69 Thatford Avenue in the Brownsville section of Brooklyn.
1906	Family moves to 312 Rugby Road, Brooklyn, in the Flatbush area. Attends PS 139.
1913	Begins playing piano for silent films at Cortelyou Theater in Flatbush.
1916	Graduates from Boys High School in Brooklyn at age 16.
1916–1920	Attends and graduates from New York University with B.A. in English, earning Phi Beta Kappa and a New York Public School teacher's certificate. At N.Y.U., composes fight song for football, "Smash, Crash Right Through."
1921	Graduates from Columbia University with a Master of Arts in Literature.
1923	Publishes first song, "Baltimore Md., That's the Only Doctor for Me," with lyrics by Eli Dawson.
1921–1924	Attends and graduates from New York University Law School, passes the New York State Bar and joins a private law practice at 299 Broadway.
1923	Writes songs at upstate Brant Lake Camp with Ted Goodman for *Surprises of 1923*.
1924	Meets Lorenz Hart, a fellow counselor at Brant Lake. They write "I Love to Lie Awake in Bed," a melody to be used later in a Schwartz show. They sell a song, "I Know My Girl by Her Perfume."
06/15/1926	Contributes to his first New York show, *The Grand Street Follies of 1926*, at the Neighborhood Playhouse. His lyricists include Albert Carroll, Theodore Goodwin, and Agnes Morgan.
Fall/1926	Works as rehearsal pianist for *Peggy-Ann*, a Rodgers and Hart musical.

Appendix A

Date	Occurrence
03/10/1927	*The New Yorkers* opens with several songs by Schwartz and lyricist Henry Myers.
1927–1929	Working with various lyricists, gets songs interpolated into shows including *The Red Robe, Ned Wayburn's Gambols, Wake Up and Dream,* and *The Grand Street Follies of 1929.*
1928	Gives up law practice for songwriting career and begins work with lyricist Howard Dietz.
04/30/1929	*The Little Show*, his first hit, runs for 321 performances. He and Dietz write seven songs included in the revue and have their first hit with "I Guess I'll Have to Change My Plan."
1930	Works on three shows in London—*Here Comes the Bride, The Co-Optimists of 1930,* and *Little Tommy Tucker*—mostly with lyricist Desmond Carter. After London, lives on E. 38th Street in Manhattan.
08/13/1930	Leaves hospital after week of recuperation from surgery for an acute appendicitis.
09/02/1930	Writes eleven songs with Howard Dietz for *The Second Little Show,* which flops.
10/13/1930	Collaborates on music with Albert Sirmay for adaptation of an operetta, *Princess Charming*, with lyrics by Arthur Swanstrom. Runs fifty-six performances.
10/15/1930	*Three's a Crowd* opens and includes "Something to Remember You By," with Dietz lyrics.
06/03/1931	*The Band Wagon*, starring Adele and Fred Astaire, opens with all Schwartz / Dietz songs, including "Dancing in the Dark," "Confession," and "New Sun in the Sky." A big hit.
09/15/1932	Collaborates with Dietz on *Flying Colors*, a revue that includes the hits "Alone Together," "Louisiana Hayride," and "A Shine on Your Shoes."
Fall/1932	Meets singer / actress Katherine Carrington during her work on *Music in the Air.*
09/13/1933	Writes several songs with various lyricists for London show, *Nice Goings On.*
11/20/1933	Writes "After All You're All I'm After" and title song for Howard Lindsay play, *She Love Me Not*, with lyricist Edward Heyman. Play runs 360 performances.
1934	Feels composing career is at a standstill, gives himself until September of the year to improve the situation or return to law practice.
07/07/1934	Marries Katherine Wright Carrington in Great Neck, Long Island at home of Lawrence Fertig.

Appendix A. Arthur Schwartz Chronology

Date	Occurrence
11/28/1934	With Dietz, works on his first book musical, *Revenge with Music*. "If There Is Someone Lovelier Than You" and "You and the Night and the Music" emerge from the mediocre show.
1934–1935	Writes over 100 songs with Dietz for a weekly radio series, *The Gibson Family*. Show runs only six months, but allows Schwartz to continue his songwriting career.
02/21/1935	Contributes songs with Howard Dietz to London revue, *Stop Press*.
09/19/1935	Returns with Dietz to the revue with *At Home Abroad*, starring Beatrice Lillie, Ethel Waters, and Eleanor Powell. Waters scores with "Thief in the Night" and "Got a Bran' New Suit."
10/09/1935	Leaves for England with wife Katherine to work on C. B. Cochran show, *Follow the Sun*. It opens February 4, 1936, with old songs with Howard Dietz and new ones with Desmond Carter.
12/25/1936	He and Dietz contribute "Prologue," a Shakespearean spoof, to *The Show Is On*.
09/02/1937	*Virginia* opens, a large-scale production at Rockefeller Center, lyrics by Albert Stillman. Show flops due to Laurence Stallings book. Schwartz score praised, especially "You and I Know."
12/22/1937	The second Schwartz / Dietz attempt at a book musical, *Between the Devil*, flops but includes hits "By Myself" and "I See Your Face before Me."
06/28/1938	Son Jonathan is born to Schwartz and Katherine Carrington.
02/09/1939	Collaborates with Dorothy Fields on *Stars in Your Eyes*, with Ethel Merman and Jimmy Durante. Closes after 127 performances.
1940	Collaborates with Oscar Hammerstein II on *American Jubilee*, a program written for the second year of the New York World's Fair of 1939–40. Their best song is "Tennessee Fish Fry."
1941	Writes four songs with Johnny Mercer for film *Navy Blues*, a Warner Bros. production.
1942	Writes songs with E.Y. Harburg for *Cairo* with soprano Jeanette MacDonald.
1943	Receives Academy Award nomination for "They're Either Too Young or Too Old" from *Thank Your Lucky Stars*, lyrics by Frank Loesser. Score also includes "Love Isn't Born (It's Made)."
1944	Produces *Cover Girl* for Harry Cohn at Columbia Pictures. Persuades Jerome Kern and Ira Gershwin to do the score. The film becomes a hit starring Rita Hayworth and Gene Kelly.
1946	Produces *Night and Day*, a Cole Porter biopic, starring Cary Grant and Alexis Smith. Although criticized for its lack of accuracy, it does well at the box office.

Appendix A

Date	Occurrence
11/04/1946	Collaborates with Ira Gershwin, George S. Kaufman, and Max Gordon on the unsuccessful *Park Avenue*. It is Gershwin's last Broadway effort and leaves Schwartz depressed and uncertain.
1947	Receives second Academy Award nomination for "A Gal in Calico" from *The Time, the Place and the Girl* with lyrics by Leo Robin. Film includes "A Rainy Night in Rio," a hit for Dinah Shore.
June/1947	Sells house at 723 North Crescent Drive, Beverly Hills for $75,000 and heads back to New York.
04/30/1948	Returns to the revue genre with Dietz for *Inside U.S.A.* The show includes "Blue Grass," "Haunted Heart," and "Rhode Island Is Famous for You," and enjoys a run of 399 performances. It is Schwartz's last revue.
Fall/1948	Living in penthouse at 94th Street and Lexington Avenue.
1950–1953	Works with the League of New York Theatres and the Council for the Living Theatre.
04/19/1951	Writes successful score with Dorothy Fields on *A Tree Grows in Brooklyn*, with Shirley Booth. Includes "Make the Man Love Me," "I'm Like a New Broom," and "I'll Buy You a Star."
1951–1952	With Dorothy Fields, writes songs for *Excuse My Dust*, and with Johnny Mercer, for *Dangerous When Wet*, both M-G-M films. Latter one includes "I Got Out of Bed on the Right Side."
1953	With Dietz, writes the show business anthem, "That's Entertainment," for movie *The Band Wagon*. It is an Arthur Freed production employing numerous Schwartz / Dietz songs. Stars Fred Astaire and Cyd Charisse and includes their famous duet on "Dancing in the Dark."
05/02/1953	Wife of nineteen years, Katherine, dies of a cerebral hemorrhage.
11/09/1953	Becomes lead plaintiff in *Schwartz v. BMI*, a class action suit by songwriters against BMI, NARTB, and several networks and music publishing houses. Testifies at two separate Congressional hearings regarding the suit.
04/08/1954	Again teams with Dorothy Fields and Shirley Booth on *By the Beautiful Sea*. It runs 270 performances with best songs "Happy Habit" and "More Love Than Your Love."
06/13/1954	Marries actress / dancer Mary O'Hagan Scott, also known as Mary Grey.
1954	On silver anniversary of his Broadway debut, awarded a citation from the Council of New York University for "his contribution to the music of America."
1955	Begins collaboration with lyricist Alan Jay Lerner to write a film score for *Paint Your Wagon*, but completes little as Lerner difficult to work with.

Appendix A. Arthur Schwartz Chronology

Date	Occurrence
Mar-Jun/1956	Produces *Twentieth Century*, *High Tor*, and *A Bell for Adano* for *Ford Star Jubilee* on CBS TV. Writes score for *High Tor* with lyrics by Maxwell Anderson and for *A Bell for Adano* with Dietz.
1956	A son, Paul, born to Schwartz and Mary Grey, while they are living at 300 Central Park West.
09/27/1958	Appears on *The Perry Como Show*, mostly devoted to Schwartz songs. Como, Ann Sheridan, Ray Walston, and the Everly Brothers perform fourteen songs. Schwartz at piano chats with Como.
1958	Elected as a director of ASCAP, a post he would hold until 1983.
1959	With Dietz and Howard Teichmann, writes *Mrs. 'Arris Goes to Paris*, a musical that never gets produced. Moves into apartment at 95th Street and Fifth Avenue.
11/18/1961	Returns to a book musical with Dietz on *The Gay Life*. It runs only 113 performances despite Barbara Cook and "Magic Moment." Dietz suffering from Parkinson's Disease during work on it.
10/17/1963	Another Broadway star, Mary Martin, cannot save another Schwartz / Dietz book musical, *Jennie*. Only "Before I Kiss the World Goodbye" stands out. It is the final effort for Schwartz and Dietz.
1967	Elected to the board of the Dramatists' Guild, a three-year stint and continues ASCAP duties.
1969	Moves to London but will cross Atlantic Ocean over 100 times to do business back in America over the next ten years, much of it for ASCAP.
1971	Federal judge rules on *Schwartz v. BMI*, dismissing the suit with prejudice, thereby ending it.
1971–1974	Works on versions of a book musical of Dickens' *Nicholas Nickleby*, to no avail.
1972	Inducted into the Songwriters Hall of Fame along with Howard Dietz.
1977–1978	Works with Sammy Cahn on various projects, including a musical *YEAH!* and a film, *Golden Memories*. None of these gets produced.
March/1978	*An Evening with Arthur Schwartz* is presented at the 92nd Street YM-YWHA, part of the *Lyrics & Lyricists* series with singers J.T. Cromwell, Anita Darian, and Barbara Lea.
1978	Writes new songs for a revised version of *A Tree Grows in Brooklyn*, with a new book by Mary Grey. Entitled *Looks Who's Dancing*, it plays summer stock in Stockbridge, Massachusetts.
1979	Living at 26 Walton Street, London, SW3.
1981	Inducted into the American Theatre Hall of Fame.

Appendix A

Date	Occurrence
1984	Receives, along with Harold Arlen, the second annual ASCAP Foundation Richard Rodgers Award for a lifetime of achievement in musical theatre.
09/03/1984	Dies in Kintnersville, Pennsylvania, of complications from a stroke.
10/22/1984	Musical tribute to Schwartz held at the Majestic Theater in New York, sponsored by ASCAP. Sons Jonathan and Paul participate as emcee and musical conductor, respectively.

Appendix B

Chronology of Produced Shows[1]

Opening	Show	Final City / Performances
06/15/26	The Grand Street Follies of 1926 (3rd ed.)	New York / 55
03/10/27	The New Yorkers	New York / 52
09/05/28	Good Boy	New York / 253
12/10/28	Well! Well! Well![2]	New Haven*
12/25/28	The Red Robe	New York / 167
01/15/29	Ned Wayburn's Gambols	New York / 31
04/30/29	The Little Show	New York / 321
05/01/29	The Grand Street Follies of 1929 (6th edition)	New York / 93
11/08/29	The House That Jack Built	London / 270
12/30/29	Wake Up and Dream	New York / 136
02/11/30	Ripples	New York / 55
02/20/30	Here Comes the Bride	London / 175
04/04/30	The Co-Optimists of 1930	London / 129
09/02/30	The Second Little Show	New York / 63
10/13/30	Princess Charming	New York / 56
10/15/30	Three's a Crowd	New York / 276
11/19/30	Little Tommy Tucker	London / 83
06/03/31	The Band Wagon	New York / 260
09/15/32	Flying Colors (The Howard Dietz Revue)	New York / 188
09/13/33	Nice Goings On	London / 221
11/20/33	She Loves Me Not[3]	New York / 360
10/22/34	Bring On the Girls	Washington, D.C.*

Appendix B

Opening	Show	Final City / Performances
11/28/34	*Revenge with Music*	New York / 58
02/21/35	*Stop Press*	London / 148
09/19/35	*At Home Abroad (A Musical Holiday)*	New York / 198
02/04/36	*Follow the Sun*	London / 204
12/25/36	*The Show Is On*	New York / 253[4]
09/02/37	*Virginia (The American Musical Romance)*	New York / 60
12/22/37	*Between the Devil*	New York / 93
02/09/39	*Stars in Your Eyes*	New York / 127
05/12/40	*American Jubilee*	New York**
11/04/46	*Park Avenue*	New York / 72
04/30/48	*Inside U.S.A.*	New York / 399
04/19/51	*A Tree Grows in Brooklyn*	New York / 267
04/08/54	*By the Beautiful Sea*	New York / 270
11/18/61	*The Gay Life*	New York / 113
10/17/63	*Jennie*	New York / 82

* Show closed before New York.
** Written for the New York World's Fair of 1939–40 as a patriotic pageant and did not play on Broadway.

  1. The following references were used to compile this list of shows.
    (1) Steven Suskin, *Show Tunes: The Songs, Shows, and Careers of Broadway's Major Composers*, 3rd ed. (New York: Oxford University Press, 2000).
    (2) Richard C. Norton, *A Chronology of American Musical Theater* (Oxford: Oxford University Press, 2002).
  2. Parts of this show became *Pleasure Bound*, which opened on Broadway in 1929, with music credited to Muriel Pollock and Maurice Rubens, but all Schwartz songs cut.
  3. Nonmusical play which had two Schwartz/Edward Heyman songs.
  4. Show had an original run of 236 performances—a two-month hiatus—then 17 more for a total of 253.

Appendix C

Songs Composed by Schwartz with Various Lyricists

NB: These songs were not all published, but comprise a list of the songs Schwartz worked on with 40 different lyricists. The number of songs, more than 650, should give the reader an idea of the scope of his work. The sources used are cited on the Addendum at the end of the list.[1] Programs from the various shows were also used. When not indicated in parentheses, titles in italics are from musical shows done either in New York or London. Songs listed as written for a show or movie may have been cut or never used, but these are not specifically indicated.

Lyricists

Stanley Adams: Independent songs[15]: 1981: The American Way; The Canadian Way; Fam'ly Trouble

Maxwell Anderson: *High Tor*: 1956 (*Ford Star Jubilee* / television): John Barleycorn; A Little Love, a Little While; Living One Day at a Time; Once Upon a Long Ago; Sad Is the Life of the Sailor's Wife; When You're in Love

Herbert Benjamin: Independent song: 1922: Tell Me Again

Irving Caesar: *The Mark of Zorro*: 1936 (unproduced movie): Dancing Conversation; I Remember a Dream; Lolita; My Saddle Is My Throne; The Night Has Lost the Moon; Serpentine

Sammy Cahn: *You're Never Too Young*: 1955 (movie): Face the Music; I Know Your Mother Loves You; I Like to Hike; Love Is All That Matters; Relax-Ay-Voo; Simpatico; You're Never Too Young; *Golden Memories*: 1978 (unproduced movie): Astaire, Kelly, and Me!; Golden Memories; You Can't Win a War Without a Song

Albert Carroll: *Grand Street Follies of 1926*: 1926: If You Know What I Mean (co-lyricist Theodore Goodwin)

Desmond Carter: *Here Comes the Bride*: 1930: Bang! There Goes My Heart; Congratulations; High and Low (co-lyricist Howard Dietz); Hot (co-lyricist Lew Levenson); I'm Like a Sailor Home from the Sea; I'll Always Remember (co-lyricists Max and Nathaniel Lief); Impossible Men; No One to Blame But You; A Rose in My Hair; Why Not Have a Little Party? (instrumental)—*Follow the Sun*: 1936: Dangerous You; Follow the Sun (instrumental); Nicotina; *Little Tommy Tucker*:

1930: I Have No Words³; Out of the Blue (co-composer Vivian Ellis); *Runaway Queen / The Queen's Affair*: 1934 (movies): Tonight⁵

Eli Dawson: *Surprises of 1923*: 1923 (Brant Lake Camp show): Baltimore, Md., You're the Only Doctor for Me

Howard Dietz: *The Little Show*: 1929: Get Up on a New Routine; Hammacher Schlemmer, I Love You; I Guess I'll Have to Change My Plan¹⁰; I've Made a Habit of You; Little Old New York; Man About Town; The Theme Song; *The Second Little Show*: 1930: Foolish Face; Good Clean Sport; I Like Your Face; I Started on a Shoestring; Lonely Hearts' Ball; Lucky Seven; My Intuition; New New York; Swing Your Tails; What a Case I've Got on You⁴; You're the Sunrise; *Three's a Crowd*: 1930: Je T'Aime; The Moment I Saw You (co-lyricist Greatrex Newman); Night after Night; Right at the Start of It; Something to Remember You By³; *The Band Wagon*: 1931: The Beggar Waltz (dance / instrumental); Confession; Dancing in the Dark; The Flag (instrumental); For Dear Old Nectar; Hoops; I Love Louisa; It Better Be Good; Miserable with You; Nanette; New Sun in the Sky; Nice Place to Visit; When the Rain Goes Pitter Patter (instrumental); Where Can He Be?; White Heat; *Flying Colors*: 1932: All's Well; Alone Together; Celebration; Day after Day; Fatal Fascination; It Was Never Like This; Just Around the Corner; Lost in the Crowd; Louisiana Hayride; Mein Kleine Acrobat; Mother Told Me So; My Heart Is Part of You; A Rainy Day; Riding Habit; A Shine on Your Shoes; Smokin' Reefers; Triplets; Two-Faced Woman; Independent songs: 1932: Is It All a Dream?²²;1933: Love Lost; 1934: What About Me?; *Nice Goings On*: 1933: What a Young Girl Ought to Know⁴; *Revenge with Music*: 1934: Flamenco (dance / instrumental); If There Is Someone Lovelier Than You; In the Middle of the Night; In the Noonday Sun; Maria; Moorish Dance (dance / instrumental); My Father Said; Never Marry a Dancer; Once-in-a-While; That Fellow Manuelo; Think It Over; Wand'ring Heart; When You Love Only One; You and the Night and the Music⁵; *The Girl from Missouri*: 1934 (movie): Born to Be Kissed; *The Gibson Family*: 1934–35 (radio): NB: Several of these songs may be found among the musical shows. They were written around the same time, usually for the musical show, but then were sung on *The Gibson Family*. Also, a few songs written for the *The Gibson Family* were later put into musical shows: Absent Minded; Algernon the Prodigy; All Russians Don't Wear Beards; All the Comforts of Home; The Auction Opera; The Best Things in Life Cost a Lot; Blue Eyes; Born to Be Kissed; Break the Rhythm; The Butler Carries On; Carnival Serenade; Christmas Carol; Circus Parade; Colored Weddin'; Coming from the Bar-X Ranch; Cowboy, Where Are You Riding?; Dancing on the Lake; Do You Feel a Thrill?; Dot's Song; Dustin' thru Town; Everything; Flirting with Dynamite; Floatin' Down the River on a Raft; Floating Through the Air; Flying in the Air; Foolish Face; Football Weather; Front Page; Glory Road; Got a Bran' New Suit; Great America; Grounds for Divorce; Handy Manny; Hi De Home Sweet Home; Hoops; Hot; Houseboat on the Harlem; How Can I Tell You?; How Low Can a Little Worm Go?; How High Can a Little Bird Fly?; How Many Ribbons on a Maypole?; The Hurdy Gurdy Man; I'm Glad It's Raining; I'm Half Crazy; I'm Like a Sailor Home from the Sea; I'm Ridin' High; I Belong to the Glee Club; I Con-

Appendix C. Songs Composed by Schwartz with Various Lyricists 321

fess; I've Got a Foolish Face; I Might As Well Be Miserable with You; I Want to Get Away from It All; I'll Make You Happy; If You Don't Wear Your Rubbers; Jungle; Jungle Jubilee; Just a Little Love, a Little Kiss; Kinky; Liza Lou; Local Girl Makes Good; Lonesome in a Crowd; A Lot of Places I Can't Go Back to; The Maestro's Getting Hot; Man About Town; Mein Kleine Acrobat; Midnight Kiss; Mother's Wedding Gown; Music in the Breeze; The Music Teacher; My Little Mule Wagon; A Quiet Evening at Home; Rhythm Makes the World Go 'Round; Rockabye Baby; Romany Caravan; 'Round the World; Shoestring; Silver Spoon in Your Mouth; Skating on the Lake; Sleigh Bells; Slightly Different Rhythm; The South South; Southern Cooking; Spring Is Here; Square Dance; The Steamboat Whistle; Sunday Picnic; Sweet Music; Tell It to Aunt Liza; There Must Be Room for You; Thief in the Night; Traveling Along; Trouble Song; Two by Two; Under the Stars; Under Your Spell; Watching the Sun Go Down; Water Boy; What a Case I've Got on You; What a Morning; When You Are Far Away from Me; Why Am I Singin' in the Mornin'?; Why Does Everyone Want to Sing?; With You Here and Me Here; You Are Free; You Are the Sunrise; You're Worth Waiting For; You Can't Win; You May Be Far Away from Me; Your Eyes Have Told Me So; *At Home Abroad*: 1935: Alt Wien; Death in the Afternoon (ballet / instrumental); Farewell, My Lovely; Get Away from It All[6]; Get Yourself a Geisha; Got a Bran' New Suit; The Hottentot Potentate; The Lady with the Tap[6]; Loadin' Time; Love Is a Dancing Thing; O Leo; O What a Wonderful World; Paree; The Steamboat Whistle; Thief in the Night; That's Not Cricket; The Toast of Vienna; What a Wonderful World; *Under Your Spell*: 1936 (movie): Amigo; I'm Going to Buy Low and Sell High; My Little Mule Wagon[9]; Under Your Spell[9]; *Follow the Sun*: 1936: How High Can a Little Bird Fly?; The Lady with the Tap; Love Is a Dancing Thing; Mein Kleine Acrobat; Sleigh Bells; *The Show Is On*: 1936: Josephine Waters; Prologue (Shakespearean Opening)[6]; *Between the Devil*: 1937: By Myself; Bye Bye Butterfly Lover; Celina Couldn't Say No; The Cocktail; Don't Go Away, Monsieur; Double Trouble; Experience; Five O'clock; Fly By Night; Front Page News; The Gendarme; How Do You Do?; I'm Against Rhythm; I've Made Up My Mind; I See Your Face before Me; The Night before the Morning After; Triplets; The Uniform[6]; Wand'ring Lover; Why Did You Do It?; You Have Everything; *Crossroads*: 1942 (movie): 'Til You Return; *Inside U.S.A.*: 1948: At the Mardi Gras; Atlanta; Better Luck Next Time; Blue Grass; Come, Oh Come (to Pittsburgh); Feller from Indiana; First Prize at the Fair; Forty Winks; Haunted Heart; If We Had a Little More Time; Inside U.S.A.; Leave My Pulse Alone; Massachusetts Mermaid; My Gal Is Mine Once More; Protect Me; Rhode Island Is Famous for You; A Song to Forget; Tiger Lily (dance / instrumental); We Won't Take It Back; *The Band Wagon*: 1953 (movie)[12]: The Egg (instrumental); The Girl Hunt (ballet / instrumental); The Private Eye; Penny Arcade (instrumental); That's Entertainment; *A Bell for Adano*: 1956 (television): A Bell for Adano; Fish; I'm Part of You; Okay, Mister Major; Why Not Surrender?; *Northwest Passage*: 1958 (television): Make Way for the Rangers; *Mrs. 'Arris Goes to Paris*: 1959 (unproduced show): Au Revoir, Paree; Before I Kiss the World Goodbye[23]; Diplomacy; Don't Go Away Monsieur; The Gendarme Never Loses His Head; I Don't Want to Go Home; I

Never Get Anywhere on Time; I'll Make You Happy; Montage—Musical Scene (dance / instrumental); The Sewing Circle on the Seine; Toujours Gai (Always Cheerful); Who Can? You Can![23]; Wonderful World; Song for publication party for *Act One*: 1959: Once in a Lifetime; *The Gay Life*: 1961: The Bloom Is Off the Rose; Bring Your Darling Daughter; Come A-Wandering with Me; Come Away; Drink the Waters; The Fair Sex; For the First Time; A Girl Like That; I'm Glad I'm Single; I Lost the Love of Anatol; I Love a Wedding; I Never Had a Chance; I'll Gladly Help You; I Wouldn't Marry You; If It Hadn't Been for You; The In-law Song; It's the First Time; Just What They Wanted; The Label on the Bottle; Magic Moment; Marriage; Now I'm Ready for a Frau; Oh, Mein Leibchen; Something You Never Had Before; This Kind of Girl; Who Can? You Can![23]; Why Go Anywhere at All?; A Wonderful Life; You're Not the Type; You Will Never Be Lonely; *Jennie*: 1963: Before I Kiss the World Goodbye[23]; Born Again; Close Your Eyes; Dinner Is Served; Femme Fatale; For Better or Worse; Harem Girls Dance (dance / instrumental); High Is Better Than Low; I Believe in Takin' a Chance; I Still Look at You That Way; I Think I'm Going to Like It Over Here; I Thought I Was Free; I'll Never Tell; It Isn't What You Have; Jennie; The Jig; Lonely Nights; A Mother Who's Really a Mother; Needle and Thread; The Night May Be Dark; No Hope for the Human Race; O'Connor; On the Other Hand; On the Thomas J. Muldoon; Put Yourself in My Hands; See Seattle; Sauce Diable (dance / instrumental); Sewing Waltz (instrumental); Waitin' for the Evening Train; Welcome; What a Charming Couple; When You're Far Away from New York Town; Where You Are

Edward Eliscu: *Queen High*: 1930 (movie): I'm Afraid of You (co-composer Ralph Rainger)

Frank Eyton: *Nice Goings On*: 1933: My Sweet One; Place in the Sun; 'Twixt the Devil and the Deep Blue Sea; Whatever You Do; With You Here and Me Here

Dorothy Fields: *Stars in Your Eyes*: 1939: All the Time; As of Today; Court Ballet (instrumental); He's Goin' Home; I'll Pay the Check; It's All Yours; Just a Little Bit More; A Lady Needs a Change; Mr. Blake; Never a Dull Moment; Night Club Ballet (instrumental); Okay for Sound; One Brief Moment; Places, Everybody; Self Made Man; Terribly Attractive; This Is It; Where Do I Go from You?[7]; *A Tree Grows in Brooklyn*: 1951: The Bride Wore Something Old; Call on Your Neighbor; Don't Be Afraid (of Anything); Growing Pains; He Had Refinement; Halloween Ballet (instrumental); I'm Like a New Broom; I'll Buy You a Star; If You Haven't Got a Sweetheart; Is That My Prince?; Look Who's Dancing; Love Is the Reason; Make the Man Love Me; Mine 'til Monday; Oysters in July; Payday; That's How It Goes; Tuscaloosa[8]; *Excuse My Dust*: 1951 (movie): Get a Horse; Goin' Steady; I'd Like to Take You out Dreaming; It Couldn't Happen to Two Nicer People; Lorelei Brown; Spring Has Sprung; That's for Children; Where Can I Run from You?; (Where Is There) One More You; *The Big Song and Dance*: 1952 (unproduced movie): Boys Are Better Than Girls; Dance Me Around; Goin' with the Birds; I'm Proud of You; I Did It and I'm Glad; Now Is Wonderful; The Profezzor; *By the Beautiful Sea*: 1954: Alone Too Long; Cake Walk (instrumental); Coney Island Boat; Good Time Charlie; Hang Up!; Happy

Appendix C. Songs Composed by Schwartz with Various Lyricists

Habit; Hooray for George the Third; I'd Rather Wake Up by Myself; It's All Mine; It's Not Where You Start[17]; It's Up to You; Lottie Gibson Specialty (Please Don't Send Me Down a Baby Brother); Me and Pollyanna; Mona from Arizona; More Love Than Your Love; Old Enough to Love[8]; The Sea Song; Thirty Weeks of Heaven; Throw the Anchor Away

Douglas Furber: *Nice Goings On*: 1933: I Know the Kind of Girl; Nice Goings On; *Wake Up and Dream*: 1929: She's Such a Comfort to Me[11] (co-lyricists Max and Nathaniel Lief and Donovan Parsons); *The House That Jack Built*: (London):1929: She's Such a Comfort to Me (see entry above)

Ira Gershwin: *Princess O'Rourke*: 1941(movie): Honorable Moon[19] (co-lyricist E.Y. Harburg); *Park Avenue*: 1946: The Dew Was on the Rose; Don't Be a Woman If You Can; Echo (dance / instrumental); For the Life of Me; The Future Mrs. Coleman; Goodbye to All That; Heavenly Day; Hope for the Best; Land of Opportunitee; My Son-in-Law; Remind Me Not to Leave Town; Stay As We Are; Sweet Nevada; There's No Holding Me; There's Nothing Like Marriage for People; Tomorrow Is the Time

David Goldberg: *Grand Street Follies of 1929*: 1929: I Need You So (co-lyricist Howard Dietz)

Ted Goodman: *Surprises of 1923*: 1923 (Brant Lake Camp show): The Big Surprise; Candy Contrabandit; Ding Dong; Post Office Blues; Seenyah!; Twilight; *Palula Island*: 1923 (Brant Lake Camp show with some lyrics contributed by Arthur Freund): Adirondack History; Injuns of the Togo Togo; Let's Whoop It Up for Brant Lake Camp; Let's Wish; Mountain Trail; Palula Moon; Spooks; Trip, Trip, Trip!

Theodore Goodwin: *Americana*: 1926: Mountain Trail; *Grand Street Follies of 1926*: 1926: If You Know What I Mean (co-lyricist Albert Carroll)

Oscar Hammerstein II: *American Jubilee*: 1940 (a pageant of Americana for the New York World's Fair of 1939–40): Another New Day; By the People; The Fireman's Serenade; How Can I Ever Be Alone?; Jenny Lind; My Bicycle Girl; One in a Million; Tennessee Fish Fry; We Like It Over Here

Otto Harbach: *Good Boy*: 1928: You're the One

E.Y. Harburg: *Queen High*: 1930 (movie) and *Follow the Leader*: 1930 (movie): Brother, Just Laugh It Off[21] (co-composer Ralph Rainger); Independent song: 1934: Then I'll Be Tired of You; *Cairo*: 1942 (movie): Cairo (The Moon Looks Down on Cairo); In Times Like These; Keep the Light Burning Bright (co-lyricist Howard Dietz); A Man Without a Woman; The Waltz Is Over; Political songs[13]: 1942: Don't Look Now, Mr. Warren; 1944: Don't Look Now Mr. Dewey (But Your Record Is Showing)

Lorenz Hart: Independent song: 1924: I Know My Girl by Her Perfume; *Dream Boy*: 1924 (Brant Lake Camp show): I Love to Lie Awake in Bed[10]; Last Night

Edward Heyman: *She Loves Me Not*: 1933 (play): After All You're All I'm After; She Loves Me Not; *That Girl from Paris*: 1936 (movie): The Call to Arms; Love and Learn; Moon Face; My Nephew from Nice; Seal It with a Kiss

Inside U.S.A. with Chevrolet[20]: *Inside U.S.A. with Chevrolet* : 1948–49 (television): Dearie; Hammock on the Porch; Inside U.S.A. with Chevrolet; Latin from Manhattan; Make a Miracle; Me and Marie; Pass the Peace Pipe; Wealthy Widow; You Can Call Me Peter; Ta-Ra-Ra (commercial)

Alan Jay Lerner: *Paint Your Wagon*[18]: Bonanza!; Californey Never Looked So Good; Kentucky; Noah Was a Wisdom Man; Over the Purple Hills; Paint Your Wagon; There's Always One You Can't Forget

Lew Levenson: *The Little Show*: 1929: Song of the Riveter

Max and Nathaniel Lief: *Well! Well! Well!* 1928: I Love You and I Like You (also in *Grand Street Follies of 1929* and *Here Comes the Bride*); I'll Always Remember (co-lyricists with Desmond Carter)

Frank Loesser: *The Moon Is Down*: 1942 (oratorio): The Moon Is Down; Independent songs: 1942 (patriotic): Buy a Bond; 1943: Way Up North; *Thank Your Lucky Stars*: 1943 (movie): The Dreamer; Good Night, Good Neighbor; How Sweet You Are; I'm Goin' North; I'm Riding for a Fall; Ice Cold Katy; Love Isn't Born (It's Made); No You, No Me; Thank Your Lucky Stars; That's What You Jolly Well Get; They're Either Too Young or Too Old; We're Staying Home Tonight

Brat Martin: Independent Song; 1922: I Am Getting Better All the Time

Johnny Mercer: *Navy Blues*: 1941 (movie): Hawaiian Party; In Waikiki; Navy Blues; Turn Out the Light (and Call the Law); When Are We Going to Land Abroad?; You're a Natural; *All Through the Night*: 1942 (movie): All Through the Night; *Dangerous When Wet*: 1953 (movie): Ain't Nature Grand; C'est la Guerre; Fifi; I Got Out of Bed on the Right Side; I Like Men; In My Wildest Dreams; Liquapep

Agnes Morgan: *Grand Street Follies of 1926*: 1926: Little Igloo for Two; Uncle Tom's Cabin (co-composer Randall Thompson); *Grand Street Follies of 1929*: 1929: Age of Innocence (dance / instrumental); The Amoeba's Lament; Don't Do It; The Double Standard; The Jolly Troubadour (instrumental); My Dynamo; Rome Is Burning; The Vineyards of Manhattan (instrumental / sketch); What Did Della Wear (When Georgie Came Across?)

Henry Myers: *The New Yorkers*: 1927: Floating Through the Air; He Who Gets Slapped; Here Comes the Prince of Wales; I Can't Get into the Quota; Indian Chant (instrumental); 99 Per Cent Pure; Romany; Self-Expression; A Song About Love; *The Little Show*: 1929: What Every Little Girl Should Know

Greatrex Newman: *The Co-Optimists of 1930*: 1930: Dancing Town; The Moment I Saw You (both with co-lyricist Howard Dietz); Nothing Up Our Sleeves (instrumental); Steeplejack; The Stuff to Give the Troops (instrumental); Sunday Afternoon

Muriel Pollock: Independent Song: 1929: I Can't Forget

Leo Robin: *Casablanca*: 1970 (unproduced show)[16]: Casablanca; Everybody Comes to Rick's; The Way Things Are; Why Should I Care?; *The Time, the Place and the Girl*: 1946 (movie): A Gal in Calico; I Happened to Walk Down First Street; Oh, But I Do; A Rainy Night in Rio; A Solid Citizen of the Solid South; Through a Thousand Dreams; The Time, the Place and the Girl; Unproduced / untitled show: 1982: A Silent Song

Harry Ruskin: *The Little Show*: 1929: High Finance

Morrie Ryskind: *Ned Wayburn's Gambols*: 1929: Gypsy Days; The Sun Will Shine; *Bring on the Girls*: 1934 (play): Down on the Old-Time Farm

Appendix C. Songs Composed by Schwartz with Various Lyricists 325

Arthur Schwartz (as composer and lyricist): *Grand Street Follies of 1926*: 1926: The Polar Bear Strut; *Glad Tiding*: 1928 (tabloid show): College Hop; Glad Tidings; *By the Beautiful Sea*: 1954 (unproduced English version): Come to Blackpool; Independent songs: circa 1920: I'm Getting Better Every Day; 1923: Promise!!; 1969: Quiet on the River; 1976: One Two Three Four Five; 1978: The World Is Turning Fast[14] (composer George Balanchine / Schwartz did lyrics only); *Dancing in the Dark*: 1979 (Manhattan Theatre Club revue): The Jog; Love Should Be Free

Alexander Slavitt: Fraternity song: 1920: Shine On, Pi Lambda Phi; New York University fight song: 1920: Smash, Crash Right Through; *Junior Show* (New York University): 1920: There's a Whole Lot of Moonlight and a Pretty Rustic Seat Independent song: 1922: Moon Dreams

Harry B. Smith: *The Red Robe*: 1928: Believe in Me

Albert Stillman: *Virginia*: 1937: Fee-Fie-Fo-Fum; Good and Lucky; Goodbye, Jonah; I'll Be Sittin' in De Lap o' de Lord; If You Were Someone Else; It's Our Duty to the King; Meet Me at the Fair; My Bridal Gown (co-lyricist Laurence Stallings); My Heart Is Dancing; An Old Flame Never Dies (co-lyricist Laurence Stallings); Send One Angel Down; Virginia; We Had to Rehearse; Why Must I Play the Lady?; You and I Know (co-lyricist Laurence Stallings); Independent song: 1938: How Can We Be Wrong? (co-lyricist Howard Dietz); *Inside U.S.A. with Chevrolet*[20]: 1948–49 (television): I'm Looking Down on the Moon

Arthur Swanstrom: *Princess Charming*[2]: 1930: First Sunbeam; Here Is a Sword; I'm Designed for Love; I Must Be One of the Roses; I'll Be There; I'll Never Leave You; Just a Friend of Mine; Never Mind How; One for All; Palace of Dreams; The Panic's On; Take a Letter to the King; Trailing a Shooting Star; Wings in the Morning; A Wonderful Thing for the King; You

Eddie Ugast: Independent song: 1924: Say Uncle! Say Uncle!

Addendum to Songs

1. In addition to programs from shows, the following sources were used for the above list:
    (a) Richard C. Norton, *A Chronology of American Musical Theater* (Oxford: Oxford University Press, 2002).
    (b) Steven Suskin, *Show Tunes: The Songs, Shows, and Careers of Broadway's Major Composers*, 4th ed. (New York: Oxford University Press, 2010).
    (c) Roger D. Kinkle, *The Complete Encyclopedia of Popular Music and Jazz: 1900–1950* (New Rochelle, NY: Arlington House Publishers, 1974).
    (d) Ken Bloom, *The American Songbook: The Singers, the Songwriters, and the Songs* (New York: Black Dog & Leventhal Publishers, 2005.)
    (e) Ken Bloom, *American Song: The Complete Companion to Tin Pan Alley Song: Volume 3: Songwriters* (New York: Schirmer Books, 2001).
    (f) Ken Bloom, *American Song: The Complete Musical Theatre Companion*, 2nd ed., 1877–1995 (New York: Schirmer Books, 1996).
    (g) Arthur Schwartz Papers, ML31.S38, Musical Division, Library of Congress, Boxes 1–21.
    (h) "*Gibson Family*: 9/15/34–6/2/35 Titles," notes on songs from *The Gibson Family*, unpublished, ASP.
    (i) Dan Dietz, *Off Broadway Musicals, 1910–2007: Casts, Credits, Songs, Critical

Reception and Performance Data of More Than 1,800 Shows (Jefferson, NC: McFarland & Company, Inc., 2010).

    (j) *IMDb* website.

  2. Music for this show was written by both Schwartz and Albert Sirmay with no specific song credited to either one of them. All lyrics were by Arthur Swanstrom.

  3. "Something to Remember You By" with Howard Dietz lyrics from *Three's a Crowd* and "I Have No Words" with Desmond Carter lyrics written for *Little Tommy Tucker,* have the same melody.

  4. "What a Case I've Got on You" was re-titled and revised as "What a Young Girl Ought to Know" for *Nice Goings On* in London.

  5. The melody for "You and the Night and the Music" was written for the 1934 British film, *The Queen's Affair,* released in America as *Runaway Queen.* For the movie, it was entitled "Tonight," with lyrics by Desmond Carter.

  6. These songs were used for a USO show, *At Ease,* with lyric revisions not written by Howard Dietz:

Original Song	From	Became
"The Lady with the Tap"	At Home Abroad	"The Soldier with the Tap-Tap-Tap"
"Get Away from It All"	At Home Abroad	"Come Along to Our Show"
"Prologue" ("Shakespearean Opening")	The Show Is On	"Shakespearean Opening"
"The Uniform"	Between the Devil	"The Uniform"

  7. This song is listed in Steven Suskin's *Show Tunes* as being recorded at the time of *Stars in Your Eyes,* the Schwartz / Fields show from 1939, although it was not in that show and no recordings around that time could be found. It was first recorded by Jonathan Schwartz for his album *Alone Together: Jonathan Schwartz Sings Arthur Schwartz* in 1977.

  8. "Tuscaloosa," cut from *A Tree Grows in Brooklyn,* and "Old Enough to Love," from *By the Beautiful Sea,* are the same melody but with different lyrics, both by Dorothy Fields. The latter song was used.

  9. "My Little Mule Wagon" and "Under Your Spell" were written for *The Gibson Family,* and the latter became the show's theme song. Both were sung by Lawrence Tibbett in the film, *Under Your Spell.* The other two songs listed were new for the film.

  10. "I Guess I'll Have to Change My Plan" was originally titled "I Love to Lie Awake in Bed," lyrics by Lorenz Hart, written for a show at Brant Lake Camp, circa 1924, where Hart and Schwartz worked.

  11. "She's Such a Comfort to Me" was interpolated into a musical revue written mostly by Cole Porter, *Wake Up and Dream,* 1929.

  12. Songs are listed as *The Band Wagon* (movie) only if written specifically for the movie and not those songs taken from *The Band Wagon* and other Schwartz / Dietz musicals for use in the movie.

  13. These two songs were the same melody used for two political campaign songs with both lyrics written by E.Y. Harburg. Earl Warren was running for Governor of California, and Thomas Dewey for President, against Harry Truman.

  14. This was a song for no particular show or dance program with music written by Balanchine.

  15. Titles designated "Independent songs" were written for no known show. These are listed mostly in the song compendium *American Song: The Complete Companion to Tin Pan Alley Song: Volume 3: Songwriters* by Ken Bloom, but also in several other sources.

  16. *Casablanca* was a musical based on the movie. Schwartz and Leo Robin worked on it for a few years in the late sixties, but it was never produced. Schwartz also wrote a score for a musical, also called *Casablanca,* with Howard Dietz, which also went unproduced, but song titles were not available.

Appendix C. Songs Composed by Schwartz with Various Lyricists

17. "It's Not Where You Start" was not used in *By the Beautiful Sea*. The same title with a different melody was used by Fields for her show with Cy Coleman, *Seesaw*, and it became a hit.

18. The Schwartz / Alan Jay Lerner songs were never used in the movie, *Paint Your Wagon*, but are available in the Arthur Schwartz Papers at the Library of Congress.

19. "Honorable Moon" was written for a fund raiser for United China Relief and introduced on national radio by Connie Boswell. It was then used two years later in *Princess O'Rourke*, sung by Nan Wynn.

20. *Inside U.S.A. with Chevrolet* was a television show which aired on CBS from September 29, 1949 through March 16, 1950, for which Schwartz, as producer, used mostly his old songs. With most of the songs written for the show, the lyricist is unclear, although the program lists Dietz, Ira Gershwin, Oscar Hammerstein II, and Albert Stillman.

21. "Brother, Just Laugh It Off" was used in two films, the first time in *Queen High*, then in *Follow the Leader*, both from Paramount in 1930.

22. "Is It All a Dream?" was ballet music, "The Beggar Waltz," from *The Band Wagon*, later turned into an independent song when Howard Dietz added lyrics. It was published in 1932.

23. *Mrs. 'Arris Goes to Paris* (1959) was never produced. Two songs written for that show were used in later shows: "Who Can? You Can!" in *The Gay Life* (1961) and "Before I Kiss the World Goodbye" in *Jennie* (1963).

Appendix D

Tribute Albums

This listing of tribute albums is arranged in entries that include performer(s), album title, year, and label.

Various; The Arthur Schwartz Songbook; 2013; Goldenlane Records CD

Meredith D'Ambrosio; By Myself; 2012; Sunnyside Communications CD SSC 1285

Ray Kennedy Trio; The Ray Kennedy Trio Plays the Music of Arthur Schwartz; 2007; Arbors Records CD LC 02732

Herb Geller; Herb Geller Plays the Arthur Schwartz Songbook; 2006; Hep Records HEP CD 2089

Arthur Schwartz, Nancy Dussault, Edward Evanko, and Judy Kaye; The Songwriters: Arthur Schwartz and Charles Strouse; 2005; Lance Entertainment Inc. DVD KOC-DV-6624

Cheryl Parker; The World Is Turning Fast: The Songs of Arthur Schwartz; 1999; Parker Productions CAP0952

Various; Dancing in the Dark: The Songs of Arthur Schwartz: Centenary Issue; 2000; ASV Ltd CD AJA 5301

Various; The Great American Composers: Howard Dietz and Arthur Schwartz; 1996; The Columbia House Company CD C21-2 8654

Jonathan Schwartz; Alone Together: Jonathan Schwartz Sings Arthur Schwartz; 1995; Muse Records CD MCD 5143 (originally released in 1977 as a LP)

Margaret Whiting; Too Marvelous for Words: A Tribute to Johnny Mercer, Richard Whiting, Arthur Schwartz & Alec Wilder; 1995; Audiophile Records CD

Various; Arthur Schwartz: American Songbook Series: Smithsonian Collection of Recordings; 1995; Smithsonian / Sony Music CD DIDP-085165

Various; Ben Bagley's Arthur Schwartz Revisited; 1992; Painted Smiles Records CD PSCD-137

Various; Dancing in the Dark: The Music and the Songs of Arthur Schwartz; 1992; Conifer Records Limited CD CDHD 180

Dave McKenna; Dancing in the Dark and Other Music of Arthur Schwartz; 1986; Concord Jazz CD CCD-4292

Arthur Schwartz; from the pen of...Arthur Schwartz; 1976; RCA Records LP LPL1-5121

Appendix D. Tribute Albums

Robert Clary; Robert Clary Sings Arthur Schwartz, Howard Dietz, and Dorothy Fields; 2003; CD (no label)

Various; The Great British Dance Bands Play the Music of Arthur Schwartz; 1978; World Records SH 274 LP Vinyl

Tommy Dorsey and His Orchestra; You and the Night and the Music: Tommy Dorsey and His Orchestra Plays the Musical Comedy Hits of Howard Dietz and Arthur Schwartz; 1951; Decca Records DL 5317 / LP Vinyl Album 839

Appendix E

Schwartz Songs on *Your Hit Parade*

This listing of *Your Hit Parade* is arranged in entries that include song, singer and / or orchestra, year and date, and highest rank on *Your Hit Parade*.

"A Gal in Calico"; Johnny Mercer and the Pied Pipers with Paul Weston and His Orchestra; 1946: December 21, 28; 1947: January 4, 11, 18, 25, February 1, 8, 15, 22, March 1, 8, 22; #1

"Haunted Heart"; Perry Como with Russ Case and His Orchestra; 1948: April 10, May 15, 22, 29, June 5, 12, 19, 26, July 3, 10, 17; #4

"How Sweet You Are"; Kay Armen and the Balladiers; 1943: September 25, November 13, December 4; #9

"I See Your Face before Me"; Carmen Lombardo with Guy Lombardo and His Royal Canadians; 1938: March 12; #9

"Oh, But I Do"; Margaret Whiting with orchestra conducted by Jerry Gray; 1947: January 18, 25, February 1, 8, 15, 22, March 1, 8, 22, 29; #3

"They're Either Too Young or Too Old"; Kitty Kallen with the Jimmy Dorsey Orchestra; 1943: October 16, 23, 30, November 6, 13, 20, 27, December 11, 18, 25; 1944: January 8, 15; #2

"This Is It"; Jack Leonard with the Tommy Dorsey Orchestra; 1939: March 18, April 1; #6

"You and I Know"; Ray Eberle and the Glenn Miller Orchestra; 1937: November 6; #10

Chapter Notes

The following refer to large collections or sources of information regarding Arthur Schwartz: ASP—Arthur Schwartz Papers, ML31.S38, Musical Division, Library of Congress, http://hdl.loc,gov/loc.music/eadmus.mu012021.

DFP—Dorothy Fields Papers, 8-MWEZ+n.c. 27914, Billy Rose Theatre Collection, New York Public Library for the Performing Arts.

HDP—Howard Dietz Papers, JPB 06-31, Music Division, The New York Public Library for the Performing Arts.

HDATBW—"Aboard the Band Wagon: A Few Verbal Snapshots from an Album of Long Association with a Popular Composer," unpublished essay, ASP, Box 51 / Box 9.

ROAS—"Reminiscences of Arthur Schwartz: Oral history, November, 1958," Columbia University Rare Book and Manuscript Library, NXCP87-A1387.

Introduction

1. Final Draft, The Perry Como Show, Show #119, September 27, 1958, ASP, Box 40 / Folder 6, 21-1-3.

Chapter 1

1. Frederick Nolan, *Lorenz Hart: A Poet on Broadway* (New York: Oxford University Press, 1994), 52.
2. Certification of Birth for Arthur Schwartz, November 4, 1900, Department of Health, Bureau of Records and Statistics, City of New York, ASP, Box 49 / Folder 7.
3. Arthur Schwartz, "THE FACTS," unpublished notes, ASP, Box 51 / Folder 1, 3.
4. Radio script, *The Songwriters: Arthur Schwartz*, ASP, Box 41 / Folder 8, 2.
5. "News and Gossip of the Broadway Front," *New York Times*, July 29, 1935; Richard Rodgers, *Musical Stages* (New York: Random House, 1975), 10.
6. Schwartz, "HOW I GOT TO PRODUCE FILMS," unpublished notes, ASP, Box 51 / Folder 2, 4.
7. Phyllis Cerf, "What's New...by Phyllis Cerf," *Newsday*, January 31, 1957.
8. Gene Lees, "The Distinctive Style of Arthur Schwartz," *High Fidelity*, September / 1976, 20.
9. Radio script, 3, 15.
10. Nolan, 48.
11. Jonathan Schwartz, *All in Good Time: A Memoir* (New York: Random House, 2004), 4.
12. Kyle Crichton, "One Easy Lesson," *Collier's*, October 14, 1944, 46.
13. Wilfrid Sheed, *The House That George Built: With a Little Help from Irving, Cole, and a Crew of About Fifty* (New York: Random House, 2008), 298.
14. Cerf, "Arthur Schwartz's First Job," *Good Housekeeping*, November / 1956.
15. Howard Dietz, HDATBW, 5.
16. "Notable Alumni—Pi Lambda Phi—WI," http://sites.google.com/site/pilambdaphiwi/notable-alumni/notable-alumni (accessed February 11, 2013), 2.
17. Schwartz, "Memo for Mr. Dietz," typed notes, undated, ASP, Box 51 / Folder 2, 1.
18. *Webster's New Universal Unabridged*

Dictionary, s.v. "Coue," "Coueism" (New York: Barnes & Noble Books, 2003).
19. Schwartz and Al Slavitt, "Smash, Crash Right Through," New York University fight song, *New York University Song Book*, Rev Ed 1921, ASP.
20. "Jubilee Composer Schwartz," *The Frater*, Pi Lambda Phi Fraternity, October / 1940, Vol. XXIII / No. 1, ASP, Box 50 / Folder 1, 6.
21. Schwartz, "THE FACTS," 1.
22. Ibid., 2.
23. Benny Green, *Let's Face the Music: The Golden Age of Popular Song* (London: Pavillion Books Unlimited, 1989), 98.
24. Schwartz, "THE FACTS," 2.
25. Nolan, 86.
26. Jack D. Brinkley, "Behind the Music," *Radio Guide*, October 20, 1934, 21.
27. Dominic Symonds, *We'll Have Manhattan: The Early Work of Rodgers and Hart* (New York: Oxford University Press, 2015), 34.
28. Program, *Surprises of 1923*, Brant Lake Mirror, daily publication, n.d., ASP, Box 41 / Folder 15.
29. *Brant Lake Mirror*, Brant Lake Camp, Horicon, New York, July 22, 1923, ASP, Box 13/ Folder 9.
30. Dorothy Hart, *Thou Swell! Thou Witty!: The Life and Lyrics of Lorenz Hart* (New York: Harper & Row, 1976), 35.
31. *The Complete Lyrics of Lorenz Hart*, Hart and Robert Kimball, eds. (New York: Alfred A. Knopf, 1986), 7–10.
32. Hart, *Thou Swell! Thou Witty!*, 35.
33. Nolan, 51–2.
34. Green, 98.
35. Benjamin Welles, "In Re: Arthur Schwartz," *New York Times*, July 7, 1940.
36. Rodgers, 51.
37. Laurence Maslon, *Broadway to Main Street: How Show Tunes Enchanted America* (New York: Oxford University Press, 2018), 15–6.
38. Frank Rasky, "Broadway Songwriter Entertains Students," *Toronto Star*, June 22, 1976, E10.
39. Hart, 36.
40. *Ibid*.
41. Nolan, 52.
42. Schwartz, "THE FACTS," 3.
43. Dietz, *Dancing in the Dark: Words by Howard Dietz: An Autobiography* (New York: Quadrangle / New York Times Book Co., Inc., 1974), 132.
44. Gary Marmorstein, *A Ship Without a Sail: The Life of Lorenz Hart* (New York: Simon & Schuster, 2012), 111.
45. Nolan, 53.

Chapter 2

1. Howard Dietz, HDATBW, 6.
2. Dorothy Hart, *Thou Swell! Thou Witty!: The Life and Lyrics of Lorenz Hart* (New York: Harper & Row, 1976), 36.
3. Gary Marmorstein, *A Ship Without a Sail: The Life of Lorenz Hart* (New York: Simon & Schuster, 2012), 69.
4. Dan Sullivan, "Arthur Schwartz Goes His Way By Himself," *Los Angeles Times*, October 17, 1976, 46.
5. Arthur Schwartz, "HOW I GOT TO PRODUCE FILMS," unpublished notes, ASP, Box 51 / Folder 2, 4; Marmorstein, 120.
6. Rodney Greenberg, *George Gershwin* (London: Phaidon Press, 1998), 37.
7. Thomas S. Hischak, *Off-Broadway Musicals Since 1919* (Toronto: The Scarecrow Press, Inc., 2011), 10.
8. Alice Lewisohn Crowley, *The Neighborhood Playhouse: Leaves from a Theatre Scrapbook* (New York: Theatre Arts Books, 1959), 117.
9. Robert Baral, *Revue: A Nostalgic Reprise of the Great Broadway Period* (New York: Fleet Publishing Corporation, 1962), 180–81; Cecil Smith and Glenn Litton, *Musical Comedy in America* (New York: Routledge / Theatre Arts Books, 1981), 133–4.
10. Crowley, 119.
11. Dominic Symonds, *We'll Have Manhattan: The Early Work of Rodgers and Hart* (New York: Oxford University Press, 2015), 66.
12. Steven Suskin, *Show Tunes: The Songs, Shows, and Careers of Broadway's Major Composers* (New York: Dodd, Mead & Company, Inc., 1986), 234. NB: This is the first edition of Suskin's *Show Tunes*. All the citations of *Show Tunes* in this chapter are from that edition. For the remainder of the book, the 4th edition is used.
13. Smith, 133.
14. Elliot Forbes, "Randall Thompson: Brief Life of a Choral Composer: 1899–1984," *Harvard Magazine*, July 1, 2001, http://harvardmagazine.com/2001/

07/randall-thompson.html (accessed March 13, 2017), 1–2.

15. Virginia L. Grattan, *American Women Songwriters: A Biographical Dictionary* (Westport, CT: Greenwood Press, 1993), 85–6.

16. Suskin, 234.

17. Schwartz, "The FACTS," unpublished notes, ASP, Box 51 / Folder 1, 4.

18. Dietz, 6–7.

19. Avis Caminez, "Americans Abroad," *The Tatler*, June / 1977.

20. Dietz, *Dancing in the Dark: Words by Howard Dietz: An Autobiography* (New York: Quadrangle / The New York Times Book Co., 1974), 132.

21. Schwartz, "The FACTS," 4.

22. Florabel Muir, "Florabel Muir Reports: Schwartz Heading East for Broadway Musical," *Hollywood (CA) Citizen-News*, April / 1947, unspecified date from incomplete article, ASP, Box 40 / Folder 2.

23. Dietz, HDATBW, 6.

24. *Ibid.*, 1.

25. "The Ins and Outs of Composing for Broadway," *Canadian Composer*, September / 1976, 12.

26. *Encyclopaedia Britannica*, s.v. "Saint John Ervine," http://www.britannica.com/biography/Saint-John-Ervine (accessed March 13, 2017), 1.

27. "Hit Writer Says Successful Song Is 50 Percent Talent and the Rest Digging and Logic," *Boston Globe*, January 12, 1947.

28. *Current Biography*, November / 1979, Vol 40 / #11, s.v. "Schwartz, Arthur"; Stanley Green, *The World of Musical Comedy: The Story of the American Musical Stage As Told Through the Careers of Its Foremost Composers and Lyricists* (Chicago: Ziff Davis Publishing Company, 1960), 185.

29. Benjamin Welles, "In Re: Arthur Schwartz," *New York Times*, July 7, 1940.

30. Miles Kreuger, *Show Boat: The Story of a Classic American Musical* (New York: Oxford University Press, 1977), 108, 110.

31. Schwartz, unpublished notes to Howard Dietz, ASP, Box 51 / Folder 2, 3–4.

32. Suskin, 235–6.

33. Broadside for *1928*, Intimate Playhouse, ASP.

34. Suskin, 235.

35. Hart, 27.

36. Charles Brackett, untitled item, *The New Yorker*, March 26, 1927.

37. "'New Yorkers' a Merry Crew," *Zits*, March 26, 1927.

38. "The New Yorkers," *Variety*, March 16, 1927.

39. *New York Mirror*, item, March 19, 1927.

40. "New Yorkers," *Deseret News* (Salt Lake City, UT), March 19, 1927.

41. Suskin, 235.

42. Ken Bloom, *American Song: The Complete Musical Theatre Companion*, 2nd ed., 1877–1995, Vol. 1: A–S (New York: Schirmer Books, 1996), 407–8.

43. Dietz, HDATBW, 7.

44. Bloom, 898, 1188.

45. Program, *The Red Robe*, December 25, 1928, Shubert Archive.

46. John Franceschina, *Harry B. Smith: Dean of American Librettists* (New York: Routledge, 2003), 273.

47. Barbara Stratyner, *Ned Wayburn and the Dance Routine: From Vaudeville to the Ziegfeld Follies: Studies in Dance History No. 13* (Oak Creek, WI: Society of Dance History Scholars, 196), 11.

48. Mark N. Grant, *The Rise and Fall of the Broadway Musical* (Boston: Northeastern University Press, 2004), 122, 230–1; Gerald Bordman, *American Musical Revue: From the Passing Show to Sugar Babies* (New York: Oxford University Press, 1985), 43–4.

49. Stratyner, 11.

50. *Ibid.*, 81.

51. Deena Rosenberg, *Fascinating Rhythm: The Collaboration of George and Ira Gershwin* (New York: Dutton, 1991), 117–18.

52. Wilfrid Sheed, *The House That George Built: With a Little Help from Irving, Cole, and a Crew of About Fifty* (New York: Random House, 2008), 49.

53. Suskin, 236.

54. Lee Davis, *Scandals and Follies: The Rise and Fall of the Great Broadway Revue* (New York: Limelight Editions, 2000), 258.

55. Sheet music for "Down on the Old-Time Farm," Arthur Schwartz and Morrie Ryskind (New York: Harms, 1934).

56. Malcolm Goldstein, *George S. Kaufman: His Life, His Theater* (New York: Oxford University Press, 1979), 233.

57. Review of *Bring on the Girls*, *Variety*, November 27, 1934, 55.

58. Jon Bradshaw, *Dreams That Money Can Buy: The Tragic Life of Libby Holman*

(New York: William Morrow and Company, Inc., 1985), 69.
59. Bloom, 418–9; Suskin, 237–8.
60. Suskin, 238.
61. Gerald Bordman, *American Musical Theatre: A Chronicle*, 3rd ed. (New York: Oxford University Press, 2001), 508; Suskin, 60; *Wikipedia*, s.v. "Ripples," https://en.wikipedia.org/wiki/Ripples_(musicals) (accessed September 1, 2019).
62. Bloom, 1179.

Chapter 3

1. David Ewen, *Popular American Composers from Revolutionary Times to the Present* (New York: H.W. Wilson Company, 1962), 152.
2. Caryl Brahms and Ned Sherrin, *Song by Song: The Lives and Work of 14 Great Lyric Writers* (Egerton, Bolton, Engalnd: Ross Anderson Publications, 1984), 248.
3. *Ibid.*, 107.
4. Deena Rosenberg, *Fascinating Rhythm: The Collaboration of George and Ira Gershwin* (New York: Dutton, 1991), 17–9; Howard Dietz, *Dancing in the Dark: Words by Howard Dietz: An Autobiography* (New York: Quadrangle / The New York Times Book Co., 1974), 21.
5. Arthur Schwartz reply to queries from Howard Dietz, ASP, Box 51 / Folder 2, 4.
6. Dietz, 73.
7. *Ibid.*
8. Steven Suskin, *Show Tunes: The Songs, Shows, and Careers of Broadway's Major Composers*, 4th ed. (New York: Oxford University Press, 2010), 7.
9. *Ibid.*; Graham Payn with Barry Day, *My Life with Noel Coward* (New York: Applause Books, 2000), 103–4; Brahms, 108.
10. Brahms, 108.
11. Ewen, 152.
12. Jack D. Brinkley, "Behind the Music," *Radio Guide*, October 20, 1934, 21.
13. Dietz, 274.
14. Ira Gershwin, *Lyrics on Several Occasions* (New York: Alfred A. Knopf, Inc., 1959), 120.
15. Schwartz, "You Have to Do More Than Rhyme," program book for *Inside U.S.A.*, ASP, 12.
16. Dietz, 76.
17. "Dietz and Schwartz," pre-publication notes for souvenir program for *Jennie*, ASP, Box 50 / Folder 1, 2.
18. Avis Caminez, "American Abroad," *The Tatler*, June / 1977.
19. Gene Lees, "The Distinctive Style of Arthur Schwartz," *High Fidelity*, September / 1976, 20.
20. Dietz, 39.
21. Herbert Keyser, *Geniuses of the American Musical Theatre: The Composers and Lyricists* (New York: Applause Theatre & Cinema Books, 2009), 60.
22. Stanley Green, *The World of Musical Comedy: The Story of the American Musical Stage As Told Through the Careers of Its Foremost Composers and Lyricists* (Chicago: Ziff Davis Publishing Company, 1960), 185.
23. Dietz, 17.
24. Benny Green, *Let's Face the Music: The Golden Age of Popular Song* (London: Pavillion Books Limited, 1989), 96.

Chapter 4

1. David A. Jasen, *Tin Pan Alley: The Composers, the Songs, the Performers and Their Times: The Golden Age of Popular Music from 1886 to 1956* (London: Omnibus Press, 1990), 236.
2. Jonas Westover, *The Shuberts and Their Passing Shows: The Untold Tale of Ziegfeld's Rivals* (New York: Oxford University Press, 2016), 8–9.
3. *Current Biography*, November / 1979, Vol. 40 / #11, H.W. Wilson Company, s.v. "Schwartz, Arthur."
4. George Jean Nathan, "The Season's Showers Bring April Flowers," *New York Post*, April 19, 1946.
5. Gary Marmorstein, *A Ship without a Sail: The Life of Lorenz Hart* (New York: Simon & Schuster, 2012), 180.
6. Caryl Brahms and Ned Sherrin, *Song by Song: 14 Great Lyric Writers* (Bolton, Lancashire: Ross Anderson Publications, 1984), 103.
7. Stanley Green, *The World of Musical Comedy: The Story of the American Musical Stage As Told Through the Careers of Its Foremost Composers and Lyricists* (Chicago: Ziff Davis Publishing Company, 1960), 186.
8. Robert Taylor, "The Roving Eye: One of the Mostly Boys," *Boston Herald*, July 24, 1963, 35.
9. Howard Dietz, *Dancing in the Dark:*

Words by Howard Dietz: An Autobiography (New York: Quadrangle / The New York Times Book Co., 1974), 121–2.

10. Alan Jay Lerner, *The Musical Theatre: A Celebration* (New York: McGraw-Hill Book Company, 1986), 107; Hamilton Darby Perry, *Libby Holman: Body and Soul* (Boston: Little Brown and Company, 1983), 50–51.

11. Dietz, 122.

12. Jack Burton, *The Blue Book of Tin Pan Alley* (New York: Century House, 1950), 477.

13. Arthur Schwartz, unpublished notes to Howard Dietz, ASP, Box 51 / Folder 2, 2.

14. Dietz, HDATBW, 9–10.

15. Dietz, *Dancing in the Dark*, 123.

16. Schwartz, ROAS, 3–4.

17. Frederick Nolan, *Lorenz Hart: A Poet on Broadway* (New York: Oxford University Press, 1994), 51–2.

18. Dietz, 124.

19. Dietz, hand-written notes for *Lyrics and Lyricists: An Evening with Howard Dietz*, HDP, Series I, Box 1 / Folder 19.

20. Dietz, *Dancing in the Dark*, 125.

21. Dwight Blocker Bowers, James R. Morris, and J.R. Taylor, *American Popular Song: Six Decades of Songwriters and Singers* (Washington, D.C.: Smithsonian Institution Press, 1984), 96–7.

22. Philip Furia and Michael Lasser, *America's Songs: The Stories Behind the Songs of Broadway, Hollywood, and Tin Pan Alley* (New York: Routledge, 2006), 75.

23. Benny Green, *Let's Face the Music: The Golden Age of Popular Song* (London: Pavillion Books Limited, 1989), 99.

24. Dietz, *Dancing in the Dark*, 126.

25. Ken Bloom, *The American Songbook: The Singers, the Songwriters, and the Songs* (New York: Black Dog & Leventhal, 2005), 298.

26. Script for *Lyrics and Lyricists*, 92nd Street YM-YWHA, ASP, Box 24 / Folder 10, 3.

27. Allen Forte, *The American Popular Ballad of the Golden Era: 1924–1950* (Princeton, NJ: Princeton University Press, 1995), 284.

28. Dan Sullivan, "Arthur Schwartz Goes His Way By Himself," *Los Angeles Times*, October 17, 1976, 46.

29. Jack D. Brinkley, "Behind the Music," *Radio Guide*, October 20, 1934, 21.

30. Bloom, 298.

31. Gerald Bordman, *American Musical Revue: From the Passing Show to Sugar Babies* (New York: Oxford University Press, 1985), 89.

32. Schwartz, ROAS, 2.

33. Brahms, 111.

34. Dietz, *Dancing in the Dark*, 128–9.

35. Ethan Mordden, *Sing for Your Supper: The Broadway Musical in the 1930's* (New York: Palgrave MacMillan, 2005), 23.

36. David Ewen, *American Songwriters: An H.W. Wilson Biographical Dictionary* (New York: The H.W. Wilson Company, 1987), 349.

37. Jasen, 236.

Chapter 5

1. Manuel Seff, "London Show Hits to Be Seen in New York Later in Season," *New York Herald Tribune*, August 3, 1930.

2. Ward Morehouse, "Piccadilly after Dark," *New York Sun*, April 25, 1930.

3. Arthur Schwartz, "Memo for Mr. Dietz," typed notes, undated, ASP, Box 51 / Folder 2, 1.

4. Schwartz, ROAS, 8–9; "Long Frocks Bring in Slower Music," *London Daily Chronicle*, March 15, 1930.

5. Program for *Here Comes the Bride*, Liverpool Empire [theatre], week of October 14, 1929, ASP.

6. Benny Green, *Let's Face the Music: The Golden Age of Popular Song* (London: Pavillion Books Limited, 1989), 102.

7. John Murray Anderson, *Out Without My Rubbers: The Memoirs of John Murray Anderson* (New York: Library Publishers, 1954), 131.

8. Steven Suskin, *Show Tunes: The Songs, Shows, and Careers of Broadway's Major Composers*, 4th ed. (New York: Oxford University Press, 2010), 29, 65–6, 155.

9. Gary Marmorstein, *A Ship Without a Sail: The Life of Lorenz Hart* (New York: Simon & Schuster, 2012), 134.

10. Program.

11. Kurt Ganzl, *The British Musical Theatre: Volume 2: 1915–1984* (Oxford: Oxford University Press, 1987), 331.

12. Alan Parsons, "1,200 Critics at Play," *London Daily Mail*, February 21, 1930.

13. Ivor Brown, "Here Comes the Bride," *London Observer*, February 23, 1930.

14. Ganzl, 331.

15. Seff.

16. "Long Frocks Bring in Slower Music."
17. Robert Baral, *Revue: A Nostalgic Reprise of the Great Broadway Period* (New York: Fleet Publishing Corporation, 1962), 235.
18. *Ibid.*; Keith Garebian, *The Making of My Fair Lady* (Toronto: ECW Press, 1993), 39.
19. Arthur B. Minikes, "Arthur Schwartz—Master of Melody," *New York University Alumnus*, November 2, 1932, 51.
20. Vernon Duke, *Listen Here!: A Critical Essay on Music Depreciation* (New York: Ivan Obolensky, Inc., 1963), 259.
21. Unidentified London newspaper review, circa April 5, 1930, ASP.
22. "The Co-Optimists," *London Daily Mirror*, circa April 5, 1930, ASP.
23. Parsons, *London Daily Mail*, circa April 5, 1930, ASP.
24. Baral, 235.
25. Morehouse.
26. Ken Bloom, *American Song: The Complete Musical Theatre Companion*, 2nd ed., 1877–1995, Vol. 1: A–S (New York: Schirmer Books, 1996), 650–1; Ganzl, 323–4, 339.
27. Green, 102.
28. Dwight Blocker Bowers, James R. Morris, and J.R. Taylor, *American Popular Song: Six Decades of Songwriters and Singers* (Washington, D.C.: Smithsonian Institution Press, 1984), 70.
29. Ganzl, 324.
30. Green, 102.

Chapter 6

1. Cecil Smith and Glenn Litton, *Musical Comedy in America* (New York: Routledge / Theatre Arts Books, 1981), 148.
2. Howard Dietz, *Dancing in the Dark: Words by Howard Dietz: An Autobiography* (New York: Quadrangle / New York Times Book Co., Inc., 1974), 132.
3. Stanley Green, *The World of Musical Comedy: The Story of the American Musical Stage As Told Through the Careers of Its Foremost Composers and Lyricists* (Chicago: Ziff Davis Publishing Company, 1960), 187.
4. Don McDonagh, *George Balanchine* (Boston: Twayne Publishers, 1983), 83.
5. Jo Mielziner, *Designing for the Theatre: A Memoir and a Portfolio* (Seaton, Devon, UK: Bramhall House, 1965), 21, 70.
6. Ken Bloom, *American Song: The Complete Musical Theatre Companion*, 2nd ed., 1877–1995, Vol. 1: A–S (New York: Schirmer Books, 1996), 989; programs for *The Second Little Show*, Royale Theatre, week of October 6, 1930, and week of September 22, 1930.
7. Programs.
8. "'Little Show' at the Wilbur," *Boston Traveler*, August 12, 1930.
9. Louis Botto, *At This Theatre: 100 Years of Broadway Shows, Stories and Stars* (New York: Applause Theatre & Cinema Books, 2002), 232.
10. Dietz, HDATBW, 14–15.
11. "The Second Little Show," *Life*, September 9, 1930.
12. "'Little Show' at the Wilbur."
13. Ruth Benjamin and Arthur Rosenblatt, *Who Sang What on Broadway, 1866–1996, Volume 1: The Singers A–L* (Jefferson, NC: McFarland, 2005), 307; Sandra Burlingame, *JazzBiographies.com*, s.v. "Grafton, Gloria," www.jazzbiographies.com/Biography.aspx?ID=159 (accessed March 18, 2018).
14. Edward Harold Crosby, "Another Brady Hit at Wilbur," *Boston Post*, August 12, 1930; programs.
15. Crosby.
16. Caryl Brahms and Ned Sherrin, *Song by Song: 14 Great Lyric Writers* (Bolton, Lancashire: Ross Anderson Publications, 1984), 111.
17. "Evolution of 'Three's a Crowd' from Idea to Revue Is Traced," *New York Herald Tribune*, March 22, 1931; Dietz, *Dancing in the Dark*, 132.
18. Margaret Case Harriman, *Take Them Up Tenderly: A Collection of Profiles* (New York: Alfred A. Knopf, 1945), 31–43; *Notable Names in the American Theatre*, s.v. "Gordon, Max" (Clifton, NJ: James T. White & Company, 1976).
19. Max Gordon, *Max Gordon Presents* (New York: Bernard Geis Associates, 1963), 125, 122.
20. Roy Hemming, *The Melody Lingers On: The Great Songwriters and Their Movie Musicals* (New York: Newmarket Press, 1986), 205; Edward Eliscu, *With or Without a Song: A Memoir* (Lanham, MD: The Scarecrow Press, Inc., 2001), 97; Arthur Schwartz, Ralph Rainger, and E.Y. Harburg,

"Brother, Just Laugh It Off" (Hollywood, CA: Famous Music Corporation, 1930).

21. David Ewen, *The Life and Death of Tin Pan Alley: The Golden Age of American Popular Song* (New York: Funk & Wagnall's, 1964), 296–7.

22. *The New Grove Dictionary of Music and Musicians*, 2nd ed., Stanley Sadie, ed. (London: Macmillan Publishers Limited, 2001), s.v. "Friml, Rudolf"; "Herbert, Victor"; "Romberg, Sigmund."

23. *Wikipedia*, s.v. "operetta," https://en.wikipedia.org/wiki/Operetta (accessed June 18, 2017), 1–5.

24. *New Grove Dictionary*, s.v. "operetta," 493.

25. Vernon Duke, *Listen Here! A Critical Essay on Music Depreciation* (New York: Ivan Obolensky, Inc., 1963), 259.

26. Alan Jay Lerner, *The Musical Theatre: A Celebration* (New York: McGraw-Hill Book Company, 1986), 84.

27. *Wikipedia*, 5.

28. Lee Davis, *Scandals and Follies: The Rise and Fall of the Great Broadway Revue* (New York: Limelight Editions, 2000), 179–80; *New Grove Dictionary*, s.v. "Szirmai, Albert."

29. "Here and Abroad: An Operetta Reaches the Sunlight," *New York Times*, October 26, 1930.

30. Ibid.

31. Ibid.

32. Bloom, 914.

33. "'Princess Charming' Is Big Hit," *Times Union* (New Haven, CT), October 7, 1930.

34. Walter Brown, "The Observation Post," *Courant* (Hartford, CT), October 11, 1930.

35. Charles Darnton, "The New Plays," *New York Evening World*, October 14, 1930; "'Princess Charming' Is Big Hit."

36. "The Three Schwartz Shows," *New York Sun*, October 11, 1930.

37. "Theater: Color and Dash Mark Romance Given at Shubert," *New Haven Evening Register*, October 7, 1930.

38. "'Princes Charming' Is Big Hit."

39. John Mason Brown, "The Play," *New York Evening Post*, October 14, 1930.

40. "The Theatre: Hurrah for Us!," *The New Yorker*, October 25, 1930, 34.

41. Douglas Gilbert, "Arthur Schwartz, Erstwhile Attorney, Now Packs His Torts in a D-Flat Chord," *New York Telegram*, October 20, 1930.

42. Gordon, 129.

43. Samuel Marx and Jan Clayton, *Rodgers and Hart: Bewitched, Bothered, and Bedeviled* (New York: G.P. Putnam's Sons, 1976), 48–9.

44. "Two Is Company—," *New York Times*, November 23, 1930.

45. Program, *Three's a Crowd*, Selwyn Theatre, week of June 1, 1931, 15–21.

46. Arnold Shaw, *Let's Dance: Popular Music in the 1930s* (New York: Oxford University Press, 1998), 33.

47. John Green, letter to Joe Thompson, KQED-FM, March 8, 1982, collection of the author, 1–2.

48. Ibid., 2.

49. Jon Bradshaw, *Dreams That Money Can Buy: The Tragic Life of Libby Holman* (New York: William Morrow and Company, Inc., 1985), 85–6; Gordon, 130–1.

50. Dietz, 134.

51. Bradshaw, 86–7; Gordon, 131.

52. Program, 15–21.

53. "Evolution."

54. Dwight Blocker Bowers, James R. Morris, and J.R. Taylor, *American Popular Song: Six Decades of Songwriters and Singers* (Washington, D.C.: Smithsonian Institution Press, 1984), 70.

55. Dan Sullivan, "Stage: Arthur Schwartz Goes His Way by Himself," *Los Angeles Times*, October 17, 1976.

56. Dietz, 132–3.

57. Gordon, 129.

58. John Bush Jones, *The Songs That Fought the War: Popular Music and the Home Front* (Boston: Brandeis University Press, 2006), 242–3.

59. Wilfrid Sheed, *The House That George Built: With a Little Help from Irving, Cole, and a Crew of About Fifty* (New York: Random House, 2007), 303.

60. "The Theater at Random," *New York Morning World*, February 8, 1931.

61. Dominic Symonds, *We'll Have Manhattan: The Early Work of Rodgers and Hart* (New York: Oxford University Press, 2015), 26.

62. "The Theater at Random."

63. Program, 19.

64. Robert Baral, *Revue: A Nostalgic Reprise of the Great Broadway Period* (New York: Fleet Publishing Corporation, 1962), 193.

65. Richard Lockridge, "Three's a Crowd," *New York Sun*, October 16, 1930.

66. "Three's Good Company," *Brooklyn Citizen*, October 16, 1930.
67. Bradshaw, 87.
68. Smith, 148.
69. "The Theatre," *Evening Wall Street Journal*, October 18, 1930.
70. "Evolution."
71. Kelcey Allen, "'Three's a Crowd' Scores Quick Success," *Women's Wear Daily*, October 16, 1930.
72. Ibid.
73. "The Three Schwartz Shows."

Chapter 7

1. Olin Downes, "News and Commentary: Original Musical Comedy," *New York Times*, June 7, 1931, X8.
2. Julian Mates, *America's Musical Stage: Two Hundred Years of Musical Theatre* (Westport, CT: Greenwood Press, 1985), 188.
3. Stanley Green, *Ring Bells! Sing Songs! Broadway Musicals of the 1930's* (New York: Arlington House, 1971), 46.
4. Malcolm Goldstein, *George S. Kaufman: His Life, His Theater* (New York: Oxford University Press, 1979), 189.
5. Max Gordon, *Max Gordon Presents* (New York: Bernard Geis Associates, 1963), 132–3.
6. "That Hit in 42D Street," *New York Times*, June 14, 1931, X2.
7. Program, *The Band Wagon*, New Amsterdam Theatre, beginning June 3, 1931, ASP, 20–1.
8. Christopher Palmer, *Dimitri Tiomkin: A Portrait* (London: T.E. Books, 1984), 31.
9. Robert Baral, *Revue: A Nostalgic Reprise of the Great Broadway Period* (New York: Fleet Publishing Corporation, 1962), 194.
10. Charles B. Cochran, *I Had Almost Forgotten...* (London: Hutchinson & Co., Ltd., 1932), 284.
11. Cochran, *Showman Looks On* (London: J.M. Dent & Sons, Ltd., 1945), 139.
12. Gordon, 133.
13. Michael Freedland, *Fred Astaire* (New York: Grosset & Dunlap, 1976), 36.
14. Goldstein, 189.
15. Gordon, 134.
16. Ibid., 134–5.
17. Howard Dietz, *Dancing in the Dark: Words by Howard Dietz: An Autobiography* (New York: Quadrangle / New York Times Book Co., Inc., 1974), 137–8.
18. Robert Russell Bennett, *The Broadway Sound: The Autobiography and Selected Essays of Robert Russell Bennett* (Rochester, NY: University of Rochester Press, 1999), 128.
19. Gordon, 135.
20. Dietz, 138.
21. Gordon, 135.
22. Howard Teichmann, *George S. Kaufman: An Intimate Portrait* (New York: Atheneum, 1972), 139–40.
23. Goldstein, 190–1.
24. George S. Kaufman, "Music to My Ears," *Stage* 15 (August 1939), 27–30 in Howard Pollack, *George Gershwin: His Life and Work* (Berkeley, CA: University of California Press, 2006), 396.
25. Michael Freedland, *Irving Berlin* (London: W.H. Allen, 1974), 118–9.
26. Fred Astaire, *Steps in Time* (New York: Harper and Brothers, 1959), 167.
27. "That Hit in 42D Street."
28. Green, *Broadway Musicals: Show by Show*, 6th ed. (New York: Applause Theatre & Cinema Books, 2008), 74.
29. Gerald Bordman, *American Musical Revue: From The Passing Show to Sugar Babies* (New York: Oxford University Press, 1985), 92; Green, *Ring Bells!*, 46.
30. Script for *Lyrics and Lyricists*, 92nd Street YM-YWHA, ASP, Box 24 / Folder 10, 1.
31. Lee Davis, *Scandals and Follies: The Rise and Fall of the Great Broadway Revue* (New York: Limelight Editions, 2000), 288.
32. Bordman, 91.
33. Baral, 195.
34. Gary Marmorstein, *A Ship Without a Sail: The Life of Lorenz Hart* (New York: Simon & Schuster, 2012), 184.
35. Ibid., 183–4.
36. "That Hit in 42D Street."
37. Goldstein, 189.
38. Program, 27.
39. Gordon, 135.
40. Bordman, 92.
41. "That Hit in 42D."
42. Green, *Ring Bells!*, 46.
43. Gordon, 136.
44. Cecil Smith and Glenn Litton, *Musical Comedy in America* (New York: Routledge / Theatre Arts Books, 1981), 149.
45. Davis, 288.
46. Ethan Mordden, *Broadway Babies: The People Who Made the American Musical* (New York: Oxford University Press, 1983), 100.

47. Bordman, 93.
48. Lincoln Barnett, *Writing on Life: Sixteen Close-Ups* (New York: William Sloane Associates, 1951), 26-7.
49. Larry Stempel, *Show Time: A History of the Broadway Musical Theater* (London: W.W. Norton & Company, 2010), 218.
50. Alec Wilder, *American Popular Song: The Great Innovators, 1900-1950* (New York: Oxford University Press, 1972), 315.
51. David Lennick, liner notes for *"Night and Day": Fred Astaire: Complete Recordings: Volume 2: 1931-1933* (Franklin, TN: Naxos Nostalgia, 2001), 3.
52. Ibid.; Kathleen Riley, *The Astaires: Fred & Adele* (New York: Oxford University Press, 2012), 145.
53. Frank Rasky, "Broadway Songwriter Entertains Students," *Toronto Star*, June 22, 1976, E10.
54. Rodney Greenberg, *George Gershwin* (London: Phaidon Press Limited, 1998), 81.
55. Ken Bloom, *American Song: The Complete Musical Theatre Companion*, 2nd ed., 1877-1995, Vol. 1: A-S (New York: Schirmer Books, 1996), 74.
56. Arthur Schwartz and Howard Dietz, "Confession" (Hollywood: Warner Bros. Inc, 1931, renewed).
57. Wilder, 316.
58. Abel, "Phi Beta Kappa Leer-ics," *Variety*, October 31, 1956.
59. Martha Wright, *Censored*, LP, B01DQ5MMVU (New York: Jubilee Records, 1956).
60. Gordon, 135; "That Hit in 42D."
61. Schwartz reply to queries from Howard Dietz, ASP, Box 51 / Folder 2, 6.
62. Dietz in script notes for *Lyrics & Lyricists* Series, November 3, 1974, HDP, Series I, Box 1 / Folder 19, dated August 1, 1974. NB: Dietz may have misremembered where he and Schwartz had done their work. The Essex House did not open until October 1931, four months after *The Band Wagon* opened.
63. Ibid.
64. Schwartz, reply to queries, 8.
65. "The Theatre: Dawn," *The New Yorker*, June 13, 1931, 28.
66. Mordden, *Sing for Your Supper: The Broadway Musical in the 1930s* (New York: Palgrave MacMillan, 2005), 29.
67. Kelcey Allen, "Amusements: 'The Band Wagon' Achieves Success of First Magnitude," *Women's Wear Daily*, June 4, 1931, 18.
68. Baral, 195.
69. William Cross, *Tilly Losch: 'Schlagobers' Sweet Fragments from Her Life*, 2nd ed. (Newport, Gwent, UK: Book Midden Publishing, 2015), 42.
70. Telegram, Audray Dale to Arthur Schwartz, July 17, 1931, ASP, Box 44 / Folder 22.
71. Downes.
72. Dietz, HDATBW, 22.
73. Benny Green, *Let's Face the Music: The Golden Age of Popular Song* (London: Pavillion Books Limited, 1989), 105.
74. Robert Taylor, "The Roving Eye: One of the Mostly Boys," *Boston Herald*, July 24, 1963, 35.
75. Radio script, *The Songwriters: Arthur Schwartz*, ASP, Box 41 / Folder 8, 6.
76. Benny Green, *Let's Face the Music*, 105.
77. Radio script, 7.
78. Philip Furia and Michael Lasser, *America's Songs: The Stories Behind the Songs of Broadway, Hollywood, and Tin Pan Alley* (New York: Routledge, 2006), 95.
79. William E. Studwell, *The Popular Song Reader: A Sampler of Well-Known Twentieth-Century Songs* (New York: The Haworth Press, 1994), 118.
80. David A. Jasen, *Tin Pan Alley: The Composers, the Songs, the Performers and Their Times: The Golden Age of Popular Music from 1886 to 1956* (London: Omnibus Press, 1990), 359.
81. Morris Dickstein, *Dancing in the Dark: A Cultural History of the Great Depression* (New York: W.W. Norton & Company, 2009), 416.
82. Ibid., 415.
83. Ibid., 416.
84. William Zinsser, *Easy to Remember: The Great American Songwriters and Their Songs* (Boston: David R. Godine, Publishers, 2001), 67.
85. Dickstein, xix.
86. Mordden, *Broadway Babies*, 47.
87. David McClintick, "A Revival of America's Great Songs," *Wall Street Journal*, December 16, 1971.
88. Charles Hamm, *Yesterdays: Popular Song in America* (New York: W.W. Norton and Company, 1979), 489-92.

89. Wilder, 314.
90. Downes.
91. Ibid.
92. Downes to Schwartz, June 4, 1931, ASP, Box 25 / Folder 1, 1–2.
93. Caryl Brahms and Ned Sherrin, *Song by Song: 14 Great Lyric Writers* (Bolton, Lancashire: Ross Anderson Publications, 1984), 103.
94. Smith, 170.
95. Schwartz, ROAS, 5–6.
96. Arthur B. Minikes, "Arthur Schwartz—Master of Melody," *New York University Alumnus*, November 2, 1932, 51.
97. Davis, 289.

Chapter 8

1. Jeremy Wilson, "Alone Together (1932)," *JazzStandard.com,* http://www.jazzstandards.com/compositions-0/alonetogether.htm (accessed December 17, 2012), 2.
2. Arthur B. Waters, "Forrest Theatre," *Philadelphia Public Ledger*, August 24, 1932.
3. Max Gordon, *Max Gordon Presents* (New York: Bernard Geis Associates, 1963), 158–9.
4. Cecil Smith and Glenn Litton, *Musical Comedy in America* (New York: Routledge / Theatre Arts Books, 1981), 171.
5. Gordon, 159.
6. Larry Adler, *It Ain't Necessarily So* (New York: Grove Press, 1984), 32.
7. Ibid., 33.
8. Wikipedia, s.v. "Buddy Ebsen," (accessed September 19, 2017).
9. Program for *Flying Colors*, The Imperial Theatre, New York, beginning September 15, 1932, 12.
10. Gordon, 159–61.
11. Carol Easton, *No Intermissions: The Life of Agnes de Mille* (Boston: Little, Brown and Company, 1996), 89–90.
12. Gerald Bordman, *American Musical Theatre: A Chronicle*, 3rd edition (New York: Oxford University Press, 2001), 529.
13. Gordon, 161.
14. Agnes de Mille, *Speak to Me, Dance with Me* (Boston: Little, Brown and Company, 1973), 35.
15. Gordon, 158.
16. Jerry Stagg, *The Brothers Shubert* (New York: Random House, 1968), 341.
17. Gordon, 160.
18. Adler, 33.
19. Gilbert W. Gabriel, "'Flying Colors,'" *New York American*, September 16, 1932.
20. Gordon, 162.
21. Ibid., 162–3.
22. Brooks Atkinson, "Flying the Band Wagon Colors," *New York Times*, October 9, 1932.
23. Caryl Brahms and Ned Sherrin, *Song by Song: The Lives and Work of 14 Great Lyric Writers* (Egerton, Bolton, England: Ross Anderson Publications, 1984), 112.
24. Wilella Waldorf, "Forecasts and Postscripts," *New York Evening Post*, August 24, 1932.
25. Richard Lockridge, "'Flying Colors,'" *New York Sun*, September 16, 1932.
26. Waters.
27. Arthur Pollock, "The Theaters," *Brooklyn Eagle*, September 16, 1932.
28. Gabriel.
29. Franklin P. Adams, *The Diary of Our Own Samuel Pepys, Vol. 2—(1926-1934)* (New York: Simon & Schuster, 1935), 1107.
30. Henry Starr Richardson, "Flying Colors," *Philadelphia Star*, August 24, 1932.
31. Bordman, 529.
32. Arthur Schwartz, reply to queries from Howard Dietz, ASP, Box 51 / Folder 2, 6.
33. Background materials for *Dancing in the Dark*, typewritten, author uncertain, HDP, Box 2 / Folder 6, 21.
34. Alec Wilder, *American Popular Song: The Great Innovators, 1900-1950* (New York: Oxford University Press, 1972), 318–19.
35. Wilson, 1.
36. Program, 17.
37. Arnold Shaw, *Let's Dance: Popular Music in the 1930's* (New York: Oxford University Press, 1998), 113;
38. YouTube, s.v. "Reefer Man" (accessed October 24, 2019); www.complex.com/music/2012/04/the-50-best-weed-songs/ (accessed October 1, 2017).
39. Harold Arlen and Ted Koehler, "The Wail of the Reefer Man" (New York: Mills Music, Inc., 1932); Walter Rimler, *The Man That Got Away: The Life and Song of Harold Arlen* (Urbana, IL: University of Illinois Press, 2015), 32.
40. Pollock.
41. John Anderson, "Old Favorites in New Revue Operate at High Speed in Gordon-Dietz Offering," *New York Journal*, September 16, 1932.

42. Robert Baral, *Revue: A Nostalgic Reprise of the Great Broadway Period* (New York: Fleet Publishing Corporation, 1962), 197.
43. Easton, 484.
44. Adler, 33; Stanley Green, *Ring Bells!: Broadway Musicals of the 1930's* (New York: Arlington House, 1971), 67.
45. Green, 67.
46. Burns Mantle, "Revue Studded with Showy Dance Numbers, Spotted with Comedy," *New York News*, September 16, 1932.
47. Dave A Epstein, publicist to Guy McCoy, editor, *Etude*, April 10, 1953, ASP, Box 44 / Folder 29, 1.
48. Benny Green, *Let's Face the Music: The Golden Age of Popular Song* (London: Pavillion Books Limited, 1989), 107.
49. Wilder, 319.
50. "The Ins and Outs of Composing for Broadway," *Canadian Composer*, September / 1976, 12.
51. Anderson.
52. Dwight Blocker Bowers, CD album notes, *Smithsonian Collection of Recordings: American Songbook Series: Arthur Schwartz* (Washington, D.C.: Smithsonian Institution, 1995), 6.
53. Anderson.
54. Baral, 197.
55. Bordman, 529.
56. Radio script, *The Songwriters: Arthur Schwartz*, ASP, Box 41 / Folder 8, 8.
57. Philip Furia, *The Poets of Tin Pan Alley: The History of America's Greatest Lyricists* (New York: Oxford University Press, 1990), 201.
58. Bowers, James R. Morris, and J.R. Taylor, *American Popular Song: Six Decades of Songwriters and Singers* (Washington, D.C.: Smithsonian Institution Press, 1984), 71.
59. Thomas S. Hischak, *Word Crazy: Broadway Lyricists from Cohan to Sondheim* (New York: Praeger Publishers, 1991), 74.
60. Wilson, 2.
61. Allen Forte, *The American Popular Ballad of the Golden Era: 1924-1950* (Princeton, NJ: Princeton University Press, 1995), 289–90.
62. Wilder, 318.
63. Steven Suskin, *Show Tunes: The Songs, Shows, and Careers of Broadway's Major Composers*, 4th ed. (New York: Oxford University Press, 2010), 50, 70, 79.
64. Stanley Green, 68.
65. Jonathan Schwartz, *All in Good Time: A Memoir* (New York: Random House, 2004), 86.
66. "Arthur Schwartz Weds Actress in L.I. Ceremony," *New York Sunday News*, July 8, 1934; Suskin, 33; "'Madame Sherry' To Be Next Municipal Opera Offering," *St. Louis Globe-Democrat*, June 16, 1935; "Miss Carrington of Stage, 43, Dies," obituary, *New York Times*, May 3, 1953; Ruth Benjamin and Arthur Rosenblatt, *Who Sang What on Broadway, 1866-1996, Volume 1: The Singers A-L* (Jefferson, NC: McFarland, 2005), 123.
67. "Mrs. Arthur Schwartz," obituary, *Variety*, May 6, 1953.
68. Jonathan Schwartz, 3–4.
69. Michael Freedland, *Jerome Kern* (New York: Stein & Day, 1981), 112.
70. Dietz, HDATBW, 16.
71. Schwartz, "HOW I GOT TO PRODUCE FILMS," unpublished notes, ASP, Box 51 / Folder 2, 4.
72. "Miss Carrington of Stage, 43, Dies."
73. Jonathan Schwartz, 17, 4.

Chapter 9

1. Benny Green, *Let's Face the Music: The Golden Age of Popular Song* (London: Pavillion Books Limited, 1989), 107.
2. "Radio: Air Operettas," *News Week* (New York), August 4, 1934.
3. Howard Dietz, HDATBW, 17–8.
4. "'Nice Goings On' at The Pavillion Next Week," *Torquay Times*, August 24, 1934.
5. Kurt Ganzl, *The British Musical Theatre*, Vol. 2 (Oxford: Oxford University Press, 1987), 379.
6. Program for *Nice Goings On*, Theatre Royal, Birmingham, England, week commencing August 28, 1933, ASP, Box 38 / Folder 10, 8.; Steven Suskin, *Show Tunes: The Songs, Shows, and Careers of Broadway's Major Composers*, 4th ed. (New York: Oxford University Press, 2010), 136.
7. Program for *Nice Goings On*, Theatre Royal, Birmingham, England (different from Chapter Note #6), week commencing August 29 (1933), ASP, Box 38 / Folder 10, unnumbered page.
8. Ganzl, 379; Ken Bloom, *American Song: The Complete Musical Theatre Companion*, 2nd ed., 1877-1995, Vol. 1: A-S (New York: Schirmer Books, 1996), 1098.

9. "'Nice Goings On' at Torquay Pavillion Next Week."
10. Ganzl, 379.
11. Dietz to Schwartz, August 9, 1933, ASP, 3.
12. Program for *She Loves Me Not*, Forty-Sixth Street Theatre, week of November 20, 1933, title page.
13. Arthur Schwartz and Edward Heyman, "After All You're All I'm After" (New York: Harms Incorporated, 1933).
14. Thomas S. Hischak, *The Tin Pan Alley Song Encyclopedia* (Westport, CT: Greenwood Press, 2002), 3.
15. Schwartz reply to queries from Dietz, ASP, Box 51 / Folder 2, 5.
16. Radio script, *The Songwriters: Arthur Schwartz*, ASP, Box 41 / Folder 8, 13.
17. *Broadway & Hollywood Legends: The Songwriters: Charles Strouse and Arthur Schwartz*, DVD, ASIN: B0001Z4OTC (New York: Lance Entertainment, Inc. / Wellspring Media, Inc., 2004).
18. ASCAP, ACE Repertory, s.v. "Then I'll Be Tired of You," https://ascap.com/repertory (accessed January 28, 2020).
19. Schwartz, at sea, to Katherine Carrington, New York, December 11, 1933, ASP, Box 44 / Folder 18.
20. Schwartz, Beverly Hills, to Carrington, New York, January 14, 1934, ASP, Box 44 / Folder 18, 1–2.
21. Dietz, HDATBW, 17.
22. Green, 107.
23. Dietz, *Dancing in the Dark: Words by Howard Dietz: An Autobiography* (New York: Quadrangle / The New York Times Book Co., 1974), 172.
24. "Music: Radio Musicomedy," *Time*, September 24, 1934.
25. "Radio: Air Operettas."
26. Jonathan Schwartz, *All in Good Time: A Memoir* (New York: Random House, 2004), 5, 27–8.
27. Green, 107; Frederick Nolan, *Lorenz Hart: A Poet on Broadway* (New York: Oxford University Press, 1994), 208; John Dunning, *On the Air: The Encyclopedia of Old-Time Radio* (New York: Oxford University Press, 1998), 471.
28. Rodney Greenberg, *George Gershwin* (London: Phaidon Press Limited, 1998), 173–4.
29. Howard Pollack, *George Gershwin: His Life and Work* (Berkeley, CA: University of California Press, 2006), 157.
30. Wilfrid Sheed, *The House That George Built: With a Little Help from Irving, Cole, and a Crew of About Fifty* (New York: Random House, 2008), 49.
31. Nolan, 208.
32. Dunning, 378.
33. Ibid., 613–4.
34. Miles Kreuger, *Show Boat: The Story of a Classic American Musical* (New York: Oxford University Press, 1977), 233; *Wikipedia*, s.v. "Maxwell House Show Boat," http://broadcastarchive-umd.tumblr.com/post/74951530421/maxwell-house-showboat (accessed November 6, 2017).
35. Alton Cook, "Scan 'The Gibson Family,'" *New York World-Telegram*, September 12, 1934.
36. Greenberg, 89.
37. Cook; Dietz in script notes for *Lyrics & Lyricists Series*, November 3, 1974, HDP, Box 1 / Folder 19, dated August 1, 1974.
38. "Major Sponsor, Heavy Publicity Equals Big Bust," http://wwww.oldtime.com/commercials/1930's/The%20Gibson%20Family.htm (accessed June 27, 2013), 1–2.
39. The Listener, "As I Hear It: 'The Gibson Family' Is a 'New Art Form,'" *Albany (NY) News*, September 17, 1934.
40. Samuel Kaufman, "The 'Gibsons' Made to Order," *New York Sun*, September 22, 1934; "Radio: Air Operettas."
41. "Four Original Songs in First Ivory Program," *Radio Dial* (Cincinnati, OH), September 20, 1934; The Listener.
42. Peter B. Flint, "Donald Voorhess, 85, Conductor Who Led 'Bell Telephone Hour,'" obituary, *New York Times*, January 11, 1989.
43. "The Gibson Family," *Variety*, September 18, 1934, 40.
44. "Radio: Air Operettas."
45. Ibid.; "The Gibson Family"; "Four Original Songs"; Dunning, 282–3; "Romantic Gibson Family Team," *Racine (WI) Journal Times*, March 15, 1935, 26. NB: There were discrepancies among the sources used for this table. The author made the best effort to get the list accurate and when uncertain, listed all names for a particular role.
46. The Listener; "Major Sponsor, Heavy Publicity Equals Big Bust," 1.
47. "The Gibson Family."
48. Kaufman.
49. Jack D. Brinkeley, "Behind the Music," *Radio Guide*, October 20, 1934, 9.

50. "The Gibson Family."
51. Kaufman.
52. "Four Original Songs."
53. David Ewen, *American Songwriters: An H.W. Wilson Biographical Dictionary* (Hackensack, NJ: H.W. Wilson Company, 1987), 351.
54. Kaufman.
55. Dietz interview with Joan Taylor, April 22, 1971, HDP, Box 2 / Folder 4, 25-6.
56. Kaufman.
57. Brinkeley, 21.
58. *Ibid.*, 9, 21.
59. Michel Mok, "2 Songsmiths Hammer on Melody Anvil; Coat, Vest, Pants! A Tune That Enchants!," *New York Evening Post*, December 20, 1934.
60. "Sheet Music Sales of 'Gibson Family,'" *Billboard* (Cincinnati, OH), October 27, 1934.
61. The Listener.
62. A.D.H., "'Gibson Family' Musical Radio Show Found Living Up to Its Publicity," *Christian Science Monitor*, September 29, 1934.
63. Schwartz, ROAS, 10.
64. "Major Sponsor, Heavy Publicity Equals Big Bust," 1.
65. *Ibid.*; Dunning, 283.
66. Dunning, 282-3, 614.
67. The Listener.
68. Leonard Maltin, *The Great American Broadcast: A Celebration of Radio's Golden Age* (New York: Dutton, 1997), 262.
69. "Dollars for Words," *Melody*, May / 1935.
70. "Brother, Can You Spare a Rhyme?," *Melody*, July / 1935, 6.
71. "Write a Song with Vernon Duke," *Melody*, August / 1935, 13-14.
72. "Prize Winners," *Melody*, August / 1935, 15.
73. Sheed, 21-2.
74. Robert Baral, *Revue: A Nostalgic Reprise of the Great Broadway Period* (New York: Fleet Publishing Corporation, 1962), 286; Bloom, 1068.
75. Kathleen Riley, *The Astaires: Fred & Adele* (New York: Oxford University Press, 2012), 142.
76. "Adelphi Theatre London," http://www.thisistheatre.com/londontheatre/adelphitheatre.html (accessed October 28, 2019).

Chapter 10

1. Benny Green, *Let's Face the Music: The Golden Age of Popular Song* (London: Pavillion Books Limited, 1989), 108.
2. Thomas S. Hischak, *Word Crazy: Broadway Lyricists from Cohan to Sondheim* (New York: Praeger Publishers, 1991), 73.
3. Philip Furia and Michael Lasser, *America's Songs: The Stories behind the Songs of Broadway, Hollywood, and Tin Pan Alley* (New York: Routledge, 2006), 123.
4. Cecil Smith and Glenn Litton, *Musical Comedy in America* (New York: Routledge / Theatre Arts Books, 1981), 171.
5. Hamilton Darby Perry, *Libby Holman: Body and Soul* (Boston: Little, Brown and Company, 1983), 246.
6. Howard Dietz to Arthur Schwartz, August 9, 1933, ASP, 4.
7. Jon Bradshaw, *Dreams That Money Can Buy: The Tragic Life of Libby Holman* (New York: William Morrow and Company, Inc., 1985), 192.
8. Perry, 246.
9. IBDB, s.v. "Georges Metaxa," http://www.imdb.com/name/nm0582386/ (accessed November 25, 2017).
10. Bradshaw, 191.
11. Wilella Waldorf, "Forecasts and Postscripts," *New York Evening Post*, September 24, 1934.
12. Ken Bloom, *American Song: The Complete Musical Theatre Companion*, 2nd ed., 1877-1995, Vol. 1: A-S (New York: Schirmer Books, 1996), 944; Green, 107.
13. "A Drama with Music by Schwartz and Dietz," *The Theatre*, October, 1934, No. 4.
14. Ethan Mordden, *Sing for Your Supper: The Broadway Musical in the 1930s* (New York: Palgrave MacMillan, 2005), 45.
15. Bloom, 944.
16. Advertisement for Harms Incorporated in *Melody: The Magazine of Words and Music*, n.d., 1934, ASP; sheet music for "Wand'ring Heart," Arthur Schwartz and Howard Dietz (New York: Harms Incorporated, 1934), cover.
17. Advertisement.
18. Dietz, HDATBW, 19; "GIBSON FAMILY 9/15/34–6/2/35," listing of music used in *The Gibson Family*, ASP; Dwight Blocker Bowers, CD album notes, *Smithsonian Collection of Recordings: American Songbook Series: Arthur Schwartz*

(Washington, D.C.: Smithsonian Institution, 1995), 9.

19. Stanley Green, *The World of Musical Comedy: The Story of the American Musical Stage As Told Through the Careers of Its Foremost Composers and Lyricists* (Chicago: Ziff Davis Publishing Company, 1960), 190.

20. Maurice Levine, transcript of taped interview with Howard Dietz, January 15, 1975, for *Lyrics & Lyricists Series*, HDP, Series I: Events and Exhibitions (1959–1976), Box 1 / Folder 15, W.

21. Alec Wilder, *American Popular Song: The Great Innovators, 1900–1950* (New York: Oxford University Press, 1972), 320.

22. Bowers, 9.

23. Benny Green, 108.

24. *IMDB*, s.v. "Runaway Queen," imdb.com/tit/e/tt0025694 (accessed November 29, 2017).

25. Benny Green, 108.

26. Furia, 123.

27. Bradshaw, 192.

28. Schwartz in script for *Lyrics & Lyricists Series*, ASP, Box 24 / Folder 10, 5.

29. Bowers, 6.

30. Hischak, 416.

31. Schwartz reply to queries from Howard Dietz, ASP, Box 51 / Folder 2, 4.

32. Stanley Green, *Ring Bells! Sing Songs!: Broadway Musicals of the 1930's* (New York: Arlington House, 1971), 107; Gerald Bordman, *American Musical Theatre: A Chronicle*, 3rd ed. (New York: Oxford University Press, 2001), 542.

33. Bradshaw, 192–3.

34. Perry, 247.

35. Hischak, 73.

36. Caryl Brahms and Ned Sherrin, *Song by Song: 14 Great Lyric Writers* (Bolton, Lancashire: Ross Anderson Publications, 1984), 112–3.

37. Bordman, 543.

38. Schwartz, ROAS, 5.

39. Schwartz reply to queries, 7.

40. L.N., "The Play: Spanish Number," *New York Times*, November 29, 1934, 33.

41. Alan Jay Lerner, *The Musical Theatre: A Celebration* (New York: McGraw-Hill Book Company, 1986), 130.

42. Mordden, 46.

Chapter 11

1. Souvenir program, *At Home Abroad*, Shubert Archive, 2.

2. Tighe E. Zimmers, *Lyrical Satirical Harold Rome: A Biography of the Broadway Composer-Lyricist* (Jefferson, NC: McFarland, 2014), 59. Author's note: chart modified to include *Hitchy Koo* series.

3. Caryl Brahms and Ned Sherrin, *Song by Song: 14 Great Lyric Writers* (Bolton, Lancashire: Ross Anderson Publications, 1984), 103.

4. Charles B. Cochran, *Showman Looks On* (London: J.M. Dent & Sons Ltd., 1945), 201.

5. Donald Bogle, *Heat Wave: The Life and Career of Ethel Waters* (New York: Harper, 2011), 261.

6. Souvenir program, 5.

7. Fred Astaire, *Steps in Time* (New York: Harper & Brothers, 1959), 242.

8. Bogle, 260.

9. J.J. Shubert to William Klein, August 2, 1935, Shubert Archive.

10. Bogle, 261–4.

11. Howard Dietz to Beatrice Lillie, September 9, 1935, HDP, Box 2 / Folder 8, 1–2. NB: This is probably a draft copy, and it is difficult to tell if sent in this form.

12. Souvenir program, 2.

13. "The New Play," Richard Lockridge, *New York Sun*, September 20, 1935.

14. Ethan Mordden, *Better Foot Forward: The History of American Musical Theatre* (New York: Grossman Publishers, 1976), 126; Stanley Green, *Ring Bells! Sing Songs!: Broadway Musicals of the 1930's* (New York: Arlington House, 1971), 114.

15. Mordden, *Sing for Your Supper: The Broadway Musical in the 1930s* (New York: St. Martin's Press, 2005), 143.

16. Vincente Minnelli, *I Remember It Well* (London: Angus and Robertson, 1975), 70–71.

17. Dwight Blocker Bowers, CD album notes, *Smithsonian Collection of Recordings: American Songbook Series: Arthur Schwartz* (Washington, D.C.: Smithsonian Institution, 1995), 5.

18. Bogle, 262–3.

19. "News and Gossip of the Broadway Front," *New York Times*, September 29, 1935.

20. Maryann Chach, Shubert Archive, email to author, January 18, 2017.

21. E. de S. Melcher, "Beatrice Lillie Stars in Excellent Revue," *Washington, D.C. Star*, March 24, 1936.

22. J.H. Keen, "Observation the Morning After," *Philadelphia Daily News*, March 10, 1936.
23. Minnelli, 70–71.
24. Robert Baral, *Revue: A Nostalgic Reprise of the Great Broadway Period* (New York: Fleet Publishing Corporation, 1962), 201.
25. "News and Gossip of the Broadway Front."
26. Advertisement, Gramophone Shop, Inc., *Playbill* for *At Home Abroad*, Winter Garden, week of December 9, 1935, Shubert Archive, 30.
27. Bruce Laffey, *Beatrice Lillie: The Funniest Woman in the World* (New York: Wynwood Press, 1989), 136.
28. Arthur Schwartz, ROAS, 10.
29. Steven Suskin, *Show Tunes: The Songs, Shows, and Careers of Broadway's Major Composers*, 4th ed. (New York: Oxford University Press, 2010).
30. Contract between Select Operating Corporation and Eleanor Powell, February 7, 1936, Shubert Archive, 1.
31. Schwartz, London, telegram to L.C. Kaufman, Shubert Theatre Network, October 21, 1935, Shubert Archive.
32. Laffey, 110.

10. Jonathan Schwartz, *All in Good Time: A Memoir* (New York: Random House, 2004), Prologue.
11. Baral, 113.
12. Jonas Westover, *The Shuberts and Their Passing Shows: The Untold Tale of Ziegfeld's Rivals* (New York: Oxford University Press, 2016), 18–20.
13. Steven Suskin, *Show Tunes: The Songs, Shows, and Careers of Broadways Major Composers*, 4th ed. (New York: Oxford University Press, 2010), 3, 40, 94, 145.
14. Programs for *The Show Is On*, Boston and New York, 1936, Shubert Archive.
15. Elinor Hughes, "The Theater," *Boston Herald*, November 9, 1936.
16. Gerald Bordman, *American Musical Revue: From the* Passing Show *to* Sugar Babies (New York: Oxford University Press, 1985), 104.
17. Richard Watts, Jr., "The Theaters: Lillie-Lahr," *New York Herald Tribune*, December 26, 1936; Robert Coleman, "'The Show Is On'—Gaily—at Winter Garden," *New York Daily Mirror*, December 26, 1936; John Mason Brown, "Two on the Isle," *New York Evening Post*, December 12, 1936.
18. Lee Davis, *Scandals and Follies: The Rise and Fall of the Great Broadway Revue* (New York: Limelight Editions, 2000), 327.

Chapter 12

1. "Variety in Records," *Leyton Express*, February 22, 1936.
2. Colvin McPherson, "'Madame Sherry' Popular at Opera," *St. Louis Post-Dispatch*, June 19, 1935; "'Madame Sherry' to Be Next Municipal Opera Offering," *St. Louis Globe-Democrat*, June 16, 1935.
3. "News of the Stage," *New York Times*, October 8, 1935, 26.
4. Arthur Schwartz reply to queries from Howard Dietz, ASP, Box 51 / Folder 2, 7.
5. "*Follow the Sun*," *Theatre World*, March, 1936, 116.
6. Robert Baral, *Revue: A Nostalgic Reprise of the Great Broadway Period* (New York: Fleet Publishing Corporation, 1962), 230.
7. Howard Reinheimer to Stanley Joseloff, January 11, 1936, Shubert Archive, 1; William Klein to Joseloff, March 24, 1936, Shubert Archive.
8. "Variety in Records."
9. C. B. Cochran to Schwartz, March 16, 1936, ASP, Box 44 / Folder 20, 1.

Chapter 13

1. Elinor Hughes "'Between the Devil,' New Musical Play, Opens at the Shubert," *Boston Herald*, December 8, 1937.
2. Souvenir program for *Between the Devil*, unidentified theater, late 1937, ASP, 1, 11.
3. Robert Coleman, "Shuberts Offer Dietz-Schwartz Musical," *New York Daily Mirror*, December 27, 1937.
4. Steven Suskin, *Show Tunes: The Songs, Shows, and Careers of Broadway's Major Composers* (New York: Dodd, Mead & Company, 1986), 247.
5. William Morris Agency, Inc. promotional brochure from 1936, ASP, Box 44 / Folder 25.
6. Arthur Schwartz to Katherine Carrington, July 7, 1936, ASP, Box 44 / Folder 18, 1.
7. Schwartz to Carrington, July 16, 1936, ASP, Box 44 / Folder 18, 1–2.
8. *Lily Pons: A Centennial Portrait,*

James A. Drake and Kristin Beall Ludecke, eds. (Portland OR: Amadeus Press, 1999), 127–8; *That Girl from Paris*, VCR, directed by Leigh Jason, 1936 (Atlanta, GA: Turner Entertainment Co., 1990).

9. Howard Barnes, "'That Girl From Paris'—Music Hall," *New York Herald Tribune*, January 1, 1937.

10. Schwartz to Howard Dietz, August 17, 1936, ASP, Box 44 / Folder 25, 1.

11. Dietz to Schwartz, circa September 1, 1936, ASP, Box 44 / Folder 25, 2.

12. Schwartz to Dietz, August 17, 1936, 2.

13. "Schwartz Off for Hollywood," *New York Herald Tribune*, March 6, 1936; Rudy Behlmer, *Memo From Darryl F. Zanuck: The Golden Years at Twentieth-Fox* (New York: Grove Press, 1993), 65.

14. Schwartz to Dietz, August 24, 1936, ASP, Box 44 / Folder 25, 1.

15. Schwartz to Dietz, August 25, 1936, ASP, Box 44 / Folder 25.

16. Dietz to Schwartz, circa September 1, 1936.

17. Gerald Bordman, *American Musical Theatre: A Chronicle*, 3rd ed. (New York: Oxford University, 2001), 559.

18. Wilella Waldorf, "Forecasts and Postscripts," *New York Post*, December 9, 1937.

19. Howard Teichmann, *George S. Kaufman: An Intimate Portrait* (New York: Atheneum, 1972), 119.

20. Edwin H. Schloss, "Footlights," *Philadelphia Record*, October 20, 1937.

21. J.J. Shubert to Lee Shubert, October 15, 1937, Shubert Archive, 1.

22. Helice Koffler, "More About Ma: The E.R. Simmons Papers," *The Passing Show*, Volume 32, 2015/2016, 31.

23. Edwin Gilbert to Messrs. Shubert; [E.R.] Simmons to J.J. Shubert; John Kenley to Shuberts; J.J. Shubert to Lee Shubert. All are dated October 15, 1937 or circa that date, and all are in the Shubert Archive.

24. Gilbert to Messrs. Shubert.

25. Kenley to Shuberts, 2.

26. J.J. Shubert to Lee Shubert, 2.

27. James Ross Moore, *André Charlot: The Genius of Intimate Musical Revue* (Jefferson, NC: McFarland, 2005), 53, 56.

28. Dietz to Schwartz, June 4, 1936, ASP, Box 44 / Folder 25, 1.

29. "Hit Writer Says Successful Song Is 50 Percent Talent and the Rest Digging and Logic," *Boston Sunday Globe*, January 12, 1947.

30. Schwartz to Dietz, August 17, 1936, 1. NB: There are two Schwartz to Dietz letters dated August 17, 1936 in the ASP. One deals with problems concerning *Between the Devil*, while the other focuses on *Under Your Spell*, Lawrence Tibbett, and goings on in Hollywood.

31. Dietz to Schwartz, March 23 and July 29, 1936; Dietz to Schwartz, circa September 1, 1936; Schwartz to Dietz, August 24, 1936. All in ASP, Box 44 / Folder 25.

32. Dietz to Schwartz, March 23, 1936.

33. Dietz to Schwartz, telegram, September 1, 1936, ASP, Box 44 / Folder 25.

34. Dietz to Schwartz, circa April 1, 1936, ASP, Box 44 / Folder 25, 2–3.

35. John Anderson, "'Between the Devil' Placid and Old-Fashioned," *New York Journal*, December 23, 1937.

36. Dietz to Schwartz, March 23, 1936, 2–3.

37. Anderson; Hughes; Brooks Atkinson, "The Play," *New York Times*, December 23, 1937; *Review of Revues & Other Matters*, CB (Charles B. Cochran), ed. (London: Jonathan Cape, 1930), 81.

38. Hughes.

39. Program for *Between the Devil*, The Imperial Theatre, New York, week of December 21, 1937; Suskin, *The Sound of Broadway Music: A Book of Orchestrators and Orchestrations* (New York: Oxford University Press, 2007), 339.

40. Program for *Between the Devil*, Shubert Theatre, Boston, December 7, 1937.

41. Waldorf.

42. Dietz to Schwartz, circa April 1, 1936, 1.

43. Anderson.

44. Ethan Mordden, *Sing for Your Supper: The Broadway Musical in the 1930s* (New York: Palgrave MacMillan, 2005), 251.

45. Atkinson.

46. Anderson.

47. Agreement, Schwartz and Dietz with Elmer Harris, January 4, 1938, collection of the author.

48. Agreement between Schwartz, Dietz, and Tanis Dietz with Select Operating Corporation, January 17, 1938, collection of the author.

49. Program for *Between the Devil*,

National Theatre, Washington, D.C., January 23, 1938, Shubert Archive.

50. Robert Coleman, "'Command Performance' Is a Great Success," *New York Daily Mirror*, January 25, 1938.

51. Tighe E. Zimmers, *Lyrical Satirical Harold Rome: A Biography of the Broadway Composer-Lyricist* (Jefferson, NC: McFarland, 2014), 23–4.

52. Atkinson.

53. Elliot Norton, "Top Hit of Season at Shubert," *Boston Post*, December 8, 1937.

54. Caryl Brahms and Ned Sherrin, *Song by Song: The Lives and Work of 14 Great Lyric Writers* (Egerton, Bolton, England: Ross Anderson Publications, 1984), 113.

55. Alan Jay Lerner, *The Musical Theatre: A Celebration* (New York: McGraw-Hill Book Company, 1986), 143.

56. Atkinson.

57. Coleman, "Shuberts Offer Dietz-Schwartz Musical."

58. Hughes.

59. Linton Martin, "New Music Show at the Chestnut," *Philadelphia Inquirer*, October 20, 1937.

60. Dan Dietz, *Off Broadway Musicals, 1910–2007: Casts, Credits, Songs, Critical Reception and Performance Data of More Than 1,800 Shows* (Jefferson, NC: McFarland, 2009), 448.

61. Norton.

62. Radio script, *The Songwriters: Arthur Schwartz*, ASP, Box 41 / Folder 8, 12.

63. Dwight Blocker Bowers, J.R. Taylor, and James R. Morris, *American Popular Song: Six Decades of Songwriters and Singers* (Washington, D.C.: Smithsonian Institution Press, 1984), 80.

64. William Zinsser, *Easy to Remember: The Great American Songwriters and Their Songs* (Boston: David R. Godine, Publishers, Inc., 2001), 67.

65. Alec Wilder, *American Popular Song: The Great Innovators, 1900–1950* (New York: Oxford University Press, 1972), 314, 318, 324.

66. Radio script, 10–11.

67. Programs for *Between the Devil*, Shubert Theatre, Boston and The Imperial Theatre, New York.

68. Bordman, 559.

69. Wilder, 323.

70. Dan Sullivan, "Stage: Arthur Schwartz Goes His Way by Himself," *Los Angeles Times*, October 17, 1976.

71. Jonathan Schwartz, *All in Good Time: A Memoir* (New York: Random House, 1974), 9.

72. Mordaunt Hall, "At the Play," *Boston Evening Transcript*, December 8, 1937.

73. Wikipedia, s.v. "I See Your Face Before Me," http://en.wikipedia.org/w/index.php?title=I_See_Your_Face_Before_Me&oldid=81438449 (accessed January 20, 2018).

74. Radio script, 11.

75. Frank Rasky, "Broadway Songwriter Entertains Students," *Toronto Star*, June 22, 1976, E10.

Chapter 14

1. Kyle Crichton, "One Easy Lesson," *Collier's*, October 14, 1944, 46.

2. Robert Coleman, "'Virginia' Opens Center," *New York Mirror*, September 4, 1937; "'Virginia,' Rockefeller Show, Begins Rehearsals at Center," *New York World-Telegram*, August 3, 1937; "On Broadway," *Variety*, September 8, 1937.

3. Walter Karp, *The Center: A History and Guide to Rockefeller Center* (New York: American Heritage Publishing Company, Inc., 1982), 120.

4. Carol Herselle Krinsky, *Rockefeller Center* (New York: Oxford University Press, 1978), 190–2.

5. "On Broadway"; Richard Watts, Jr. "The Theater," *New York Herald Tribune*, September 12, 1937.

6. Watts, Jr.

7. Krinsky, 192.

8. Watts., Jr.

9. Steven Suskin, *Show Tunes: The Songs, Shows, and Careers of Broadway's Major Composers*, 4th ed. (New York: Oxford University Press, 2010), 131.

10. Ken Bloom, *American Song: The Complete Musical Theatre Companion*, 2nd ed., 1877–1995 (New York: Schirmer Books, 1996), 1199–1200.

11. Arthur Schwartz, "History Needs No Makeup for Musical Role," *New York Herald Tribune*, August 29, 1937.

12. Ibid.

13. Schwartz, untitled notes, ASP, Box 44 / Folder uncertain, 8.

14. Ethan Mordden, *Make Believe: The Broadway Musical in the 1920s* (New York: Oxford University Press, 1997), 140.

15. Gerald Bordman, *American Musical Theatre: A Chronicle* (New York: Oxford University Press, 2001), 556.
16. Schwartz, "History."
17. "'Virginia,' Rockefeller Show, Begins Rehearsals at Center."
18. Ibid.
19. "On Broadway: Virginia."
20. Ibid.
21. Suskin, *The Sound of Broadway Music: A Book of Orchestrators and Orchestrations* (Oxford: Oxford University Press, 2007), 570.
22. "The Ins and Outs of Composing for Broadway," *Canadian Composer*, September 1976, 12.
23. Schwartz, reply to queries from Howard Dietz, ASP, Box 51 / Folder 2, 1.
24. "The Ins and Outs of Composing for Broadway."
25. *Songwriters Hall of Fame*, s.v. "Al Stillman," http://www.songwritershalloffame.org/exhibits/bio/C282 (accessed February 12, 2013), 1.
26. Schwartz, "History."
27. Milton Esterow, "The Ambulatory Arthur Schwartz," *Musical America*, Vol. 83 / #10, October 1963, 17. NB: Harold Arlen was another composer and inveterate walker, usually going on foot from his residence to the offices of his publisher and back, in Walter Rimler, *The Man That Got Away: The Life and Songs of Harold Arlen* (Urbana, IL: University of Illinois Press, 2015), 24.
28. Ward Morehouse, "Broadway After Dark," *New York Sun*, July 27, 1937.
29. Schwartz, "History."
30. Morehouse.
31. "'Virginia,' Rockefeller Show, Begins Rehearsals at Center."
32. Morehouse.
33. Schwartz, "History."
34. "'Virginia,' Rockefeller Show, Begins Rehearsals at Center."
35. Douglas Gilbert, "'Virginia' Is a Page of Colonial History," *New York World-Telegram*, September 3, 1937; Bordman, 556.
36. Schwartz, "History."
37. Ibid.
38. Morehouse.
39. Coleman.
40. Watts, Jr.
41. John Mason Brown, "Two on the Aisle," *New York Evening Post*, September 4, 1937.
42. David Jenness and Don Velsey, *Classic American Popular Song: The Second Half-Century, 1950–2000* (New York: Routledge, 2006), 83.
43. Gilbert.
44. Arthur Pollock, "The Theater," *Brooklyn Eagle*, September 3, 1937.
45. "'Virginia' Opens N.Y. Season; Fails to Win B'Way Favor," *Hollywood Reporter*, September 3, 1937.
46. Burns Mantle, "Centre Theatre Opens Season with Expansive Musical Comedy," *New York Daily News*, September 4, 1937; "On Broadway: Virginia"; Jack Anderson, "Patricia Bowman, a Ballerina Who Linked Two Eras of Dance," obituary, *New York Times*, April 27, 1999.
47. Brooks Atkinson, "America to Music," *New York Times*, September 12, 1937.
48. Gilbert.
49. Karl Helm, "The Reporter at the Play," *New York Evening Post*, September 3, 1937.
50. *The Hi De Ho Blog*, www.thehidehoblog.com/blog/tagged/avis%20andrews (accessed July 9, 2018).
51. Watts, Jr.
52. "On Broadway: Virginia."
53. Watts, Jr., "The Theaters," *New York Herald Tribune*, September 3, 1937.
54. Mordden, *Sing for Your Supper: The Broadway Musical in the 1930s* (New York: Palgrave MacMillan, 2005), 112.
55. John Anderson, "'Virginia' Opens Season with Lavish Splendor," *New York Evening Journal*, September 3, 1937.
56. "On Broadway: Virginia."
57. Mantle.
58. Bordman, 556.
59. Watts, Jr., "The Theater," September 12, 1937.
60. Brown.
61. Ron Fassler, "Swingin' the Dream," https://medium.com/@ronfassler/swingin-the-dream-a08b82311994, (accessed October 12, 2019) 1–2; Christopher A. Coppula, *Jimmy Van Heusen: Swinging on a Star* (Nashville, TN: Twin Creek Books, 2014), 133–43.
62. Howard Pollack, *The Ballad of John Latouche: An American Lyricist's Life and Work* (New York: Oxford University Press), 139; Krinsky, 194.
63. Stanley Green, *The World of Musical Comedy: The Story of the American Musical Stage as Told Through the Careers of Its*

Foremost Composers and Lyricists (Chicago: Ziff Davis Publishing Company, 1960), 191.
64. "'Virginia' Opens N.Y. Season; Fails to Win B'Way Favor."
65. Atkinson, "Marrying an Angel," *New York Times*, May 22, 1938, 151.
66. Anderson.
67. Mordden, *Sing for Your Supper*, 113.
68. Schwartz reply to queries from Dietz, ASP, Box 51 / Folder 2, 5.
69. Bruce C. Elrod, ed., *Your Hit Parade and American Top 10 Hits*, 4th ed., s.v. "You and I Know" (Ann Arbor, MI: Popular Culture Ink, 1994), 42.
70. *Discography of American Historical Recordings*, s.v. "You and I Know" and "An Old Flame Never Dies," (accessed October 1, 2019); *Discogs*, https://www.discogs.com/Claude-Thornhill-In-Disco-Order-Volume-1/release/11167424 (accessed October 1, 2019).
71. Bordman, 556.
72. Mantle.
73. Anderson.
74. *Ibid.*
75. Watts, Jr., "The Theater," September 12, 1937.
76. Crichton, 46.
77. Schwartz, untitled notes, 8.

Chapter 15

1. Arthur Schwartz, "The Evolution of a Gay Musical: Collaborators Hardly Know It," *New York Herald Tribune*, February 12, 1939, VI 5.
2. *Ibid.*
3. Brian Kellow, *Ethel Merman: A Life* (New York: Viking, 2007), 72.
4. Tighe E. Zimmers, *Lyrical Satirical Harold Rome: A Biography of the Broadway Composer-Lyricist* (Jefferson, NC: McFarland, 2014), 10–25.
5. Deborah Grace Winer, *On the Sunny Side of the Street: The Life and Lyrics of Dorothy Fields* (New York: Schirmer Books, 1997), 119.
6. Michael Freedland, *Irving Berlin* (London: W.H. Allen, 1974), 190, 210.
7. Wilfrid Sheed, *The House That George Built: With a Little Help from Irving, Cole, and a Crew of About Fifty* (New York: Random House, 2008), 180.
8. Publicity program for *Stars in Your Eyes*, ASP, Box 41 / Folder 10, 10.
9. Leonard Lyons, *New York Post*, September 9, 1938 in Eric A. Gordon, *Mark the Music: The Life and Work of Marc Blitzstein* (New York: St. Martin's Press, 1989), 174.
10. Publicity program, 10.
11. Steven Moore, "The Avant-Pop Novels of J. P. McEvoy," *Numero Cinq*, March / 2017, Vol. VIII, No.3; *IMDb*, s.v. "J. P. McEvoy," https://www.com/title/tt0025318/?ref_=nm_knf_2 (accessed April 29, 2018); IBDB, s.v. "J. P. McEvoy," https://www.ibdb.com/broadway0-cast-staff/j-p-ncebvoy-6521 (accessed April 24, 2018); Cladriteradio, http://www.cladriteradio.com/images/authors/jpmcevoy2.jpg (accessed April 24, 2018).
12. Winer, 117.
13. Kellow, 72.
14. Charlotte Greenspan, *Pick Yourself Up: Dorothy Fields and the American Musical* (New York: Oxford University Press, 2010), 126.
15. Schwartz.
16. Kellow, 73.
17. Deborah Jowitt, *Robbins: His Life, His Theater, His Dance* (New York: Simon & Schuster, 2004), 40; Don McDonagh, *George Balanchine* (Boston: Twayne Publishers, 1983), 51.
18. Publicity program, 8.
19. Winer, 119.
20. Steven Suskin, *The Sound of Broadway Music: A Book of Orchestrators and Orchestrations* (Oxford: Oxford University Press, 2009), 547.
21. Publicity program, 10.
22. Greenspan, 121.
23. Joshua Logan, *Josh: My Up and Down, In and Out Life* (New York: Delacorte Press, 1976), 114.
24. Schwartz.
25. Greenspan, 122.
26. Schwartz.
27. Logan, 115.
28. Kellow, 74.
29. Schwartz.
30. Winer, 119.
31. Ethel Merman, *Merman* (New York: Simon & Schuster, 1978), 99.
32. Winer, 119.
33. Ethan Mordden, *Sing for Your Supper: The Broadway Musical in the 1930s* (New York: Palgrave MacMillan, 2005), 253.
34. Kellow, 74.
35. *Ibid.*
36. Schwartz.

37. Logan, 115.
38. Mordden, 252.
39. Merman, 100.
40. Ibid., 102.
41. Kellow, 73-4.
42. Script for *Lyrics & Lyricists*, 92nd Street YM-YWHA, ASP, Box 24 / Folder 10, 6.
43. Dwight Blocker Bowers, CD album notes, *Smithsonian Collection of Recordings: American Songbook Series: Arthur Schwartz* (Washington, D.C.: Smithsonian Institution, 1995), 12.
44. Hugh Martin, *Hugh Martin: The Boy Next Door* (Encinitas, CA: Trolley Press, 2010), 84-5.
45. Mordden, *Make Believe: The Broadway Musical in the 1920s* (New York: Oxford University Press, 1997), 194.
46. Logan, 115.
47. Gerald Bordman, *American Musical Theatre: A Chronicle*, 3rd ed. (New York: Oxford University Press, 2001), 566.
48. Ken Bloom, *American Song: The Complete Musical Theatre Companion*, 2nd ed., 1877-1995, Vol. 1: A-S (New York: Schirmer Books, 1996), 1063; Winer, 124; Program for *Stars in Your Eyes*, Majestic Theatre, week of April 17, 1939, 29, 31; Typescript of *Stars in Your Eyes*, Wisconsin Historical Society Archives, Papers, 1922-1950, Wiman, Dwight Deere, U.S. Mss25AN, Box 5 / Folder 6, 2-3.
49. Reviewers comments noted in Greenspan, 124.
50. *Ibid.*
51. Merman, 102.
52. Schwartz.
53. *Ibid.*
54. Logan, 115.
55. Kellow, 74.
56. Logan, 115.
57. Schwartz, ROAS, 11-12.
58. Cecil Smith and Glenn Litton, *Musical Comedy in America* (New York: Routledge / Theatre Arts Books, 1981), 172.
59. Schwartz, "The Evolution of a Gay Musical."
60. Schwartz, reply to queries from Howard Dietz, ASP, Box 51 / Folder 2, 3.
61. Dietz, HDATBW, 12.
62. Schwartz, reply to queries, 3.
63. Deems Taylor, *Some Enchanted Evenings: The Story of Rodgers and Hammerstein* (New York: Harper & Brothers, 1953), 141.

64. Frederick Nolan, *Lorenz Hart: A Poet on Broadway* (New York: Oxford University Press, 1994), 253.
65. Hugh Abercrombie Anderson, *Out Without My Rubbers: The Memoirs of John Murray Anderson* (New York: Library Publishers, 1954), 178-9.
66. Hugh Fordin, *Getting to Know Him: A Biography of Oscar Hammerstein II* (New York: Random House, 1977), 172.
67. Nolan, *The Sound of Their Music: The Story of Rodgers and Hammerstein* (New York: Applause Theatre and Cinema Books, 2002), 73; Taylor, 141.
68. Taylor, 141; Suskin, 318.
69. Bloom, 29.
70. Fordin, 172.
71. Nolan, *Lorenz Hart*, 252-3.
72. Schwartz and Oscar Hammerstein II, "Tennessee Fish Fry" (New York: Chappell & Co., Inc., 1940).
73. Nolan, *The Sound of Their Music*, 73; Taylor, 141.
74. Benjamin Welles, "In Re: Arthur Schwartz," *New York Times*, July 7, 1940.

Chapter 16

1. Allen L. Woll, *The Hollywood Musical Goes to War* (Chicago: Nelson-Hall, 1983), 49.
2. Irene Thirer, "Screen News and Views," *New York Post*, July 1, 1946.
3. Michael Freedland, *Irving Berlin* (London: W.H. Allen, 1974), 240-1.
4. Deena Rosenberg, *Fascinating Rhythm: The Collaboration of George and Ira Gershwin* (New York: Dutton, 1991), 324.
5. Freedland, 236-7.
6. Christopher Palmer, *Dimitri Tiomkin: A Portrait* (London: T.E. Books, 1984), 41.
7. archives.nypl.org, s.v. "United China Relief records," http://archives.nypl.org/mss/3078 (accessed July 22, 2018).
8. "Music: Honorable Moon," *Time*, July 21, 1941, 40.
9. IMDb, s.v. "Princess O'Rourke," https://www.imdb.com/title/tt036277/soundtrack?ref_=ttgf_ql_7 (accessed July 22, 2018); Arthur Schwartz, Ira Gershwin, and E.Y. Harburg, "Honorable Moon" (New York: Chappell & Co., Inc., 1941); *Princess O'Rourke* [1943], directed by Norman Krasna, DVD (Burbank, CA: Turner

Notes—Chapter 16

Entertainment Co. and Warner Bros. Entertainment, Inc., 2009).

10. Johnny Mercer, unpublished autobiography, Johnny Mercer Collection, George State University Library, http://digitalcollections.library.gsu.edu/cdm/ref//collection/music/id/1361 pp 42–3 (accessed March 9, 2019), 42–3.

11. Gene Lees, *Portrait of Johnny: The Life of John Herndon Mercer* (New York: Pantheon Books, 2004), 64.

12. Schwartz and Mercer, "You're a Natural" (Hollywood: Warner Bros. Pictures, Inc., 1941).

13. *Another Old Movie Blog*, s.v. "Navy Blues – 1941," https://anotheroldmovieblog (accessed July 23, 2018).

14. Ibid.

15. Joseph I. Breen to Jack L. Warner, Warner Bros. Pictures, Inc., letters dated April 24, April 28, and May 7, 1941, Margaret Herrick Library, Digital Collections, s.v. "Navy Blues, 1941," 14, 23, 27.

16. Script for *Lyrics and Lyricists*, 92nd St YM-YWHA, ASP, Box 24 / Folder 10, 4.

17. Robert Kimball, Barry Day, Miles Kreuger, and Eric Davis, *The Complete Lyrics of Johnny Mercer* (New York: Alfred A. Knopf, 2009), 115.

18. *Ace Repertory*, s.v. "All Through the Night," https://www.ascap.com/repertory (accessed July 25, 2018); Meredith d'Ambrosio, *By Myself*, CD, SSC 1285 (New York Sunnyside Communications, 2012).

19. *Cairo*, directed by Maj. W.S. Van Dyke, II, 1942, DVD (Burbank, CA: Warner Home Video, 2012).

20. Agreement among E.Y. Harburg, Howard Dietz, and Schwartz with Leo Feist, Inc. and Loew's Incorporated regarding "Keep the Light Burning Bright," April 29, 1942, collection of the author.

21. Roy Hemming, *The Melody Lingers On: The Great Songwriters and Their Movie Musicals* (New York: Newmarket Press, 1986), 13.

22. Jonathan Schwartz, *All in Good Time: A Memoir* (New York: Random House, 2004), 20.

23. Sidney Skolsky, "Watching Them Make Pictures," unidentified article, probably *Photoplay*, circa August, 1942, ASP.

24. Wilfrid Sheed, *The House That George Built: With a Little Help from Irving, Cole, and a Crew of About Fifty* (New York: Random House, 2008), 276.

25. Susan Loesser, *A Most Remarkable Fella: Frank Loesser and the Guys and Dolls in His Life: A Portrait by His Daughter* (New York: Donald I. Fine, Inc., 1993), 43.

26. IMDb, s.v. "Thank Your Lucky Stars (1943)," https://www.imdb.com/title/tt0036422/soundtrack?ref_=ttgf_ql_7 (accessed July 30, 2018).

27. Woll, 49.

28. Don Tyler, *Hit Songs, 1900–1955: American Popular Music of the Pre-Rock Era* (Jefferson, NC: McFarland & Company, Inc., 2007), 277.

29. *Thank Your Lucky Stars*, directed by David Butler, 1943, DVD, ASIN: B001KY-8JHG (Burbank, CA: Warner Home Video, 2008).

30. John Bush Jones, *The Songs That Fought the War: Popular Music and the Home Front* (Boston: Brandeis University Press, 2006), 213.

31. Kathleen E.R. Smith, *God Bless America: Tin Pan Alley Goes to War* (Lexington, KY: The University Press of Kentucky, 2003), 31.

32. Jones, 225.

33. Freedland, 190.

34. Hazel Meyer, *The Gold in Tin Pan Alley* (Philadelphia: J.B. Lippincott Company, 1958), 110.

35. Ibid.

36. Woll, 70.

37. Jonathan Schwartz, 23.

38. Meyer, 111.

39. Jones, 263.

40. Bruce C. Elrod, ed., *Your Hit Parade and American Top 10 Hits*, 4th ed., s.v. "They're Either Too Young or Too Old" (Ann Arbor, MI: Popular Culture Ink, 1994).

41. Gail Kinn and Jim Piazza, *The Academy Awards: The Complete Unofficial History* (New York: Black Dog & Leventhal Publishers, 2014), 71.

42. John Stewart, *Broadway Musicals, 1943–2004* (Jefferson, NC: McFarland, 2006), 463.

43. *ACE Repertory*, s.v. "They're Either Too Young or Too Old," https://www.ascap.com/repertory (accessed August 1, 2018).

44. Caryl Brahms and Ned Sherrin, *Song by Song: The Lives and Work of 14 Great Lyric Writers* (Egerton, Bolton, England: Ross Anderson Publications, 1984), 1.

Chapter 17

1. Jon Pareles, "Tribute to Arthur Schwartz Fills Theater with His Music," *New York Times*, October 24, 1984, D27.
2. Arthur Schwartz, "HOW I GOT TO PRODUCE FILMS," unpublished notes, ASP, Box 51 / Folder 2, 5.
3. Michael Freedland, *Jerome Kern* (New York: Stein and Day, 1981), 162–3.
4. Gerald Bordman, *Jerome Kern: His Life and Music* (New York: Oxford University Press, 1980), 397.
5. David Ewen *The World of Jerome Kern: A Biography* (New York: Henry Holt and Company, 1960), 8, 4.
6. Douglas Watt, "Bugs Bunny Gets a Brush-off from a Songwriting Lawyer," *New York News*, June 27, 1946.
7. Bordman, 383.
8. Philip Furia, *Ira Gershwin: The Art of the Lyricist* (New York: Oxford University Press, 1996), 180.
9. William G. Hyland, *The Song Is Ended: Songwriters and American Music, 1900–1950* (New York: Oxford University Press, 1995), 257.
10. Deena Rosenberg, *Fascinating Rhythm: The Collaboration of George and Ira Gershwin* (New York: Dutton, 1991), 107.
11. Saul Chaplin, *The Golden Age of Movie Musicals and Me* (Norman, OK: University of Oklahoma Press, 1994), 56.
12. Freedland, 163.
13. Wilfrid Sheed, *The House That George Built: With a Little Help from Irving, Cole, and a Crew of About Fifty* (New York: Random House, 2008), 120.
14. Alvin Yudkoff, *Gene Kelly: A Life of Dance and Dreams* (New York: Back Stage Books, 1999), 125.
15. *Wikipedia*, s.v." Phil Silvers," (accessed June 22, 2018).
16. Yudkoff, 127–8.
17. Pareles.
18. Yudkoff, 124.
19. Freedland, 163.
20. John S. Wilson, "Broadway Report: A Tunesmith Comes Back," *PM*, June 28, 1946.
21. Furia, 182.
22. Bordman, 398.
23. Freedland, 163–4.
24. Jonathan Schwartz, *All in Good Time: A Memoir* (New York: Random House, 2004), 24.
25. Bordman, 398.
26. Kyle Crichton, "One Easy Lesson," *Collier's*, October 14, 1944, 46.
27. Furia, 180–1.
28. Ira Gershwin, *Lyrics on Several Occasions* (New York: Alfred A. Knopf, Inc., 1959), 274.
29. Bordman, 398.
30. Hyland, 257; Furia, 181.
31. Gershwin, 276.
32. Yudkoff, 128.
33. *Ibid.*, 129–30; Chaplin, 51.
34. Bob Thomas, *King Cohn: The Life and Times of Hollywood Mogul Harry Cohn* (Beverly Hills: New Millenium Press, 2000), 248.
35. Yudkoff, 129.
36. Crichton, 46.
37. Yudkoff, 130.
38. Arthur Schwartz, ROAS, 12–13.
39. Yudkoff, 130.
40. Mrs. F.D. Moffett, "Versatile Voiced Moberlyan 'Dubs' for Unmusical Star," *Moberly* (MO) *Monitor-Index*, February 19, 1952 (from *St. Louis Post-Dispatch*.).
41. Schwartz, "HOW I GOT TO PRODUCE FILMS," 5.
42. Crichton, 44.
43. Schwartz, "Music, Maestro, Please!," *The Hollywood Reporter*, September 23, 1946.
44. Freedland, *Irving Berlin* (London: W.H. Allen, 1974), 207.
45. William McBrien, *Cole Porter: A Biography* (New York: Alfred A. Knopf, 1998), 275.
46. Richard G. Hubler, *The Cole Porter Story* (Cleveland, OH: The World Publishing Company, 1965), ix.
47. Robert Kimball, ed., *The Complete Lyrics of Cole Porter* (New York: Alfred A. Knopf, 1983), various.
48. McBrien, 275.
49. Charles Schwartz, *Cole Porter: A Biography* (New York: The Dial Press, 1977), 214–5.
50. *Ibid.*, 215; George Eells, *The Life That Late He Led: A Biography of Cole Porter* (New York: G.P. Putnam's Sons, 1967), 213.
51. Arthur Schwartz to Jack Warner, July 30, 1951, ASP.
52. Freedland, *Irving Berlin*, 274.
53. "'Night and Day': Smash Hit for Warners," *Box Office Digest*, undated, 1946, ASP, Box 39 / Folder 6.
54. Neil Rau, "Visiting the Studios,"

Pittsburgh Sun-Telegraph, September 7, 1946.
 55. McBrien, 290.
 56. Rau.
 57. Roy Hemming, *The Melody Lingers On: The Great Songwriters and Their Movie Musicals* (New York: Newmarket Press, 1986), 169.
 58. Arthur Schwartz to J.L. Warner, April 13, 1944, Warner Bros. Archives, School of Cinematic Arts, University of Southern California, Box 2877 / Folder 2533, "Night and Day" Legal – "Cole Porter," 1–2.
 59. McBrien, 291.
 60. Hemming, 170.
 61. Charles Schwartz, 222.
 62. "The Current Cinema: Songs, No Witty Patter," *New Yorker,* July 27, 1946.
 63. William Hawkins, "Movies: 'Night and Day' Fine Story of Cole Porter," *New York World-Telegram,* July 25, 1946.
 64. Critics' comments in Irving Hoffman, "'Night' Topnotch Musical; Critics Call 'Time' Adult," *The Hollywood Reporter,* July 29, 1946, 6.
 65. "The Picture of the Week: Cole Porter Music Given Thrilling Life in Magnificent 'Night and Day,'" *Hollywood Reporter,* July 9, 1946.
 66. Irene Thirer, "Screen News and Views," *New York Post,* July 1, 1946.
 67. Freedland, *Irving Berlin,* 144; Stanleigh P. Friedman, attorney, to Roy Obringer, Warner Bros. Studios, March 6, 1946, Warner Bros. Archives, School of Cinematic Arts, University of Southern California, Box 2877 / Folder 2532, "Night and Day" Legal—"Cole Porter".
 68. McBrien, 274.
 69. Watt.
 70. Leslie Halliwell, *Halliwell's Film and Video Guide,* Revised and Updated, s.v. "Night and Day" (New York: HarperPerennial, 1997).
 71. Charles Schwartz, 222; http://www.answers.com/topic/night-and-day-1946-film (accessed February 13, 2013), 1–2.
 72. Hubler, xi.
 73. Cole Porter to Arthur Schwartz, May 28, 1946, ASP, Box 39 / Folder 5.
 74. Charles Schwartz, 223.
 75. Jonathan Schwartz, 25–6.
 76. Florabel Muir, "Florabel Muir Reports: Schwartz Heading East for Broadway Musical," *Hollywood Citizen-News,* April 1947, n.d., from incomplete article, ASP, Box 40 / Folder 2. NB: Ms. Muir's article, although valuable for its content, has information that is untimely. By April 1947, Schwartz had long been back to New York and working on *Park Avenue.*
 77. Arthur Schwartz to Col. J.L. Warner, July 17, 1946, ASP, Box 39 / Folder 5.
 78. Schwartz reply to queries from Howard Dietz, ASP, Box 51 / Folder 2, 2.
 79. Schwartz, ROAS, 13–6.
 80. Muir.
 81. Jonathan Schwartz, 23.
 82. Muir.
 83. Howard Dietz, HDATBW, 3.

Chapter 18

 1. Dave A. Epstein, notes to Guy McCoy, editor of *Etude,* April 10, 1953, ASP, Box 44 / Folder 29, 1.
 2. Arthur Schwartz, handwritten notes regarding songwriting, undated, unpublished, ASP, Box 51 / Folder 1, 1.
 3. Schwartz, 3.
 4. Rose Heylbut, "How to Write Good Tunes," *Etude,* October / 1954, 10.
 5. Epstein.
 6. Howard Dietz, *Dancing in the Dark: Words by Howard Dietz: An Autobiography* (New York: Quadrangle / New York Times Book Co., Inc., 1974), 31.
 7. "Hit Writer Says Successful Song Is 50 Percent Talent and the Rest Digging and Logic," *Boston Sunday Globe,* January 12, 1947.
 8. Heylbut.
 9. Jonathan Schwartz, *All in Good Time: A Memoir* (New York: Random House, 2004), 15–6.
 10. Dietz, HDATBW, 13.
 11. Frederick Nolan, *Lorenz Hart: A Poet on Broadway* (New York: Oxford University Press, 1994), 86.
 12. Dietz, HDATBW, 9.
 13. Schwartz, reply to queries from Dietz, ASP, Box 51 / Folder 2, 1.
 14. Dietz, HDATBW, 22.
 15. Benny Green, *Let's Face the Music: The Golden Age of Popular Song* (London: Pavillion Books Limited, 1989), 97.
 16. Alec Wilder, *American Popular Song: The Great Innovators, 1900–1950* (New York: Oxford University Press, 1972), 313.
 17. John Tasker Howard, *Our American*

Music: Three Hundred Years of It, 3rd ed. (New York: Thomas Y. Cromwell Company, 1946), 671.

18. Heylbut, 11.

19. Wilder, 313.

20. Ken Bloom, *The American Songbook: The Singers, the Songwriters and the Songs* (New York: Black Dog & Leventhal, 2005), 296.

21. Jon Pareles, "Tribute to Arthur Schwartz Fills Theater with His Music," *New York Times*, October 24, 1984, D27.

22. Stanley Green, *The World of Musical Comedy: The Story of the American Musical Stage as Told Through the Careers of Its Foremost Composers and Lyricists* (Chicago: Ziff-Davis Publishing Company, 1960), 184.

23. William Zinsser, *Easy to Remember: The Great American Songwriters and Their Songs* (Boston: David R. Godine, Publishers, Inc., 2001), 67.

24. Heylbut, 11.

25. Wilfrid Sheed, *The House That George Built: With a Little Help from Irving, Cole, and a Crew of About Fifty* (New York: Random House, 2007), 301–3.

26. Schwartz, handwritten notes, 4.

27. Schwartz, notes on article for *Redbook*, ASP, Box 51 / Folder 3, 1.

28. Arthur B. Minikes, "Arthur Schwartz—Master of Melody," *New York University Alumnus*, November 2, 1932, 52.

29. Wilder, 320.

30. Schwartz, "HOW I GOT TO PRODUCE FILMS," unpublished notes, ASP, Box 51 / Folder 2, 4.

31. Jack D. Brinkley, "Behind the Music," *Radio Guide*, October 20, 1934.

32. Deena Rosenberg, *Fascinating Rhythm: The Collaboration of George and Ira Gershwin* (New York: Dutton, 1991), 62.

33. Sheed, 17.

34. Dietz, HDATBW, 4.

35. Dietz, *Dancing in the Dark*, 132.

36. Florabel Muir, "Florabel Muir Reports: Schwartz Heading East for Broadway Musical," *Hollywood* (CA) *Citizen-News*, April 1947, unspecified date from incomplete article, ASP, Box 40 / Folder 2.

37. "The Ins and Outs of Composing for Broadway," *Canadian Composer*, September / 1976, 12.

38. Jonathan Schwartz, 16.

39. James Aswell, "My New York," *Columbia* (MO) *Tribune*, September 20, 1964.

40. *Broadway & Hollywood Legends: The Songwriters: Charles Strouse and Arthur Schwartz*, DVD, ASIN: B0001Z4OTC (New York: Lance Entertainment, 2004).

41. "Dietz and Schwartz," pre-publication notes for souvenir program for *Jennie*, ASP, Box 50 / Folder 1, 4.

42. Alton Cook, "Scan 'The Gibson Family,'" *New York World-Telegram*, September 12, 1934.

43. "Dietz and Schwartz."

44. Avis Caminez, "Americans Abroad," *The Tatler*, June / 1977.

45. Schwartz, ROAS, 3.

46. Sheed, 306.

47. Jonathan Schwartz, Preface to *That's Entertainment: The Great Songs of Dietz & Schwartz* (Secaucus, NJ: Warner Bros. Publications Inc., 1990).

Chapter 19

1. Jonathan Schwartz, *All in Good Time: A Memoir* (New York: Random House, 2004), 35.

2. Edward Jablonski, *Gershwin* (New York: Doubleday, 1987), 346.

3. Philip Furia, *Ira Gershwin: The Art of the Lyricist* (New York: Oxford University Press, 1996), 199.

4. Craig Lloyd, "Nunnally Johnson (1897–1977)," *New Georgia Encyclopedia*, https://www.georgiaencyclopedia.org/articles/arts-culture/nunnally-johnson-1897-1977 (accessed September 16, 2018); Tom Stempel, *Screenwriter: The Life and Times of Nunnally Johnson* (San Diego, CA: A.S. Barnes & Co., Inc., 1980), 118.

5. Malcolm Goldstein, *George S. Kaufman: His Life, His Theater* (New York: Oxford University Press, 1979), 397.

6. Ibid.

7. Jablonski, 345.

8. Stanley Green, *The World of Musical Comedy: The Story of the American Musical Stage As Told Through the Careers of Its Foremost Composers and Lyricists* (Chicago: Ziff Davis Publishing Company, 1960), 193.

9. Arthur Schwartz to Max Gordon, January 26, 1946, ASP, Box 40 / Folder 1.

10. Ibid.

11. George S. Kaufman to Ira Gershwin, January 1946, n.d., Gershwin Collection,

New York Public Library for the Performing Arts, Box 28 / Folder 22.

12. Furia, 195–7.

13. Howard Teichmann, *George S. Kaufman: An Intimate Portrait* (New York: Atheneum, 1972), 220.

14. Jonathan Schwartz, 31.

15. Douglas Watt, "Bugs Bunny Gets a Brush-Off from a Songwriting Lawyer," *New York News*, June 27, 1946.

16. Goldstein, 398.

17. Kaufman, "Music to My Ears," *Stage 15*, August / 1938, 27–30, in Howard Pollack, *George Gershwin: His Life and Work* (Berkeley, CA: University of California Press, 2006), 396.

18. Deena Rosenberg, *Fascinating Rhythm: The Collaboration of George and Ira Gershwin* (New York: Dutton, 1991), 199.

19. Kaufman, "Music to My Ears."

20. Furia, 199–200.

21. Jablonski, *Irving Berlin: American Troubadour* (New York: Henry Holt and Company, 1999), 115.

22. Robert Coleman, "The Theatre: Stromberg to Scout Strawhat Talent," *New York Mirror*, June 28, 1946.

23. Kaufman to Gershwin.

24. Program for *Park Avenue*, Sam S. Shubert Theatre, New York, week of November 11, 1946, 47; John Stewart, *Broadway Musicals, 1943-2004* (Jefferson, NC: McFarland, 2006), 462.

25. Reviews of *Park Avenue*, November 5, 1946: John Chapman, *New York Daily News*; Brooks Atkinson, *New York Times*; and William Hawkins, *New York World-Telegram*.

26. Chapman.

27. Coleman, review of *Park Avenue*, *New York Daily Mirror*, November 5, 1946.

28. Howard Barnes, review of *Park Avenue*, *New York Herald Tribune*, November 5, 1946.

29. David Jenness and Don Velsey, *Classic American Popular Song: The Second Half-Century, 1950-2000* (New York: Routledge, 2006), 83.

30. Ethan Mordden, *Beautiful Mornin': The Broadway Musical in the 1940s* (New York: Oxford University Press, 1999), 191.

31. Jenness, 83.

32. Jablonski, "What About Ira?," in *The Gershwin Style: New Looks at the Music of George Gershwin*, Wayne Schneider, ed.

(New York: Oxford University Press, 1999), 261.

33. Ira Gershwin, *Lyrics on Several Occasions* (New York: Alfred A. Knopf, Inc., 1959), 312.

34. "Park Avenue / Gershwin Music," http://www.gershwin.com/shows/park-avenue (accessed December 17, 2012).

35. Gershwin, 121.

36. Jablonski, "What About Ira?," 261.

37. Caryl Brahms and Ned Sherrin, *Song by Song: The Lives and Work of 14 Great Lyric Writers* (Egerton, Bolton, England: Ross Anderson Publications, 1984), 59.

38. Jablonski and Lawrence D. Stewart, *The Gershwin Years: George and Ira* (New York: Da Capo Press, 1996), 302.

39. Goldstein, 398.

40. Gershwin, 80.

41. Jenness, 83–5.

42. Jablonski, *Gershwin*, 345.

43. John Stewart, 462.

44. Goldstein, 398.

45. Hawkins.

46. Jablonski, *The Gershwin Years*, 303.

47. Jablonski, "What About Ira?," 261.

48. Stewart, 462.

49. Rick Simas, *The Musicals No One Came to See: A Guidebook to Four Decades of Musical-Comedy Casualties on Broadway, Off-Broadway and in Out-of-Town Try-out, 1943-1983* (New York: Garland Publishing, Inc., 1987), 228–9.

50. Gershwin, 349–50.

51. Gershwin to Jablonski, November 1946, in Jablonski, "What About Ira?," 261.

52. Jonathan Schwartz, 35.

Chapter 20

1. Gerald Bordman, *American Musical Revue: From The Passing Show to Sugar Babies* (New York: Oxford University Press, 1985), 120.

2. Wilfrid Sheed, *The House That George Built: With a Little Help from Irving, Cole, and a Crew of About Fifty* (New York: Random House, 2008), 89.

3. Arthur Schwartz to Katherine Carrington, July 16, 1936, ASP, Box 44 / Folder 18, 2.

4. Schwartz in script for *Lyrics & Lyricists*, ASP, Box 24 / Folder 10, 6.

5. Don Tyler, *Hit Songs, 1900–1955:*

American Popular Music in the Pre-Rock Era (Jefferson, NC: McFarland, 2007), 463.

6. PRODUCTION NOTES on *The Time, the Place and the Girl*, Warner Bros. Studio, Margaret Herrick Library, Production Files, 2.

7. Gary Marmorstein, *Hollywood Rhapsody: Movie Music and Its Makers: 1900-1975* (New York: Schirmer Books, 1997), 259.

8. Herbert Cohn, "Screen," *Brooklyn Eagle*, December 27, 1946.

9. Howard Pollack, *The Ballad of John Latouche: An American Lyricist's Life and Work* (New York: Oxford University Press), 141, 150.

10. Bruce C. Elrod, ed., *Your Hit Parade and American Top 10 Hits*, 4th ed., s.v. "Oh, But I Do" (Ann Arbor, MI: Popular Culture Ink, 1994).

11. PRODUCTION NOTES, 4.

12. Marmorstein, 361.

13. Philip K. Scheuer, "New Musical Has Pleasing Song Score," *Los Angeles Times*, January 18, 1947.

14. *ACE Repertory*, s.v. "A Gal in Calico," https://www.ascap.com/repertory (accessed September 27, 2018).

15. Elrod, s.v. "A Gal in Calico."

16. Jonathan Schwartz, *All in Good Time: A Memoir* (New York: Random House, 2004), 36–7.

17. Schwartz to Beatrice Lillie, August 12, 1947, ASP, Box 47 / Folder 8.

18. Schwartz to Lillie, September 27, 1947, ASP, Box 47 / Folder 8, 5.

19. Jonathan Schwartz, 38.

20. Schwartz to Lillie, September 27, 1947, 1–2.

21. Various correspondences to Schwartz; Schwartz to Lillie, September 27, 1947, 1; Fred Allen to Schwartz, October 15, 1947; and Charles Lederer to Schwartz, October 27, 1947. All these are in ASP, Box 30 / Folder 10.

22. P.G. Wodehouse to Schwartz, December 24, 1947, ASP, Box 30 / Folder 10.

23. Schwartz to Wodehouse, December 30, 1947, ASP, Box 30 / Folder 10..

24. Steven Suskin, *Show Tunes: The Songs, Shows, and Careers of Broadway's Major Composers*, 4th ed. (New York: Oxford University Press, 2010), 190, 410; "Arnold Howitt Dies at 59," *New York Times*, October 23, 1977, 40.

25. Schwartz to Lillie, August 12, 1947.

26. Schwartz to Lillie, September 27, 1947, 2.

27. Ibid., 2–3.

28. Actors' Equity Association Standard Run-of-the Play Contract and Rider, January 9, 1948, collection of the author; Schwartz to Lillie, addendum to Contract and Rider, January 9, 1948, collection of the author.

29. Schwartz to Lillie, October 8, 1947, ASP, Box 47 / Folder 8, 2.

30. Schwartz, "Memo for Mr. Dietz," typed notes, ASP, Box 51 / Folder 2, 1.

31. Wikipedia, s.v. "Jack Haley," https://en.wikipedia.org/wiki/Jack_Haley (accessed October 22, 2018); Eric Pace, "Jack Haley, Actor, 79, Dead; Was Tin Woodman in 'Oz,'" *New York Times*, June 7, 1979, D95.

32. Schwartz to Lillie, August 12, 1947.

33. Lawrence Van Gelder, "Thelma Carpenter, 77, Singer with Big Bands," obituary, *New York Times*, May 17, 1997.

34. Dwight Blocker Bowers, CD album notes, *Smithsonian Collection of Recordings: American Songbook Series: Arthur Schwartz* (Washington, D.C.: Smithsonian Institution, 1995), 7.

35. Unpublished lyrics for "Rhode Island Is Famous for You," ASP, Box 7 / Folder 20.

36. Howard Dietz to Schwartz, July 9, 1947, ASP, Box 44 / Folder 25.

37. Caryl Brahms and Ned Sherrin, *Song by Song: 14 Great Lyric Writers* (Bolton, Lancashire: Ross Anderson Publications, 1984), 115.

38. Alec Wilder, *American Popular Song: The Great Innovators, 1900-1950* (New York: Oxford University Press, 1972), 326.

39. Bordman, 130.

40. Wodehouse to Dietz, May 16, 1948, HDP, Series I, Box 2 / Folder 8.

41. Laurence Maslon, *Broadway to Main Street: How Show Tunes Enchanted America* (New York: Oxford University Press, 2018), 82.

42. Bordman, *American Musical Theatre: A Chronicle* (New York: Oxford University Press, 1978), 615.

43. *Inside U.S.A.*, CD Sepia 1056 (United Kingdom: Sepia Records Limited, 2005).

44. Handwritten program notes for *Lyrics & Lyricists Series*, HDP, Series I, Box 1 / Folder 19.

45. Schwartz replies to queries from Dietz, ASP, Box 51 / Folder 2, 3.
46. Suskin, *Opening Night on Broadway: A Critical Quotebook of the Golden Era of the Musical Theatre*, Oklahoma! *(1943)* to Fiddler on the Roof *(1964)* (New York: Schirmer Books, 1990), 335–7; Bruce Laffey, *Beatrice Lillie: The Funniest Woman in the World* (New York: WYNWOOD Press, 1989), 138.
47. Lee Davis, *Scandals and Follies: The Rise and Fall of the Great Broadway Revue* (New York: Limelight Editions, 2000), 364.
48. Robert Baral, *Revue: A Nostalgic Reprise of the Great Broadway Period* (New York: Fleet Publishing Corporation, 1962), 213.
49. Bordman, *American Musical Revue*, 120.
50. Laffey, 138–45; Actors' Equity Contract Rider, 1.
51. Laffey, 143–4.
52. Jonathan Schwartz, 45.
53. Ethan Mordden, *Beautiful Mornin': The Broadway Musical in the 1940s* (New York: Oxford University Press, 1999), 185.
54. Schwartz, ROAS, 17.

Chapter 21

1. "Speaking of Television," press release, Columbia Broadcasting System, October 19, 1949, ASP, Box 30 / Folder 9, 4.
2. Richard Irvin, *The Early Shows: A Reference Guide to Network and Syndicated Prime-Time Television Series from 1944 to 1949* (Albany, GA: BearManor Media, 2018), 155, 161, 170–2.
3. "Arthur Schwartz Doing Christmas Eve Video Show Costing $30,000," *Variety*, December 15, 1948.
4. "CBS Will Use Films as Video Background," *Motion Picture Daily*, December 24, 1948.
5. "Less TV Depends on Radio, Better Off It Will Be, Sez Arthur Schwartz," *Variety*, December 29, 1948.
6. "Arthur Schwartz," Playbill for Inside U.S.A. with Chevrolet, for CBS Studio No. 52, ASP, Box 30 / Folder 9, 4.
7. Arthur Schwartz, "Television for Tomorrow," *Playbill*, 2.
8. "Speaking of Television," 4.
9. Charles B. Cochran, *Showman Looks On* (London: J.M. Dent & Sons, 1945), 303.
10. Howard Dietz, HDATBW, 21.
11. Schwartz, "INSIDE U.S.A.," early notes, n.d., ASP, Box 30 / Folder 9, 1–2.
12. Irvin, 38.
13. W.E. Fish, general sales manager of Chevrolet Motor Division, "Chevrolet and Television," *Playbill*, 3.
14. "Inside U.S.A. with Chevrolet," *Playbill*, 1.
15. Irvin, 150.
16. John Crosby, "Radio in Review," *New York Herald Tribune*, October 20, 1949.
17. THE STARS OF INSIDE U.S.A., typed notes, ASP, Box 30 / Folder 9.
18. "INSIDE U.S.A. TELEVISION SHOWS," typed notes, ASP, Box 30 / Folder 9.
19. Crosby.
20. "Television Reviews," *Variety*, October 5, 1949.
21. "Inside U.S.A with Chevrolet.," *Playbill*, 16.
22. "OTHER SKETCHES AVAILABLE," ASP, Box 48 / Folder 2, 1–2.
23. "Television Reviews."
24. *Ibid*.
25. *Variety*, March 22, 1950.
26. Crosby.
27. *Variety*, March 22, 1950.
28. W.E. Fish to Schwartz, April 13, 1950, ASP, Box 31 / Folder 1.
29. Winslow H. Case to Schwartz, March 20, 1950, ASP, Box 31 / Folder 1.
30. "Arthur Schwartz Gives Views on Current Contract Trouble," *Theatre News Weekly*, July 28, 1950.
31. Samson Raphaelson to Schwartz, June 27, 1950, ASP, Box 47 / Folder 8, 1.
32. Lewis Funke, "News and Gossip Gathered on the Rialto," *New York Times*, October 15, 1950.
33. "Arthur Schwartz Gives Views on Current Contract Trouble," 2.
34. *Ibid*.
35. "A Plan and a Leader," editorial, *Theatre News Weekly*, September 29, 1950.
36. "Main Street to Broadway," *Theatre Arts*, July 1953, 17.
37. Schwartz, "*Main Street to Broadway*: Giving the Theatre a New Lease on Life," *Theatre Arts*, July 1953, 19.
38. Schwartz to Dietz, January 29, 1953, ASP, Box 44 / Folder 25, 1.

39. Tighe E. Zimmers, *Tin Pan Alley Girl: A Biography of Ann Ronell* (Jefferson, NC: McFarland, 2009), 108–9.
40. "'Main Street' Paving Easier Legit Path," *Daily Variety* (Hollywood), May 8, 1953.
41. Schwartz, "The Theatre: Stage Struck Audiences," *Playbill* for *Stage Struck,* October 2, 1953.
42. Brooks Atkinson, review of *Hilda Crane,* Coronet Theatre, *New York Times,* November 2, 1950, 38.
43. IBDB, s.v. *"Hilda Crane,"* https://www.idbd/broadway-production/hilda-crane-1878 (accessed September 16, 2018).
44. Luther Davis to Schwartz, November 17, 1950, ASP, 1–2.
45. Davis telegram to Schwartz, October 2, 1951, ASP, 1–2.
46. *Wikipedia,* s.v. "Grand Hotel (musical)," https://en.wikipedia.org/wiki/Grand_Hotel_(musical) (accessed June 16, 2018).

Chapter 22

1. William Zinsser, *Easy to Remember: The Great American Songwriters and Their Songs* (Boston: David R. Godine, Publishers, Inc., 2001), 69.
2. Ken Mandlebaum, liner notes for *A Tree Grows in Brooklyn,* CD SK 48014 (1951; New York: Sony Music Entertainment Inc., 1991), 11; George Abbott, *"Mister Abbott"* (New York: Random House, 1963), 228.
3. Deborah Grace Winer, *On the Sunny Side of the Street: The Life and Lyrics of Dorothy Fields* (New York: Schirmer Books, 1997), 167.
4. Mandelbaum, 11.
5. Jonathan Schwartz, *All in Good Time: A Memoir* (New York: Random House, 2004), 50–1.
6. Charlotte Greenspan, *Pick Yourself Up: Dorothy Fields and the American Musical* (New York: Oxford University Press, 2010), 181.
7. Mandelbaum, 10.
8. Jim Manago, *Love Is the Reason for It All: The Shirley Booth Story* (Albany, GA: BearManor Media, 2008), 94.
9. Mandelbaum, 11.
10. Arthur Schwartz, "Music Tries to Recapture the Brooklyn of Yesterday," *New York Herald Tribune,* April 17, 1951. NB: A Schwartz draft of this article, close to the printed edition, is contained in ASP, Box 41 / Folder 27.
11. Stanley Green, *The World of Musical Comedy: The Story of the American Musical Stage As Told Through the Careers of Its Foremost Composers and Lyricists* (Chicago: Ziff Davis Publishing Company, 1960), 194.
12. John Chapman, "That Tree from Brooklyn," *New York Daily News,* April 29, 1951, Section Two, 3; Mandelbaum, 12.
13. Ethan Mordden, *Broadway Babies: The People Who Made the American Musical* (New York: Oxford University Press, 1983), 146.
14. Howard Teichmann, *George S. Kaufman: An Intimate Portrait* (New York: Atheneum, 1972), 54.
15. Leonard Sillman, *Here Lies Leonard Sillman: Straightened Out at Last* (New York: The Citadel Press, 1959), 105–6.
16. "The Trouper," *Time,* August 10, 1953, in David C. Tucker, *Shirley Booth: A Biography and Career Record* (Jefferson, NC: McFarland, 2008), 62.
17. John McClain, "The Drama," *New York Journal American,* April 1, 1951.
18. "TV Talent and Show Tips," *The Billboard,* May 5, 1951, 7.
19. Brooks Atkinson, "That Brooklyn Tree," *New York Times,* circa late April, 1951, ASP.
20. Manago, 98.
21. Betty Smith, postcard to Schwartz, December 12, 1950, ASP, Box 44 / Folder 2.
22. Abbott to Schwartz, December 19, 1950, ASP, Box 44 / Folder 2.
23. Abbott, *"Mister Abbott,"* 256.
24. Schwartz, "Music Tries to Recapture the Brooklyn of Yesterday."
25. Winer, 171.
26. Schwartz.
27. Ibid.
28. *A Tree Grows in Brooklyn,* CD SK 48014 (1951; New York: Sony Music Entertainment Inc., 1991).
29. Alec Wilder, *American Popular Song: The Great Innovators, 1900–1950* (New York: Oxford University Press, 1972), 326.
30. ACE Repertory, s.v. "Make the Man Love Me," http://www.ascap.com/repertory (accessed November 18, 2018).
31. *Alone Together: Jonathan Schwartz Sings Arthur Schwartz,* CD MCD 5143 (New York: Muse Records, 1995).
32. Program for *A Tree Grows in*

Brooklyn, Forrest Theatre, Philadelphia, week of March 26, 1951.
33. Mandelbaum, 13.
34. Ken Bloom, *American Song: The Complete Musical Theatre Companion*, 2nd ed., 1877–1995, Vol. 1: A–S (New York: Schirmer Books, 1996), 1144.
35. Dorothy Fields, lyrics for "I'm Old Enough," DFP, Box 2 / Folder 11.
36. John Stewart, *Broadway Musicals, 1943–2004* (Jefferson, NC: McFarland, 2006), 614.
37. Schwartz.
38. Mandelbaum, 14.
39. Atkinson.
40. Manago, 97.
41. Tucker, 62.
42. Schwartz.
43. Manago, 98.
44. Schwartz.
45. Mordden, *Better Foot Forward: The History of American Musical Theatre* (New York: Grossman Publishers, 1976), 238.
46. Mandelbaum, 14.
47. Chapman, review of *A Tree Grows in Brooklyn*, Alvin Theatre, *New York Daily News*, April 20, 1951.
48. Linton Martin, review of *A Tree Grows in Brooklyn*, Forrest Theatre, *Philadelphia Enquirer*, April 1, 1951.
49. Laurence Maslon, *Broadway to Main Street: How Show Tunes Enchanted America* (New York: Oxford University Press, 2018), 130.
50. Winer, 170–1.
51. Vernon Duke, *Listen Here! A Critical Essay on Music Depreciation* (New York: Ivan Obolensky, Inc., 1963), 266; Gerald Bordman, *American Operetta: From H.M.S. Pinafore to Sweeney Todd* (New York: Oxford University Press, 1981), 171; Mel Tormé, *My Singing Teachers* (New York: Oxford University Press, 1994), 124; Mordden, *Coming Up Roses: The Broadway Musical in the 1950s* (New York: Oxford University Press, 1998), 42; Martin, Atkinson, review of *A Tree Grows in Brooklyn*, *New York Times*, April 20, 1951; Herbert H. Keyser, *Geniuses of the American Musical Theatre: The Composers and Lyricists* (New York: Applause Theatre & Cinema Books, 2009), 65, 83; Otis L. Guernsey, Jr., review of *A Tree Grows in Brooklyn*, *New York Herald Tribune*, April 20, 1951; Winer, 171; Green, 194.
52. Winer, 174.

53. Max Wilk, *They're Playing Our Song* (New York: Atheneum, 1973), 45.
54. Manago, 93.
55. Financial statements of THE BROOKLYN TREE COMPANY, March 24 through May 12, 1951, ASP, Box 41 / Folder 27.
56. John Rosenfield, "Stage in Review," *Dallas Morning News*, June 24, 1952, 8.
57. Mandelbaum, 13.
58. Marjory Adams, "'Tree Grows in Brooklyn' Stars Gay Joan Blondell," *Boston Daily Globe*, October 14, 1952.
59. Manago, 99.
60. Robert Emmet Long, *Broadway, The Golden Years: Jerome Robbins and the Great Choreographers-Directors: 1940 to the Present* (New York: Continuum, 2001), 87; Amanda Vaill, *Somewhere: The Life of Jerome Robbins* (New York: Broadway Books, 2006), 181–2.
61. Mordden, *Coming Up Roses*, 46.
62. Rosenfield.
63. "The Golden Dozen," *New York Daily News*, April 29, 1951, Section Two, 3.
64. TCM.com, "Excuse My Dust (1951)," http://www.tcm.com/tcmbd/title/138/Excuse-My-Dust/article.html (accessed February 11, 2013).
65. Greenspan, 166.
66. ARTHUR SCHWARTZ: EXCUSE MY DUST song list, DFP, Box 1 / Folder 1.
67. Greenspan, 167.
68. David Jenness and Don Velsey, *Classic American Popular Song: The Second Half-Century, 1950–2000* (New York: Routledge, 2006), 85.
69. Wikipedia, s.v. "Esther Williams" (accessed April 22, 2019), 1–6; IMDb, s.v. "Ester Williams" (accessed April 22, 2019), 2–4.
70. Esther Williams and Digby Diehl, *Million Dollar Mermaid: An Autobiography* (New York: Simon & Schuster, 1999), 238.
71. William R. Weaver, "Reviews: 'Dangerous When Wet,'" *Motion Picture Daily*, May 11, 1953.
72. *Dangerous When Wet*, directed by Charles Walters, 1953, VCR (Burbank, CA: Turner Entertainment Co. and Warner Home Video, 2000).
73. Williams, 227–8.
74. Weaver.
75. Jenness, 86–7.
76. Gary Marmorstein, *Hollywood Rhapsody: Movie Music and Its Makers*

1900–1975 (New York: Schirmer Books, 1997), 260.
77. Lynn Bowers, "Novel Plot in Swim Musical," *Los Angeles Examiner*, July 2, 1953.
78. Maslon, 113.
79. Dominic McHugh, *Loverly: The Life and Times of* My Fair Lady (New York: Oxford University Press, 2012), 6–7, 13–4.
80. Lawrence Langner to Gabriel Pascal, February 15, 1952, Theatre Guild Collection, Yale University, 137; Jared Brown, *Moss Hart: A Prince of the Theatre* (New York: Back Stage Books, 2006), 334; Stephen Citron, *The Wordsmiths: Oscar Hammerstein 2nd and Alan Jay Lerner* (New York: Oxford University Press, 1995), 242.
81. Frank Rasky, "Broadway Songwriter Entertains Students," *Toronto Star*, June 22, 1976, E10.
82. Zinsser, 68–9.

Chapter 23

NB: The details of this suit and the long-term fight between ASCAP and BMI are covered in far more detail in two books, both of which are cited in these Chapter Notes: (1) *American Popular Music Business in the 20th Century*, by Russell and David Sanjek, and (2) *The B Side: The Death of Tin Pan Alley and the Rebirth of the Great American Song* by Ben Yagoda. Their books go into much more detail on all matters discussed in Chapter 23 and are recommended for interested readers. Russell Sanjek was a longtime employee of BMI but seems to have been a reliable and fair-minded historian.

1. Arthur Schwartz to Jack Cummings, October 8, 1952, ASP, Box 44 / Folder 21, 1.
2. John Schneider, "This Boycott Changed American Music," *Radio World*, May 4, 2015, https://www.radioworld.com/columns-and-views/this-boycott-changed-american-music (accessed January 24, 2019), 1.
3. *Ibid.*, 2.
4. Schwartz, 2.
5. *Schwartz v. Broadcast Music, Inc.*, 180 F. Supp. 322 (S.D.N.Y. 1959), ASP, Box 47 / Folder 7, 24–5.
6. Schwartz, 1–2.
7. Richard Rodgers and Oscar Hammerstein II, joint statement, circa November 9, 1953, ASP, Box 47 / Folder 5.
8. *Schwartz v. BMI, Inc.*, 1.
9. *Ibid.*, 24.
10. Milton Lewis, "33 Top Song Writers File $150,000,000 Trust Suit," *New York Herald Tribune*, November 10, 1953; Val Adams, "Composers Sue for $150,000,000; Allege Radio-TV-Record Monopoly," *New York Times*, November 10. 1953.
11. Adams.
12. Schwartz, 3.
13. Irving Berlin to Schwartz, December 14, 1953, ASP, Box 44 / Folder 15.
14. Schwartz to Berlin, circa December 21, 1953, ASP, Box 44 / Folder 15, 2–3.
15. Berlin to Schwartz, December 28, 1953, ASP, Box 44 / Folder 15.
16. Wilfrid Sheed, *The House That George Built: With a Little Help from Irving, Cole, and a Crew of About Fifty* (New York: Random House, 2008), 57–8.
17. *Schwartz v. BMI*, 3, 21–2.
18. Lewis.
19. *Ibid.*
20. "Don't Sing Any 'Dirty' Blues," *Variety*, November 18, 1953.
21. Schwartz to Miriam Stern, October 20 [1953], collection of the author, 1–2.
22. Ben Yagoda, *The B Side: The Death of Tin Pan Alley and the Rebirth of the Great American Song* (New York: Riverhead Books, 2015), 186.
23. Russell Sanjek and David Sanjek, *American Popular Music Business in the 20th Century* (New York: Oxford University Press, 1991), 128.
24. *Ibid.*, 158.
25. Yagoda, 188–91.
26. Bob Chandler, "Celler Winds Probe with No Major Net Monopoly Findings, but Trouble is Still Looming on D. of J. Front," *Variety*, October 3, 1956.
27. Yagoda, 192–3.
28. *Ibid.*, 193.
29. *Ibid.*, 194–5.
30. *Ibid.*, 196–7, 220.
31. Jack Lawrence, *They All Sang My Songs: The Life and Times of Jack Lawrence* (Fort Lee, NJ: Barricade Books, 2004), 205–6.

Chapter 24

1. Dan Sullivan, "Arthur Schwartz Goes His Way by Himself," *Los Angeles Times*, October 17, 1976.

2. Gerald Mast, *Can't Help Singin': The American Musical on Stage and Screen* (Woodstock, NY: The Overlook Press, 1987), 239.
3. Wilfrid Sheed, *The House That George Built: With a Little Help from Irving, Cole, and a Crew of About Fifty* (New York: Random House, 2007), 221.
4. Mast, 239.
5. Frank Miller, *TCM.com*, s.v. "The Band Wagon (1953)," http://www.tcm.com/tcmdb/title/3539/The-Band-Wagon/articles.html (accessed February 11, 2013), 3.
6. Hugh Fordin, *M-G-M's Greatest Musicals: The Arthur Freed Unit* (New York: Da Capo Press, 1996), 397.
7. "Dancing in the Dark," *Variety*, November 9, 1949.
8. David Jasen, *Tin Pan Alley: The Composers, the Songs, the Performers and Their Times* (New York: Donald I. Fine, 1988), 359.
9. Stanley Green, *Encyclopaedia of the Musical Film* (New York: Oxford University Press, 1981), 21; THE BANDWAGON [sic] SYMPOSIUM, USC Cinematic Arts Library, Arthur Freed Papers, "The Band Wagon," Box 47:12, 4.
10. Kurt Ganzl, *The Encyclopedia of the Musical Theatre*, 2nd ed., s.v. "Comden, Betty" and "Green, Adolph" (New York: Schirmer Books, 2001).
11. Vincente Minnelli, *I Remember It Well* (London: Angus & Robertson, 1974), 261.
12. Kenneth Jones, "Think Pink: Songwriter Roger Edens Heard in Return of NYC Cabaret Show," *Playbill*, October 7, 2002, http://www.playbill.com/article/think-pink-songwriter-roger-edens-heard-in-return-of-NYC-cabaret-show-oct-7-com-108749 (accessed March 15, 2019); Wikipedia, s.v. "Roger Edens" (accessed March 18, 2019); Walter Rimler, *The Man That Got Away: The Life and Songs of Harold Arlen* (Urbana, IL: University of Illinois Press, 2015), 25.
13. Interview of Betty Comden and Adolph Green, *The Band Wagon*, directed by Vincente Minnelli, DVD, two-disc set (Burbank, CA: Warner Home Video, 2005), Disc Two.
14. Irving Paul Lazar to Arthur Freed, October 6, 1952, USC Cinematic Arts Library, Arthur Freed Papers, "The Band Wagon," Box 3:14.

15. Tom Mikotowicz, *Oliver Smith: A Bio-Bibliography* (Westport, CT: Greenwood Press, 1993), 174.
16. Minnelli, 261.
17. Howard Dietz, HDATBW, 23.
18. Interview of Michael Kidd, *The Band Wagon*, DVD, Disc Two.
19. Michael Freedland, *Fred Astaire* (New York: Grosset & Dunlap, 1976), 134–5.
20. Dietz, *Dancing in the Dark: Words by Howard Dietz: An Autobiography* (New York: Quadrangle / The New York Times Book Co., 1974), 295.
21. Fordin, x.
22. Ibid., 398; Ganzl, s.v. "Kidd, Michael."
23. Gary Marmorstein, *Hollywood Rhapsody: Movie Music and Its Makers: 1900–1975* (New York: Schirmer Books, 1997), 259.
24. Green and Burt Goldblatt, *Starring Fred Astaire* (Garden City, NY: Doubleday and Company, Inc., 1977), 381; *The Band Wagon*, DVD, Disc One.
25. Metro-Goldwyn-Mayer Pictures, Picture Estimate, Production #1610, September 23, 1952, USC Cinematic Arts Library, Arthur Freed Papers, "The Band Wagon," Box 3:12, 4, 12–13.
26. Green and Goldblatt, 381; Fordin, *The World of Entertainment! Hollywood's Greatest Musicals* (Garden City, NY: Doubleday and Company Inc., 1975), 532.
27. Nick Thomas, "India Adams and Annette Warren," *Boomer*, January 29, 2019; India Adams, phone discussion with author, July 23, 2019.
28. https://search.proquest.com/afi/printviewfile?accountid=14749, 5.
29. Fordin, *The World of Entertainment!*, 532; Miller, 5.
30. USC Cinematic Arts Library, Roger Edens Collection, "The Band Wagon," Box 5:6.
31. Mast, 269.
32. Jonathan Schwartz, *All in Good Time: A Memoir* (New York: Random House, 2004), 76–7.
33. Carol J. Oja, *Bernstein Meets Broadway: Collaborative Art in a Time of War* (New York: Oxford University Press, 2014), 61–2.
34. Minnelli, 263.
35. Ronald E. Franklin, "Real Shoeshine Man Leroy Daniels Danced with Fred Astaire in 'The Band Wagon,'" https://

reelrundown.com/movies/Real-Shoemine-Man-Leroy-Daniels-Danced-with-Fred-Astaire-in-The-Band-Wagon (accessed March 16, 2019), 1–7; Mark Knowles, *The Man Who Made the Jailhouse Rock: Alex Romero, Hollywood Choreographer* (Jefferson, NC: McFarland, 2013), 82–3, 182–3.

36. Mikotowicz, 176.
37. Miller, 1.
38. Dietz, "Subj: That's Entertainment," dated August 1, 1974, in script notes for *Lyrics & Lyricists Series*, November 3, 1974, HDP, Series 1, Box 1 / Folder 19, 2–3.
39. Interview of Jonathan Schwartz, *The Band Wagon*, DVD, Disc Two.
40. Sullivan.
41. Mast, 271–2.
42. Marmorstein, 259.
43. Kathleen Riley, *The Astaires: Fred & Adele* (New York: Oxford University Press, 2012), 141.
44. Interview of Jonathan Schwartz.
45. Marmorstein, 258.
46. Mast, 274.
47. Alec Wilder, *American Popular Song: The Great Innovators, 1900–1950* (New York: Oxford University Press, 1972), 313.
48. Miller, 3.
49. Interview of Alexander Courage, *The Band Wagon*, DVD, Disc Two.
50. Miller, 3.
51. *Ibid.*, 5.
52. Sheed, 59–60.
53. Rodney Greenberg, *George Gershwin* (London: Phaidon Press Limited, 1998), 92.
54. Fordin, *M-G-M's Greatest Musicals*, 411.
55. Miller, 2, 5.
56. Fordin, *M-G-M's Greatest Musicals*, 413.
57. *Ibid.*, 407.
58. INTERVIEW WITH NANETTE FABRAY, USC Cinematic Arts Library, Arthur Freed Papers, "The Band Wagon," Box 47:12, 3, 4.
59. Fordin, *M-G-M's Greatest Musicals*, 416.
60. THE BANDWAGON [sic] SYMPOSIUM, 1.
61. Miller, 2.
62. Fred Astaire, *Steps in Time* (New York: Harper & Brothers, Publishers, 1959), 301.
63. Miller, 5.
64. Freedland, 134.
65. Astaire, 301.
66. Interview of Cyd Charisse, *The Band Wagon*, DVD, Disc Two.
67. Interview of Ava Astaire McKenzie, *The Band Wagon*, DVD, Disc Two.
68. Miller, 4; Fordin, *M-G-M's Greatest Musicals*, 409.
69. Fordin, *M-G-M's Greatest Musicals*, 402–7.
70. Freedland, 134.
71. INTERVIEW WITH NANETTE FABRAY, 1.
72. Astaire, 302–3.
73. Lazar to Floyd Hendrickson, M-G-M, December 3, 1952, USC Cinematic Arts Library, Arthur Freed Papers, "The Band Wagon," Box 3:14.
74. Dietz to Schwartz, January 17, 1953, USC Cinematic Arts Library, Arthur Freed Papers, "The Band Wagon," Box 3:14.
75. "Miss Carrington of Stage, 43, Dies," obituary, *New York Times*, May 3, 1953.
76. Jonathan Schwartz, *All in Good Time*, 58–9, 50.
77. Marmorstein, 260.
78. Marjory Adams, "Dietz-Schwartz Week in Boston Brings Couplet for Mayor Hynes," *The Boston Daily Globe*, July 14, 1953.
79. Dietz, "Music Makers Beat 'The Band Wagon's' Drum," unidentified newspaper, Cleveland, Ohio, circa August 1953, ASP.
80. Minnelli, 272.
81. Fordin, *M-G-M's Greatest Musicals*, 403.
82. Interview of Jonathan Schwartz.
83. Gail Kinn and Jim Piazza, *The Academy Awards: The Complete Unofficial History* (New York: Black Dog & Leventhal Publishers, 2014), 113.
84. Don Tyler, *The Great Movie Musicals: A Viewer's Guide to 168 Films That Really Sing* (Jefferson, NC: McFarland, 2010), 21.
85. Max Gordon to Fred Astaire, August 6, 1953, Max Gordon Papers, TC024, Manuscripts Division, Department of Special Collections, Princeton University Library.

Chapter 25

1. Brooks Atkinson, "The Theatre: 'By the Beautiful Sea,'" *New York Times*, April 9, 1954.

2. *The Complete Lyrics of Alan Jay Lerner*, Dominic McHugh and Amy Asch, eds. (Oxford: Oxford University Press, 2018), xix, 203; Ethan Mordden, *Love Song: The Lives of Kurt Weill and Lotte Lenya* (New York: St. Martin's Press, 2012), 252.

3. Thomas M. Pryor, "Cinerama Slates Full-Length Film: *Paint Your Wagon*, with New Music and Lyrics, on Tap as First Feature in Process," *New York Times*, February 11, 1953, 35; Edwin Schallert, "Cinerama Start Looms," *Los Angeles Times*, February 11, 1953, B9.

4. McHugh, *Loverly: The Life and Times of* My Fair Lady (New York: Oxford University Press, 2012), 18.

5. Stephen Citron, *The Wordsmiths: Oscar Hammerstein 2nd and Alan Jay Lerner* (New York: Oxford University Press, 1995), 243.

6. Edward Jablonski, *Alan Jay Lerner: A Biography* (New York: Harry Holt and Company, 1996), 85–6.

7. Gene Lees, *Inventing Champagne: The Worlds of Lerner and Loewe* (New York: St. Martin's Press, 1990), 252.

8. Louis Calta, "*Li'l Abner* Bagged by Two Showmen," *New York Times*, March 17, 1953, 26, in *Alan Jay Lerner: A Lyricist's Letters*, McHugh, ed. (Oxford: Oxford University Press, 2014), 32.

9. Alan Jay Lerner telegram to Arthur Schwartz, July 21, 1953, ASP.

10. Doris Shapiro, *We Danced All Night: My Life Behind the Scenes with Alan Jay Lerner* (New York: William Morrow and Company, Inc., 1990), 16.

11. *Alan Jay Lerner: A Lyricist's Letters*, 36–7.

12. "Ina Claire to Star in 'Clerk'; Schwartz to Write 'Sea' Score," *New York Daily News*, November 12, 1953.

13. Jonathan Schwartz, *All in Good Time: A Memoir* (New York: Random House, 2004), 91.

14. *The Complete Lyrics of Alan Jay Lerner*, xx.

15. John Stewart, *Broadway Musicals, 1943–2004* (Jefferson, NC: McFarland, 2006), 338.

16. Ibid., 85.

17. William Hawkins, review of *By the Beautiful Sea*, Majestic Theatre, *New York World-Telegram and Sun*, April 9, 1954.

18. *By the Beautiful Sea*, originally released in 1954 as Capitol Records S 531, CD (New York: DRG Records, Incorporated, 2003).

19. David Jenness and Don Velsey, *Classic American Popular Song: The Second Half-Century, 1950–2000* (New York: Routledge, 2006), 86.

20. Cyrus Durgin, "The Stage," *Boston Daily Globe*, February 24, 1954.

21. Alta Maloney, "'By the Beautiful Sea,' Shirley Booth, Shubert," *Boston Traveler*, February 24, 1954.

22. Stephen Holden, "Mae Barnes, 89, Jazz Singer Famous for Charleston," *New York Times*, January 18, 1997.

23. Souvenir program for *By the Beautiful Sea*, ASP, 12.

24. Durgin.

25. Atkinson, "Magnetic Lady," *New York Times*, circa April 15, 1954, ASP.

26. Durgin.

27. Jim Manago, *Love Is the Reason for It All: The Shirley Booth Story* (Albany, GA: BearManor Media, 2008), 130–1.

28. David C. Tucker, *Shirley Booth: A Biography and Career Record* (Jefferson, NC: McFarland, 2008), 86.

29. Gregory Katz, "Lunch with the FT: Theatre of Dreams," *Financial Times*, October 28, 2005, in Tucker, 86.

30. Stewart, 85.

31. Mordden, *Coming Up Roses: The Broadway Musical in the 1950s* (New York: Oxford University Press, 1998), 123.

32. Suskin, *The Sound of Broadway Music: A Book of Orchestrators and Orchestrations* (Oxford: Oxford University Press, 2007), 154.

33. Ibid., 194–5.

34. Lee Moselle to Arnold Weissberger, September 24, 1954, ASP.

35. Weissberger to Moselle, October 19, 1954, ASP, 1.

36. Schwartz to The Hon. Hugh M. Burns, Chairman, California Legislative Committee on Un-American Activities, January 28, 1954, ASP, Box 44 / Folder 16, 1–2.

37. Durgin; Deborah Grace Winer, *On the Sunny Side of the Street: The Life and Lyrics of Dorothy Fields* (New York: Schirmer Books, 1997), 187; Atkinson, "The Theatre: 'By the Beautiful Sea.'"

38. Atkinson, "The Theatre: 'By the Beautiful Sea.'"

39. Charlotte Greenspan, *Pick Yourself Up: Dorothy Fields and the American*

Musical (New York: Oxford University Press, 2010), 188.
40. Atkinson, "Magnetic Lady."
41. Maloney.
42. Mordden, *Coming Up Roses*, 123.
43. Manago, 134.
44. Durgin.
45. Atkinson, "Magnetic Lady."
46. Greenspan, 189–90.
47. Mordden, 120.
48. Lawrence Perry, "Footlights of Broadway—Composer Talks of Books," *Springfield* (MA) *Republican*, May 2, 1954.
49. *Ibid*.
50. *Ibid*.
51. Martin Denton, "By the Beautiful Sea," *NYTheatre.com*, June 16, 1999.
52. BIO. ON MARY," unpublished, ASP, Box 51 / Folder 5.
53. Jonathan Schwartz, 87–8, 93.
54. Mary Grey to Schwartz, letters dated November 25, 1952 and February 3 and 8, 1953, ASP.
55. Ben Yagoda, *The B Side: The Death of Tin Pan Alley and the Rebirth of the Great American Song* (New York: Riverhead Books, 2015), 26–7.
56. *Ibid.*, 28.
57. *Ibid.*, 16–7.

Chapter 26

1. Howard Dietz to Paul Gallico, October 16, 1959, ASP, Box 38 / Folder 3, 10.
2. Jerome Weidman to Arthur Schwartz, July 25, 1954, ASP.
3. Weidman to Schwartz, August 10, 1954, ASP, 1–3.
4. Tighe E. Zimmers, *Lyrical Satirical Harold Rome: A Biography of the Broadway Composer-Lyricist* (Jefferson, NC: McFarland, 2014), 127–41.
5. Roy Fjastad, York Pictures, to Sidney Justin, et al., June 24 and August 31, 1954, Margaret Herrick Library, Academy of Motion Picture Arts and Sciences, Paramount Pictures Contract Summaries, Folder 1450 / Schwartz, Arthur (composer).
6. Jonathan Schwartz, *All in Good Time: A Memoir* (New York: Random House, 2004), 85.
7. Stephen Holden, "Sammy Cahn, Word Weaver of Tin Pan Alley, Dies at 79," *New York Times*, January 16, 1993.
8. *IMDb*, s.v. "You're Never Too Young (1955)," "Soundtracks" (accessed September 22, 2019).
9. *You're Never Too Young*, directed by Norman Taurog, DVD (Hollywood, CA: Paramount Pictures, 1955).
10. "Picture: You're Never Too Young," *Variety*, June 15, 1955.
11. Sheet music for "Relax-Ay-Voo," Schwartz and Sammy Cahn (London: Pickwick Music, Ltd., 1955).
12. *Getty Images*, s.v. "Orson Welles," https://www.gettyimages.com/detail/news-photo/from-left-american-actor-orson-welles-american-director-news-photo/83077693 (accessed June 29, 2019); *Wikipedia*, s.v. "Ford Star Jubilee" (accessed March 26, 2013).
13. Robert Windeler, *Julie Andrews: A Life on Stage and Screen* (New York: Birch Lane Press, 1997), 42.
14. *Ibid.*, 41; Oscar Godbout, "Historic Peak," *New York Times*, November 27, 1955, X9.
15. Julie Andrews, *Home: A Memoir of My Early Years* (New York: Hyperion, 2008), 185.
16. High Tor, CD Stage 2420, Ford Star Jubilee / CBS Television Production, March 10, 1956 (London: Stage Door Records, 2017).
17. *Ibid*.
18. *Ibid*.
19. Andrews, 186.
20. Alan Jay Lerner to Andrews, December 5, 1955 in Dominic McHugh, ed., *Alan Jay Lerner: A Lyricist's Letters* (Oxford: Oxford University Press, 2014), 62.
21. Windeler, 42.
22. Niles Marsh, album notes for *Four Television Musicals (Original Cast)*, LP album, BP 1019 (Longwood, FL: Blue Pear Records, n.d.).
23. Mary Cremmen, "TV Notebook," *Boston Evening Globe*, June 4, 1956.
24. Marsh; Ethan Mordden, *Coming Up Roses: The Broadway Musical in the 1950S* (New York: Oxford University Press, 1998), 204–5; David A. Jasen, *Tin Pan Alley: An Encyclopedia of the Golden Age of American Song* (New York: Routledge, 2003), 388.
25. Marsh.
26. Bob Williams, "Around the Dials," *Philadelphia Bulletin*, June 4, 1956.
27. Cremmen.
28. John Crosby, "Television and Radio:

Bell with Music," *New York Herald Tribune*, June 6, 1956.
  29. Carla Reynolds, "Clearing the Air," *Moline Dispatch*, June 2, 1956.
  30. Ben Gross, "What's On?," *New York Daily News*, June 2, 1956.
  31. *A Bell for Adano*, songs by Arthur Schwartz and Howard Dietz, part of *Four Television Musicals (Original Cast)*.
  32. IMDb, s.v. "Anna Maria Alberghetti," https://www.imdb.com/name/nm0016402/bio (accessed August 16, 2019).
  33. Jack Gould, "TV: 'A Bell for Adano,'" *New York Times*, June 4, 1956; Gross, "What's On?: 'A Bell for Adano' Rings Again—This Time in Color," *New York Daily News*, June 4, 1956.
  34. "First Night Ball Chairman Named by Theater Wing," *New York Herald Tribune*, November 13, 1956.
  35. Tom Donnelly, "Menu Will Run from Cal to Roz," *New York World-Telegram & Sun*, January 7, 1957.
  36. "American Theatre Wing Command Performance," notes on proposed talent and production ideas, December 7, 1956, ASP, Box 41 / Folder 6, 1–2.
  37. Burt Boyar, "Beau Broadway," *New York Morning Telegraph*, January 29, 1957.
  38. Bill Smith, "News and Views," *Show Business*, February 4, 1957.
  39. "The Theatre: For (Not By) Brooks Atkinson," *New York Times*, March 3, 1958.
  40. "Blowout for Brooks," *Time*, March 17, 1958, 55.
  41. Dietz, *Dancing in the Dark: Words by Howard Dietz: An Autobiography* (New York: Quadrangle / New York Times Book Co., Inc., 1974), 333–4.
  42. "The Theatre: For (Not By) Brooks Atkinson."
  43. Dietz, 330–1.
  44. Kitty Carlisle Hart, *Kitty: An Autobiography* (New York: Doubleday, 1988), 193.
  45. Jo Mielziner to Schwartz and Dietz, April 9, 1958, ASP, Box 38 / Folder 3.
  46. Martin Benson, "Paul Gallico – A Biography," http://www.paulgallico.info/lit_gallicobiog.html (accessed March 21, 2019); Wikipedia, s.v. "Paul Gallico," http://en.wikipedia.org/wiki/Paul_Gallico (accessed March 21, 2019).
  47. Saint Subber to Kay Brown, March 23, 1959, ASP, Box 38 / Folder 3.
  48. Minimum Basic Production Contract between World Enterprises, Inc. and Schwartz, Dietz, and Howard Teichmann, April 21, 1959, collection of the author.
  49. *Notable Names in the American Theatre*, s.v. "Teichmann, Howard" (Clifton, NJ: James T. White & Company, 1976).
  50. Minimum Basic Production Contract.
  51. Dietz to Gallico, June 30, 1959, ASP, Box 38 / Folder 3, 1.
  52. Gallico to Dietz and Schwartz, July 12, 1959, ASP, Box 38 / Folder 3, 1–2.
  53. Dietz and Schwartz to World Enterprises, c/o Ray Stark, August 6, 1959, ASP, Box 38 / Folder 3.
  54. Gallico to Katharine Brown, August 29, 1959, ASP, Box 44 / Folder 39, 1.
  55. Helen Hayes to Dietz, September 30, 1959, and Dietz to Hayes, October 1, 1959, ASP, Box 38 / Folder 3.
  56. Gallico to Brown, 3–8.
  57. Dietz to Hayes.
  58. Dietz to Gallico, October 16, 1959, ASP, Box 38 / Folder 3, 1–2, 6.
  59. *Ibid.*, 7–10.
  60. IMDb, s.v. "Mrs. 'Arris Goes to Paris," https://www.imdb.com/title/tt0104930/?ref=fn_al_tt_1 (accessed February 26, 2019).

Chapter 27

  1. Arthur Schwartz to Henry Kaufman and Eugene Lerner, January 4, 1962, ASP, 2.
  2. Johnny Loeb telegram to Schwartz, November 17, 1961, ASP. NB: There were several typos or misspellings in the original telegram. Rather than put several [sic] designations into the text, the errors were corrected.
  3. Program for *The Gay Life*, directed by Gerald Freedman, Sam. S. Shubert Theatre, New York, premier performance, November 18, 1961.
  4. Jonathan Schwartz, *All in Good Time: A Memoir* (New York: Random House, 2004), 143.
  5. Lerner to Kermit Bloomgarden, October 3, 1961, ASP, 2.
  6. Ethan Mordden, *Open a New Window: The Broadway Musical in the 1960s* (New York: Palgrave, 2001), 60.
  7. Lerner.
  8. Jonathan Schwartz, 143.
  9. Mordden, 60.
  10. Dennis McGovern and Deborah

Grace Winer, *Sing Out, Louise!* (New York: Schirmer Books, 1993), 70.

11. Schwartz to Kaufman and Lerner, 2.

12. Josef Mossman, "Gorgeous 'Gay Life' Becomes Even Better," *Detroit News*, October 19, 1961.

13. McGovern, 70.

14. Alec Wilder, *American Popular Song: The Great Innovators, 1900–1950* (New York: Oxford University Press, 1972), 328.

15. *The Gay Life*, Howard Dietz and Arthur Schwartz, original-cast recording, Capitol SWAO 1560 / WAO 1509 (Los Angeles: Capitol Records, 1962).

16. Mordden, *Broadway Babies: The People Who Made the American Musical* (New York: Oxford University Press, 1983), 160.

17. "The Theater: Amorous Buffoon," review of *The Gay Life*, *Wall Street Journal*, November 20, 1961.

18. Schwartz to Dorothy Morrison, *The New Yorker*, December 26, 1961, ASP.

19. Norman Nadel, "Theater: 'The Gay Life' Invades Stage at Shubert Theater," review of *The Gay Life*, *New York World Telegram*, November 20, 1961.

20. Steven Suskin, *The Sound of Broadway Music: A Book of Orchestrators and Orchestrations* (New York: Oxford University Press, 2007), 109.

21. John Chapman, "Show Business," review of *The Gay Life*, *New York Daily News*, November 20, 1961.

22. Richard Watts, Jr., "Two on the Aisle: The Amorous Life in Old Vienna," review of *The Gay Life*, *New York Post*, November 20, 1961.

23. Gerald Bordman, *American Musical Theatre: A Chronicle* (New York: Oxford University Press, 2001), 680.

24. Stanley Green, "On the Town in Old Vienna," *HIFI / STEREO*, April / 1962, 61.

25. Vernon Duke, *Listen Here! A Critical Essay on Music Depreciation* (New York: Ivan Obolensky, 1963), 278.

26. John McClain, "Colorful and Melodic Evening of Good Fun," review of *The Gay Life*, *New York Journal*, November 20, 1961.

27. Chapman.

28. Nadel.

29. Louis Cook, "'The Gay Life' CAN Be a Great One," review of *The Gay Life*, *Detroit Free Press*, October 4, 1961, 12.

30. Thomas R. Dash, "'Gay Life,' Wiener Schnitzel: Savory, Succulent, Spicy," review of *The Gay Life*, *Women's Wear Daily*, November 20, 1961.

31. Wilder, 329.

32. Ibid., 327.

33. Schwartz to Max Gordon, December 11, 1961, Max Gordon Papers, TC024, Manuscripts Division, Department of Special Collections, Princeton University Library.

34. Schwartz to Kaufman and Lerner, 1.

35. "Glad Rags for a Gay Life," *Life*, January 19, 1962, 49–51.

36. Schwartz to Kaufman and Lerner, 2.

37. Lerner to Schwartz, February 8, 1962, ASP, Box 33 / Folder 4.

38. Dietz, *Dancing in the Dark: Words by Howard Dietz: An Autobiography* (New York: Quadrangle / The New York Times Book Co., 1974), 335.

39. Suskin, *Show Tunes: The Songs, Shows, and Careers of Broadway's Major Composers*, 4th ed. (New York: Oxford University Press, 2010).

40. Wilder, 326–7, 330.

41. Dietz, 329.

42. Joan Taylor interview with Dietz, April 27, 1971, HDP, Box 2 / Folder 4, 31.

43. Wilfrid Sheed, *The House That George Built: With a Little Help from Irving, Cole, and a Crew of About Fifty* (New York: Random House, 2008), 288.

44. Jonathan Schwartz, 144.

Chapter 28

1. Howard Dietz and Arthur Schwartz to Cheryl Crawford and Richard Halliday, August 9, 1963, ASP, Box 33 / Folder 3, 2.

2. Jonathan Schwartz, *All in Good Time: A Memoir* (New York: Random House, 2004), 166.

3. Schwartz to Albert I. DaSilva of Reinheimer & Cohen, two memos, both dated February 13, 1963, collection of the author.

4. Stuart W. Little, "Theater News: Mary Martin Picks Laurette Play," *New York Herald Tribune*, September 24, 1962.

5. Josef Mossman, "Melody Lingers on for *The Gay Life*," *Detroit News*, January 21, 1962.

6. Dietz, "AUTOB 'Jennie,'" notes regarding *Jennie*, ASP, 3.

7. Ibid.

8. Ronald L. Davis, *Mary Martin, Broadway Legend* (Norman, OK: University of Oklahoma Press, 2008), 226.
9. Bill Rosenfield, liner notes for *Jennie*, CD 09026-06189-2 (New York: RCA Victor / BMG Classics, 1993), 7,10; Ken Mandelbaum, *Not Since Carrie: Forty Years of Broadway Musical Flops* (New York: St. Martin's Press, 1991), 53.
10. Max Shulman to Schwartz and Dietz, February 5, 1962, ASP, Box 33 / Folder 4; confirmed by Richard Halliday to Schwartz, February 5, 1962, ASP, Box 33 / Folder 4.
11. Publicity program for *Jennie*, 1962, ASP, Box 33 / Folder 8, 8.
12. Davis, 227.
13. Yvonne Petrie, "Home on the Road: Wives Follow 'Jennie,'" *Detroit News*, September 27, 1963.
14. Halliday, in Brazil, to Dietz, February 5, 1963, Vincent J. Donehue Papers, Series I: General Correspondence, 1946–1966, New York Public Library for the Performing Arts, Billy Rose Theatre Collection, Dorothy and Lewis B. Cullman Center, Box 1 / Folder 15, 1–2.
15. Program notes for *Lyrics & Lyricists* series, HDP, Box 1 / Folder 19, 1–3.
16. John Stewart, *Broadway Musicals, 1943–2004* (Jefferson, NC: McFarland, 2006), 303–4; Mandelbaum, 53.
17. Dietz, *Dancing in the Dark: Words by Howard Dietz: An Autobiography* (New York: Quadrangle / New York Times Book Co., Inc., 1974), 274.
18. Dietz to Howard E. Reinheimer, attorney, October 10, 1963, collection of the author.
19. Cheryl Crawford, *One Naked Individual: My Fifty Years in the Theatre* (Indianapolis, IN: The Bobbs-Merrill Company, 1977), 181–2.
20. Ethan Mordden, *Make Believe: The Broadway Musical in the 1920s* (New York: Oxford University Press, 1997), 135.
21. Earl Wilson, "Mary Martin To Prove What Everybody Knows," *Boston Traveler*, July 24, 1963, 40.
22. Davis, 227.
23. Dietz and Schwartz to Crawford and Halliday, 1–2.
24. Davis, 226.
25. Dietz and Schwartz to Crawford and Halliday, 2.
26. Kevin Kelly, "'Jennie' Is Ponderous, Very Nearly Witless," *Boston Globe*, July 30, 1963.
27. Mandelbaum, 53.
28. "Song Writer Suing Boston Stage Critic," *New York Times*, August 14, 1963, 29.
29. Herman Kogan, "The Cry Is Heard: 'Critic, Keep Away!,'" *Chicago Daily News*, September 7, 1963.
30. Rosenfield, 11.
31. Elinor Hughes, "The Theaters: Second Trip Shows Changes in 'Jennie,'" *Boston Herald*, August 31, 1963, 20.
32. Dietz and Schwartz to [Crawford and Halliday], September 7, 1963, ASP, Box 33 / Folder 3, 2.
33. Dietz and Schwartz to Halliday, Crawford, Vincent Donehue, and Carol Haney, September 8, 1963, ASP, Box 33 / Folder 3, 1–2.
34. Halliday to Arnold Schulman, Dietz, and Schwartz, submitted by Herman Bernstein in the presence of Cheryl Crawford, September 10, 1963 at 5:15 P.M., ASP, Box 33 / Folder 3.
35. Mandelbaum, 53; Davis, 229; "'Jennie' Closing after 82 Shows," *New York Times*, December 20, 1963; Mary Martin, *My Heart Belongs* (New York: William Morrow and Company, 1976), 196.
36. Schulman, Dietz, and Schwartz, legal document directed to Crawford, Halliday and The Jennie Company, September 11, 1963, ASP, Box 33 / Folder 3, 1–2.
37. Schulman, Dietz, and Schwartz to Crawford, September 13, 1963, Box 33 / Folder 3, 1–2.
38. Jonathan Schwartz, 166.
39. Schwartz to Crawford, September 26, 1963, ASP, Box 33 / Folder 4.
40. Crawford, 181.
41. Mordden, *Open a New Window: The Broadway Musical in the 1960s* (New York: Palgrave, 2001), 81.
42. Mandelbaum, 55.
43. Ken Bloom, *American Song: The Complete Musical Theatre Companion*, 2nd ed., 1877–1995, Vol. 1: A–S (New York: Schirmer Books, 1996), 559; program for *Jennie*, the Fisher Theatre, Detroit, week of September 29, 1963; liner notes for *Jennie*, CD 09026-06189-2 (New York: RCA Victor / BMG Classics, 1993), 3.
44. Harold Rogers, "Mary Martin Arrives in 'Jennie,'" *Christian Science Monitor*, July 30, 1963.

45. Louis Cook, "'Jennie' a Ponderous Melodrama," *Detroit Free Press*, September 10, 1963, 8-C.
46. Milton Esterow, "The Ambulatory Arthur Schwartz: He Composes While Walking," *Musical America*, Vol 83 / #10, October / 1963, 16.
47. Martin, 193.
48. Alec Wilder, *American Popular Song: The Great Innovators, 1900–1950* (New York: Oxford University Press, 1972), 329.
49. Esterow, 17.
50. *Jennie*, CD 09026-06189-2 (New York: RCA Victor / BMG Classics, 1993).
51. Mandelbaum, 55; Stewart 304; "Statement of Cash Receipts and Disbursements and Summary of Cash Position as at December 31, 1963," Jennie Company, Exhibit 'A', ASP, Box 33.
52. Dietz, *Dancing in the Dark*, 337.
53. Davis, 228.
54. David Kaufman, *Some Enchanted Evenings: The Glittering Life and Times of Mary Martin* (New York: St. Martin's Press, 2016), 223–4.
55. *Ibid.*, 219.
56. Jonathan Schwartz, 167.
57. Crawford, 181–2.

Chapter 29

1. Jonathan Schwartz, album notes, *Alone Together: Jonathan Schwartz Sings Arthur Schwartz*, LP (New York: Muse Records, 1977). This album was re-released by Muse Records in 1995 as a CD.
2. Frances C. Breeding to Hugh Downs, March 24, 1963, ASP, Box 44 / Folder 31.
3. Unidentified writer to Downs, March 22, 1963, ASP, Box 44 / Folder 31.
4. Sam Zolotow, "'Casablanca' to Begin New Life As a Broadway Musical in Fall," *New York Times*, February 21, 1967; "Musical Stage for 'Casablanca,'" *New York Daily News*, February 21, 1967.
5. Arthur Schwartz, London, to Julie [Epstein], August 19 and September 29, 1967, ASP.
6. Schwartz, Saint-Jean-Cap-Ferrat, France to Mr. [Hugh] Beaumont, July 17, 1970, ASP, Box 44 / Folder 13.
7. Lyric sheets for *Casablanca* songs, ASP, Box 4 / Folder 6.
8. John S. Wilson, "'Night and the Music' and Arthur Schwartz at 'Y,'" *New York Times*, March 17, 1978.
9. Jonathan Schwartz, *All in Good Time: A Memoir* (New York: Random House, 2004), 23.
10. Wilson.
11. "Show Tune Composer on Board," *QE2 Express*, May 16, 1979 and shipboard brochure, "A Festival of Life on QE2," May 14, 1979, both in ASP, Box 50 / Folder 5; T.J. Conroy, Executive Cruise Director to Schwartz, March 14, 1978, ASP, Box 44 / Folder 17.
12. Arthur Schwartz to Ken McCormick, September 22, 1971, ASP, 1–2.
13. Benny Green, *Let's Face the Music: The Golden Age of Popular Song* (London: Pavillion Books Limited, 1989), 110.
14. Schwartz to Ned Sherrin, November 28, 1971, ASP, Box 38 / Folder 12. NB: All correspondence regarding a musical stage version of *Nicholas Nickleby* in which Schwartz was involved is in ASP, Box 38 / Folder 12
15. "Nickleby—Stigwood's New Super Star?," *Evening News* (London), October 3, 1972, 12.
16. Schwartz to Caryl Brahms, July 29, 1973.
17. Brahms and Sherrin to Schwartz, November 6, 1973.
18. Schwartz to Brahms and Sherrin, November 18, 1973.
19. Hobe Morrison, "Schwartz Writes Dickens Musical Lyrics," *Herald-News* (North Jersey), July 10, 1975.
20. Harold Fielding to Schwartz, December 9, 1976 and January 13, 1977.
21. Jonathan Schwartz, *All in Good Time*, 168.
22. Dick Kleiner, "Melody Man Lured to Lyrics," *News-Herald* (Panama City, FL), December 3, 1976.
23. Peter Hepple, "From the Pen of Arthur Schwartz," *The Stage*, March 25, 1976.
24. Martin Bookspan, "Americana," *Consumers' Union*, March / 1977, 173.
25. *from the pen of...Arthur Schwartz*, RCA LPL15121 (New York: RCA Limited, Records Division, 1976).
26. Schwartz, album notes, *from the pen of...Arthur Schwartz*.
27. Howard Dietz to Schwartz, June 22, 1976, ASP, Box 44 / Folder 25.
28. Schwartz to Dietz, July 1, 1976, ASP, Box 44 / Folder 25, 1–3.

29. Dietz to Schwartz, July 19, 1976, ASP, Box 44 / Folder 25.

30. Dietz to Schwartz, October 12, 1976, ASP, Box 44 / Folder 25.

31. *That's Entertainment: The Great Songs of Dietz & Schwartz* (Secaucus, NJ: Warner Bros. Publications, 1990).

32. Dan Sullivan, "Arthur Schwartz Goes His Way by Himself," *Los Angeles Times*, October 17, 1976, 46.

33. Jonathan Schwartz, album notes.

34. Album notes for *Frank Sinatra Sings for Only the Lonely*, CD (Hollywood, CA: Capitol Records, Inc., 1998).

35. Sammy Cahn Papers, Margaret Herrick Library (MHL), Academy of Motion Picture Arts and Sciences (AMPAS), Folder 1095 / Schwartz, Arthur, 1-2.

36. Wilson.

37. Cahn to Schwartz, December 17, 1977, ASP, Box 41 / Folder 3, 1.

38. Canadian Broadcasting Company interview with Yip Harburg, November 26, 1979, typed manuscript, 7, in Harriet Hyman Alonso, *Yip Harburg: Legendary Lyricist and Human Rights Activist* (Middleton, CT: Wesleyan University Press, 2012), 105.

39. Schwartz to Cahn, September 27, 1977, Sammy Cahn Papers, Folder 1095 / Schwartz, Arthur, 1-2.

40. Schwartz to Cahn, January 2, 1978, Sammy Cahn Papers, Folder 1095 / Schwartz, Arthur.

41. Schwartz to Cahn, September 28 and October 6, 1977, and January 2 and 23, 1978; Ann Beckham to Cahn, Schwartz, et al., MEMORANDUM regarding *The Adventures of Don Quixote and Sancho Panza*, May 26, 1977. All of these are in Sammy Cahn Papers, Folder 1095 / Schwartz, Arthur.

42. Schwartz to Cahn, September 28, 1977.

43. Program for *The Lyrics & Lyricists Series: An Evening with Arthur Schwartz*, 92nd Street YM-YWHA, March 19-20, 1978.

44. Wilson.

45. *Current Biography*, s.v. "Schwartz, Arthur," November / 1979, Vol 40 / #11, H.W. Wilson Company.

46. Jonathan Schwartz, *All in Good Time*, 247.

47. Allen Hughes, "Turning a Career Into a Revue," *New York Times*, January 5, 1979, C3.

48. Program for *Dancing in the Dark*, January 3–February 3, 1979, Manhattan Theatre Club, ASP.

49. Hughes.

50. "ALL ABOUT LOVE", promotional piece, unpublished, ASP, Box 24 / Folder 2.

51. Schwartz to Mr. [Norman] Lear, June 19, 1982 and Mrs. [Leona] Helmsley, July 14, 1982. Both in ASP, Box 24 / Folder 2.

52. Green, 104, 111.

53. Jonathan Schwartz, 259-62.

54. *Ibid.*, 280-1.

Bibliography

Adler, Larry. *It Ain't Necessarily So: An Autobiography*. New York: Grove Press, 1984.

Alonso, Harriet Hyman. *Yip Harburg: Legendary Lyricist and Human Rights Activist*. Middleton, CT: Wesleyan University Press, 2012.

Anderson, John Murray. *Out Without My Rubbers: The Memoirs of John Murray Anderson*. New York: Library Publishers, 1954.

Andrews, Julie. *Home: A Memoir of My Early Years*. New York: Hyperion, 2008.

Astaire, Fred. *Steps in Time*. New York: Harper and Brothers, 1959.

Baral, Robert. *Revue: A Nostalgic Reprise of the Great Broadway Period*. New York: Fleet Publishing Corporation, 1962.

Bennett, Robert Russell. *The Broadway Sound: The Autobiography and Selected Essays of Robert Russell Bennett*. Rochester, NY: University of Rochester Press, 1999.

Bloom, Ken. *American Song: The Complete Musical Theatre Companion*, 2nd ed., 1877–1995. New York: Schirmer Books, 1996.

_____. *The American Songbook: The Singers, the Songwriters, and the Songs*. New York: Black Dog & Leventhal Publishers, 2005.

Bogle, Donald. *Heat Wave: The Life and Career of Ethel Waters*. New York: Harper, 2011.

Bordman, Gerald. *American Musical Revue: From the Passing Show to Sugar Babies*. New York: Oxford University Press, 1985.

_____. *American Musical Theatre: A Chronicle*. New York: Oxford University Press, 1978.

_____. *American Operetta: From H.M.S. Pinafore to Sweeney Todd*. New York: Oxford University Press, 1981.

_____. *Jerome Kern: His Life and Music*. New York: Oxford University Press, 1980.

Botto, Louis. *At This Theatre: 100 Years of Broadway Shows, Stories and Stars*. New York: Applause Theatre and Cinema Books, 2002.

Bowers, Dwight Blocker, James R. Morris, and J.R. Taylor. *American Popular Song: Six Decades of Songwriters and Singers*. Washington, D.C.: Smithsonian Institution Press, 1984.

_____. *Smithsonian Collection of Recordings: American Songbook Series: Arthur Schwartz*. Washington, D.C.: Smithsonian Institution, 1995.

Bradshaw, Jon. *Dreams That Money Can Buy: The Tragic Life of Libby Holman*. New York: William Morrow and Company, Inc., 1985.

Brahms, Caryl, and Ned Sherrin. *Song by Song: The Lives and Work of 14 Great Lyric Writers*. Bolton, Great Britain: Ross Anderson Publications, 1984.

Burton, Jack. *The Blue Book of Tin Pan Alley: A Human Interest Anthology of American Popular Music*. Watkins Glen, NY: Century House, 1950.

Chaplin, Saul. *The Golden Age of Movie Musicals and Me*. Norman, OK: University of Oklahoma Press, 1994.

Citron, Stephen. *The Wordsmiths: Oscar Hammerstein 2nd and Alan Jay Lerner*. New York: Oxford University Press, 2012.

Cochran, Charles B. *I Had Almost Forgotten...*. London: Hutchinson & Co., Inc., 1932.

_____, ed. *Review of Revues*. London: Jonathan Cape, 1930.

_____. *Showman Looks On.* London: J.M. Dent & Sons, Ltd., 1945.
Coppula, Christopher A. *Jimmy Van Heusen: Swinging on a Star.* Nashville, TN: Twin Creek Books, 2014.
Crawford, Cheryl. *One Naked Individual: My Fifty Years in the Theatre.* Indianapolis, IN: The Bobbs-Merrill Company, Inc., 1977.
Cross, William. *Tilley Losch: 'Schlagobers': Sweet Fragments from Her Life.* Newport, Gwent, UK: Book Midden Publishing, 2015.
Crowley, Alice Lewisohn. *The Neighborhood Playhouse: Leaves from a Theatre Scrapbook.* New York: Theatre Arts Books, 1959.
Current Biography. November 1979. New York: The H.W. Wilson Company, 1979.
Davis, Lee. *Scandals and Follies: The Rise and Fall of the Great Broadway Revue.* New York: Limelight Editions, 2000.
Davis, Ronald L. *Mary Martin, Broadway Legend.* Norman, OK: University of Oklahoma Press, 2008.
de Mille, Agnes. *Speak to Me, Dance with Me.* Boston: Little, Brown and Company, 1973.
Dickstein, Morris. *Dancing in the Dark: A Cultural History of the Great Depression.* New York: W.W. Norton & Company, 2009.
Dietz, Dan. *Off Broadway Musicals, 1910–2007: Casts, Credits, Songs, Critical Reception and Performance Data of More than 1,800 Shows.* Jefferson, NC: McFarland, 2010.
Dietz, Howard. "Aboard the Band Wagon: A Few Verbal Snapshots from an Album of Long Association with a Popular Composer," unpublished notes, Box 51 / Folder 9. Arthur Schwartz Papers, ML31.S38, Musical Division, Library of Congress.
_____. *Dancing in the Dark: Words by Howard Dietz: An Autobiography.* New York: Quadrangle / The New York Times Book Co., 1974.
Duke, Vernon. *Listen Here! A Critical Essay on Music Depreciation.* New York: Ivan Obolensky, Inc., 1963.
_____. *Passport to Paris: An Autobiography of Vernon Duke.* Boston: Little, Brown and Company, 1955.
Dunning, John. *On the Air: The Encyclopedia of Old-Time Radio.* New York: Oxford University Press, 1998.

Easton, Carol. *No Intermissions: The Life of Agnes de Mille.* Boston: Little, Brown and Company, 1996.
Eells, George. *The Life That Late He Led: A Biography of Cole Porter.* New York: G.P. Putnam's Sons, 1967.
Eliscu, Edward. *With or Without a Song: A Memoir.* Lanham, MD: The Scarecrow Press, Inc., 2001.
Elrod, Bruce C., ed. *Your Hit Parade and American Top 10 Hits,* 4th ed. Ann Arbor, MI: Popular Culture Ink, 1994.
Ewen, David. *All the Years of American Popular Song.* Englewood Cliffs, NJ: Prentice-Hall, Inc., 1977.
_____. *American Songwriters: An H.W. Wilson Biographical Dictionary.* New York: The H.W. Wilson Company, 1987.
_____. *The Life and Death of Tin Pan Alley: The Golden Age of American Popular Song.* New York: Funk & Wagnall's, 1964.
_____. *The World of Jerome Kern: A Biography.* New York: Henry Holt and Company, 1960.
Fordin, Hugh. *M-G-M's Greatest Musicals: The Arthur Freed Unit.* New York: Da Capo Press, 1996.
_____. *The World of Entertainment! Hollywood's Greatest Musicals.* Garden City, NY: Doubleday and Company, Inc., 1975.
Forte, Allen. *The American Popular Ballad of the Golden Era: 1924–1950.* Princeton, NJ: Princeton University Press, 1995.
Franceschina, John. *Harry B. Smith: Dean of American Librettists.* New York: Routledge, 2003.
Freedland, Michael. *Fred Astaire.* New York: Grosset & Dunlap, 1976.
_____. *Irving Berlin.* London: W.H. Allen, 1974.
_____. *Jerome Kern.* New York: Stein & Day, 1981.
Furia, Philip. *Ira Gershwin: The Art of the Lyricist.* New York: Oxford University Press, 1996.
_____. *The Poets of Tin Pan Alley: The History of America's Greatest Lyricists.* New York: Oxford University Press, 1990.
_____. *Skylark: The Life and Times of Johnny Mercer.* New York: St. Martin's Press, 2003.
_____, and Michael Lasser. *America's Songs: The Stories Behind the Songs of Broadway, Hollywood, and Tin Pan Alley.* New York: Routledge, 2006.
Ganzl, Kurt. *The British Musical Theatre:*

Volume 2: 1915–1984. Oxford: Oxford University Press, 1987.
_____. *The Encyclopedia of the Musical Theatre*, 2nd ed. New York: Schirmer Books, 1994.
Garebian, Keith. *The Making of My Fair Lady*. Toronto: ECW Press, 1993.
Gershwin, Ira. *Lyrics on Several Occasions*. New York: Alfred A. Knopf, 1959.
Goldstein, Malcolm. *George S. Kaufman: His Life, His Theater*. New York: Oxford University Press, 1979.
Gordon, Max. *Max Gordon Presents*. New York: Bernard Geis Associates, 1963.
Gottfried, Martin. *Broadway Musicals*. The Netherlands: Harry N. Abrams, B.V., 1984.
Grant, Mark N. *The Rise and Fall of the Broadway Musical*. Boston: Northeastern University Press, 2004.
Green, Benny. *Let's Face the Music: The Golden Age of Popular Song*. London: Pavillion Books Limited, 1989.
Green, Stanley. *Broadway Musicals: Show by Show*, 6th ed. New York: Applause Theatre & Cinema Books, 2008.
_____. *Encyclopaedia of the Musical Film*. New York: Oxford University Press, 1981.
_____. *Ring Bells! Sing Songs!: Broadway Musicals of the 1930's*. New Rochelle, NY: Arlington House, 1971.
_____. *The World of Musical Comedy: The Story of the American Musical Stage As Told Through the Careers of Its Foremost Composers and Lyricists*. Chicago: Ziff Davis Publishing Company, 1960.
_____, and Burt Goldblatt. *Starring Fred Astaire*. Garden City, NY: Doubleday and Company, Inc., 1977.
Greenberg, Rodney. *George Gershwin*. London: Phaidon Press Limited, 1998.
Greenspan, Charlotte. *Pick Yourself Up: Dorothy Fields and the American Musical*. New York: Oxford University Press, 2010.
Halliday, Mary Martin. *My Heart Belongs*. New York: William Morrow and Company, Inc., 1976.
Halliwell, Leslie. *Halliwell's Film and Video Guide*. New York: HarperPerennial, 1997.
Hamm, Charles. *Yesterdays: Popular Song in America*. New York: W.W. Norton and Company, 1979.
Harriman, Margaret Case. *Take Them Up Tenderly: A Collection of Profiles*. New York: Alfred A. Knopf, 1945.
Hart, Dorothy. *Thou Swell! Thou Witty!: The Life and Lyrics of Lorenz Hart*. New York: Harper & Row, 1976.
Hart, Kitty Carlisle. *Kitty: An Autobiography*. New York: Doubleday, 1988.
Hemming, Roy. *The Melody Lingers On: The Great Songwriters and Their Movie Musicals*. New York: Newmarket Press, 1986.
Hischak, Thomas S. *Off-Broadway Musicals Since 1919*. Toronto: The Scarecrow Press, Inc., 2011.
_____. *The Tin Pan Alley Song Encyclopedia*. Westport, CT: Greenwood Press, 2002.
_____. *Word Crazy: Broadway Lyricists from Cohan to Sondheim*. New York: Praeger Publishers, 1991.
Howard, John Tasker. *Our American Music: Three Hundred Years of It*, 3rd ed. New York: Thomas Y. Cromwell Company, 1946.
Hubler, Richard G. *The Cole Porter Story*. Cleveland, OH: The World Publishing Company, 1965.
Hyland, William G. *The Song Is Ended: Songwriters and American Music, 1900–1950*. New York: Oxford University Press, 1995.
Irvin, Richard. *The Early Shows: A Reference Guide to Network and Syndicated Prime-Time Television Series from 1944 to 1949*. Albany, GA: BearManor Media, 2018.
Jablonski, Edward. *Alan Jay Lerner: A Biography*. New York: Henry Holt and Company, 1996.
_____. *Gershwin*. New York: Doubleday & Co., Inc., 1987.
_____. *Harold Arlen: Happy with the Blues*. Garden City, NY: Doubleday & Company, Inc., 1960.
Jasen, David A. *Tin Pan Alley: An Encyclopedia of the Golden Age of American Song*. New York: Routledge, 2003.
_____. *Tin Pan Alley: The Composers, the Songs, the Performers and Their Times: The Golden Age of Popular Music from 1886 to 1956*. London: Omnibus Press, 1990.
Jenness, David, and Don Velsey. *Classic American Popular Song: The Second Half-Century, 1950–2000*. New York: Routledge, 2006.
Jones, John Bush. *The Songs That Fought the War: Popular Music and the Home Front,*

1939–1945. Waltham, MA: Brandeis University Press, 2006.

Kaufman, David. *Some Enchanted Evenings: The Glittering Life and Times of Mary Martin.* New York: St. Martin's Press, 2016.

Kennett, Lee. *For the Duration... The United States Goes to War: Pearl Harbor–1942.* New York: Charles Scribner's Sons, 1985.

Keyser, Herbert H. *Geniuses of the American Musical Theatre: The Composers and Lyricists.* New York: Applause Theatre & Cinema Books, 2009.

Kimball, Robert, ed. *The Complete Lyrics of Cole Porter.* New York: Alfred A. Knopf, 1983.

Kinkle, Roger D. *The Complete Encyclopedia of Popular Music and Jazz: 1900–1950.* New Rochelle, NY: Arlington House Publishers, 1974.

Kinn, Gail, and Jim Piazza. *The Academy Awards: The Complete Unofficial History.* New York: Black Dog & Leventhal Publishers, Inc., 2014.

Laffey, Bruce. *Beatrice Lillie: The Funniest Woman in the World.* New York: Wynwood Press, 1989.

Lawrence, Jack. *They All Sang My Songs: The Life and Times of Jack Lawrence.* Fort Lee, NJ: Barricade Books, 2004.

Lees, Gene. *Inventing Champagne: The Worlds of Lerner and Loewe.* New York: St. Martin's Press, 1990.

_____. *Portrait of Johnny: The Life of John Herndon Mercer.* New York: Pantheon Books, 2004.

Lerner, Alan Jay. *The Musical Theatre: A Celebration.* New York: McGraw-Hill Book Company, 1986.

Loesser, Susan. *A Most Remarkable Fella: Frank Loesser and the Guys and Dolls in His Life: A Portrait by His Daughter.* New York: Donald I. Fine, Inc., 1993.

Logan, Joshua. *Josh: My Up and Down, In and Out Life.* New York: Delacorte Press, 1976.

Long, Robert Emmet. *Broadway, The Golden Years: Jerome Robbins and the Great Choreographers-Directors: 1940 to the Present.* New York: Continuum, 2001.

Manago, Jim. *Love Is the Reason for It All: The Shirley Booth Story.* Albany, GA: BearManor Media, 2008.

Mandelbaum, Ken. *Not Since Carrie: Forty Years of Broadway Musical Flops.* New York: St. Martin's Press, 1991.

Marmorstein, Gary. *Hollywood Rhapsody: Movie Music and Its Makers: 1900–1975.* New York: Schirmer Books, 1997.

_____. *A Ship Without a Sail: The Life of Lorenz Hart.* New York: Simon & Schuster, 2012.

Martin, Hugh. *Hugh Martin: The Boy Next Door.* Encinitas, CA: Trolley Press, 2010.

Marx, Samuel, and Jan Clayton. *Rodgers and Hart: Bewitched, Bothered, and Bedeviled.* New York: G.P. Putnam's Sons, 1976.

Maslon, Laurence. *Broadway to Main Street: How Show Tunes Enchanted America.* New York: Oxford University Press, 2018.

Mast, Gerald. *Can't Help Singin': The American Musical on Stage and Screen.* Woodstock, NY: The Overlook Press, 1987.

Mates, Julian. *America's Musical Stage: Two Hundred Years of Musical Theatre.* Westport, CT: Greenwood Press, 1985.

McBrien, William. *Cole Porter: A Biography.* New York: Alfred A. Knopf, 1998.

mcclung, bruce d. *Lady in the Dark: Biography of a Musical.* New York: Oxford University Press, 2007.

McDonagh, Don. *George Balanchine.* Boston: Twayne Publishers, 1983.

McGovern, Dennis, and Deborah Grace Winer. *Sing Out, Louise!.* New York: Schirmer Books, 1993.

McHugh, Dominic. *Alan Jay Lerner: A Lyricist's Letters.* Oxford: Oxford University Press, 2014.

_____. *Loverly: The Life and Times of My Fair Lady.* New York: Oxford University Press, 2012.

_____, and Amy Asch, eds. *The Complete Lyrics of Alan Jay Lerner.* Oxford: Oxford University Press, 2018.

Meyer, Hazel. *The Gold in Tin Pan Alley.* Philadelphia: J.B. Lippincott Company, 1958.

Mielziner, Jo. *Designing for the Theatre: A Memoir and a Portfolio.* Seaton, Devon, U.K.: Bramhall House, 1965.

Mikotowicz, Tom. *Oliver Smith: A Bio-Bibliography.* Westport, CT: Greenwood Press, 1993.

Minnelli, Vincente. *I Remember It Well.* London: Angus and Robertson, 1975.

Moore, James Ross. *André Charlot: The Genius of Intimate Musical Revue.* Jefferson, NC: McFarland, 2005.

Mordden, Ethan. *Better Foot Forward: The*

History of American Musical Theatre. New York: Grossman Publishers, 1976.

———. *Broadway Babies: The People Who Made the American Musical.* New York: Oxford University Press, 1983.

———. *Coming Up Roses: The Broadway Musical in the 1950s.* New York: Oxford University Press, 1998.

———. *Make Believe: The Broadway Musical in the 1920s.* New York: Oxford University Press, 1997.

———. *Sing for Your Supper: The Broadway Musical in the 1930s.* New York: Palgrave MacMillan, 2005.

The New Grove Dictionary of Music and Musicians, 2nd ed., Stanley Sadie, ed. London: Macmillan Publishers Limited, 2001.

Nolan, Frederick. *Lorenz Hart: A Poet on Broadway.* New York: Oxford University Press, 1994.

———. *The Sound of Their Music: The Story of Rodgers and Hammerstein.* New York: Applause Theatre and Cinema Books, 2002.

Norton, Richard C. *A Chronology of American Musical Theater.* Oxford: Oxford University Press, 2002.

Oja, Carol J. *Bernstein Meets Broadway: Collaborative Art in a Time of War.* New York: Oxford University Press, 2014.

Palmer, Christopher. *Dimitri Tiomkin: A Portrait.* London: T.E. Books, 1984.

Perry, Hamilton Darby. *Libby Holman: Body and Soul.* Boston: Little Brown and Company, 1989.

Pollack, Howard. *The Ballad of John Latouche: An American Lyricist's Life and Work.* New York: Oxford University Press, 2017.

———. *George Gershwin: His Life and Work.* Berkeley, CA: University of California Press, 2006.

Riley, Kathleen. *The Astaires: Fred & Adele.* New York: Oxford University Press, 2012.

Rimler, Walter. *The Man That Got Away: The Life and Songs of Harold Arlen.* Urbana, IL: University of Illinois Press, 2015.

Rosenberg, Deena. *Fascinating Rhythm: The Collaboration of George and Ira Gershwin.* New York: Dutton, 1991.

Sanjek, Russell, and David Sanjek. *American Popular Music Business in the 20th Century.* New York: Oxford University Press, 1991.

Schwartz, Arthur. "THE FACTS," unpublished notes, Box 51 / Folder 1. Arthur Schwartz Papers, ML31.S38 Musical Division, Library of Congress.

———. "Reminiscences of Arthur Schwartz: Oral history, November, 1958." Columbia University Rare Book and Manuscript Library. NXCP87-A1387.

———. Reply to queries from Howard Dietz, Box 51 / Folder 2. Arthur Schwartz Papers.

———. *The Songwriters: Arthur Schwartz,* radio script, Box 41 / Folder 8. Arthur Schwartz Papers.

Schwartz, Charles. *Cole Porter: A Biography.* New York: The Dial Press, 1977.

Schwartz, Jonathan. *All in Good Time: A Memoir.* New York: Random House, 2004.

———. *The Man Who Knew Cary Grant.* New York: Plume, 1989.

Shapiro, Doris. *We Danced All Night: My Life Behind the Scenes with Alan Jay Lerner.* New York: William Morrow and Company, Inc., 1990.

Shaw, Arnold. *Let's Dance: Popular Music in the 1930's.* New York: Oxford University Press, 1998.

Sheed, Wilfrid. *The House That George Built: With a Little Help from Irving, Cole, and a Crew of About Fifty.* New York: Random House, 2007.

Sillman, Leonard. *Here Lies Leonard Sillman: Straightened Out at Last.* New York: The Citadel Press, 1959.

Simas, Rick. *The Musicals No One Came to See: A Guidebook to Four Decades of Musical-Comedy Casualties on Broadway, Off-Broadway and in Out-of-Town Try-out, 1943–1983.* New York: Garland Publishing, Inc., 1987.

Smith, Cecil, and Glenn Litton. *Musical Comedy in America.* New York: Routledge / Theatre Arts Books, 1981.

Smith, Kathleen E.R. *God Bless America: Tin Pan Alley Goes to War.* Lexington, KY: The University Press of Kentucky, 2003.

Stagg, Jerry. *The Brothers Shubert.* New York: Random House, 1968.

Stempel, Larry. *Showtime: A History of the Broadway Musical Theater.* London: W.W. Norton & Company, Ltd., 2010.

Stempel, Tom. *Screenwriter: The Life and Times of Nunnally Johnson.* San Diego, CA: A.S. Barnes & Company, Inc., 1980.

Stewart, John. *Broadway Musicals, 1943–2004*. Jefferson, NC: McFarland, 2006.

Stratyner, Barbara. *Ned Wayburn and the Dance Routine: From Vaudeville to the Ziegfeld Follies: Studies in Dance History No. 13*. Oak Creek, WI: Society of Dance History Scholars, 1996.

Studwell, William E. *The Popular Song Reader: A Sampler of Well-Known Twentieth-Century Songs*. New York: The Haworth Press, 1994.

Sullivan, Dan. "Stage: Arthur Schwartz Goes His Way by Himself." *Los Angeles Times*, October 17, 1976.

Suskin, Steven. *Show Tunes: The Songs, Shows, and Careers of Broadway's Major Composers*, 4th ed. New York: Oxford University Press, 2010.

_____. *Show Tunes: The Songs, Shows, and Careers of Broadway's Major Composers*. New York: Dodd, Mead & Company, Inc., 1986.

_____. *The Sound of Broadway Music: A Book of Orchestrators and Orchestrations*. Oxford: Oxford University Press, 2009.

Symonds, Dominic. *We'll Have Manhattan: The Early Work of Rodgers and Hart*. New York: Oxford University Press, 2015.

Teichmann, Howard. *George S. Kaufman: An Intimate Portrait*. New York: Atheneum, 1972.

Thomas, Bob. *King Cohn: The Life and Times of Hollywood Mogul Harry Cohn*. Beverly Hills: New Millenium Press, 2000.

Tormé, Mel. *My Singing Teachers*. New York: Oxford University Press, 1994.

Tucker, David C. *Shirley Booth: A Biography and Career Record*. Jefferson, NC: McFarland, 2008.

Tyler, Don. *The Great Movie Musicals: A Viewer's Guide to 168 Films That Really Sing*. Jefferson, NC: McFarland, 2010.

_____. *Hit Songs, 1900–1955: American Popular Music of the Pre-Rock Era*. Jefferson, NC: McFarland, 2007.

Vaill, Amanda. *Somewhere: The Life of Jerome Robbins*. New York: Broadway Books, 2006.

Westover, Jonas. *The Shuberts and Their Passing Shows: The Untold Tale of Ziegfeld's Rivals*. New York: Oxford University Press, 2016.

White, Mark. *"You Must Remember This...": Popular Songwriters 1900–1980*. New York: Charles Scribner's Sons, 1985.

Wilder Alec. *American Popular Song: The Great Innovators, 1900–1950*. New York: Oxford University Press, 1972.

Williams, Esther, and Digby Diehl. *The Million Dollar Mermaid: An Autobiography*. New York: Simon & Schuster, 1999.

Windeler, Robert. *Julie Andrews: A Life on Stage and Screen*. New York: Birch Lane Press, 1997.

Winer, Deborah Grace. *On the Sunny Side of the Street: The Life and Lyrics of Dorothy Fields*. New York: Schirmer Books, 1997.

Woll, Allen L. *The Hollywood Musical Goes to War*. Chicago: Nelson-Hall, 1983.

Yagoda, Ben. *The B Side: The Death of Tin Pan Alley and the Rebirth of the Great American Song*. New York: Riverhead Books, 2015.

Yudkoff, Alvin. *Gene Kelly: A Life of Dance and Dreams*. New York: Back Stage Books, 1999.

Zimmers, Tighe E. *Lyrical Satirical Harold Rome: A Biography of the Broadway Composer-Lyricist*. Jefferson, NC: McFarland, 2014.

_____. *Tin Pan Alley Girl: A Biography of Ann Ronell*. Jefferson, NC: McFarland, 2009.

Zinsser, William. *Easy to Remember: The Great American Songwriters and Their Songs*. Boston: David R. Godine, Publishers, Inc., 2001.

Index

Numbers in **_bold italics_** indicate pages with illustrations

Abbott, George 219–24, 229
"Absent Minded" 91, 94, 320
Academy Award nominations 162, 200, 313–4
Adams, Franklin P. 28, 31
Adams, India 245–6, 249
Adams, Stanley 115, 238, **_299_**, 303, 319
Adler, Larry 76, 80
Adler, Richard 232, 272
"After All You're All I'm After" 86, 119, 312, 323
Ager, Milton 88, 235
"Ain't Nature Grand" 231, 324
Alberghetti, Anna Maria 272–3
Alexander's Ragtime Band 12, 115, 172
All About Love 298, 308–9
All Through the Night 155, 157, 183, 324
"All Through the Night" 155, 157, 183, 324
Allen, Elizabeth 284
Allen, Fred 35, 39, 44, 46, 48, **_56_**–59, 202
"Alone Together" 75–6, 81–2, 127, 181–2, 225, 246, 303, 305, 312, 328
"Alone Too Long" 183, 259, 322
American Federation of Musicians (AFM) 206–7
American Jubilee 151–2, 213, 313, 318, 323
American Popular Song 1, 3, 7, 10–1, 170
American Theatre Hall of Fame 315
Anderson, John Murray 6, 19, 105
Anderson, Maxwell 131, 270–2, 307, 315, 319
Andrews, Avis 136, 138
Andrews, Julie 270–1
Arden, Eve 166, 173–4
Arlen, Harold 1, 25, 49, 54, 80, 88, 106, 115, 135, 153, 158, 185, 232, 291, **_297_**, 304
Artists and Models 105, 143
ASCAP 7, 103, 138, 150–1, 206, 233–40, **_297_**, **_299_**, 300, **_303_**, 306, 315–6
Astaire, Adele 62–3, **_62_**, 65, 67–8, 243–7, 249–53, 255, 312
Astaire, Fred 38, 62–5, **_62_**, 67–8, 70, 107, 127–8, 173, 312, 314
At Home Abroad 6, 30, 105–11, 113–4, 118, 201, 244, 246, 250, 313, 318, 321, 326
Atkinson, Brooks 125–6, 137, 227, 262, 274–5
Auerbach, Arnold **_197_**, 202

Bailey, Robin 290, 294–5
ballads 7, 25, 30, 58, 81, 101, 128, 182–4, 192, 205–6, 226, 256, 283, 304
Ballard, Lucinda 151, 280, 283–4, 289, 296
ballet 63, 68, 70, 77, 97, 135, 148, 182, 184–5, 193, 208, 244–5, 251–2, 261, 275, 321–2, 327
"Baltimore, Md., You're the Only Doctor for Me" 13, 181, 311, 320
The Band Wagon (film) 6, 38, 70, 79–81, 127–8, 217, 241–55, **_242_**, 314, 321, 326
The Band Wagon (revue) 6, 38, 42, 61–75, **_62_**, 81, 96, 106, 118, 144, 206, 241–3, 245–6, 284, 312, 317, 320, 326–7
Barker, John 68, 72, 206
Barnes, Mae 258–60, 262
"Before I Kiss the World Goodbye" 183, 277, 279, 290, 294–5, 315, 321–2, 327
"The Beggar Waltz" 67–8, 70–1, 96, 184, 245, 284, 320, 327
Behrman, S.N. 288
Bel Geddes, Norman 76–7, 80
A Bell for Adano 183, 271–3, 315, 321
Bender, Milton "Doc" 13, 22–3
Benjamin, Herbert 319
Bennett, Robert Russell 79, 99, 132, 262
Berlin, Irving 1, 6, 65, 71, 82, 88, 96, 105–6, 115, 135, 141, 150, 153–4, 171–2, 175, 185, 191, 196, 208, 219, 232, 236–7, 248, 266
Bernstein, Leonard 1, 232, 253
Bettis, Valerie 204, 206, 208
Between the Devil 7, 76, 117–29, **_121_**, 122, 133, 135, 139, 204, 245–6, 250, 277, 313, 318, 321, 326
biopic (film biography) 171–2, 175–6, 241
Blane, Ralph **_299_**
Blitzstein, Marc 142, 145
Bloom, Rube 88
Bloomgarden, Kermit 278–9, 280–1
"Blue Grass" 183, 204–5, 284, 314, 321
"The Blue Pajama Song" 15, 36–8, 250
BMI, Inc. (BMI) 7, 233–40, 314
Bock, Jerry 268
"Body and Soul" 54–5, 57–8, 99
Bond, Sheila 212–3

377

Booth, Anne 134, 136–7
Booth, Shirley 217, **221**–2, 225–9, 232, 258–63, 314
Brady, William A., Jr. 37, 40
Brahms, Caryl 298, 301–2
Brandt, Eddie 54
Brant Lake Camp 13–15, 20, **37,** 311, 320, 323, 326
Bring On the Girls 26, 317, 324
Brodszky, Nicholas 269
Brooklyn **9–10,** 311
"Brother, Just Laugh It Off " 49, 323, 327
Brown, Nacio Herb 85, 241, 248
Brownsville **9–10,** 311
Bubbles, John W. 136, 138
Buchanan, Jack 27, 38, 46, **121**–29, **122,** 204, 245–6, 250–1, 253
Buck, Ford L. 136, 138
burlesque 5, 19, 22, 33, 36, 40, 47, 115, 122
Butterworth, Charles 75, 78
"Buy a Bond" 158
"By Myself " 117, 126–9, 182, 245–7, 250, 303–5, 313, 321, 323, 328
By the Beautiful Sea 6, 183, 225–6, 232, 256, 258–64, 267, 314, 318, 322, 325–7

Caesar, Irving 27, 49, 88, 118, 120, 131, 319
Cahn, Sammy 266, 269, 272, **297,** 298, 304, 306–7, 315, 319
Cairo 155, 157–9, 313, 323
Caldwell, Anne 2
Calloway, Cab 80, 136, 306
camp shows 13–14
Cantor, Eddie 160–1, 198
Capp, Al 257–8
Carmichael, Hoagy 1, 88, 156, 159
Carpenter, Thelma 204–5, 284
Carrington, Katherine "Kay" 82–3, 86–7, 112–4, 118, 128, 139, **141,** 178, 195, 200, 208, 220, 252, 254–5, 258, 300, 312–4
Carroll, Albert 19–20, 25–6, 311, 319
Carroll, Earl 6, 19, 33–4, 46, 105, 130
Carroll, Leo G. 122–4
Carson, Jack 198–200
Carter, Desmond 41–2, 44–5, 55, 68, 101, 112, 201, 214, 313, 319, 324, 326
Casablanca 298–300, 302, 324, 326
casting 121, 133–4, 137
CBS 88, 210, 217, 219, 233, 236, 270, 272, 275, 297, 315, 327
Celler, Emanuel, Representative 238–9
censorship 69, 102, 156–7, 161
Center Theater 130–1, 133, 135–7
Cerf, Bennett 28–9, 220
Chaplin, Saul 155, 269
Charig, Philip 49, 54, 88, 156
Charisse, Cyd 70, **242,** 244–6, 249, 251–3, 314
Charlot, André 6, 34, 43, 46, 106, 123
Chevrolet Motor Division 212–4
Chiari, Walter 280–2, 284–5

Christie, Ken 90, 132, 151
coat, vest, and pants 94, 185–6
Coca, Imogene 75, 78, 127, 251
Cochran, C.B. 6, 27, 34, 43–4, 63, 66, 104, 106, 111, 112–3, 118, 173, 211, 313
Cohan, George M. 1, 6, 172, 237
Cohn, Harry 164, 166, 168–70, 176–7, 313
Colby, Marion 212–3
Coleman, Cy 11, 141
Columbia Pictures 164, 313
Columbia Records, Inc. 68, 236, 239, 264
Columbia University 5, 12, 21, 31, 110, 311
Comden, Betty 232, 242–3, 246–7, 251, 255, 264
"Come A-Wandering with Me" 283–4, 322
Command Performance 125–6
Como, Perry 5, 133, 206–7, 305, 315, 330
"Confession" 68–9, 312, 320
Connelly, Marc 25, 28, 47–8, 100, 107, 213
The Conning Tower 28–9, 31
Cook, Barbara 279, 280–6, 315
Cooper, Courtney Ryley 84, 90, 92, 95
The Co-Optimists of 1930 43–4, 55, 118, 312, 317, 324
Coots, J. Fred **299**
Cornwell, Ardon 124, 132
Council of the Living Theatre (CLT) 215–7, 314
Courage, Alexander 245, 250
Cover Girl 164–71, 173–5, 190, 313
Coward, Noël 29, 38, 59, 63, 99, 117, 124, 190, 232
Crawford, Cheryl 287, 289–94, 296
Crosby, Bing 72, 129, 200, 206, 247, 270–1
Crossroads 155, 321
Curtiz, Michael **173**–4, 199–200

Dancing in the Dark (anthology/revue) 308, 325
Dancing in the Dark (book) 2–3, 30, 35, 79, 295, 301
Dancing in the Dark (film) 241–2
"Dancing in the Dark" 30, 61, 64, 66, 71–2, 81–3, 127, 137, 182, 206, 242, 245, 249, 252–4, 303, 308, 312, 314, 320, 328
Dangerous When Wet 230–1, 314, 324
Daniels, LeRoy 245, 247
Davis, Bette 160, 162
Davis, Luther 218
Davis, Owen 95, 134–5
Dawson, Eli 13, 311, 320
Day, Doris 199–200
"Death in the Afternoon" 109, 184–5, 321
delayed hit 57–8
de Mille, Agnes 76–7, 80, 166, 261
de Paul, Gene 258, 269
depression 178, 195, 220, 260
Depression 68, 72, 75, 77, 82, 87, 97, 130
DeSylva, B.G. "Buddy" 25, 29, 49, 85, 88, 185
Deutsch, Adolph 245, 252, 255

Dietz, Howard 1, 6–7, 15, 20–1, 25–32, 34–9, **37,** 41, 44–5, 46–9, 53–9, 61, 64–5, 68–73, 75–81, 83–5, 87–95, 105–13, 115, 117–27, 133, 135, 137, 143, 149–50, 155, 158, 169, 177–8, 180–1, 183, 185–6, 189–90, 196–7, **197,** 199–208, **199, 201,** 211–2, 217–8, 232, 241–55, **242,** 264, 271–9, 280, 282–96, **288,** 298–300, 302, 304–5, 307, 312–5, 317, 319–20, 323–29
Dixon, Adele **121**–4, **122,** 126
"Dollars for Words" 95
Donaldson, Walter 2, 184
Donehue, Vincent J. 288–9, 291, 302
"Don't Be a Woman If You Can" 192–3, 323
Dowdey, Clifford 82–3
Downes, Olin 71, 73
Dramatists' Guild 290, 300, 315
"The Dreamer" 155, 160–2, 324
Dreyfus, Max 15, 20, 29, 39, 49, 51, 156, 196, 251
Dubin, Al 2, 248
Duke, Vernon 1, 42, 49, 50, 54, 88, 95, 114, 185, 227, 283, 305
Durante, Jimmy 89, 144, 146–8, 173, 219, 313

Earl Carroll's Vanities 105, 107
Ebsen, Buddy 76, 80, 126
Ebsen, Vilma 76, 80, 126
Ed Sullivan Show—210, 227, 273, 284
Edens, Roger 243, 246–7, 250–3, 255
Eisenhower, Pres. Dwight D. 261, 274
Eliscu, Edward 49, 202, 322
Ellington, Duke 1
Epstein, Julius J. 202, 298–9
Evans, Ray 272
Evans, Wilbur 258–60, 262
An Evening with Arthur Schwartz 307
evolution of songs 36–7, 55
Excuse My Dust 229–30, 314, 322
Eyton, Frank 54, 84, 322

Fabray, Nanette 79, 127, 223, 245–6, 250–1, 253
farce 85, 117, 121, 125
"Farewell, My Lovely" 109, 321
Fertig, Lawrence 87, 220, 313
Fields, Dorothy 1, 6, 53, 118, 140–50, 183, 190, 219–30, **220,** 232, 235, 256, 258–60, 262–3, 272, 282, 298, 302, **303,** 305–7, 313–4, 322–3
Fields, Herbert 18, 24, 53–4, 143, 219, 258
Fields, Lew 18, 24, 33, 53–4, 143, 229
"First Prize at the Fair" 204, 206, 213, 321
"Fish" 273, 313, 321
Flying Colors 6, 75–82, 106, 113, 118, 126–7, 245–6, 250–1, 312, 317, 320
Follow the Leader 49, 323, 327
Follow the Sun 112–3, 118, 201, 313, 318–9, 321
"For Better or Worse" 294–5, 322
Ford Star Jubilee 270–2, 315, 319
Freed, Arthur 241, 243–4, 247–8, 250–5, 258, 314

Freedman, Gerald 280–1, 283
Freeman, Everett 160, 164
Freund, Arthur 14, 323
Friml, Rudolf 49–50, 103–4, 150, 182
from the pen of…Arthur Schwartz 38, 303–4, 328
Fryer, Robert 219, 260
Furber, Douglas 27, 84, 323

"A Gal in Calico" 79, 200, 303–4, 314, 324, 330
Gallico, Paul 275–9
Gardiner, Reginald 109, 114–5
Garland, Judy 147, 198, 223, 243, 252
The Gay Life 6, 183, 279, 280–6, 315, 318, 322, 327
George White's Scandals 57, 105
Gershwin, George 1, 6, 25, 41–2, 49, 51, 54, 70–1, 82, 88, **103,** 111, 114–5, 153, 156, 165, 167, 172, 181, 185, 191, 229, 251, 266
Gershwin, Ira 1, 6, 28, 30, 41–2, 88, 106, 111, 115, 118, 153, 155, 159, 165–9, 173, 183, 189–95, 212, 235, 251, 302, 307, 313–4, 323
Geva, Tamara 59, 75, 81
The Gibson Family 84–5, 87–95, 100, 113, 119, 132, 134, 185, 191, 212, 277, 312, 320, 325–6
Gilbert, Edwin 122–3
Gilbert, W.S. 50, 82, 259
"The Girl Hunt" 246, 251–2, 254, 321
Goldberg, David 27, 323
Goldwater, Barry, Senator 240
Good Boy 22–4, 317, 323
"Goodbye to All That" 183, 192–4, 323
Goodman, Ted 13, 311, 323
Goodwin, Theodore "Ted" 20, 311, 319, 323
Gordon, Max 6, 48–9, 53–6, 61, 63–4, 66–7, 75–8, 82, 123–4, 131, 189, 194, 255, 284, 314
"Got a Bran' New Suit" 109–10, 113, 246, 313, 320–1
Graham, Ronald 134, 136–7
The Grand Street Follies 19–20, 27–9, 43, 48, 263
The Grand Street Follies of 1926 19–20, 22, 311, 317, 319, 323–5
The Grand Street Follies of 1929 20, 22, 25–6, 312, 317, 323–4
Grant, Cary 173–4, 176, 313
Green, Adolph 232, 242–3, 246–7, 251, 255
Green, Johnny 54–5, 88, 96, 119, 243
Greenwich Village Follies 48, 105, 120
"Growing Pains" 224, 322
Gunther, John **197,** 200–1

Haakon, Paul 109, 114–5
Haley, Jack 156, 201, 204, 207–8, 213
Halliday, Robert 52–3, 59, 287–93, 302
"Hammacher Schlemmer, I Love You" 36, 39, 181, 320
Hammerstein, Oscar, II 1, 83, 111, 131, 151–3, 156, 186, 188, 212–3, 225, 232, 239, 272, 274–5, 292, 302, 313, 323

Index

"Happy Habit" 260, 314, 322
Harbach, Otto 23, 41, 112, 150, 238–9, 263, 323
Harburg, E.Y. "Yip" 1, 25, 28, 49, 86, 88, 96, 106, 115, 142, 145, 153, 155, 157–9, 232, 298, 305–7, 313, 323, 326
Harms, T.B. 15, 49, 51, 94, 100, 156, 196
Harris, Sam H. 26, 48, 105
Hart, Lorenz 1, 13–20, 22–3, 28–30, 34, 36–7, **37**, 42, 47–8, 53, 66, 69, 81, 88–9, 111, 115, 130, 141–2, 147, 151, 153, 172, 180, 183, 186, 202, 205, 229, 241, 250, 307, 311, 323, 326
Hart, Moss 64, 96, 114, 202, 213, 274–5, 292, 300
"Haunted Heart" 182, 204, 206, 208, 314, 321, 330
Haverlin, Carl 236–9
Hayes, Helen 216, 223, 274, 278
Hayes, Peter Lind 212–3
Hayworth, Rita 164–6, 169, 173, 190, 313
"He Had Refinement" 226, 228, 322
Herbert, Victor 23, 49–50, 54, 150, 156, 170, 172, 182, 185, 263
Here Comes the Bride 41–4, 68, 101, 118, 245, 312, 317, 319, 324
Heyman, Edward 54–5, 86, 118–9, 196, 312, 323
"High and Low" 42, 68, 245, 249, 319
High Tor 270–2, 315, 319
Hilda Crane 177, 214, 217–8
Hitchy-Koo 105
Hollywood 6, 35, 86, 140–1, 152, 153–63, 164–78, 190, 196–8, 201, 210, 229–30, 233, 241–55, 262, 269–70, 273, 280, 288
Holman, Libby 25–6, 35, 39, 44–5, 54–59, **56**, 58, 66, 83, 98–104, 284
"Honorable Moon" 155–6, 323, 327
"Hoops" 67–8, 70, 320
Horwitt, Arnold B. 202
The House That Jack Built 27, 317, 323
"How High Can a Little Bird Fly?" 94, 113, 320–1
"How Sweet You Are" 155, 160–2, 183, 324, 330

I Can Get It for You Wholesale 140, 267–9
"I Got Out of Bed on the Right Side" 230–1, 314, 324
"I Guess I'll Have to Change My Plan" 15, 33, 36–8, **37**, 245, 249–50, 303, 305, 312, 320, 326
"I Happened to Walk Down First Street" 198, 324
"I Have No Words" 45, 55, 320, 326
"I Know My Girl by Her Perfume" 15–16, 311, 323
"I Love Louisa" 64, 67–70, 242, 245, 249, 253, 311, 320
"I Love to Lie Awake in Bed" 14–15, 36–8, **37**, 311, 323, 326
"I Love You and I Like You" 26, 42, 324

"I See Your Face Before Me" 117, 126, 128–9, 182, 305, 313, 321, 330
"I Still Look at You That Way" 183, 294–5, 322
"Ice Cold Katy" 155, 160–1, 324
"If There Is Someone Lovelier Than You" 100–2, 182, 186, 303, 313, 320
"If You Haven't Got a Sweetheart" 225, 284, 322
"I'll Buy You a Star" 183, 225–6, 314, 322
"I'll Never Leave You" 52, 59, 325
"I'll Pay the Check" 147–8, 322
"I'm Like a New Broom" 225, 305, 314, 322
"I'm Part of You" 183, 273, 321
Inside U.S.A. 6, 177, 183, 185, 196–7, **197**, 199–209, **201**, 211–3, 219, 258, 261, 284, 314, 318, 321
Inside U.S.A. with Chevrolet 210–4, 323–5, 327
interpolations 23–5, 36, 38, 41, 54, 60–1, 96, 114–5, 203
intimate revue 19, 33–5, 40, 46–8, 53, 75, 106, 211
"Is It All a Dream?" 68, 320, 327
Ivory Soap 84, 89–90, 94

"Je T'aime" 55, 59, 320
Jennie 6, 183, 279, 286–96, **288**, 297, 300, 302, 315, 318, 322, 327
Johnson, Albert 61, 66–7, 70, 99–100, 124, 136, 151
Johnson, Nunnally 188–90, 192, 194
Johnston, Johnny 219, **221**, 223–7

Kahn, Gus 2
Kanin, Fay 280–3
Kanin, Michael 280–3
Kaufman, George S. 26, 28, 61, 63–5, 73, 122, 124, 188–94, 202, 213, 223, 262, 268, 276, 292, 314
"Keep the Light Burning Bright" 155, 158, 323
Kelly, Gene 165–9, 173, 190, 231, 313
Kelly, Kevin 292
Kenley, John 122–3
Kern, Jerome 2, 6, 23, 27, 29, 42, 49, 51, 54, 59, 77, 83, 88–9, 92, 99, **103**–4, 115, 138, 143–4, 150–1, 153, 156, 160, 164–9, 172–3, 180–2, 186, 229, 241, 250–1, 266, 284, 313
Kidd, Michael 244, 249–52
Koehler, Ted 80, 115

"A Lady Needs a Change" 146, 148, 322
"The Lady with the Tap" 109, 113, 321, 326
Lahr, Bert 114–5
Lamas, Fernando 230–1
"Land of Opportunitee" 192–3, 323
Lane, Burton 2, 54, 88, 240, 257–8, 272
Laska, Edward 115
law practice 5, 7, 16–17, 20–1, 30, 84, 87, 150, 311–2
law school 13–14, 16, 80, 311
Lawrence, Gertrude 46, 124, 173, 227

Lawrence, Jack 235, 238, 240
Laye, Evelyn 51, *121*–124, 126, 128
League of New York Theatres (LNYT) 215–7, 261, 314
Leonard, Warren 76, 80
Leonidoff, Leon 132, 151
Lerner, Alan Jay 2, 51, 104, 126, 232, 235, 252, 256–8, 271, 292, 304, 314, 324, 327
Lerner, Eugene 281–2, 284–5
Leslie, Lew 6, 19, 105–6
Levant, Oscar 27, 88, 156, 212, 245–6, 250, 252
Levenson, Lew 38, 319, 324
Levine, Maurice 100–1
Levy, Newman 28, 213
Lew Leslie's Blackbirds 105–6
Lief, Max 26, 27, 42, 183, 324
Lief, Nathaniel 26, 27, 42, 183, 324
Li'l Abner 245, 257–8
Lilley, Edward Clark 123–4, 132
Lillie, Beatrice 46, 106–10, 114–5, 127, **199**, 201–8, 313
"A Little Love, a Little While" 270–1, 319
The Little Show 6, 15, 22, 26, 30, 33–41, **37**, 44, 46, 49, 55, 59, 74–5, 83, 99, 106, 118, 144, 181, 245, 250, 312, 317, 320, 324
Little Shows 44, 46–7
Little Tommy Tucker 44–5, 55, 312, 317, 319, 326
Loeb, Philip 75, 78, 127, 251
Loesser, Frank 2, 6, 65, 153, 155, 158–63, 183, 198, 230, 232, 292, 305, 307, 313, 324
Loewe, Frederick 2, 232, 256, 258
Logan, Joshua 145–9, 219, 299
London shows 41–5, 111, 311–2
"Long Ago and Far Away" 167–9
Look Who's Dancing 298, 307–8, 315
"Look Who's Dancing" 225, 322
Losch, Tilly 27, 62–3, 65–7, 70, 72, 81, 96, 144, 206
"Louisiana Hayride" 79, 245, 250, 312, 320
"Love Is a Dancing Thing" 110, 113, 303, 321
"Love Is the Reason" 226, 322
"Love Isn't Born (It's Made)" 155, 160–1, 313, 324
lyric writing 20, 22, 30, 119
Lyrics & Lyricists Series 38, 69, 100–2, 290, 304, 307, 315
Lyrics on Several Occasions 30, 168, 192

MacDonald, Jeanette 157–8, 313
MacMurray, Fred 56, **58**
made-for-television movie 270
"Magic Moment" 182, 280, 283–4, 315, 322
Main Street to Broadway 216–7
"Make the Man Love Me" 182, 219, 224–5, 268, 314, 322
The Mark of Zorro 118, 120, 319
marriage 86–8, 264–5
Martin, Brat 324
Martin, Dean 269

Martin, Hugh 2, 147–8, 272
Martin, Lynn 160
Martin, Mary 173–5, 216–7, 274, 279, 287–96, 302, 315
Martin, Tony 102, 200
Mattox, Matt 289, 291
McEvoy, J.P. 140–6, 149–50, 202, 213, 219
McHugh, Jimmy 2, 143, **297**
Mears, Martha 169
Melody magazine 95
Menotti, Gian Carlo 232, 235
Mercer, Johnny 2, 6, 153–7, **154**, 159, 230–1, 200, 248, 258, **299**, 304, 307, 313–4, 324, 328, 330
Merman, Ethel 48–9, 68, 142, 144, 146–9, 173–4, 219, 227, 243, 273–4, **303**, 313
Merrill, Bob 292
Metaxa, Georges 99–102
Meyer, Joseph (Joe) 49, 235
M-G-M Studios 31, 35, 85, 87, 107, 117, 122, 143, 153, 155, 158, 166, 218, 229–31, 241–2, 244, 246, 248–9, 255, 286, 314
Mielziner, Jo 46–7, 262, 275
Miller, Mitch 239, 264–6
Miller, Woods 109
"Mine 'til Monday" 224, 322
Minnelli, Vincente 107–10, 114, 242–4, 247, 249–50, 252–3
minor key 75, 81, 102, 181, 206
Mississippi Belle 171–2
Mitty, Nomi 223
"Moanin' Low" 39, 55, 99
Mollison, Clifford 42
"The Moment I Saw You" 44, 55, 320, 324
"The Moon Is Down" 155, 159, 324
The Moon Is Down 155, 159, 188, 324
"The Moon Looks Down on Cairo" 155, 158, 323
Moore, Monette 80
Mordden, Ethan 40, 70, 72, 100, 104, 125, 131, 136, 146, 208–9, 226–7, 229, 282
"More Love Than Your Love" 183, 259, 265, 314, 323
Morgan, Agnes 19–20, 26–7, 311, 324
Morgan, Dennis 160–1, 197–200
Motion Picture Production Code 154, 156–7, 250
Mrs. 'Arris Goes to Paris 267, 275–9, 315, 321, 327
multi-picture deals 169–70, 177–8
Murray, Wynn 23, 152
Music Box Revues 53, 105
Music by Gershwin 88
Music in the Air 83, 86, 300, 312
musical comedy 3, 5, 32, 34, 36, 40–1, 47, 51, 65, 84, 88, 91, 95, 101, 125, 142, 148, 153, 165, 181, 191, 194, 219, 228, 232, 257, 260, 263, 275, 278, 287, 329
musical spectacles 130, 136–7, 288
musical travelogue 108–9, 112, 114, 201, 204

"My Bicycle Girl" 151–2, 323
"My Gal Is Mine Once More" 204, 207, 321
"My Little Mule Wagon" 94, 119, 321, 326
"My New Kentucky Home" 145–6, 149
Myers, Henry 18, 23, 38, 54, 312, 324

National Association of Radio and Television Broadcasters (NARTB) 235–7, 314
National Film Registry 255
Navy Blues **154**–7, 313, 324
NBC 84–5, 89–90, 233–4, 236, 297
Ned Wayburn's Gambols 22, 24–6, 312, 317, 324
Neighborhood Playhouse 19–20, 28–9, 311
New Faces 105
"New Sun in the Sky" 64, 67–8, 242, 245, 249, 305, 312, 320
New York State Bar 16, 311
New York University (NYU) 12–13, 311, 314, 325
The New Yorkers 22–3, 38, 312, 317, 324
Newman, Greatrex 44, 55, 96, 320, 324
Nice Goings On 84–5, 312, 317, 320, 322–3, 326
Nicholas Nickleby 298, 301–2, 305, 315
Night and Day 170–8, **173**, 313
1939 New York World's Fair 138, 144, 148–9, 151–2, 313, 318, 323
Nyberg, Mary Ann 253, 255

"Oh, But I Do" 183, 198–9, 324, 330
O'Hagan Scott, Mary (AKA Mary Grey) 264, **265**, 298, 307–9, 314–5
"Old Enough to Love" 225, 323, 326
"An Old Flame Never Dies" 137–8, 325
"Once Upon a Long Ago" 270–1, 319
operetta 5, 34, 49–53, 73, 97, 99–100, 103–4, 131–2, 137–8, 181–2, 232, 312
oral history 74, 110, 149, 331
oratorio 159, 324
orchestrations 55, 79, 120, 132, 277, 283, 304

pageant of American history 151–2, 318, 323
Paige, Janis 198–200
Paint Your Wagon 256–7, 314, 324, 327
Pakula, Alan 287, 289
Paley, William S. 236, 238
Palula Island 14, 323
Paramount Pictures 49
Park Avenue 6, 178, 183, 188–95, 284, 314, 318, 323
Parkinson's Disease 286, 288–9, 295–6, 305, 315
Parsons, Donovan 27, 323
The Passing Show (1894) 33
The Passing Shows (Shuberts) 33, 105
Peggy-Ann 18–19, 21, 42, 54, 311
Perry Como Show 5, 315
Petrillo, James C. 206–7
Phi Beta Kappa 12, 16, 178, 311
Pi Lambda Phi 12, 325

piano accompanist 26, 64, 83, 191
piano playing 6, 10–2, 113, 185, 309
Pins and Needles 126, 140, 142, 202
Pitot, Genevieve 260–1
plugged songs 57–8, 94, 161–2
"The Polar Bear Strut" 20, 325
Pollock, Muriel 324
Pons, Lily 118–9, 143, 196
popular songs 36, 71, 93, 170, 179–82, 222, 234, 239, 285
Porter, Cole 2, 27, 49, 51, 69, 82, 84, 88, 111, 135, 146, 157, 170–6, 182, 203, 205, 232, 248, 272, 291, 313, 326
Porter, Linda 173–4, 176
Powell, Edward B. 79, 124
Powell, Eleanor 106–14, 313
Previn, André 11, 71, 128–9, 232, 257
Princess Charming 49–53, 59, 138, 312, 317, 325
Princess O'Rourke 155–6, 323, 327
Prinz, Leroy 198–200
"The Private Eye" 246, 251–2, 321
Procter & Gamble 84, 89, 94
producing 164–78, 200, 202–4, 208, 210–4, 217–8
prologs 25
"Put Me to the Test" 167

Queen High 49, 322–3, 327
The Queen's Affair 101, 214, 320, 326

radio 57, 84–5, 87–95, 102, 113, 119, 137, 156, 161, 185, 189, 191, 206, 211, 217, 233–7, 239, 255, 260
Radio City Music Hall 130, 132, 135
Rainger, Ralph 39, 49, 55, 196–7, 322–3
"A Rainy Night in Rio" 199–200, 303–4, 314, 324
Raphaelson, Samson 48, 214, 216, 218
Rasch, Albertina 59, 61–3, 70, 77
rationing songs 161
Raye, Martha **154,** 156
Razaf, Andy 80, 114
RCA Victor 68, 234, 295
The Red Robe 22, 24, 312, 317, 325
rehearsal pianist 18, 21, 54, 83, 300, 311
Reinheimer, Howard 189, 207, 278
"Relax-Ay-Voo" 269, 319
repeated notes 72, 109, 128
Revenge with Music 7, 96, 97–104, 117–8, 135, 211, 245–6, 313, 318, 320
revolving stage 66–7
revue 2–3, 5–7, 13, 15, 19, 22–5, 27, 30, 33–40, 43–4, 46–8, 51, 53, 56–9, 62–70, 73–4, 80, 96–9, 104–12, 114–6, 118, 120, 123, 126–7, 131, 135, 140–1, 143, 145, 150, 159, 163, 171, 177, 181, 184, 191, 195–6, 199–202, 207–11, 213, 219, 222–3, 227, 241–2, 244, 250, 254–5, 261, 279, 306–8, 312–4, 317, 325–6
"Rhode Island Is Famous for You" 204–6, 208, 213, 303–4, 314, 321

Index

Richard Rodgers Award 316
Ripples 27, 317
Robbins, Jack 35
Robin, Leo 2, 118, 183, 196–200, 272, 298–9, 304–5, 307, 314, 324, 326
Rockefeller family 130–3, 137–9
Rodgers, Richard 2, 13–16, 18–9, 28, 42, 47–9, 51, 53–4, 66, 69, 88–9, 102, 111, 115, 130, 141–2, 147, 151, 153, 172, 186, 188, 191, 217, 225, 229, 232, 235, 241, 250, 257, 266, 272, 274–5, 292, 294, 311, 316
Rogers, Gingers 49, 107, 223, 249
"Romany" 23, 321
Romberg, Sigmund 2, 49–50, 52–3, 57, 92, *103*–4, 111, 156, 172, 182, 222
Rome, Harold 1–2, 126, 140–2, 198–9, 202, 232, 268, *297*
Ronell, Ann 1, 88, 216–7
Roosevelt, Pres. Franklin D. 125–6, 262
Rose, Billy 89, 130, 144, 151, 230, 238
Ross, Jerry 232
Ruby, Harry 49, 88
Rule, Jimmy *299*
Runaway Queen 101, 214, 320, 326
Ruskin, Harry 324
Ryskind, Morrie 25–6, 28–9, 324

Saddler, Donald 260–1
Saidy, Fred 142, 232
Salinger, Conrad 124, 245, 248–9
Sargent, Jean 76, 81
Sarnoff, David 236, 238
Schoenfeld, Mr. (law partner) 16, 20
Schulman, Arnold 289, 291, 293–4
Schutt, Arthur 79
Schwab, Laurence *103*
Schwartz, Dora Grossman *9*–10, 311
Schwartz, Jonathan 2, 3, 7, 11, 71, 82–3, 87–8, 102, 113, 128, 141, 158–9, 162, 176, 178, 180, 185, 187, 190, 195, 200–1, 208, 220, 225, 228, 246–9, 254–5, 258, 264, *265*, 269, 281, 286–7, 293, 296, *297*, 300, 302, 305–6, 308–10, 313, 326, 328
Schwartz, Paul 3, 7, 264, 266, 295, 309–10, 315
Schwartz, Solomon Samson *9*–12, 311
Schwartz, William 10
Schwartz/Dietz songbook 187, 304–5
Schwartz v. BMI, Inc. 233–40, 314–5
Schwartzophrenia 18, 21
Scott, Madeleine 264, *265*
"Seal It with a Kiss" 119, 323
The Second Little Show 40, 44, 46–9, 59, 312, 317, 320
"Send One Angel Down" 136, 138, 325
Serenade to the President 274
"Shakespearean Opening" 115, 321, 326
Sharaff, Irene 132, 135, 262, 289, 294
She Loves Me Not 86, 119, 312, 317, 323
Sheed, Wilfrid 57, 88, 142, 165, 184, 186, 237, 241, 286

Sheridan, Ann *154*, 156, 160–1, 315
Sherrin, Ned 193, 298, 301–2
Sherwood, Robert 202, 216
"She's Such a Comfort to Me" 27, 84, 323, 326
"A Shine on Your Shoes" 76, 80, 126, 245, 247, 303, 312, 320
Shore, Dinah 57, 160–2, 199, 210, 314
Short, Hassard 53–5, 58–9, 61, 66–7, 70, 99–100, 124, 136
show business anthems 7–9, 217, 248, 314
show doctor 21, 100, 122–5, 188, 219, 229
The Show Is On 111, 114–6, 313, 318, 321, 326
Shubert, J.J. 6, 105, 107, 122–3
Shubert, Lee 6, 77, 105, 107, 215
Shubert brothers 19, 24, 33–4, 40, 77, 105–7, 111, 113–4, 122–6
Shulman, Max 289
Shutta, Ethel 294–5
Sillman, Leon 105, 223
Silvers, Phil 165–6
Simms, Ginny 174–5
"Simpatico" 269, 319
Sinatra, Frank 38, 72, 102, 129, 305
Sirmay, Albert 27, 49, 51–2, 138, 312, 326
"Skating on the Lake" 93–4, 185–6, 321
Slavitt, Alexander 12, 325
"Smash, Crash Right Through" 12, 311, 325
Smith, Alexis 160, 173–4, 313
Smith, Betty 219–23, 225–6, 229, 308
Smith, Harry B. 2, 24, 156, 325
Smith, Oliver 244–5, 247, 249, 250, 253, 255, 280, 283–4
"Smokin' Reefers" 79–80, 320
"Something to Remember You By" 45–6, 55–9, *56*, 58, 99, 182, 242, 245, 249, 284, 303–5, 312, 320, 326
"Something You Never Had Before" 183, 284, 322
Sondheim, Stephen 2, 193, 304
song demonstrator 64
song dubbing 90, 160, 162, 169, 199, 230, 242, 245–6, 249
"Song of the Riveter" 38, 324
songs on spec 86
Songwriters Hall of Fame 315
Songwriters of America 235
songwriting 2, 6, 12–3, 15, 18, 21, 32, 37, 88, 92–5, 104, 117, 137–8, 150, 153, 179–87, 232, 241, 312
sophistication 36, 39, 59, 65, 79, 92, 184
special occasion songs 274–5
Spialek, Hans 79, 124, 131–2, 144, 151
"Spring Has Sprung" 230, 322
Stafford, Jo 81, 206
Stallings, Laurence 131–7, 183, 313, 325
Stark, Ray 276–9
Stars in Your Eyes 140–51, 153, 183, 190, 306, 313, 318, 322, 326
Steinbeck, John 159
Stewart, Martha 192

384 Index

Stillman, Albert 28, 132–3, 136–8, 183, 212–3, 313, 325
Stop Press 96, 313, 318
story writing 160, 164
Strauss, Johann 50, 70, 131, 284
Strayhorn, Billy 2
Styne, Jule 2, 11, 219, 269, 272, **299**
Suesse, Dana 88, 95
Sullivan, Arthur 50, 82, 259
Sullivan, Barry 272–3
"The Sun Will Shine" 25, 324
"Sunday Afternoon" 44, 324
Surprise from Santa 210–1
Swanstrom, Arthur 51–2, 312, 325–6
"Sweet Music" 246, 321
"Sweet Nevada" 192–3, 284, 323
Sweetland, Sally 160, 199–200
Swift, Kay 2, 39, 88, 189–90
Swing to the Left 144, 146, 149

tabloid shows 21–2, 263, 321
Tamiris, Helen 194, 208, 260–1
Tandy, Jessica 214, 217–8
tap dancing 24, 106–7, 109–10, 247
Taylor, Laurette 287–9, 294
teaching 5, 12–13, 300, 311
Teichmann, Howard 64, 276–9, 315
television 76, 90, 137, 143, 166, 176, 183, 205, 209–14, 227, 229, 234–9, 247, 255, 270–3, 276, 279, 289, 297, 300, 303, 319, 321, 323, 325, 327
television musicals 272–3
"Tennessee Fish Fry" 151–2, 213, 313, 323
Thank Your Lucky Stars 155, 159–63, 183, 198–9, 313, 324
That Girl from Paris 118–9, 196, 323
Thatford Avenue **9–10,** 311
That's Entertainment! (films) 246, 249
"That's Entertainment" (song) 7, 217, 241–2, **242,** 245, 249, 253, 255, 303, 314
That's Entertainment: The Great Songs of Dietz & Schwartz 187, 305
"That's for Children" 230, 322
"Then I'll Be Tired of You" 86, 182, 305, 323
"There's No Holding Me" 192, 323
"They're Either Too Young or Too Old" 155, 160, 162–3, 200, 313, 324, 330
"Thief in the Night" 109–10, 313, 321
The Third Little Show 106
"This Is It" 147–8, 183, 322, 330
Thompson, Randall 20, 235, 324
Three's a Crowd 6, 44, 46–8, 52–61, **56,** 58, 66, 73, 75, 78, 106, 245, 284, 312, 317, 320, 326
Tibbett, Lawrence 94, 118–20, 159, 326
"Tiger Lily" 185, 204
The Time, the Place and the Girl 183, 197–200, 304, 314, 324
Tin Pan Alley 1, 12, 15, 49, 72, 84, 110, 159, 165, 170, 185, 238, 259, 326

Tiomkin, Dimitri 62, 154–5
"Tonight" 101–2, 155, 320, 326
torch song 39, 47, 53–4, 147, 147
Toumanova, Tamara 144–5, 148
A Tree Grows in Brooklyn 6, 183, 219–30, **220,** 221, 232, 234, 258–9, 262, 268, 284, 292, 295, 298, 301, 307–8, 314–5, 318, 322, 326
"Triplets" 126–7, 246, 250–1, 253, 303, 320–1
trunk songs 36, 80, 101
"Tuscaloosa" 225, 322, 326
"Two-Faced Woman" 246, 320
Tyers, John 204, 206

Ugast, Eddie 15–16, 325
Uncle Charlie's Tent Show 95, 134
Under Your Spell 94, 118–20, 321, 326
"Under Your Spell" 91, 94, 118–20, 321, 326
United China Relief 155–6, 327

Van Dyke, Marcia **221,** 223, 225–7
Van Dyke, Maj. W.S. 158–9
Van Heusen, Jimmy 2, 137, 266, 269, 272, 306
Van Vechten, Carl 98–9
vaudeville 5, 15, 21–2, 26, 33–5, 106, 143–4, 166, 243, 248, 269
versatility 93, 274
Vickers, Martha 197–200
Vidor, Charles 168
Virginia 130–9, 183, 211, 222, 281, 301, 313, 318, 325
Voorhees, Donald 87, 90, 120, 124, 132, 151

Wake Up and Dream 22, 27, 84, 312, 317, 323, 326
Walker, Don 132, 144, 283
Wall, Phil 124, 132
Wallace, George 292–5
Walters, Charles 126, 260
Warner, Jack 170–3, 175, 177
Warner Bros. 154, 156–7, 159, 170–1, 173–4, 177, 313
Warren, Harry 2, 88, 232, 248
wartime psychology 153, 160, 162
Washington, Ned **299**
Waters, Ethel 106–11, 158, 313
Wayburn, Ned 24–6
"We Won't Take It Back" 204, 207, 321
Weatherly, Tom 6, 34–7, 39–40, 46, 48
Webb, Clifton 35–9, 44, 46, 48, 55–9, **56,** 75, 81, 122, 127, 250–1
Weidman, Jerome 267–9
Weill, Kurt 2, 141, 185, 190
Well! Well! Well! 22, 24, 183, 317, 324
Welles, Orson 141, 168, 250, 270, 276
"What a Young Girl Ought to Know" 85, 320, 326
"What Did Della Wear (When Georgie Came Across?)" 27, 324
"When Are We Going to Land Abroad?" 155–7

"When You're in Love" 270-1, 319
"Where Do I Go from You?" 183, 305-6, 322, 326
"Where You Are" 183, 290, 294-5, 322
White, George 6, 19, 33-4, 46, 105
"White Heat" 67-8, 320
White Horse Inn 131, 135-7
Whiting, Richard A. 85, **103**, 196, 248, 328
"Who Can? You Can!" 276-7, 279, 284, 322, 327
"Why Go Anywhere at All?" 282, 322
Wilder, Alec 54, 68-9, 72, 79-80, 82, 101, 127-8, 182, 184, 206, 225, 250, 272, 284-6, 295, 328
William Morris Agency 117-9
Williams, Esther 230-1
Williamsburg, Virginia 130, 132, 134, 139, 222, 301
Willson, Meredith 292
Wiman, Dwight Deere 6, 34-5, 37, 39-40, 46-8, 102, 140, 144-6, 148
Winninger, Charles 89, 95, 99

Wodehouse, P.G. 202, 206
Woodward, Joanne 260
Woolley, Monty 173
working methods 179, 186, 191, 207, 224, 286, 294-5, 301-2, 306-7
Wright, Martha 69, 223
writing for a specific performer 106, 123, 146

Yaconelli, Frank 273
"You and I Know" 137-8, 183, 313, 325, 330
"You and the Night and the Music" 97, 101-3, 181-2, 186, 245, 249, 303, 305, 313, 320, 326, 329
Youmans, Vincent 2, 25, 49, 54, 82, 88, 131, 156, 184, 196
Young, Rida Johnson 2
Your Hit Parade 138, 144, 162, 199-200, 330
"You're a Natural" 155-6, 324
You're Never Too Young 269, 306, 319

Ziegfeld, Florenz, Jr. 6, 24, 33-4, 46, 105
Ziegfeld Follies 25, 54, 105, 107, 111-2, 143

www.ingramcontent.com/pod-product-compliance
Lightning Source LLC
Chambersburg PA
CBHW051250300426
44114CB00011B/966